AMERICAN GOVERNMENT

Second Edition

UNIVERSITY PRESS OF FLORIDA

Florida A&M University, Tallahassee
Florida Atlantic University, Boca Raton
Florida Gulf Coast University, Ft. Myers
Florida International University, Miami
Florida State University, Tallahassee
New College of Florida, Sarasota
University of Central Florida, Orlando
University of Florida, Gainesville
University of North Florida, Jacksonville
University of South Florida, Tampa
University of West Florida, Pensacola

ORANGE GROVE TEXT *PLUS*

FAU | FLORIDA ATLANTIC UNIVERSITY

AMERICAN GOVERNMENT

SECOND EDITION

TIMOTHY O. LENZ

FLORIDA ATLANTIC UNIVERSITY

AND

MIRYA HOLMAN

TULANE UNIVERSITY

University Press of Florida

Gainesville · Tallahassee · Tampa · Boca Raton

Pensacola · Orlando · Miami · Jacksonville · Ft. Myers · Sarasota

ISBN 978-1-61610-218-0

Orange Grove Texts *Plus* is a joint imprint of the University Press of Florida, which is the scholarly publishing agency for the State University System of Florida, comprising Florida A&M University, Florida Atlantic University, Florida Gulf Coast University, Florida International University, Florida State University, New College of Florida, University of Central Florida, University of Florida, University of North Florida, University of South Florida, and University of West Florida.

University Press of Florida
15 Northwest 15th Street
Gainesville, FL 32611-2079
http://orangegrovetexts.org

CONTENTS

CHAPTER 1: WHY GOVERNMENT? WHY POLITICS?

1.0 | What is Government?

Government can be defined as the institutions and processes that make and implement a society's legally authoritative decisions. The government unit can be a city, a school board, a county, a state, a multi-state regional compact, a national government, or even an international body. In the U.S., government includes the **national** government institutions—Congress, the presidency, the federal courts, and the federal bureaucracies; the 50 **state** governments—state legislatures, governors, courts, and bureaucracies; and the thousands of **local** governments—cities, counties, and other special government districts such as school boards and the transportation authorities that govern airports, seaports, and mass transit. These governments make legally authoritative decisions that include legislation, administrative regulations, executive orders, case law rulings, and other public policy actions that are authoritative because individuals and organizations are obligated to obey them or face some kind of legal sanction.

1.10 | *Why Government*

Is government necessary? Do people need governing—or is it possible for people to live without government? What should governments do—what are the appropriate or legitimate functions of government? Why do governments exist all over the world even though people everywhere are so critical of government? These are political questions that were first asked in ancient times when people began thinking about life in organized societies. They are still asked today. The answers to questions about the need for government, and the legitimate role of government, reflect contemporary thinking about fundamental human values and goals, including freedom, order, morality and ethics, equality, justice, individualism, economic security, and national security. Although these are widely shared values and goals, their relative importance varies a great deal among the countries of the world. The *why government* questions are especially relevant in the United States because of its strong tradition of anti-government rhetoric.

The strong strain of anti-government thinking is evident in public policy. For example, most Americans think that employees should get paid family leave to care for babies or family members who are sick or injured. However, the U.S. is the only developed country that does not mandate paid family leave. What explains this disconnect between public opinion and public policy? One explanation is the general public skepticism about government mandates and social programs. A PEW Research Center survey revealed strong public support for paid family leave, but also differences of opinion about whether the family leave should be required by the government or whether employers should merely be encouraged to provide it.[1] A federal law—The Family and Medical Leave Act—provides for 12 weeks of unpaid leave, but only about 60% of workers are eligible for it. Furthermore, the Bureau of Labor Statistics (BLS) data indicate that only 13% of employees have employer paid leave—and these are upper income workers, not the low-paid workers who have the greatest need for it. Organizations such as The Center for WorkLife Law at the

"I believe that all government is evil, and that trying to improve it is largely a waste of time"
– H.L. Mencken (1880-1956)

"Democracy is the worst form of government except for all those others that have been tried."
-Winston Churchill (1874-1965)

University of California Hastings advocate for employment policies that accommodate employees with family caregiving responsibilities, and laws that target family responsibilities discrimination (FRD)—discrimination against workers with family caregiving responsibilities. The comparatively strong anti-government political culture in the U.S. is the primary reason for the comparatively limited family leave policy in the U.S.

1.11 | *Why Politics*

Government is not the only way to organize life in a political community. Life is also organized by **civil society**. The term civil society refers to the private sector individuals that voluntarily cooperate with others, the families, the political parties and interest groups, the professional associations, schools, and religious institutions or faith-based organizations. These **civil society** organizations and institutions are not government entities. Life is also organized by **business**. Business is also the private sector, but it is the private *for-profit* sector rather than the *not-for-profit* sector. Figure One below illustrates the three sectors of society that organize life in a community: **government** (the public sector); **civil society** (the private sector); and **business** (the for-profit sector). In American politics, anti-government rhetoric commonly reflects the belief that the growth of government (the public sector) is taking over political functions that were traditionally (and perhaps better) performed by the private sector (civil society and business). Public policy debates about education, job training, health care or other social services, highways, parks, and protection from crime are often about whether these functions and services should be provided by government or the private sector. Although politics is often associated with government, it is important to remember that government does not have a monopoly of politics. There is a great deal of non-government politics in civil society and business.

Figure 1.11: The Three Sectors of Society

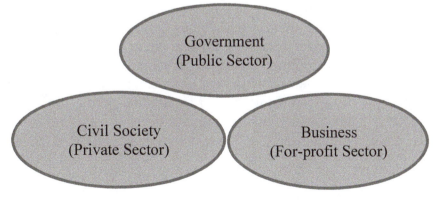

1.12 | *The Power Problem*

The ***power problem*** is at the foundation of thinking about good government. The power problem is the need to *grant* government enough power to effectively address the problems that people expect government to address, while also *limiting* power enough so that government officials can be held accountable for their actions. Finding the right balance between grants and limits is difficult—and imbalances either way are political power problems. A good system of government is one where government is given enough power to provide public safety, protect national security, promote economic prosperity, and establish justice—but not so much power that government cannot be held accountable by the people. Too much power can be a problem because strong government can threaten individual rights and become corrupt. Too little power can be a problem because weak or ineffective governments are likely to be unable to provide economic security, national security, or justice. Criminal enterprises and terrorists can also take advantage of the opportunities created by fragile governments and "failed states." Finding the right balance between granting *and* limiting power is difficult because people have conflicting beliefs about what government should do. In constitutional democracies such as the U.S. individual, ideological, and partisan differences of opinion about the power problem are resolved in both the political system (primarily elections) and the legal system (court rulings).

One recurring political problem in democracies is the tension between freedom and order. Individual freedom (or liberty) is an essential element of democracy because self-government requires liberty. The American political tradition places a high value on individual liberty. For instance, the First Amendment to the U.S. Constitution provides that "Congress shall make no law…" restricting freedom of religion, speech, press, or association. But order is also an important political value. Creating and maintaining good public order is a primary responsibility of government. Governments are expected to provide public safety—protection from crime, foreign invasions, and domestic disturbances—and to regulate behavior that members of the political community consider inappropriate. The laws that are passed to achieve good public order, such as laws that prohibit disturbing the peace, limit individual freedom.

Political debates are often about whether people should have freedom of choice about how to live their lives, or whether government should have the power to regulate behavior in order to maintain good public order. In American politics, these debates are often framed as a conflict between freedom and order because the relationship between individual freedom and government power is considered a zero-sum relationship. In a zero-sum relationship, an increase in one thing (e.g., government power to regulate behavior) means a corresponding decrease in the other thing (e.g., individual freedom): so more government means less freedom. However, democratic values include **equality** as well as freedom and order, and more government can mean more equality. Civil rights laws, for instance, increase the government's power to promote political, economic, and social equality by decreasing the freedom to discriminate.

1.13 | *Politics*

People have different opinions about whether their political system allows too much freedom or provides too little public order. They also have different opinions about what government should be doing. The U.S. Constitution does not provide many specific answers to questions about where to strike the right balance between individual rights and government powers. The Fourth Amendment declares the right "against unreasonable searches and seizures," but does not say when a police officer's search or seizure is unreasonable or whether the right applies to non-citizens. The Fifth and Fourteenth Amendments guarantee due process of law, but do not specify what it means. The Eighth Amendment prohibits "cruel and unusual punishment" but does not define such punishment. And Article I, Section 8 of the Constitution grants Congress power to provide for the "general Welfare of the United States," but does not specify what the general welfare means.

Anyone familiar with politics expects conservatives and liberals, Republicans and Democrats, libertarians, socialists, and populists to have different ideas about government power. Less attention is paid to *conditions and events*. Events and conditions have a major impact on ideological and partisan thinking about where to strike the right balance between individual rights and government power. Is it a time of war or peace? Is the economy good or bad? Is the country experiencing a crime wave, or are crime rates stable or declining? What is the terrorism threat level? The Department of Homeland Security (DHS) used to provide color-coded threat levels, but now uses the National Terrorism Advisory System (NTAS) to communicate threat levels to the general public.

The Constitution does not say very much about government power during times of crisis or emergency. Article I Section 9 of the Constitution *does* provide that Congress may suspend the writ of habeas corpus "when in Cases of Rebellion or Invasion the public Safety may require it." But most questions about striking the right balance between granting and limiting power are political questions more than legal questions. Questions about the right size and role of government are left for each generation to decide according to the particular circumstances or conditions they face.

American politics is often framed as debates about the *size* of government but political differences of opinion are more likely to be about the *role* of government. Describing politics as a debate between those who support *big government* and those who support *small government* tends to overlook ideological differences of opinion about what government should be doing. Debates about the appropriate role of government are arguments about whether government is doing the right things or the wrong things, whether certain public policies should be changed or reformed or ended, and whether the government needs to change its priorities. So politics is about beliefs about the *right size* and the *proper role* of government.

1.14 | *Justice*

Ideally, politics is about establishing a just political system. The Preamble to the U.S. Constitution declares that its purpose is "to form a more perfect Union" and to "establish Justice." Justice is a concept that is central to thinking about politics and government but it is a concept that is hard to precisely define. A simple definition is that justice means *fair treatment*. Defining justice *as fairness* means that individuals or groups should get what they deserve: good or appropriate behavior is recognized, encouraged, and rewarded, while bad or inappropriate behavior is also recognized, discouraged, and even punished. This understanding of justice as fairness is a universal value in the sense that *all societies* value fair treatment. However, the definition of fairness and the commitment to living up to ideals of justice vary a great deal from one country to another. In the U.S., the Bill of Rights and civil rights statutes are the primary sources of legal protection for justice defined as fair treatment by the government.

One way to think about justice is that it is about the proper ordering of individuals, values, things, and groups within a society. The nature of a just society or political system has been the subject of political thought since people first began thinking about living a good life in an organized society. Justice is a familiar subject in works of politics, philosophy, theology, and law. The Ancient Greek philosophers Plato and Aristotle described what they believed to be the attributes of a just society and the best form of government to achieve justice.

The Founders of the American political system thought a great deal about the best form of government to create a just society. For instance, the Declaration of Independence explains why the American colonists were justified in fighting the Revolutionary War against Great Britain. It includes a long list of charges that the "king of Great Britain" acted so unjustly that the colonists were justified in taking up arms and breaking their political bonds with what John Q. Adams called our "parent state." In a July 4th, 1821 *Independence Day Speech*, Adams explained that as British subjects, the colonists were initially "nurtured" and "educated" about human rights, but then subject to "parental neglect, harshness, and injustice" so that finally "the hand of the parent" was scarcely felt except as the hand wielding the whip.

The interest in establishing a more perfect, just political system did not end with the founding era. Both sides in the Civil War claimed to be fighting for justice. The North fought against slavery and for preservation of the Union. The South fought for the preservation of slavery and the power of states, as sovereign entities within a federal system of government, to leave the Union. The various primarily liberal civil rights movements that began in the latter years of the 19th Century and developed during the 20th Century were organized efforts to achieve a more just society for blacks, women, and other minorities. Most recently, the Black Lives Matter movement was inspired by the belief that police use of force against young black males and other people of color was unjust.

There is also a conservative civil rights movement that has had a profound impact on public policy. It consists of conservative movements including the pro-life movement (to limit abortion rights), the gun rights movement (to limit gun control policy), and the property rights movement (to limit environmental and other zoning laws). Tea Party Movement is another conservative movement working to, among other things, reduce federal taxes and spending and increase border control

Politics is usually inspired by efforts to create a more just political order. The pursuit of justice continues to inspire political action because, as John Rawls argued in *A Theory of Justice*, "justice is the first virtue of social institutions, as truth is of systems of thought."[2] Justice is a universal human value that is recognized as an important value in virtually all political communities. Politics is often about competing ideas about what justice is.

Political science studies both individuals and systems. At the individual level of analysis, justice can be defined as a person's expectation that she or he will be treated fairly, that they will get what they deserve. Is a person recognized and rewarded for doing well or behaving appropriately, or sanctioned for not doing well or behaving inappropriately? The system level of analysis examines the workings of institutions. A just political system is one that maintains institutions that treat people fairly. This is why justice is closely related to government legitimacy. Legitimacy is the belief that a political order is just. Government legitimacy reflects the political community's acceptance of government authority and therefore the obligation to obey the law. Justice as fair treatment is a universally accepted concept valued in all cultures and countries, but beliefs about what justice requires in a particular situation is a subjective value judgment.

Retributive justice is probably the kind of justice that is most familiar to the general public because it is closely related to thinking about punishment. Retributive justice is concerned with the proper response to wrongdoing, particularly criminal sentencing policy. The *law* of retribution—*lex talionis*—is based on the principle of retributive *justice*—the belief that the punishment should fit the crime. The biblical verse "life for life, eye for eye, tooth for tooth, hand for hand, foot for foot, wound for wound, stripe for stripe," embodies the principle of retributive justice. However, there is no consensus that the "an eye for an eye" principle of retributive justice should be interpreted **literally** to mean that retributive justice requires taking the eye of a person who took another's eye, taking a hand from a person who took another's hand, taking a tooth from a person who took another's tooth, taking the life of a person who took another's life, and so on for all crimes or wrongful injuries. The alternative to literally reading the "an eye for an eye" biblical verse is the metaphorical interpretation. The metaphorical interpretation is that retributive justice requires **proportionality**: the punishment must fit the crime. A just punishment must be proportionate to the crime, but it does not require that punishment be identical to the crime.

A second way of thinking about justice is *restorative justice*. Unlike retributive justice, restorative justice is not primarily concerned with punishing an offender. Restorative justice emphasizes the importance of restoring the victim—making the victim whole again—AND rehabilitating the offender.

Distributive justice is another kind of justice. It is most relevant to thinking about the economic order rather than criminal justice. *Distributive justice* is concerned with the proper distribution of values or valuables among the individuals or groups in a society. The valuables can be things of material value (such as income, wealth, food, health care, tax breaks, or property) or non-material values (such as power, respect, or recognition of status). Distributive justice is based on the assumption that values or valuables can be distributed equitably based upon merit. Political debates about economic inequality, a fair tax system, access to education, and generational justice (whether government policies benefit the elderly more than the young) are often conducted in terms of distributive justice: who *actually gets* what and who *should be* getting what.

1.2 | The Social Contract Theory of Government

The social contract theory of government is the most influential modern democratic theory of government. Thomas Hobbes, John Locke, and Jean-Jacques Rousseau were social contractarians whose thinking about human nature, the origin of government, and the obligation to obey the law influenced the American founders' thinking about government. The social contract continues to profoundly influence the American public's thinking about government. According to social contract theory, people create governments by entering into agreements—whether written or unwritten—to live together under a particular form of government. The agreement is *social* because the members of a community decide to create a binding agreement to live together under a form of government. If the form of government is a democracy or a republic, the agreement is to create a form of self-government. The agreement is a *contract* because it includes terms and conditions that bind both parties—the people and the government. The contract specifies the rights and obligations of citizens (e.g., freedom of expression; obey the laws), and the powers and limits of government (e.g., to provide public safety and good public order). The social contract theory of government was revolutionary for its time because it is based on the idea of *popular sovereignty*—the belief that legitimate governing authority comes from the people—the people as sovereigns—rather than either the divine right to rule or the government itself.

In western political thought, *the state of nature* is used to explain the origin of government. The 17th Century English political philosopher Thomas Hobbes (1588-1679) believed that life in a state of nature (that is, life without government), would be "solitary, poor, nasty, brutish, and short" because human beings are self-interested actors who will take advantage of others if given the opportunity. Hobbes thought that it was human nature for the strong to take advantage of the weak. The continual competition for economic and political advantage created a constant "war of all against all" that threatened life. Hobbes believed that government was created when people decided to enter into a social contract that created an authority with enough power to maintain order. The social contract is a contract in the sense that it includes specific terms and conditions that bind both parties: the people give up a measure of individual freedom in exchange for the government providing public safety and security. Hobbes' classic work *Leviathan* (1651) describes a strong government with power to create and maintain order. The word Leviathan comes from the biblical reference to a great sea monster—an image that critics of today's big government consider appropriate.

Beliefs about human nature are the foundation of all ideologies. Some ideologies have a basically negative view of human nature: people are considered by nature to be basically self-interested or even quite capable of evil, and therefore need government and civil society institutions such as organized religion to keep them from harming others. Some ideologies have a more positive view of human nature: people can learn to be public-spirited, cooperative, and even benevolent. These different views of human nature directly affect thinking about the size and scope of government. Anarchists think that people are capable of getting along well without government. Libertarians think only minimal government is necessary. Conservatives and liberals think government is necessary and useful—but for different purposes. Authoritarians think human nature makes Leviathan necessary.

1.21 | *John Locke (1632–1704) and Jean-Jacques Rousseau (1712–1778)*

In *An Essay Concerning the True Original, Extent and End of Civil Government*, the English political philosopher John Locke described life in the pre-government "state of nature" as a condition where "all men" are in "a state of perfect freedom to order their actions and dispose of their possessions and persons, as they think fit, within the bounds of the law of nature, without asking leave, or depending upon the will of any other man."[3] Locke did not mean that "perfect freedom" gave people license to do whatever they wanted. He believed that the natural state of man is to live free from oppression and the will of man—"living together according to reason without a common superior on earth" and "to have only the law of Nature for his rule." The law of nature mandated that "no one ought to harm another in his life, health, liberty, or possessions." But history teaches that some people inevitably gain power over others and that the stronger use that power to harm the weaker. Locke believed that free individuals decide to leave the state of nature and live under government in order to prevent the misuse of power.

In *The Social Contract*, Jean-Jacques Rousseau wondered why people are born free everywhere but everywhere live under the obligation to obey government. As he succinctly put it, "Man is born free, and everywhere he is in chains." This puzzle remains relevant in contemporary politics. Is it possible to live under government, where an individual is legally obligated to obey the law, and still be free? Has democracy solved the problem by creating self-government?

1.22 | *Influences on the American Founders*

John Locke believed that individuals decided to leave the state of nature and live under government because government offered greater protection of the right to life, liberty, and property. This natural rights-based thinking understanding greatly influenced the writers of the Declaration of Independence. The Declaration of Independence explains and justifies the Revolutionary War as the right and duty of a free people to assert their natural or "unalienable Rights" to "Life, Liberty, and the Pursuit of Happiness" against government tyranny. Some of the most important words and ideas in the Declaration of Independence can be traced to Locke:

- Natural rights. The concept of natural rights as rights that individuals have because they are human beings—rights that are not created by government;
- Social contract theory. The idea that the Constitution created rights and obligations for both the people and government; and
- Popular sovereignty. The idea that the people are sovereign and government legitimacy must be based on the consent of the governed.

The social contract theory that government is based on the consent of the governed explains why it is rational for an individual to voluntarily give up the freedom of living in the state of nature and agree to live under a government that can tell them what they can and cannot do, a government with the power to take a person's life, liberty, and property.

The English political philosopher John Stuart Mill (1806–1873) elaborated on these ideas about government power in liberal democracies—those western-style governments that are based on limited government, individualism, and equality. His classic book *On Liberty* reflected the increased importance of individual liberty in the 19th Century. While generally supportive of popular sovereignty and the contract theory of government, Mill advocated for stronger protection of individual liberty from the majority rule. For example, Mill is remembered today for advocating the *Harm Principle* as a way to answer the question "What is government for?" According to the Harm Principle, the only legitimate reason for government to use law is to prevent someone from harming someone else.

The Harm Principle is libertarian. It considers moral regulatory policies—that is, laws that legislate morality or which are primarily intended to promote morality—illegitimate uses of government power. The Harm Principle is also libertarian because it considers laws that are intended to prevent people from harming themselves inappropriate. The Harm Principle does not allow paternalistic legislation such as laws requiring the wearing of seatbelts or motorcycle helmets, or laws that prohibit drug or alcohol use or gambling in order to protect people from harming themselves.

The contract theory of government still strongly influences thinking about government. In *A Theory of Justice* (1971), John Rawls argues that it makes sense for individuals to give up their individual preferences—or, to put it another way, their personal freedom to do as they please—and agree to obey laws enacted by the members of the political community. Like Locke and Mill, Rawls believes that people create governments because they believe that life will be more secure and more just than life without government.

Support for the social contract theory is especially strong in the U.S. The social contract was originally appealing because the founders' political experiences included creating governing documents. The British colonists created governing documents such as the Mayflower Compact of 1620 and the Massachusetts Bay Charter of 1629 when they came to North America. The founders also created two forms of government: the Articles of Confederation and the Constitution. They actually created social contracts based on self-government. Popular sovereignty is the belief that government authority ultimately comes from the people. This belief remains strong in contemporary thinking about government. The social contract theory is also especially strong in the U.S. because the U.S. has a capitalist economy. Capitalism is based on economic contracts where individuals and organizations enter into legal agreements to provide goods and services for money. An economic culture where people regularly enter into contracts to buy and sell is likely to support a political culture where people think of government as a social contract that specifies the terms and conditions for managing public affairs.

1.3 | Modern Government

The U.S. has a strong tradition of anti-government politics but criticism of government does not extend to anarchism. Anarchism is the political philosophy that government should be abolished because it is unnecessary *and* illegitimate. Anarchists believe that government is unnecessary because people can freely organize their own lives.

And they believe government is illegitimate because it is based on power, force, or compulsion rather than consent. The word *anarchism* derives from a Greek word meaning *without bosses*. Does this mean that anarchists advocate complete freedom? The symbol of anarchism—the Anarchism Flag—is variously depicted as a slashed black "A" embedded in a black circle. Is anyone really an anarchist? Jonnie Rotten, The former Sex Pistols singer whose real name is John Lydon, explains why he is an anarchist: "I am a natural-born anarchist. I've never in my life supported any government anywhere, and I never will." One song in his songbook is "Anarchy in the U.K."

Critics of anarchism associate it with anarchy—chaos or extreme disorder. But anarchists do not advocate chaos or disorder. They simply believe that individuals should be able to freely and voluntarily organize their lives to create social order and justice without being forced to do so by the government. Ideologies are based on beliefs about human nature. Anarchists have an optimistic view of human nature. They believe that the human reasoning capacity makes it possible for individuals to exercise self-control AND to realize the benefits of voluntarily working together for the common good. Anarchists also believe in the ability of the private sector to provide the goods and services—including good public order—that people have come to be dependent on government to provide.

Americans love to hate government, but the U.S. tradition of anti-government politics does not include anarchism. The anti-government politics is commonly expressed as a *libertarian* belief that the size and scope of government ought to be greatly reduced but not eliminated entirely. The general consensus that government is necessary—if a *necessary evil*—does not mean there is widespread agreement on the size and role of government. American politics includes lively debates about the *right size* and the *appropriate role* for government.

> **Think About It!**
> Are people by nature good or bad? Read President Abraham Lincoln's First Inaugural Address. Lincoln describes people as capable of good OR evil, stresses the importance of education and socialization to develop the better instincts and moral conscience, and he appeals to Americans to be guided by "the better angels of our nature."

1.31 | *Market Failures*

Governments everywhere are expected to maintain good public order, provide national security, maintain public safety, and provide material prosperity and economic stability. What is the best way to decide what the government should do? The U.S. has a democratic political system that is based on limited government and a capitalist economic system that is based on a market economy. So for political and economic reasons, the default answer to the question what should government do is that goods and services should be provided by the private sector where possible. The preference for goods and services to be provided by the private sector rather than the public sector (government) is sometimes called the *Subsidiary Principle*. According to the subsidiary principle, wherever possible decisions should be made by the private sector rather than the government, and wherever possible decisions should be made by the lowest possible level of government. In terms of the level of government, this means that a decision should be the responsibility of the lowest level of government—local, state, or national. The Subsidiary Principle directs that government action should be limited to those situations where the private marketplace is unable to efficiently or equitably provide a good or service. For example, market failures justify government provision of a good or service. The following describes some of the market failures that are commonly considered justifications for government action despite the preference for private action.

The first market failure is the fact that markets do not always provide for public goods. A public good is one whose benefits cannot be limited to those who have paid for it once the good is provided. Clean air, clean water, safe streets, national security, and an educated citizenry are often considered public goods. The government provides national security because the benefits of being safe from foreign attacks or terrorism cannot easily be limited to those who have been willing to pay the costs of providing national security. The government regulates air pollution because it is hard to limit the breathing of clean air to those individuals who have voluntarily paid for it. The benefits of safe streets are hard to limit to those who have paid for police forces. The fact that it is hard or even impossible to limit the benefits of a good or a service to those who have paid for it creates the *free rider* problem: individuals have an economic incentive to freely enjoy the benefit without paying the cost. One solution to the free rider problem is that government provides public goods such as clean air, national security, and crime control by requiring everyone to pay taxes to pay for the public good. Is health care an example of a market failure? Medicare and Medicaid are federal government programs that provide health care for the elderly and the poor because of the belief that the marketplace cannot provide affordable health care insurance for these two populations of consumers. The extended debates over the Affordable Care Act (Obamacare) and its reform or replacement are essentially between those who think that the free market can provide affordable health insurance and those who think that health insurance is an example of a market failure that requires government intervention in some form or another.

A second market failure is **externalities**. In a perfect market, an economic transaction—that is, the buying or selling of something—will include the total cost of producing and consuming the good or service. In a perfect market, the only people who are affected by a market transaction are the buyer and seller. Therefore, these agreements to buy or sell something are private agreements that do not involve the government. However, sometimes private market transactions do affect people who are not party to the agreement. An externality occurs when a market transaction affects individuals who are not a party to the transaction. There are **negative externalities** and **positive externalities**. An example of a negative externality is the pollution that is caused by making or using a product but which is not reflected in its price. The price of a gallon of gasoline does not include the environmental degradation caused by burning a gallon of gas to run a lawnmower or drive a car. The purchase price of a plastic toy or a steel car does not include the cost of the air pollution or water pollution that is caused by mining the raw materials, manufacturing the steel or plastic, playing with the battery-powered toy, or driving the gasoline-powered car if the mining company or the factory are able to externalize some of the cost of production. Externalities occur when a factory (or an electrical power plant, for that matter) is able to discharge polluted water into a river if the plant is located along a waterway, or the plant is able to send some of the cost of production up the smokestack where the Jetstream disperses the air pollution when the prevailing winds carry it away from the site. Under these conditions, the price of a gallon of gas or a car or an electrical watt does not capture all of the cost of making or consuming the product. Neither the manufacturer nor the consumer pays the full price when the costs of production and consumption do not include water and air pollution.

Those who live downstream or downwind pay some of the price by living with dirtier air or dirtier water. These are negative externalities because the producer and consumer agree on a purchase price that negatively affects third parties—people who are not the parties to the market transaction. These negative externalities are one justification for government intervention in the marketplace. So one answer to the question, what should government do, is that government action should prevent negative externalities.

Not all market failures are negative. Positive externalities include education, **vaccination**, and crime control. A person who pays for an education can benefit from it. And education could be limited to those who actually pay for it. But the benefits of education are not necessarily limited to the student who pays the tuition and receives the education), or the school that receives the tuition. The positive externalities include employers, who are able to hire from a qualified workforce without having to pay for the cost of education or training, and society, because democracy requires an educated citizenry. These have historically been arguments for public education paid by taxpayers rather than solely by students.

A third example of a market failure is a **monopoly**. Free-market economic theory is based on competition. If a single business monopolizes a particular sector of the market, the lack of competition likely results in market inefficiency. Capitalism assumes competition results in fair pricing, product innovation, and good customer service. The absence of competition is likely to result in high pricing, a lack of innovation, and poor customer service. This is why the development of sectors of the economy that are dominated by fewer and fewer, larger and larger companies is usually a concern. The Industrial Revolution resulted in large corporations that monopolized sectors of the economy such as oil, steel, and other commodities. Congress passed the Sherman Antitrust Act in 1890, which prohibited monopolies or restraints on trade that limited competition. At one time, the Standard Oil Company controlled about 90% of the oil refining in the U.S. The law was passed during the Progressive Era, a time when there was support for creating *big government* to keep *big business* in check. Currently, corporate mergers in the information economy have raised concerns about Microsoft's domination of the software market or telecommunications companies dominating television, radio, and the internet.

The fourth market failure justifying government intervention is **equity**. Economics is about the efficient allocation of resources. In a capitalist system, people get what they can pay for. Goods and services are available on the basis of the ability to pay. Politics is about equity or fairness or justice. Equity is the perception that people are getting what they deserve. Collective goods (or social goods) are those that *could* be delivered in the private sector based solely on a person's ability to pay for the good or service, but which are often provided by the government or subsidized by taxes as a matter of public policy. Public utilities such as water and sewage and electricity and telephone service, for example, could be provided by the private sector solely on the basis of an individual's ability to pay for them, but the political system considers these goods and services, including basic education and perhaps health care, social goods.

1.4 | What is Politics?

Government involves politics, and it is hard to talk about government without talking about politics, *but government is not the same thing as politics*. Politics happens wherever people interact with one another—in families, organized religions, schools, sports teams, and the workplace. Political scientists focus on certain kinds of politics, the kinds that involve government and public policy, for example.

1.41 | *Two Basic Conceptions of Politics?*

There are two basic conceptions of politics: a ***material*** conception and a ***values*** conception. The political scientist Harold Lasswell defined politics as the determination of "who gets what, when, how."[4] This materialistic definition focuses on politics as the authoritative allocation of scarce resources such as money, land, property, or other valuable things. Politics is also about values.

David Easton defined politics as "the authoritative allocation of values for a society."[5] These non-material **values** include freedom, order, patriotism, honor, duty, religious belief, ethics, and conceptions of

morality. Politics includes organized efforts to enact public policies that support values and behaviors that are considered desirable and worthy of government support. Examples include public policies that support marriage by providing tax breaks for married persons, support child rearing with policies that provide employees with parental and family leave and parents with food stamps, support education by providing income tax deductions for educational and professional training expenses, and support work by requiring those who receive unemployment compensation or other social welfare programs to be looking for work. These are all examples of how the government can subsidize desirable values and behaviors. Politics also includes efforts to regulate or even prohibit values or behaviors that are considered undesirable. Public policies control idleness, tobacco use, alcohol consumption, gambling, prostitution, pornography, abortion, and hate crimes—just to mention a few behaviors that are considered undesirable for reasons of health or morals.

Politics also includes the *processes* by which decisions about allocating scarce resources and subsidizing or regulating values are made. After all, democracy is the process of self-government. So politics includes campaigns and elections, public opinion formation, voting behavior, interest groups lobbying, and government decision making—the behavior of local government officials (school boards, city councils, and county commissions), legislators (state legislators and members of Congress), members of the executive branch (governors, the President, and members of the bureaucracy), and judges. The following provides basic definitions and explanations of some of the terms that are essential to understanding American government and politics.

1.42 | *What is Political Science?*

Political Science is the branch of the social sciences that systematically studies the theory and practice of government. Political scientists describe, analyze, explain, and predict 1) the political behavior of individuals and organizations such as political parties and interest groups; and 2) the workings of political systems. As an academic discipline, political science has historical roots in moral philosophy, political philosophy, political economy, and even history. The historical or traditional roots in moral and political philosophy included making normative or value-based statements about how individuals *should* live *good and meaningful lives* in *good and meaningful societies*. However, modern political science strives to be less political and more scientific, less prescriptive and more descriptive, less normative and more empirical. As a result, contemporary political science values gathering empirical evidence about politics and government in order to further understanding of the way things work more than making arguments about how political things ought to work.

1.5 | Political Values

Politics and government are not limited to material values or valuables such as money, property, or other forms of wealth and possessions. Government and politics are also concerned with important political values including individual freedom, social order, equality, public safety, ethics and morality, and justice.

1.51 | *Individual Liberty*

One of the most important changes in American politics since the founding era is the increased emphasis on individual liberty. The colonial era is remembered as the Puritans' search for religious freedom. The Revolutionary War is remembered as the fight for the natural rights mentioned in the Declaration of Independence—principally "Life, Liberty, and the pursuit of Happiness." And the Constitution is remembered as a document inspired by the need to protect individual liberty—principally in the Bill of Rights. However, the politics of the colonial era emphasized the need to obey authority figures in order to maintain good moral order, and the Constitutional Convention was called in 1787 in order to give the federal government more power to create and maintain order. During the founding era, individual obedience was *relatively* more important than individual freedom. Over time, individual liberty became a more important value in American political culture. Today, individual liberty seems to be the paramount political value defined as a person's right to make decisions about his or her own life without some authority figure limiting, restricting, or interfering with their freedom of choice. Individual liberty is considered an aspect of personal autonomy or self-determination.

This conception of individual liberty as the absence of external constraints is sometimes called the *negative conception* of liberty because it defines freedom as the absence of *government limits* on a person's freedom to do whatever they want. There is, however, a *positive conception* of liberty that defines freedom as the right to personal development rather than the absence of external limits. In this sense, *negative* means the absence of legal limits and *positive* means the opportunity to do something. Isaiah Berlin elaborated on the distinction between positive and negative liberty in *Two Concepts of Liberty*. Negative liberty refers to the condition where an individual is protected from (usually) government limits on freedom. Positive liberty refers to having the means, the resources, or the opportunity to do what one wants to do, to become what one wants to become, and to develop abilities and interests and identities.

The American political and legal tradition reflects the negative conception of liberty as the absence of government limits. The negative conception is evident in the Bill of Rights. The First Amendment provides that "Congress shall make no law" restricting freedom of religion, speech, or press. The Fifth Amendment prohibits the government from taking a person's life, liberty, or property without providing due process of law. And the Fourteenth provides that "No state shall…" deny to any person within its jurisdiction the equal protection of the laws. In fact, the courts have read the provisions of the Bill of Rights to apply only to the way government treats individuals. These civil liberties guaranteed in the Constitution do not, as a rule, give individuals rights as much as they limit government power to limit individual freedom. Figure 15.1 below describes how in the U.S. civil liberties—defined here to mean the *constitutional* protections of rights—apply only to the way the government treats individuals. This is the public sector. Civil liberties do not apply to the way individuals treat other individuals. This is the private sector.

Figure 1.51: The Negative and Positive Conceptions of Liberty

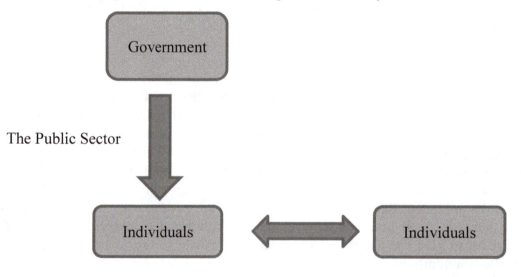

The fact that the U.S. Constitution reflects the negative conception of liberty is one reason why the U.S. Constitution has fallen out of favor as a model for other countries to follow when they write new constitutions. Contemporary political cultures value individual liberties more than they did over 200 years ago when the U.S. Constitution was written. The negative conception of liberty seems old-fashioned or even outdated.

Modern expectations of justice include constitutions that guarantee positive rights and liberties.[6] Section 2 of The Canadian Charter of Rights and Freedoms provides that everyone has fundamental freedoms of "thought, belief, opinion and expression, including freedom of the press and other media of communication." South Africa's Constitution provides that everyone has the right to "freedom of artistic expression," human dignity, the right to life, and freedom from all forms of violence and torture. Article 1(1) of Germany's Constitution guarantees everyone the right "to the free development of his personality" and "the right to life." These are all examples of positive conceptions of individual rights that are not stated negatively as the absence of government limits. They assert positive rights that also apply to the way that individuals (and organizations such as businesses) treat other individuals.

> Think About It!
> Should the U.S. Constitution guarantee positive liberty?

1.52 | Social Order

Order is an important political value because one of the major responsibilities of government is to create and maintain good social order. The public expects government to fight crime, manage public demonstrations and protests, and prevent social unrest including civic disturbances, riots, or even domestic rebellions, and national security from foreign threats. The government's role in providing these aspects of physical order or conditions is less controversial than its role in providing good social order as it relates to standards of moral, ethical, or religious behavior. Moral regulatory policy can be very controversial because it involves values about which people may strongly disagree. The term culture wars refers to ideological battles over values related to public policies concerning issues such as abortion, gay rights, the definition of marriage, welfare, religion in public life, and patriotism.

1.53 | Justice

Justice is a basic concept that is central to most assessments of the legitimacy of a society. While it is hard to precisely define justice or a just society or political order, the concept of justice as fair treatment is a universal value shared by people everywhere. Justice means being treated fairly or getting one's just deserts whether they are rewards for doing well or sanctions for inappropriate behavior or punishment for illegal behavior.

1.54 | Equality

Equality is an important value in democratic political systems. Equality is an essential element of democracy. However, equality is actually a complicated and controversial concept whose meaning and significance has been debated from the founding era until today. Equality does not mean that

everyone must be treated the same, or that it would be a good thing if everyone were treated the same. The words of the *Declaration of Independence* assert that we are all created equal and endowed by our creator with certain unalienable rights. But this has never been understood to mean that everyone is the same (in terms of abilities, for example) and should be treated the same as everyone else (regardless of merit). The natural inequality of age and ability, for instance, are contrasted with the political equality that is expressed by references to egalitarian principles such as "one person one vote" or equality under the law. This concept of political and legal equality is expressed in the Fourteenth Amendment, which prohibits the state governments from denying to any person within their jurisdiction the "equal protection of the laws." The Fourteenth Amendment was initially intended to prohibit racial discrimination, but its scope has been broadened to include prohibition against legal discrimination on the basis of gender or age. Government can treat people differently, but it cannot discriminate against individuals, which means inappropriately treating individuals differently.

1.55 | *Political Power, Authority, and Legitimacy*

Power, authority, and legitimacy are important concepts that are central to the study of politics and government. **Power** is the ability to *make* another person do what you want, to force others to do what you want. It is the use of coercion or force to make someone comply with a demand. This definition of power is value neutral. It does not say whether power is good or bad, proper or improper, legal or illegal, legitimate or illegitimate. **Authority** is the right to make other people do what you want. A person who is authorized to issue orders that require others to comply with or obey demands has authority to require obedience or compliance with the order. The authority could be based upon a person's position as a duly elected or appointed government official. The word *authority* derives from the Latin word "auctoritas." In modern usage, authority is a type of power: po*wer which is recognized as legitimate, justified, and proper.* The difference between authority and power is often illustrated by the example of a gunman who has power to make a person comply with an order to give up a wallet or open the safe. Such commands, while powerful, are not legitimate.

The sociologist Max Weber identified three types of authority: traditional, charismatic, and rational-legal. Traditional authority is based on long-established customs, practices, and social structures and relationships. Tradition means the way things have always been done. Power that is passed from one generation to another is traditional authority. Traditional authority historically included the hereditary right to rule, the claim of hereditary monarchs that they had a right to rule by either blood-lines (a ruling family) or divine right. The concept of a ruling family is based on traditional authority. The rise of social contract theory, where government is based on the consent of the governed, has undermined traditional authority and challenged its legitimacy. Democracies generally require something more than a ruler's claim that their family has, by tradition, ruled the people./

The second type of authority is charismatic authority. Charisma refers to special qualities, great personal magnetism, or the distinct ability to inspire loyalty or confidence in the ability to lead. Charismatic authority is therefore personal. In politics, charismatic authority is often based on a popular perception that an individual is a strong leader. The

Spanish word *caudillo* refers to a dynamic political-military leader, a strong man. Charismatic leadership is sometimes associated with the cult of personality, where neither tradition nor laws determine power.

The third type of authority is rational (or legal) authority. Rational-legal authority depends on formal laws for its legitimacy. A constitution or other kind of law gives an individual or an institution power. A government official has power by virtue of being duly elected or appointed to office. Most modern societies rely upon this kind of legal-rational authority to determine whether power is legitimate. In the U.S., for example, the power of the presidency is vested in the office, not the individual who happens to be president.

Legitimacy refers to the appropriate ability to make others do what you want, the legal right to make others comply with demands. It is a normative or value-based word that indicates something is approved of. Political legitimacy is the foundation of governmental authority as based on the consent of the governed. The basis of government power is often subject to challenges to its legitimacy, the sense that the action is authorized and appropriate. Authority remains a contested concept because, while the conceptual difference between authority and power is clear, the practical differences may be hard to identify because of disagreements about whether a law is legitimate. In the U.S., the tradition of civil disobedience recognizes that individuals have some leeway to refuse to comply with a law that they consider illegitimate.

1.6 | Citizenship

A citizen is a member of the political community. Citizenship confers certain rights, duties, and obligations. Citizenship can be bestowed in a variety of ways. In some countries, a person becomes a citizen by being born on the territory of the country or being born to parents who are citizens. The U.S. has this *jus soli* or the "right of soil" citizenship. The other way to become a citizen is by naturalization. This involves passing a basic test about the U.S. political system, meeting a residency requirement, and taking an oath. Other countries have different rules about citizenship. In Germany, citizenship was by blood (or 'right of blood') until the 1990s. A person's parents had to be ethnically German to receive citizenship, and there was no method by which a non-German could become a citizen until the late 1990s, when the law was changed to allow naturalization. Other countries require citizens to pass certain economic requirements to become citizens.

Citizens have responsibilities as full members of a country. U.S. citizens are expected to obey the laws, pay taxes, vote, serve on juries, and if required submit to military service. Government actions are binding on all residents whether citizens or not. Citizens also have rights. Rights are what differentiate between citizens and *subjects*. Subjects do not have rights; it is their duty to do what the government tells them to do—to obey the law without the right to make it or to control the government. Controlling government is important because government has the power to take a person's life, liberty, and property. Criminal law powers include the power to sentence convicted offenders to prison or to death. The government's civil justice powers include the power to take a person's property by fines, eminent domain, or withdrawal of business or occupational licenses. In democratic systems, the sense of civic responsibility to participate in public affairs is one way that the citizenry controls government.

1.7 | Forms of Government

One subject of interest to political science is the different forms of government. A simple description of the different forms of government is that there is government of the one, the few, and the many. Each of these three forms of government has a good variation and a bad variation.

Table 1.7 Forms of Government

Form of Government	Good Variation	Bad Variation
The One	Monarchy	Tyranny/Autocracy
The Few	Aristocracy	Oligarchy (rich or powerful)
The Many	Republic/Representative Democracy	Direct Democracy Mob Rule/Ochlocracy (tyranny of majority)

The three forms of government refer to the basic system of government, the government institutions that are established by a political community. The U.S. system of government was intended by its founders to be a mixed form of government because it includes elements of all three forms: monarchy (the presidency); aristocracy (the Senate, the Electoral College, and the Supreme Court); and democracy (the House of Representatives; elections). The founders created a mixed form of government as part of the institutional system of checks and balances.

The system of checks and balances was designed to create a political system where institutions and political organizations provided a measure of protection against corruption and abuse of power. The Founders thought that the mixed form of government was the best way to avoid what historical experience seemed to indicate was inevitable: the tendency of a political system to become corrupt. The Founders were acutely aware of the problem of corruption and the tendency of political systems to become corrupt over time. Their worries about centralizing power were succinctly expressed by the 19th Century Italian-British figure, Lord Acton (1834–1902), whose aphorism is still widely quoted today: "Power tends to corrupt; absolute power corrupts absolutely."

The Founders believed the power problem of corruption could be avoided by dividing power so that no one person or institution had complete power. But they also realized the tendency of all forms of government to become corrupt or decay over time. Monarchy—the good form of government of one—tended to decay into tyranny—the bad form of government of one. Aristocracy—the good form of government of the few (best and brightest)—tended to decay into oligarchy—government of the rich or powerful. And democracy—the good form of government of, by, and for the many—tended to decay into mobocracy, tyranny of the majority, ochlocracy, or rule by **King Numbers**. So they created a mixed form of government with elements of each to guard against the bad forms.

The roots of American thinking about democracy can be traced to Classical Greece and the Roman Republic; the Age of Enlightenment; the Protestant Reformation, and colonial experiences under the British Empire. The ancient Greeks in the city-state Athens created the idea of the democratic government and practiced a kind of democracy. The Romans developed the concept of the representative democracy or republican government where citizens elect representatives to act on their behalf.

The United States is a republic or **representative democracy**. The diagram below describes the difference between direct and representative democracy.

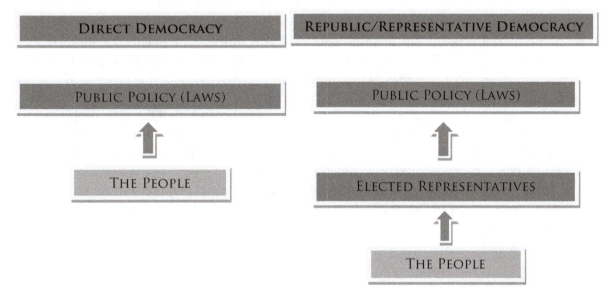

In a republic, individuals do not directly govern themselves. Voters elect representatives who, as government officials, make laws for the people. This contrasts with a **direct democracy,** where voters choose public policies themselves. Today, however, the term democracy is used generically to include direct and indirect democracy (or republican systems of government). The Constitution's original design provided for only limited democracy in the way the national government worked. The members of the House of Representatives were directly elected by the people, but the members of the Senate were selected by state legislators, the president was chosen by the Electoral College (not by popular vote of the people), and federal judges were nominated by the president and confirmed by the Senate to serve life terms. And only a small percentage of citizens (white male property owners) were originally allowed to vote in elections. The Constitution provided only limited popular control over government because the Founders were skeptical of direct democracy. Over time, the Constitution, the government, and politics became more democratic with the development of political parties, the direct election of senators, and an expansion of the right to vote.

Think About It!
In the past, direct democracy was considered impractical and undesirable because of geographical constraints, limited forms of travel and communications, and an uneducated and ill-informed public. Technology and public policy have changed these conditions. Should the U.S. now use technology to expand direct democracy by having the voters directly vote in referenda on national issues?

1.8 | Summary: Why government and politics?

Politics occurs almost everywhere. Governments exist almost everywhere. This is because they are ways that individuals organize themselves to more effectively achieve their *individual goals* such as public safety, good public order, education, health care, and economic prosperity and income security. Government and politics are also ways to achieve *social goals* such as a sense of belonging to a community, national or cultural identity, protection of national security, and the establishment of a just society. Governments are created to be one of the ways to provide and maintain these material and non-material goals. But governments can also threaten or even take these things away from people. The Fifth Amendment to the U.S. Constitution prohibits the government from taking a person's life, liberty, or property without due process of law. Is this a limit on government power? Yes. Is it a grant of government power? Yes—because it means that the Constitution gives the government power to take life, liberty, and property IF it provides due process of law before doing so. The fact that government can protect or threaten important values is one of the reasons why government and politics are almost continually debated and sometimes even fought over. Individuals and groups have different ideas about what government should be doing, and are willing to fight for control of government so that their ideas and beliefs can be acted upon or implemented in public policy.

1.9 | Other Resources

1.91| *Internet*

The Library of Congress: http://memory.loc.gov/ammem/index.html

For more information on the political theory of Thomas Hobbes and John Locke: http://www.iep.utm.edu/hobmoral/ and http://www.iep.utm.edu/locke/

The Declaration of Independence: http://avalon.law.yale.edu/18th_century/declare.asp

The U.S. Constitution: http://avalon.law.yale.edu/18th_century/usconst.asp

U.S. Government: http://www.usa.gov/

The Center for Voting and Democracy has links to articles related to elections and democracy, and links to organizations and ideas related to reforming the electoral system, and analysis of electoral returns. www.fairvote.org/

1.92 | In the Library

Berlin, Isaiah. 1958. *Two Concepts of Liberty*. Oxford: Clarendon Press.

Hobbes, Thomas. 1996. *Leviathan.* Richard Tuck (Ed.) New York: Cambridge University Press.

Locke, John. 1773. *An essay concerning the true original extent and end of civil government.* Boston: Edes and Gill.

Locke, John. 1988. *Two Treatises of Government.* Peter Laslett (Ed.) New York, Cambridge University Press.

Mill, John Stuart. 1869. *On Liberty.* London: Longman, Roberts & Green.

Plato. 1995. *The Last Days of Socrates.* Hugh Tredennick (Ed.) New York: Penguin.

Rawls, John. 1971. *A Theory of Justice.* Cambridge, MA: Belknap Press.

Rousseau, Jean-Jacques. 1762. *The Social Contract.*

Weber, Max. 1958. "The three types of legitimate rule." *Berkeley Publications in Society and Institutions*, 4 (1): 1-11. Translated by Hans Gerth.

Xenophon. 1990. *Conversations of Socrates.* Hugh Tredennick (Ed.) New York: Penguin.

[1] http://www.pewsocialtrends.org/2017/03/23/americans-widely-support-paid-family-and-medical-leave-but-differ-over-specific-policies/

[2] John Rawls. 1971. *A Theory of Justice*. Cambridge, MA: Belknap Press of Harvard University Press.

[3] Locke, John. 1689. *Second Treatise of Civil Government*. "Chapter 2: Of the State of Nature."

[4] Harold Dwight Lasswell. 1935. *Politics Who Gets What, When and How*. Gloucester, MA.: Peter Smith Publisher Inc.

[5] *The Political System*. 1953. New York: Knopf, p.65.

[6] Law, David S., and Versteeg, Mila. 2012. "The Declining Influence of the United States Constitution." 87 New York University Law Review 3(June):762-858. Available at http://papers.ssrn.com/sol3/papers.cfm?abstract_id=1923556

KEY TERMS

Public Good

Power

Authority

Legitimacy

Government

Politics

Citizen

Justice

Social Contract

Direct Democracy

Representative

Democracy

Oligarchy

Monarchy

Polity

Tyranny

Aristocracy

Personal Liberty

1.0 | STUDY QUESTIONS

1.) What are the basic questions to be asked about American (or any other) government?

2.) Why do governments exist everywhere if governments everywhere are widely criticized?

3.) What is politics?

4.) What is meant by *power?*

5.) *What is political power?*

6.) Explain the concepts authority, legitimacy, justice, and democracy.

7.) Distinguish among the three concepts of democracy mentioned in the chapter, explaining in which of these senses the textbook refers to American government as *democratic*.

CHAPTER 2: THE U.S. SYSTEM OF CONSTITUTIONAL GOVERNMENT

Image courtesy of www.blueridge.edu

2.0 |The Constitution and Constitutional Government

American support for the Constitution is so strong that it has been described as reverence for a sacred text that is, along with the Declaration of Independence, the foundation of American civil religion that treats these founding documents as *American Scripture*.[1] Americans are also very critical of politics, political parties, government in general. Is the Constitution, which created the political system, at least partly to blame for the modern system of government and politics? This chapter examines the Constitution and the system of government that it created. The primary goals are to

- Describe the origin and the development of the constitutional system of government;
- Explain the functions of a constitution; and
- Assess how the system of constitutional government works today. This includes comparing how it was intended to work with how it actually works today, and comparing the Constitution with the constitutions of other countries.

The main theme of the chapter is that there is tension between the exceptionally strong commitment to the Constitution as *a sacred political text* and the strong, almost constant pressures to change and adapt to the modern world in a country whose national identity is defined by political, economic, social, technological, and scientific change. The tensions between *continuity*—remaining true to basic founding principles and political ideals and values—and *change*—the need to adapt to meet contemporary needs and desires and conditions—exist in all political systems. But the tension between desiring to stay true to founding values while responding to a dynamic, changing world is especially strong in the U.S. because of the strong commitment to the Constitution and the values it embodies. The commitment to founding values is a kind of legal fundamentalism. It gets stronger during times of great change, challenges, and crises. In fact, a recurring theme in American politics is the belief that contemporary problems can be solved by "going back to the future," by reviving the nation's founding values and the original understanding of how government and politics were intended to work.

"We are under a Constitution but the Constitution is what the Court says it is."

-Charles Evans Hughes

"For as in absolute governments the king is law, so in free countries the law ought to be king; and there ought to be no other."

Thomas Paine,

Common Sense (1776)

The image below is Carin Goldberg's variation of John Trumbull's 1817 painting *Declaration of Independence*. The <u>original painting</u>, which was commissioned by Congress, did not have the Christ figure.

Carin Goldberg's Montage of John Trumbull's
Declaration of Independence (The Bridgeman Art Library)

> Talk About It!
> "How Christian Were the Founders?"[1]

2.1 | The Constitution and Constitutional Government

A constitution is a governing document that sets forth a country's basic rules of politics and government. Constitutions are today almost universally recognized as an appropriate foundation for a political system, therefore most countries have constitutions. The expectation that a modern political system will have a constitution originates from the political belief that constitutional government is a good form of government—that constitutional government is a legitimate, rightful, or appropriate form of government. Constitutions are today considered essential for good government because they promote the rule of law, government accountability, and political legitimacy. As a basic law, a constitution provides the foundation for the rule of law, the expectation that government power must be based on law. The rule of law makes it possible to hold government officials legally accountable for their actions. The rule of law thereby fosters the sense of political legitimacy—the public acceptance of government as the appropriate authority. Political legitimacy is important in a democracy because people are more likely to accept government and obey law if it is considered legitimate.

Constitutional government is *government according to the rule of a basic or fundamental law*. Constitutional government is not merely government based on the rule of law. It is government based on a particular kind of the rule of law: the rule of a basic or fundamental law. The constitution provides the foundation for the system of government. Political systems based on constitutional government have a legal hierarchy of laws. In the U.S. system of constitutional government, the hierarchy of laws includes constitutional law, legislative or statutory law, and administrative or regulatory law. The legal hierarchy means that not all laws are created equal. Constitutional law trumps the other kinds of laws. Legislation—statutes that are passed by Congress or state legislatures—cannot conflict with the Constitution. Administrative law—the rules and regulations that are created by administrative or bureaucratic agencies—cannot conflict with the legislation that created and authorized the administrative agency *or* the Constitution. The Constitution is the basic or fundamental law: it establishes the basic framework of government, allocates government powers, and guarantees individual rights. The Constitution cannot be changed by majority vote. Statutes can be passed by majority vote. Statutes are considered *ordinary* laws because they can be created or changed by simply majority vote. The Constitutional law is basic or fundamental law: constitutional amendments require super majority votes: two-thirds vote to propose an amendment and three-quarters vote to ratify an amendment. Diagram 2.1 below illustrates the hierarchy of laws in the U.S.

Diagram 2.1
The U.S.
Hierarchy of Law

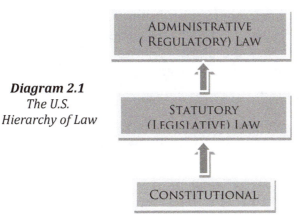

2.2 | Rule of Law

The rule of law (ROL) is defined as the principle that governmental authority is exercised only in accordance with public laws that are adopted and enforced according to established procedures. The principle is intended to be a safeguard against arbitrary governance by requiring that those who make and enforce the law are also bound by the law. Government based on the rule of law is contrasted with government according to the rule of man. The rule of man describes a political system where government officials determine their own powers without reference to pre-existing laws.

The idea of government according to the rule of law has ancient roots. One source is classical Greek and Roman political thought. The writings of the ancient Greek political philosophers Plato and Aristotle described and analyzed different forms of good and bad government. Plato believed that the best form of government was the rule of man, specifically rule by a philosopher-king. He described a philosopher-king as a wise and good ruler—think of someone like Solomon, a wise person who not only *knew* what to do but was a *good* person who could be trusted to do what is right. Plato believed that rule by such a philosopher-king was the best form of government because the wise and good leader would be free to do what was right without being limited by laws or other government institutions with which power was shared.

Aristotle described a good form of government as one with institutions and laws. His description of a good form of government is more closely identified with the modern concept of government according to the rule of law. For example, Aristotle's good government was less dependent on a leader's character. He described a system of government that did not depend on getting a leader as good and wise as Solomon. Aristotle made government power less personal and more institutional: a leader's power was based on the authority of the office held rather than personal attributes such as physical strength, charismatic leadership, heredity or blood-lines, or some other personal attribute.

Western thinking about the rule of law also includes English and French political philosophers. The English political philosopher Samuel Rutherford's *Lex, Rex* (1644) advocated using law (*Lex*) to control the power of a monarch or other ruler (*Rex*). The English political struggles to bring the king under the law influenced American thinking about good government. The French political philosopher Montesquieu's *The Spirit of the Laws* (1748) provided the American Founders with specific ideas about how to create a system of government that guarded against the abuse of power. Montesquieu's main contribution to the U.S. system of constitutional government is the principle of the separation of powers—dividing government into three branches (the legislative, the executive, and the judicial branches).

During the colonial and revolutionary eras, Thomas Paine's *Common Sense* (1776) drew upon these sources for inspiration about how law could be used to control the power of the king, and indeed all government power. In this sense, Paine's political theory reflected the development of the rule of law to displace the rule of man. According to Paine,

> . . . the world may know, that so far as we approve of monarchy, that in America THE LAW IS KING. For as in absolute governments the King is law, so in free countries the law OUGHT to be King; and there ought to be no other.

This was an extremely bold assertion—for which a person could lose one's life. Thomas Paine earned his reputation as a radical for claiming that the king was not the sovereign ruler—that the king was *not above* the law but rather *subject to* the law. This claim could be considered treason, for which the penalty was death. It was also revolutionary because it challenged the English monarchy's claim to the divine right to rule. One of the best statements of what the rule of law meant to the Founders is John Adams' statement in *The Constitution of the Commonwealth of Massachusetts*:

> "In the government of this commonwealth, the legislative department shall never exercise the executive and judicial powers or either of them: the executive shall never exercise the legislative and judicial powers, or either of them: the judicial shall never exercise the legislative and executive powers, or either of them: to the end it may be a government of laws and not of men."
> (*The Constitution of the Commonwealth of Massachusetts*, Part The First; Art. XXX)

Support for the rule of law continued to develop during the 19th century. The legal scholar Albert Venn Dicey's *Law of the Constitution* (1895) how it meant that everyone was under the law and no one was above it:

> "... every official, from the Prime Minister down to a constable or a collector of taxes, is under the same responsibility for every act done without legal justification as any other citizen. The Reports abound with cases in which officials have been brought before the courts, and made, in their personal capacity, liable to punishment, or to the payment of damages, for acts done in their official character but in excess of their lawful authority. [Appointed government officials and politicians, alike] ... and all subordinates, though carrying out the commands of their official superiors, are as responsible for any act which the law does not authorise as is any private and unofficial person." (at 194)

2.3 | Is the Rule of Law Part of an American Creed?

The rule of law has become so important in American thinking about government that it is considered part of an ***American Creed***. A creed is a statement of basic beliefs. The American Creed refers to the widely-shared set of political beliefs about the country's basic governing principles: the rule of law; popular sovereignty; checks and balances (principally the separation of powers and federalism); individual rights; and judicial review.

Most governments today are at least officially committed to the ROL even if they do not live up to the ideal. The importance of the ROL is reflected in the fact that non-governmental organizations (NGOs) such as the World Bank consider it an essential condition for political, social, and economic development. The World Bank's Law & Development/Law and Justice Institutions Programs link the ROL with national development. The almost worldwide acceptance of the ROL as a basic principle of governing has made law one of the factors determining whether a government is legitimate. ROL values make government action *authority* rather than *power*. The ROL gives government action legitimacy. In Western political development is closely related to the development of law as an alternative to the traditional sources of power and authority: heredity or family blood lines; the divine right to rule; or personal charisma (the strongman appeal).

2.31 | *Constitutional Democracy*

The U.S. is commonly called a democracy or a republic but it is actually a constitutional democracy or constitutional republic. The *constitutional* limits the *democracy*! The Constitution limits democracy as defined as majority rule. Congress may pass popular laws that ban flag burning or punish radical political speech or prohibit certain religious practices but even laws that have widespread public support can be declared unconstitutional. In the U.S. legal hierarchy, the Constitution trumps statues (even if they are popular). Democratic politics may be about popularity contests and majority rule but constitutional law. The Bill of Rights protects individual rights from majority rule. In fact, the Constitution is a counter-majoritarian document in the sense that it cannot be changed by a simple majority vote. Changing the Constitution requires extra-ordinary majorities. A constitutional amendment requires a two-thirds vote to propose an amendment and a three-quarters vote to ratify it.

2.32 | *Three Eras of Development*

American government can be divided into three eras or stages of political development: the founding era; the development of the system of government; and the emergence of the modern system of government.

- The *founding* era includes the colonial experience culminating with the Declaration of Independence and the Revolutionary War; the Articles of Confederation, which was the first form of government; and the creation of the republican system of government in 1787.

- The *development* era is much longer and not as clearly defined as the founding era. It includes the early 1800s when the Marshall Court (1801–1835) issued landmark rulings that broadly interpreted the powers of the national government; the post-Civil War constitutional amendments that abolished slavery, prohibited denial of the right to vote on account of race, and prohibited states from denying equal protection and due process of law; and the Progressive Era (from 1890 to around the end of WWI) policies regulating monopolies and working conditions (e.g. enacting child labor laws, workplace safety laws, and minimum wage and maximum hours laws). These developments changed the system of government and politics. Political parties were organized. The national government's power was expanded. And the political culture changed. There was an increased expectation of the right to participate in politics and greater popular control over government.

- The *modern* era of American government is usually traced to the 1930s response to the Great Depression. The Great Depression was a national—indeed, a global—economic crisis that the American public expected the national government to address. The development of a national economy further strengthened public expectations that the national government was responsible for managing the economy. The public began to look to the federal government for solutions to problems. Organized crime was perceived as a national problem that required federal action. World War II and the subsequent Cold War also increased the power of the national government, which has primary responsibility for foreign affairs and national defense. The creation of a social welfare state and a national security or warfare state changed politics and governance. It changed the distribution of power between the national and state governments, it expanded the power of the presidency, contributed to the rise of the administrative state—the federal bureaucracy that Americans love to hate.

The following sections examine the founding era. The development and modern eras are examined in greater detail in the chapters on congress, the president, the judiciary, and federalism.

2.4 | Founding Era

2.41 | Colonial Era

People came to the new world primarily from England and Europe for a variety of reasons. Some came looking for greater political freedom. Some came for economic opportunity with the promise of free land. Some were entrepreneurs who saw the New World as a place to make money. Some were seeking a new start in life. Some fled religious persecution in their home land and were searching for freedom to practice their religion. In the 16th and 17th centuries, English joint-stock companies were formed under charters from the crown to promote commercial and territorial expansion in North America. The Virginia Company of London founded the Jamestown settlement in 1607. In New England, the Massachusetts Bay Company charter described explicitly religious political purposes. The First Charter of Virginia (1606), The Mayflower Compact (1620) and The Charter of Massachusetts Bay (1629) are documentary evidence of the colonial era belief that politics and government had explicitly religious purposes.[2] The colonial experience with charters creating communities also provided colonists with personal experiences creating or "constituting" governments. These experiences are one reason why the social contract theory of government has been so influential in shaping American thinking about government.

2.42 | *Spirit of Independence*

Several factors fostered a spirit of independence in the colonies. The first factor is the **character** of the people who came to "the New World." In the seventeenth century, crossing the Atlantic Ocean was a long, difficult, and dangerous undertaking. The people who made the trip tended to be the hardier, more adventurous, or more desperate individuals, so the colonies were populated with people who had an independent streak. A second factor is **geography**. The large ocean between the rulers and the ruled created conditions that allowed a sense of colonial identity to develop. King James I (1600-1625) increased the independent spirit by allowing the colonists to establish assemblies such as the Virginia House of Burgesses. Each of the 13 colonies had a constitution. These conditions fostered expectations of individual liberty in self-government, religious practices, and economic activity. By the mid-1700s, local traditions and distance weakened colonial ties to the Crown. A third factor is **ideas**. The political philosophy of the Age of Enlightenment included an emphasis on reason, self-government, liberty, and equality. These ideas appealed to the colonists' and were used to challenge British imperial power in the New World.

A fourth factor is **economics**. The colonial economies differed from the British economy. Changes in the economic ties between England and the colonies increased support for political independence. During the colonial era the British economic policy was mercantilist. **Mercantilism** is the theory that the government controls and directs economic activity, particularly foreign trade, in order to maximize the state's wealth. The British controlled colonial industries and trade to increase imperial wealth. The British prohibited their colonies from trading with other imperial powers like the Dutch to ensure that British colonial gold and silver stayed within the empire. The American colonies initially benefited economically from this mercantilist arrangement. They had a buyer for

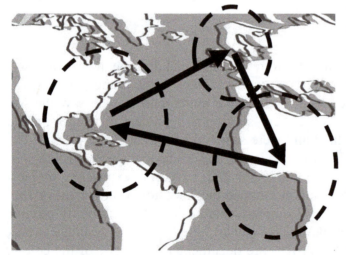

the raw materials and other goods produced by the colonies. The American colonies produced wood for ships for the British fleet as well as tobacco, cotton, rice, and sugar for export. In return, the colonists could buy finished products like ships and rum. Mercantilism was responsible for the **triangle** trade: slaves were brought to America from Africa; sugar, cotton, and tobacco were exported to England; and manufactured goods, textiles, and rum were sent to Africa to pay for slaves.

This mercantilist arrangement changed as the colonial economy developed. The colonies started chafing against mercantilist policies as they believed they were no longer receiving competitive prices for their goods. Furthermore, as the New England economy developed into a manufacturing and trade economy, New England started taking England's place in the trade triangle, thereby reducing the need for the British Empire.

2.43 | *Trade and Taxation*

Despite the complaints about trade policies, the colonists were generally content with British governance until the **Seven Years War** (1756—1763). The long and expensive war with the French and Indians ended with the British in control of most of North America. The colonists thought this would open up even more cheap frontier land for them to settle but the British had other ideas. The Crown decreed in 1763 that there would be no further westward movement of British subjects because the Crown did not want to pay to defend settlers against Indians. The British Parliament taxed the colonists to pay for the very expensive war. **The Sugar Act** of 1764 taxed sugar, wine, coffee, and other products commonly exported to the colonies. The colonists resented these taxes and began to cry "no taxation without representation!"

Parliament further angered the colonists by passing **the Stamp Act** in 1765, which required all printed documents to bear a stamp. The printer had to pay for the stamp. In the same year, the Parliament passed the **Mutiny (Quartering) Act** that forced colonists to either provide barracks for British soldiers or house them in their homes. The colonists, who were already mad about paying taxes, started protesting that they have to pay for soldiers to live in their homes. The Sons of Liberty, which were organized by Samuel Adams and Patrick Henry to act against the Crown, looted the Boston tax collectors home. Violence spread throughout the colonies and the stamp act became virtually unenforceable.

In 1767, Parliament enacted **the Townshend Acts** that imposed duties on many products including tea. The Sons of Liberty started a boycott which prompted the British to send troops to Boston. When British soldiers fired on a crowd of protesters, killing five people, the event was depicted as the Boston Massacre. Paul Revere portrayal of the British captain ordering the troops to fire on the crowd inflamed colonial passions.

Paul Revere's engraving of the Boston Massacre

In 1772, still upset by the tea tax, Samuel Adams suggested the creation of Committees of Correspondence to improve communication among colonists. By 1774, twelve colonies had formed such committees which organized protests prior to the revolution and coordinated actions during the revolution. Despite colonial opposition, Parliament passed another tax on tea in 1773 and, consistent with mercantilist economic policy, granted a monopoly to the East India Company. The colonists responded by dumping tea into Boston Harbor. The "Boston Tea Party" enraged King George, who declared that it was time to force the colonies to fall into line. The King persuaded Parliament to pass **the Coercive Acts** or the Intolerable Acts, which allowed Britain to blockade Boston harbor and placed 4,000 more soldiers in Boston. These actions increased resentment on both sides of the Atlantic. All but one colony (Georgia) agreed to send delegates to a new continental congress to present a united message to the King.

2.44 | First and Second Continental Congresses

The First Continental Congress that met in Philadelphia in September and October 1774 consisted of 56 delegates from every colony except Georgia. They adopted a statement of rights and principles, including colonial rights of petition and assembly, trial by peers, freedom from a standing army, and the selection of representative councils to levy taxes. The statement provided that the Congress would meet again in May 1775 if the King did not agree with their requests. King George refused the request of the Continental Congress. A second Continental Congress called a meeting in May of 1775, but before the delegates could meet fighting broke out at Lexington and Concord, Massachusetts. When the delegates at the Second Continental Congress convened on May 10, 1775 the atmosphere was more hostile toward Britain. King George sent 20,000 more troops. The Revolutionary War had begun in earnest.

Think About It!
Anti-war movements in the Revolutionary Era? Not everyone in the colonies supported the Revolutionary War. And not everyone in Britain thought it was a good idea to send troops to put down colonial rebellions. See the British political cartoon from 1775 describing King George's decision as being led by obstinacy and pride:
http://www.loc.gov/pictures/item/97514880/

2.45 | The Declaration of Independence (1776)

The Declaration of Independence was written to justify the colonists' taking up arms to overthrow an existing political system. It is a philosophical defense of the right of revolution. Thomas Jefferson, a Virginia farmer and lawyer, was the main author of the Declaration of Independence. The language that Jefferson used in the Declaration reflected John Locke's words and ideas about natural or God-given rights, popular sovereignty, the social contract theory of government based on the consent of the governed, and even a people's right to revolt against an unjust government. The following language from the Declaration of Independence explains these ideas:

> *"When in the course of human events, it becomes necessary for one people to dissolve the political bands which have connected them with another, and to assume among the powers of the earth, the separate and equal station to which the laws of nature and of nature's God entitle them, a decent respect to the opinions of mankind requires that they should declare the causes which impel them to the separation.*
>
> *We hold these truths to be self-evident: That all men are created equal; that they are endowed by their Creator with certain unalienable rights; that among these are life, liberty, and the pursuit of happiness; that, to secure these rights, governments are instituted among men, deriving their just powers from the consent of the governed; that whenever any form of government becomes destructive of these ends, it is the right of the people to alter or to abolish it...."*

The Declaration acknowledges that people should not be quick to revolt against a government. It is only after *"a long train of abuses"* intended to reduce the people to despotism that *"it is their right, it is their duty, to throw off such government, and to provide new guards for their future security..."* The Declaration listed the King's actions that aimed to establish "absolute tyranny" over the states. It then declared *"**That these**"*

United Colonies are, and of right ought to be, FREE AND INDEPENDENT STATES; that they are absolved from all allegiance to the British crown and that all political connection between them and the state of Great Britain is, and ought to be, totally dissolved..."

> Think about it!
> Does the *spirit* of the Declaration of Independence give Americans the right to revolt against the government?

2.5 | Articles of Confederation

The first American form of government was the Articles of Confederation. The Continental Congress approved the Articles of Confederation and they took effect in 1781 upon ratification by all thirteen states. A confederation is a loose association of sovereign states that agree to cooperate in a kind of voluntary "league of friendship." The Second Article of Confederation provided that "Each state retains its sovereignty, freedom, and independence, and every power, jurisdiction, and right, which is not by this Confederation expressly delegated to the United States, in Congress assembled." The Third Article provided that "The said States hereby severally enter into a firm league

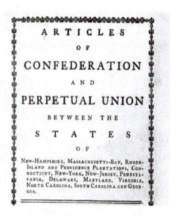

of friendship with each other, for their common defense, the security of their liberties, and their mutual and general welfare, binding themselves to assist each other, against all force offered to, or attacks made upon them, or any of them, on account of religion, sovereignty, trade, or any other pretense whatever."

In a **confederation,** political power is decentralized because the central (or national) government is weak and the state or regional governments are strong. The Articles of Confederation had major defects which were exposed during the Revolutionary War. The defects became more apparent after the Revolutionary War when the states no longer felt the need to work together to face the threat of the common enemy. The Articles had five major defects related to taxing power, an executive official, commerce, amendment, and the power to maintain domestic order.

- **Taxing**. The national government did not have the power to tax, which meant that congress (the main institution of the national government) had to beg the states to pay for the war and other government functions. It is hard today to imagine a government without the power to tax.

- **Executive**. The Articles did not provide a chief executive. The Revolutionary War was fought against a monarchy (an executive figure), and the natural reaction of the Founders was to create a new political system which did not have a single leader or executive figure who could become a monarch. The Declaration of

Independence lists the colonists' grievances against King George. The Revolutionary War was fought against a monarch who was accused of tyrannical abuse of power. It was logical for the Founders to create a form of government where a representative body, a legislative institution more closely identified with democratic government, had the most power.

- **Commerce**. The Articles did not give the national government power much economic power. The states had power to regulate interstate and foreign commerce. Some states enacted laws which benefited economic interests in their state and discriminated against out of state or foreign business interests. These kinds of economic protectionist legislation limited trade. States could also coin money. Critics eventually saw state power over commerce and economics as a barrier to the development of a national economy and advocated giving the national government power over interstate and foreign commerce.

- **Amendment**. One of the most important challenges facing any political system is how to provide for change in response to different economic, social, or political circumstances. The Articles could be amended only by unanimous consent of congress and the state legislatures. This made it very difficult if not impossible for the government to adapt to circumstances that it faced.

- **Domestic Order**. Because power was decentralized, the national government did not have power to act to ensure domestic tranquility and order. Maintaining good public order is one of basic responsibilities of any government. The national government's ineffectual response to domestic disturbances such as Shays' Rebellion and secessionist movements in some parts of the country exposed the weakness of the national government under the Articles.

The most famous of these domestic threats to public order were armed marches in Massachusetts. In the fall of 1786 and winter of 1787, Daniel Shays, a Revolutionary War veteran, lead around 1500 supporters on an armed march to stop mortgage foreclosures. Economic conditions were bad. High state taxes and high interest rates caused farmers to face bankruptcy and mortgage foreclosures. Shays and his supporters marched on the government to demand that it provide them with some relief from the bad economic conditions. The State of Massachusetts appealed to the national government for help in putting down **Shays' Rebellion**, but the national government could not act without the consent of the other states, which rejected the request for money to establish a national army. Order was finally restored when the governor of Massachusetts called out the state militia.

A scene at Springfield, during Shay's Rebellion, when the mob
attempted to prevent the holding of the Courts of Justice
—E. Benjamin Andrews, 1895

Shays' Rebellion alarmed government officials and political leaders who believed the national government needed to be given more power to respond to such threats to good public order. A constitutional convention was held in the summer of 1787 to "revise" the Articles of Confederation to correct its defects. However, the delegates to the convention decided to abolish the Articles of Confederation and create a new form of government. After lively debate, the delegates drafted a new constitution which created a new system of government, a federal republic with a stronger national government. Modern Americans tend to forget the central role that Shays' and other "unruly" individuals played in the creation of the republic. (Holton 2007) Radical popular action has been a part of the American political experience and tradition from the founding of the republic, through the civil war fought to preserve the union, to modern efforts to create a government that is responsive to the people.

2.5 | U.S. Constitution

Although the delegates to the Constitutional Convention met in secret, the records of the convention debates reveal lively debates about what form of government to create. The convention debates and the subsequent debates over ratification of the new constitution were generally organized as a debate between the Federalists and the Anti-federalists. The Federalists supported ratification because they believed that the country needed a stronger national government. Their arguments for ratification were made in a series of famous essays written by James Madison, Alexander Hamilton, and John Jay called The Federalist Papers. The Anti-federalists opposed ratification of the Constitution because they believed that it gave the national government too much power. They preferred a political union where the states had more power. The Anti-federalists tend to be overlooked because they lost the argument. The Constitution was ratified. But the Anti-federalist Papers are worth reading in an era when American politics includes criticism of the size of the federal government.

The Declaration of Independence and the Constitution were written for two very different purposes. The Declaration is a philosophical defense of a people's right to overthrow an unjust government. The Constitution is a practical, working document that was written to create a more effective form of government. The Preamble of the Constitution states that "We, the people…" establish the Constitution "in order to form a more perfect Union, establish justice, insure domestic tranquility, provide for the common defense, promote the general welfare, and secure the blessings of liberty to ourselves and our posterity…" The Constitution created a new form of government, a "more perfect Union" that was more capable of accomplishing the things that the people expect government to do. Alexander Hamilton explained this purpose in Federalist *Number One*:

> AFTER an unequivocal experience of the inefficiency of the subsisting federal government, you are called upon to deliberate on a new Constitution for the United States of America. The subject speaks its own importance; comprehending in its consequences nothing less than the existence of the UNION, the safety and welfare of the parts of which it is composed, the fate of an empire in many respects the most interesting in the world.

Considering the passionate motives of those who supported or opposed the new Constitution, Hamilton worried that a spirit of self-righteous passion would make compromise and cooperation difficult, and that the intolerant spirit would tempt one side to attempt to dominate the other side by physical force rather than the force of argument. In *To Secure These Rights: The Declaration of Independence and Constitutional Interpretation* (1995), Douglas Gerber argues that the purpose of the Constitution was to effectuate or make possible the Lockean liberal principles that were asserted in the *Declaration of Independence*. The *Declaration* asserted the existence of certain unalienable or natural rights; the Constitution created a system of constitutional government that provided the means to achieve the rights and protect them.

The main body of the Constitution establishes the basic framework of government. It provides for a republican system of government; elections and representation; and it grants and limits the powers of government. Article I provides the powers of the legislative branch. Article II provides the powers of the executive branch. Article III provides the powers of the judicial branch. The first ten amendments to the Constitution, commonly referred to as the Bill of Rights, provide for individual rights. The Bill of Rights includes important limits on the powers of government.

2.51 | *Three Functions of the Constitution*

The U.S. Constitution does three things. It establishes the basic framework of the government; it allocates government powers; and it declares or guarantees individual rights.

Establish the basic framework of government. The Constitution creates a **republican** form of government, a **federal** system of government, and a system of government with the **separation of powers**. A republic is a type of democracy. It is an indirect democracy. Elected representatives make public policy for the people. The people control government by electing government officials.

A federal system is a two-tiered system of government where power is divided between a central government—the national or federal government—and the regional or state governments. Federalism is a *geographic* division of power between the national government and the state governments. The actual division of powers is specific in some areas of public policy. For instance, the national government has exclusive power over interstate commerce, coining money, foreign affairs, and declaring war. But there are other areas of public policy where both the national and state governments make policy. These include crime, education, the environment, and taxes. The division has also changed over time as the federal government became involved with more and more areas of public policy. Federalism is part of the system of institutional checks and balances whereby the national and state governments check one another's powers.

The separation of powers is the functional division of power among the legislative, executive, and judicial branches of government. The separation of powers was created for two reasons. The first reason is the system of institutional checks and balances. Dividing power among three branches was intended to prevent the concentration of power in the hands of one individual or one institution. The separation of powers is often cited as evidence that the Founders intended to create an inefficient system of government.

The three branches were not intended to be completely independent of one another. The French political philosopher Montesquieu, who was the main inspiration for the tripartite separation of powers, believed that each branch had to be sufficiently independent of the others so that one branch could not create, or abolish, any other branch, but not completely separate of each another. The system of institutional jealousy depends on some overlap so that each branch will guard against another branch poaching on its turf. Congress' power to enact laws can be checked by the president's veto. The president's veto can be overridden by a two-thirds majority vote in both houses of congress. The president is delegated power as commander-in-chief, but only congress has the power to declare war and to raise and support an army. The president has the power to nominate federal judges, ambassadors, and other high government officials, but the nominations must be confirmed by the Senate. And the Supreme Court has final authority to strike down both legislative and presidential acts as unconstitutional. The president nominates federal judges but they must be confirmed by the Senate. Congress determines the federal judiciary's budget and the organization of the federal court system. Over time, the president has become such an important participant in the legislative process that it is common today to refer to *the administration's budget* or *the administration's bill* or even presidential legislation (e.g., executive orders). In order to understand how government works today, it is necessary to understand presidential legislation and judicial policy making, two terms that the separation of powers did not originally provide for.

The second reason for the separation of powers is that it contributes to good governance. The Founders considered the separation of powers a modern, innovative, political scientific contribution to good government. In *Federalist 47*, Madison praised the "celebrated" Montesquieu for popularizing the "invaluable precept in the science of politics." Each of the three branches is designed with a special institutional competence that makes a unique contribution to good government. Congress is designed as a representative institution that makes laws. The presidency is designed for both decisive action in emergencies and to fairly implement the laws passed by Congress. The judiciary is well-designed to decide conflicts involving the interpretation of the laws. The legislative branch's institutional competence is **representation** of districts, states, and interests, deliberation, negotiation, and ultimately compromise to make laws for the nation. The executive branch's institutional competence is **action**, the ability to act swiftly when needed, and the just **administration** of the laws passed by Congress. The executive is to ensure that the laws passed by Congress are uniformly applied, not enforced selectively against the minority party, racial or ethnic minorities, or the political opponents of the people who made the laws. The judiciary's institutional competence is **dispute resolution**. This includes both conducting trials and interpreting the laws when there are legal disputes about what the laws mean.

> Think About It!
> Was the separation of powers intended to make government *inefficient*, or was it intended to make government *better*?

The Founders intended the legislative branch to make laws, the executive to carry them out, and the judicial branch to interpret the laws. But this is not exactly the way the system works. The modern national government does have three separate institutions but they actually share *law making* power. For instance, the terms *presidential legislation* and *legislating from the bench* are commonly used to describe what the modern presidency and judiciary actually do. Descriptions of how the modern government works typically include legislative policymaking, executive policymaking, and judicial policymaking.

The study of comparative government and politics reveals that the separation of powers is not essential for democracy. Modern democracies include presidential government and parliamentary government. The separation of powers is more common to presidential systems than parliamentary systems. Parliamentary systems typically fuse the legislative and executive powers by making the prime minister—the executive governing officer—an elected member of the legislative body or parliament. In parliamentary systems, one institution, the elected legislature or parliament, is the supreme governing body; the other institutions (the prime minister or the courts) are inferior to it. In separation of powers, each branch is largely independent of the other branches in the sense that the other branches are not created by, or dependent on, another branch for its existence. Congress cannot abolish the judiciary; the president cannot abolish congress. In parliamentary systems where the legislative and executive powers are fused, the people typically elect the members of the representative assembly (i.e., the parliament), who then select the prime minister from among the body's members. The fact that a prime minister is selected by the legislative body, and is an elected member of that body, fuses rather than separates institutional power.

In the U.S., Congress does not select the president, and the president is not a member of congress. The president is selected independent of Congress. In a parliamentary system, the tenure of a prime minister selected by a legislature is likely to end when the term of the legislature ends and a new parliament selects a new executive. In a presidential system the executive's term may or may not coincide with the legislature's term. The legislative and executive powers can be informally fused by party loyalty. Party loyalty means that members of Congress may be more loyal to a president of their party than to Congress. Party loyalty can undermine the system of institutional checks and balances.

Allocate Power. The second function of a Constitution is to allocate power. The Constitution *both* grants *and* limits government powers. The main grants of power to the national government are provided in Article I (legislative), Article II (executive), and Article III (judicial). Article one I, Section 8 provides a list of powers delegated to Congress. The main limits on the power of the national government are provided in the Bill of Rights. The challenge when writing a constitution is to strike the right balance between granting and limiting government power: a government that is too weak can be ineffectual or result in a failed state; a government that is too strong can threaten individual liberty.

Guarantee Individual Rights (or Freedoms). The third function of a constitution is to provide for individual rights. The U.S. Constitution, the 50 state constitutions, and the constitutions of other countries include provisions declaring or guaranteeing rights. In the U.S. Constitution, the Bill of Rights provides for freedom of speech, religion, and press, as well as providing protection against unreasonable search and seizure, due process of law, the right to a trial by jury, and protection against cruel and unusual punishment. These constitutionally protected rights are sometimes called civil liberties. Civil liberties are distinct from civil rights, which is a term that usually refers to individual rights that are provided in legislation rather than the Constitution.

Civil Liberties are the constitutional rights that limit the government's power to restrict individual freedom. Civil liberties are often called individual rights or individual liberties because they limit government power over individuals. Civil liberties include the First Amendment guarantees of freedom of religion, speech, and press; the Second Amendment right to keep and bear arms; the Fourth Amendment right against unreasonable search and seizure; the Fifth Amendment guarantee of due process of law; the Eighth Amendment prohibition against cruel and unusual punishment; and the Fourteenth Amendment guarantee of equal protection of the laws. Some of the most important civil liberties provisions are described in very general language: the protection against unreasonable search and seizure; the guarantee of due process of law; and the prohibition against cruel and unusual punishment. The meanings of these vague words are not precise. People disagree about their meaning. As a result, conflicts between individuals who claim a civil liberties freedom from government restriction and government claims that they have the power to restrict the freedom are often decided by the Supreme Court.

The term *civil rights* is often used generically to refer to individual rights and individual liberties. But there are two significant differences between civil liberties and civil rights. First, civil rights are statutory rights. They are provided in legislation, not the Constitution. Second, civil rights protect individuals against discrimination. Civil rights laws promote equality by prohibiting discrimination on the basis of race, gender, religion, ethnicity, or some other status or characteristic. Two examples of landmark civil rights laws are the 1964 Civil Rights and the 1965 Voting Rights Act.

2.52 | *Bill of Rights*

When the Constitution was submitted to the states for ratification, it did not include a provision declaring or guaranteeing individual rights. The Federalists, who supported the Constitution, argued that a bill of rights was unnecessary because the powers of the newly formed national government were so carefully limited that individual rights did not have to be specifically mentioned in the Constitution. In fact, some Federalists argued that adding a bill of rights could actually be dangerous because listing specific individual rights that the government could *not* limit would inevitably be interpreted to mean that the government *could limit* any rights that were not actually mentioned in the bill of rights. Nevertheless, legislators in some states threatened to withhold ratification of the Constitution unless a bill of rights was added to the document.

The Anti-federalist George Mason, a constitutional convention delegate from Virginia, opposed the new constitution because it did not include a bill of rights. The Anti-federalist worries that the new constitution created a stronger national government but did not include a bill of rights threatened the ratification of the Constitution. In order to ease Anti-federalist worries, a bill of rights was proposed to limit the power of the national government. The first ten amendments were based on Mason's *Virginia Declaration of Rights*. In 1789, the First Congress of the United States adopted the first ten amendments to the Constitution. These amendments were ratified by the required number of states in 1791. The following is an edited version of the first ten amendments to the Constitution (the Bill of Rights):

First Amendment: *"Congress shall make no law respecting an establishment of religion, or prohibiting the free exercise thereof; or abridging the freedom of the speech, or of the press....."*

Second Amendment: *"A well-regulated Militia, being necessary to the security of a free State, the right of the people to keep and bear Arms, shall not be infringed."*

Fourth Amendment: *"The right of the people to be secure in their persons, houses, papers, and effects, against unreasonable searches and seizures, shall not be violated...."*

Fifth Amendment: *"No person shall...be subject for the same offence to be twice put in jeopardy of life or limb, nor shall be compelled in any criminal case to be a witness against himself, nor be deprived of life, liberty, or property, without due process of law; nor shall private property be taken for public use, without just compensation."*

Sixth Amendment: *"In all criminal prosecutions, the accused shall enjoy the right to a speedy and public trial, by an impartial jury of the State and district wherein the crime shall have been committed.....and to have the assistance of counsel for his defence."*

Seventh Amendment: *"In suits at common law, where the value in controversy shall exceed twenty dollars, the right of trial by jury shall be preserved..."*

Eighth Amendment: *"Excessive bail shall not be required, nor excessive fines imposed, nor cruel and unusual punishment inflicted."*

Ninth Amendment: *"The enumeration in the Constitution, of certain rights, shall not be construed to deny or disparage others retained by the people."*

Tenth Amendment: *"The powers not delegated to the United States by the Constitution, nor prohibited by it to the States, are reserved to the States respectively, or to the people"*

Until 2008, the Supreme Court had interpreted the Second Amendment as guaranteeing the states the power to maintain a well-regulated militia. As such, the Second Amendment was read as a *federalism* amendment: it protected the states from the federal government—particularly its military power. In *District of Columbia v. Heller*, the Supreme Court ruled that the Second Amendment guaranteed an individual right to keep and bear arms. As a result, the right to keep and bear arms has now been added to the list of civil liberties that individuals and organizations, such as the National Rifle Association, can use to challenge gun control and other regulatory policies enacted by the federal, state, or local governments.

Most of the provisions in the Bill of Rights apply to criminal justice. They list specific rights. The Ninth Amendment is different. It was added to the bill of rights to ease Anti-federalist worries that *not* listing a right mean that the right did not exist. What if the men who made up the list forgot to include a basic right? What if a future generation considered a right a fundamental right? The Ninth Amendment was intended as a statement that the Bill of Rights should not be read as an exhaustive list.

2.53 | Civil Rights and Civil Liberties

The relationship between religion and politics is one of the most controversial issues in American politics. During the colonial era, government and politics had explicitly religious purposes. The *First Charter of Virginia* (1606), the *Mayflower Compact* (1620), and *The Book of the General Lawes and Libertyes Concerning the Inhabitants of the Massachusetts* (1648), for example, describe government and politics as organized efforts to make people moral—as defined by organized religious beliefs. Some colonies had an established church—an officially recognized and government supported church. Massachusetts established the Congregational Church as the official church and some southern colonies established the Anglican Church as the official religion. Over time, the colonies moved away from establishing an official denomination and toward establishing Christianity or Protestantism.

The Constitution changed the relationship between church and state—or at least the relationship between religion and the federal government. Article VI of the Constitution provides that "no religious Test shall ever be required as a Qualification to any Office or public Trust under the United States." More important, the First Amendment prohibits Congress from making any law "respecting an establishment of religion or prohibiting the free exercise" of religion. The First Amendment guarantees freedom of religion, which includes the right of individuals and organizations to actively participate in politics, but it limits government support for religion. Political and constitutional debates involve providing public aid to religious schools, policies allowing or requiring organized prayer in public schools, religious displays of the Ten Commandments or crèches in public places, laws related to the teaching of evolution or creation science, and legislating morality. Civil liberties claims have been made to challenge the constitutionality of using law to promote morality by regulating obscenity, to prohibit certain sexual behavior, and to define marriage as a relationship between one man and one woman.

2.6 | Constitutionalism

This chapter began with an acknowledgement that having a constitution is today almost universally accepted as the best form of government. But having a document called a constitution does not mean that a political system is committed to constitutional government. Constitutionalism refers to the public and government officials' commitment to the values that are expressed in the Constitution. Without the commitment, a constitution is merely paper or words without much to back them up. With the commitment, a constitution acquires real political and legal force. Americans have an especially strong commitment to the Constitution. Support for the Constitution remains strong even in tough times of economic hardships, domestic disorder, or national security threats. In contrast, public support for the government varies a great deal, and in fact support for government institutions has declined over time. The enduring appeal of the Constitution and the belief in the founding values that are embodied in it (e.g., freedom; limited government; equality) remain a political constant even in times of great political change, conflict, and even turmoil. What explains the enduring appeal of the Constitution?

One explanation is that the enduring public support reflects a general commitment to the Constitution or to constitutional government rather than support for specific provisions of the Constitution or particular interpretations of them. This explanation is supported by studies of public opinion that reveal consistently low levels of knowledge about what is actually in the Constitution. A public opinion survey conducted by the Constitution Center revealed surprisingly low levels of public knowledge about the Constitution: less than five percent of the American public could correctly answer even basic questions about the constitution.

The consistently high levels of public support for the Constitution do not mean there is general consensus about *what* specific provisions of the Constitution actually mean. In fact, the general consensus supporting the Constitution masks political conflict about what specific provisions of the Constitution mean and how to interpret them. For instance, both conservatives and liberals profess support for the Constitution and the values embodied in it. But they consistently disagree about the government's criminal justice powers, its economic regulatory powers, its moral regulatory powers, and its war powers. For instance, both sides in the debates about the role of religion in American government and politics appeal to the Constitution as supporting their side of the debate about school prayer.

Liberals and conservatives also disagree about *how* the Constitution should be interpreted. A Pew Research survey of public opinion about the Constitution revealed major differences between conservatives and liberals, an ideological divide that was so wide that it was described as a chasm. Conservatives believe the Constitution should be interpreted according to the original meaning of the words or the original intentions of those who wrote them. Liberals believe that the Constitution should be interpreted according to contemporary societal expectations. These differences reflect the tension between continuity and change, between adhering to certain beliefs and changing with the times. Particularly during hard times or times of crisis, conservatives are apt to blame political problems on departing the republic's political and constitutional founding values, and to call for a return to them as the solution to the problems.

2.61 | *Relationship between the Constitution and the Political System*

The relationship between the political system that was established by the Constitution and modern governance is both interesting and complicated. Public opinion reflects such strong support for the Constitution *and* such strong criticism of the government that it could be said that Americans love the Constitution but hate the government (that it created). Although it may seem surprising, venerating the Constitution can create governance problems. Reverence for the Constitution can create problems. Take, for example, constitutionalists. Constitutionalists believe the Constitution should be strictly or literally interpreted. Some religious constitutionalists believe that the Constitution was a divinely-inspired document. The belief that a document is divinely-inspired makes reasoned political analysis, including assessment of the problems of modern governance, difficult. Secular constitutionalists merely believe that the Constitution should be strictly interpreted. Some of the individuals who call themselves constitutionalists are advocates of the Tenth Amendment. The motto of these "Tenthers" is *"The Constitution. Every Issue. Every Time. No Exceptions, no Excuses."* These constitutionalists believe the solution to the nation's problems is to return to the *original* Constitution, not the Constitution as it has come to be understood. This is one of the main points of the Tea Party movement.

Political and legal scholars disagree about whether the nation's problems can be solved by returning to the original understanding of the Constitution and how the government was intended to work. Appeals to return to "the" Founders views are misleading insofar as it presumes that there was one, single, unified voice. At a minimum there were basic differences between the Federalists and the Anti-federalists.

The bicentennial of the Constitution in 1987 produced a number of scholarly works that identified governance problems that could be traced to the Constitution, and recommended constitutional reforms to create "a more workable government."[3] Constitutionalists and some conservatives reject the argument that the constitutional design of government is flawed or that modern challenges require modernizing the Constitution. Those who advocate change write in the Jeffersonian tradition.

2.62 | *Should Laws, Like Food Products, Have Expiration Dates?*

Thomas Jefferson argued that laws, including the Constitution, should have sunset provisions. He thought that laws should last only twenty years—the lifespan of a generation—because one generation should not bind a succeeding generation. No society "can make a perpetual constitution, or even a perpetual law," because just as the earth "belongs always to the living generation," people are masters "of their own persons, and consequently may govern them as they please." The constitution and laws "naturally expire at the end of 19 years." the life span of a generation. Laws that are enforced longer are enforced as "an act of force, and not of right." Jefferson did not think that the problem of one generation binding another could be solved by claiming that each succeeding generation's decision not to repeal a law was tacit consent to it. This tacit consent might apply if the form of government "were so perfectly contrived that the will of the majority could always be obtained fairly and without impediment." But no form of government is perfect. Representation is likely to be "unequal and vicious," various checks limit proposed legislation, factions control government bodies and bribery corrupts them, and personal interests cause government officials lose sight of "the general interests of their constituents." So practically speaking, "a law of limited duration is much more manageable" than one that needs to be repealed.[4]

This chapter began by describing references to the Constitution as a sacred text. Sanford Levinson is a legal scholar who is very critical of the constitutional design of American government. He also thinks that venerating the founding era and the system of government created by the Constitution is, ironically, not in keeping with the founding values of the republic. In "Our Imbecilic Constitution," Levinson reminds us that the authors of the *Federalist Papers* advocated ratification of the new Constitution by "mock[ing] the 'imbecility' of the weak central government created by the Articles of Confederation." Levinson scolds those who call the modern American political system "dysfunctional, even pathological" but fail to even mention the Constitution's role "in generating the pathology." According to Levinson, slavery, the Senate system of providing equal representation to North Dakota and California, the Electoral College, and the separation of powers, all created problems—but "the worst single part of the Constitution…is surely Article V, which has made our Constitution among the most difficult to amend of any in the world." Amendment is so difficult that the mere discussion of possible reforms is considered a waste of time. He considers it unfortunate that "most contemporary Americans" have lost the ability to "think seriously" about whether the Constitution's provisions for governance still serve us very well" and instead "envelope" the Constitution "in near religious veneration."

Levinson blames the modern dysfunctional government on the decision to make the Constitution so hard to amend. Most of the 50 state constitutions are much easier to amend—fourteen states give the voters the opportunity call a constitutional convention at regular intervals; there have been more than 230 state constitutional conventions, and "each state has had an average of almost three constitutions." Levinson describes the framers' "willingness to critique, indeed junk, the Articles of Confederation" truly admirable, and he thinks that "we are long overdue for a serious discussion about [the Constitution's] own role in creating the depressed (and depressing) state of American politics."[5]

2.63 | Continuity and Change

The U.S. Constitution is the world's *oldest* continuing governing document and it is a very *brief* document. The Constitution's longevity is related to its brevity. The Constitution has lasted as long as it has partly because it is such a short document. It is a short document that is filled with general phrases describing government and politics. The Preamble declares its purpose as "to form a more perfect Union" and "establish Justice." creating "a more perfect Union." Article I gives Congress power to use whatever means "necessary and proper" to accomplish the things that Congress has power to do. The Bill of Rights has especially memorable but flowery phrases. The 5th Amendment prohibits government from denying any person **due process of law**. The 4th Amendment prohibits **unreasonable searches and seizures**. The 8th Amendment prohibits **cruel and unusual punishment**. These general provisions of the Constitution allow for, or perhaps require, interpretation to give them concrete meaning, interpretation to determine how they are to be applied in specific instances. Interpretation is a way to informally change the meaning of the Constitution—to accommodate change without requiring formal amendment or an entirely new constitution. The short and general Constitution has endured for more than 200 years with only 27 amendments—and the first ten amendments were adopted as the bill of rights in 1791. This means that the Constitution has undergone only minimal formal changes despite more than two centuries of major political, economic, social, technological, and scientific changes.

Which raises a question: Is the Constitution, an Eighteenth Century document, still relevant to Twenty-first Century government and politics? It is. But the informal accommodation to reflect change means that it is no longer possible to read the Constitution to understand how modern American government and politics actually work. The following are just some of the major political developments that are not even mentioned in the Constitution.

- **Political Parties**. The Constitution does not say anything about political parties even though parties play a central role in politics and government. Parties have also changed the way the Electoral College works.
- **Corporations**. The Constitution does not say anything about corporations even though they are important economic organizations that the Supreme Court has said are "persons" for the purposes of the Fourteenth Amendment.
- **The Fed**. The Constitution does not say anything about the Federal Reserve Board even though "the Fed" is a very important government body with control over monetary policy.
- **The Fourth Branch**. The Constitution creates three branches of government but the development of the federal bureaucracy has created a fourth branch of government.
- **Presidential Government**. The Founders created a system based on legislative government but presidential power expanded over time and the system developed into presidential government.
- **Presidential Legislation**. This term applies to, among other things, executive orders and executive agreements as forms of presidential lawmaking.
- **Judicial Review**. The Constitution does not explicitly give courts the power of judicial review, but this implied power to review the acts of other government officials to determine whether they are constitutional has greatly expanded the power of courts.
- **The Congressional Committee System**. It is impossible to understand how Congress works without describing the committee system and the party leadership system.
- **The Sole Organ Doctrine**. This doctrine is one of the key concepts for understanding the modern president's role in foreign affairs and national security policy.
- **A National-centered System**. The Founders created a state-centered political system, but the government has developed into a national-centered system.

> Think About It!
> Can a person read the Constitution to get a good understanding of how American government and politics work today?

> Act on It!
> Contact a local, state, or national government official (e.g., your member of Congress), and ask them whether they support any constitutional amendments.

2.7 | Comparative Constitutional Law

One way to better understand the U.S. Constitution is to compare it to other constitutions. The constitutions of the 50 states are very different than the U.S. Constitution. Among other things, the state constitutions are much younger, longer and more detailed than the U.S. Constitution. The constitutions of other countries are even more varied. The ready electronic access to the constitutions of other countries makes it easy to compare the constitutions of the countries of the world. Reading a country's constitution to determine what form of government the country has, and to determine what civil rights and liberties it includes, provides insights into the political history of a nation. It is especially interesting to compare the civil rights and liberties provisions in the newer constitutions with those of older constitutions such as the U.S. Constitution because the U.S. played an important role in writing the constitutions of Germany and Japan after World War I and, more recently, the constitutions of Iraq and Afghanistan.

2.8 | Summary

This chapter examines the origins and development of the U.S. system of constitutional government. It includes the various factors that fostered colonial independence and the subsequent development of American government and politics, and the system of civil liberties and civil rights. Two main themes are the tension in American political culture between granting and limiting power, and the tension between *continuity* (preserving the original understanding of the Constitution and the founding era values) and *change* (adapting to the political, social, economic, and technological conditions of the times). One aspect of self-government is thinking about the system of government and politics so that the general public, as informed citizens, can answer two basic questions. How is it working for us? How can we help to form "a more perfect Union?"

2.9 | Additional Resources

2.91 | INTERNET SOURCES:

Primary documents are available at
http://www.loc.gov/rr/program/bib/ourdocs/Constitution.html

Montesquieu. *The Spirit of the Laws.* http://www.constitution.org/cm/sol.htm

Paine, Thomas. 1776. *Common Sense*
http://www.ushistory.org/paine/commonsense/singlehtml.htm

Rutherford, Samuel. 1644. *Lex Rex: Law Is King, or The Law & The Prince.*
http://www.lonang.com/exlibris/rutherford/

The Constitution of the Commonwealth of Massachusetts
http://www.netstate.com/states/government/ma_government.htm

The First Charter of Virginia (1606)
http://www.lonang.com/exlibris/organic/1606-fcv.htm

The Mayflower Compact (1620)
http://avalon.law.yale.edu/17th_century/mayflower.asp

The Charter of Massachusetts Bay (1629)
http://avalon.law.yale.edu/17th_century/mass03.asp

The Lawes and Libertyes of Massachusetts (1648)
http://www.commonlaw.com/Mass.html

The National Constitution Center: http://www.constitutioncenter.org/

The constitutions of countries of the world: www.constitution.org/cons/natlcons.htm

2.92 | IN THE LIBRARY

Amar, Akhil Reed. 2005. *America's Constitution: A Biography.* New York: Random House.

Beard, Charles. 1913. *An Economic Interpretation of the Constitution of the United States.* New York: Macmillan.

Berkin. Carol. 2003. *A Brilliant Solution: Inventing the American Constitution.* New York : Harcourt.

Bowler, Shaun and Todd Donovan. 2001. *Demanding Choices and Direct Democracy.* Ann Arbor, MI: University of Michigan Press.

Breyer, Stephen. 2006. *Active Liberty: Interpreting our Democratic Constitution.*

Dicey, Robert A. and Albert Venn. 1895. *Law of the Constitution.* 9th Edition, 1950. London: MacMillan.

Gerber, Douglas. 1995. *To Secure These Rights: The Declaration of Independence and Constitutional Interpretation.* New York: New York University Press.

Holton, Woody Holton. 2007. *Unruly Americans and the Origins of the Constitution.* New York: Hill and Wang.

Ketcham, Ralph. 2003. *The Anti-Federalist Papers and the Constitutional Convention Debates.* Signet Classics.

Kyvig, David E. 1998. *Explicit and Authentic Acts: Amending the U.S. Constitution, 1776- 1995.* University Press of Kansas.

Maier, Pauline. 1997. *American Scripture: Making the Declaration of Independence.* New York: Knopf.

KEY TERMS:

Constitutions
Rule of Law
Mercantilism
The triangle trade
Seven Years War
The Sugar Act
The Stamp Act
Mutiny Act
The Townshend Acts
The Coercive Acts
Confederation
Shays' Rebellion
A republican system of government
Federalism
Separation of powers
Checks and balances
The Bill of Rights

[1] "American Scripture," *God in America* (2010). PBS Frontline. http://www.pbs.org/godinamerica/american-scripture/.

[2] A repository of these historical documents is available at http://avalon.law.yale.edu/

[3] See, for example, *A Workable Government? The Constitution after 200 Years*. 1987. Ed. by Burke Marshall. New York: W.W. Norton & Company; *Reforming American Government: The Bicentennial Papers of the Committee on the Constitutional System*.1985. Ed. by Donald L. Robinson. Boulder, CO: Westview Press.

[4] Letter to James Madison," (September 6, 1789) In *The Papers of Thomas Jefferson*, Edited by Julian P. Boyd, et al. Princeton: Princeton University Press. 1950. http://press-pubs.uchicago.edu/founders/documents/v1ch2s23.html

[5] Sanford Levinson, "Our Imbecilic Constitution," *The New York Times* (May 8, 2012). Accessed at www.nytimes.com

CHAPTER 3: CONGRESS

3.0 | Congress

Congress has been called the *broken branch* of government. Public opinion polls that consistently indicate lower levels of confidence in Congress than almost all other government and non-government institutions are evidence the Congress is an institution that *everyone loves to hate*. Congress is called the broken branch of government because nothing seems to make Congress less capable of action than the need for action. The only reason there are more lawyer jokes than congressmen jokes is there are so many more lawyers than members of Congress. Why does the modern Congress get so little respect? During the early years of the republic, representative institutions such as Congress were considered part of the modern trend toward democracy as a progressive alternative to monarchy. The 19th Century Senate was considered the greatest deliberative body in the world! What changed? Congress still sometimes debates important issues, but the rhetoric rarely rises to the level of greatness. Congressional speeches are usually delivered to an almost empty chamber where the speaker talks to a camera that delivers the message to the speaker's home state, district, or political party. The televised congressional hearings that attract public attention more closely resemble Kabuki theatre than good lawmaking. Kabuki theatre is highly stylized stage drama performed by actors wearing elaborate make-up and costumes. Calling televised congressional hearings Kabuki theatre, because the hearings are posturing and posing rather than substantive lawmaking, is actually an insult to Kabuki theatre, an ancient stage tradition.

Former Attorney General Loretta Lynch began her career in the 1990s as an Assistant U.S. Attorney in Brooklyn. Speaking at a dinner for alums of that office, Lynch said that her priorities as Attorney General came from ideals shaped by her experiences in the Brooklyn office. After reminding the audience that the Department of Justice is "the only Cabinet agency named after an ideal," she said that testifying before Congress "made me wistful for my days in Brooklyn in interview rooms, talking to murderers and getting honest answers."[1] Why is testifying before Congress compared unfavorably with interviewing or interrogating murderers? Why can Congress be insulted by complimenting it for being a perfectly good 19th Century institution!

Did Congress decline—and public opinion merely reflect its decline? Or did changes in public opinion cause Congress to change? The argument presented in this chapter explains the fact of congressional decline as primarily caused by a major, long-term shift in thinking about government—a shift away from legislative governance toward executive (presidential) governance. The chapter focuses on the following issues:

- The **Power Problem** with Congress. Individual members of Congress and Congress as an institution are more accountable than effective. As a result, power has flowed to institutions that are generally considered more effective for governance.
- The **Functions** of Congress. The political development of the American system of government includes major changes in Congress's roles.
- The **Organization** of Congress. The internal organization of Congress—particularly bicameralism, the committee system, and the party structure—affects what Congress does well and what it does not do very well.

3.1 | The Power Problem

The power problem is the need to **grant** government enough power to effectively address the problems that people expect government to solve, while also **limiting** power so that it can be held accountable. A successful government is one that strikes the right balance between granting and limiting power. The main power problem with Congress is effectiveness: Congress is often unable to get anything done. Congress has been called "the broken branch" of government because the public and many political scientists consider it an inefficient or ineffective institution. Congress has plenty of critics. Public opinion polls generally reflect that the public does not hold Congress in very high regard because Congress does not seem to be making much headway toward solving the nation's problems. Congress ranks low in measures of public confidence in institutional effectiveness. This is not surprising because Congress is not designed to be an especially effective institution. It is designed as a representative institution where different interests and perspectives are represented, and decision-making requires negotiating, bargaining, and compromise. These democratic values (representation, bargaining, and compromise) are sometimes at odds with effective or decisive action.

> Think about It!
> Are members of Congress sophomoric? Are they smarter than a 5th grader? Analysis of speech patterns indicates that they *talk* like 10th graders
> http://www.npr.org/blogs/itsallpolitics/2012/05/21/153024432/sophomoric-members-of-congress-talk-like-10th-graders-analysis-shows

GALLUP 2010 Confidence Poll; "Now I am going to read you a list of institutions in American society. Please tell me how much confidence you, yourself, have in each one–a great deal, quite a lot, some, or a little.

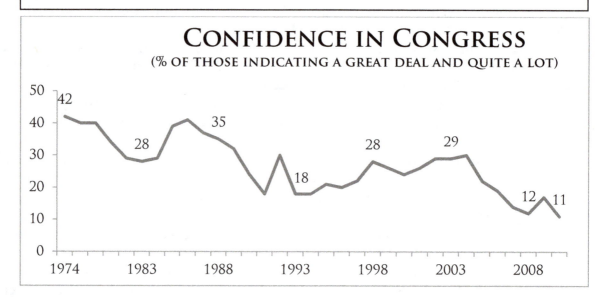

Are members of Congress smarter than tenth graders? A study of congressional speeches on the floor of the House and Senate concluded that the level of speech was at the tenth grade level— *and declining*! Descriptions of "sophomoric" talk do not instill public confidence in Congress.

3.2 | Change over Time

Congress' role in the U.S. system of government has changed a great deal over time. Congress does not play the same role that it did during the founding era. The Founders made Congress **the** law-making branch of the federal government. Article I Section I of the Constitution provides that "all legislative Powers herein granted shall be vested in a Congress of the United States, which shall consist of a Senate and House of Representatives." Congress was intended to be the *first branch* of government in the sense that it was intended to be the primary branch of the federal government. Congress was the most powerful (and therefore also the most dangerous) branch of government.

The political experiences of the Founders made it logical for them to create a political system where the legislative branch was most powerful. The Revolutionary War was fought against a monarchy. Many of the Founders remained wary of executive power. And the Founders believed that the legislative branch was more democratic, that it was a republican or representative institution during a time when republican or representative government seemed to be the wave of the future. Representative government was considered modern, one of the then-recent advances in the "science" of good government.

The Founders did not create three branches of government with equal power. The legislative, executive, and judicial branches were created equal in the sense that they have the same constitutional status. The Founders created a system of legislative government, not executive government or judicial government. But as the U.S. political system developed, the presidency accumulated a great deal of power in absolute terms and relative to Congress. Congress is still the **first** branch but it is not necessarily the **primary** branch of government. The modern system has developed into a political system based on executive governance rather than legislative governance.

This change has occurred over time. The 19th Century was the golden age of representative assemblies as governing bodies. The 20th Century was not kind to representative assemblies which lost favor to executive government—particularly parliamentary systems headed by prime ministers—in most countries of the world. The decline of congressional power relative to the president is certainly one of the most importance changes in the way the U.S. system of government works. Congress is no longer "the central institution" of the national government.[2] Congress is still a powerful institution. Compared to the representative assemblies in many other countries, Congress is a powerful institution because it plays both a lawmaking and a representative role. In most modern parliamentary systems, the representative body (the parliament) is largely limited to representation, with a prime minister who actually governs the country and makes policy for the nation.

Congress still performs many important functions, but its primary role, to be the lawmaker for the nation, has diminished. The modern Congress focuses less on making laws for the nation and more on **representation** and **oversight** of the administration. Representation of constituents (i.e., individuals in the district or state) and organized interests is a very important function of individual members of Congress and Congress as an institution. The importance of legislative oversight of the administration (and the bureaucracy) has increased as Congress has delegated more and more power to the president and the size of the federal bureaucracy has increased. But the president has taken the lead in many areas of public policy making—particularly global affairs such as national defense and foreign policy but also areas of domestic policy such as fiscal policy (the setting of budget priorities).

Congress lost power relative to the executive for a broad range of reasons. One of the general reasons is related to the nature of power in the U.S. system of government.

Power is dynamic, not static. It is not a solid or fixed quantity. It is more like a liquid that flows to wherever it seems to be most effective. Power will flow to whichever *level* or government (national or state) seems more effective at addressing the problems facing the nation. And power will flow to whichever *branch* of government (legislative, executive, or judicial) which seems most effective. Or power will flow to the private sector if the public considers the private sector more effective at solving a problem than the public sector. Today, the general public sees the president as the nation's leader because the presidency seems to be a more effective institution.

3.3 | The Separation of Powers

In order to describe the way Congress works today, it is necessary to understand how the separation of powers works today. The separation of powers doctrine does not provide for a watertight separation of legislative, executive, and judicial powers. Although the Constitution delegates to Congress *all* legislative powers, Congress is not the only government body that makes laws. According to the Congress website, "The legislative branch is the law making branch of the government made up of the Senate, the House of Representatives, and agencies that support Congress." Congress is the only source of federal statutes or legislation, but there are other kinds of law, including executive orders, executive agreements, administrative regulations, and even case law. Presidents *make law* when they sign executive orders. The Supreme Court *makes law* when it interprets what the Fourth Amendment prohibition against "unreasonable searches and seizures" actually means when police officers are investigating individuals who are suspected of crimes. And administrative agencies such as the Federal Communications Commission and the Internal Revenue Service *make laws* through rulemaking actions that define indecency or determine whether a religious organization should be granted tax exempt status.

Just as the executive and judicial branches have some lawmaking powers, Congress also has powers over the other branches. The House of Representatives controls **appropriations** or the budget. Without funding, the other branches – particularly the executive branch – are hamstringed in their ability to act. The House also has the power of **impeachment**, or the formal charging of a government official with treason, bribery, other high crimes and misdemeanors. The Senate then acts as a court for the impeachment, with the Chief Justice of the Supreme Court presiding. The Senate also has the power to approve (or fail to approve) the most important of the presidential appointments, including federal judgeships, ambassadorships, and cabinet level posts. The Senate also approves all treaties. Congress also has the power to declare war.

3.4 | Constitutional Powers

Congress has two types of constitutional powers: enumerated powers and implied powers. **Enumerated powers** are those that are specifically mentioned. Enumerated powers are sometimes called delegated powers because they are powers that the Constitution actually delegates to government. **Implied powers** are those that are not specifically mentioned but which can be logically implied to flow from those that are enumerated.

3.41 | *Enumerated Powers*

The following are some of the enumerated powers granted in Article I, Section 8:

"The Congress shall have power
to lay and collect taxes, duties, imposts and excises, to pay the debts and provide for the common defense and general welfare of the United States; but all duties, imposts and excises shall be uniform throughout the United States;

To borrow money on the credit of the United States;
To regulate commerce with foreign nations, and among the several states, and with the Indian tribes;
To establish a uniform rule of naturalization, and uniform laws on the subject of bankruptcies throughout the United States;
To coin money, regulate the value thereof, and of foreign coin, and fix the standard of weights and measures;
To establish post offices and post roads;
To promote the progress of science and useful arts, by securing for limited times to authors and inventors the exclusive right to their respective writings and discoveries;
To constitute tribunals inferior to the Supreme Court;
To define and punish piracies and felonies committed on the high seas, and offenses against the law of nations;
To declare war, grant letters of marque and reprisal, and make rules concerning captures on land and water;
To raise and support armies, but no appropriation of money to that use shall be for a longer term than two years;
To provide and maintain a navy;
To make rules for the government and regulation of the land and naval forces;
To provide for calling forth the militia to execute the laws of the union, suppress insurrections and repel invasions; ... And
To make all laws which shall be necessary and proper for carrying into execution the foregoing powers, and all other powers vested by this Constitution in the government of the United States, or in any department or officer thereof."

Think about It!
The Senate must confirm presidential nominees. When did time the Senate last reject a presidential nominee to head an executive department? Or a Supreme Court nominee?

http://www.senate.gov/artandhistory/history/common/briefing/Nominations.htm

---

3.42 | *Implied Powers*

Article I Section 8 is a list of Congress's enumerated powers. The list of specifically mentioned powers ends with the **necessary and proper** clause. (See above). The necessary and proper clause has been interpreted to mean that Congress can make "all laws which shall be necessary and proper" to achieve its enumerated powers. In effect, the necessary and proper clause gives Congress power to choose the means it considers necessary to achieve its legislative ends. For example, Congress has the enumerated power to raise an army, and the implied power to use a military draft to raise the army. Congress has enumerated power to regulate commerce and coin money, and the implied power to create the Federal Reserve System and the Department of the Treasury to perform these functions. The necessary and proper clause is sometimes called **the elastic clause** because it has been interpreted very broadly to allow Congress to choose the best means to accomplish its specifically mentioned powers. Supreme Court established the precedent for broadly interpreting the necessary and proper clause to give Congress implied powers in _McCulloch v. Maryland_ (1819). This landmark case involved a legal challenge to Congress' power to charter a national bank. Congress created a national bank. Maryland taxed the Baltimore branch of the national bank. The Supreme Court was asked to decide whether Congress had the power to create a national bank and whether a state could tax a branch of the bank. Chief Justice John Marshall ruled that the power to create a national bank was an implied power that flowed from Congress' delegated powers, including the power to regulate commerce. Congress could decide whether a national bank was a "necessary and proper" way to regulate commerce. Marshall, incidentally, was a prominent member of the Federalist Party, which supported a strong national government to promote economic development. The _McCulloch_ ruling established a precedent that the Court would broadly interpret the powers of Congress. As a result, Congress today legislates on many areas of public policy that are not actually mentioned in the Constitution as grants of power.

3.5 | What Does Congress Do?

Congress has four main roles or functions:

- **Lawmaking** for the nation (legislating)

- **Representation** (of constituents and interests)

- **Legislative Oversight** (overseeing the administration and investigating scandals)

- **Constituency service** (solving constituent problems)

3.51 | _Law-making for the nation_

The Constitution delegates all legislative power to Congress. It therefore is the only branch of government that can "make laws." Both the House and the Senate must pass a bill for it to become a law but they have different roles in the law making process. For instance, tax bills must originate in the House of Representatives. This provision of the Constitution reflects the Founders' belief that decisions to tax the people should originate with the government institution that was closest to the people. The members of the House are closer to the people than members of the Senate. Members of the House are directly elected by the people to serve two-year terms. The members of the Senate were originally chosen by state legislatures and served six-year terms.

3.52 | Representation

Congress is a representative institution. The members of the House and Senate are elected representatives of the people. Congress is institutionally designed to represent geographic districts. In the House of Representatives, the legislative districts are 435 geographic areas with about 650,000 people in each district. In the Senate, the districts are the 50 states. Representation is not limited to geography. Members of Congress also represent individuals and organized interests. In a large, populous nation such as the United States, representative institutions increase *political efficacy*. Political efficacy is the belief that it is possible for a person to participate effectively in government and politics. Representative institutions are one of the ways that government is designed to be responsive to public demands and interests. Efficacy is related to the belief that individuals and organizations can have an impact on government. In the U.S. system of republican government, congress is the institution that is designed to represent the people, deliberate on public policy options, and enact make laws for the nation.

There are three theories of representation: the **delegate** theory; the **trustee** theory; and the **politico** theory. The delegate theory is that members of Congress *should* act as instructed delegates of their constituents. According to this theory, elected representatives are not free agents: representatives have a political obligation to do what their constituents want. A legislator who votes on bills based strictly on public opinion polls from the district, for example, is acting as a delegate. The trustee theory is that members of Congress *should* do what they think is in the best interest of their constituents. According to this theory, elected representatives are free agents: they can vote according to what they think is right or best regardless of public opinion in the district. A trustee uses his or her judgment when deciding how to vote on a bill, for example. A trustee does not feel obligated to vote based on public opinion polls from the district.

Studies of Congress indicate that legislators are not typically either delegates or trustees. The **politico** theory of representation suggests that representatives *are* rational actors whose voting behavior reflects the delegate or trustee theory of representation depending on the situation.

Members of Congress are expected to represent their districts. The representation of districts includes representing individuals and organized constituents such as business interests that are located in the district. Members from agricultural districts are expected to represent agricultural interests. Members from urban districts are expected to represent urban interests. Members from manufacturing districts are expected to represent manufacturing interests, and members from districts where mining, forestry, or other natural resource interests are located are expected to represent those interests. Where one industry is especially important to a district, particularly in the House of When one interest is the dominant interest in a districts, a representative may be strongly identified with that single interest. For example, Congressman Norm Dicks represents Washington State's 6th Congressional District. The 6th District includes Tacoma's port district, the Puget Sound Naval Yard and other military installations, and a number of defense contractors. One of the companies, Boeing, which is the world's largest aerospace manufacturer, was headquartered in Washington State until it relocated to Chicago.

Representative Dicks serves on three key House Appropriations Subcommittees dealing with defense, Interior and the Environment, and Military Construction/Veterans.

Representative Dicks' came to be called "The Representative from Boeing" because of his strong advocacy for Boeing. His representation of American Defense Contractors included strong opposition to the U.S. military's decision to award a major defense contract to build the new generation of airplane refueling tankers to a European and American consortium of airplane builders.

3.53 | Constituency Service

The third congressional role is related to representation. Constituency service is helping constituents solve problems that they may have with the government. All the Web sites of the members of the House of Representatives prominently list constituency service as one of the things that the member of congress does for the individuals or organizations in the district. Members of Congress maintain offices in their districts to help solve constituent problems: getting government benefits such as Social Security checks; getting Veteran's services; problems with government regulations of business; or who have kinds of problems or issues that constituents have with the government. This constituency *casework* often involves helping individuals or organizations cut through government red tape or bureaucratic procedures.

> **Act on It!**
> Contact one of your member of congress (a representative or one of your two senators) and ask them about a political issue of concern to you. How can you find a member of Congress?
> Go to the www.usa.gov
> Click on Government Agencies and Elected Officials
> Select Branches of Government; then Legislative Branch;
> Select House of Representatives or Senate.
>
> Or go to https://www.senate.gov/ and http://www.house.gov/

3.54 | Legislative Oversight

The fourth congressional role is oversight. Congress's oversight role consists of two primary functions:

- Oversight of the Laws

- Investigation of Scandals

The first oversight function is overseeing the way the laws are being administered by the president and the bureaucracy. The oversight of the laws is important because Congress makes the laws but the executive branch administers or implements the laws. Congress oversees the administration of the laws by conducting hearings to determine how public policy is being implemented, to determine whether the president is implementing the laws the way Congress intended, or to determine whether the law needs to be changed based on information about how it is working—especially whether it is working well or not. The primary method of legislative oversight is congressional hearings at which members of the executive branch or independent regulatory agencies may be called to testify about how they are carrying out the laws that Congress passed.

Congressional hearings are the principal formal method by which committees collect and analyze information in the early stages of legislative policymaking. But there are other kinds of hearings as well: confirmation hearings (for the Senate, not the House), legislative hearings, oversight hearings, investigative hearings, or a combination of them. Hearings usually include oral testimony from witnesses, and questioning of the witnesses by members of Congress.

There are several types of congressional hearings. Congressional Standing (or Policy) committees regularly hold legislative hearings on measures or policy issues that may become public law. Agriculture committees hold hearings on proposed legislation related to agriculture policy. Banking and financial services committees hold hearings on bills related to the financial services sector of the economy. The armed services committees hold hearings on legislative proposals related to national defense and the military. The health, education, and labor committees hold hearings on bills related to these aspects of domestic policy. Sometimes a committee holds hearings on several bills before deciding on one bill for further committee and chamber action. Hearings provide a forum where witnesses from a broad range of backgrounds can appear to provide facts and opinions to the committee members. The witnesses include members of Congress, other government officials, representatives of interest groups, academics or other experts, as well as individuals directly or indirectly affected by a proposed bill. Most congressional hearings are held in Washington, but field hearings are held outside Washington.

Oversight hearings are intended to review or study a law, a public policy issue, or an activity. Such hearings often focus on the quality of federal programs and the performance of government officials. Hearings are also one way for Congress to ensure that executive branch is implementing laws consistent with legislative intent. A significant part of a congressional committee's hearings workload is dedicated to oversight. Committee oversight hearings might include examination of gasoline price increases, lead paint on toys imported from China, the safety of the food supply in the wake of e. coli contamination, indecent programming broadcast over the television or radio airwaves, the government's response to natural disasters, terrorism preparedness, Medicare or Medicaid spending or access to health care, or matters related to crime policy.

The second oversight function is investigation of scandals. Investigative hearings are similar to legislative hearings and oversight hearings, but they are specifically convened to investigate when there is suspicion of wrongdoing on the part of public officials acting in their official capacity, or suspicion of

private citizens whose activities or behavior may warrant a legislative remedy. Congress might conduct investigate hearings to get additional information about use of steroids in professional sports such as baseball, or to determine whether tobacco companies are "spiking" the nicotine content in cigarettes or whether tobacco company executives think nicotine is addictive. Congress has broad power to investigate. Some of its most famous investigative hearings are benchmarks in American political history:

- The Teapot Dome Scandal in the 1920s.
- The Army-McCarthy Hearings during the Red Scare in the 1950s.
- The Watergate scandal in the 1970s.
- The Church Committee Hearings on the CIA and illegal intelligence gathering in the 1970s
- The Iran-Contra Affair Hearings in 1987.
- The National Commission investigating the 9/11 terrorist attacks.
- The National Commission investigating the financial crisis.
- The investigation of Trump campaign and administration officials' contacts and financial relationships with Russian officials.

Investigative hearings gather information and issue reports that are often used to pass legislation to address the problems that the hearings examined. The National Commission on Terrorist Attacks Upon the United States was created to "investigate the facts and circumstances" relating to the terrorist attacks. The National Commission's Report was used to increase coordination of intelligence about terrorism. The Financial Crisis Inquiry Report submitted by the National Commission on the Causes of the Financial and Economic Crisis in the United States in January 2011 included among its recommendations regulation of certain financial transactions.

Confirmation hearings on presidential nominations are held in fulfillment of the Senate's constitutional role to "advise and consent." Senate committees hold confirmation hearings on presidential nominations to executive and judicial positions within their jurisdiction. When the President nominates the head of an executive agency—such as the Secretary of State, Interior, Department of Homeland Security, or Defense—the Senate must confirm the nomination. The Senate also must confirm the president's nominees for federal judgeships.

Confirmation hearings offer an opportunity for oversight into the activities of the nominee's department or agency. The vast majority of confirmation hearings are routine, but some are controversial. The Senate may use the confirmation hearing of a nominee for Attorney General to examine how the Administration has been running the Department of Justice and provide some guidance on how the Senate would like the Department to function. The Constitution also requires that the Senate consent to the ratification of treaties negotiated by the executive branch with foreign governments. Arms control treaties have historically been controversial. Recently, the Senate used the ratification of the Strategic Arms Reduction Treaty between the U.S. and Russia to exert power over the executive branch and to influence the foreign policy choices of the President.[3] Therefore, hearings provide an opportunity for different points of view to be expressed as a matter of public record. So confirmation hearings are one of the ways that the Senate performs its constitutional responsibilities in an important area of public policy.

One of Congress' implied powers is the power to issue subpoenas and to hold individuals in contempt of Congress for not complying with demands to testify or provide requested information. Most of the time individuals welcome an invitation to testify before Congress because it can be a valuable opportunity to communicate, publicize, and advocate their positions on important public policy issues. However, if a person declines an invitation, a committee or subcommittee may require an appearance by issuing a subpoena.

CONGRESSIONAL POWER IN ACTION: THE INDICTMENT OF ROGER CLEMENS

"Let me be clear. I have never taken steroids or HGH"

- Roger Clemens, to House Committee on Oversight and Government Reform

Roger "The Rocket" Clemens was indicted on August 19th, 2010, by the House Committee on Oversight and Government Reform for lying about using performance enhancing drugs during his long baseball career. Clemens' celebrated career has been called into question by the subpoena and indictment powers by the House of Representatives. In response, Clemens Tweeted "I look forward to will keep an open mind until trial," the message said. "I appreciate all the support I have been getting. I am happy to finally have my day in court." A jury ultimately found Mr. Clemens not guilty of criminal charges. Mr. Clemens and his lawyers before the House Committee:

Committees also may subpoena correspondence, books, papers, and other documents. Subpoenas are issued infrequently, and most often in the course of investigative hearings. The subpoena power is an implied power of Congress. Congress has the enumerated power to legislate, and hearings and subpoenas are implied powers that are logically related to Congress' need for information related to legislation it is considering. But when Congress requests records from the executive branch, the president cite executive privilege as a constitutional power to refuse to give Congress the information it requests during an oversight investigation. In 2012, the House Oversight and Government Reform Committee demanded records related to Operation "Fast and Furious," a Bureau of Alcohol, Tobacco, Firearms and Explosives sting operation that was intended to track illegal gun running on the Mexican border. The operation lost track of guns that it had provided, and the guns ended up in the possession of a Mexican drug cartel. Congress demanded information about the program and how it went wrong.

> The House of Representative Oversight Committee held hearings on Operation "Fast and Furious" a botched undercover operation to investigate gun smuggling along the Mexican border.
> http://www.pbs.org/newshour/rundown/justice-dept-gives-congress-documents-on-fast-and-furious/
> https://oversight.house.gov/report/committee-releases-fast-furious-report-obstruction-congress-department-justice/

3.55 | *Lawmaking, Representation, or Oversight?*

Today, Congress devotes more time to representation and oversight and less time making laws for the nation. This shift has occurred more in some areas of public policy than in others. In foreign affairs and national security, for example, Congress generally follows the president's lead in formulating public policy. In domestic affairs, Congress typically exerts more influence over public policy. As individual members of Congress pay more attention to representation, oversight, and constituency service, they pay less attention to law making for the nation. As a result, Congress as an institution also focuses less on its traditional lawmaking role. This change is reflected in the congressional work schedule. Today's Congress spends much less time in session. For an interesting perspective by a member of the House of Representatives who left Congress and then returned after 33 years, listen to Congressman Rick Nolan's (Democrat-Minnesota) thoughts about why Congress no longer works (well).

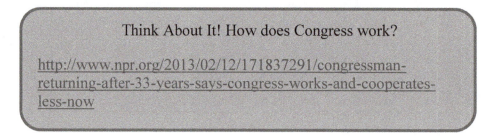

> Think About It! How does Congress work?
>
> http://www.npr.org/2013/02/12/171837291/congressman-returning-after-33-years-says-congress-works-and-cooperates-less-now

3.6 | The Internal Organization of Congress

How an institution is organized affects *what* it does. The three most important aspects of the way Congress is organized are bicameralism, the committee system, and the party system.

3.61 | *Bicameralism*

Congress is a bicameral or two-house body. <u>Bicameralism</u> is part of the system of checks and balances and part of the functional differences in legislative governance. The House of Representatives and the Senate have different sizes, roles, and rules of operation. The House is larger and therefore has more formal rules of operation to govern debate. The Senate is smaller and relies more on informal rules, a tradition of open debate (including the infamous filibuster), and personal relationships. In order for a bill to become a law it must pass both houses of Congress—a fact that makes lawmaking in bicameral bodies much more complicated than in unicameral bodies.

3.62 | *The Committee System*

The key to understanding how Congress works is the committee system. Congress does most of its work in committees. The committee system is a form of division of labor. Most modern organizations operate with a system of division of labor where individuals are assigned different tasks in order to take advantage of specialization or expertise. The standing committees in Congress are an example of specialization. The jurisdiction of congressional committees such as the House of Representatives committee on agriculture, the committee on education and labor, the committee on financial services, and the committee on foreign affairs reflects their area of legislative expertise and authority. There are four basic kinds of committees: **standing committees, joint committees, conference committee,** and **select or special committees.** The House of Representatives committee system and the Senate committee system are similar but each body creates its own committee system.

- **Standing** committees are the most prominent of the committees. These are the permanent committees that focus on specific area of legislation, such as the House Committee on Homeland Security or the Senate Committee on Armed Forces. The majority of the day-to-day work in Congress occurs in these standing committees. Generally, sixteen to twenty members serve on each committee in Senate and thirty-one members serve on committees in the House. The majority party determines the number of committee members from each party on each committee, which ensures that the majority party will have the majority of committee members. Standing committees also have a variety of **subcommittees** that cover more precise subsections of the legislative issues addressed by the committee. Generally, subcommittee members have considerable leeway in shaping the content of legislation.
- **Joint** committees have members from the House and the Senate and are concerned with specific policy areas. These committees are set up as a way to expedite business between the houses, particularly when pressing issues require quick action by Congress.
- **Conference** committees are created to reconcile differences between the House and Senate versions of a bill. The conference committee is made up of members from both the House and the Senate who work to reach compromises between similar pieces of legislation passed by the House and the Senate.
- **Select** or special committees are temporary committees that serve only for a very specific purpose. These committees conduct special investigations or studies and report back to whichever chamber established the committee.

Senate Committee Hearing on the Banking Industry Subprime Mortgage
Crisis

Russian interference in the 2016 elections became a major issue late in the 2016 campaign season and then became one of the major stories during the Trump administration. The investigations expanded in scope after President Trump fired James Comey, the Director of the FBI. The non-criminal investigations included intelligence agency reports on Russian interference that led to House and Senate Intelligence Committee investigative hearings, Senate Judiciary Committee hearings, and House Oversight hearings. Evidence that President Trump tried to get the FBI to "back off" its counterespionage investigations resulted in criminal investigations for obstruction of justice and the appointment of a special counsel (Robert Mueller) to investigate the affair. The Senate Judiciary Committee Subcommittee on Crime and Terrorism held hearings on "Russian Interference in the 2016 United States Elections." The video of the May 8, 2017 hearings provide a good example of Congress performing its investigatory role. The two witnesses appearing before the Subcommittee are Sally Q. Yates, former Acting Attorney General, and James Clapper, former Director of National Intelligence.

Senate Judiciary Committee Subcommittee on Crime and Terrorism, Hearings on Russian Interference in the 2016 United States Election (May 8, 2017). Senator Graham (R-South Carolina), Chair, and Senator Whitehouse (D-Rhode Island), Ranking Member. Senator Whitehouse is holding the exhibit "The Kremlin Playbook."

The special counsel has some independence from the White House and can therefore conduct an investigation that follows all leads—which is why the appointment of a special counsel is such a serious threat to the Trump administration. The investigation can examine Russian interference with the election. It can investigate to determine whether Trump campaign officials, such as the digital campaign director, helped the interference by providing useful information so that the Russians could deploy armies of Twitter bots that targeted specific Congressional districts in swing states. The special counsel can also follow its investigative leads to Trump campaign and Trump family business relationships, particularly financial dealings with Russian oligarchs, banks, and other individuals and entities. The original focus of the oversight—Russian interference in the elections—is probably a less serious threat to the Trump administration that the risks of financial disclosures resulting from criminal investigations that followed the money.

The Trump June Tweetstorms

After 7 months of investigations & committee hearings about my "collusion with the Russians," nobody has been able to show any proof. Sad!

I am being investigated for firing the FBI Director by the man who told me to fire the FBI Director! Witch Hunt

You are witnessing the single greatest WITCH HUNT in American political history - led by some very bad and conflicted people!

3.63 | *The Political Party System*

The third organization characteristic that is essential for understanding how Congress operates is the party system. The House and the Senate are organized differently but both houses have party leadership structures. The **majority party** is the party with the most seats; the **minority party** is the party with second number of seats. The majority party in each house organizes the sessions of Congress and selects its leadership. The majority party in the House of Representatives selects the Speaker of the House and the majority party in the Senate choses the Majority Leader. The House of Representatives leaders are chosen by the members of the House. The Senate leaders are chosen by the members of the Senate.

Leadership in the House of Representatives

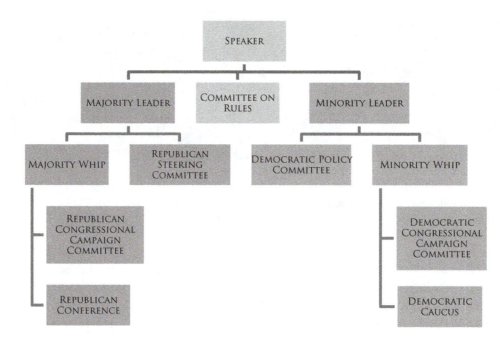

The House is a much larger body than the Senate therefore the House relies more heavily on formal rules to function. Loyalty to the party organization, party leadership, and voting along party lines are also all more common in the House than in the Senate. The most powerful position in the House of Representatives is the **Speaker of the House,** which is the only leadership position in the House that is created by the Constitution. The Speaker is a member of the majority party and is elected by their party to oversee House business, interact with the Senate and the President, and is the second in line of presidential succession. In addition to the Speaker, the House leadership includes majority and minority leaders; majority and minority whips; party policy committees that the Republicans call a Steering Committee and Democrats call a Democratic Policy Committee; Republican and Democratic congressional campaign committees; and the Republican Conference and Democratic Caucus.

The Senate's presiding officer is determined by the Constitution, which sets forth that the vice-president of the United States is the ranking officer of the Senate. The vice-president is not a member of the Senate, so he votes only in the case of a tie. The **president pro tempore**, or the official chair of the Senate, is a largely honorary position awarded to the most senior senator of the majority party. The leader with power in the Senate is the majority leader, who is elected to their position by their party. The Senate, with far fewer members than the House, is a more causal organization that relies much less on formal structures of power for organization. As such, the majority party leader in the Senate has less power than the Speaker of the House. The Senate also lacks a rule committee, but has a largely similar structure to the House, in terms of the positions of power within each party.

LEADERSHIP IN THE SENATE

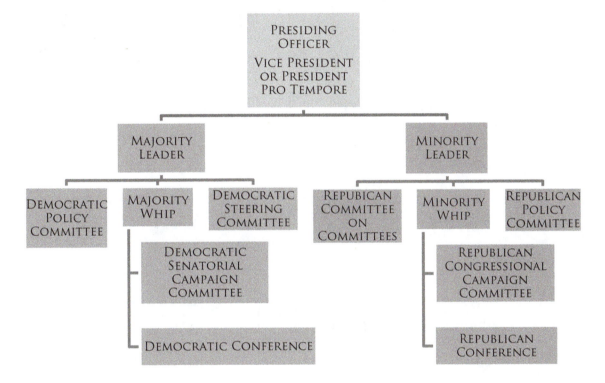

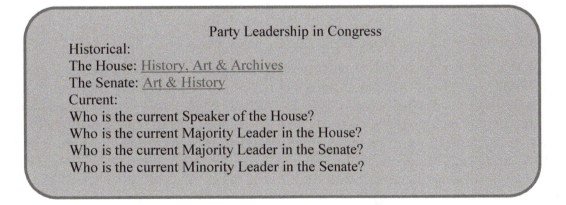

Party Leadership in Congress
Historical:
The House: History, Art & Archives
The Senate: Art & History
Current:
Who is the current Speaker of the House?
Who is the current Majority Leader in the House?
Who is the current Majority Leader in the Senate?
Who is the current Minority Leader in the Senate?

3.64 | *How a Bill Becomes a Law*

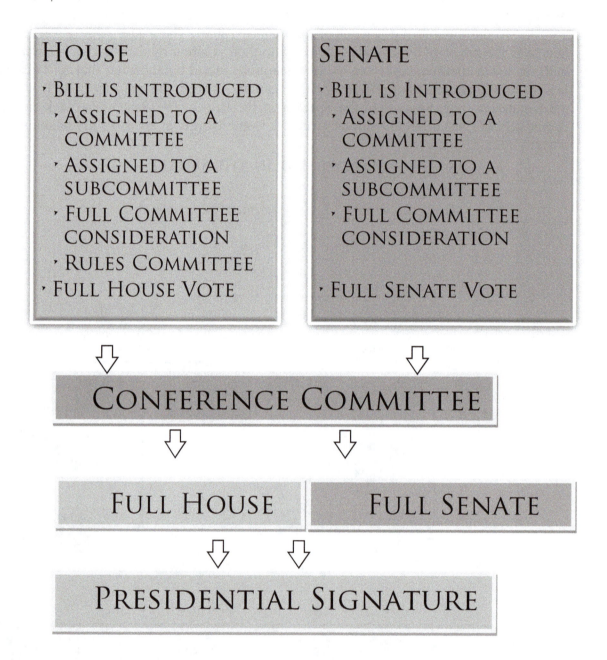

The process by which Congress makes legislation is complex and drawn out, involving a series of procedural steps that have been institutionalized overtime. The first formal step in either the House of Representatives or the Senate is to introduce the bill for consideration in the legislative body. The bill is introduced and assigned to a committee for consideration; once in the committee, the bill is assigned to an appropriate subcommittee. The subcommittee will study the bill, hold hearings for those individuals and interest groups concerned with the bill, and debate and edit provisions of the bill. The subcommittee sends the bill back to the full committee, who votes on whether to send the bill to the full House or Senate for consideration. In the House (and *only* in the House), the bill is then sent to the House Rules committee, where the rules governing debate and amendments on the bill are decided. Both the House and the Senate debate and vote on the bill. If the bills considered by the House and Senate differ, the bills are sent to a Conference committee, which crafts a single bill that both houses of Congress will find acceptable. The bill from the Conference committee is then sent back to both the House and the Senate for a final vote. If the bill passes both houses, the legislation is sent to the president for either approval (through signing) or a veto. If the president vetoes a bill, a two-third vote by both the House and the Senate can override the veto.

> **Think About It!**
> The British Parliamentary System provides for Prime Minister's Question Time as a way form members of parliament to ask the prime minister questions. Would this tradition help presidential-congressional relations in the U.S?
> https://www.c-span.org/series/?PrimeMinisterQue

3.65 | *Sessions of Congress*

A term of Congress is divided into two sessions, one for each year. Congress has occasionally also been called into an extra or special session. A new session commences on January 3 (or another date, if Congress so chooses) each year.

> Think the Senate doesn't have a sense of humor?
> Senate history, art, and political cartoons are available at the Senate website:
> http://www.senate.gov/pagelayout/art/g_three_sections_wi th_teasers/exhibits.htm

3.7 | **Summary**

The power problem with Congress—effective governance—explained the diminished and changed roles. The modern Congress pays less attention to legislating for the nation and more attention to its other functions—particularly representation and administrative oversight. Congressional scholars Ornstein and Mann (2012) attribute the low regard for Congress to a mismatch between Congress's constitutional design—the separation of powers—and its modern parliamentary form—ideologically distinct parties where one is the majority and has power to enact its policies. According to this analysis, the separation of powers model requires negotiating, bargaining, and compromise to enact legislation. But partisanship has introduced a parliamentary element without the capacity for majoritarian power to legislate. The result is gridlock perceived as ineffective leadership. Ornstein and Mann also blame congressional dysfunction on the modern Republican Party, which has become so ideologically extremist that it refuses to compromise. Ideological extremism is a source of the party's electoral strength. The Republican Party is a coalition whose elements are members of movements or causes such as the anti-tax movement, the religious right (pro-life), national security, and crime control. These causes motivate voters such as members of the Tea Party movement that have made Republicans see themselves as insurgents fighting the established political norms in and out of Congress. By contrast, the modern Democratic Party (at least since the civil rights era) has functioned more like a collection of interests who are merely trying to get something from government rather than mobilizing a movement to change politics and government. The result is "asymmetrical polarization." Donald Trump's successful insurgency campaign has created an opportunity to test the theory that Congress deserves its reputation as the broken branch of government because it is institutionally unable to act decisively on issues of national political interest.

3.9 | Additional Resources

3.91 | INTERNET RESOURCES

USA.gov provides information about Congress:
https://www.usa.gov/branches-of-government

Senate.gov:
https://www.senate.gov/
House.gov:
http://www.house.gov/

In order to get a sense of how important constituency service is to members of Congress, visit the website of your congressional representative or the site of another member of the House of Representative: http://www.house.gov/house/MemberWWW.shtml

C-SPAN.org:
https://www.c-span.org/congress/

A user friendly website for information about Congress is http://www.opencongress.org/

Want to find a federal law? Congress legislates on an extremely broad range of subjects ranging from domestic policy (clean air, clean water, obscenity or indecency on radio or television or the Internet, crime, health care) to foreign affairs (international trade, defense policy). One way to find a federal law is through http://thomas.loc.gov/. Select Multiple Previous Congresses; select Bill Summary Status; select Congress (of your choice); select Advance Search; type in search phrase (e.g. Venezuela, for legislation related to that country; or terrorism for legislation related to national security); select date, or date range; and hit search.

The *Washington Post*'s "Today in Congress" section including committee hearings and votes. www.washingtonpost.com

3.92 | *IN THE LIBRARY*

Arnold, R. Douglas. 2006. *Congress, the Press, and Public Accountability*. Princeton University Press.

Dodd, Lawrence and Bruce Oppenheimer (Eds). 2001. *Congress Reconsidered*, 7th ed. Washington, D.C.: Congressional Quarterly.

Mayhew, David. 2000. *America's Congress*. New Haven: Yale University Press.

O'Connor, Karen (Ed). 2002. *Women and Congress: Running, Winning, Ruling*. Haworth.

Ornstein, Norman, and Mann, Thomas E. 2012. *It's Even Worse than It Looks*. New York: Basic Books.

Tate, Katherine. 2003. *Black Faces in the Mirror: African Americans and their Representatives in the U.S. Congress*. Princeton University Press.

---

[1] Quoted in Jeffrey Toobin, *The New Yorker*, "The Bench: Tipped Scales," (February 27, 2017).Accessed at http://www.newyorker.com/magazine/2017/02/27/loretta-lynchs-ideal-of-justice

[2] Theodore J. Lowi and Ginsberg, Benjamin (1996). *American Government*. Fourth Edition. New York: W.W. Norton & Company. p. 153.

[3] http://dosfan.lib.uic.edu/acda/treaties/salt2-1.htm

TERMS:

Appropriations
Impeachment
Enumerated powers
Implied powers
Necessary and proper clause
Delegate
Trustee
Politico
Majority party
Minority party
Speaker of the House
President pro tempore
Standing committees
Joint committees
Conference committee
Select or special committees
Legislative oversight
Constituency service

STUDY QUESTIONS

1) Discuss the powers of Congress and the differences between the House and Senate.
2) What are the constitutional powers of Congress?
3) What roles do political parties play in the organization of Congress?
4) To what extent do the various leadership positions in the House and Senate make some leaders more powerful than others?
5) Describe a typical day of a member of Congress.
6) How representative is Congress? Discuss both the theories of representation and the demographic make-up of Congress. How has this changed over time?
7) What is the traditional process by which a bill becomes a law?

CHAPTER 4: THE PRESIDENCY

4.0 | Introduction

When the American public thinks of the presidency, they think of the president—the ***person*** whose name, face, character, and personality are prominently featured during the presidential campaign, and the ***person*** who upon taking office dominates media coverage of the federal government. The president *personifies* the federal government. The media report on the *Trump* administration, the *Obama* administration, the *Bush* 41 administration, and so on. Political scientists reinforce the personal perspective by emphasizing the importance of presidential character and style. In one sense, Article II of the Constitution created a personal presidency by providing that "The executive Power shall be vested in a President of the United States of America." In contrast with the legislative and judicial branches, one individual has all the executive power. The modern president personifies the federal government, but the presidency is actually a vast institution that consists of a large number of offices, executive departments, and agencies. So the presidency consists of an *individual* and an *office*. Understanding the presidential role in government and politics requires learning about the person who is *president* and the *presidency*, the individual who happens to occupy the Office of the President of the United States and the institution. This chapter examines three main issues that are central to the presidency:

- The power problem: Accountability.
- The increase in presidential power: Presidential government?
- Management of the executive branch: Controlling the bureaucracy.

The accountability problem is directly raised by the question whether a president can be indicted for a crime. During the 2016 campaign, Donald Trump claimed that his supporters were so smart and so loyal to him that he could stand in the middle of 5th avenue and shoot someone and not lose any of his voters. This political claim was surprising and debatable. What may be even more surprising and debatable is the legal claim that a president cannot be indicted for a crime. Whether a sitting president has immunity from prosecution for a crime is an *open question* in the sense that the U.S. Supreme Court has never decided the question. Presidents have claimed that they are immune from prosecution. And legal scholars have explained the constitutional theory justifying immunity, but the Court has not yet agreed with them. The claim seems to be incompatible with what is taught in American government 101 and civics about the American commitment to the rule of law (rather than the rule of man) and the belief that no one, not even the president, is above the law.

4.1 | The Unprecedented President

Political scientists describe "change elections" as elections when voters want different public policies and therefore put a different party in control of government. The desire for change also applies to presidential character and style. President George W. Bush had an informal style that relied on gut instincts more than careful analysis of the issues. President Obama's rational character sometimes made him seem *too cool for school*, too rational, and too aloof to enjoy or engage in the back-slapping give-and-take of legislative politics. *No drama* Obama was a Spockian rationalist. Spock was the hyper-rational character in *Star Wars* (1966–69), the science fiction television series that became a cult phenomenon, who described human behavior with the catch phrase "highly illogical." President Trump is a political phenomenon who has swung the pendulum back toward drama. His character and style thrive on drama—even high political melodrama. Did the presidential pendulum swing from *too cool* to *too hot*?

The Trump presidency is unprecedented in many ways. During the presidential campaign he broke all the conventional rules and established norms but he still survived and even thrived as an unconventional candidate to become an unconventional president. He denigrated and bullied individual opponents—even breaking Ronald Reagan's Eleventh Commandment, "Thou Shalt Not Speak Ill of Another Republican," by insulting virtually all of the Republican candidates during the primary. He is a master practitioner of *political jiu jitsu*! *Jiu jitsu* is using an opponent's strength or momentum, or one's own weakness, against the opponent. Trump accused Hillary Clinton of being a liar, of being corrupt, of being plagued by scandals, and of being in the pocket of Wall Street *because* these were his own political weaknesses. He accused the news media of being fake news *because* he had a record of playing fast and loose with the facts. He very effectively used his weaknesses against his opponent to throw them off balance. This is not easy to do.

He criticized individual government officials, including judges. He criticized government and politics in general. Scandals involving bad personal behavior that probably would have ended most presidential campaigns did not end his. His first 100 days in office included a major scandal involving his and his associates' relations with Russia. He did not keep his word about releasing his income tax records. He is the only president to have never held a prior elective office or served in the military. He is the first real estate developer-president. And the legal and ethical questions about the conflicts of interest between his official duties as president, and his and his family's business interests, are unprecedented. President Trump's son Eric's casual comment that in his business world "[n]epotism is kind of a factor of life" seems an affront to basic American beliefs about meritocracy as well as norms and laws against using public office for private profit.

The Trump administration's blurring of the line between private profit and public interest is unprecedented. This is particularly the case with his and his associates' business and political relations Russia. A military report prepared for President-elect Trump named Russia the greatest threat to U.S. national security interests. President Trump's flattering description of Vladimir Putin as a strong leader, and Trump's campaign and administration officials with financial ties to Putin, raised concerns and prompted counter-intelligence investigations by the Federal Bureau of Investigation and intelligence agencies. Against this background, President Trump's strong criticism of U.S. intelligence agencies and his remarks at CIA headquarters the day after his inauguration were particularly unprecedented. President Trump began his presidency with an unprecedented low public opinion approval rating. And the Trump administration's rocky relationship with the media has also been unprecedented.

Donald Trump the 45th President of the United States

4.11 | The Personal Presidency

In other ways, however, the Trump president is not unprecedented as much as it takes normal to the extremes. It is the culmination of the long-term trend toward the *personal presidency*. The personal presidency may be the most significant development in the American system of government. The term personal presidency originates with works such as Lowi's *The Personal President* (1985). It refers to a presidency whose political legitimacy is based on popular support and whose power is characterized by executive discretion. The political legitimacy is reflected in presidential claims of electoral mandates that support their agendas. The executive discretion is evident in claims that the president has the power to do whatever he or she thinks is necessary and appropriate, and statutes that actually give presidents that power.

Taken together, the personal power and the executive discretionary power make it hard to hold presidents legally accountable for their actions. In fact, both features of the modern presidency are part of the shift away from the model of legal accountability toward the model of political accountability. The model of legal accountability relies on rule of law values to hold presidents and other government officials accountable. The model of political accountability relies on elections as referenda on presidential actions. The classic defense of the political model of accountability is former President Richard Nixon's argument that if a president orders something that is plainly illegal to be done—for example, a burglary, a forgery, a robbery, perhaps even a murder—then it is not illegal.

Think About It!
Is this claim consistent with the American commitment to the rule of law?
"If the president does it, that means it is not illegal." (The Nixon-Frost Interviews, April 6, 1977)
Former President Nixon, in his own words.

The term *personal presidency* also refers to power that is personal rather than institutional. Personal bases of power increase a president's independence from institutional checks and balances by Congress, the courts, or the political parties. The deregulation of campaign finance makes it easier for candidates to run self-financed campaigns that are not dependent political parties for fund-raising and campaign workers. The increase in the percentage of voters who consider themselves Independents rather than Republicans or Democrats makes it easier for candidates to be more independent of partisan support. Party loyalty strengthens congressional creates stronger ties to the president and weaker institutional loyalty. The diminished public confidence in Congress and the declining party identification have created a void that the personal presidency is occupying. President Obama's eight years in office provided evidence of the personal presidency. Obama's support was personal more than partisan. Democratic voter turnout was higher when he was on the ballot in the 2008 and 2012 elections than when he was not on the ballot. Democrats lost 69 congressional seats in the mid-term elections in 2010 and 22 seats in 2014, and Hillary Clinton lost the 2016 presidential election.

4.12| *The Postmodern Presidency*

The personal nature of the presidency requires scholars to reassess presidential theories with each new president in order to determine whether the new president confirms theories or signals the beginning of a new presidential era. Presidential scholars have identified the traditional presidency of the 19th Century and the modern presidency that began in 1932 with Franklin

Roosevelt. The main difference between the two is the modern presidency's activism with a popular electoral base. Some scholars think the era of the modern presidency ended with President Nixon, who resigned the presidency rather than face impeachment and removal from office. These scholars maintain that the personal presidency enabled the development of a third presidential era—the postmodern presidency.

The term postmodern presidency was originally was coined to describe a new era of a diminished presidency. (Rose) Stark (1993) describes Bill Clinton as the first postmodern president. Miroff (2000: 106) defines the postmodern president as "a political actor who lacks a stable identity associated with ideological and partisan values and who is, thereby, free to move nimbly from one position to another as political fashion dictates." Ironically, the postmodern presidency is the result of a governing style that increasingly depends on public approval as a base of support. It is ironic because the popular support was originally considered solely a strength of the modern presidency. Public approval dependency creates an incentive for presidents to stage-manage spectacles in order to create and reinforce presidential images. Daniel Boorstin's *The Image: A Guide to Pseudo-Events in America* (1962) describes how spectacles became part of managing the president's image. Presidential "debates" and press conferences have become public performance events that are staged for the media to report, rather than regularly scheduled opportunities for the general public to gain information about candidates, parties, or presidential administrations. The images and events are staged reality.

President Trump began his tenure in office as a new kind of postmodern president. The first reason he is a new postmodern president is his effective appropriation of the original meaning of postmodern. Postmodernism began as a primarily liberal belief that facts, values, and reality are relative or subjective because they are almost entirely dependent upon an individual's or a culture's perspective. This academic belief in subjectivity provided the foundation for the popular cultural belief that most of the news media and much of science (e.g., theories of evolution and climate change) is biased. This conditioning enabled President Trump to call media criticism of him or his administration fake news. In fact, conservative Republicans called CBS News correspondent and anchor Dan Rather "Dan Rather Biased" for his liberal bias in covering Presidents Reagan and presidential candidate George W. Bush.

The second reason Trump is a new kind of postmodern president is because his ideology seems a mash-up of conventional ideas, and political base of support reflects ideological and partisan cross cutting. This creates the opportunity to form a new presidential coalition that realigns the political system. These unconventional developments in presidential politics are hard to explain using conventional political science literature about political systems, government institutions, and scholarship on the presidency. Therefore the following analysis looks at these developments and the <u>postmodern presidency of Donald Trump</u> through the lens of popular culture.

4.13| *The Popular Culture Lens*

Julian Barnes is an award-winning English writer. His satirical postmodern novel *England, England* (1998) is about a rich entrepreneur with a big ego, Sir Jack Pitman, who decides to create a theme park called England England that is filled with all the things and figures that tourists consider quintessentially or stereotypically English—Big Ben, Harrods, the Queen, pubs, the White Cliffs of Dover, etc. The Disneyland-style theme park England England becomes tremendously popular and successful because all things English are so conveniently located, so clean, and so well-run. So many people leave the real "old" England to live in the fake England England that the real England suffers a great decline. Spoiler alert: the satire ends in a sex scandal!

Was the appeal of Donald Trump's campaign promise to *Make America Great Again* based on the desire to recreate an *America, America* where all the things that are part of the distinctive American national identity were preserved? The campaign slogan did echo Patrick Buchanan's call for a culture war in his Culture Wars Address at the Republican Party Convention in 1992. Buchanan called upon his fellow conservative Republicans *to fight* to take back *our* cities, *our* culture, and *our* country. The audience—an overwhelmingly white, upper class, older America—enthusiastically supported his call because they felt that they were still losing their country despite having elected Presidents Reagan and George H. W. Bush in 1980, 1984, and 1988. Donald Trump renewed this call to take back the country—but for a different, more populist demographic.

Donald Trump's character and style complement the postmodern variation of the personal presidency. His personality-centric politics accelerated the political system's momentum away from institution-centric politics and toward personality politics. Trump's personal campaign style then became a personal style of governance. As President, he spends a great deal of time every day watching television to see how the media are portraying him and his administration. Media reports about him, his family, and his administration produce Tweet storms. All presidents pay close attention to grooming their image in the media. The Reagan administration was famously attuned to how television visuals conveyed images because it brought Madison Avenue advertising and Hollywood Boulevard sensibilities to managing the president's image. Michael Deaver, Reagan's Deputy Chief of Staff responsible media relations, and Dick Darman, a presidential aide responsible for budget issues among other, realized that the masterful use of pictures—particularly presidential photo ops—reinforced in the public's mind favorable images of President Reagan. Deaver was one of the White House officials whose backgrounds in Hollywood entertainment and Madison Avenue marketing taught them that good visuals could trump critical words.

A case study is a 1984 story that CBS aired on the evening news. The report by Lesley Stahl's exposed the apparent hypocrisy of President Reagan speaking at a nursing home and a Special Olympics event while his administration's budget reduced spending on disabled children and health care. Stahl worried that the critical story would hurt her access to the White House, but Dick Darman called her to say "Great story, kiddo." He explained, "You guys in Televisionland haven't figured it out, have you? ....*Nobody heard you.*"[1] [Emphasis added.] Powerful emotional pictures or images of the president being presidential by getting on or off Air Force One are more important than the critical words accompanying the story. Michael Deaver reinforced this point by explaining that he did not care if a news reporter's voice-over was critical of President Reagan's policy, as long as the news report had good visuals, because "the eye trumps the ear every time." Good pictures were more important than bad words.

The Reagan administration was innovative because it applied Madison Avenue marketing strategies to politics. The voting public was considered consumers of political information the way customers were considered consumers of commercial information. President Trump has used commercial popular culture—his reputation as a dealmaker—and added elements of entertainment popular culture—celebrity status—to politics and governance. This combination of commercial and entertainment appeal is apparent in an Associated Press interview where he repeatedly claims that he gets great ratings whenever he is on television—whether it is the inauguration, an address to Congress, a news program, or a press conference. Exaggerating the size of crowds and audiences reinforces his supporters' belief that the mainstream or Fake News media are biased against both him and them. Insulting the CBS news program *Face the Nation* by calling it "Deface the Nation" similarly plays to a conservative Republican base that has been referring to "the lame-stream" media for years.

4.14 | *Framing Theory*

Media scholars developed framing theory to describe and explain the mass media's influence on public opinion. According to framing theory, the way the news media present an issue to the audience—the way facts and stories are framed—influences what people think about the subject. Framing theory also applied to fiction. For example, legal fiction is a universally popular genre for television and film. How police procedurals frame their crime stories shapes what people think about criminal justice officials, the causes of crime, and the appropriate public policies to prevent crime and to punish offenders. Print and electronic news stories similarly influence thinking about public affairs. Framing theory is crucial to understanding both the Trump presidency and the news media's reporting and analysis of the administration.

Understanding the unconventional Trump campaign and presidency requires thinking outside the conventional political frames provide by presidential scholars. It requires looking at popular culture. Terry Gross, the host of the NPR radio program *Fresh Air*, describes President Trump as living and working "at the intersection of politics and popular culture." A real estate developer who became a television celebrity on *The Apprentice*, Trump greatly accelerated the speed with which politics was becoming popular culture by bringing a "reality show sensibility to the office." It is not surprising that the popular cultural obsession with movie stars and other celebrities brought a celebrity figure to the White House. What unsettling is how he got there by conspicuously breaking all the rules and then he continued to break the rules about presidential conduct.

Frank Rich, a writer for *New York* magazine, describes Trump as brilliant at creating the drama that all good showmen master to get and keep the audience's attention. According to Rich, Trump makes outrageous statements and then contradicts them with more outrageous statements two hours later; streams the public from all media platforms and angles including television and Twitter; and continually "gins up" the suspense and the drama in order to keep the spotlight and all the eyeballs focused on him and what he is doing.[2] He used one form of entertainment— reality television—to get to the White House, then continued to use it in the White House, and then added drama by changing the location to Mar-a-Lago, the National Historic Landmark in Palm Beach, Florida that is an even more exotic setting than the White House. Reality television was a popular culture stop along the way. Television does not merely mirror society, politics, or culture. It provides insightful commentary that tells us a great deal about modern American culture. Accordingly, *The Apprentice* is as revealing about Donald Trump as it is revealing about us.

4.15 | *Political Personalities or Personas*

Professional wrestling is another popular culture phenomenon that provides a useful alternative frame for understanding President Trump and his loyal base of support. President Trump has used his long relationship with professional wrestling to develop his larger-than-life persona. In fact, wrestling explains conservative personalities such as Alex Jones and Donald Trump.[3] Professional wrestling fans know that the contests are not *real* athletic contests even though the wrestlers are athletes performing in the ring. The fans get genuine emotional feelings from matches that are elaborated staged contests between characters portrayed as heroes and villains. This may help explain why as a candidate and as president, Trump is not expected to state facts or tell the truth. The conventional wisdom is that politicians and government officials are expected to tell the truth, to state facts, and to stand firm by not flip-flopping on the issues.

Donald Trump's pattern of not telling the truth, not stating facts, and flip-flopping on major issues has kept fact-checkers busy, but it has not been as politically damaging as expected of a conventional candidate or president. His unconventional behavior seems to violate the civic moral of the story about young George Washington and the cherry tree! It is also hard to reconcile with President John Adams's blessing that is carved into the fireplace in the State Dining Room: "I pray God to bestow "May none but an honest and wise men rule under this roof."

Think About It!

An early civics lesson?

One of the most enduring and endearing stories about George Washington is the cherry tree story. Young George Washington used a hatchet that he received as a gift to damage a cherry tree. Confronted by his father who angrily asked whether he had damaged the tree, young George admitted it saying "I cannot tell a lie." His father was overjoyed because his son's honesty was worth more than a thousand trees. The moral of the story is part of the American national myth about private virtue being the foundation for political character.

Presidential scholars pay a great deal of attention to presidential character and style. Occasionally, this includes the touchy study of mental health. Americans believe that the process for selecting a president is well designed to weed out individuals who are politically or psychologically unsuited for the job. This faith might be shaken by the results of a Duke University study of 37 presidents from Washington to Nixon. The results were published in the Journal of Nervous and Mental Disease in 2006. Almost half of the 37 presidents studied met the criteria for a psychiatric disorder at some time in their lives—mostly depression, nervousness, and substance abuse. Presidents have often obscured disease and disorder. President John F. Kennedy's obvious tan was called a sign of vigor when it actually was a symptom of Addison's disease. In *Landslide* (1988), Jane Mayer and Doyle McManus describes White House concerns about President Reagan' health. Reagan was 76 years old in 1987 during the stress of the Iran-Contra scandal. When Howard Baker became Reagan's Chief of Staff he was so worried about a dysfunctional White House that he asked an aide to gather information about the President. The staff reported that Reagan did not want to work—he just wanted to stay in the residence and "watch movies and television." Subsequent studies of Reagan's speech patterns reveal changes that are linked with Alzheimer's disease, with which he was diagnosed four years after leaving office.

Think About It!
Read the DSM criteria for the Narcissistic Personality Disorder
http://www.mayoclinic.org/diseases-conditions/narcissistic-personality-disorder/basics/symptoms/con-20025568
Is it relevant to politics?
https://www.psychologytoday.com/blog/brainstorm/201701/shrinks-battle-over-diagnosing-donald-trump

Have the civics rules changed? Or is Trump just a special case to whom the rules about probity do not apply? There is another explanation, one that ties Trump's character and style to his political constituency. Popular culture once again provides good insights. Alex Jones is the host of a right-wing radio program and contributor to the website *InfoWars.com*. In a custody hearing, his ex-wife claimed that his statements denying the 2012 mass shooting at Sandy Hook Elementary School, and his claims that Hillary Clinton was running a sex-trafficking operation out of a pizza parlor, were evidence that he was unstable and therefore an unfit parent. Jones replied that his outrageous comments are all *just for entertainment value*. Jones's claim that his conservative persona was just an act will not likely hurt his standing in the radical right community because the audience knows that the persona is artifice. They don't expect or even want factual truth. Jones's rhetoric and persona, like President Trump's rhetoric and persona, validate basic political feelings and perhaps even provide a cathartic release of pent-up frustrations with politics.

Spectacle or political theater is a hallmark of the postmodern presidency. Professional wrestling presents fake matches that are treated as real matches so that audiences can experience "genuine emotion." This allows the real and the fake to coexist side-by-side in the minds of the wrestlers and the fans. The wrestlers genuinely care about the fan's experience. Both the wrestlers and the fans care more about the "emotional fidelity" of the matches—the meaning of the dramatic conflict—than the "facts." President Trump's political success is an indication that the aesthetic of World Wrestling Entertainment has spread outside the ring into the real world of political conflict. Taking the fight outside is familiar to anyone who has seen professional wrestling matches. Some of the most dramatic matches have one wrestler throwing his opponent out of the ring where the fighting continues among the fans. Donald Trump's repeated promise to build a big, high, strong and beautiful wall along the southern border is not necessarily intended to be taken literally. The political significance of the promise is catharsis: the promise to take concrete action releases the anger and sense of betrayal some of his supporters feel about the loss of control over immigration policy, southern border anxiety, and worries about the loss of American national identity after a period of increased and uncontrolled immigration. The repeated pledges to repeal Obamacare can be similarly explained as political catharsis as much as literal descriptions of promised actions. This rhetorical style has worked well for Donald Trump because he is such a good showman capable of producing high drama.

Read About It!
The Tweeter-in-Chief?
President Trump's Tweeting habits have been a major source of political drama
http://www.trumptwitterarchive.com/

4.2 | The Power Problem

The power problem is the difficulty striking the right balance between granting government enough power to be effective while also limiting power so that government can be held accountable. The power problem with Congress is effectiveness. Congress is institutionally designed for representation and deliberation rather than effective or decisive action. The power problem for the presidency is accountability. The executive power was vested in the hands of one individual to promote effectiveness. The discretionary nature of modern presidential power makes it hard to hold a president legally accountable for the use of government power.

4.21 | *Is the Presidency Imperial or Imperiled?*

Best Presidents	Worst Presidents
1. Abraham Lincoln	1. James Buchanan
2. Franklin D. Roosevelt	2. Andrew Johnson
3. George Washington	3. Franklin Pierce
4. Teddy Roosevelt	4. Warren Harding
5. Harry Truman	5. William Harrison

Source: C-SPAN Survey of Historians on Presidential Leadership

George Washington
1st President of the United States
(1789-1797)

Presidents
John Adams   Thomas Jefferson   James Madison

The power of the president has greatly increased over time, and that the increased power of the president has presented some challenges. The modern presidency is much more powerful than the Founders intended it to be. In the early decades of the 19th Century, great political figures including Henry Clay, Daniel Webster, and John C. Calhoun, served in the Senate, a body that was described as the "greatest deliberative body in the world." Abraham Lincoln did not aspire to be president. His ambition was to serve in the Senate. The antebellum presidency was by contrast "a mundane administrative job that offered little to a man of Lincoln's oratorical abilities."[4] The modern president is not only more powerful than the president was in the early years of the republic but the modern president is more powerful relative to Congress. The Founders created a system of legislative governance in the sense that

Congress was intended to be the primary branch of government. But the system has developed into presidential government. The presidency has become the primary branch of government, the most powerful branch of government—the first among equals. Presidents accumulated power for a variety of reasons but the main reason is crises. Domestic and foreign crises, wars and other threats to national security, and hostage rescue missions have concentrated power in the branch of government that was designed to act quickly.

The personal nature of the presidency has caused presidential scholars to regularly take the pulse of the presidency to determine whether it is too strong, too weak, or just about right. The term **Imperial Presidency** describes presidents who are too strong, too powerful for their and our own good. The term **Imperiled Presidency** describes presidents who are too weak to govern effectively. The term Imperial Presidency was coined to describe a presidency that had grown too powerful, and resembled a monarchy insofar as it was becoming hard to control.[5] The imperial label was initially applied to the presidencies of Lyndon Johnson (1963-1968) and Richard Nixon (1969-1974).

The Imperiled Presidency label was initially applied to the presidencies of Gerald Ford (1973-1976) and Jimmy Carter (1977-1980). President Ford seemed incapable of responding effectively to a domestic economic crisis. The Organization of the Petroleum Exporting Countries (OPEC) oil embargo shocked the economy with gas shortages and inflation.[6] The Ford administration's response to the threat included distributing "WIN" buttons, but the Whip Inflation Now buttons seemed a pathetically weak response to the economic threat of gas shortages. President Carter seemed incapable of responding effectively to either the domestic or foreign crises. The Soviet invasion of Afghanistan in 1978, an anti-American Iranian Revolution in 1979 that included holding Americans hostage in Teheran, created the impression that the presidency had become too weak.

RONALD REAGAN, 40TH PRESIDENT OF THE UNITED STATES

Ronald Reagan campaigned for the presidency pledging to return to a stronger presidency, and his election as president (1981–1988) marked a return to a strong presidency with confidence in American leadership in foreign affairs and national security. However, Reagan's successor, George H. W. Bush (Bush the Elder or "41"), who served from 1989 to 1992, revived worries about an imperiled presidency. Bill Clinton's presidency (1993–2000) was described as both imperial and imperiled. The presidency of George W. Bush (or Bush "43") revived worries about an imperial presidency. Conservatives and Republicans criticized President Obama for being both imperial and imperiled, both too strong and too weak! The dynamic nature of presidential power, the fact that it fluctuates greatly from one president to the next, makes it hard to take the pulse of the presidency to see whether it is too weak or too strong.

> "The whole government is so identified in the minds of the people with his personality that they make him….responsible for society itself."
>
> William H. Taft
> 27th President of the United States

> "All the president is, is a glorified public relations man who spends his time flattering, kissing, and kicking people to get them to do what they are supposed to do anyway."
>
> Harry S. Truman
> 33rd President of the United States

4.21 | *Presidential Power*

The delegates at the constitutional convention of 1787 extensively debated whether the new government should have a single executive. The opponents of a single executive worried that it would betray the Revolutionary War had been fought against monarchy. But the constitutional convention was called to remedy defects in the Articles of Confederation, and it was agreed that the lack of an executive figure was one of the defects. The extended debate over executive power concluded with the creation of a unitary executive with both considerable powers and considerable checks and balances.

The following diagram shows the president's formal (or *legal*) and informal (or *political*) powers.

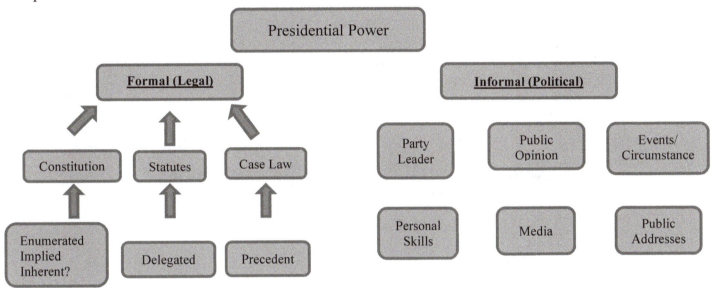

The formal powers are provided in the Constitution, statutes, and case law. The president's *constitutional* powers are set forth in Article II. Article II is a short article that only generally mentions presidential power. It is much shorter than Article I, which specifically lists congressional powers. The Article II statement that "the executive Power shall be vested in a President" is followed by brief descriptions of how the president is selected, eligibility to serve as president, a statement that the president is commander-in-chief, and a description of the president's appointment and treaty making powers. The president's *statutory* powers are very extensive. From the earliest years of the republic, Congress has delegated broad powers to the president. These statutory delegations have greatly increased presidential power. The president's *case law* powers come from court rulings, primarily Supreme Court decisions interpreting the law. The president's formal constitutional powers have changed very little since the founding of the republic, but presidential power has increased a great deal. This is one of the reasons why presidential scholars refer to the development of the personal presidency. The major changes have occurred in the president's statutory, case law, and political powers.

The rule of law is so widely accepted as an essential element of good government that it can be considered the successor doctrine to democracy as the measure of good government. The rule of law principle is considered part of the American "creed." Courses on Introduction to American government and civics education contrast political systems based on the rule of law with those based on the rule of man, and describe the rule of law as the good form of government and the rule of man as the bad form of government. The rule of law is the principle that government authority is legitimately exercised only in accordance with written, publicly disclosed laws that are adopted in accordance with established procedure. The rule of law is a safeguard against arbitrary governance by requiring those who make and enforce the law to be bound by the law. The modern presidency is difficult to reconcile with this principle.

4.3 | Legal Sources

In order to understand the presidency, it is very important to recognize the difference between legal and political powers. In fact, the difference is one of the keys to explaining the modern presidency. The president's constitutional powers have remained surprisingly constant (or steady) for more than 200 years. In fact, the major amendment affecting presidential power is the 22nd Amendment and it actually reduced presidential power by limiting a president to serving two full terms in office—thereby making a president a lame duck as soon as the second term begins.

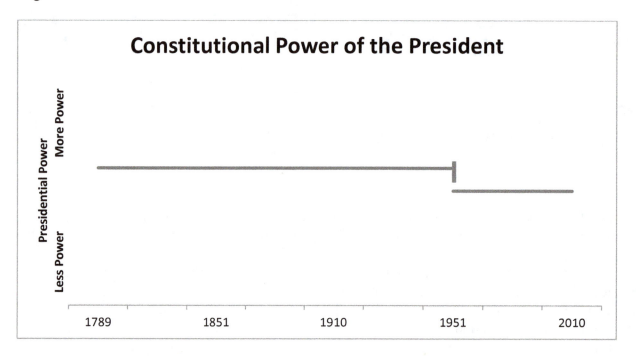

But presidential power has increased a great deal since the founding of the republic, *and* presidential power fluctuates considerably from one president to another. The president's constitutional powers have been static, but presidential power has been very dynamic: it has increased over time, and it varies from one president to the next with some presidents considered strong and others weak. The fact that presidential power changes while the constitution remains the same means that the key to understanding presidential power is not the Constitution but statutory law, case law, and politics.

4.31 | *The Article II Constitutional Power*

Presidents claim three kinds of constitutional powers: enumerated, implied, and inherent powers. The **enumerated** powers are those that are actually mentioned in Article II:

- The chief executive;
- The commander in chief;
- The veto power (to veto legislation);
- The pardon power;
- The power to make treaties;
- The power to appoint ambassadors and other government officials including Supreme Court justices;
- The power to from time to time report to Congress on the state of the union; and
- The power (or duty) to "*take Care that the Laws be faithfully executed....*"

Some of these enumerated powers are shared with Congress. For instance, the Senate must ratify treaties and confirm the appointment of federal judges, high-ranking administrators such as the secretaries of the executive departments, and the commissioners of the independent agencies such as the Federal Reserve Board.

Implied powers are powers that are not actually mentioned in the Constitution, but which are logically related to them. The president is not limited to those powers that are specifically granted. The following are implied powers of the president.

- Firing Officials. The power to hire implies the power to fire. If the president has the enumerated power to appoint an official, then it is implied that the president has the power to fire that official because the power to fire is logically related to the president's responsibility as chief executive to manage the executive branch.
- Executive Privilege. Executive privilege is a president's power to refuse to disclose to Congress, the courts, or the public certain communications with advisors or other individuals. The Supreme Court has held that the president needs executive privilege to ensure that the president can get candid advice about public policy matters. Executive privilege limits the power of Congress or the courts to compel the president or his subordinates or advisors to disclose communications.
- Executive Agreements. Executive Agreements are international agreements between the leaders of countries. Executive agreements function like treaties but they do not require Senate ratification. Therefore the president has more control over executive agreements than treaties. The Supreme Court has held that the president's constitutional power over foreign affairs implies the power to enter into executive agreements.
- Executive Orders. An executive order is a presidential directive, usually issued to an executive branch official, which provides specific guidelines on how a policy is to be implemented. Executive orders are a way for the president to manage the executive branch. Executive orders are a form of presidential legislation.

Inherent power is the most controversial kind of presidential power. The Supreme Court has never official recognized inherent powers, but presidents regularly claim they have inherent powers. Inherent powers are powers that presidents claim as inherent in the office, powers that the president has simply because the president is the president. Presidents have historically claimed that they have the power to do something (e.g., use military force) simply because they are President. The argument for inherent powers is that certain powers are inherent in the office and therefore do not require any specific legal authorization.[7] The inherent powers doctrine is controversial because it is practically impossible to hold Presidents legally accountable if they can claim that their actions do not need legal authorization.

4.32 | *Statutory Powers*

The president also has powers that are conferred by statutes. Congress has delegated a broad range of powers to the president to act in domestic policy and global affairs. In fact, Congress has delegated so much policy making power to the president that political scientists refer to *presidential legislation* and call the modern president the *chief legislator*. The following is just a short list of statutory delegations of broad discretionary power to the president.

The Hostage Act of 1868. This 19th Century Act authorized the president to take "all actions necessary and proper, not amounting to war, to secure the release of hostages." It provided that the president may act quickly to secure the release of "any citizen of the United States has been unjustly deprived of his liberty by or under the authority of any foreign government." Furthermore, the president has the duty to attempt to secure the release of any hostage and can "use such means, not amounting to acts of war, as he may think necessary and proper to obtain or effectuate the release; and all the facts and proceedings relative thereto shall as soon as practicable be communicated by the president to Congress."[8]

Employment Act of 1946. This Act declared that it was the federal government's responsibility to manage the economy. It also delegated to the president the power "to foster and promote free competitive enterprise, to avoid economic fluctuations or to diminish the effects thereof, and to maintain employment, productivity, and purchasing power."[9] The Act was passed because of the significant increase in unemployment in the early 1930s and the perceived "planlessness" of economic policy.

Gulf of Tonkin Resolution (1964). This Act authorized the president "to take all necessary measures to repel any armed attack against the forces of the United States and to prevent further aggression." Congress gave the president a "blank check" to fight the war in Vietnam.[10]

Economic Stabilization Act of 1970. This Act authorized the president "to stabilize prices, rents, wages, and salaries by issuing orders and regulations he deems appropriate."[11]

Emergency Economic Stabilization Act of 2008. This Act authorized the president, acting through the secretary of the treasury, to spend up to $700 billion dollars to "rescue" or "bailout" distressed financial institutions.[12]

Authorizations for the Use of Military Force in Afghanistan and Iraq (2002) In response to the terrorist attacks on September 11, 2001, Congress authorized the president "to use all means that he deems appropriate, including the use of military force, in order to enforce the UN resolutions, defend the national security interests of the United States against the threat posed by Iraq, and restore international peace and security in the region."[13]

The cumulative effect of all these congressional delegations has been a great increase in the statutory powers of the president. Modern presidents have much more statutory power than early presidents. The chart below, "Statutory Powers of the President Over Time," describes the statutory powers of the president over time. The stepped increases indicate the statutory delegations of power.

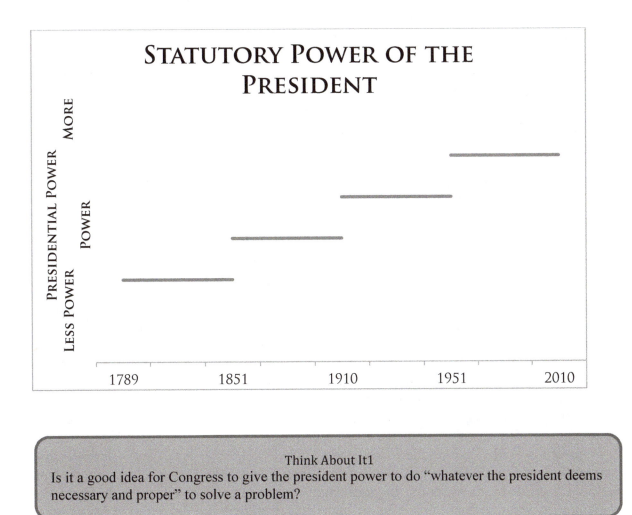

> **Think About It1**
> Is it a good idea for Congress to give the president power to do "whatever the president deems necessary and proper" to solve a problem?

4.33 | *Case Law Sources of Presidential Power*

Case law is the third source of formal power. The Supreme Court's rulings in cases involving war, national security, foreign affairs, and emergency powers are an especially important source of presidential power. The Court has generally supported an expansive reading of presidential power in these areas of law so there is a large body of case law that supports presidential power. *U.S. v. Curtiss-Wright Export Corporation* (1936) is one of the most important cases. Curtiss-Wright Export Corporation was a major U.S. company that, among other things, was an international arms dealer. The company challenged the president's power to issue an executive order banning companies from selling arms to two South American countries that were fighting over a border region. The Court upheld the president's power, saying that the **Sole Organ** doctrine gave the president power complete power over foreign affairs. The **Sole Organ** doctrine originates from a statement that Representative John Marshall made in the House of Representatives in 1799: "The President is the sole organ of the nation in its external relations, and its sole representative with foreign nations."[14]

Presidents have relied on this and other expansive readings of presidential power in national security and foreign affairs. World War II, the Cold War, and the War on Terror provided presidents with many opportunities to use the Sole Organ doctrine to assert control over foreign affairs—particularly when challenged by Congress or in court. For example, President George W. Bush claimed that the president, not Congress or the Supreme Court, had the power to decide how to treat the unlawful enemy combatants that were detained in the war on terror. The enemy combatant cases that the Supreme Court decided in 2002, 2004, and 2008 were exceptions to the general rule that the courts defer to presidential power over national security affairs because they established constitutional limits on the president's power as commander-in-chief to decide how best to wage the war on terror.

4.4 | Political Sources of Presidential Power

Presidents also have a variety of informal or political sources of power. In contrast with the legal sources, which have remained fairly constant over time, the political sources change a great deal.

4.41| *Party Leader*

The emergence of political parties fundamentally changed politics and government. Political parties changed government by making the president the de facto leader of the president's party. The Republican and Democratic Parties have official leaders, but the president is the most politically visible member of the party and its highest elected official. Presidents use the parties to build public support for their policies, to build political support in Congress for their policies, and to organize support for electoral campaigns.

President Andrew Jackson was the first president to use a mass membership party as a base of political support. He served during the time when political parties changed from legislative caucuses—meetings of like-minded members of Congress—to mass membership organizations—parties with whom members of the public identified. The development of mass political parties created a new source of presidential power. In the past, presidents were not always willing to use the party as a base of support. President Rutherford B. Hayes was a Republican but he did not consider himself beholden to either public opinion or the Republican Party.

Is President Trump Jacksonian? Is he channeling Andrew Jackson, populist with a reputation for being a fighter and a strong leader? Trump may find Jackson appealing, but his identification with Jackson comes from his advisor, Steve Bannon, who called Trump's election Jacksonian. Since then, President Trump has on numerous occasions identified himself with Jackson as, for example, a strong leader who might have prevented the Civil War in the way that being a strong leader today may prevent political violence.

> **Think About It!**
> Is President Trump's suggestion that he could have done a deal to prevent the Civil War a sign of developing narcissism? Some presidential scholars think that the man makes the office, while others think that the office makes the person? Robert Caro's study of Lyndon Johnson, *Master of the Senate*, writes that *power reveals*—possessing power reveals a person's character and even exaggerates their characteristics.

Partisanship has undermined the system of institutional checks and balances. The separation of powers was supposed to help solve the problem of corruption. Congress would protect its power from the executive or judicial branch; the president would protect executive power from encroachment by the congress or the courts; and the courts would protect their power from Congress or the president. Party loyalty has undermined the system of institutional checks because party loyalty often trumps institutional loyalty. Members of Congress may support a president of their party, and oppose a president of the other party, more than they support Congress as an institution. The voting records of Supreme Court Justice also indicate strong support for the views of the political party of the president who nominated them. The congressional investigations of President Trump's firing of Michael Flynn (President Trump's National Security Advisor), FBI counter-terrorism investigations of Russian interference in the 2016 elections intended to help Trump, and congressional investigation of President Trump's firing of the Director of the FBI, illustrate how partisanship has eroded institutional checks and balances. The Chair of the House of Representatives Permanent Select Committee on Intelligence, Devin Nunes (R-California), seemed more loyal to President Trump than to congressional investigative and oversight powers. The expansion of presidential power was enabled by the diminished institutional loyalty of members of Congress.

4.42 | *Personal Skills*

The fact that the Constitution vests the executive power in one person means that a president's power will depend on personal skills, native intelligence, experience, character, leadership, and management styles. Presidential manage skills have become more important because the executive branch has become so large and complex. Presidents cannot assume that government bureaucrats, particularly the professional or career civil service employees, will automatically do what the President wants or even tells them what to do. Presidential political skills can also be effective by using powers of persuasion to get members of Congress to support them. The fact that personal skills vary from one incumbent to another is one reason why presidential power fluctuates even while formal power remains the same.

4.43 | *Inaugural Addresses and Annual Messages*

The President has formal occasions to communicate with Congress, the American people, and the rest of the world. The Inaugural Address is an opportunity to state goals and set the national agenda. The State of the Union address originates from the constitutional requirement that the President "shall from time to time give to the Congress Information of the State of the Union, and recommend to their Consideration such Measures as he shall judge necessary and expedient." President Obama's 2013 Inaugural Address

ANNUAL STATE OF THE UNION ADDRESS

described globalism as a positive development that moved politics forward to a future world "without borders." Present Trumps 2017 Inaugural Address was very different in tone and substance. It promised a new nationalism that would end the "American carnage" caused by globalism.[15] The State of the Union address an annual occasion to recount highlights of the past year and announce goals for the upcoming year.

4.44 | *Events, Circumstances, Conditions*

Presidential power is also affected by the political events, circumstances, and conditions facing the nation. A president whose political party also controls Congress is usually in a better position than one who has to deal with a Congress controlled by the other party. Divided control of the federal government sometimes produces **gridlock**, an inability of the House of Representative, the Senate, and the president to agree on public policies.

Crises have historically resulted in an increase in presidential power. In times of crisis, the public and other government officials look to the president for leadership and give him leeway to select the appropriate policy responses to the crisis. Wars and other threats to national security, economic crises, and other emergency conditions have also tended to increase presidential power. The Great Depression of the 1930s created an expectation that the national government respond to a national economic emergency. The president became the person held responsible for maintaining economic prosperity. The modern president who does not appear to be acting decisively to address problems is likely to suffer a loss of political support or public approval.

Public opinion polling records the effects of events or circumstances on public approval of the president. George W. Bush is a good example of the impact of events on presidential popularity. He began his tenure in office with approval ratings of around 50%. His approval rating soared to nearly 90% immediately after the 9/11 terrorist attacks, his approval rating soared to nearly 90%. Then it sank to historic lows as the wars in Afghanistan and Iraq dragged on and the Great Recession began. His approval rating was around 34% when he left office. President Obama's approval rating increased as the economy recovered. Another reason why President Trump is unprecedented is because he began office with unprecedented low public approval ratings.

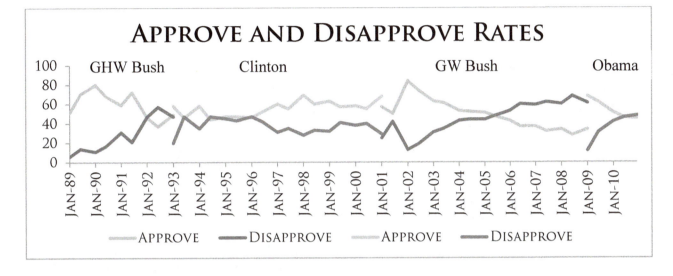

4.45 | Public Opinion

In a democracy, public opinion can serve as an important source of presidential power or an important limit on it. Strong public support adds to a president's formal powers, while weak public support subtracts from it. One of the most widely reported measures of public opinion about the president is the regular survey of job approval ratings. The president's popularity as measured by job approval is regularly measured and widely reported as a kind of presidential report card.[16] Unlike the constitutional and statutory powers, which are fairly constant, public opinion is dynamic.

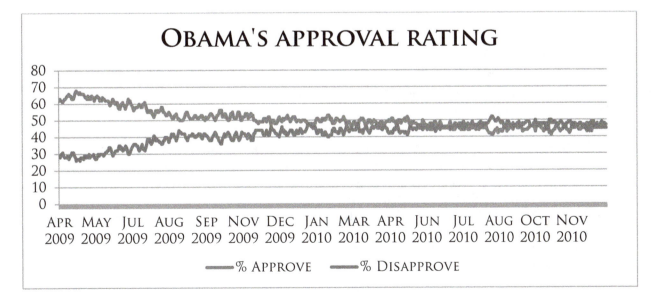

President Obama's approval ratings followed the familiar pattern of high initial approval, with eventual declines in approval ratings. Approval ratings are considered important indicators of a president's ability to get their agenda enacted into law.

4.46 | *MediA*

Presidents typically have a love-hate relationship with the media. Presidents love to use the media to get their message out, and presidents love favorable coverage of themselves and their administration. But presidents also hate *bad* press, which they tend to define as any critical media coverage of them or their administration. The *love* side of the relationship is evident in the eagerness of any administration to provide favorable photo opportunities that reinforce the image of presidential leadership. The *hate* side of the relationship is apparent in statements by presidents from Thomas Jefferson to Richard Nixon. *President Jefferson's Second Inaugural Address* (March 4, 1805) included strong criticism of press coverage of his administration:

> "During this course of administration, and in order to disturb it, the artillery of the press has been levelled against us, charged with whatsoever its licentiousness could devise or dare. These abuses of an institution so important to freedom and science, are deeply to be regretted, inasmuch as they tend to lessen its usefulness…[T]hey might, indeed, have been corrected by the wholesome punishments reserved and provided by the laws of the several States against falsehood and defamation; but public duties more urgent press on the time of public servants, and the offenders have therefore been left to find their punishment in the public indignation…..No inference is here intended, that the laws, provided by the State against false and defamatory publications, should not be enforced; he who has time, renders a service to public morals and public tranquility, in reforming these abuses by the salutary coercions of the law; but the experiment is noted, to prove that, since truth and reason have maintained their ground against false opinions in league with false facts, the press, confined to truth, needs no other legal restraint; the public judgment will correct false reasonings and opinions, on a full hearing of all parties; and no other definite line can be drawn between the inestimable liberty of the press and its demoralizing licentiousness. If there be still improprieties which this rule would not restrain, its supplement must be sought in the censorship of public opinion."

(Courtesy of *The American Presidency Project*, John Woolley and Gerhard Peters.)

Richard Nixon had a famously difficult relationship with the media during his entire political career. President Nixon's relationship with the press became especially difficult when the press began investigating criminal activity related to Watergate and then reported on the widening scandal. The following excerpt from President Nixon's News Conference on Oct. 26th 1973 reveals his disdain for the press corps:

> Q. Mr. President, you have lambasted the television networks pretty well. Could I ask you, at the risk of reopening an obvious wound, you say after you have put on a lot of heat that you don't blame anyone. I find that a little puzzling. What is it about the television coverage of you in these past weeks and months that has so aroused your anger?
> THE PRESIDENT [to Robert C. Pierpoint, CBS News]. Don't get the impression that you arouse my anger. [Laughter]
> Q. I'm afraid, sir, that I have that impression. [Laughter]
> THE PRESIDENT. You see, one can only be angry with those he respects.

(Courtesy of The American Presidency Project: www.presidency.ucsb.edu
http://www.presidency.ucsb.edu/ws/index.php?pid=4022#ixzz1sa7xTDeJ)

4.5 | The Office: The Organization of the Executive Branch

The executive branch is organized around the various functions of the office of the presidency. The president is the head of the executive branch, with the vice-president and the white house staff under his direct supervision. The Executive Office of the President consists of the individuals who serve as the president's policy advisors. These individuals also manage the various policy offices that are located in the executive branch. The final component of the president's circle of advisors is the cabinet. The cabinet is an informal name for the heads of the fifteen executives departments—e.g., the Secretaries of State, Defense, Treasury and so on.

The growth of the executive branch has included what is commonly called the bureaucracy or the administrative state. As the chief executive officer, the president has a great deal of control over the administrative apparatus that produces regulations.

Department Head	Year	Responsibilities
Secretary of State	1789	Foreign policy
Secretary of the Treasury	1789	Government funds and regulation of alcohol, firearms, and tobacco
Secretary of Defense	1789	National defense, overseeing military
Attorney General	1870	Represents the U.S. government in federal court; investigates and prosecutes violations of federal law
Secretary of the Interior	1849	Natural resources
Secretary of Agriculture	1889	Farmers, food-quality, food stamps and food security
Secretary of Commerce	1903	Business assistance and conducts the Census
Secretary of Labor	1913	Labor programs, labor statistics, enforcement of labor laws
Secretary of Health and Human Services	1953	Health and income security
Secretary of Housing and Urban Development	1965	Urban and housing programs
Secretary of Transportation	1966	Transportation and highway programs
Secretary of Energy	1977	Energy policy and research
Secretary of Education	1979	Federal education programs
Secretary of Veterans Affairs	1989	Programs for veteran's assistance
Secretary of Homeland Security	2002	Issues relating homeland security

4.51 | *The Origins of the Office of the Presidency*

The Treaty of Paris (1783) ended the Revolutionary War. The United States emerged from the war as an independent country with the governmental structure that the Second Continental Congress drew up in 1777. The Articles of Confederation was a voluntary league of friendship among the states. The Articles government had inherent problems that became increasingly apparent with the end of the war and the defeat of the common enemy (Great Britain).

During the economic depression that followed the revolutionary war, the viability of the American government was threatened by political unrest in several states, most notably Shays' Rebellion in Massachusetts. The Articles had created a weak federal government, one that consisted of a Congress but no president. The lack of an executive office was one of the perceived weaknesses of the Articles of Confederation. Individuals who presided over the Continental Congress during the Revolutionary period and under the Articles of Confederation had the title "President of the United States of America in Congress Assembled." This title was often shortened to "President of the United States." But these individuals had no important executive power. The Congress appeared institutionally incapable of functioning as a lawmaker for the nation, which was a barrier to the nation-wide development of commerce and economic development.

The Constitutional Convention of 1787 was convened to reform the Articles of Confederation, but the delegates decided to create an entirely new system of government. The long and lively debates about the nature and power of the presidency addressed the power problem of giving the president enough power to be effective while also limiting power so that the president could be held accountable. The creation of the executive was shaped both the colonial experiences under the British monarchy, which made delegates wary of executive power, and the weakness of the Articles of Confederation, which made delegates think that executive power was necessary. They ultimately created an executive with both considerable power and substantial limits within a legislative-centered system of government. They believed that this was how the executive was made safe for republican government.

4.52 | *Washington Averts a Threat*

At the close of the Revolutionary War, officers of the Continental Army met in Newburgh, New York, to discuss grievances and consider a possible insurrection against Congress. The army officers were angry about Congress's failure to honor its promises to provide salaries, bounties and life pensions. The

officers heard rumors that they might not receive any compensation because the American government was going broke.

On March 10, 1783, an anonymous letter was circulated among the officers addressing those worries and calling for an unauthorized meeting of officers to be held the next day to consider possible military solutions to the problems of the civilian government and its financial woes. General Washington forbade the officers to attend the unauthorized meeting and suggested they meet a few days later, on March 15th, at the regular meeting of his officers. Meanwhile, another anonymous letter was circulated that suggested Washington was sympathetic to the claims of the disgruntled officers. On March 15, 1783, Washington's officers gathered in a church building in Newburgh. General Washington unexpectedly showed up, personally addressed the officers, and appealed to their sense of responsibility to protect the young republic. See the Appendix, "George Washington Prevents the Revolt of the Officers." Washington helped the U.S. avoid having a political military and a political commander in chief as president.

4.6 | The [S]election of the President

The constitutional qualifications to become president include being a natural-born citizen of the United States, at least thirty-five years old, and a resident in the United States for at least fourteen years. The Twenty-second Amendment also limits a president to serving two terms in office. The "natural-born" qualification means that some prominent individuals and successful politicians such as California Governor Arnold Schwarzenegger are not eligible to be president. And members of the "birther" movement question President Barack Obama's eligibility to serve as president. There is some discussion today of whether the requirement that a president be a natural-born citizen should be changed so that naturalized citizens who have lived in the country for a long time would be eligible to become president.

The informal, political requirements include having some government experience. The majority of presidents had prior experience as vice presidents, members of Congress, governors, or generals. Thirty-one of forty-two presidents served in the military. President Ulysses Grant's Civil War service as General-in-Chief and President Eisenhower's distinguished military career as Allied Commander during WWII are examples of how military service is seen as a political qualification for the presidency. During presidential campaigns government experience, or in an anti-government political climate, the lack of government experience is presented as a political qualification for office. Membership in one of the two major political parties is also an informal political qualification. Candidates usually must receive the backing of either the Republican Party or the Democratic Party because the U.S. has a two-party system that makes it hard for third or minor party candidates to be successful. In 1992, third-party candidate Ross Perot received nearly 19% of the popular vote.

4.61 | *Is This Any Way to [S]elect the President?*

People commonly refer to the **election** of the president, but the Electoral College officially

selects the president. The process of choosing the president is complicated. It involves both election—popular votes cast in the elections in fifty states—and selection—Electoral College votes. The United States is a republic or indirect democracy, but the voters do not directly elect the President. Presidents are chosen indirectly by the **Electoral College**. This process is complicated and has been criticized for years.

4.61 | *ELECTIONS*

Elections take place every four years on the Tuesday after the first Monday in November. Many states do provide early and absentee voting several weeks before the day of the election. The U.S. does not have a single, national election for President. Presidential elections are actually 50 separate elections because each state conducts an election for President.

4.62 | *The Campaign*

Presidential campaigns begin well before primary elections. A **primary election** is an election to determine party candidates for office. The two major political parties use primary elections to reduce the number of candidates in advance of their national nominating conventions. There was no incumbent in the 2016 presidential campaign, so there was an unusually large number of Republicans and Democrats running for their party nominations. There was an especially large

number of Republicans running for the Republican nomination. The Republican Party held primary elections and caucuses to determine who would be the Republican Party's nominee. Each party's nominating convention formally selects the party nominee for president. The party's presidential candidate chooses a vice presidential nominee and this choice is rubber-stamped by the convention. The party also establishes a platform on which to base its campaign. Although nominating conventions have a long history in the United States, their importance in the political process has greatly diminished.

From L to R: Ronald Reagan (40st), Gerald Ford (38th), Jimmy Carter (39th), and Richard Nixon (37th)

The fact that primaries determine which candidate has the most delegates to the party convention means that modern conventions usually merely ratify the results of the primary elections, rather than actually choosing the party's nominee. However, the national party conventions remain important for focusing public attention on the nominees and for energizing the parties for the general election.

Party nominees participate in nationally televised debates that are sponsored by the Commission on Presidential Debates. The Commission negotiates the terms of presidential debates, including determining the number of debates and the rules determining which candidates are allowed to participate in the debates. The rules typically exclude candidates other than the nominees of the two major parties. Ross Perot was a third party candidate who was allowed to participate in the 1992 debates, but the Libertarian Party candidates Gary Johnson and William Weld were excluded from the 2016 debates. Modern presidential campaigns rely heavily on the media.

Campaigns rely on a variety of communications media to communicate their messages. Radio and television ads "package" and "sell" candidates and parties to the general public. The Museum of the Moving Image shows campaign ads from the 1952 presidential campaign between Republican Dwight Eisenhower and Democrat Adlai Stevenson until today. These ads show how campaigns have changed over time. Changes in technology change campaign strategies. The development of social media has been incorporated into campaigns. President Obama's campaigns relied heavily on new technologies to reach younger voters. Donald Trump's campaign strategy incorporated traditional campaign events, the free media coverage he attracted, and direct or unfiltered communications using Twitter.

Trump's style made the 2016 presidential election unusual. He ran as an outsider who defeated both the Republican Party establishment and the Democratic Party establishment. As a wealthy businessman, he claimed the financial resources to be independent of special interests by "self-funding" his campaign. A savvy marketer, Trump attracted media attention that he did not have to pay for. He mastered the social media style of sending out short but punchy comments about other candidates. This unorthodox, unfiltered style of communication exposed his political inexperience and revealed his strategy to appeal to voters by being politically incorrect rather than being controlled by professional campaign handlers and message massagers.

4.63 | *Working the Refs*

One of Donald Trump's political strategies is *working the refs*. This phrase describes players or coaches who complain about, or complain to, the referees in order to get more calls to go their team's way. Trump worked the refs during his presidential campaign and continues to do so for governing. During a campaign, the refs are the media and campaign analysts who report on who is ahead and who is behind, who has failed to meet expectations, met expectations, or exceeded expectations. As president, Trump famously worked the refs by calling some of the news media the "fake news" media. Working the refs also includes challenging the objectivity and credibility of the intelligence agencies (most prominently, the Central Intelligence Agency and the FBI), the Federal Reserve Board, the Bureau of Labor Statistics, the Environmental Protection Agency (on climate change), and the Congressional Budget Office, the nonpartisan office responsible for assessing the impact that the Republican replacement of Obamacare would have on the budget deficit. Challenging the objectivity of individual officials and agencies questions their legitimacy. This is different than saying that the FBI tends to be conservative because it is biased toward law enforcement, or that the Environmental Protection Agency or the Department of Education tend to be liberal because they support environmental protection and education. Working the refs obviously applies to the courts, who ultimately decide the legality of many government policies. But working the refs also applies to the public and the press. President Trump's social media strategy is intended to work around the mainstream or institutional press to communicate unfiltered with Twitter followers.

4.64 | *The End of the Gaffe*

The traditional expectation that presidents will be articulate and well-spoken individuals who can use language to clearly communicate ideas and arguments, supported by evidence, is weakening. These are less important components of what it means to be presidential. President Ronald Reagan earned his reputation as *the great communicator*. Presidents George H. W. Bush and George W. Bush earned their reputations as not gifted communicators because of their tendency to mangle syntax. After leaving office, George W. Bush jokingly acknowledged his reputation for malapropisms and making up words such as "strategery." Technology changes the way people communicate. Electronic communications such as email and social media such as Twitter have made communication less formal and more casual. Traditionally, public communication from presidents meant that the president was *speaking*. *Speaking* meant a formal address as distinct from casual and personal communication. Donald Trump's campaign rhetoric and his unconventional Tweeting presidency have been effective because the populist, anti-establishment mood made the official, formal *speaking* style seem contrived verbiage written by speech writers and political advisors. His casual speaking style and even bad English come across to his core supporters as "talking" straight from the heart rather than speaking. (McWhorter)

Stephen Wayne's 10th edition of *The Road to the White House 2016* describes the ways to get to the White House. It is now apparent that Madison Avenue and Hollywood Boulevard can take you to 1600 Pennsylvania Avenue. The PBS program <u>*American Experience: Reagan*</u> (1998) describes how President Reagan's road to the White House included Hollywood Boulevard—his experience in film and television and the public image of him—and Madison Avenue—his advisors' application of advertising and marketing skills to politics, particularly during the 1984 reelection campaign. The entertainment business and the advertising industry understood the political importance of creating and burnishing images. Reagan explained his appeal to voters: They look at me and they see themselves." President Reagan's fixation on imagery did have a cost. During his second term, Reagan functioned more like a master of the ceremonial presidency than the chief executive—although this was partly due to medical problems such as Alzheimer's rather than a political strategy. <u>Donald Trump's road to the White House</u> also relied on celebrity status for name recognition. He then used the mainstream media to keep the media spotlight on him.

Presidential campaigns are long—and getting longer. Do the long campaigns contribute to voter fatigue? Do the long campaigns contribute to the comparatively low turnout in presidential elections? The large audiences for the Republican primary debates and the general election debates between Trump and Clinton can be interpreted as evidence of voter interest, not voter fatigue. The U.S. has by far the longest campaign season for selecting the head of government. Senator Ted Cruz announced that he was running <u>on March 23, 2015</u> so the presidential campaign lasted 597 days. During that time, there could have been four <u>Mexican elections</u>, seven <u>Canadian elections</u>, 14 <u>British elections</u>, 14 <u>Australian elections</u> or 41 French elections.

4.65 | *The Electoral College*

With the possible exception of the Federal Reserve Board, the <u>Electoral College</u> may be the least-known government institution. The Founders disagreed on the way to select the president. Some favored a national popular vote; others wanted Congress to choose the president. The Electoral College was created because the Founders did not trust people enough to allow them to directly elect the president. In a time of limited public education, limited communication, and a fear of sectionalism in American politics, the Founders believed that the average voter could not be trusted to judge which of the presidential candidates would be best for the country. The Electoral College was intended to be a council of wise elders who would choose the best person from among

those who received the most popular votes in the presidential election. The College would review the people's choices and then decide for itself which of their preferences would be best. The Electoral College no longer performs this role because of the development of political parties.

Although the Constitution would allow state legislators to select the members of the Electoral College, the states have provided for the members of the Electoral College to be chosen by popular vote. At state party conventions, the state political parties choose party loyalists to serve as members of the Electoral College. Whichever party's candidate wins the most popular votes in the state gets to have its members cast the state's Electoral College votes. The members of the Electoral College almost always cast their vote for their party's candidate because the members of the Electoral College are chosen by the political party whose candidate received the most popular votes in that state.

Voters in each of the 50 states actually cast their votes for a slate of Electors chosen by the candidates' political parties. The Electoral College actually selects the President. Each state has the same number of Electoral College votes as it has members in the Congress. There are 535 members of Congress, so the Electoral College consists of 535 members plus three for the District of Columbia so there is a total of 538 members of the Electoral College. When citizens cast their votes, the names of the presidential and vice presidential candidates are shown on the ballot. The vote, however, is actually cast for a slate of Electors chosen by the candidate's political party. In most states, the ticket (the candidates for president and vice-president) that wins the most popular votes in a state wins all of that state's Electoral College votes. Maine and Nebraska are the two exceptions to the winner-take-all rule. They give two electoral votes to the statewide winner and one electoral vote to the winner of each congressional district.

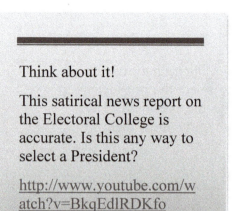

Think about it!

This satirical news report on the Electoral College is accurate. Is this any way to select a President?

http://www.youtube.com/watch?v=BkqEdlRDKfo

The winning set of electors meets at their state's capital on the first Monday after the second Wednesday in December, a few weeks after the election, to vote, and sends a vote count to Congress. The vote count is opened by the sitting vice president, acting in his capacity as President of the Senate, and read aloud to a joint session of the incoming Congress, which was elected at the same time as the president. Members of Congress can object to any state's vote count, provided that the objection is supported by at least one member of each house of Congress. A successful objection will be followed by debate; however, objections to the electoral vote count are rarely raised.

In the event that no candidate receives a majority of the electoral vote, the House of Representatives chooses the president from among the top three contenders. However, each state delegation is given only one vote, which reduces the power of the more populous states.

4.64 | *Is It Time for a Change?*

The Constitution originally provided that the U.S. Electoral College would elect both the President and the Vice President in a single election. The person

From L to R: George H.W. Bush (41st), Barack Obama (44th), George W. Bush (43rd), William (Bill) Clinton (42nd), and Jimmy Carter (39th)

Think About It!

What is the best way to choose a leader? Are there differences between "insiders" who are promoted up through the organizational ranks and "outsiders?" Is it a good idea to "roll the dice" with an outsider?

http://www.npr.org/2012/10/25/163626172/decision-time-why-do-some-leaders-leave-a-mark

with a majority would become President and the runner-up would become Vice President. The elections of 1796 and 1800 exposed the problems with this system. In 1800 the Democratic-Republican plan to have one elector vote for Jefferson and not Aaron Burr did not work; the result was a tie in the electoral votes between Jefferson and Burr. The election was then sent to the House of Representatives, which was controlled by the Federalist Party. Most Federalists voted for Burr in order to block Jefferson from the presidency. The result was a week of deadlock. Jefferson, largely as a result of Hamilton's support, ultimately won. The Twelfth Amendment (ratified in 1804) required electors to cast two distinct votes: one for president and another for vice president. It explicitly precluded from being vice president those ineligible to be president: people under thirty-five years of age, those who have not inhabited the United States for at least fourteen years, and those who are not natural-born citizens.

The Electoral College remains controversial today because it is inconsistent with basic democratic principles. In a democracy, voters should have the right to choose their leaders. In a democracy, the candidate who gets the most popular votes should win the office. In 2000, the Democratic candidate Al Gore received the most popular votes, but Republican George Bush became president because he received the most Electoral College votes. In 2016, Democrat Hillary Clinton won the popular vote by almost three million votes, but Republican Donald Trump won the presidency by receiving the most Electoral College votes. The Electoral College also distorts representation because it is biased in favor of less populous states and against more populous states. The most populous state, California, only has one electoral vote for every 660,000 residents, while the least populous state, Wyoming, has one electoral vote for about every 170,000 residents. This means that a vote cast in one state is worth much more than a vote cast in another state. So how much is a vote for president worth? It varies a great deal depending on the state. *The New York Times* story "How Much is Your Vote Worth?" provides a chart describing the different vote values in the 50 states.[17]

> **Check It Out!**
> *270towin* is a website that provides interactive maps of national elections, information about historical and current presidential and other elections, and other basic information about U.S. politics.
> http://www.270towin.com/

One of the more innovative ways use technology to make the selection of the president more democratic is the creation of an electronic national primary election. The Americans Elect organization describes the current political system for choosing leaders as lacking democratic legitimacy and failing to serve the people very well. Their solution is to create an electronic, national primary election that gives voters more control over the selection of candidates and the political parties less control. What do you think of the idea? Or perhaps we could create an "Assembly of Experts for the Leadership?"

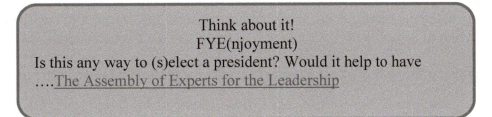

> **Think about it!**
> FYE(njoyment)
> Is this any way to (s)elect a president? Would it help to have
> ....The Assembly of Experts for the Leadership

4.7 | The Bureaucracy

Americans love to hate the government bureaucracy—particularly the federal bureaucracy. Much of the federal bureaucracy is located within the executive branch, so it is the part of the federal government that the president as Chief Executive is responsible for managing. The following provides a brief definition of bureaucracy, a description of the federal bureaucracy, and explanation of who controls the federal bureaucracy.

4.71 | *What is a Bureaucracy?*

A bureaucracy is a large organization whose mission is to perform a specific function or functions. Bureaucracies are organizations with three distinctive characteristics:

- Hierarchy. A bureaucracy structured hierarchically. It has a chain of command. At the top of the hierarchy are the policy makers. At the bottom of the hierarchy are the policy followers. Individuals in organizations have supervisors with higher ranks within the chain of command.
- Division of Labor. A bureaucracy is based on the division of labor. Individuals perform specific tasks rather than having everyone do everything the organization does. The division of labor allows organizations to develop expertise.
- Rules. A bureaucracy works according to written rules and regulations that determine what tasks individuals are assigned. An organization that is overly bureaucratic, which has too many strict rules and regulations, is sometimes said to have too much "red tape." Too many rules and regulations can limit an organization's performance of its mission.

It is important to note that this definition of a bureaucracy is not limited to government. Bureaucracy is the most common way of organizing individuals to perform functions in the private sector and the public sector. Corporations in the for-profit sector and the non-profit sector are bureaucracies. Political parties and interest groups are private sector bureaucracies.

In the public sector (i.e., government), the bureaucracy is the term for some of the officials who are responsible for administering the laws. The elected officials (the president and members of Congress) are not considered members of the federal bureaucracy. The political appointees that run the 15 executive departments (e.g., the departments of state, treasury, commerce, defense, and justice) are not the bureaucracy. The federal bureaucracy is the professionals or career officials who work in the mid and lower tiers of an organization. These individuals are not elected or appointed: they typically receive their jobs based on civil service tests. The federal bureaucracy consists of the people who carry out the organization's policies that are made by the upper management levels are the political appointees. Click on the organizational chart of any of the 15 executive departments to see the bureaucratic structure of the department.

The following figure represents a typical executive department bureaucratic organization.

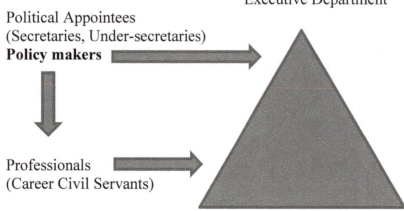

Executive Department

Political Appointees
(Secretaries, Under-secretaries)
Policy makers

Professionals
(Career Civil Servants)

Policy followers

4.72 | *Controlling the Bureaucracy*

There are several reasons why it is important to control the bureaucracy. The most important reason for controlling the bureaucracy is because it is an unelected "fourth branch" of government with a great deal of policymaking (or rule making) power. The bureaucracy does not fit easily into the tripartite separation of powers into the legislative, executive, and judicial branches. The bureaucracy makes "laws." Government agencies such as the Federal Communications Commission do not make *legislation* but administrative agencies do issue legally binding *rules* that have the same legal effect as laws passed by Congress.

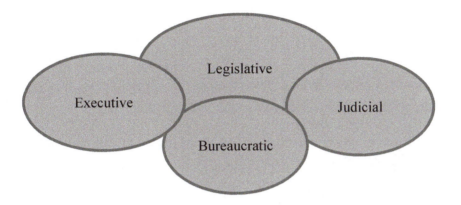

So control of the bureaucracy is very important in a democracy. Congress creates the bureaucracy—the departments and agencies and commissions—therefore Congress can abolish it. Congress also uses its budget power to control agencies. The Senate exerts some control over the bureaucracy because presidential nominations for upper-level management positions require Senate confirmation. The president's power as chief executive includes the power of appointment, which is the main tool for managing the federal bureaucracy.

It is also increasingly important to control the bureaucracy because of its size and complexity. The federal bureaucracy epitomizes the idea of big government! The U.S. still has only one president. The size of Congress has been fixed at 535 for more than a century. And the number of states has remained at 50 since Hawaii joined the union in 1959. But the federal government is now much bigger than it was a century ago because of the increase in the number of executive departments, agencies, bureaus, and independent regulatory commissions—and the regulations they produce. In organizational theory, the saying that *personnel is power* describes the importance of using the appointment power to staff the government in order to steer the government, staffing to control public policy. A president who is gifted with the ability to give great speeches can inspire support, but effective leadership requires paying attention to personnel policy, including the appointment of administrative officials.

4.8 | Summary

The development of the U.S. system of government from a congress-centered system to a president-centered system is one of the most important changes that have occurred over the more than 200 years of the existence of the republic. The increased power of the president, and the personal nature of modern presidential power, makes the power problem with the presidency even more important. The challenge is to find ways to hold executive power accountable. The personal and political nature of presidential power, and its roots in events, character, personal skills, and public opinion, presents a challenge for a system of government committed to the rule of law.

4.8 | Additional Resources

4.81 | *Internet Resources*

USA.gov provides information about the federal government, including the executive branch: https://www.usa.gov/branches-of-government#Executive_Departments

C-SPAN's "The Executive Branch" provides information about the president and the presidency: https://www.c-span.org/executiveBranch/

The official Website of the White House is https://www.whitehouse.gov/

Brief biographies of your favorite or least favorite president and first lady are available at https://www.whitehouse.gov/1600/Presidents

The American Presidency Project hosted at the University of California, Santa Barbara, provides a great deal of useful information and original documents related to the presidency: http://www.presidency.ucsb.edu/

The Avalon Project at Yale provides a broad range of documents, including the Annual Messages to Congress and Inaugural Addresses: http://avalon.law.yale.edu/subject_menus/sou.asp.

4.82 | *In the Library*

Abbott, Philip. 2008. *Accidental Presidents: Death, Assassination, Resignation, and Democratic Succession (The Evolving American Presidency)*. Palgrave Macmillian.

Boorstin, Daniel. 1962. *The Image: A Guide to Pseudo-Events in America*. Vintage.

Bradley, Richard. 2000. *American Political Mythology from Kennedy to Nixon*. Peter Lang Publishing.

Dionne, E.J. and William Kristol (Eds). 2001. *Bush v. Gore: The Court Cases and the Commentary*. Brookings Institution.

Mayer, Jane and Doyle McManus. 1988. *Landslide: The Unmaking of the President, 1984–1988*. Boston: Houghton Mifflin Company.

Lowi, Theodore. 1985. *The Personal President*. Ithaca, NY: Cornell University Press.

McWhorter, Jan. "How to Listen to Donald Trump Every Day for Years." *The New York Times* (January 21, 2017). Accessed at www.nytimes.com.

Miroff, Bruce. 2000. "Courting the Public: Bill Clinton's Postmodern Education," In *The Postmodern Presidency: Bill Clinton's Legacy in U.S. Politics*. Pittsburgh: University of Pittsburgh Press.

Pika, Joseph A. and John Anthony Maltese (Eds). 2006. *The Politics of the Presidency*. Sixth Edition. Washington, DC: CQ Press.

Rose, Richard. 1988. *The Postmodern President*. Chatham, NJ: Chatham House Publishers.

Sauer, Patrick. 2000. *The Complete Idiot's Guide to the American Presidents*. Alpha Books.

Schlesinger, Arthur M. 2004. *War and the American Presidency*. New York: W. W. Norton & Company.

Stark, Steven. "The First Postmodern Presidency." *The Atlantic* (April 1993). Accessed at https://www.theatlantic.com/past/docs/politics/polibig/postmod.htm

Taranto, James and Leonardo Leo (Eds). 2004. *Presidential Leadership: Rating the Best and the Worst in the White House*. New York: The Free Press.

Woodward, Bob. 2002. *Bush at War*. New York: Simon and Schuster.

TERMS

The rule of law
Imperial
Presidency
Delegated powers
Implied powers
Electoral College
Primary elections

STUDY QUESTIONS

1. How has the power of the president changed relative to Congress?
2. What is the role of the president in the legislative process?
3. What factors caused the expansion of presidential power?
4. How has the president's role as commander in chief of the military changed over time?
5. How do the president's cabinet and staff assist the president in exercising his duties and achieving his goals?
6. How does public opinion affect the presidency? How does the president use public opinion to achieve his policy goals?
7. If you were redesigning the Constitution from scratch, what existing presidential powers would you retain, which would you get rid of, and which would you modify? Why?

---

[1] Quoted in Jay Rosen, "Pressthink," *A Project of the Arthur L. Carter Journalism Institution at New York University.* Accessed at http://archive.pressthink.org/2004/06/09/reagan_words.html

[2] Quoted in NPR *Fresh Air* interview with Terry Gross (April 26, 2017). Accessed at http://www.npr.org/2017/04/26/525575857/veep-executive-producer-on-making-a-show-about-the-craven-desire-for-power

[3] Nick Rogers, "How Wrestling Explains Alex Jones and Donald Trump," *The New York Times* (April 25, 2017).

[4] Stephen B. Oates, 1994. *Abraham Lincoln: The Man Behind the Myths.* New York: HarperPerennial, p.76.

[5] Arthur M. Schlesinger, Jr. 1973. *The Imperial Presidency.* Boston and New York: Houghton Mifflin.

[6] http://www.opec.org/aboutus/history/history.htm

[7] Louis Fisher provides an excellent description of presidential claims of inherent powers. See http://loc.gov/law/help/usconlaw/pdf/Inherent-March07.pdf

[8] Quoted in *Dames & Moore v. Regan*, 453 U.S. 654 (1981). The Hostage Act was codified at 22 U.S.C. Sect. 1732 (1976).

[9] http://research.stlouisfed.org/publications/review/86/11/Employment_Nov1986.pdf

[10] http://avalon.law.yale.edu/20th_century/tonkin-g.asp

[11] http://www.presidency.ucsb.edu/ws/index.php?pid=3273

[12] http://www.house.gov/apps/list/press/financialsvcs_dem/press092808.shtml

[13] http://www.gpo.gov/fdsys/pkg/PLAW-107publ243/content-detail.html

[14] See *U.S. v. Curtiss-Wright Export Corp.*, 299 U.S. 304, 319 (1936).
http://supreme.justia.com/us/299/304/case.html
[15] http://www.npr.org/2017/01/20/510629447/watch-live-president-trumps-inauguration-ceremony
[16] See http://www.presidency.ucsb.edu/data/popularity.php
[17] "How Much is Your Vote Worth?" The New York Times (November 2, 2008). Accessed at
www.Nytimes.com

CHAPTER 5: THE COURTS

5.0 | The Courts

The above image is a picture of the U.S. Supreme Court Building. What does the building remind you of? It is intended to remind you of <u>a temple of justice</u>. The design of the building and the black robes that the Justices wear are intended to instill reverence for the courts and the law. All countries have courts. Courts are considered an essential element of good government because they administer justice and uphold the rule of law.

But courts do not have the same role in all countries. Courts have a very limited role in some countries and a very broad role in others. Courts play a broad role in modern American government, politics, and society. They rule on everything from "A" (abortion and agriculture and airlines) to "Z" (zoning and zoos and zygotes). In fact, the broad role that courts play in the U.S. political system explains why courts are considered essential for good government and the administration of justice, but they are also frequent targets of strong criticism. This chapter explains the complicated thinking about courts by examining three main issues related to the role courts play in the U.S. system of government and politics:

- The Power Problem for the Federal Courts;
- The Increased Power of the Judiciary; and
- The Relationship between Law and Politics.

"Presidents come and go, but the Supreme Court goes on forever." President William Howard Taft

"It is emphatically the province and duty of the judicial department to say what the law is." Chief Justice John Marshall in *Marbury v. Madison*

The *power problem* for the federal courts is legitimacy. In a democracy, there is a preference for policymaking by elected government officials. Federal judges are appointed to life terms. The tensions between democratic values and rule of law values are evident in court rulings. The *increased power* of the judiciary is a source of criticism because the courts have over time become much more powerful than originally intended. The judiciary was originally called the "least dangerous" branch of government. Today, court critics talk about an "imperial judiciary." The charge that the courts have become imperial is based on claims that judges have assumed powers previously held by the political branches of government. The issue of courts as *government institutions* is ultimately about the relationship between law and politics, the legal system and the political system. The Constitution created a political system where three separate institutions share power, and the courts are not immune from political criticism any more than Congress and the president.

The Supreme Court's decisions in cases about abortion, the death penalty, school prayer, obscenity and indecency, sexual behavior, and marriage have made the Court one of the primary targets in the **culture wars**. The term culture wars refers to *political fights* over values rather than valuables, but the fights are also legal conflicts. The chapter's primary focus is the U.S. Supreme Court, but some attention is paid to organization and operation of the federal court system and the state court systems. The American legal system also provides a prominent role for juries, so some attention is paid to jury justice.

5.1 | The Power Problem For the Federal Courts

Previous chapters examined the power problem for Congress (effectiveness) and the presidency (accountability). The power problem for the federal courts is **legitimacy**. The problem is rooted in a basic democratic principle: the preference for policy making by elected government officials. Federal judges are appointed to life terms. This makes the federal judiciary an undemocratic or even counter-majoritarian government institution. The legitimacy problem arises when individual judges or the courts as an institution make decisions that affect or in effect make public policy.

The federal courts are not the only non-elected government institution with policymaking power. The Federal Reserve Board is not elected and it has substantial power to make economic policy related to inflation and employment. The U.S. is not a pure democracy; it is a constitutional democracy. The Constitution actually places a number of very important limits on majority rule. In fact, the Constitution (particularly the Bill of Rights) is a counter-majoritarian document. The fact that courts interpret the Constitution means that courts sometime perform a counter-majoritarian role in the constitutional democracy. Much of the controversy surrounding the role of the courts in the U.S. system of government and politics is about the legitimacy of courts making policy. Judicial policymaking or legislating from the bench is considered inappropriate in a political system where the elected branches of government are expected to have the primary policymaking power. The power problem for the courts is about the boundaries between the political system and the legal system, the separation of politics and law. Keeping law and politics separate is complicated by the fact that the judiciary is expected to have some degree of independence from the political system so that courts can perform one of their most important roles: enforcing basic rule of law values in a constitutional democracy.

Think About It!

C-SPAN presents *Constitutional Role of Judges* in the American republic and democratic systems, and *Legal Scholars Examine Role of Courts in Democracy*:
https://www.c-span.org/video/?301909-1/constitutional-role-judges
https://www.c-span.org/video/?305745-1/role-courts-us-democracy

---

5.2 | Political History of the Supreme Court

Judicial power is also controversial because courts have historically taken sides in many of the most important and controversial issues facing the nation. The Supreme Court has had four distinct eras based on the kinds of issues the Court decided during the era: the Founding Era (1790–1865); the Development Era (1865–1937); the Liberal Nationalism Era (1937–1970); and the Conservative Counter-revolution (1970–). The specific issues that the Court decided during these four eras changed, but the Court consistently addressed many of the major political controversies and issues of the day. The Supreme Court Timeline marks some of these eras and issues.

5.21 | *The Founding Era (1790–1865)*

During the Founding Era the Court issued major rulings explaining how the new system of government worked. Its federalism rulings broadly interpreted the powers of the national government. The Marshall Court (1801-1835) established the power of judicial review in *Marbury v. Madison* (1803). It ruled that Congress had complete power over interstate commerce in *Gibbons v. Ogden* (1824). And it broadly interpreted Congress's power under the Necessary and Proper Clause in *McCulloch v. Maryland* (1819).

Chief Justice Roger B. Taney replaced Marshall. The Taney Court (1836–1864) was less concerned about establishing the new powers of the national government, so it issued a number of rulings upholding the powers of the states using the doctrine of **dual federalism**. Dual federalism is the idea that both levels of government are supreme in their respective fields. The national government is supreme in matters of foreign affairs and interstate commerce. The states are supreme in intrastate policies such as commerce, education, the regulation of morality, and criminal justice. The Taney Court's ruling in *Dred Scott v. Sandford* (1857) limited Congress's power to limit the spread of slavery, thereby contributing to the inevitability of the Civil War. The *Dred Scott* ruling struck down the Missouri Compromise of 1820, a law passed by Congress to limit the spread of slavery in the territories.

5.22 | *Development and Economic Regulation (1865-1937)*

During this era, the Court decided cases challenging the government's power to regulate the economy. Government regulation of the economy increased during the Progressive Era (roughly 1890 to WWI) and the New Deal Era (1930s) in order to ease some of the problems created by the Industrial Revolution. The government regulations included anti-trust laws, child labor laws, minimum wage and maximum hour laws, and workplace safety regulations. However, the Court saw its role as protecting business from government regulation so it used its power of judicial review to strike down many of these laws. In 1934 and 1935 it declare unconstitutional many of the major provisions of the Roosevelt Administration's New Deal. This exposed a major conflict between the political system and the legal system. The political system supported government regulation of business and social welfare policies that were intended to end the Great Depression and provide more income security. But the Court saw its role as protecting business from government regulation.

One reason for the New Deal era conflict between the political branches and the Court was an accident of history. President Franklin D. Roosevelt was unlucky in that he did not have the opportunity to appoint a member of the Supreme Court during his entire first term in office. Political change occurs regularly with the election calendar: every two years. But the Justices are appointed to life terms so vacancies occur irregularly with retirements or death. President Roosevelt and congressional Democrats saw the election of 1932 as a critical election that gave them a mandate to govern. They became increasingly frustrated with Supreme Court rulings where a conservative majority (often by 6–3 or 5–4 margins) struck down major New Deal programs in 1935 and 1936. Roosevelt eventually proposed legislation to add another member to the Court for every sitting justice over the age of seventy, up to a maximum of six more members—which would have increased the size of the Court from nine to 15 members. This proposal was very controversial because it was a presidential plan to "pack" the Court with new Justices who would support his New Deal policies. Although the Court's rulings striking down New Deal policies were unpopular, President Roosevelt's court packing plan was considered an inappropriate attempt to exert political control over the Court. The proposal died in Congress.

But in 1937 the Court seemed to get the political message. It abruptly changed its rulings on economic regulation and began to uphold New Deal legislation. The Court announced that it would no longer be interested in hearing cases challenging the government's power to regulate the economy. The Court indicated that it would henceforth consider questions about the government's power to pass economic regulations matters for the political branches of government to decide. The Court also announced that in the future it was going to take a special interest in cases involving laws that affected the political liberties of individuals. In effect, the Court announced that it would use judicial restraint when laws affected economic liberties but judicial activism when laws affected political liberties. The Court further explained that it was especially interested in protecting the rights of "discrete and insular" minorities. This 1937 change is called **the constitutional revolution of 1937** because it was such an abrupt, major change in the Court's reading of the Constitutional and its understanding of its role in the system of government and politics.

5.23 | *The Era of Liberal Nationalism (1937-1970)*

In the middle years of the 20th Century, the Court participated in debates about civil liberties and civil rights by assuming a new role: 1) protector of individual liberties; and 2) supporter of equality. The Court's interest in civil liberties cases marks the beginning of the Court's third era. It began protecting civil liberties in cases involving freedom of expression (including freedom of religion, speech, and press); the rights of suspects and criminals in the criminal justice system; racial and ethnic minorities to equal protection of the laws; and the right to privacy. The Warren Court (1953-1969) is remembered for its judicial activism on behalf of civil liberties. Chief Justice Earl Warren presided over the Court's important civil liberties cases supporting individual freedom and equality in both **civil** law and **criminal** law. In the 1950s and 1960s, the Court's civil liberties rulings ordering school desegregation put the Court in the middle of debates about racial equality.

The Warren Court's civil law rulings included the landmark school desegregation case *Brown v. Board of Education* (1954), and landmark right to privacy cases such as *Griswold v. Connecticut* (1965). In *Griswold v. Connecticut* the Court held that the U.S. Constitution included an implied right to privacy that prohibited states from passing laws that made it a criminal offense to disseminate information about birth control devices— and by implication, the implied right to privacy limited government power to regulate other aspects of sexual behavior. The Warren Court also issued rulings that affected the freedom of religion. In *Engel v. Vitale* (1962), the Court ruled that it was unconstitutional for government officials to compose a prayer and require that it be recited in public schools. The prayer was "Almighty God, we acknowledge our dependence upon Thee, and beg Thy blessings upon us, our teachers, and our country." In *Abington School District v. Schempp* (1963) the Court held that mandatory Bible reading in public schools was unconstitutional.

The Warren Court's criminal law rulings were no less controversial than its civil law rulings. The Court broadened the rights of suspects and convicted offenders in the state criminal justice systems. *Gideon v. Wainwright* (1963) broadened the right to the assistance of counsel by holding that anyone charged with a felony had a right to be provided an attorney if he or she could not afford to pay for one. *Mapp v. Ohio* (1961) held that the Exclusionary Rule applied to state courts. The Exclusionary Rule prohibited the use of evidence seized in violation of the Constitution in order to obtain a conviction. *Miranda v. Arizona* (1966) may be the most famous of the Warren Court rulings on criminal justice. It required police officers to notify suspect of their constitutional rights before questioning them. These rights include the right to remain silent, the right to have the assistance of counsel, and notified that anything said can be used in a court of law against them.

These Warren Court rulings, and the Burger Court's ruling in *Roe v. Wade* (1973) that the right to privacy included the right to an abortion, put the Court in the middle of "the culture wars"—the political conflicts over value as opposed to economics. Judicial decisions about state laws defining marriage continue the tradition of judicial participation in the leading controversies of the day.

5.24 | *The Conservative Counter-Revolution*

One indication that the era of liberal nationalism has ended is the fact that today's Court has a different agenda than the Warren Court. The conservatives have had working majorities on the Burger, Rehnquist, and now the Roberts Courts. They are interested in different issues than the Warren Court. President Nixon's election in 1968 marked the beginning of the rightward change in the country's *political* direction. His appointment of four Justices marked the beginning of the rightward change in the Court's *legal* direction. Crime became a national issue in the 1968 presidential campaigns. Richard Nixon portrayed judges as being soft on crime, and pledged to appoint judges who would get-tough-on-crime. President Nixon appointed four members of the Court, including Chief Justice Warren Burger. The Burger Court's (1969–1986) conservatism was first evident in criminal law. Crime fighting is a core function of government. All levels of government participate in making and implementing crime policy.

The election of conservative Republican presidents (Nixon, Ford, Reagan, Bush 41 and Bush 43)—and even the election of Democratic Presidents Carter and Clinton who came from the conservative wing of the Democratic Party—solidified the Court's rightward movement. Federal judges are appointed by political figures through a political process: the president nominates and the Senate confirms. So it is not surprising that political changes are reflected in the judiciary because the selection of federal judges is an obvious contact point between law and politic, between the legal system and the political system.

The Rehnquist Court (1986–2005) had a conservative working majority. It revived federalism to limit Congress's Commerce Clause powers. In *U.S. v. Lopez* (1995) and it struck down the Gun Free School Zones Act of 1990. In *U.S. v. Morrison* (2004), the Court struck down provisions of the Violence Against Women Act of 2000. The Roberts Court (2005–present) has also generally been a conservative Court. Chief Justice Roberts and Justice Samuel Alito were nominated in part because their lower court rulings supported business interests. Business issues had been overshadowed by higher profile issues such as abortion, school prayer, affirmative action, and the death penalty. But the Roberts Court has issued a number of rulings that are favorable to business interests. A 2010 ruling struck down provisions of federal law regulating independent campaign contributions. The <u>Citizens United v. Federal Election Commission</u>) ruling eased restrictions on corporate campaign contributions. The Roberts Court has also adopted the *Accommodationist* interpretation of the Establishment Clause of the First Amendment. It allows much more government support for, or accommodation of, religion than the *Wall of Separation* interpretation. And on matters of national security and counterterrorism policy, the conservative working majority on the current Court supports broad interpretations of the president's power as Commander-in-Chief.

5.3 | The Increased Power of the Courts: Going from Third to First?

The judiciary is called the third branch of government for two reasons. First, the judiciary is provided for in Article III of the Constitution. Second and more important,

the legislative and executive branches were intended to be more powerful than the judiciary. The judiciary was intended to be the weakest of the three branches of government. In *Federalist No. 78*), Alexander Hamilton described the judiciary as the "least dangerous" branch of government because the courts had neither the power of the purse (Congress controlled the budget) nor the power of the sword (the executive branch enforced the laws). The following describes ho
But courts have always played an important role in American society. In *Democracy In America*, Alexis de Tocqueville (1835) famously said, "There is hardly a political question in the United States which does not sooner or later turn into a judicial one." Today, critics call the courts an imperial judiciary.

5.31 | *The Early Years*

In the early years of the republic the Court initially lacked power or prestige. Early presidents had a hard time finding people who were willing to serve on the Court because it was not considered an important or prestigious institution. And the Justices' duties included travel to the circuit courts and a time when frontier travel was very difficult.
The Supreme Court first met in February 1790 at the Merchants Exchange Building in New York City, which then was the national capital. When Philadelphia became the capital city later in 1790 the Court followed Congress and the President there. After Washington, D.C., became the capital in 1800 the Court occupied various spaces in the U.S. Capitol building until 1935, when it moved into its own building.
The Court acquired prestigious during the Marshall Court Era. Chief Justice John Marshall's ruling in *Marbury v. Madison* (1803) established the doctrine of judicial review. The Marshall Court also ended the practice of each judge issuing his or her own opinion in a case and began the tradition of having the Court announce a single decision for the Court. This change created the impression that there was one Court with one view of what the Constitution meant, rather than a Court that merely consisted of individuals with differing points of view. The Marshall Court enhanced the Court's prestige as an authoritative body with special competence to interpret the Constitution when disputes arose over its meaning. But the main reason for the expansion of the power of the courts is the power of judicial review.

5.32 | *Judicial Review*

Judicial review is the power of courts to review the actions of government officials to determine whether they are constitutional. It is a power that all courts have, not just the Supreme Court, and it is a power to review the actions of *any* government official: laws passed by Congress; presidential actions or executive orders; regulations promulgated by administrative agencies; laws passed by state legislatures; actions of governors; county commission decisions; school board policies; city regulations; and the rulings of lower courts. The Constitution does not explicitly grant the courts the power of judicial review. Judicial review was established as an implied power of the courts in the landmark case *Marbury v. Madison* (1803), where the Court for the first time ruled that a law passed by Congress was unconstitutional. The case was a minor dispute. President John Adams signed a judicial appointment for William Marbury. His commission was signed but not delivered when a new President (Thomas Jefferson) took office. When the new administration did not give Marbury his appointment, Marbury used the Judiciary Act of 1789 to go to the Supreme Court asking for an order to deliver his commission as judge. Chief

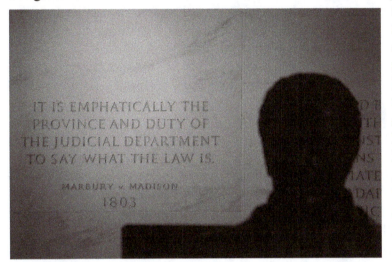

Statute of John Marshall in the foreground, shadowed, quotation from Marbury v. Madison (written by Marshall) engraved into the wall. United States Supreme Court Building.

Justice John Marshall's ruling in *Marbury v. Madison* used syllogistic reasoning to explain why it was logical to read the Constitution as implying that courts have the power to review laws and declare them unconstitutional if they conflicted with the Constitution. Syllogistic logic is a form of reasoning that allows inferring true conclusions (the "then" statements) from given premises (the givens or "if" statements). Marshall structured the logical argument for judicial review as follows:

> [If] the Constitution is a law,
> [and if] the courts interpret the laws,
> [then] the courts interpret the Constitution.

Marshall further reasoned that courts have the power to declare a law unconstitutional:

> [If the] Constitution is the supreme law of the land,
> [and if] a law, in this case the Judiciary Act of 1789, conflicts with the Constitution,
> [then] that law is unconstitutional.

Judicial review is the court's power to review and declare unconstitutional laws passed by Congress, executive orders or other actions of the President, administrative regulations enacted by bureaucracies, lower court judges, laws passed by state legislatures, or the actions of state governors, county commissioners, city officials, and school board policies. Judges have used judicial review to declare unconstitutional a federal income tax law, presidential regulations of the economy, state laws requiring that black children be educated separate from white children in public schools, school board policies requiring the recitation of organized prayer in public schools, and laws making flag burning a crime.

Some of the Founding Fathers, particularly Federalists such as Alexander Hamilton, accepted the notion of judicial review. In *Federalist No. 78* Hamilton wrote: "A constitution is, in fact, and must be regarded by the judges, as a fundamental law. It therefore belongs to them to ascertain its meaning, as well as the meaning of any particular act proceeding from the legislative body. If there should happen to be an irreconcilable variance between the two, that which has the superior obligation and validity ought, of course, to be preferred; or, in other words, the Constitution ought to be preferred to the statute." The Antifederalists (e.g., Brutus in *Antifederalist #XV*) feared the judicial power would be exalted above all other, subject to "no controul," and superior even to Congress. Nevertheless, judicial review has become a well-established power of the courts.

5.33 | *Limits on Judicial Power*

Does judicial review make the courts more powerful than the legislative and executive branches of government because the courts can rule presidential and congressional actions unconstitutional? The courts do have the power to strike down presidential and congressional actions. Does this make the judiciary the most powerful, not the least powerful, branch of government? There are limits on judicial power. The courts cannot directly enforce their rulings. Judges rely on individuals or other government officials to enforce their rulings. And judges cannot expect automatic compliance with their rulings. Opposition to desegregation of public schools after the 1954 *Brown v. Board of Education* was widespread. In 1957 the Florida Legislature passed an Interposition Resolution that asserted that the U.S. Supreme Court did not have the authority to order states to desegregate public schools therefore Florida government officials did not have to comply with the Brown ruling.

Interposition is a doctrine that asserts the power of a state to refuse to comply with a federal law or judicial decision that the state considers unconstitutional. Compliance with the Court's rulings outlawing organized prayer in public schools has also been mixed. And police officer compliance with Court rulings on search and seizure is not automatic. The courts depend on compliance by executive branch officials, such as school board members, teaching, and police officers.

5.34 | *Judicial Restraint and Judicial Activism*

The legitimacy of judicial power is usually described in terms of two concepts of the appropriate rule for the judiciary: judicial restraint and judicial activism. **Judicial restraint** is defined as a belief that it is appropriate for courts to play a limited role in the government, that judges should be very hesitant to overturn decisions of the political branches of government, and that judges should wherever possible defer to legislative and executive actions. **Judicial activism** is defined as a belief that it is appropriate for courts to play a broad role in the government—that judges should be willing to enforce their view of what the law means regardless of political opposition in the legislative or executive branches. There are three main elements of judicial restraint.

- **Deference** to the Political Branches of Government. Judicial deference to legislative and executive actions is a hallmark of judicial restraint. When judges are reluctant to overturn the decisions of the political branches of government they are exercising judicial restraint. Judges who bend over backwards to uphold government actions are exercising judicial restraint. Judicial activists are less deferential to the political branches of government. Activist judges are more willing to rule that the actions of government officials—whether the president, the Congress, lower court judges, the bureaucracy, or state government officials—are unconstitutional.

- Uphold **Precedent**. Precedent is a legal system where judges are expected to use past decisions as guides when deciding issues that are before the court. Precedent means that judges should decide a case the same way that they have decided similar cases that have previously come before the court. When judges decide cases based on established precedent, they are exercising judicial restraint. Judges who rely on "settled law" are using judicial restraint. Activists are not as committed to uphold precedent. They are more willing to overturn precedents or create new ones that reflect changes in contemporary societal attitudes or values. Activist judges are less bound by what has been called the "dead hand of the past."

- Only **Legal** Issues. Courts are institutions that are designed to settle legal disputes. Advocates of judicial restraint believe that courts should only decide legal questions, that courts should not become involved with political, economic, social, or moral issues. One indicator of judicial restraint is when a court limits its cases and rulings to legal disputes. It is not always clear, however, whether an issue is a legal or a political issue. Cases that address campaigns, voting, and elections, for instance, involve both law and politics because voting is considered a right, rather than merely a political privilege. Judicial activists are less concerned about getting the courts involved with cases or issues that affect politics, economics, or social issues. They are willing to issue rulings that affect politics because they don't necessarily see a bright dividing line between politics and law.

5.35 | Ideology and Roles

The above definitions of restraint and activism do not mention ideology even though restraint is commonly considered conservative and activism is commonly considered liberal. Judicial restraint and activism are not intrinsically conservative or liberal. For most of the Supreme Court's history, its activism has been conservative. The Marshall Court was a conservative activist court. During the 1930s the Court was a conservative activist court. Today's identification of liberalism as activism can be traced to the period

1937– 1970 when the Court's activism was generally liberal. Since then, the Court has once again become a primarily conservative activist Court. The Rehnquist Court used federalism and the separation of powers to strike down federal legislation such as the Violence Against Women Act, the Gun Free School Zones Act, and provisions of the Brady Handgun Control Act. The Rehnquist Court's ruling in _Bush v. Gore_ (2000) ensured that George W. Bush became President despite receiving fewer votes than Al Gore. The Roberts Court has continued the trend toward conservative activism by striking down campaign finance regulations. Its rulings have most notably ignored established precedent to overturn existing campaign finance laws and to create a new individual right to keep and bear arms.

5.4 | Courts as Government Institutions

A court can be defined as a government body designed for settling legal disputes according to law. In the U.S. courts have two primary functions: **dispute resolution** and **law interpretation**.

5.41 | *Dispute Resolution*

The dispute resolution function of courts is to settle disputes according to law. This is a universal function associated with courts. Courts provide a place and a method for peaceably settling the kinds of disputes or conflicts that inevitably arise in a society. These disputes or conflicts could be settled in other ways, such as violence (vendettas, feuds, duels, fights, war, or vigilantism) or political power. One justice problem with these methods of dispute resolution is that the physically strong, or the more numerous, or the more politically powerful will generally prevail over the physically weaker, the less numerous, or the less politically powerful. These alternative methods of dispute resolution tend to work according to the old maxim that Might Makes Right. The modern preference for settling disputes peaceably according to law rather than violence or political power has made the dispute resolution function of courts a non-controversial function because they are associated with justice.

Dispute resolution is the primary function of *trial courts*. A trial is a fact-finding process for determining who did what to whom. In a civil trial, the court might determine whether one individual (the respondent) did violate the terms of a contract to provide another individual (the plaintiff) with specified goods or services, or whether a doctor's treatment of a patient constituted medical malpractice, or whether a manufacturer violated product liability laws. In a criminal trial, the court might determine whether an individual (the defendant) did what the government (the prosecution) has accused him of doing.

The dispute resolution function of courts is familiar to most people as a courtroom trial where the lawyers who represent the two sides in a case try to convince a neutral third party (usually a jury) that they are right. In one sense, a trial is nothing more than a decision making process, a set of rules for making a decision. But a trial is a distinctive decision making process because it relies so heavily on very elaborate procedural rules. The rules of evidence (what physical or testimonial evidence can and cannot be introduced) are very complicated. The rules of evidence are important because the decision (the trial verdict) is supposed to be based solely on the evidence introduced at trial. Trials have captured the political and cultural imagination so much so that famous trials are an important part of the political culture of many countries including the U.S.

5.42 | *Law Interpretation*

The second function of courts is law interpretation. Courts decide what the law means when there is a disagreement about the meaning of words or when two provisions of law conflict. Courts decide whether a police officer's search of a person's car constitutes a violation of the Fourth Amendment's prohibition against "unreasonable search and seizure." Courts decide whether imposing the death penalty on children or mentally handicapped persons with an I.Q. below 70 violates the Eighth Amendment prohibition against "cruel and unusual punishment." Courts interpret the meaning of due process of law.

Law interpretation is primarily the function of *appellate courts*. Appeals courts do not conduct trials to determine facts; they decide the correct interpretation of the law when a party appeals the decision of a trial court. Law interpretation is a much more controversial function than dispute resolution because it involves judges making decisions about what the law means. The Supreme Court "makes" legal policy when it decides whether police practices related to search and seizure or questioning suspects are consistent with the Fourth Amendment warrant requirements or the Fifth Amendment due process of law. It makes legal policy when it decides whether the death penalty constitutes cruel or unusual punishment. It makes policy when it decides whether laws restricting abortion violate the right to privacy. It makes policy when it reads the Fourteenth Amendment Equal Protection Clause to require "one person, one vote." It also makes policy when it decides whether the traditional definition of marriage as the union of one man and one woman deprives gays and lesbians of the Equal Protection of the laws. The law interpretation function is often political and often controversial because it gets the courts involved with making policy.

The dispute resolution function is not very controversial. There is broad public support for the idea of government creating courts to peaceably settle conflicts according to law. Law interpretation is the controversial function of courts because it gets courts involved with policy making.

5.43 | *The U.S. Court Systems*

The U.S. has a federal system of government that consists of one national government and fifty state governments. The U.S. has two court systems: the federal court system and the state court systems. But it can also be said that the U.S. has 51 courts systems and 51 systems of law because each state has substantial autonomy to create its own court system and its own system of criminal and civil laws.

5.44| *The Organization of the Federal Court System*

The main federal court system consists of one Supreme Court, 13 Courts of Appeals, and 94 District Courts. These are the Article III courts with general jurisdiction over all criminal and civil cases raises questions federal law. But they are not the only federal courts. There also are special or legislative courts that Congress has created with jurisdiction over special kinds of cases: the U.S. Court of Federal Claims; the U.S. Court of Appeals for Veterans Claims; the Foreign Intelligence Surveillance Courts; and Immigration Courts.

5.45 | *The 50 State Court Systems*

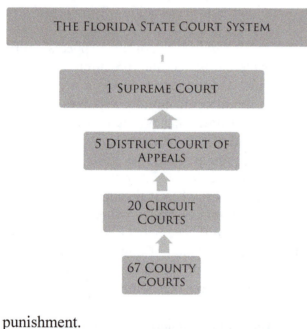

The U.S. system of federalism gives each state substantive power to establish its own court systems and its own system of civil and criminal laws. Therefore the U.S. does not have two court systems (one federal and one state). It has fifty-one systems: one federal and 50 separate state court systems.

The Florida Supreme Court administers or manages the entire state court system. This includes budgeting and allocation of judicial resources. It also hears appeals from death penalty sentences, cases in which a defendant receives capital punishment.

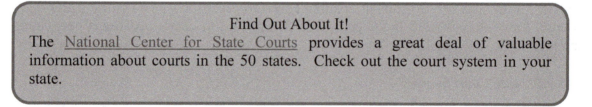

Find Out About It!
The National Center for State Courts provides a great deal of valuable information about courts in the 50 states. Check out the court system in your state.

5.46 | *The Supreme Court of the United States*

The Supreme Court (SCOTUS) is the highest court in the United States. It is also the head of the judicial branch of the federal government and as such has administrative and legal responsibilities for managing the entire federal court system. The Supreme Court consists of nine Justices: the Chief Justice and eight Associate Justices. The Justices are nominated by the President and confirmed with the "advice and consent" of the Senate to serve terms that last a lifetime or during "good behavior." Federal judges can be removed only by resignation, or by impeachment and subsequent conviction.

The Supreme Court is the only court established by the Constitution. All other federal courts are created by Congress. Article III of the Constitution provides that:

> The judicial Power of the United States, shall be vested in one supreme Court, and in such inferior Courts as the Congress may from time to time ordain and establish. The Judges, both of the supreme and inferior Courts, shall hold their Offices during good Behavior, and shall, at stated Times, receive for their Services a Compensation which shall not be diminished during their Continuance in Office.

5.47 | *Supreme Court Jurisdiction*

The term *jurisdiction* refers to a court's authority to hear a case. The Supreme Court's jurisdiction is provided in the Constitution, statutes, and case law precedents.

Constitutional. Article III provides that judicial power "shall extend to all Cases…arising under this Constitution, the Laws of the United States, and Treaties…." The Court has both original and appellate jurisdiction, but the Court is primarily an appellate court. The Court's original jurisdiction (that is its authority to sit as a body hearing a case for the first time, as a kind of trial court) is limited to cases "affecting Ambassadors, other public Ministers and Consuls, and those in which a State shall be Party…" The Founders gave the Supreme Court original jurisdiction over cases where states are parties in order to remove the case from the geographic jurisdiction of a state. They believed it served the interests of justice to have a legal dispute between two states be decided by a federal court that was not physically located in a state. In all other cases, the Court has appellate jurisdiction; that is, it reviews the decisions of lower courts.

Statutory. Congress also has statutory authority to determine the jurisdiction of federal courts. The Federal Judicial Center lists "Landmark Judicial Legislation" related to the organization and jurisdiction of the federal courts from the Judiciary Act of 1789 to the creation of the federal circuit in 1982. Congress has attempted to prohibit the courts from hearing controversial issues by passing *court stripping* laws that prohibit federal courts from hearing cases involving flag burning or school prayer for instance. The Detainee Treatment Act limited the jurisdiction of courts to hear cases involving habeas corpus application of a Guantanamo Bay detainee.[1] The Constitution specifies that the Supreme Court may exercise original jurisdiction in cases affecting ambassadors and other diplomats, and in cases in which a state is a party. In all other cases, however, the Supreme Court has only appellate jurisdiction. The Supreme Court considers cases based on its original jurisdiction very rarely; almost all cases are brought to the Supreme Court on appeal. In practice, the only original jurisdiction cases heard by the Court are disputes between two or more states.

The Judiciary Act of 1789 gave the Supreme Court jurisdiction over appeals from state courts. Article III of the U.S. Constitution gives federal courts jurisdiction over all "cases" or "controversies" arising under federal law. This means that federal courts do not have jurisdiction to hear hypothetical disputes or to give advisory opinions about whether a proposed law would be constitutional.

Case Law Precedents. The Supreme Court also has authority to determine the jurisdiction of the federal courts. Its case law rulings and its administrative rules describe the kinds of cases or issues that federal courts hear. The Court's Rule 10 provides that a petition for certiorari should be granted only for "compelling reasons." One such reason is to resolve lower court conflicts. A lower court conflict occurs when different courts interpret the same law differently. An example of lower court conflict is the rulings upholding and striking down the Affordable Care Act. Other compelling reasons to accept an appeal are to correct a clear departure from judicial procedures or to address an important question of law. A writ of certiorari is a request to a higher court to review the decision of a lower court. The Court receives around 7,000 petitions each year, but issues only 75 or so decisions each year, so the Court has an elaborate screening process for determining which writs will be accepted. After the Court grants the writ of certiorari, the parties file written briefs and the case is scheduled for oral argument. If the parties consent and the Court approves, interested individuals or organizations may file amicus curiae or friend of the court briefs which provide the Court with additional information about the issues presented in a case.

5.48 | *The Supreme Court Term*

The Supreme Court meets in the United States Supreme Court building in Washington D.C. Its annual term starts on the first Monday in October and finishes sometime during the following June or July. Each term consists of alternating two-week intervals. During the first interval, the court is in session, or "sitting," and hears cases. During the second interval, the court is recessed to consider and write opinions on cases it has heard. The Court holds two-week oral argument sessions each month from October through April. Each side has half an hour to present its argument—but the Justices often interrupt them as you can tell when listening to the Oyez audio recordings.

      After oral argument, the Justices schedule conferences to deliberate and then take a preliminary vote. Cases are decided by majority vote of the Justices. The most senior Justice in the majority assigns the initial draft of the Court's opinion to a Justice voting with the majority. Drafts of the Court's opinion, as well as any concurring or dissenting opinions, circulate among the Justices until the Court is prepared to announce the ruling.[2]

5.5 | **The Selection of Federal Judges**

Article II grants the president power to nominate federal judges, whose appointments must be confirmed by the Senate. The individual Justices and the Court as an institution are political, but judicial politics is different than the politics of members of Congress or the president. The politics is less overt; partisan politics is less apparent. But individual Justices and the Court are described in political terms primarily as conservative, moderate, or liberal rather than as members of a political party. Media accounts of the Court refer to the right wing, the left wing, and the swing or moderate Justices. Presidents nominate individuals who share their ideology and usually their party identification. Senators also consider party and ideology when considering whether to ratify a nominee. Presidents generally get Justices who vote the way they were expected to vote but there are some prominent exceptions to the rule that presidents get what they expected from their nominees:

- Oliver Wendell Holmes disappointed President Theodore Roosevelt;
- Chief Justice Earl Warren disappointed President Eisenhower who expected Warren to be a traditional conservative but he presided over the most liberal Court in the Court's history;
- Justice Harry Blackmun became more liberal than President Nixon expected him to be; and
- Justice David Souter's voting record was more liberal than President George H. W. Bush expected.

The Constitution does not provide any qualifications for federal judges. A Supreme Court Justice does not even have to be a lawyer. The President may *nominate* anyone to serve and the Senate can reject a nominee for any reason. But most members of the Court have been graduates of prestigious law schools, and in recent years presidents have nominated individuals with prior judicial experience.

5.51 | *Demographics*

In addition to political factors such as party and ideology, and legal factors such as legal training, legal scholars examine demographic factors such as race, ethnicity, age, gender, and religion. The Supreme Court is not a representative institution. For the first 180 years, the Court's membership almost exclusively white male Protestant. In 1967 Thurgood Marshall became the first black member of the Court. In 1981, Sandra Day O'Connor became the first female member of the Court. It is interesting that the first black Justice was a liberal who was replaced by a conservative black Justice (Clarence Thomas) and the first female Justice was a conservative who was succeeded by a liberal (Ruth Bader Ginsburg). Justice Brandeis became the first Jewish Justice in 1916. In 2006 Samuel Alito became the fifth sitting Catholic Justice, which gave the Court a Catholic majority. This is significant because the conservative majorities on the Burger, Rehnquist, and Roberts Courts have changed First Amendment freedom of religion law by relying less on the *Wall of Separation* doctrine when deciding church and state cases, and relying more on the *Accommodation* doctrine, which allows much more government accommodation of and support for religion.

5.52 | *Senate Hearings*

As the courts have played a broader role in our system of government and politics, the confirmation process has attracted more attention from interest groups, the media, political parties, and the general public. The nomination of Supreme Court Justices is now an opportunity to participate in the political process. The Senate Judiciary Committee conducts hearings where nominees are questioned to determine their suitability. At the close of confirmation hearings, the Committee votes on whether the nomination should go to the full Senate with a positive, negative or neutral report.

The practice of a judicial nominee being questioned by the Senate Judiciary Committee began in the 1920s as efforts by the nominees to respond to critics or to answer specific concerns. The modern Senate practice of questioning nominees on their judicial views began in the 1950s, after the Supreme Court had become a controversial institution after the *Brown v. Board of Education* decision and other controversial rulings. After the Senate Judiciary Committee hearings and vote, the whole Senate considers the nominee. A simple majority vote is required to confirm or to reject a nominee. Although the Senate can reject a nominee for any reason, even reasons not related to professional qualifications, it is by tradition that a vote against a nominee is for cause. It is assumed that the President's nominee will be confirmed unless there are good reasons for voting against the nominee. And so rejections are relatively rare. The most recent rejection of a nominee by vote of the full Senate came in 1987, when the Senate refused to confirm Robert Bork. A President who thinks that his nominee has little chance of being confirmed is likely to withdraw the nomination.

5.53 | *Vacancies*

The Constitution provides that Justices "shall hold their Offices during good Behavior." A Justice may be removed by impeachment and conviction by congressional vote. In 1805, Justice Samuel Chase became the only Justice to have been impeached by the House—he was acquitted by the Senate. His impeachment was part of the era's intense partisan political struggles between the Federalists and Jeffersonian-Republicans. As a result, impeachment gained a bad reputation as a partisan measure to inappropriately control the Court rather than as a legitimate way to hold judges accountable as public officials. Court vacancies do not occur regularly. There are times when retirement, death, or resignations produce vacancies in fairly quick succession. In the early 1970s, for example, Hugo Black and John Marshall Harlan II retired within a week of each other because of health problems. There have been other lengthy periods when there have been no Court vacancies. Eleven years passed between Stephen Breyer's appointment in 1994 and Justice O'Connor's retirement in 2005. Only four presidents have been unable to appoint a Justice: William H. Harrison, Zachary Taylor, Andrew Johnson, and Jimmy Carter.

The Chief Justice can give retired Supreme Court Justices temporary assignments to sit with U.S. Courts of Appeals. These assignments are similar to the senior status, the semi-retired status of other federal court judges. Justices typically plan their retirements so that a president who shares their ideological and partisan ties will appoint their successor.

5.54 | *Republicans Playing Hardball*

Justice Antonin Scalia died on February 13, 2016. Shortly after his death, Senate Majority Leader Mitch McConnell (R-Kentucky) issued the following statement: "The American people should have a voice in the selection of their next Supreme Court Justice. Therefore, this vacancy should not be filled until we have a new President." On March 16, President Obama nominated Merrick Garland, the Chief Judge of the U.S. Court of Appeals for the District of Columbia, to fill the vacancy. The Republican majority in the Senate refused to even consider the Garland nomination. The Republican strategy was to stonewall the nomination. Majority Leader McConnell also "slow-walked" the confirmation of other judicial nominees to "run out the clock" so that the Obama nomination game would over with the 2016 elections. The refusal to act on the

Supreme Court nomination and the slowing of the confirmation process were a political gamble that a Republican would win the presidency. The gamble paid off.

During the campaign, Donald Trump consulted with two very prominent conservative organizations, The Federalist Society and the Heritage Foundation, to create a list of people from whom he promised to select judicial nominees if elected. The campaign strategy worked: it became one of the reasons for conservatives and republicans to vote for Trump because the names on the list were supporters of gun rights and critics of the constitutional right to abortion. President Trump nominated and the Senate confirmed Neil Gorsuch to the Supreme Court. President Trump described Gorsuch as a judge in the Scalia model: a legal conservative who believed that Originalism is the appropriate method of deciding cases. The strategy to run out the clock greatly reduced the number of Obama appointees to the federal courts. Compare the judicial appointments for the following presidents who faced a Senate controlled by the other party during their last two years in office:

Table 5.541: Number of Judges Appointed During Last Two Years of Term with Opposition Party Controlling Senate

	Number of Judges Appointed
President	During Last Two Years With Opposition Party
Reagan	83
Clinton	72
George W. Bush	68
Obama	20

The Republican slow-walk strategy resulted in more than 120 judicial vacancies when President Trump took office, which was a great opportunity for President Trump to have a significant, long-term impact on legal policy. President Obama appointed a total of 329 Article III judges. Article II judges are those that are nominated by the president and confirmed by the Senate.

Table 5.542: Total Number of Obama Judicial Appointments to Article III Courts

	Obama Appointments
2	Supreme Court Justices
55	Court of Appeals Judges
268	District Court Judges
4	U.S. Court of International Trade Judges
329	Total

In addition to these Article III courts, President Obama appointed judges to Article I (or legislative courts): Tax Court; Court of Appeals for Veterans Claims; Court of Military Commission Review; Court of Federal Claims; and Court of Appeals for the Armed Forces. He also appointed Immigration Court Judges.

5.55 | *The Size of the Supreme* Court

The Constitution does not specify the size of the Supreme Court. Congress determines the number of Justices. The Judiciary Act of 1789 set the number of Justices at six. President Washington appointed six Justices—but the first session of the Supreme Court in January 1790 was adjourned because of a lack of a quorum. The size of the Court was expanded to seven members in 1807, nine in 1837, and ten in 1863. In Judicial Circuits Act of 1866 provided that the next three Court vacancies would not be filled. The Act was passed to deny President Johnson the opportunity to appoint Justices. The Circuit Judges Act of 1869 set the number at nine again where it has remained ever since. In February of 1937 President Franklin D. Roosevelt proposed the Judiciary Reorganization Bill to expand the Court by allowing an additional Justice for every sitting Justice who reached the age of seventy but did not retire (up to a maximum Court size of fifteen). The Bill failed because members of Congress saw it as a court packing plan. Roosevelt was in office so long that was able to appoint eight Justices and promote one Associate Justice to Chief Justice.

The New Supreme Court (2017)

5.6 | Deciding Cases: Is it Law or Politics?

One of the most frequently asked questions about the courts is whether judges decide cases based on law or politics. This question goes to the heart of the legitimacy problem. To answer the question let's look first at the Supreme Court as an institution. The Supreme Court has almost complete control over the cases that it hears. The Supreme Court controls its docket. It decides only 80-90 of the approximately 10,000 cases it is asked to decide each year. This means that the Court decides which issues to decide and which issues not to decide. This is, in a sense, political power.

The role of law and politics in an individual Justice's decision making is of more direct interest. Legal scholars identify a variety of influences or factors that explain judicial decisions. But there are two general models of judicial decision making: a legal model and a political (or extra-legal) model. The legal model of deciding cases explains judicial decisions as based on legal factors (the law and the facts of the case). The political model explains decisions as based on behavioral factors (demographics such as race, gender, religion, ethnicity, age), attitudinal factors (political, ideological, or partisan), or public opinion. The legal methods include the plain meaning of the words, the intentions of the framers, and precedent. The most political method is interpretation, where judges decide cases based on their own beliefs about what the law is or should be, or contemporary societal expectations of justice.

5.61 | *The Methods of Deciding Cases*

The U.S. is a system of government based on the rule of law. Judges are expected to decide cases based on the written law: the Constitution, statutes, and administrative law. The following is the logical order in which judges decide cases, beginning with the most legal method (the plain meaning of the words) and ending with the most political method (interpretation).

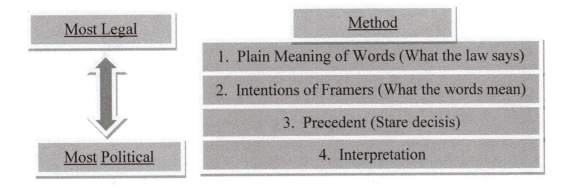

Most Legal	Method
	1. Plain Meaning of Words (What the law says)
	2. Intentions of Framers (What the words mean)
	3. Precedent (Stare decisis)
Most Political	4. Interpretation

5.62 | *Plain Meaning of the Words*

A judge reads the law to determine whether the case can be decided by the plain meaning of the words. Sometimes the meaning of the law is plain. The Constitution requires that a President be 35 years old and a native born citizen. But some provisions of the Constitution are ambiguous. The Fifth Amendment provides that "No person shall be... deprived of life, liberty, or property, without due process of law..." The Eighth Amendment prohibits "cruel and unusual punishments." It is impossible to read the phrases "due process" or "cruel and unusual punishment" and arrive at a plain meaning of the words. Judges must use other methods to determine the meaning of these general provisions of the Constitution.

Statutes can present a similar problem. The Communication Decency Act of 1996, for instance, made it a felony to "knowingly" transmit "obscene or indecent" messages to a person under age 18. It is easy to determine whether a person who was sent a message was under age 18; it is virtually impossible to define with any precision the meaning of "indecent." Therefore judges use the second method: they try to determine what the people who wrote the law intended the words to mean.

5.63 | Intentions of the Framers

Judges have several ways to determine the intention of the framers of the law. In order to determine what a provision of the Constitution was intended to mean, judges examine the Records of the Constitutional Convention, the writings or letters of the delegates to the Constitutional Convention of 1787, the *Federalist Papers* (a series of essays by James Madison, Alexander Hamilton, and John Jay supporting the adoption of the new Constitution), or the writings of the Anti-federalists (authors who opposed the ratification of the new constitution). In order to determine the meaning of the words in a constitutional amendment, judge examine the Congressional Record for evidence of the intentions of the framers. The congressional debates surrounding the adoption of the 13th, 14th, and 15th Amendments, for example, can help understand what these three post-Civil War Amendments were intended to mean.

5.64 | Precedent

The U.S. legal system is based on **precedent** or *stare decisis*. *Stare decisis* is Latin for "let the previous decision stand." The system of precedent means a judge is expected to decide a current issue the way a previous issue was decided. Although precedent may seem like a legalistic way to decide cases, it is actually based on a common sense expectation of justice: an expectation that an individual will be treated the way other similarly situated individuals were treated. In this sense, precedent is a basic element of fairness.

Precedent is a system where the past guides the present. But courts cannot always decide a case by looking backward at how other courts decided a question or legal issue. Sometimes a judge may think it is inappropriate to decide a current question the same way it was decided in the past. Attitudes toward equality and the treatment of women for example may have changed. Or attitudes toward corporal punishment may have changed. Rigidly adhering to precedent does not readily allow for legal change. And sometimes courts are presented with new issues for which there is no clearly established precedent. Advances in science and technology, for instance, presented the courts with new issues such as patenting new life forms created in the laboratory or the property rights to discoveries from the Human Genome Project. When the plain meaning of the words, the intentions of the framers, and precedent do not determine the outcome of a case, then judges sometimes turn to another method: interpretation.

5.65 | Interpretation

Interpretation is defined as a judge deciding a case based on 1) her or his own understanding of what the law should mean; or 2) modern societal expectations of what the law should mean. Determining the meaning of the Eighth Amendment prohibition against "cruel and unusual punishment" illustrates how judges use interpretation. Should it mean what people considered cruel and unusual punishment in the 18th Century? Or should judges refer to the standards of modern or civilized society when determining what punishments the Eighth Amendment prohibits? Interpretation is controversial because it gives judges power to decide what the law means. This is why interpretation is called political decision-making, legislating from the bench, or judicial activism. Judicial restraint usually means judicial deference to the other branches of government, upholding precedent, and deciding only legal (not economic, social, or political) issues. Interpretation raises the power problem with the courts. In a democracy, the legitimacy of judicial interpretation of the laws is controversial.

5.66 | *Two Models of Decision Making*

The following flow charts depict two models of legal decision making: the Classical or Legal Model and the Legal Realist (or Political) Model. Which do you think describes how judges and jurors decide cases? Which do you think describes how judges and jurors should decide cases?

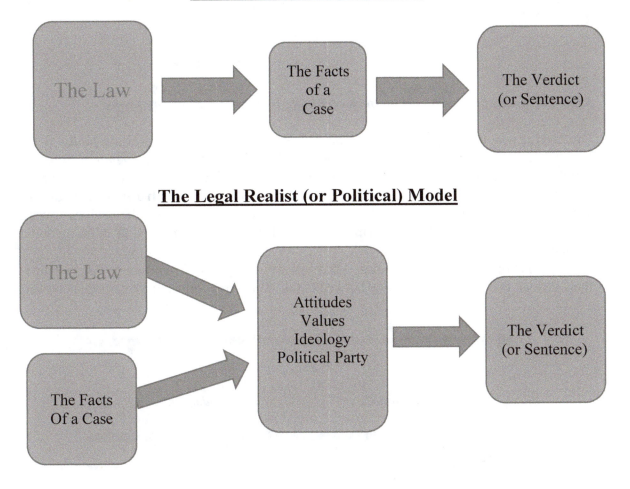

The Classical or Legal Model

The Law → The Facts of a Case → The Verdict (or Sentence)

The Legal Realist (or Political) Model

The Law, The Facts Of a Case → Attitudes, Values, Ideology, Political Party → The Verdict (or Sentence)

5.67 | Three Models of Legal Systems

The methods that judges use to decide cases, and the role that juries play in the administration of justice, reflect different beliefs about the relationship between the political system and the legal system. A *Responsive Legal System* is one where the legal system is almost completely responsive to politics so that law and politics are basically the same thing. At the other end of the spectrum, an *Autonomous Legal System* is one where law and politics are almost completely separate: politics does not affect law. The Politico-Legal System is one where legal institutions are separate from political institutions but isolated from political institutions—for example, politicians select judges but they have lifetime tenure and cannot be removed except for cause. Politics often involves debates about the merits of an issue AND debates about whether the issue should be decided by politics or by law, by the legal system (courts) or by the political system.

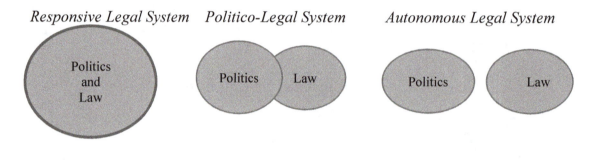

Responsive Legal System   *Politico-Legal System*   *Autonomous Legal System*

5.68 | *The Crime Control Model of Justice and The Due Process Model of Justice*

One useful way to understand liberal and conservative thinking about crime policy is the two models of justice described by Herbert Packer *The Limits of the Criminal Sanction* (1968). The models describe two ways of thinking about how best to achieve or administer justice. The two models represent the **ends of a spectrum or a range of views**, not two categories. Liberals and conservatives tend to locate themselves toward one or the other value in the following five sets of paired values related to thinking about justice.

Four of the pairs are familiar. The *Individual Rights v. Government Power* pair is the familiar civil liberties conflict between individual freedom and government power.

Think about it!
Should judges make policy?
What does Justice Antonin Scalia say about reading the law?
http://www.pbs.org/newshour/bb/law/july-dec12/scalia_08-09.html

Rehabilitation v. Punishment reflects the preference for criminal sentencing policy that emphasizes rehabilitation or punishment. Sentencing law looks very different depending on which value is emphasized. The *Justice **with** Law v. Justice **without** Law* pair reflects describes the difference between thinking that law (e.g., elaborate rules of evidence and procedure) is the best way to achieve justice and thinking that justice is best achieved without law (e.g., executive discretion rather). *Legal Autonomy v. Responsive Law* describes legal systems that are relatively separate from the political system or fairly responsive to it. In responsive legal systems, sheriffs, prosecutors, and judges are elected officials who are held politically accountable rather than legally accountable.

The fifth pair of values—**Law** and **Order**—are less familiar because "law and order" are often described as a single value.

Due Process (Liberal) Model   Crime Control (Conservative) Model

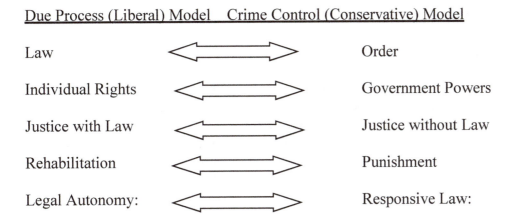

Law	Order
Individual Rights	Government Powers
Justice with Law	Justice without Law
Rehabilitation	Punishment
Legal Autonomy:	Responsive Law:

5.69 | *Popular Legal Culture*

Most Americans have fairly strong opinions about crime. Where does the general public get information about the legal system? Some people have direct personal experience: they are arrested and tried for a felony, for example, or they have sued someone or they have been sued. Some people have served on juries. People also get indirect information from family, friends, and colleagues. The media are also an important source of public thinking about crime. The media effect applies to the news media and legal fiction. Trials certainly have captured the public's imagination. The nation's history is marked by famous "trials of the century." Fictional TV judges are familiar figures in the public imagination: *The People's Court*; *Judge Judy*; Judge Joe Brown; Judge Mathis; Judge Alex; and even Judge Wapner's *Animal Court*. Police procedurals are staples of television programming. The media frame crime stories in terms of the crime control and due process models of justice.

5.7 | Jury Justice

The relationship between law and politics is complicated in the U.S. because of political culture (democratic theory); legal culture (the strong commitment to popular justice as the will of the people); and constitutionalism (limits on popular justice).

5.71 | *The Jury as a Political Institution*

The founders intended juries to function as a political institution. The jury was intended to be part of the elaborate system of institutional checks and balances. Juries were composed of lay people who could *check* government power. The Trial of John Peter Zenger (1735) established the tradition of jurors refusing to convict a defendant despite the judge's directive to do so. The Declaration of Independence consists of a list of charges accusing the King of violating the rights of colonists—including the right to trial by jury. Article III, Section 2 of the Constitution, the Sixth Amendment, and the Seventh Amendment provide for the right to trial by jury in criminal and civil cases. In *Democracy in America* (1835), Alexis de Tocqueville wrote: "The jury is, above all, a political institution, and it must be regarded in this light in order to be duly appreciated." He also described the jury system as a "public school, ever open" to teach people about the culture of rights and responsibilities.

Individual jurors are also political in the sense that their attitudes and values influence decision-making. This is why so much attention is paid to the demographics of a jury—its racial, ethnic, gender, age, income, religion, and other demographic composition. Juror selection is an extremely important stage of the legal process because empirical evidence of decision making indicates that demographic and attitudinal factors influence decisions. This is why jury consulting has become a profession. It is also one of the reasons why the Black Lives Matter movement put police accountability for the use of force on the agendas of the national government and local government.

5.72 | *Trials as Fact-finding processes*

A trial is a fact-finding process with elaborate procedural rules governing the kinds of evidence that can be considered. The U.S. uses the adversarial system of justice. Each side—the two adversaries—presents its side of the story to a neutral third party decision-maker—judge or jury. The adversarial system is based on the belief that the best way to discover the truth of "what happened" is to have each side tell its story to a neutral third party which then determines which set of facts is most believable. The burden of proof in a criminal trial is proving "beyond a reasonable doubt" that the accused did what they were accused of. There is a lower burden of proof in a civil trial: "the greater weight of the evidence."

Determining the facts can be hard. In *Courts on Trial: Myth and Reality in American Justice*, Judge Jerome Frank explains that fact-finding is hard because "facts are guesses." This seems an astonishing statement because it means that the question whether a defendant is guilty of murder is a guess. The *fact* is that a person was killed; the guess is whether the killing was murder. Why is it so hard for jurors to determine what happened after a lengthy trial where both sides have presented evidence and made arguments? Why is it so hard to determine who did what to whom, or why they did it? There are several reasons.

- Hard cases. Easy cases are settled; they don't actually go to trial. More than 90% of criminal cases are settled by plea bargains.

- The adversarial process. The adversarial process itself may contribute to the difficulty of determining who is telling the truth. Each side in a trial has an incentive to exaggerate its version of what happened rather than to tell the truth, each attorney has an incentive to portray their client as a regular Mother Theresa and the opponent as a regular Ted Bundy. The prosecution and the defense may hire expert witnesses who are paid to testify in support of their side. After listening to conflicting/competing expert witnesses, a jury is left to decide what happened. Is the adversarial system the best way to design a fact-finding process? Many other countries do not use the adversarial system. Most European countries, for example, use the inquisitorial system: judges play an active role in investigating, questioning, and determining what happened rather than just presiding over a trial where the two lawyers tell their sides of the story.

- Eyewitness testimony. Even one of the most compelling types of testimony—eyewitness testimony—is notoriously faulty. And research indicates that police line-ups have structural flaws that produce false positive identifications that result in wrongful convictions.

- Human psychology. The study of how people make decisions indicates that fact-finding is intertwined with value judgments. Jurors tend to accept as fact evidence that supports their beliefs. This is confirmation bias. In criminal trials, jurors believe or give credibility to witnesses that support their predisposition to support the police or the accused. That is, jurors use the crime control or due process model of justice to frame the question of guilt or innocence. In civil cases, confirmation bias means that jurors who think that people need to assume more personal responsibility for their injuries, and jurors who think that people need to be compensated for their injuries, will accept evidence that supports their predisposition and discount evidence that challenges their predisposition. The concept of cognitive dissonance helps explain juror decisions. *Cognitive dissonance* occurs when a person faces ideas or information or evidence that conflict with their strongly held beliefs. The conflict/contradiction creates discomfort and is unsettling. Logically, one might expect that a rational person would *adjust their beliefs to fit the facts/evidence.* But the evidence indicates that this is not always what happens. When faced with cognitive dissonance, people often contort the facts, interpret the facts, or construct the facts to fit into (confirm or conform to) their belief system. This means that jurors affirm their own group identity (including ideology) when confronted with a different identity. This "us" versus "them" dynamic produces bias in the administration of justice.

What do these aspects of human psychology mean for "judging" the evidence presented at trial? How does a juror weigh the testimony of a defendant, a character witness, a child who testifies, an eyewitness, or an expert? These psychological questions are central to the story lines and theme of legal fiction, including the classic film *12 Angry Men* (1957) and many television police procedurals.

5.73 | *Demographics: You think who you are?*

The belief that juries are political institutions and the belief that legal facts are guesses means that the composition of the jury is central to the administration of justice! **What you think** about the facts of a case involving the use of deadly force, for example, depends to a great extent on **who you are**. This is why scientific or social scientific jury selection (jury consulting) has grown as a profession.

5.74 | *Race*

In the early decades of the 20th Century, the U.S. Supreme Court began to intervene in state and local criminal justice to remedy racial discrimination in the administration of justice. This included the problem all-white juries.

The Scottsboro Boys (1931-1937). The story of the Scottsboro Boys case is also told in the PBS article. Click on the link for defense counsel Samuel Liebowitz to get a sense of the difference between the world of a northern, Jewish New York lawyer and the southern political culture of the day. Why did the U.S. Supreme Court intervene in the local political/legal culture? The book and film *To Kill a Mockingbird*, which are legal fiction based loosely on the Scottsboro Boys case, expose the problem of racial discrimination in the administration of local jury justice.

Smith v. Texas, 311 U.S. 128, 130 (1940). The Court mentioned the need to make the jury "truly representative of the community," but did not declare that a defendant had a right to a representative jury.

The Men Accused of Murdering Emmett Till (1955). The white sheriffs did not seem worried about being accused of a crime because they believed the local political-legal system would not convict them.

Representation, pluralism, and diversity have become important factors in determining whether political decisions are legitimate. They have also become important factors determining the legitimacy of legal decisions. At one time, laws stole prohibited women from serving on juries. Today, it is unconstitutional to exclude women from jury duty. The representative ideal does not mean that juries must have the same number of women and men; it simply means that the jury pool must not systematically exclude or be biased against women. The jury pool must include a "fair cross-section" of the community.

The original ideal of trial by a jury of peers did not mean trial by an impartial jury. In fact, it meant trial by a *partial* jury. A jury of peers was *partial* in the sense that the jurors would be familiar with the community, its values, and maybe even the defendant and the victim. The jury of peers was intended to achieve "local justice." Professionals run the criminal justice system: the police; the prosecutors; the judges; and the lawyers. Jurors provide the lay perspective on the administration of justice. Juries do have a different perspective than judges: jurors **do** justice while judges **do** law.

> Think About It!
> What should be the goal of jury selection? The voir dire is used to exclude "biased" or "prejudiced" jurors. Is the composition of the jury relevant in cases where white police officers fatally shoot black men? What about cases where civilians claim that they are immune from prosecution und a state's Stand Your Ground Law?

5.75 | *Trials as Morality Plays*

Trials are not just fact-finding processes. Trials are also morality plays. In a morality play, the characters represent values that are in dramatic conflict: good versus evil; heroes versus villains; freedom versus order; law versus violence; and even law versus justice. These are the themes of the dramatic conflicts in the famous trials of Socrates, Jesus, Peter Zenger, John Brown, Timothy McVeigh, and O.J. Simpson or any of the other more contemporary Famous Trials. These dramatic conflicts explain why some trials become media spectacles that attract national attention as the trial of the century, decade, or year. Fictional trials also serve as morality plays that teach us about law and justice. Legal fiction is such a universally popular form of fiction that it can be considered a form of world literature.

5.8 | Summary

All countries have courts. In the U.S. courts decide legal disputes and interpret the laws. Interpretation is often controversial because it means that judges are deciding what the law means in ways that are often considered judicial policymaking or legislating from the bench. The legitimacy of judicial policymaking is questionable in a democracy where laws are supposed to be made by the elected representatives of the people. As judicial power has expanded over time, the legitimacy of judicial power has become even more contentious. The controversy is at root a controversy about the appropriate relationship between politics and law, between the political system and the legal system. The chapter focused on the role of the courts in the administration of justice, but it also described some aspects of jury justice because the jury is an important institution in the administration of justice.

5.9 | Additional Resources

5.91 | *Internet Resources*

Information about the Supreme Court is available at http://www.supremecourt.gov/. Information about the federal court system is available at http://www.uscourts.gov/Home.aspx and the Federal Judicial Center.

Information about the organization and functions of the federal court system, including a court locator to find the federal courts in your area or information about serving as a juror, is available at http://www.uscourts.gov/

The full text and summaries of Supreme Court opinions, as well as audio recordings of the oral arguments before the U.S. Supreme Court are available at the Oyez Project: http://www.oyez.org/

Landmark Supreme Court cases are available at www.landmarkcases.org

A gallery of famous trials (e.g., Socrates, Galileo, the Salem Witch Trials, John Peter Zenger, and the Oklahoma City Bomber) are available at htt://www.law.umkc.edu/faculty/projects/ftrials/ftrials.htm

Videos of the Justices explaining their views on how they see their individual job as Justices and the Court's role as an institution in their own words are available at the C-SPAN Web site: http://supremecourt.c-span.org/Video/TVPrograms.aspx

Information about the 50 state court systems is available at The National Center for State Courts: http://www.ncsconline.org/

For Information about Florida's death row, a virtual tour of a prison cell, or other information about convicted offenders on the death row roster is available at the My Florida Web site (click Government, Executive Branch, Department of Corrections): www.myflorida.gov The link to death row fact sheets is http://www.dc.state.fl.us/oth/deathrow/

Additional information about the Supreme Court is available at http://www.pbs.org/wnet/supremecourt/educators/lp4b.html and http://www.pbs.org/wnet/supremecourt/educators/lp4c.html

Demographic information about the Supreme Court Justices is available at http://www.fas.org/sgp/crs/misc/R40802.pdf

5.82 | *In the Library*

Ball, Howard. 2004. *Supreme Court and the Intimate Lives of Americans: Birth, Sex, Marriage, Childrearing, and Death.* New York University Press.

Bugliosi, Vincent et. al. 2001. *The Betrayal of America: How the Supreme Court Undermined Our Constitution and Chose Our President.* Thunder's Mouth Press.

Breyer, Stephen. 2016. *The Court and the World: American Law and the New Global Realities.* Knopf.

Carmon, Irin, and Shana Knizhnik. 2015. *Notorious RBG: The Life and Times of Ruth Bader Ginsburg.* Dey Street Books.

Cohen, Adam. 2016. *Imbeciles: The Supreme Court, American Eugenics, and the Sterilization of Carrie Buck.* Penguin Press.

Cooper, Philip. 1999. *Battles on the Bench: Conflict Inside the Supreme Court.* University Press of Kansas.

Dworkin, Ronald (Ed). 2002. *Badly Flawed Election: Debating Bush v. Gore, the Supreme Court, American Democracy.* The New Press.

Frank, Jerome. 1967. *Courts on Trial: Myth and Reality in American Justice*. New York: Athenium.

Gottlieb, Stephen. 2016. *Unfit for Democracy: The Roberts Court and the Breakdown of American Politics*. New York University Press.

Gregory, Leland H. 1998. *Presumed Ignorant! Over 400 Cases of Legal Looniness, Daffy Defendants, and Bloopers from the Bench*. Bantam Books.

Hall, Kermit (Ed). 2000. *Conscience and Belief: The Supreme Court and Religion*. Garland Publishers.

Hammond, Thomas H., Chris W. Bonneau, and Reginald S. Sheehan. 2005. *Strategic Behavior and Policy Choice On The U.S. Supreme Court*. Stanford University Press.

Hansford, Thomas G. and James F., II Spriggs. 2006. *The Politics of Precedent on the U.S. Supreme Court*. Princeton University Press.

Hitchcock, James and Robert P. George (Ed). 2004. *The Supreme Court and Religion in American Life: From Higher Law to Sectarian Scruples* (New Forum Books Series), Vol. 2. Princeton University Press.

Lazarus, Edward. 1998. *Closed Chambers: The First Eyewitness Account of the Epic Struggles Inside the Supreme Court*. Times Books.

Lipkin,, Robert. 2000. *Constitutional Revolutions: Pragmatism and the Role of Judicial Review in American Constitutionalism*. Duke University Press.

Lopeman, Charles S. 1999. *The Activist Advocate: Policy Making in State Supreme Courts*. Praeger.

McCloskey, Robert and Sanford Levinson. 2000. *The American Supreme Court*. Third Edition. University of Chicago Press.

Noonan, John T. 2002. *Narrowing the Nation's Power: The Supreme Court Sides with the States*. University of California Press.

Peppers, Todd C. 2006. *Courtiers of the Marble Palace: The Rise and Influence of the Supreme Court Law Clerk*. Stanford University Press.

Raskin, Jamin B. 2004. *Overruling Democracy: The Supreme Court Versus the American People*. Taylor and Francis, Inc.

Rehnquist, William H. 2001. *The Supreme Court*. Knopf.

Schwartz, Herman. 2002. *The Rehnquist Court*. Hill and Wang.

Starr, Kenneth. 2002. *First Among Equals: The Supreme Court in American Life*. Warner.

Toobin, Jeffery. 2008. *The Nine: Inside the Secret World of the Supreme Court*. Anchor.

Yarbrough, Tinsley. 2001. *The Rehnquist Court and the Constitution*. Oxford University Press.

---

[1] http://jurist.law.pitt.edu/gazette/2005/12/detainee-treatment-act-of-2005-white.php

[2] The Court's annual case schedule and docket are available at http://www.supremecourtus.gov/

5.83 | TERMS

Legitimacy
Judicial restraint
Judicial activism
Judicial review
Dispute resolution
Law interpretation
Precedent
Jury Justice
Jury of Peers

5.84 | DISCUSSION QUESTIONS

1. Discuss the importance of the Marshall Court.
2. Explain *stare decisis* and the role it plays in the American judicial system. What did William Rehnquist mean when he called *stare decisis* "a cornerstone of our legal system" but said that "it has less power in constitutional cases?" Do you agree with him?
3. Describe the racial, ethnic, and gender makeup of the federal courts. Does it matter that some groups are underrepresented and other groups are overrepresented? Why?
4. Discuss the criteria for nominating Supreme Court justices and the process by which the nominees are confirmed. How has the process changed in recent years?
5. Discuss the advantages and disadvantages of judicial activism and judicial restraint.
6. Compare and contrast the attitudinal, behavioral, and strategic models of judicial decision making. Explain which of these models most accurately captures how judges make their decisions.
7. What factors affect the implementation of court rulings? Should courts be given additional power to implement decisions?

CHAPTER 6: Federalism

OUT OF MANY, ONE.

6.0 | Why Federalism?

What is federalism? Why have a federal system of government? How does the U.S. system of federalism work today? These are some of the questions that will be answered in this chapter. The chapter
- Defines federalism.
- Explains the logic of the U.S. system of federalism.
- Describes how the U.S. system of federalism works today, and
- Examines the power problem with federalism.

The general public does not think about federalism very much and therefore does not have much to say one way or another about federalism itself.[1] The average voter has stronger opinions about criminal justice policy, education, abortion, immigration, or national security policy than opinions about federalism. Federalism tends to be considered a technical matter of interest to government officials or political insiders more than the general public. Americans do, however, have strong opinions about "big government"—and opinions about big government are often directly related to federalism because "big government" is a euphemism for the federal government of "Washington." In fact, political opinion about public polices related to crime, education, abortion, the environment, health care, and immigration is usually related to opinions about federalism because they include opinions about whether the policies should be state or national government policies.

Federalism is a two-tiered system of government in which power is divided between a national (or central) government and the subnational units (states, provinces, or regional governments). Therefore federalism is a geographic division of power. In the U.S., power is distributed between the national government and state governments. The number of states has grown from the original 13 to 50 today with the addition of Hawaii in 1959. In other countries with federal systems (e.g., Argentina, Australia, Canada, Germany, and India) the regional governments are called provinces. Constitutional federalism means that neither the national nor the state governments can abolish one another because both levels of government are the creatures of the constitution. A state such Alabama or Vermont or Wyoming is not a creature of the national government or a mere local administrative unit of the national government. In the U.S. system of federalism, both the national and state governments are sovereign political entities. Federalism is based on the concept of dual sovereignty: both the national and state governments have sovereignty. Sovereignty is defined as having the ultimate or highest authority. Is it possible to have two sovereigns with authority over the same geographic area and people? The idea of dual sovereigns does seem to conflict with the concept of sovereignty as ultimate government authority. In fact, this is the source of the power problem with federalism. The image below depicts political fighting over federalism in Australia, which is analogous to the 50 states fighting with one other in the U.S.

The **power problem with federal systems** of government is the need to strike the right balance of power between the state governments and the federal government. The Constitution provides for a federal system but with a few notable exceptions, such as the power to coin money and the power to regulate interstate commerce, which are exclusively federal powers, the Constitution does not specify what powers each has. As a result, American politics has historically included debates about which level of government should do what, and whether the federal government is getting too big. Finding the right balance of powers is both a legal (or constitutional) matter **and** a political matter. It is about law and politics. In fact, federalism is a good example of the challenge of adapting a Constitution that is more than 200 years old to modern times, the challenge of maintaining continuity with the federal system established by the Constitution while accommodating major economic, political, technological, scientific, and social changes.

"The question of the relation of the States to the Federal Government is the cardinal question of our constitutional system. At every turn of our national development, we have been brought face to face with it, and no definition either of statesmen or of judges has ever quieted or decided it."
Woodrow Wilson, 28th President of the United States

Federalism is not the most common type of political system in the world. Most of the world's approximately 190 countries have unitary systems of government (that is one unit), not federal systems. So why does the U.S. have a federal system? The answer to this question is provided in the very origins of the word *federalism*. The word federalism comes from the Latin *foedus*, or covenant, where individuals or groups agree to join a political union with a government body to coordinate their interests and represent them. In the American political experience, the colonists had strong attachments to their colonial governments, just as people now have attachments to their state governments. The colonists were wary of giving too much power to a central government. Federalism was a way for government power to be divided between the states and a national government as part of the system of checks and balances.

Federalism serves three main purposes. First, it is part of the system of institutional checks and balances that was designed to control government power by dividing it between two levels of government. Second, creates a political system where interests can be represented in the national government. Members of Congress represent states and districts within states. Third, federalism creates a governance system where the states can serve as "laboratories of experimentation." If one or more states try a policy (e.g., education reform or health care reform) that works, the successful policy experiment can be adopted by other states. If one state's policy experiment fails then the costs are limited to one state—unlike what happens when the national government adopts a policy that fails.

6.1 | Comparing Systems of Government

One way to better understand federalism is to compare it with other types of government. There are three basic types of systems of government: unitary systems, confederal systems, and federal systems.

6.11 | Unitary Systems

A **unitary system** is, as the term suggests, a political system with one level of government. Power concentrated in one central government. The central government has sovereignty or the highest governing authority. The central government may create local or regional units to help govern but these units are "creatures" of the national or unitary government. They are created by the national government and they can be abolished by the national government—and the national government also can determine how much power the local units have because the local units do not have sovereignty.

In France, for example, the national government can abolish local governments or change their boundaries. This kind of national control over state governments does not exist in the United States, because the Constitution created a federal system where both the federal (national) government and the state governments have independent constitutional status. The Constitution provides for both a national government and state governments. The American states, however, are unitary systems. The states can create, alter, or abolish local governments such as cities, counties, school districts, port authorities, as well as the other kinds of special governments that states create.

Canada has a federal system that divides power between the federal parliament and provincial governments. Under the Constitution Act, Section 91 of the Canadian Constitution provides for federal legislative authority and Section 92 provides for provincial powers. One difference between Canadian and U.S. federalism is that the Canadian system provides that the provincial governments have specifically delegated powers and all the national government retains all residual powers. In the U.S. the national government has specifically delegated powers and the states retain all residual powers. All federal systems have political conflicts over which level of government has power over which areas of policy. Areas of Canadian conflict include legislation with respect to regulation of the economy, taxation, and natural resources. The actual distribution of powers evolves over time. The Australian system of federalism resembles the U.S. system in terms of the division of power between the national and state governments but Australia has a parliamentary system rather than the separation of powers.

6.12 | Confederal Systems

A **confederal system** (or a confederation) is a political system where the constituent units (the states, provinces, or regional governments) are more powerful than the central (or national) government. Power is decentralized. The central government is comparatively weak, with fewer powers and governing responsibilities than the units.

6.13 | *American Federalism*

The Founders decided to create a federal system rather than a unitary or confederal system because of their political experience. The Revolutionary War was fought against the British monarchy, a unitary system with power concentrated in the national government. And the first U.S. form of government, the Articles of Confederation, was a confederal system that was widely viewed as flawed because it left the national government with too little power to address the problems facing the new nation. They considered federalism a form of government that was between the extreme centralization of a unitary system and the extreme decentralization of a confederation.

6.2 | The Articles of Confederation

The first U.S. government after the colonial era was a confederation: The Articles of Confederation. Congress adopted The Articles of Confederation in 1777 and they became effective upon ratification by the states in 1781. The following are some of the most important provisions of the Articles of Confederation.

Articles of Confederation

"To all to whom these Presents shall come, we the undersigned Delegates of the States affixed to our Names send greeting.

Articles of Confederation and perpetual Union between the states of New Hampshire, Massachusetts-bay Rhode Island and Providence Plantations, Connecticut, New York, New Jersey, Pennsylvania, Delaware, Maryland, Virginia, North Carolina, South Carolina and Georgia.

I. The Stile of this Confederacy shall be "The United States of America."

II. Each state retains its sovereignty, freedom, and independence, and every power, jurisdiction, and right, which is not by this Confederation expressly delegated to the United States, in Congress assembled.

III. The said States hereby severally enter into a firm league of friendship with each other, for their common defense, the security of their liberties, and their mutual and general welfare, binding themselves to assist each other, against all force offered to, or attacks made upon them, or any of them, on account of religion, sovereignty, trade, or any other pretense whatever."

X. [Authorizes a committee of the states to carry out the powers of Congress when Congress is in recess.]

The above language from the Articles of Confederation describes a union where most power resides with the constituent units, the states. It specifically refers to the political system as a union of states that join together in "a league of friendship." It stipulates that each state retains its "sovereignty, freedom, and independence." Article X authorizes a committee of the states to act for Congress when Congress is in recess. The language of the Articles suggests that the each state that joined the Confederation remained free to decide whether to leave the Confederation. Slavery and the nature of the union, specifically whether states could leave it, were the two main causes of the Civil War.

6.21 | *The Second Confederation*

Eleven southern states believed that secession was one of the powers retained by the states as sovereign and independent entities in the federal system created by the Constitution. The Constitution created a federal system, but it did not define whether states could leave the union. Political divorce was not mentioned. The North argued that the union was permanent—that once a state decided to join ***the*** United States the marriage was permanent. The South argued that the states retained the power to decide to leave the union. Their view of federalism left more power in the hands of the states which were united as ***these*** United States," a term that reflects their belief that federalism left considerable power with the states.

The Confederate States of America (1861-1865), or the Confederacy, was the government formed by eleven southern states. The United States of America ("The Union") believed that secession was illegal and refused to recognize the Confederacy as a legal political entity. The North considered the South a region in rebellion. The end of the Civil War in the spring of 1865 began a decade-long process known as <u>Reconstruction</u>. This "second civil war" involved extensive efforts to exert federal control over the states of the confederacy. Political resistance against federal authority was quite strong, and the struggle for the civil rights of newly freed slaves and Black citizens continued into the 20th Century as part of the civil rights movement. Determining the appropriate balance of power between the national and state governments remains a controversial political and legal issue.

6.3 | Federalism and the Constitution

The Constitution created a federal government with more power than the national government had under the Articles of Confederation. Specific powers were **delegated** to the national government. Article I, Section 8 of the Constitution lists powers granted to Congress. The list of powers delegated to Congress includes the power to coin money, tax, regulate interstate commerce, and raise and support armies.

The Constitution also took some powers that had belonged to the states under the Articles of Confederation and gave them to the federal government. The states were specifically prohibited from coining money and regulating interstate commerce because the Founders—principally the Federalists—believed that the national government had to direct the nation's economic development. Then there is the infamous Supremacy Clause, which provides that federal laws "shall be the supreme Law of the Land." The Supremacy Clause does not prohibit states from having laws that differ from the federal laws, but it does prohibit states from passing laws that conflict with federal laws.

All other powers—those not delegated to the national government, or prohibited to the states—were to be reserved (or left with) the states or the people. These are the **reserved** powers. The reserved powers are dictated by the 10th Amendment: "The powers not delegated to the United States by the Constitution, nor prohibited by it to the States, are reserved to the states respectively, or to the people." The language of the 10th

Amendment reflects the fact that there was some uncertainty about exactly which powers the Constitution delegated to a stronger national government. The Anti-Federalists worried that the new Constitution betrayed the Revolutionary War cause of fighting against a monarchy or strong central government. The Constitution did significantly increase the power of the national government. The 10th Amendment reassured the Anti-federalists that the states retained their traditional powers.

Figure 6.3: The State Powers, Federal Powers, and Shared Powers

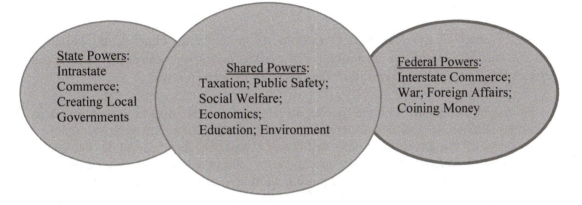

State Powers: Intrastate Commerce; Creating Local Governments

Shared Powers: Taxation; Public Safety; Social Welfare; Economics; Education; Environment

Federal Powers: Interstate Commerce; War; Foreign Affairs; Coining Money

The first U.S. government after the colonial era was a confederation: The Articles of Confederation. Congress adopted The Articles of Confederation in 1777 and they became effective upon ratification by the states in 1781. The following are some of the most issues related to federalism.

The Constitution does not define or explain federalism because the states were pre-existing units of government. The Constitution also did not define the nature of the union, whether the union was permanent or states could decide to secede. The Constitution also did not provide specifics on the actual division of power between the national and state governments. The balance of power between the national and state governments was left to be determined by politics and by subsequent generations. In fact, the balance of power between the national and state governments has historically been determined more by politics than by the actual language of the Constitution. This is apparent in the way that federalism has been an important aspect of political events throughout the history of the United States. Federalism was a central element of the Civil War; the Civil Rights movements; the expansion of the rights of suspects and prisoners in the criminal justice system; the controversy over the right to privacy as it applies to abortion policy; and most recently, federalism has been an underlying issue involving the controversy over the definition of marriage.

6.4 | Why Federalism?

Federalism is part of the Madisonian system of institutional checks and balances. In *Federalist No 51*, Hamilton explained how dividing power between two levels of government in a "compound republic" checked government power:

> In a single republic, all the power surrendered by the people is submitted to the administration of a single government; and the usurpations are guarded against by a division of the government into distinct and separate departments. In the compound republic of America, the power surrendered by the people is first divided between two distinct governments, and then the portion allotted to each subdivided among distinct and separate departments. Hence a double security arises to the rights of the people. The different governments will control each other at the same time that each will be controlled by itself.

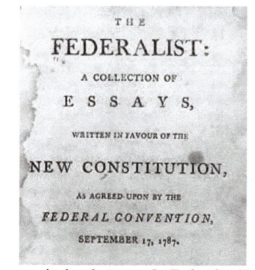

Hamilton was an ardent Federalist. He believed that one of the lessons of history was that threats to good public order came from a government that was too strong to hold government officials accountable and from government that was too weak to create or maintain good public order. Hamilton believed that federalism solved some of the problems of a weak national government under the Articles of Confederation, weaknesses that were exposed by Shays' Rebellion and other domestic disturbances by creating a stronger national government. Federalists also supported a strong national government to direct economic development. In *Federalist Number Nine*, Hamilton wrote:

A FIRM UNION WILL BE OF THE UTMOST MOMENT TO THE PEACE AND LIBERTY OF THE STATES, AS A BARRIER AGAINST DOMESTIC FACTION AND INSURRECTION. IT IS IMPOSSIBLE TO READ THE HISTORY OF THE PETTY REPUBLICS OF GREECE AND ITALY WITHOUT FEELING SENSATIONS OF HORROR AND DISGUST AT THE DISTRACTIONS WITH WHICH THEY WERE CONTINUALLY AGITATED, AND AT THE RAPID SUCCESSION OF REVOLUTIONS BY WHICH THEY WERE KEPT IN A STATE OF PERPETUAL VIBRATION BETWEEN THE EXTREMES OF TYRANNY AND

ANARCHY....[THE CRITICS OF REPUBLICAN GOVERNMENT] HAVE DECRIED ALL FREE GOVERNMENT AS INCONSISTENT WITH THE ORDER OF SOCIETY....THE SCIENCE OF POLITICS, HOWEVER, LIKE MOST OTHER SCIENCES, HAS RECEIVED GREAT IMPROVEMENT. THE EFFICACY OF VARIOUS PRINCIPLES IS NOW WELL UNDERSTOOD, WHICH WERE EITHER NOT KNOWN AT ALL, OR IMPERFECTLY KNOWN TO THE ANCIENTS. THE REGULAR DISTRIBUTION OF POWER INTO DISTINCT DEPARTMENTS; THE INTRODUCTION OF LEGISLATIVE BALANCES AND CHECKS; THE INSTITUTION OF COURTS COMPOSED OF JUDGES HOLDING THEIR OFFICES DURING GOOD BEHAVIOR; THE REPRESENTATION OF THE PEOPLE IN THE LEGISLATURE BY DEPUTIES OF THEIR OWN ELECTION: THESE ARE WHOLLY NEW DISCOVERIES, OR HAVE MADE THEIR PRINCIPAL PROGRESS TOWARDS PERFECTION IN MODERN TIMES.

> Think About It!
> Do you agree with Hamilton's analysis of the threats to freedom in Federalist No.8, "The Consequences of Hostilities Between the States"?
> http://thomas.loc.gov/home/histdox/fed_08.html

Hamilton's call for a national government with enough power to create and maintain good public order as well as to promote economic development stands in sharp contrast with the Anti-federalists. The Anti-federalists were a loosely-organized group of individuals who advocated for what would today be called states' rights. They believed that the powers of the national government should be limited and that the states should be the primary political unit within the American system of federalism.

6.5 | The Political Effects of Federalism

Federalism has two principal effects on government and politics. First, it creates a large number of governments. Second, complicates government and politics.

6.51 | The Surprisingly Large Number of Governments

Although federalism is a two-tiered system of government, the U.S. actually has a large number of governments: one national government; 50 state governments; and thousands of local governments.

The Number of Governments in the United States	
Type	Number
Federal Government	1
States	50
Counties	3,043
Municipalities	19,372
Townships or Towns	16,629
School districts	13,726
Special Districts*	34,683
• Mosquito Control	
• Child Protective Services	
• Port Authority	
• Airport	
• Beach Taxing	
• Health Care	
• F.I.N.D (Florida Inland Navigation District)	
TOTAL NUMBER OF GOVERNMENT UNITS:	87,504
*Examples of Special Districts in Palm Beach County, Florida	

Source: U.S. Department of Commerce, Statistical Abstract of the United States, 2003 (Washington, D.C.: U.S. Government Printing Office, 2003), 261

Think About It! What's in a name? Does it matter whether a municipality is a city or a town? Yes, it does.

Niagara Falls in Danger of Losing Status as City, Aid"
http://www.npr.org/2012/10/25/163653935/niagara-falls-in-danger-of-losing-city-status-aid

Act on it!

One good thing about having a large number of governments is the increased access to government. Contact a local government official and ask a question about a public policy issue of interest to you.

6.52 | Complicated Government and Politics

Federalism also complicates American government and politics. In unitary political systems, political debates focus on the substance of public policy. The debates focus on *what* public policy should be concerning foreign affairs, economics, crime, education, the environment, moral regulatory policy, or religion. All countries debate public policy on these controversial issues. In the U.S., federalism means that political debates are about *what* public policy should be and about *who* should be making public policy. We debate whether abortion should be legal, whether there a right to die, whether global warming exists and what public policy should be, whether the death penalty should be used for sentencing, whether organized prayer be allowed in public schools. We also debate who should make the policy—whether it should be made by the national government or state governments. Federalism makes American politics doubly complicated: we debate what policy should be and who should make it.

The distribution of power between the national and state governments has been part of many of the nation's most important political developments: the Civil War; the Progressive Era; the Great Depression of the 1930s; and the 20th Century Civil Rights movements. Federalism also inspired the modern conservative movement beginning in the latter 1960s as a backlash against the New Deal and Great Society expansions of national government power.

Debates about federalism are debates about one aspect of the **power problem**: how much power to centralize in the national government and how much power to leave decentralized with the states. The Constitution does not solve the power problem in the sense that it does not specify, except for certain areas such as coining money and regulating interstate commerce, whether the national government or the state governments have power to act in an area of public policy. The federalism dimension of the power problem has been dynamic. The actual distribution of power between the national and state governments changes depending on conditions and circumstances. Crises usually result in centralization of power in the national government. Shays' Rebellion, the Great Depression; World War II and the Cold War, and terrorist threats to national security were all crises that resulted in increased power for the national government.

6.6 | Federalism is Dynamic

The balance of power between the national and state governments is dynamic. It is always changing, with the balance sometimes tilting toward the national government and sometimes tilting toward the states. But modern federalism does not work the way the Founders intended. The Founders created a political system where most government power was left in the hands of the states and the national government's powers were limited. It was a state-centered system. Over time, however, the powers of the national government expanded, and expanded relative to the states. The following describes the major historical changes in federalism.

6.61 | *Dual Federalism*

The first era of federalism is described as dual federalism. **Dual federalism** is a theory of federalism that describes both the federal government and the state governments as co-equal sovereigns. Each is sovereign in its respective areas of policymaking. The Supreme Court endorsed this understanding of federalism in an early case *Cooley v. Board of Port Wardens* (1851). The question in this case was whether a state government could require that ships entering or leaving the Philadelphia harbor hire a local pilot. The Constitution gives the national government exclusive power to regulate commerce among the states. The Philadelphia Port traffic involved more than one state, so it was interstate commerce. The Court developed the **Cooley Doctrine** to decide whether a matter was for local or national regulation. According to the Cooley Doctrine, subjects that are "in their nature national, or admit only of one uniform system, or plan of regulation, may justly be said to...require exclusive legislation by Congress." Subjects that are not national and require local diversity of regulation are left to the states. The Cooley Doctrine assumes that the national and state governments have separate areas of responsibility. For example, the national government would have exclusive power over interstate commerce, national security, and foreign affairs, while the state governments would have exclusive power over schools, law enforcement, and road building.

The Cooley Doctrine still serves as a guide for determining whether the national or state governments have power to regulate, but it does not provide specific answers to questions about whether something required a single, uniform system of regulation. In fact, as both the national and state governments shared responsibility over more areas of public policy, debates about highway speed limits, legal drinking ages, educational policy, the regulation of airports, and immigration issues have challenged the idea that each level of government is supreme in it respective field.

6.62 | *Cooperative Federalism*

Cooperative federalism describes the national and state governments as sharing power over areas of public policy. Dual federalism is an outdated concept in the sense that there are so few areas of public policy that are exclusively either state or national, and so many areas of public policy where the federal government now acts. For example, all levels of government are involved in education, economics, transportation, crime, and environmental policy. The term **intergovernmental relations** is useful for understanding how modern federalism works because it captures how the national, state, and local governments interact with one another to make and administer policy.

One way to better understand the forces of change in the American political system is to examine economics. Economic changes have prompted the expansion of the federal government. The Industrial Revolution in the mid-19th Century fundamentally changed the American economy. The emergence of large national corporations created support for national government action to regulate these new centers of private power. During the Progressive Era (1890s until the World War I) the national government began to regulate industries such as the railroads, steel, banking, and mining. The federal government also passed social welfare legislation including child labor laws and minimum wage and maximum hour laws. In fact, today the federal government redistributes resources from wealthier states to poorer states. In today's economy, population mobility, the ability to relocate to states where the jobs are is an important economic indicator.

The PEW Research Center's Economic Mobility Project
Provides data on economic mobility in the U.S. and in the states:
http://www.pewtrusts.org/en/multimedia/data-visualizations/2012/economic-mobility-of-the-states

6.63 | *Expansion of Federal Power*

One measure of big government is the increased size and influence of the national government relative to the state governments. As the country changed from a local economy to a national economy, where businesses made and sold products and services across the country, public opinion shifted toward seeing the national government as the appropriate level of government to regulate business. During the 20th Century the power of the national government continued to expand relative to the states. The modern era of the U.S. political system began in the 1930s partly in response to an economic crisis. The Great Depression created popular support for national government activism to remedy the problem of the economic depression. The trend toward centralizing power and responsibility for maintaining material prosperity has accelerated with the further development of a global economy, where businesses buy and sell in a world economy.

A second source of expansion of federal power is civil rights. The Civil War Amendments—the 13th, 14th, and 15th Amendments—expanded the federal government's role in promoting racial equality. The Fourteenth Amendment, which was ratified in

1868, prohibits a state from denying to any person within its jurisdiction the equal protection of the laws. This Amendment was intended to protect the rights of newly freed slaves from state laws that discriminated against them on account of race. The Fourteenth Amendment gave Congress power to pass "appropriate legislation" to enforce the provisions of the Amendment. Congress used this power to pass civil rights legislation such as the Civil Rights Act of 1875 which outlawed racial discrimination in public accommodations. However, in the *Civil Rights Cases* (1883), the Supreme Court declared the law unconstitutional because it regulated private behavior—the decisions of owners of hotels and restaurants not to serve Black customers. According to the Court, the

Fourteenth Amendment, which was the basis for the Act, prohibited state action. The Court's landmark ruling in *Plessy v. Ferguson* (1896) also limited the scope of federal civil rights laws by upholding state laws that required racial segregation.

The Civil Rights Movement of the 1950s and 1960s also relied on federal efforts to secure the civil rights of individuals who were the victims of discrimination. Some of these efforts relied on Congress, which passed laws such as the 1964 Civil Rights Act and the 1965 Voting Rights Act. Some of the efforts relied on the United States Supreme Court. Decisions in landmark cases such as Brown v. Board of Education (1954) made state actions supporting racial discrimination in public schools unconstitutional. In many parts of the country the use of federal power to enforce equal protection of the laws prompted strong resistance. The constitutional argument against this use of federal power to promote equality, particularly racial equality, was the states' rights argument.

Federalism was part of the background of the civil rights movement. The U.S. Supreme Court rulings in cases such as *Brown v. Board of Education*, in which they outlawed racial segregation in public schools, prompted a political backlash in the states, particularly in the South. The principal reason for the backlash was opposition to integration. However, there was also a strong **states' rights** opposition to integration. States' rights can be defined as a belief that a policy is the responsibility of a state government not the national or federal government. Florida was one of the southern states that cited states' rights reasons for opposing

court-ordered desegregation. In 1957, the Florida Legislature passed an Interposition Resolution in response to *Brown v. Board of Education*. **Interposition** is a political doctrine that a state can interpose itself between the people of the state and the federal government when the federal government exceeds its authority. The Interposition Resolution declared that the U.S. Supreme Court exceeded its power when it declared racially segregated public schools unconstitutional.

Advocates of states' rights opposed the use of federal power to achieve greater racial equality in state politics, government, and society. George Wallace is an important political figure in the states' rights movement. He was a precursor of the modern conservative movement's criticism of big government, by which he meant a federal government with the power to order states to change their laws regarding race relations. He is a good example of how thinking about federalism is interwoven with thinking about civil rights in the U.S. Wallace was a forceful and articulate spokesperson for the conservative belief that the federal government's powers were limited to those specifically enumerated. He gave impassioned campaign speeches defending states' rights against a civil rights movement that relied heavily on "outside agitators" to bring about change. The outsiders were the federal government in general and the courts in particular.

> **Think About It!**
> Listen to one of Governor George Wallace's states' rights speech against the civil rights movement:
> http://www.youtube.com/watch?v=QW6ikSCDaRQ&feature=endscreen&NR=1

A third reason for the expansion of federal power is criminal justice policy. The development of a national economy made state borders less relevant for legitimate business and economic activity because goods were no longer made, marketed, and sold entirely within one state. Illegitimate businesses were also organized nationally. Organized crime, in particular, did not operate exclusively within a single state. The rise of organized crime presented a challenge to law enforcement which was historically state and local law enforcement. The rise of nationally organized criminal enterprises provided one of the justifications for the creation of the Federal Bureau of Investigation (FBI). The FBI has jurisdiction across the country, unlike local law enforcement whose jurisdiction (or legal authority) is geographically limited. Historically, criminal justice has been one of the areas of public policy reserved to the states under the U.S. system of federalism. The rise of organized crime, the war on crime, and the war on drugs made crime and policing a national political issue to be addressed by the federal government. Congress responded by passing more and more anti-crime legislation—a trend toward federalizing crime that continued throughout the 20th Century and into the 21st Century.

Think about it! Why does the U.S. have a federal law enforcement agency? The FBI tells the story of its creation and expansion in "A Brief History of the FBI."http://www.fbi.gov/about-us/history/brief-history

A fourth reason for the expansion of federal power is national security, national defense, and foreign policy. World War II and the Cold War increased the power of the national government. Threats to national security have historically been considered the primary responsibility of the federal government. The war on terror has continued to shift power to the national government relative to the states. For instance, the federal government increasingly uses the resources and information on local governments to find and track terrorist suspects. Terrorism is often an international threat—its support networks, funding, and training involve other countries, and terrorists seek to move easily across national borders—therefore the threat of terrorism typically increases the power to the federal government.

The economy, civil rights, national security, and crime are not the only reasons for the expansion of federal power. In environmental policy, Congress has passed major legislation such as the Clean Air Act and the Clean Water Act and established bureaucratic agencies the Environmental Protection Agency to implement the new federal environmental policies. In educational policy, Congress passed the No Child Left Behind Act. The Act increased the federal government's role in an area of public policy that was traditionally left to the states. In health care, President Obama signed the Patient Protection and Affordable Health Care Act on March 23, 2010. Twenty-eight states filed lawsuits claiming that parts of the Act, which critics called Obamacare, were unconstitutional because they exceeded the federal government's power. The Supreme Court upheld most provisions of the Act, including the mandate that individuals buy health insurance or pay a penalty/tax, in National Federation of Independent Business v. Sebelius (2012), but ruled that state sovereignty protected the states from certain provisions of the law that required states to adopt certain health care policies or lose federal Medicaid funding.

6.7 | The Conservative Backlash: New Federalism

Beginning in the latter 1960s, conservatives began criticizing the expansion of the federal government and the idea of cooperative federalism. Their criticism of "big government" included calls for returning some power to the states. Their advocacy of states' rights was intended primarily as a check on the expansion of the national government's power in domestic affairs. The Nixon administration's policies to support returning some powers to the states were called New Federalism.

> **Think about it!**
>
> *Do we still need states? In a global economy, are political boundaries such as states merely an additional business expense?*

The political support for New Federalism was also reflected in changes in the Supreme Court's rulings. The Court began to limit the powers of the federal government. From 1938 until 1995, the Court did not invalidate any federal statute on the grounds that the law exceeded Congress' power under the Interstate Commerce Clause. But in *United States v. Lopez* (1995), the Court ruled that some provisions of the Gun-Free School Zones Act, a federal law enacted in 1990 to curb gun violence, exceeded Congress's commerce powers and infringed on the states' reserved powers to provide safe schools. A conservative majority on the Rehnquist Court issued a number of important rulings that enforce constitutional provisions that limit congressional power in fields of public policy where the states have power to act. These rulings are based on the political conservative belief that federalism is a legal arrangement that protects the states and is part of the system of checks and balances that protects individual freedom.

The challenge is to adapt a more than 200 year old system of federalism to a modern environment that has experienced a great deal of political, economic, technological, and social change. Take, for example, economic change. The U.S. economy has changed from local to state to national and now, with globalism, international trade. How does a global economy affect the distribution of power between the national and state governments? How has the U.S. assumption of the role as the world's policeman, the Cold War, and the war on terror affected the distribution of power between the national and state governments? These economic and national security developments have increased federal power—an increase that sometimes, but not always, means a decrease in state powers.

Federalism is one aspect of the conservative backlash against the liberal centralization of power that occurred during the New Deal and Great Society eras. The backlash has not been inspired by opposition to big government in general. Conservatives supported big government for national security purposes, getting tough on crime, and moral regulatory purposes (e.g., sexual behavior, marriage, obscenity and indecency, and the definition of marriage). Even in economic policy, business groups with ties to conservative and Republican politics such as the U.S. Chamber of Commerce and the National Association of Manufacturers lobbied for the passage of federal laws that explicitly preempt state tort laws. Tort laws govern wrongful injury lawsuits such as product liability and medical malpractice litigation. The states traditionally had primary responsibility for tort laws as part of their reserved powers. The tort reform movement, of which the Chamber of Commerce and the National Association of Manufacturers are prominent supporters, advocates taking cases out of the state courts and into the federal courts. This is evidence that liberal and conservative attitudes toward federalism tend to be strategic rather than principled. A principled position is one that is taken regardless of whether it produces a preferred outcome. A strategic position is one that is taken because it produces a preferred outcome. Liberals tend to think that policies should be decided in the states when they think the state political systems will produce liberal policy outcomes. Conservatives tend to think that policies should be decided in the states when they think the state political systems will produce conservative policy outcomes. If a liberal (or a conservative) thinks the federal government will produce a preferred policy outcome, they are likely to think that the policy should be decided by the federal government rather than the states.

6.71 | *Immigration Policy*

Immigration is one of the issues that illustrate the potential conflict between national and state policy. Controlling undocumented immigrants is a pressing issue in some states, particularly states bordering Mexico and states with large numbers of undocumented immigrants. The key constitutional doctrine for understanding whether states have the power to act in an area or policy field is **preemption**. Federal law can preempt or trump state law. The preemption doctrine is based on the Supremacy Clause, Article VI of the Constitution, which provides that the Constitution, federal laws, and treaties shall be the "supreme Law of the Land." The Supremacy Clause guarantees national union. When deciding whether a state law conflicts with a federal law the Court does a "preemption analysis" consisting of three questions. Did Congress expressly state that federal law preempted state law? Does the state law conflict with federal law? Has Congress so extensively regulated the area of policy to have "occupied the field?" If Congress has enacted a comprehensive and unified federal policy in a field, then Congress has assumed responsibility for that field and left little or no room for state action. States can experiment with health care reform, education reform, and many other reforms in other areas of public policy.

Immigration policy is a special case because it has national security implications. Illegal immigration became a political issue when some states thought the federal government was unwilling or unable to enforce immigration laws. States adopted a variety of laws that were intended to discourage illegal entry and to discourage employment of illegal immigrants or undocumented aliens. Arizona, which shares a border with Mexico, is one such state. In 2010 it passed SB1070 an immigration control law that, among things, required Arizona police officers to determine the citizenship or immigration status of a person who was lawfully detained. SB1070 served as a model for other states including Alabama, Georgia, Indiana, South Carolina, and Utah. The Arizona law was challenged on the grounds that it was preempted by federal law. In *Arizona v. U.S.* (2012), the Supreme Court upheld one provision of the law and struck down three provisions.

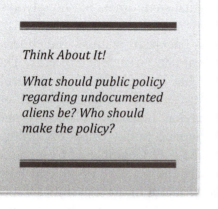

Think About It!

What should public policy regarding undocumented aliens be? Who should make the policy?

The stated purpose of SB1070 was to use state resources to help the federal government enforce its immigration laws. The law 1) required law enforcement officers to check the immigration status of persons who they have a "reasonable suspicion" are in the country illegally; 2) required the warrantless arrest of individuals that law enforcement official have probable cause to believe have committed a crime for which the person could be deported; 3) made it a crime to not carry immigration papers in the state; and 4) made it a crime for illegal immigrants to seek a job or to work in the state.

The Court upheld provision number one but struck down the other three. The Court explained that the federal government's broad power over immigration and alien status is based on 1) its enumerated power in Art I, Sect. 8 cl. 4 to "establish an uniform Rule of Naturalization;" 2) its inherent sovereign power to control and conduct foreign relations; and 3) the Supremacy clause. The fact that Congress has created a single sovereign responsible for maintaining a comprehensive and unified system to keep track of aliens within the nation limits state sovereignty to legislate in a policy field that Congress has occupied. The dissenting Justices argued that the states have their own inherent sovereignty and can legislate on immigration matters of great concern to them.

6.7 | *How Do States Still Matter?*

Rick Meyerowitz is an artist best known for his work for *National Lampoon*.
This is his interpretation of U.S. political cultural geography.

6.8 | Summary

This chapter described federalism, explained the origins of the U.S. system of federalism, and described its development over time. The division of powers between the national and state governments has been controversial throughout the nation's history. Federalism has proven to be a dynamic form of government in the sense that the actual distribution of power between the national and state governments has varied a great deal over time. The Constitution provides for a federal system but, with the notable exception of foreign affairs and interstate commerce, it does not specify exactly what each level of government has power to do. As a result, the actual balance of power between the national and state governments changes. In this sense, federalism is dynamic. The federal government's power has increased, and it has increased relative to the state governments for a variety of reasons, including the development of a global economy. Because of the central role federalism plays in the system of checks and balances, changes in federalism raise important questions about where to strike the right balance between state and federal power.

6.9 | Additional Resources

6.91 | *Internet Resources*

One valuable resource for information about the states is the PEW Center On the States which describes and analyzes state policy trends, for example. See http://www.pewcenteronthestates.org/

The Tenth Amendment Center provides a contemporary view on states' rights: http://www.tenthamendmentcenter.com/

The Urban Institute's publication "Assessing the New Federalism" is an informative look at the place for cities in the U.S. system of federalism: www.urban.org/center/anf/index.cfm

Publius: The Journal of Federalism is an academic journal dedicated to the investigation of issues related to federalism: http://publius.oxfordjournals.org/

The National Council of State Legislators provides a variety of information about state legislatures, including ideas about the relationship between the state and federal governments: www.ncsl.org/statefed/afipolcy.htm

6.92 | *In the Library*

Berman, David. 2003. *Local Governments and the States: Autonomy, Politics, and Policy*. ME Sharpe.

Burgess, Michael. 2006. *Comparative Federalism: Theory and Practice*. Routledge.

Butler, Henry N. 1996. *Using Federalism to Improve Environmental Policy*. American Enterprise Institute Press.

Cornell, Saul. 1999. *The Other Founders: Anti-Federalism and the Dissenting Tradition in America, 1788-1828*. University of North Carolina Press.

Doernberg, Donald. 2005. *Sovereign Immunity And/Or the Rule of Law: The New Federalism*. Carolina Academic Press.

Donahue, John. 1997. *Disunited States*. Basic Books.

Elkins, Stanley and Eric McKitrick. 1995. *The Age of Federalism: The Early American Republic, 1788-1800*. Oxford University Press.

Gerston, Larry N. 2007. *American Federalism: A Concise Introduction*. M.E. Sharpe.

Karmis, Dimitrios. 2005. *Theories of Federalism: A Reader*. London: Palgrave Macmillan.

Nagel, Robert F. 2002. *The Implosion of American Federalism*. Oxford University Press.

Noonan, Jr. John T. 2002. *Narrowing the Nation's Power: The Supreme Court Sides with the States*. University of California Press, 2002.

Schrag, Peter. 1999. *Paradise Lost: California's Experience, America's Future*. University of California Press.

Tarr, G. Alan, Robert F. Williams, Josef Marko (Eds.). 2004. *Federalism, Subnational Constitutions, and Minority Rights*. Praeger.

Twight, Charlotte. 2002. *Dependent on D.C.: The Rise of Federal Control over Ordinary Lives*. Palgrave.

Zimmerman, Joseph. 2002. *Interstate Cooperation: Compacts and Administrative Agreements*. Praeger.

---

[1] Larry N. Gerston. 2007. *American Federalism: A Concise Introduction*. New York: M.E. Sharpe, Inc., p.87.

TERMS:

Federalism
Unitary system
Confederation
Delegated powers
Reserved powers
The power problem
Dual federalism
Cooley Doctrine
Cooperative federalism
States' rights
Interposition

6.93 | STUDY QUESTIONS

Why have a federal system of government?

Discuss the allocation of federal and state powers.

Explain how the allocation of federal and state powers has changed over time.

Describe four areas where federal powers have grown into areas traditionally reserved for the states.

Discuss the current state of federalism in the United States.

What role did the civil rights movement play in the expansion of federal powers?

How is federalism dynamic?

Why did the Federalists believe that a strong federal government was necessary?

CHAPTER 7: THE MEDIA, POLITICS, AND GOVERNMENT

7.0 | The Media and Democracy

This chapter examines the media's role in politics and government. It includes beliefs about the relationship between democracy and freedom of the press, changes in the media communication landscape, and the power problem with the media—specifically the problem of media bias.

Freedom of the press is considered essential for democracy. Freedom House is a non-government organization that issues annual reports on the state of global democracy. Its 2017 report on freedom in the world "Populists and Autocrats: the Dual Threat to Global Democracy" concluded that 2016 "marked the 11th consecutive year of decline in global freedom." Freedom of expression is an important component of Freedom House's measure of how democratic a country is. The *Report* explains that a country's scores on freedom of expression are determined by, among other things, the following factors:

> *"Were it left to me to decide whether we should have a government without newspapers or newspapers without a government, I should not hesitate a moment to prefer the latter."*
> **Thomas Jefferson**

> *"The man who reads nothing at all is better educated than the man who reads nothing but newspapers. The press is the toxin of the nation."* **Thomas Jefferson**

> *"Why should a government which believes it is doing right allow itself to be criticized. It would not allow opposition by lethal weapons. Ideas are much more fatal things than guns."*
> **Nikolai Lenin (1920)**

> *"I'm as mad as hell, and I am not going to take this anymore."*
> *UBS Evening News* **Anchor Howard Beale in the film *Network* (USA 1976)**

• The existence of a "free and independent media and other forms of cultural expression;"

• Protection for "open and free private discussions" using social media platforms;

• Media freedom to report on government corruption; and

• The existence of free and fair elections that provide candidates for office access to the media to communicate with the electorate.

7.1 | The Media Roles

In the U.S., the media have four main roles. The **economic role** is to provide consumers with goods and services. In this sense, the media are just like any other for-profit companies in the business sector: some make cars or household appliance like toasters; some create intellectual property like films or television programming; some provide legal, financial, or medical services; all offer their products to the public for purchase. But the media are a special kind of business. The press is the only business that is given constitutional protection. The First Amendment guarantees freedom of the press because of the belief that democracy—self-government—requires an informed and educated citizenry. This is the media's **educative role**. The media are expected to provide information about public affairs and current events so that voters can make good political decisions. Reporters report politics. The television and radio broadcast media are even required by law to perform this educative role as one of the conditions for the government to issue broadcast licenses. The media also play a **watchdog role**. The institutional media are part of the system of checks and balances. The media coverage of public affairs includes investigative reporting on government affairs. The mass media also play a **socialization role**. Their news and public affairs programming and their entertainment programming shape the way media consumers think about politics and government. This is why television is watched so closely to determine the "profound" effects it has on the psychosocial development of children and youth; how family values are portrayed; how religion is portrayed; how the criminal justice system is portrayed; and the portrayal of wars and threats to national security.

7.2 | The Power Problem with the Media: Bias

Mass communication scholars have developed <u>framing theory</u> to explain "the media effect." Framing refers to the context that the media provide for the information that they provide or the stories they tell. Framing influences the consumer's thinking about the topic. The media effect is central to the power problem with the media. The power problem with the media is bias. The solution is not free press because a free press is not necessarily a fair press. Determining the media effect is important because the media play such a large and growing role in American life. The media are integrated into American society in the sense that they occupy a significant share of an individual's daily life. The media are an important sector of the American economy. The media are an important source of information about, and analysis of, politics. The media also report on government.

The media are frequently charged with bias. The media have biases. One media bias is economic: the pursuit of profits. Most media are private, for-profit corporations whose business model depends on profitability to be successful. They make money by providing entertainment and information (news) programming that the public and advertisers will pay for. Therefore, the economic role is the primary function of most media and the educative, watchdog, and socialization roles are secondary.

A second media bias is ideological. This is the most frequent charge of media bias—and the media are most frequently charged with having a liberal, progressive, or leftwing bias. This is reflected in the promotion of values such as equality, tolerance, and pluralism or diversity. A third bias is the bias toward action and conflict and drama. Stories about nothing happening are not compelling and therefore do not attract eyeballs, ears, or money. The action bias is reflected in the slogan that when it comes to news reports, "If it bleeds, it leads!" The conflict and drama bias is reflected in negative political campaign coverage—but also feel good news stories about individuals overcoming hardship or kittens being rescued from trees. A fourth bias is partisanship. Media partisanship has changed a great deal over time. During the founding era, the press was not just political; it was an overtly partisan press. Handbills and flyers and papers were distributed to convince readers to support candidates, government officials, and political parties. Over time, however, political culture changed with the development of journalism as a profession. The media kept their distance from political parties partly because an overtly partisan media seemed to conflict with the American belief in the free market of ideas from which the public could choose.

Professionalism, technology, changes in mass communications law have changed the way we communicate, but claims of media bias have remained fairly constant. There are, however, periods of heightened concern about bias. The emergence of large corporations in the railroad, banking, manufacturing, and oil sectors of the economy resulted in Progressive Era support for big government to act as a countervailing force to big business. The institutional press was also assigned an investigative or watchdog role to report on both big business and big government abuses of power. This is the media's role in the system of institutional checks and balances. Technological developments are changing this role. Technology has increased opportunities for unfiltered political communication. Compared to the mass media, the new social media provide greater opportunities for unfiltered communication between the public, candidates for office, and government officials. The media mediate less than they used to. This technological changed has diminished the mass media's socialization role. New technologies have enabled film and television producers to target a niche audience with edgier or more ideological programming rather than offering middle of the road programming that appeals to the largest national audience. This is related to a third change. Although the mainstream media and professional journalism have been less overtly committed to specific movements or political parties than when the country was founded, this is changing as advocacy journalism enters the media mainstream. Conservatives and Republicans have been supporting economic deregulation of the broadcast media since the 1980s when the Federal Communications Commission (FCC) abolished the Fairness Doctrine. Since then the FCC has allowed more concentrations of corporate media ownership in local media markets. Most recently, the FCC has begun deregulating the Internet by ending net neutrality rules and privacy rule that prohibited Internet service providers (ISPs) from selling an individual's browser history.

These professional, technological, and legal changes have resulted in more ideological and partisan perspectives in coverage of public affairs. Fox News is a company that is closely aligned with the Republican Party. The Sinclair Group is closely aligned with conservative perspectives on public affairs, and NBC's cable and satellite television network MSNBC presents a liberal perspective or framing of public affairs. Taken together, these professional, technological, and legal developments make the power problem even more central to understanding the media effect on politics and government. One of the politically interesting developments in television business is the emergence of ideological and partisan television networks and media companies. Fox News and the Sinclair Broadcast Group are competitors, but they both are right-leaning companies. Fox News is the established company. Roger Ailes, the former head of Fox News, realized that there was a large audience of conservatives and Republicans who wanted more ideological (i.e., conservative) and partisan (i.e., Republican) news. He built the network into an extremely successful political business model.

Sinclair has 72 local TV stations and plans to add 42 more by acquiring Tribune Media. Sinclair requires its local stations to air its conservative content such as Terrorism Alert Desk updates and criticism of Democrats. Fox News is best understood as partisan rather than ideological because it consistently supports Republican positions rather than conservative views or principles. This is evident in how the network frames budget deficits and presidential power. Budget deficits, and an imperial president are framed as problems when a Democrat is in the White House but not when a Republican is in the White House. During the Obama administration a recurring theme of Fox News stories was the threat of an imperial president and a weak president who compromised national security. Fox ended this media frame when President Trump was inaugurated. The network's coverage of the Russia-Trump scandal also reveals partisanship rather than ideology. Its coverage frames the story as Democratic hysteria rather than whether Russia was undermining democracy and U.S. national security.

7.21 | A Love-Hate Relationship

The media may be essential for democracy but Americans do not have a love affair with the press. The relationship with the press is more of a love-hate relationship. Which of the two Thomas Jefferson quotes about the press do you think was made before he became president, and which do you think was made after he became president? A politician's attitudes toward the press do seem to depend on whether a person is in office or not. When Donald Trump Tweeted that elements of the media were "fake news" and "the enemy of the American people" he was running a familiar play in the playbook of conservatives and Republicans.[1] The Nixon administration had strained relations with the press. In the latter 1960s, President Nixon and Vice-president Spiro Agnew attacked the press for being "nattering nabobs of negativism." One of Nixon's speechwriters, Patrick Buchanan still delights in charging the mainstream media with bias. Conservative organizations such as *Human Events* still echo these complaints about media bias. After the 2008 presidential election, a senior adviser for John McCain, the Republican presidential candidate, said that the *New York Times* "is today not by any standard a journalistic organization."

7.22 | *The Founding Era*

Freedom of the press played an important role in the founding of the American republic. The Trial of John Peter Zenger established the media's role in holding the government accountable. In 1735, Zenger, the editor and publisher of a newspaper called *The New York Weekly Journal*, was arrested for sedition and libel for publishing articles that criticized William Cosby, the governor of New York. The outcome of the case strengthened the colonists' commitment to two important concepts in American political culture: The first concept is that trial by jury is an important check on government power; the second concept is that the media are an important check on government power.

The First Amendment provides that "Congress shall make no law.... abridging the freedom.... of the press...." This special status is why the press is sometimes called "the fourth estate"—a reference to the fact that the press is a political institution like Congress, the president, and the judiciary. The early press focused on scandals and salacious stories in order to sell papers. The early press, which was sometimes called "the penny press" because the papers were very cheap, was both political and partisan. A paper was identified with a particular point of view: it openly and explicitly and strongly either supported or opposed a political party; it took strong stands on political issues, candidates, or government officials. Neither the reading public nor public officials expected a newspaper to strive for objectivity or neutrality. One of the insights that made Fox News so successful was the realization that there was a large conservative market for more opinion and less reporting. Its marketing slogan, "Fair and Balanced," slyly references objectivity.

AS GAG-RULERS WOULD HAVE IT.
—Satterfield in the Jersey City *Journal*.

7.23 | *Libel Laws*

Despite the absolutist language of the First Amendment prohibiting Congress from passing any law restricting freedom of speech or press, the First Amendment has never been interpreted to mean people can say or write whatever they want. In the early days of the republic, the *free press* was not even expected to be a *fair press*. Influential or prominent individuals and government officials who were upset by newspaper stories about them could sue for defamation. Libel and slander are false spoken or written statements that injure a person. The Alien and Sedition Acts of 1798 made it a crime (seditious libel) to publish false or scandalous statements that tended to bring government into disrepute. The Federalist Party was the majority in Congress. Members of the Federalist Party did not like what Thomas Jefferson and other anti-federalists were saying about them, so they passed the Acts. The Sedition Act was repealed when Jefferson became president and the Democratic-Republican Party became the dominant political party. The Acts are evidence that American political culture supporting a press that was free to criticize government officials was accompanied by criticism of the press for not being fair.

7.24 | *Commercial Media*

In the 1830s, the partisan press changed to a commercial press with the emergence of came to be called the penny press. Advances in printing technology allowed newspapers to be produced at a far cheaper rate (one cent rather than 6 cents). The reduced cost of producing newspapers made news profitable. Papers made money by printing sensationalized accounts of crimes and disasters and scandals. This was **yellow journalism**, a pejorative reference to journalism that features scandal mongering, sensationalism, jingoism, or other unprofessional practices and coverage.

Newspaper circulation battles between Joseph Pulitzer's *New York World* and William Randolph Hearst's *New York Journal* produced sensational stories about rising tensions in Cuba, which was a Spanish colony. When the U.S. ship *The Maine* exploded in Havana harbor, Hearst and Pulitzer blamed the Spanish and urged military retaliation. The Spanish-American war is considered the first press-driven war.

Pulitzer's coverage of the explosion   Hearst's coverage of the explosion

7.25 | *Professional Press*

The development of a professional press began around 1900 when Joseph Pulitzer started a school of journalism at Columbia University. Journalism schools trained journalists to be objective, to separate facts from of opinion, and to avoid biased coverage of public affairs. The idea of an objective press was based on a belief that facts were distinct from values: objective journalists should have "faith in *facts*" and skepticism toward *values*; objective journalists should segregate facts and opinions/values."[2] This professional ethic encouraged journalists to consider the reporter separate from the news they reported and take pride in presenting the news (the facts) as objectively or neutrally as possible. The ideal of an objective *professional* press contributed to the belief that the institutional press should assume a watchdog role investigating and publicizing wrongdoing in business and government.

The New York Times investigative reporting on The Pentagon Papers in 1971 and the *Washington Post* investigation reporting on the Watergate Scandal in 1972 are two prominent examples of the press watchdogging the government. The investigate reporting sharpened President Nixon's already famous press hostility. Listen to the following audio recording of a December 14, 1972 conversation between President Nixon and Henry Kissinger, his Secretary of State. What does President Nixon's advice about press relations, after discussing how to handle press coverage of the Vietnam War, reveal about his attitudes toward the press?

> **Think About It!**
> In the Nixon Tape "Nixon, Kissinger on 'Christmas Bombing'" President Nixon says to Kissinger:
> "Also, never forget. The press is the enemy. The press is the enemy. The press is the enemy. The establishment is the enemy. The professors are the enemy. The professors are the enemy. Write that on the blackboard 100 times. And never forget it."
> http://www.youtube.com/watch?v=h0vi2l0WxO8

7.3 | The Mass, New, and Social Media

The term mass media refers to media that are specifically designed to reach a large (that is, mass) audience such as the entire population of a nation or state. The term was coined in the 1920s with the development of nationwide radio networks and mass-circulation newspapers and magazines. The classic examples of mass media are the three television networks—ABC, CBS, and NBC—before the emergence of cable television networks (CNN and ESPN began in the late 1970s) and the Internet. The programming of the three broadcast television networks was clearly intended to appeal to a national audience. The broadcast networks and the major newspapers (e.g., *The New York Times*, *Washington Post*, *Chicago Tribune*, and *Los Angeles Times*) are sometimes referred to as the "MSM " or mainstream media. Conservative critics of the media adapted this term by labeling the liberal mainstream media the *lamestream media*.

Government officials, politicians, and the general public have been quite critical of the power of the mass media. In the 1976 film <u>Network</u>, the fictional character Howard Beale is the evening news anchor for the UBS network. His famous, award-winning rant during a television broadcast resonated with the public. Beale told viewers to go to a window, open it, and shout "I'm mad as hell and I'm not going to take it anymore!" Beale's outburst voiced public frustration with *big media* in an era when three broadcast networks—ABC, CBS, and NBC—dominated the airwaves. The proliferation of media outlets has changed the media landscape but it hasn't ended worries about the power problem and media bias.

Although it seems a paradox, the media are now both more consolidated (in terms of ownership) and more fragmented (in terms of the types of media). In 1940, 83% of newspapers were independently owned. Now less than 20% of newspapers are not a part

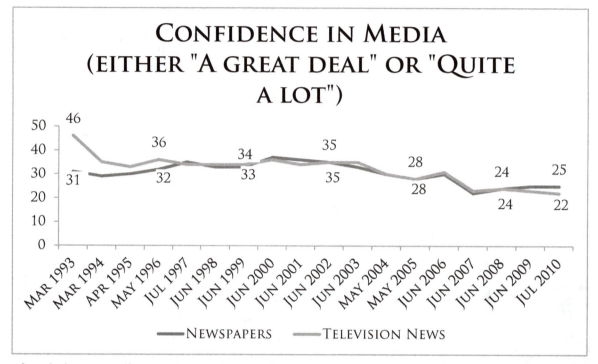

of a chain or media conglomerate. But there are now more ways to get information: 24 hour cable and satellite news programs and the Internet. The increase in the number of outlets, and the fragmentation of the media, enable consumers to seek out sources that reinforce their views.

7.31 | *The Social Media*

Developments in communication technology have changed the media landscape. Social media present alternatives to the traditional mass media (radio, television, newspapers and magazines). The term social media describes a broad range of Web-based devices for sharing information. The social media allow for more user-generated content, so the distinction between producers and consumers is diminished. This blurs the distinction between professional and amateur journalism. It also erodes the traditional mass media role as one of the "mediating" institutions. In a mass society of 300 million people, for example, the institutional press mediated between big government and the individual citizen. The effects of the social media revolution are just being assessed. As with all revolutions, there are positives and negatives. The expanded control over distribution of information is a positive development but one that also includes concerns about the changed nature of political communications.

The new forms of media have had a major impact on the way people get information and the way campaigns communicate with the electorate. A survey by the Pew Center for Internet & American Life[3] found that nearly three quarters of (74%) of internet users (55% of the general population) went online in 2008 to get involved in the political process or to get news and information about the election. 45% of internet users used the internet to watch a video related to the campaign and a third forwarded political content to others. These findings explain why campaigns increasingly rely on the new media to reach people.

Think About it!
Are the social media ruining politics?
http://www.politico.com/magazine/story/2015/09/2016-election-social-media-ruining-politics-213104

7.32 | *The End of Institutional Press?*

The social media contributed to long-term declines in newspaper subscriptions. The trend raised serious questions about the future of newspapers. In "The Report on the State of the News Media in 2007," Arthur Ochs Sulzberger Jr, the publisher and chairman of The

New York Times Company, responded to questions about the impact of technological changes on print journalism. He said, "I really don't know whether we'll be printing *The Times* in five years, and you know what? I don't care?"[4] This is a surprising statement for a newspaperman to make about the future of the print press.

The *Report* noted that technology was transforming the media in ways that may be as important the development of the television and radio, and perhaps even as important as the development of the printing press itself. Information technology changes the way people get information, but more important, it changes the relationship that people have with institutions such as government, schools, and the media. According to the *Report*, "Technology is redefining the role of the citizen—endowing the individual with more responsibility and command over how he or she consumes information—and that new role is only beginning to be understood." Information technology has empowered individuals by making them less dependent on the institutional media to *mediate*. Mediating refers to what institutions in mass societies do when they function as intermediaries between big government and individuals. As the scale of government expands—as government gets bigger and bigger—the distance between a single individual and the government increases. Mediating institutions solve some of the problems of scale, where larger scale organizations make the individual seem less important. The owners of newspaper, television, and Internet companies, and the editors who work for them, filter, edit, or otherwise decide what is newsworthy and merits reporting. Information technology is making this traditional "mediating" role less important. But eliminating the mediating institutions leaves the individual citizen or consumer with more responsibility for determining the accuracy of the electronic information that is now so widely available and either free or cheap. These new or non-institutional media are part of trend toward "de-intermediation" that includes Wikipedia, We Media, YouTube, and the blogosphere.

7.33 | *Journalism as a Profession*

The development of an independent, professional journalism began after the Civil War when newspapers were no longer as likely to be closely allied with a political party. The fact the newspapers became less partisan did not mean that the press became less political, however. Newspapers in the latter part of the 19th Century became very political during the Progressive Era (roughly the 1890s until World War I), but they tended to be political in the sense that they criticized political machines and political party bosses, or advocated on behalf of causes such as public corruption. As journalism became a profession, reporters were less partisan but still political. Investigative reporting of scandals or working conditions redefined the role of the press from a partisan press to an institutional press with the power to set the political agenda by calling public attention to an issue than needed political attention.

7.4 | Media and the Political System

The media—organizations and individuals working as reporters, editors, and producers—have a great deal of control over what the American public sees as the news. This includes what the media decide to report, how the information in framed, and what the media decide not to report. This is the essence of the power problem with the media.

7.41 | *Reporting Political News*

Reporting political news and public affairs information is one of the core functions of media outlets, particularly those with a national focus. Washington, D.C. has the largest concentration of news professionals in the United States. There are more than 8,000 reporters with Congressional press passes in Washington, covering political news for the American public.[5] Presidents hold press conferences to shape public opinion and to explain their actions. The number of formal press conferences is actually rather low. President G. W. Bush held 210 (26 per year) and President Obama held 164 (21 per year).[6] However, the White House press secretary generally meets the press daily.

Press conferences appear to be an opportunity for the media to directly ask the president a question and get an answer from the president rather than from advisers or spokespeople. But press conferences are actually carefully staged events. Government officials provide answers that they have scripted and rehearsed before the conference. As the figure below shows, presidents in the early 1900s gave many more press conferences than modern presidents.[7] Richard Nixon and Ronald Reagan gave very few press conferences; Nixon's low numbers were partially due to the fact that he had bad previous experiences with the press and partially due to the scandal of Watergate. Reagan's low numbers were largely due to the fact that he preferred alternate venues for communicating with the press. These included one-on-one interviews, answering questions on his way to or from the presidential helicopter, during a photo session, or brief interviews with local or regional television stations as a way to avoid the Washington press corp. Sam Donaldson, White House reporter for ABC News said, "The reason we yell at Reagan in the Rose Garden is that's the only place we see him."[8]

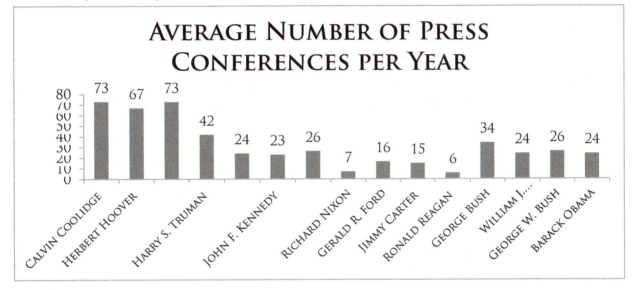

The George W. Bush administration exerted fairly strong control over information by not saying very much, by requiring prior approval to make media comments, and by limiting White House leaks. The limited press access frustrated the media. Obama preferred informal, off-the-cuff style interactions with the press and he limited the number of formal press conferences.

Media coverage of Congress is different than the coverage of the President. Congress has 535 members and is a decentralized institution. Public awareness of what Congress is doing and how it operates is rather low. Media coverage focuses on the leadership—the Speaker and majority and minority leaders. The chairs of committees engaged in reviewing important policies *may* get some attention from local stations and papers that report on local representatives.

The media **does** cover congressional committee hearings, particularly committee hearings called to investigate scandals. This kind of media coverage of Congress, the Administration, or business tends to be negative. It frames the story as institutional failures or inappropriate if not illegal behavior. The coverage is also often framed as partisan fights or highly ritualized theater more than serious attempts to solve a problem. The negative coverage is partly responsible for the public's negative perceptions of Congress as an ineffective branch of government. Media coverage of congressional committees doing their work, or federal bureaucrats doing their jobs, is not usually considered newsworthy. In fact watching committees and bureaucracies at work is considered as exciting as watching paint dry. This is, in fact, an example of a media bias for action or the drama of scandal rather than routine workings of government.

7.5 | The Media and Communications Law

There is an extensive body of law governing the media. The legal regime includes the U.S. Constitution; statutory law (federal and state legislation); regulatory law (the administrative rulings and orders promulgated by agencies such as the Federal Communications Commission); and case law (primarily federal court rulings) interpreting the First Amendment.

7.51 | *You can't always say (or post) what you want*

Perhaps the most important thing to know about freedom of the press is that you are not free to publish whatever you want to. The Supreme Court has never said that the First Amendment gives an individual the right to say anything that he or she wants to say. For instance, the First Amendment does not protect libel and slander. Libel is writing something that is false and injures another person. A person can be held responsible (financial or otherwise) for publishing something libelous and the government can punish individuals who publish factual information that is deemed harmful to national security. During the World War I era the Court upheld laws that punished individuals for criticizing U.S. participation in the war. The Supreme Court developed the Clear and Present Danger Test as a way to explain what kinds of political expression can be punished without violating the First Amendment. The government can punish individuals for saying or publishing things that raise a "clear and present danger" of causing actions that the government has the power to prevent. The application of this old doctrine is being challenged by counterterrorism policies that target Internet posts, terrorist websites, and blogging.

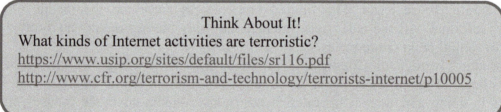

Think About It!
What kinds of Internet activities are terroristic?
https://www.usip.org/sites/default/files/sr116.pdf
http://www.cfr.org/terrorism-and-technology/terrorists-internet/p10005

7.52 | *Constitutional Law*

The First Amendment is the primary source of Constitutional protections for the media in the United States. It states that the "Congress shall make no law… abridging the freedom

of speech, or of the press." The Court has generally interpreted this right broadly and struck down attempted by the government to regulate the media. Freedom of the press has largely taken the form of protection from **prior restraint,** or the government banning expression of ideas prior to their publication. The most famous case upholding the press right to publish what it thinks is newsworthy is *New York Times v. United States* (1971).

This is the *Pentagon Papers* case. The *New York Times* and the *Washington Post* had published excerpts of classified Department of Defense documents (the Pentagon Papers) examining the conduct of the War in Vietnam, and the papers planned additional publications. The Nixon administration sought an injunction against the publication of the documents, contending that the documents would prolong the war and embarrass the government. The Supreme Court explained that the First Amendment freedom of the press placed a heavy burden of proof on the government to explain why "prior restraint" (that is, an injunction that prohibiting publication) was necessary. And the Court ruled that the government had not met the burden of proof because it did not explain why publication of the documents would lead to immediate, inevitable, and irreparable harm to national security or other interests. As a result of the Court's rulings, the U.S. has one of the freest presses in the world.

The government can limit freedom of the press if publication threatens national security interests. The government can legally prevent publication of certain strategic information such as the movement of troops during wartime. It can also legally censor publication of instructions on how build nuclear bombs. However, information technology has made such efforts to prevent publication practically difficult or even impossible. Information is now freely available on the Internet—even real time images of military actions. The War in Iraq illustrates how media technology has changed coverage of wars. The Pentagon adopted a policy of embedding journalists in military units. And soldiers with smart phones have repeatedly taken photos that exposed inappropriate or illegal behavior.

7.53 | *Statutory Laws*

The statutory basis for the federal government's media and telecommunications policy has its roots in two congressional acts, the <u>Communications Act of 1934</u> and the <u>Telecommunications Act of 1996</u>. The Communications Act of 1934 established the **Federal Communications Commission** (FCC) to oversee "interstate and foreign commerce in wire and radio communication." The FCC is considered one of the independent commissions because its members serve terms of office, can be removed only through impeachment, and no more than three of its five members can be from one political party.

The Communications Act went through a major overhaul when Congress passed the Telecommunications Act of 1996. The primary purpose of the Telecommunications Act was to deregulate the telecommunications industry. Prior to the 1996 Act, much of the telecommunications industry resembled a monopoly. People did not have a choice as to where they purchased their telephone service. The 1996 Act also relaxed laws on media ownership. Prior to the 1996 Act, a single company could not own more than twelve television stations or forty radio stations. The 1996 Act greatly relaxed this regulation, instead putting the cap of ownership at 35% of the national market for television and removing the cap entirely for radio ownership. As a result, major media companies like CBS, Fox, and Clear Channel greatly increased their shares of the media markets.

7.54 | *Administrative Regulations: The Fairness Doctrine*

In addition to the Constitution, statutes, and case law, the legal regime governing communications include administrative regulations promulgated by the FCC. The **Federal Communications Commission** is the primary source of these regulations, orders and policies. These regulations include the day-to-day actions of the FCC and the 1,899 employees that work for the FCC. This might include the approval of a merger of two telecommunications companies, fining companies for indecency, licensing amateur radio operators, and regulating some aspects of the internet.

The Fairness Doctrine is one of the rules or regulations that the Federal Communications Commission promulgated. The **Fairness Doctrine** required radio and television broadcast license holders to present controversial issues of public importance in a fair and balanced manner. The Fairness Doctrine is a good example of an administrative regulation or "law" created by an administrative agency. It is a law in the generic sense that it is an official, binding policy that individuals or organizations are not free to decide whether to comply with it. The FCC's authority to issue regulations was upheld by the Supreme Court in *Red Lion Broadcasting Co. v. FCC* (1969).[9] Red Lion Broadcasting aired on a Pennsylvania radio station a 15-minute broadcast by Reverend Billy James Hargis as part of a Christian Crusade series. The broadcast accused an author, Fred Cook, of being a Communist and of writing a book to "smear and destroy Barry Goldwater." Cook demanded free time to reply under the Fairness Doctrine. Red Lion refused. The FCC ruled that the broadcast was a personal attack that violated the Fairness Doctrine. Red Lion challenged the Fairness Doctrine in court.

The Supreme Court upheld the constitutionality of the Fairness Doctrine on the grounds that Congress had the authority to regulate broadcast media because of the scarcity doctrine. According to the scarcity doctrine, the airwaves are public and the government can regulate them by licensing to prevent signal overlap. The scarcity doctrine is what differentiates the print media, which are not licensed by the government, from the broadcast media, which are. Cable TV is not subject to the same kinds of government licensing and regulation. According to the Court, Congress had the power to regulate the airwaves and it could authorize the FCC to issue regulations such as the Fairness Doctrine.

The FCC repealed the Fairness Doctrine in 1987. Presidents nominate and the Senate confirms the five appointed commissioners who run the FCC. President Reagan appointed Republican commissioners who supported deregulating business. President Reagan appointed Mark S. Fowler as a member of the FCC. Fowler served from 1981 until 1987, including as chair of the FCC. Fowler served as FCC commissioner from 1981 until 1987. This was early in the modern era of government deregulation of various sectors of the economy. President Carter began the deregulation in energy (especially natural gas) and transportation (especially the airlines). President Reagan continued it with the deregulation of labor (e.g., collective bargaining laws) and the telecommunications industry. Fowler was a former broadcast industry lawyer who wondered why the broadcast media were treated so different than the film industry. The traditional arguments included

- The scarcity doctrine. There is a limited number of broadcast airwaves so the government licenses them to allocate the scarce resources to bring order to the airwaves.
- The public service. The broadcast media were considered a private industry that served a public purpose so government regulation was necessary.
- The protection and promotion of good civic values. The FCC regulated the broadcast industry to ensure that the licensees served "the public interest." This was part of the social responsibility to be considered when deciding whether to issue or renew a broadcast license.

Read Fowler's November 1981 interview with Reason magazine where he justifies deregulation of the broadcast media: "Television is just another appliance. It's just a toaster with pictures." Do you agree with him? Why would Fowler's views be of interest to Reason magazine? Does it have an ideological perspective? What does his claim imply about government regulation of any media devices such as smart phones or platforms or the Internet? Should government deregulate all aspects of media communication? The economic or business regulation currently includes anti-trust law which limits media consolidation and cross ownership of press, television, radio in a single media market. What about Net Neutrality? Should the government have any power to regulate mass or social media to maintain morals, to limit violence, or to police radical speech?

The FCC commissioners concluded that the Fairness Doctrine was limiting rather than enhancing public debate because the technology revolution that increased the media voices in the information marketplace made the Fairness Doctrine unnecessary. In fact, conservatives argued that the Fairness Doctrine and other government regulations, such as campaign finance laws, were unconstitutional limits on freedom of expression. Ending the Fairness Doctrine gave rise to conservative radio and television programs hosted by prominent conservative figures including Rush Limbaugh and Bill O'Reilly. Conservatives were taking to the airwaves using a style of ideological and partisan advocacy that would not have been possible under the regulatory schemes of the Fairness Doctrine. Fairness would have required broadcasters to provide airtime for the other side to reply anytime a network took a side on a controversial matter of public interest.

The current FCC continues this economic (that is, business) deregulatory policy and political (that is, ideological) deregulatory policy. It allows media mergers in the communications industry despite anti-trust laws: the FCC's position is that emerging technology and marketplace competition is preferable to government regulation of this rapidly changing sector of the American economy. Congress reflected the business deregulation perspective in the Telecommunications Act of 1996.

7.6 | Mass Media Re-regulation: Moral Regulatory policy and 'air' pollution

Media policy has traditionally divided the ideological left and right in American politics. It is not a matter of one side supporting government regulation and the other side opposing government regulation. The left and right are often divided over the purposes of government regulation. Liberals are generally more concerned about violence;

conservatives are generally more concerned about sex. During the 1960s and 1970s, the liberals on the Supreme Court began deregulating morality with civil libertarian rulings. The Court's First Amendment rulings limited the government's power to restrict access to sexually explicit materials or otherwise regulate behavior to promote morality. The deregulation was one of the reasons for the conservative backlash called the culture war over values.

The following are some of the federal statutes that attempted to re-regulate communications, particularly to protect minors.

7.61 | The Communications Decency Act of 1996[10]

This law criminalized the "knowing" transmission of "obscene or indecent messages" to any person who was under 18 years of age. It defined obscene or indecent as any message "that, in context, depicts or describes, in terms patently offensive as measured by contemporary community standards, sexual or excretory activities or organs." The Supreme Court declared these provisions of the Act unconstitutional in *Reno v. American Civil Liberties Union* (1997).[11] Justice Stevens explained that the Act restricted the ability of adults to engage in communication that is appropriate for them so much that the Act's costs outweighed its benefits.

7.62 | The Child Online Protection Act of 1998 (The "Son of CDA")[12]

This Act required commercial Web site operators to take actions to prevent persons under 18 from seeing material harmful to children by demanding proof of age from computer users. The Act provided a fine of $50,000 and 6 month prison term for allowing minors to view harmful content, which it defined as harmful using "contemporary community standards."[13] The law was challenged in court. In *Ashcroft v. American Civil Liberties Union* (2004), the Supreme Court ruled that the law

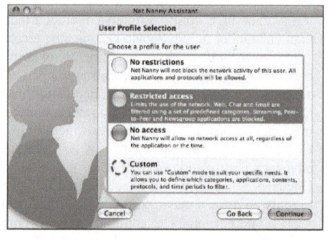

was unconstitutional because it unduly limited adults' right to freedom of expression. In 2007, U.S. District Judge Lowell A. Reed explained why he thought it was not a good idea to try to protect minors by limiting their rights as adults: "perhaps we do the minors of this country harm if First Amendment protections, which they will with age inherit fully, are chipped away in the name of their protection."[14]

7.63 | The Children's Internet Protection Act of 2000.[15]

This Act required public libraries to and public schools to take measures to limit computer access to certain Web sites in order to protect children. The law was challenged by the American Library Association on the account that it required libraries to block access to constitutionally protected information. In _United States et al. v. American Library Association_ (2003), the Supreme Court ruled that the law did not violate the First Amendment because the law did not require libraries to block access to information but simply made the government provision of financial assistance for obtaining Internet service dependent on compliance with the law.

7.62 | The FCC

Congress has authorized the FCC to enforce federal laws concerning obscenity, indecency, and profanity, as well as a broad range of illegal actions by telecommunications companies, such as "mystery fees"[16] or "pay-to-play" programs.[17] The FCC's Enforcement Bureau reviews public complaints and investigates to determine whether the facts warrant government action.[18] These investigations can result in fines, other sanctions, or even the loss of broadcast license. The difficulty determining what constitutes programming that warrants fines or other legal actions is illustrated by Michael Powell, the former Chair of the FCC, who stated the FCC's position on a television network broadcast of the popular film, _Saving Private Ryan_ without censoring the soldiers' cursing. In response to public complaints about the primetime broadcast, and in an attempt to ease broadcasting company concerns about whether they would be subject to FCC disciplinary actions (fines or broadcast licensure revocation), Powell provided the following explanation of FCC policy.

STATEMENT OF MICHAEL K. POWELL, CHAIR
FEDERAL COMMUNICATION COMMISSION

Re: Complaints Against Various Licensees Regarding Their Broadcast on November 11, 2004, of ABC Television Network's Presentation of the Film "Saving Private Ryan,"

Today, we reaffirm that content cannot be evaluated without careful consideration of context. Saving Private Ryan is filled with expletives and material arguably unsuitable for some audiences, but it is not indecent in the unanimous view of the Commission.

This film is a critically acclaimed artwork that tells a gritty story—one of bloody battles and supreme heroism. The horror of war and the enormous personal sacrifice it draws on cannot be painted in airy pastels. The true colors are muddy brown and fire red and any accurate depiction of this significant historical tale could not be told properly without bringing that sense to the screen. It is for these reasons that the FCC has previously declined to rule this film indecent.

This, of course, is not to suggest that legal content is not otherwise objectionable to many Americans. Recognizing that fact, it is the responsible broadcaster that will provide full and wide disclosure of what viewers are likely to see and hear, to allow individuals and families to make their own well-informed decisions whether to watch or not. I believe ABC and its affiliated stations made a responsible effort to do just that in this case.

Fair warning is appropriately an important consideration in indecency cases. In complaints you often find that Americans are not excessively prudish, only that they are fed up with being ambushed with content at times and places they least expect it. It is insufficient to tell consumers not to watch objectionable content, if the "shock" value is dependent on the element of surprise. This is particularly true in broadcast television, where viewers are accustomed and encouraged to order their viewing by parts of the day—morning shows, daytime TV and late night have long been the zones in which expectations are set. When those lines are blurred, the consumer loses a degree of control, a degree of choice.

Context remains vital to any consideration of whether profanity or sexual content constitutes legally actionable indecency. The Commission must stay faithful to considering complaints within their setting and temper any movement toward stricter liability if it hopes to give full effect to the confines of the First Amendment."

7.7 | Which Way Are We Going?

Since the 1980s, communication law and policy leads have been moving in two different directions at the same time. One direction supported by conservatives and Republicans is toward deregulation of the business side of communications. They support less government. But they also support more regulation to protect traditional social or moral values and national security. This is a good example of how ideological debates are usually about the use of government power not the size of government. Conservatives worry more about sex over the airwaves while liberals worry more about violence.

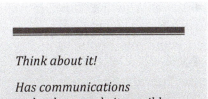

Think about it!

Has communications technology made it possible for almost anyone to claim to be a journalist?

The conflict between economic deregulation and social re-regulation/regulation is apparent in a proposal made by the Chair of the FCC to extend the FCC's regulatory authority to cable television. Interest groups such as the Parents Television Council support the proposal to give the FCC authority to regulate explicit sex and violence and indecency. Tim Winter, the President of the PTC tried to put telecommunications in proper perspective when he stated that, except for the Pentagon, the FCC has "the most important role in our nation." His argument echoed some of the earliest founding statements about the relationship between the media and democracy, particularly his claim that the way we communicate (the public airwaves, electronic communication, cable, satellite, telephone) is "the essence of our democracy."

Advocates of expanding FCC authority over the communications sector by authorizing it to regulate cable as well as broadcast companies have encountered strong opposition. Opponents of expanding the FCC's regulatory authority include the national Cable and Telecommunications Association. The Association believes that the best way to regulate the industry is to rely on the intensely competitive marketplace, not government intervention. In fact, despite the politics supporting increased government regulation of programming, the law is likely to present a significant hurdle. Blair Levin, the former chief of staff to former FCC Chairman Reed Hundt, thinks that the effort to extend the FCC's reach to include cable companies would ultimately lose in the courts. He also wryly comments that efforts to adopt a la carte service subscriptions to protect family values was likely doomed: "Every chairman of the FCC comes to realize there is a conflict between family values and market values."[19]

7.71 | Media Bias

Today's claims of media bias reflect 1) the perception that journalism is not living up to the high standards of professional objectivity; 2) the proliferation of media forms and outlets; and 3) the importance in daily personal, work, and entertainment lives. The increase in media consumption attracts scrutiny of the media effect on values, attitudes, behavior, and American culture. This includes studying ideological and partisan bias in the coverage of public affairs.[20]

7.72 | Sitcom TV Family Values

Television families provide popular cultural commentary on contemporary American values. *Father Knows Best* (1954–1960) was about the idealized American domestic life: a father with a stable, upper-middle class white-collar job and a stay-at-home mother parenting their children. Subsequent television family sitcoms showed realistic blue-collar working class families that were ideologically divided by current events such as the Vietnam War (*All in the Family*) and struggling to make ends meet during a recession (*Roseanne*). Roseanne Barr described *Roseanne* as a sitcom with an economic populist message about "the end of the working class in America." Then *The Simpsons* brought a punk music sensibility to an animated satire that poked mostly gentle fun at almost all conventional American values.

Good satire is taken seriously. *The Simpsons* was actually got into the heads in the White House. In a 1990 *People* magazine interview, First Lady Barbara Bush called *The Simpsons* "the dumbest thing I had ever seen." So the writers had the character Marge Simpson write a letter to the First Lady defending her television family. The First Lady wrote back with a pleasant letter conceding she may have been too critical of the fictional family. But then things got serious. The Republican Party was the party of traditional family values. Republican President George Herbert Walker Bush pledged at a Convention of Religious Broadcasters to continue working to strengthen American families, to make American families more like *The Waltons* and less like *The Simpsons*. This only encouraged the show's writers who incorporated the back-and-forth into episodes. Jim Brooks, one of the co-developers and executive producers of *The Simpsons* explains the running dialogue in the clip, <u>*Bush v. Simpsons*</u>.

Finally, the mockumentary-style sitcom *Modern Family* (2009–present) could have been titled *Postmodern Family*. Its portrayal of a father's gradual and begrudging acceptance of his gay son, husband, and adopted Asian child is a commentary on who seems to have won the culture wars over homosexuality and diversity.

> **Think About It!**
> <u>*The Simpsons*</u> **Predicted President Trump?**

Those who are in positions of power are likely to think the media are biased because the institutional press has historically played a watchdog role. The press does investigative reporting on those in positions of power. This includes the private for-profit sector (e.g., corporate CEOs and union officials), the private not-for-profit sector (e.g., the management of charities such as the Red Cross or Wounded Warriors), and the public sector (government officials). The media's government watchdog role makes it *the opposition* in the sense that journalists investigate whatever administration is in control of government in order to hold public power accountable.

Societies have multiple power centers. They include business (of which the media is one part), education, religion, and government. Government is not the only power center. It is merely the *elected* power center. The relationship between the media, as a business, and politics has always been complicated but the digital revolution has raised new promises and threats for political communication. In a 2009 TED talk, Clay Shirky, a scholar of interactive telecommunications, described three ways the digital revolution has changed communication. The first change was the interactive forms of mass communication. The telephone expanded *one-to-one* communication. Then television and radio expanded *"one-to-many"* communication. Now the Internet has expanded the *many-to-many* communications as new interactive form of mass communications. The second change is the digitization of all media. Digitization makes the Internet a platform for all other media as telephone calls, newspapers and magazines, and television and film all migrate to the Internet. The fact that consumers can now access information at any of their linked platforms is transforming the media from businesses that produced information or content into sites that coordinate the distribution of information. This technology may ultimately enrich politics by enabling more people to access more information and to interact with others to discuss it. However, the current concern is that it has enabled individuals to self-select information and interactions that reinforce preconceived ideas and beliefs, thereby creating even louder political echo chambers.

The third effect of the digital revolution is to make it easier for consumers or audiences to also be producers and speakers. This can increase civic engagement in ways that are good for the health of a democracy. But it can also increase cynicism in ways that undermine the health of a democracy. Digital technology and technological convergence make democratic politics vulnerable in the same way the globalism makes people, animals and plants more vulnerable to viruses. Information and misinformation can go viral because technology has made the information landscape open and fluid while also weakening the links between voters' perceptions and reality precisely at a time when the news we consume is based on emotion and identity as much as it is based on facts.

7.8 | Summary

The media have played an important role in American politics and government since the founding of the republic. Today, the media have an economic, educative, watchdog, and socialization role. The power problem with the mass media in particular is media bias. Knowledge is power, and the general public traditionally relied heavily on the mass media for information about government and politics. The digital revolution has changed power relations. Social media, for example, have created new capabilities for direct and interactive relations among the general public and between citizens and government officials.

7.9 | Additional Resources

The Center for Media and Public Affairs at http://www.cmpa.com/ provides information about the public role of the media.

The Pew Research Center's Project on Excellence in Journalism at http://journalism.org/ and the Internet & American Life Project provides interesting perspectives on the cultural effects of the reliance on the Internet: http://www.pewinternet.org/.

One useful source of information about the modern media is http://journalism.org/

One example of the new media is the fake news shows have blurred some of the distinctions between news and entertainment (Infotainment). http://www.colbertnation.com/the-colbert-report-videos/252013/october-08-2009/bend-it-like-beck

The Annenberg Public Policy Center at the University of Pennsylvania conducts content analysis on TV coverage of politics: www.appcpenn.org

Newseum.org provides information about the history of news and media. Topics include coverage of the terrorist attacks of September 11, 2001, war correspondents, editorial cartoonists, women photographers, and front-page stories from around the country. www.newseum.org

7.91 | *In the Library*

Baker, C. Edwin. 2006. *Media Concentration and Democracy: Why Ownership Matters*. Cambridge University Press.

Bennett, W. Lance. 2004. *News: The Politics of Illusion*. Longman.

Bennett, W. Lance, Regina G. Lawrence, and Steven Livingston. 2007. *When the Press Fails: Political Power and the News Media from Iraq to Katrina*. University of Chicago Press.

Cook, Timothy. 1998. *Governing with the News*. University of Chicago Press.

Eshbaugh-Soha, Matthew. 2003. "Presidential Press Conferences over Time." *American Journal of Political Science* 47 (2):348–353

Fritz, Ben et al. 2004. *All the President's Spin: George W. Bush, the Media, and the Truth*. Simon and Schuster Trade.

Goldberg, Bernard. 2001. *Bias: A CBS Insider Exposes How the Media Distort the News*. Regnery Press.

Graber, Doris A. (Ed). 1998. *The Politics of News: The News of Politics*. Congressional Quarterly Books.

Jamieson, Kathleen Hall. 2000. *Everything You Think You Know About Politics…And Why You're Wrong*. Basic Books.

Kovach, Bill and Tom Rosenstiel. 2007. *Elements of Journalism: What Newspeople Should Know and the Public Should Expect*. Crown Publishing.

Lieberman, Trudy. 2000. *Slanting the Story: The Forces that Shape the News*. New Press.

Prior, Markus. 2007. *Post-Broadcast Democracy: How Media Choice Increases Inequality in Political Involvement and Polarizes Elections*. Cambridge University Press.

Schechter, Danny. 2003. *Media Wars: News at a Time of Terror*. Rowman and Littlefield Publishers, Inc.

Shogun, Robert. 2001. *Bad News: Where the Press Go Wrong in the Making of the President*. Ivan Dee Press.

Summerville, John. 1999. *How the News Makes Us Dumb*. Intervarsity Press.

Key Terms
Educative Role
Watchdog Role
Commercial Media
Framing
Bias

STUDY QUESTIONS

1. When covering Congress, who tends to be the focus of media coverage? Why?
2. Leonard Downie, Jr., the former executive editor of the Washington Post, does not vote because he thinks voting might lead to questions about his neutrality. Explain whether you think journalists can be neutral and also vote in elections?
3. Compare and contrast the print press and electronic media.
4. How much confidence does the public have in the media? Is this level of confidence sufficient to ensure a vibrant democracy?
5. What are the major periods of the media?
6. What is the media's relationship with the president?

---

[1] http://www.trumptwitterarchive.com/archive
[2] Schudson, Michael. 1981. *Discovering the News: A social history of American newspapers*. New York: Basic Books.
[3] http://www.pewinternet.org
[4] Quoted in The State of the News Media 2007, An Annual Report on American Journalism, http://stateofthemedia.org/2007/narrative_overview_intro.asp
[5] A congressional press pass allows reporters to sit in the House and Senate press galleries, as well as providing some access to presidential press briefings. The process to get a congressional press pass is available here: http://www.senate.gov/galleries/daily/rules2.htm
[6] http://www.presidency.ucsb.edu/data/newsconferences.php

[7] Gerhard Peters. "Presidential News Conferences." *The American Presidency Project*. Ed. John T. Woolley and Gerhard Peters. Santa Barbara, CA: University of California. 1999-2010. Available at: http://www.presidency.ucsb.edu/data/newsconferences.php.

[8] Steven V. Roberts, "Washington Talk: The Presidency; Shouting Questions At Reagan," *New York Times*, October 21, 1987.

[9] http://www.oyez.org/cases/1960-1969/1968/1968_2_2

[10] http://www.fcc.gov/Reports/tcom1996.txt

[11] http://www.oyez.org/cases/1990-1999/1996/1996_96_511

[12] http://www.ftc.gov/ogc/coppa1.htm

[13] http://www.gseis.ucla.edu/iclp/coppa.htm

[14] http://www.salon.com/21st/feature/1999/02/02feature.html

[15] http://www.fcc.gov/cgb/consumerfacts/cipa.html

[16] http://www.fcc.gov/eb/News_Releases/DOC-301874A1.html

[17] http://www.fcc.gov/eb/News_Releases/DOC-300325A1.html

[18] http://www.fcc.gov/eb/

[19] http://www.npr.org/templates/story/story.php?storyId=16783080

[20] http://www.stateofthenewsmedia.org/chartland.asp?id=200&ct=col&dir=&sort=&col4_box=1

"A popular government without popular information, or means of acquiring , is but a Prologue to a Farce or a ragedy, or perhaps both. Knowledge ill forever govern ignorance, and a eople who mean to be their own Governors must arm themselves with the power which knowledge gives."

James Madison

Letter to W.T. Barry

(August 4, 1822)

8.0 | Public Opinion

In an 1822 *Letter to W. T. Barry*, James Madison applauded Kentucky for its generous appropriation for a system of public education. Madison believed that "a people who mean to be their own Governors, must arm themselves with the power knowledge gives." The belief that knowledge is power is still the foundation of the belief that democracy requires an educated, informed, and active citizenry. In fact, many collective human endeavors are based on the belief that knowledge can overcome ignorance, and that information can be applied to solve scientific, technological, medical, and political problems. Knowledge makes self-government possible but an informed public does not guarantee that a political system will be democratic. This chapter examines public opinion. Political scientists, government officials, political party leaders, candidates running in elections, and interest groups of all kinds pay a great deal of attention to public opinion in order to better understand

- What the public thinks about issues, parties, and candidates;
- Ways to measure public opinion;
- How public opinion is formed so that it can be changed or even controlled; and
- How public opinion influences public policy.

8.1 | The Power Problem

The power problem with public opinion is essentially the question whether public opinion is a cause or an effect—whether public opinion causes public policy and government action, or is a result of it. **Democratic theory** describes public opinion as the cause of public policy. It assumes that public opinion drives the political machine. The relationship between public opinion and public policy is more complicated than the simple cause and effect relationship described in Figure 8.1 (Classic Democratic System Model) below. One complication is the fact that the U.S. is not a pure or direct democracy. It is a constitutional democracy or constitutional republic that limits majoritarian government. The government is not designed to automatically or directly turn public opinion into public policy. A second complication is the nature of public opinion. Public opinion polls and political science research indicate that public opinion is not a static or fixed force in a political system. It is dynamic; events and circumstances change it; organized campaigns are based on the assumption that public opinion can be changed, managed, or even manufactured. Companies develop marketing campaigns to influence consumers' thinking about products. They are not merely responding to consumer demands or preferences; they create consumer demands and preferences.

Political campaigns are similarly designed to influence rather than merely respond to voters' thinking about issues, policies, candidates, and parties. The media effect of such campaigns complicates democratic theory describing public opinion as the cause of government action. The fact that a political system is a democracy does not make the power problem with public opinion irrelevant. Figure 8.11 (Modified Democratic System Model) below illustrates why so much attention is paid to the political forces that *create* public opinion rather than just *measuring* public opinion.

Figure 8.1 Classical Democratic Systems Model

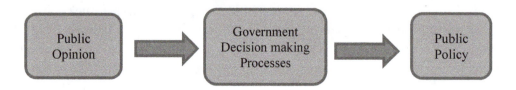

Figure 8.11 Modified Democratic System Model

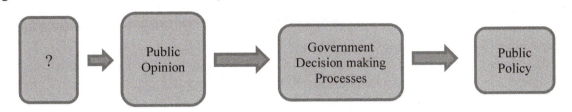

8.11 | *Presidential Approval Ratings*

Presidential approval ratings measure public opinion about how the president is doing. They are a measure of public opinion that reflects thinking about conditions and event such as the state of the economy (e.g., the unemployment rate), crime rates, and national security. Presidential approval ratings also reflect the public's perception of responses to events such as terrorist attacks or other threats to national security, economic downturns, and natural disasters such as hurricanes and earthquakes. Regardless of a president's control over some of these politically relevant events, presidents are expected to either control them or respond effectively to them. One of the clearest and most consistent examples of how events affect presidential popularity is the "rally around the flag" effect. National security threats, and presidential responses to them, almost always provide an immediate increase in presidential approval ratings. The size and the duration of the increase varies depending on the event and its duration. However, the rally around the flag effect creates a systematic bias toward taking decisive action. Presidents who face domestic opposition are tempted to travel abroad where the images of the leader of the free world generally bolster public approval ratings. Actions taken as commander-in-chief tend to have a similar effect on public approval.

The 9/11 terrorist attacks and President George W. Bush's response to them—first, by military action in Afghanistan and then by the military invasion of Iraq—produced a record rally effect. His approval rating jumped 35 points to 86%. President George H. W. Bush's approval jumped 18 points to 89% during the Gulf War and Operation Desert Storm.

> Fact Check It!
> Check out The American Presidency Project (Hosted at the University of California, Santa Barbara, and a collaboration of John Woolley and Gerhard Peters) charts on the presidential approval ratings of president.

8.12 | Wagging the Dog?

There is a saying in politics that a crisis is too important to waste. Crises create opportunities for political action because they create sudden changes in public opinion. Enemies, particularly foreign enemies, can also be politically useful because they create opportunities for action. Foreign enemies can produce the rally effect. The 1997 film *Wag the Dog* explored a fictional president's use of Madison Avenue advertising experts and Hollywood entertainment production values to produce a fake war to divert attention from a sex scandal. The film is about a president who is running for reelection when the press uncovers a sex scandal shortly before the day of the election. The president is accused of groping a young girl who is a member of an organization similar to the Girl Scouts. The president consults a seasoned spin-doctor who advises declaring a fake war (against Albania) to create a distraction from the sex scandal. Does art imitate life? The film seemed prescient. In early 1998, the public learned that President Clinton had oral sex in the Oval Office with a young intern. Then in the summer of 1998 he launched Tomahawk missile strikes against al-Qaeda in Afghanistan and Sudan in retaliation for August 7th attacks against the U.S. embassies in Kenya and Tanzania. President Trump had record low job approval ratings and problems with his domestic agenda. Then he authorized cruise missile strikes in Syria. One prominent foreign affairs commentator, Fareed Zakaria, said of the missile strikes, "I think Donald Trump became President of the United States…"

> **Think About It!**
> What lessons do presidents learn from the record of military actions producing at least short-term increases in public approval ratings?

8.2 | Two Models of Representation

Public opinion is defined as the aggregate of public attitudes or beliefs about government and politics. Popular sovereignty, the belief that the people are the ultimate source of government authority, is one of the basic principles of American government. The belief that government authority derives from the people means that public policies are supposed to be based on public opinion. Responsiveness to public opinion is one measure of a political system's legitimacy—the belief that a system of government is lawful, right, or just. The delegate model and the trustee model are two models of how government officials rely on public opinion when making public policy.

8.21 | *THE DELEGATE MODEL*

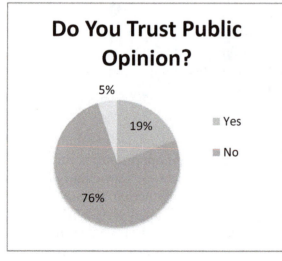

Do You Trust Public Opinion?

5%
19%
76%

■ Yes
■ No

According to the delegate model, elected government officials are obligated to do the will of the people who elected them to office. Government officials are instructed delegates in the sense that they are expected to do what the people want. The delegate model of democracy is populistic in the sense that the elected representatives of the people are obligated to enact public opinion, they are free to decide what is best for the general public or their constituents. Representatives are not free agents.

8.22 | *The Trustee Model*

The **trustee model** allows government officials more freedom of choice to decide what is in the public interest. Government officials are not expected to act solely upon public opinion. Elected representatives are considered trustees who are trusted to use their good judgment, experience, expertise, or information to do what they think is best rather than merely doing what the people want based on public opinion polls, for example. The trustee model provides that representatives are held accountable for their decisions in regular elections, but they have considerable freedom to choose courses of action. The trustee model is more elitist in the sense that elected representatives are expected to be the "better sorts" of the community, the leaders who are chosen to make good decisions about public policy without merely following public opinion.

8.23 | *The Founders' Intentions*

The Framers establishes an indirect democracy, a representative democracy, or a **republic** because they believed a republic was a better form of government than direct democracy. The Revolutionary War was fought against monarchy—rule by King George. They did not want to create a democracy that was rule by King Numbers. While generally committed to more popular government, they did not want majority rule. Their thinking about democracy and public opinion is evident in Madison's *Federalist Papers Number 10* and *Number 51*.

Federalist Number 51 elaborates on the ways to limit the abuse of government power that is made necessary by human nature. Popular sovereignty is the primary way to limit the abuse of power, and the system of checks and balances (federalism and the separation of powers) is the secondary (or "auxiliary") limit on the abuse of power. Madison famously wrote that human nature makes government necessary, and makes it necessary to control government:

> Ambition must be made to counteract ambition. The interest of the man must be connected with the constitutional rights of the place. It may be a reflection on human nature, that such devices should be necessary to control the abuses of government. But what is government itself, but the greatest of all reflections on human nature? If men were angels, no government would be necessary. If angels were to govern men, neither external nor internal controls on government would be necessary. In framing a government which is to be administered by men over men, the great difficulty lies in this: you must first enable the government to control the governed; and in the next place oblige it to control itself. A dependence on the people is, no doubt, the primary control on the government; but experience has taught mankind the necessity of auxiliary precautions.

In *Federalist Number 10*, Madison explained that the best form of government was one that was based on limited majority rule. The Constitution placed limits on the power of the people to do whatever they wanted. It protected minorities—mainly the wealthy and landowners—from majority rule. The Bill of Rights provide many important limits on majority rule. For example, the First Amendment protects freedom of expression regardless of whether a majority of the American public supports laws prohibiting burning or otherwise desecrating the American flag.

8.3 | POLITICAL SOCIALIZATION

The formation of political beliefs, attitudes, and ideology is one of the most important questions about public opinion. Political socialization is the process by which people form ideas and develop political values. The agents of socialization include family, friends, organized religion, education, life experiences, work, political parties, the media, and the government.

8.31 | FAMILY

Socialization begins early in life and continues throughout life. Children begin to form political attitudes very early in life so family is a strong influence on thinking about government and politics. Children do not always or automatically identify with their parents' ideology or political party, but there is a strong correlation between a person's party affiliation and their parent's party affiliation. However, some of the other agents of socialization actually counteract the influence of the family. Many children are now raised in families where both parents work. This means that the family's influence has decreased relative to other agents of socialization such as schools, friends, work colleagues, and the media.

8.32 | EDUCATION

Education is also a major agent of socialization. Schools teach students facts and values; students learn information and values in schools. Public schools have an educational and a socialization mission. This is why school desegregation, school busing, school prayer, mandatory flag salutes or pledges of allegiance, and curriculum issues such as civics, values, tolerance, diversity, and the teaching of evolution and creationism have been so controversial. Schools have been at the center of the culture wars over values because they are important agents of socialization and the transmission of political values.

8.33 | LIFE EXPERIENCES

Not all political attitudes are fixed early in life. Socialization occurs throughout the life span. A person's adult experiences, desires, or needs can change old beliefs and create new ones. Attitudes toward social welfare programs are influenced by a person's health or economic status, Personal experience with illness affects thinking about health care policy. Wealth and poverty affect thinking about economic policy. Income and wealth are related to ideology and partisanship.

Economics is one of the factors that have consistently divided conservatives and liberals, Republicans and Democrats. Economics includes how a person earns a living. Work experience as an entrepreneur, a business owner or manager, or as an employee influence attitudes toward the role of government, tax policies and spending policies, government regulation of business, and social welfare policy. In fact, these economic attitudes are among the most important factors determining where someone is a conservative, a liberal, a socialist, or a populist.

8.34 | *Geography*

Regionalism has played an important role in some of the country's most significant political experiences. Early in the nation's history, the regional divisions were the result of distinctive economic systems. The northeast had a manufacturing and shipping economy. The south had an agrarian and plantation economy. The interior of the country had a frontier economy. The divisions between northern industrial economies and the agricultural, slave-holding southern economy was a major cause of the Civil War. During the 20th Century, urbanization created major differences between urban and rural areas. These regional differences were expected to decrease with the increase in communication, travel, population mobility, and the development of a national economy—which created more uniformity in language, culture, and politics. National uniformity diminished the regional distinctiveness of the South and the Northeast, but political geography is still important. The elections of 2016 revealed important political differences between rural areas and the major urban centers. The Republican candidate Donald Trump had strong support in rural counties while Democratic candidate Hillary Clinton had strongest support in urban centers. In fact, the urban-rural differences in public opinion are now more important than regionalism. But there are still regional differences in thinking about politics. People in the Northeast and the West are more likely to support abortion rights, while those in the Midwest and South are more likely to favor restricting access to abortions. As the above chart shows, there are strong regional differences in thinking about social issues such as gay marriage.

8.35 | *RACE AND ETHNICITY*

The study of socialization is not limited to the individual level. Race and ethnic identity are also important. African Americans initially identified as Republicans because Abraham Lincoln freed the slave with the Emancipation Proclamation, won the Civil War, and then Republicans passed federal civil rights legislation to protect the rights of blacks from racially discriminatory laws passed by Democrats in Southern states. Then in the 1930s, Democratic Party support for New Deal legislation to end the Great Depression attracted blacks to the Democratic Party. And Democratic support for the civil rights movement further strengthened black support for liberal and Democratic policies.

In the late 1800s and early 1900s, Europeans from countries like Italy, Ireland, Germany, and Poland immigrated in large numbers to the United States. These groups became a part of Franklin Delano Roosevelt's New Deal coalition in the 1930 and they continued to be part of the Democratic Great Society coalition in the 1960s. Since then, however, white ethnic voters have changed their party identification. Republican Presidents Richard Nixon and Ronald Reagan appealed to white ethnic voters who had socially conservative attitudes about issues such as school prayer, patriotism, and sexual behavior. As white ethnics became more economically well off, they were also more likely to agree with Republican efforts to reduce social welfare. Ronald Reagan was so successful in appealing to these European ethnic groups that they were called "Reagan Democrats." In recent years, the politics of immigration has changed. The political behavior of Latinos has attracted a great deal of attention because they are the fastest growing ethnic group in the United States. Partisan appeals for Latino support are complicated by the fact that the term Latino includes such a broad range of people with different backgrounds, experiences, and attitudes. For example, Mexican-Americans and Cuban-Americans have very different political beliefs partly because they have had such different political and economic experiences.

8.36 | GENDER

Gender is correlated with political attitudes and party identification. During the last thirty years, women have been more likely to support liberal issues and the Democratic Party, while men are more likely to support conservative issues and the Republican Party. The gender difference in party identification is the **gender gap**. Women are also more likely to support affirmative action policies, welfare policies, income assistance, reproductive rights (pro-choice views on abortion), and equal rights for gays and lesbians. Women have voted for the Democratic presidential candidate at a higher rate than men in every presidential election since Jimmy Carter's 1980 bid against Ronald Reagan. Women also register more frequently as members of the Democratic Party. As the figure below shows, the gender gap in party registration fluctuates with the year, but women are consistently more likely to register as Democrats. Gender issues played an important role in the 2016 presidential election. The Democratic candidate Hillary Clinton's campaign relied heavily on the traditional liberal and Democratic appeal as better on women's issues, and attacked Donald Trump (and Republicans generally) as worse on women's issues. This campaign slogan was to fight "The War on Women" by voting Democratic. The PEW Research Data reports on gender voting in presidential elections.

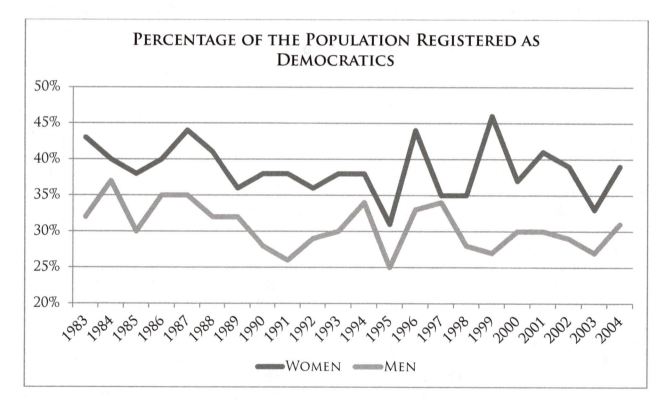

8.37 | *THE MEDIA*

The media play a large and growing role in modern American society. In 1997, adult Americans spent around thirty hours a week watching television, and children spent even more time watching television.[1] Today the U.S. Department of Health and Human Services estimates that children spend around seven hours a day in front of some electronic screen. There is a great deal of research examining how this much screen time affects children. In terms of public opinion, the consensus that media influence public opinion does not extend to agreement about the nature of that influence. The traditional mass media played an important institutional role in "mediating" between individuals and the government. This mediating role included political socialization.

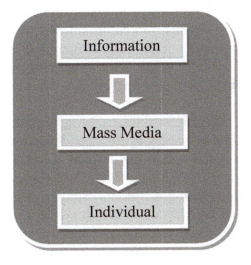

The Mediating Role of the Mass Media

The traditional mass media include the print press (especially newspapers) and the broadcast media (especially broadcast television and radio networks). One of the media effects on public opinion is *setting the agenda*: the media decide what issues the public should be thinking about. The media decide what constitutes news—the events that are worth reporting. The way media frame stories also influences public opinion. This is at the heart of charges that there is a media bias.

8.38 | *THE GOVERNMENT*

The government can influence public opinion in a variety of ways. Public schools, for example, teach civics—which included attitudes toward government politics. The government also has programs and initiatives to instill patriotic beliefs. The government also has a great deal of power to influence thinking about national security because it controls so much information about national security matters. Presidents can use their *bully pulpit* to build support for a policy or a cause. The government as agent of socialization is controversial. It seems to complicate the Classical Democratic Systems Model of democracy by describing the government as one of the factors that creates public opinion. One definition of propaganda is government efforts to influence public opinion. Propaganda is a normative term. Like democracy, conservative, liberal, bureaucracy, terrorism, and ideology, propaganda is a value-laden term. Propaganda is considered illegitimate or improper government efforts to influence individuals' thinking about politics. Propaganda is associated with brain washing or other efforts of thought control usually associated with totalitarian governments. The dictionary definition of propaganda is that it is using words or speech intended to convince someone of a political position or point of view. This definition of propaganda as persuasion or advocacy is central to politics. Political power is usually defined as a person's power to make others **do** what they want them to do. Should political power be defined more broadly as the power to make others **do or think** what you want? Given the importance of public opinion, government officials and other political actors have vested interests in influencing thought and action.

8.4 | Is Public Opinion a Cause or an Effect?

Rhetoric is one important means of political communication. Rhetoric is the art of using language—both public speaking and writing—to communicate, to persuade, or to convince. In the 19th Century rhetoric was taught using collections of memorable political speeches and even "pulpit eloquence" such as *The American Orator*. The *Orator* was an influential book that trained individuals in proper public speaking techniques the way that other books trained people in proper etiquette.

Public opinion is dynamic, not static. It changes. More important, *it can be changed*. Public opinion about the president, for example, is very dynamic and responds to a broad range of factors. Public opinion about congress is more stable, but reflects general public assessments of how congress is performing as a political institution. Public opinion polls such as the Gallup Poll regularly ask people for their opinion about government. Sixty-nine percent of Americans say they have a great deal or fair amount of confidence in the Supreme Court, compared with 50% for Congress and 43% for the president. Public confidence in Congress and the president has been trending steadily downward for decades. In contrast, public confidence in the Court has remained very stable.[2]

Political actors, such as candidates for office, government officials, party leaders, interest group leaders, and community activists are not limited to responding to public opinion. Political actors try to influence, change, and even to control public opinion. In government and politics information is power. Information about how people acquire their attitudes increases understanding of socialization and creates the opportunity to influence it.

8.41 | *THE MARKETPLACE OF IDEAS*

Understanding *how* people acquire their attitudes can make it possible to use that information to control *what* people think. This is the essence of the power problem with public opinion. Can public opinion (ideas and attitudes) be manufactured the way material products are made? Can ideas about candidates, parties, and issues be sold the way other products are sold to consumers? The marketplace is a familiar and powerful concept in the United States because the U.S. is a capitalist country where people are very familiar with the idea of a marketplace of goods and services. It is not surprising that the logic of the *economic marketplace* has been applied to politics. The *political marketplace of ideas* refers to the ability to pick and choose from among the competing ideologies and parties the way that consumers are able to pick and choose from among the competing sellers of goods and services.

The application of economic marketplace logic to the political marketplace raises some important questions about the nature of public opinion. One question is about the role of advertising. The conventional economic wisdom is that marketers and advertisers respond to consumer demands for products and services. But modern advertising also creates demand. The ability to create consumer demand, rather than just respond to consumer demands, is one reason why the government regulates the advertising of certain goods and services. The government regulates lawyer advertising, medical advertising, and tobacco products. The Federal Trade Commission's mission includes regulating business practices that are "deceptive or unfair" to consumers. The mission of the FTC's Bureau of Consumer Protection is to prevent "fraud, deceptive, and unfair business practices in the marketplace." It investigates complaints about advertising.

8.42 | *The Government in the Marketplace of Ideas*

Governments try to control what people think—about issues, candidates, political parties, government officials, and about the government itself. The pejorative term for government efforts to influence public opinion is propaganda. Propaganda is considered the inappropriate manipulation of public opinion—usually by totalitarian or authoritarian regimes. Therefore the terms *public communication* or *public relations* or *public diplomacy* are more commonly used to describe campaigns that target public opinion. In the 1930s and 1940s the government began to use new professions and methods of mass communication such as public relations, advertising, and film to influence public opinion. During the Great Depression, the Roosevelt Administration "advertised" one of its New Deal programs, the Works Progress Administration (WPA): "By the People, For the People: Posters from the WPA, 1936-1943." The extensive archives of such public relations or propaganda campaigns include some of the short films the government produced to build popular support for military service, citizenship, war policies and national security actions, and others. The archives of moving images include government films to shape the following thinking and behavior:

- For appropriate behavior for young people in the 1950s, watch "How do you do?" or "What to do on a date."
- For appropriate behavior for young people in the 1950s, watch "How to be a teenage in 1950";
- Watch the cartoon *Private Snuffy Smith* for messages about patriotism and military service; http://archive.org/details/private_snuffy_smith
- Watch *Sex Madness* for messages about health and good sexual behavior. http://archive.org/details/sex_madness
- Compare *Reefer Madness* (1936) with the current movement to legalize marijuana.

- Watch *Japanese Relocation*, produced by the Office of War Information and the Bureau of Motion Pictures: http://www.youtube.com/watch?v=_OiPldKsM5w

In terms of global public opinion, the U.S. Department of State's <u>Undersecretary for Public Diplomacy and Public Affairs</u> is responsible for a broad range of programs that are intended to influence worldwide thinking about issues that are related to U.S. foreign policy interests.

8.5 | Democratic Theory and Political Reality

The relationship between public opinion and public policy is more complicated than simply declaring that in a democracy public opinion causes or determines public policy. In most modern, western-style democracies, there are ongoing debates about how much public opinion matters, the extent to which public opinion actually determines public policy. One school of thought argues that groups of elites either control the political process or have more influence on it than the general public. The elites are variously described as the rich, the powerful, the influential, the insiders, the special interests with more resources to influence public policy. The elites could be in the private sector (e.g., business interests) or the public sector (government officials such as bureaucrats). Political systems do not have to have complete equality in order to be democratic. Democracies can have unequal access to political power. But equality is a democratic value, so great concentrations of economic power that result in great inequality of political power raise concerns. Modern democratic theories are generally pluralists who believe that it is enough to have power spread around among elites so that no single set of elites can control public opinion and dominate the political process. Pluralist democrats concede that modern democracies do not uniformly distribute political power, but they maintain that groups of elites have to compete for influence over public opinion and public policy.

8.51 | *The Premise of Democratic Theory*

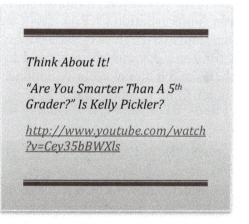

Think About It!

"Are You Smarter Than A 5th Grader?" Is Kelly Pickler?

http://www.youtube.com/watch?v=Cey35bBWXls

The premise (or basic assumption) of democratic theory is that an informed public makes choices about government officials and public policies. In other words, democratic theory assumes that elections determine who governs and what policies will be enacted into law. This is the argument that democratic government is legitimate because its authority is based on the consent of the governed. Is this assumption valid? The empirical evidence indicates that the assumption of an informed public is mistaken. Public opinion polls indicate that the American public is not well informed about public affairs, candidates, or issues. Civics knowledge is rather low. The average voter has little information about public affairs, including the names of their representatives in city government, county government, state legislature, or congress. People do not pay much attention to politics. The influence of popular culture is reflected in the fact that people pay more attention to entertainment and sports than public affairs. The low levels of information about politics are the result of apathy or disinterest. Political efficacy is the belief that political participation matters. The belief that participation in politics does not really matter very much creates low levels of efficacy. People have time constraints. They are busy with families and work and other activities. People have to establish priorities for allocating scarce resources such as time, effort, and money. It is easier for professionals who have white-collar jobs or information-related jobs such as journalism or academia to keep up with public affairs. People who have blue-collar jobs or jobs that do not involve working with information are more likely to have higher priorities than keeping up with the issues.

8.52 | *Measuring Public Opinion*

Public opinion polling is a fact of modern life. Gathering information and selling it is big business. Gallup polls are a familiar feature of modern politics. The widespread use of public opinion measurement around the world is evidence of the belief that public opinion is important for political and other purposes. Governments consider surveys useful for gathering information about what the public thinks, for guiding public information and propaganda campaigns, and for formulating public policies. The U.S. Department of Agriculture was one of the first government agencies to sponsor systematic, large-scale surveys and it still conducts them to gather information.

An opinion poll is a survey of opinion from a particular sample. Opinion polls are usually designed to represent the opinions of a population by asking a small number of people a series of questions and then extrapolating the answers to the larger group within certain confidence intervals.

8.53 | *Usable Knowledge?*

The first known example of an opinion poll was a local straw vote conducted by *The Harrisburg Pennsylvanian* in 1824. It showed Andrew Jackson leading John Quincy Adams by 335 votes to 169 in the contest for the presidency. This straw vote was not scientific. But straw votes became popular in local elections. In 1916, the *Literary Digest* conducted a national survey as part of an effort to increase circulation. The straw vote correctly predicted Woodrow Wilson's election as president. The *Digest* correctly called the following four presidential elections by simply mailing out millions of postcards and counting the returns. In 1936, the *Digest's* 2.3 million "voters" constituted a very large sample, but the sample included more affluent Americans who tended to support the Republican Party. This biased the results. The week before the election the *Digest* reported that Republican Alf Landon was far more popular than Democrat Franklin D. Roosevelt. At the same time, George Gallup conducted a much smaller, but more scientifically-based survey. He polled a demographically representative sample, and correctly predicted Roosevelt's landslide victory in the 1936 presidential election. The *Literary Digest* soon went out of business. The polling industry gained credibility and public opinion polling began to play a more important role in politics, particularly campaigning.

Thinking about public opinion polling has changed a great deal over time. In a 1968 book, *The Pulse of Democracy*, George Gallup and Saul Rae described public opinion polling as *taking* the pulse of democracy. By this, they meant that polling used social scientific methods to try to accurately measure *what the public was thinking* about public affairs. Today, polling is more likely to be conducted for the purpose of *making* the pulse of democracy by using social scientific methods to ultimately influence public opinion. This is the argument David W. Moore makes in *The Opinion Makers* (2008). The emphasis is now on usable information. These changes in thinking about how and what people think, and how to use data, are directly related to the power problem with public opinion.

> Think About It!
> What is a "push poll?" What does the American Association for Public Opinion Research think about push polls?

8.54 | *Methods*

In the early days of public opinion polling, polls were conducted mainly by face-to-face interviews (on the street or in a person's home). Face-to-face polling is still done, but telephone polls have become more popular because they can be conducted quickly and cheaply. However, response rates for phone surveys have been declining. Some polling organizations, such as YouGov and Zogby use Internet surveys, where a sample is drawn from a large panel of volunteers and the results are weighed to reflect the demographics of the population of interest. This is in contrast to popular web polls that draw on whoever wishes to participate rather than a scientific sample of the population, and are therefore not generally considered accurate.

The wording of a poll question can bias the results. The bias can be unintentional (accidental) or intentional. For instance, the public is more likely to indicate support for a person who is described by the caller as one of the "leading candidates." Neglecting to mention all the candidates is an even more subtle bias, as is lumping some candidates in an "other" category. Being last on a list affects responses. In fact, this is one reason why election rules provide for listing candidates in alphabetic order or alternating Republican and Democratic candidates. When polling on issues, answers to a question about abortion vary depending on whether a person is asked about a "fetus" or and "unborn baby."

All polls based on samples are subject to sampling error which reflects the effects of chance in the sampling process. The uncertainty is often expressed as a margin of error. The margin of error does not reflect other sources of error, such as measurement error. A poll with a random sample of 1,000 people has margin of sampling error of 3% for the estimated percentage of the whole population. A 3% margin of error means that 95% of the time the procedure used would give an estimate within 3% of the percentage to be estimated. Using a large sample reduces the margin of error. However if a pollster wishes to reduce the margin of error to 1% they would need a sample of around 10,000 people. In practice pollsters need to balance the cost of a large sample against the reduction in sampling error and a sample size of around 500-1,000 is a typical compromise for political polls.[3]

- **Nonresponse** bias. Some people do not answer calls from strangers, or refuse to respond to polls or poll questions. As a result, a poll sample may not be a representative sample from a population. Because of this selection bias, the characteristics of those who agree to be interviewed may be markedly different from those who decline. That is, the actual sample is a biased version of the universe the pollster wants to analyze. In these cases, bias introduces new errors that are in addition to errors caused by sample size. Error due to bias does not become smaller with larger sample sizes. If the people who refuse to answer, or are never reached, have the same characteristics as the people who do answer, the final results will be unbiased. If the people who do not answer have different opinions then there is bias in the results. In terms of election polls, studies suggest that bias effects are small, but each polling firm has its own formulas on how to adjust weights to minimize selection bias.

- **Response** bias. Survey results may be affected by response bias. Response bias is when a respondent gives answers that not reflect his or her actual beliefs. This occurs for a variety of reasons. One reason is that a respondent may feel pressure not to give an unpopular answer. For example, respondents might be unwilling to admit to socially unpopular attitudes such as racism, sexism, or they may feel pressure to identify with socially or politically popular attitudes such as patriotism, civic activism, or religious commitment. For these reasons, a poll might not reflect the true incidence of certain attitudes or behaviors in the population. Pollsters can engineer response bias to generate a certain result or please their clients. This is one of the reasons why the term pollster suggests huckster, or a con artist. Even respondents can manipulate the outcome of a poll by reporting more extreme positions than they actually hold. The wording of surveys and the ordering of question creates response bias.

- **Question wording**. The wording of the questions, the order in which questions are asked, and the number and form of alternative answers offered influence results of polls. Thus comparisons between polls often boil down to the wording of the question. For some issues the question wording can produce pronounced differences between surveys. One way in which pollsters attempt to minimize this effect is to ask the same set of questions over time, in order to track changes in opinion. Another common technique is to rotate the order in which questions are asked. One technique is the split-sample, where there are two versions of a question and each version presented to half the respondents.

- **Coverage** bias. Coverage bias is another source of error is the use of samples that are not representative of the population as a consequence of the methodology used, as was the experience of the *Literary Digest* in 1936. For example, telephone sampling has a built-in error because people with telephones have generally been richer than those without phones. Today an increased percentage of the public has only a mobile telephone. In the United States it is illegal to make unsolicited calls to phones where the phone's owner may be charged simply for taking a call. Because pollsters are not supposed to call mobile phones, individuals who own only a mobile phone will often not be included in the polling sample. If the subset of the population without cell phones differs markedly from the rest of the population, these differences can skew the results of the poll. The relative importance of these factors remains uncertain today because polling organizations have adjusted their methodologies to achieve more accurate election predictions.

8.6 | The 2016 Presidential Election

One of the big stories in the analysis of Trump's stunning upset victory in 2016 is the public opinion polls. Most of polls indicated that Hillary Clinton was likely to win the election. She did not. The initial explanations for Trump's surprising upset victory focused on methodological problems with the polls: systematic biases; polls as flawed measures of public opinion and voting behavior; respondents who said they would not vote for Trump but did—including Trump supporters intending to mislead the political establishment; ideological biases in interpreting polls; and last minute voting decisions that tended to go Republican. The *flawed polls story* is appealing for several reasons. First, the winners tend to write the story about elections. The Trump campaign portrayed the public opinion polls as yet another source of establishment bias that it had to overcome as an underdog. The *David versus Goliath* storyline appealed to Trump's populist base because it affirmed a core political narrative. Second, the American public has lingering suspicions about polls and pollsters and experts. Confounding the experts seems to affirm traditional democratic theory that intelligent and informed voters decide elections, not scientific or social scientific models that are used to predict (and therefore perhaps to control?) voting behavior. Third, focusing on polling methodology and interpretation is a way to avoid some of the more complicated assessments of the successful and the unsuccessful campaign strategies and tactics— specifically reading the tea leaves to determine what was going on with the electorate.

Were the polls wrong? The American Association for Public Opinion Research's Report, *An Evaluation of 2016 Election Polls in the U.S.* (May 4, 2017), describes the outcome of the election as "jarring" and "shocking" even for Trump's pollsters. But the Report also says that *the national polls* were "correct" and "accurate," while some state and regional polls (in critical upper-Midwest states under-stated Trump support. The Report also lists three reasons why polls under-stated Trump support.[4] Other post-mortem analyses include the NPR story about the impact of FBI Director James Comey's letter about a Hillary Clinton investigation.[5] More broadly, the 2016 elections raised some fundamental questions about the nature of public opinion, thinking about science and social science facts in a hyper-partisan world, and the role of the media in undermining trust in information.

Was the media coverage of the elections biased? Yes. There was a clear bias toward negative coverage. The Shorenstein Center on Media, Politics and Public Policy's "Research: Media Coverage of the 2016 Election" describes the coverage and its consequences.[6] Part 2, "News Coverage of the 2016 Presidential Primaries: Horse Race Coverage Has Consequences," summarizes the primary coverage:

- Trump received much more coverage than the others, and the coverage was positive while the primary was contested and then negative after it was decided.
- Clinton received more negative coverage than Sanders, but Sanders received little coverage.
- Character and policy received little coverage compared to the horserace coverage (chances of winning).

Part 4, "News Coverage of the 2016 General Election: How the Press Failed the Voters," describes the media coverage of the general election as having an overwhelmingly negative tone and being light on public policy. It also described the steady stream of criticism as having a corrosive effect that erodes trust in leaders and institutions and undermines confidence in government and public policy. It also noted that the media framing of coverage was also distinctive for a false equivalency that misleads voters: the coverage of Clinton and Trump had a "virtually identical" negative tone despite the fact that the records of the two candidates were different in relevant ways. For instance, fact-checkers concluded that candidate Trump was far more likely to state non-facts than Clinton. So the equally-negative media coverage contributed to the environment where candidate and then

President Trump could both not state facts AND accuse the fake news media and Democrats and the intelligence community and others of not stating facts!

The 2016 election, Russia's intervention in U.S. and other elections, and the Trump administration's accusation of fake media coverage, have contributed to the proliferation of Internet and social media conspiracy theories and fake news stories. The identification of the problem of electronic propaganda may be the first step in the organization of a political movement to minimize its negative effects on public opinion, and to increase confidence in information which is an essential condition for functioning democracies. Google and Facebook are working on logarithmic formulas that can eliminate the human factor in assessing whether information received is good or bad information, or to label information so that consumers know what they are dealing with. Educators and advocates of civic engagement have also developed news literacy programs to teach students and citizens how to differentiate the real and the fake merchandise (political information; news). The News Literacy Project is one of these programs intended to arm the public in an era where the social media have been weaponized for politics, campaigns and elections, and the recruitment of terrorists.

> "Do You Know Who Murdered Seth Rich?"
> http://www.pbs.org/video/3001223329/

8.7 | Comparative Public Opinion

Many of the issues that political scientists have identified as most important to understanding American government and politics are not unique to the United States. The comparative study of public opinion reveals the similarities and differences in how the peoples of the world think about politics and government. This is increasingly important in a world that is economically and politically wired.

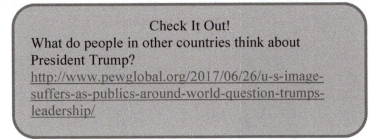

> Check It Out!
> What do people in other countries think about President Trump?
> http://www.pewglobal.org/2017/06/26/u-s-image-suffers-as-publics-around-world-question-trumps-leadership/

8.71 | *The World Values Survey*

One source of comparative information about public opinion is the World Values Survey. The World Values Survey developed from the European Values Study (EVS) in 1981 which covered only 22 countries worldwide. Ronald Inglehart (The University of Michigan) is a leading figure in the extension of the surveys around the world. The survey was repeated after an interval of about 10 years in then again in a series of "waves" at approximately five year intervals. The WVS was designed to provide a longitudinal and cross-cultural measurement of variation of values. The European origin of the project made the early waves of the WVS Eurocentric and notable for their especially weak representation in Africa and South-East Asia. In order to overcome this bias by becoming more representative, the WVS opened participation to academic representatives from new countries that met certain minimal survey standards. They could then exchange their data with the WVS in return for the data from the rest of the project. As a result, the WVS expanded to 42 countries in the 2nd wave, 54 in the 3rd wave and 62 in the 4th wave. Today the WVS is an open source database of the WVS available on the Internet. The Secretariat of the WVS is based in Sweden. The official archive of the World Values Survey is located in [ASEP/JDS] (Madrid), Spain.

The global World Values Survey consists of about 250 questions resulting in some 400 to 800 measurable variables. One of the variables measured is Happiness. The comparative "Perceptions of Happiness" are widely quoted in the popular media. Does the U.S. get a smiley face? The popular statistics website Nationmaster also publishes a simplified world happiness scale derived from the WVS data. The WVS website allows a user to get a more sophisticated level of analysis such as comparison of happiness over time or across socio-economic groups. One of the most striking shifts in happiness measured by the WVS was the substantial drop in happiness of Russians and some other Eastern European countries during the 1990s.

8.72 | *The Inglehart Map*

Another result of the WVS is the Inglehart Map. A number of variables were condensed into two

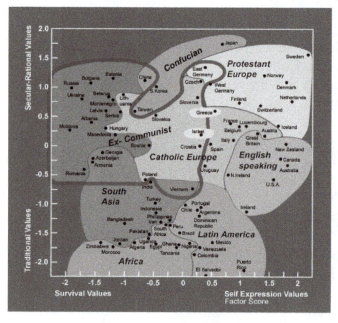

dimensions of cultural variation called the "traditional v. secular-rational" and the "survival v. self-expression" dimensions. On this basis, the world's countries could be mapped into specific cultural regions because these two dimensions purportedly explain more than 70 percent of the cross-national variance. The WVS also found that trust and democracy were values that crossed most cultural boundaries.

The Inglehart Map of the World

8.73 | *Religion and Economic Development*

The Pew Research Center's Global Attitudes Project provides data on the relationship between a country's wealth and its religiosity. The results show that countries with a high per capita income tend to score low on religiosity.[7]

8.8 | Additional Resources

One valuable source of information about American public opinion, voting, and political participation is the "American National Election Studies" information available at http://www.electionstudies.org/

The website http://www.americanrhetoric.com/ provides audio and video recordings of important public speeches—including the "top 100" American speeches. See, for example, the famous Goldwater Speech delivered at the Republican Party Convention in 1964.

8.81 | *In the Library*

Asher, Herbert. 2001. *Polling and the Public: What Every American Should Know*. Washington, DC: CQ Books.

Clem Brooks and Jeff Manza. 2007. *Why Welfare States Persist: The Importance of Public Opinion in Democracies*. Chicago: University of Chicago Press.

Katherine Cramer Walsh. 2007. *Talking About Race: Community Dialogues and the Politics of Difference*. Chicago: University of Chicago Press.

Robert Eisinger. 2003. *The Evolution of Presidential Polling*. Cambridge University Press.

Robert Erikson, et al. 1994. *Statehouse Democracy: Public Opinion and Policy in the American States*. Cambridge University Press.

Robert Erikson, Michael Mackuen, and James Stimson. 2002. *The Macro Polity*. Cambridge University Press.

Robert S. Erikson and Kent L. Tedin. 2006. *American Public Opinion: Its Origins, Content, and Impact*. Eighth Ed. Longman.

George Gallup. *The Gallup Poll Public Opinion*. Scholarly Resources, published annually.

Gallup, George, and Saul Rae. 1968. *The Pulse of Democracy*. New York: Greenwood Press.

John Hibbing and Elizabeth Theiss-Morse. 2002. *Stealth Democracy: American's Beliefs about How Government Should Work*. Cambridge University Press.

Darrell Huff. 1993. *How to Lie With Statistics*. W.W. Norton.

Helen Ingram, et al (Eds). 2004. Mediating Effect of Public Opinion on Public Policy: Exploring the Realm of Health Care. State University of New York Press.

Paul Lavrakas and Michael J. Traugott. 2000. *Election Polls, the News Media and Democracy*. Chatham House.

Walter Lippman. 1922. *Public Opinion*. Accessed at http://www.gutenberg.org/ebooks/6456

Moore, David W. 1992. *The Superpollsters: How They Measure and Manipulate Public Opinion in America*. Four Walls Eight Windows.

Moore, David W. 2008. *The Opinion Makers*. Boston: Beacon Press.

Willem E. Saris and Paul M. Sniderman (Eds). 2004. *Studies in Public Opinion: Attitudes, Nonattitudes, Measurement Error, and Change*. Princeton University Press.

James A. Stimson. 2004. *Tides of Consent: How Public Opinion Shapes American Politics*. Cambridge University Press, 2004.

Jeffrey Stonecash. 2003. *Political Polling: Strategic Information in Campaigns*. Rowman and Littlefield.

Keith Warren. 2001. *In Defense of Public Opinion Polling*. Westview Press.

Robert Weissberg. 2002. *Polling, Policy, and Public Opinion*. Palgrave.

---

[1] Statistical Abstract of the United States, 1997 (Washington, DC: Government Printing Office, 1997), 1011.

[2] Survey Methods: Results are based on telephone interviews with 1,010 national adults, aged 18 and older, conducted Sept. 14-16, 2007. For results based on the total sample of national adults, one can say with 95% confidence that the margin of sampling error is ±3 percentage points. In addition to sampling error, question wording and practical difficulties in conducting surveys can introduce error or bias into the findings of public opinion polls.

[3] Note that to get 500 complete responses it may be necessary to make thousands of phone calls.

[4] https://www.aapor.org/Education-Resources/Reports.aspx

[5] Daniel Kurtzleben "Pollsters Find 'At Best Mixed Evidence' Comey Letter Swayed Election," *NPR* (May 5, 2017). Accessed at http://www.npr.org/

[6] Thomas Patterson, "Research: Media Coverage of the 2016 Election," *Shorenstein Center on Media, Politics and Public Policy* (September 7, 2016). Accessed at https://shorensteincenter.org/research-media-coverage-2016-election/

[7] http://people-press.org/reports/display.php3?ReportID=167

9.0 | What's in a Name?

"A conservative is a man with two perfectly good legs who, however, has never learned how to walk forward."

Franklin Delano Roosevelt,
32ⁿᵈ President of the United States

"The trouble with our liberal friends is not that they are ignorant, but that they know so much that isn't so."

Ronald Reagan,
40th President of the United States

Have you ever been in a political discussion, debate, or perhaps even a heated argument where one person objected to another person's statement by responding, *"That's* not what I mean by conservative (or liberal)? If so, then join the club. Good political discussions often have to be paused when it becomes clear that the participants do not agree on the meanings of the terms that are central to the discussion. Ideologies are such conversation stoppers because familiar terms such as conservative, liberal, populist, socialist, and fascist are often used without agreeing on their meanings. This chapter has three main goals:

- Explaining what ideology is and what it does;
- Defining the major ideologies that influence American government and politics—primarily liberalism, conservatism, libertarianism, socialism, and populism.
- Describing how ideology affects modern American government and politics.

Some attention is also paid to other "isms" that are closely associated with important political movements or actions. They have some of the attributes of an ideology but are typically focused on a specific subject: feminism; environmentalism; fundamentalism; and terrorism.

9.1 | What is an ideology?

An <u>ideology</u> is a belief system that consists of a relatively coherent set of ideas about government and politics AND the public policies that are intended to implement the ideas or achieve the goals. An ideology is a belief system that consists of a *set* of ideas on a

broad range of issues as opposed to a single belief about a single issue. The belief system can help people make sense of the world around them. People go through life with "mental images" of "how the world is or should be organized." These images constitute an ideology—a way to simplify, organize, evaluate and "give meaning to what otherwise would be a very confusing world."[1] Individuals who are daily bombarded with information can use ideology to help make sense of it. When people read about a terrible crime or crime statistics, ideology can provide a ready-made explanation for the cause of the criminal behavior as well as a predisposition to support a liberal or conservative public policy response to crime. A person who sees video of police officers beating someone on the streets on Los Angeles or elsewhere is apt to use ideology to provide a handy mental image of whether the use of force is justified or a case of police brutality. A person who reads about the latest data on unemployment can use ideology to provide a framework for thinking that the unemployment rate is too high or too low. A person who thinks about taxes is apt to use ideology to conclude that taxes are too high or too low without having to spend a great deal of time learning about economic policy. And finally, individuals who view actual images of bombing or read about the use of military force can use an ideological "mental image" to react to the action based on an ideological bias for or against the use of military force.

The second part of an ideology is its action component. Ideologies include public policies that are intended to act on ideas or goals. In fact, the commitment to action differentiates an ideology from a philosophy. For example, political philosophy is the study of fundamental questions about human nature, politics and government, rights such as liberty and equality, law, justice, and what constitutes a good or moral public order. Political philosophers examine questions about the legitimacy of government; the difference between power and authority; the nature of freedom and equality; civic duties and obligations; and the nature and scope of government power to limit individual liberty. The adherents of an ideology are committed to specific sets of values and to acting to achieve them in the realm of politics and government.

9.12 | *A Coherent Set of Ideas: Human Nature and the Role of Government*

An ideology is not just a set of ideas it is a *coherent* set of ideas. This means that the components of an ideology should be consistent with one another. One idea should not conflict with others. For example, ideologies typically include beliefs about human nature and beliefs about the appropriate role for government. In terms of human nature, an ideology can describe human nature as basically 1) good or bad; and 2) fixed or flexible. The belief that human nature is basically good means that people are expected to do the right thing because they have a natural sense of right and wrong and will generally do what is right. The belief that human nature is basically bad means that people are by nature self-interested, that evil is part of human nature, and therefore people will often do wrong. The belief that human nature is fixed assumes that an individual's capacities and abilities are determined at birth: intelligence, aptitudes, and character are a matter of nature. The belief that human nature is flexible means that an individual's capacities and abilities can be developed by family, religion, culture, tradition, and education: intelligence, aptitudes, and character are a matter of nurture. Beliefs about the determinants of human behavior are of great political importance because they shape beliefs about the best form of government (e.g., whether democracy will work), the

Think about It! Watch the trailer for the 1938 film *Angels with Dirty Faces*. What do you think the film says about human nature?
http://www.youtube.com/watch?v=Nld4DcRHME0

appropriate role of government (e.g., limited or broad), and they shape public policies. For instance, they determine criminal justice policies, particularly whether sentencing policies should emphasize punishment or rehabilitation.

James Madison is called the architect of the American system of government he designed the elaborate system of institutional checks and balances. He believed that people were by nature self-interested and needed to have their ambitions checked. Thomas Jefferson wrote extensively about human nature, specifically about the question whether humans were self-interested egoists (individuals whose actions are based solely on "self-love") or whether they had a moral sense. He believed people had a natural moral sense. The question was whether it was based on religion, which would justify government support for religion, or a natural sense of moral obligation or conscience. These are some of the most profound questions about human nature and social or political behavior. In a June 13, 1814 *Letter to Thomas Law*, "The Moral Sense," Jefferson discussed his thoughts on the question. "The Creator would indeed have been a bungling artist had he intended man for a social animal without planting in him social dispositions." These social dispositions, which limit self-interest, self-love, or egoism, provide an innate sense of morality that constitutes the "Principles of Natural Religion."[2]

In his First Inaugural Address (delivered March 4, 1861), President Lincoln spoke about human nature when he closed his Address with the hope that the divisiveness of the Civil War could be ended by appeals to "the better angels of our nature." Lincoln believed that without such appeals to our good nature, appeals to the worse angels of our nature would result in division, discord, and violence.

An ideology is inconsistent if it includes positive *and* negative views of human nature, or if it includes both fixed *and* flexible views of human nature. It is harder to determine whether an ideology has consistent views on the role of government because ideologies include ideas about the appropriate *size* of government and the appropriate *use* of government power. Size refers to small or big government; use refers to the purposes of government. With the notable exception of libertarianism, ideologies typically support small government for some purposes and big government for others. For example, modern conservatives support big government for national security, morals regulation, and crime, but small government for regulating business. Liberals support big government to regulate business and to expand social and economic equality, but small government to regulate morality. Political debates tend to focus on the *size* of government: which individual, political party, or ideology supports big government and which supports small government. The focus on size overlooks the importance of the *role* of government—what government power is actually being used for.

Think About It!

Are humans Hobbesian creatures who are violent by nature?
What does Steven Pinker's 2007 TED Lecture, *The Myth of Violence*, say about human nature?
http://www.ted.com/talks/lang/en/steven_pinker_on_the_myth_of_violence.html

9.13 | *The Meaning of Terms*

Liberalism and conservatism are the two labels that are most commonly attached to individuals, political parties, interest groups, the media, public policies, and government officials—including judges. The fact that they are very familiar terms does not mean that their meanings are very clear. The absence of shared definitions of important political concepts such as freedom, order, justice, conservatism, and liberalism is problematic. A shared political vocabulary is important in a democracy where voters are expected to make informed decisions. Democracy works best when citizens know the meanings of the words used to describe government and politics. Developing shared understandings of conservatism and liberalism is complicated by the fact that they have changed a great deal over time. Ideologies are dynamic, not static. What it means to be a conservative or a liberal changes over time.

9.14 | *The Functions of Ideology*

In politics as in economics and sports, *organization* increases effectiveness. Ideologies organize interests. Ideologies can increase the effectiveness of individuals and ideas by organizing them in order to maximize their impact on public policy. In this respect, ideologies serve a purpose that is similar to political parties and interest groups. But ideologies both unite people and divide them. Ideologies do bring people together to work for shared ideas but they also move people apart by dividing them into opposing camps: believers and non-believers. The fact that ideologies both unite and divide, increase political cooperation and political conflict, is one reason why Americans are so ambivalent about ideology, why they have conflicting feelings about ideology. The ambivalent feelings about ideology can be traced to the earliest days of the republic when the Founders warned against "the mischiefs of faction." In *Federalist Number 9* Hamilton argued that a firm union was a safeguard against "domestic faction." In Federalist Number 10 Madison described how to design a political system that "cured" the "mischiefs of faction." Worries about the harmful effects of factions have not gone away. Today's worries are about ideologies or parties or special interests divided Americans into competing camps that fight hard for their views rather than working toward the common good. The later chapters describe how organization can increase an individual's feelings of efficacy, the belief that individual participation in politics matters because it can make a difference. Ideology *can* play a similar role because it unites and organizes like-minded people to work on behalf of shared ideas.

9.2 | The Major Isms

The range of ideological debates in the U.S. is very limited compared to other democracies. American politics is practically limited to liberalism and conservatism. There are occasional references to other ideologies such as libertarianism, radicalism, socialism, and fascism, but these ideologies are for the most part outside the

mainstream of political debate or they are considered the more extreme elements within liberalism or conservatism. The more extremist ideologies of the left and right ends of the political spectrum are not usually part of political discourse. In this sense, the two-ideology system mirrors the two-party system: both present voters with a limited range of political choices.

Liberalism and conservatism have changed a great deal over time. In the early 1800s, the conservative party was the Federalist Party, which advocated a strong federal government, and the liberal party was the Jeffersonian Republicans, which advocated states' rights. In the 1930s, conservatives supported states' rights while liberals supported expansion of the federal government. Since the mid-1960s four major issues have consistently divided conservatives and liberals:

- *National Security Policy.* Conservatives have generally been stronger supporters of national defense than liberals. This was the case during the Cold War and it has continued during the War on Terror.
- *Crime Policy.* Conservatives have consistently supported getting tough on crime by strengthening the police and punishment as the main goal of sentencing. Liberals have consistently supported the expansion of due process rights of suspects and rehabilitation as a main goal of sentencing.
- *Moral Regulatory Policy.* Conservatives have consistently supported moral regulatory policies related to abortion, pornography, sexual behavior, marriage, and the establishment of religion. Liberals have consistently supported moral deregulatory policies.
- *Economic Policy.* Conservatives have been more consistently pro-business and anti-tax. Liberals have generally been more pro-labor and more supportive of government regulation of business.

9.30 | Conservatism: Traditional and Modern

This is a conservative era in American politics. Conservatism has been the dominant, but not exclusive, force in national politics since the late 1960s.[3] The notable exception is the reaction to the Watergate scandal in the mid-1970s. However, conservatism is not monolithic. It might be said that wherever two or more conservatives are gathered together the discussion invariably turns to who is the real, true conservative. The following describes the two main strains of conservatism: traditional conservatism (during the period from the 1930s until the mid-1960s) and modern conservatism (from the mid-1960s until today). There are three main differences between traditional and modern conservatism—their views on change, ideology, and the role of government.

9.31 | *Views on Change*

Traditional conservatism is closest to the original meaning of the word conservative, which is derived from the Latin *conservāre*—meaning to conserve by preserving, keeping, or protecting traditional beliefs, values, customs, or ways of doing things. Traditional conservatives defend the status quo against radical or revolutionary change or the assumption that all change is reform (good change). Edmund Burke (1729-1797), the

Edmund Burke, 1771

Irish-British political philosopher, is considered the father of traditional conservatism. He did not oppose change. In fact, he argued that a government without a means of changing lacked the necessary means for its own survival. However, Burke preferred slow or incremental change and opposed radical or revolutionary change.

Modern conservatism is a much stronger advocate for *change*. In fact, some conservatives call themselves radical conservatives. A radical is someone who advocates basic, even revolutionary change. Radicals can be leftwing or rightwing. When President Reagan called his administration a bunch of radicals he reminded voters that he was a movement conservative, a person who was committed to the cause of overturning liberal social, economic, and defense policies. In contrast to traditional conservatism, which rejected radical or revolutionary change of the right or left, modern conservatism advocates major, even radical or revolutionary change. However, the change is usually described as radical change from the liberal status quo, change that will bring the country back to the basics. This usually means that the solution for many of the contemporary social, economic, and political problems is to return to the Founder's original understanding of politics, government, and the Constitution. This recurring conservative theme is one of the main points of the Tea Party movement.

Traditional conservatism's skepticism about change is related to the belief in the importance of order. Traditional conservatives consider order the necessary condition for achieving or maintaining other important values such as individual freedom, private property, and justice—and without good order, these other values and valuables are unlikely to be attained. Traditional conservatives believe that order can be created and maintained by social institutions (family, schools, churches, and civic organization) as well as by government. In this sense, traditional conservatives are not anti-government. They believe that government has a responsibility to maintain domestic order, to control crime, to preserve traditional values through moral regulatory policies, and to provide national security from foreign threats. But traditional conservatives believe that the primary responsibility for these activities lies with the private sector, the civil society, rather than the public sector (the government). The Burkean emphasis on order, social institutions, and civic responsibility made traditional conservatism less committed to other values such as individualism, individual liberty, and equality. A leading American traditional conservative is Russell Kirk (1918-1994). The Russell Kirk Center provides a good description of traditional conservative principles. They include belief in natural law, hierarchy, the connection between property rights and freedom, faith in custom and tradition, and skepticism of change.

9.32 | *Views on Ideology*

The second different between traditional and modern conservatism is that modern conservatism is much more *ideological*. Today's conservatives portray conservatism as an ideology that will solve the problems created by liberalism. The term *movement conservative* refers to those conservatives who consider themselves part of an organized cause to work for conservative ideas. These conservatives are part of a cause. Traditional conservatives were to a certain extent anti-ideological. They considered ideology problematic because it was extremism rather than moderation—and traditional conservatives were in the Aristotelian and Burkean traditions that emphasized conservatism as moderation rather than extremism. The word ideology was originally coined to refer to the scientific study of ideas. It was originally used to describe how the systematic study of ideas could lead to a better understanding of the political world the way that science increased understanding of the natural world. But by the middle of the 20th Century the word ideology was used to describe the ideas that were used to get political power, to shape public policy, and to justify government action. In fact, beginning in the latter 1950s, sociologists including Nan Aron, Seymour M. Lipset, Edward Shils, and Daniel Bell warned that in modern societies ideology was actually assuming the role that religion played in traditional societies. They did not mean this as a compliment. They considered ideology at least partly an irrational, unthinking, and therefore unreasonable force in a world where modern governments had become very powerful and even totalitarian. Their warnings about the dangers presented by modern ideology came from recent political experience. It was a reaction against the ideologies of the left (Communism in the Soviet Union and China) and the right (Fascism in Hitler's Germany and Mussolini's Italy) during the period from the 1930s to the 1960s. These critics of ideology came to be called neoconservatives, or new conservatives.

9.33 | Views on the Role of Government

The third difference between traditional and modern conservatives concerns the role of government. Modern conservative support for change and ideology has changed conservative thinking about the role of government. Conservatives are not antigovernment or even advocates of small government as much as they oppose what government has been doing. Specifically, conservatives oppose public policies that promote egalitarianism, social welfare, the due process model of justice, and the de-regulation of morals. The claim that conservatives are not antigovernment can be supported by examining conservative views on the four major policy areas that have consistently divided conservatives and liberals: national security; crime; economics; and moral regulatory policy. The conservative position is not antigovernment in these four areas. Conservatives are pro-government on national security, crime, regulation of morals, and even, to a lesser extent, economics. There *is* a libertarian strain within conservatism that is consistently antigovernment but mainstream conservatism does not take the libertarian position on the major policies.

The conservative movement's support for government is apparent in the principles and positions taken by leading conservative organizations such as The Heritage Foundation, The American Conservative Party, and The American Conservative Union. The Heritage Foundation describes itself as a leading voice for conservative ideas such as individual freedom, limited government, traditional values, and strong national defense. It promotes the latter two values by support for "big" government. The American Conservative Party's principles are more anti-government in the sense that they more consistently advocate limited government. The principles include natural rights and individual liberty, the belief that law should be used to support liberty and mediate disputes where one person has harmed another, and the reminder that "[t]he armed forces and law enforcement exist to bolster private defense, not supplant it."

Ideologies include a commitment to acting on values. Conservatives use both the government and the private sector to achieve their goals, but they are more likely than liberals to support the private sector delivery of goods and services. The free market plays a central role as a means to achieve conservative goals. In fact, the market model is often presented as an alternative to a statist or government model for organizing society. The English political philosopher Adam Smith developed the marketplace model in *Wealth of Nations*. This book, which was published in 1776, the same year as the Declaration of Independence, is one of the most influential books ever written. Smith advocated an alternative to mercantilism, the conventional economic model of the day that the government should direct economic activity for the wealth of the empire. Smith described an economic system where the prices of goods were determined by the interactions of buyers and sellers in a competitive marketplace rather than the government. Over time, however, the logic of the marketplace model has been extended beyond economics to other, non-economic areas of society. For example, the economic free marketplace of goods has been expanded to politics where the free market place of ideas is based on the same logic as the economic free market. This is controversial because the marketplace model assumes that goods and services should be available on the basis of the ability to pay—but some things are valuable even though they are not highly valued in the economic marketplace. The philosopher Michael Sandel worries about applying the logic of the marketplace to more and more non-economic settings. Listen to his argument about what money cannot buy and should not buy. Do you agree with him? What are some of the consequences of thinking about citizens as consumers?

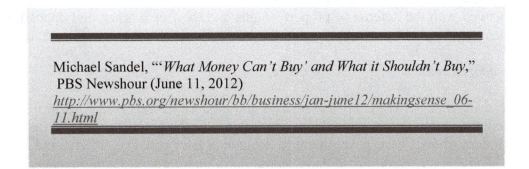

Michael Sandel, "'*What Money Can't Buy' and What it Shouldn't Buy*,"
PBS Newshour (June 11, 2012)
http://www.pbs.org/newshour/bb/business/jan-june12/makingsense_06-11.html

9.40 | Liberalism

A standard dictionary definition of a liberal is a person who believes in individual liberty. But defining liberalism as an ideology that values individual liberty is not very helpful because conservatives also profess a belief in individual liberty. Furthermore, liberals, like conservatives, value good public order. So it is more accurate to say that liberals and conservatives place different values on individual liberty and order. In general, liberals tend to place a higher priority on liberty than order, while conservatives generally tend to place a higher priority on order more than liberty.

Defining liberalism is complicated for some of the same reasons that conservatism is complicated: liberalism is a set of ideas—not just one idea; the set of ideas has changed over time; and liberalism is not monolithic. The two main strains of liberalism that are examined here are classical liberalism and modern liberalism.

9.41 | *Classical Liberalism*

Classical liberalism is rooted in the ideas of the English political philosopher John Locke (1632-1704). Locke's ideas greatly influenced the thinking of the American founders. His words about the importance of life, liberty, and property found their way into the Declaration of Independence. Locke emphasized the following five ideas:

- Reason. Humans should use their reasoning capacity to understand the natural and political world rather than *merely* relying on faith, custom, or tradition in order to organize society.
- Individualism. The importance of the individual as a political actor relative to groups, classes, or institutions included an emphasis on legal equality.
- Liberty. Freedom is valued more than order, or relative to obedience to authority.
- Social Contract Theory of Government. Individuals decide to leave the state of nature and create government based on the consent of the governed and created by a social contract.
- Property Rights. Economic rights (to property and contract) are related to political rights. The shift is toward a private sector economy rather than one run by the government is an aspect of the commitment to limited government.

Classical liberalism originated as a political theory that limited government. During much of the 20th Century classical liberalism was actually considered conservative because it was associated with the defense of property rights and the free market, and opposition to government regulation of the economy and the expansion of the social welfare state.

9.42 | *Modern Liberalism*

The main difference between classical liberals and modern liberals is that modern liberals abandoned the emphasis on limited government as the best way to protect individual rights. Modern liberals used government to achieve greater equality, liberty, and income security.

- Equality. The various civil rights movements of the 19th, 20th, and 21st centuries expanded equality for racial and ethnic minorities and women. Most recently, the gay rights movement has advocated for greater legal equality under the law. Egalitarianism became a more important goal for modern liberals. Laws were used to limit discrimination.
- Liberty. Modern liberals also used law to protect civil liberties. Radical political speech. Limits on government censorship. The right to privacy and deregulation of morals.
- Income Security. Modern liberals used government policies to pass social welfare programs (e.g., social security; Medicare; unemployment insurance; workers compensation). These policies were designed to increase income security for the young, the old, and the sick. Support for the creation of the social welfare state explains why modern liberals are called social welfare liberals to differentiate them from classical liberals.

One of the founders of modern liberalism is the 19th Century English political philosopher John Stuart Mill. In *On Liberty and Representative Government*, Mill explained a principle or rule for determining what government should be allowed to do,

> "The only purpose for which power can be rightly exercised over a member of a civilized community, against his will, is to prevent harm to others. His own good, either physical or moral, is not a sufficient warrant."

and what it should not be allowed to do, in a political system based on limited government. The rule has come to be called The Harm Principle. In fact, Mill was merely restating the liberal idea developed by Thomas Jefferson (and John Locke before him):

> "The legitimate powers of government extend to such acts only as are injurious to others. But it does me no injury for my neighbor to say there are twenty Gods or no God. It neither picks my pocket nor breaks my leg."

The Harm Principle is libertarian in the sense that it limits government power over individuals. Mill accepted the basic principles of classical liberalism, particularly individual freedom, but he was more supportive of using government power to protect liberty and to promote equality. The origins of social welfare liberalism can be traced to this shift toward greater reliance on government to provide economic and social security. In modern American politics, liberals generally support government regulation to promote equality and economic security—the social welfare state—while conservatives generally support government regulation to promote law and order, national security, and morality—the national security and moral regulatory state.

One indication that this is a conservative era in American politics is the fact that liberalism has become a pejorative term, a negative term. Liberalism has been stigmatized as the "L-word" after been blamed for being soft on crime, for being weak on national defense, for undermining traditional values, and for being unduly critical of capitalism. In fact, the word liberal is so out of political favor today that liberals call themselves progressives. Progressive is a euphemism for liberal and Progressivism is a strain of liberalism.

Think About It!
Why are conservatives happier than liberals?
http://www.pbs.org/newshour/bb/business/july-dec11/makingsense_12-09.html

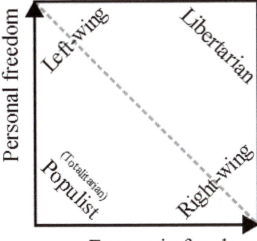

Nolan chart, 2d political spectrum. Diagonal line indicates classical 1d left-right political spectrum.

9.50 | Libertarian

Libertarianism is a simpler ideology than either conservatism or liberalism. Simply stated, libertarians value freedom and believe that individuals and groups can organize life with only minimal government. Libertarians have a positive view of human nature. The belief that government threatens freedom—that more government means less freedom—is reflected in The Libertarian Party motto: "Maximum freedom. Minimal Government." The familiar slogan, "That government is best which governs least!" is libertarian. Libertarians believe in minimal government: government should be limited to doing what is necessary to protect individuals from being harmed by others. Libertarians value freedom more than order, but they believe that order actually emerges from the competition of the marketplace. This is the basis of libertarian support for laissez faire policies in economic, political, and social affairs. Laissez faire is a French term for "let it be." In economics, laissez faire means allowing the competition of the marketplace, and the interaction of buyers and sellers, to operate without government intervention, regulation, or control. Libertarians rely on the private sector to produce order and prosperity. In politics, libertarians oppose using government power to promote values such as equality, patriotism, or morality. They also oppose immigration policies that limit the free movement of people across national borders. This is why libertarians can be conservative on some issues (opposed to using law to promote equality or create social welfare or to regulate business) and liberal on others (opposed to moral regulatory policy and opposed to laws promoting patriotism).

Libertarians take seriously the **harm principle** as a guide for limited government. The harm principle is libertarian insofar as it considers the only legitimate use of government power is preventing individuals from being harmed by others. Harm means physical harm to person or property or interests. The harm principle does not allow paternalistic legislation, using laws to prevention people from harming themselves by smoking, drinking alcohol or using drugs, eating unhealthy food, riding motorcycles without a helmet, or riding in a car without a seatbelt.

9.60 | Other Isms

9.61 | *Socialism and Communism*

Socialism is the belief that economic power is the basis of political power and that economic equality is essential for political equality. The belief that economic inequality causes political inequality provides the socialist justification for using government to actively promote equality through extensive government regulation or even government control of the economy. In order to achieve political equality, the government as redistributes resources through progressive taxation and social welfare program, at a minimum, and government control of the economy (both the means of production and the distribution of goods and services) at a maximum. Karl Marx is the most famous figure associated with socialism because he developed a comprehensive, systematic analysis of the relationship between economics and politics, thereby giving earlier socialist thinking an ideology or world view. For an American economist's critique of the rise and fall of socialism as an economic model read Robert Heilbroner's analysis.

Like conservatism and liberalism, there are many variations of socialism. In fact, in American politics the term socialist is often used in a generic sense to refer to any "big government" taxing and spending policies. In this sense, government spending as a share of the nation's Gross Domestic Product is a measure of how *socialistic* the country is. Socialists do support expansive government. But so do non-socialists. For example, the federal government's response to the Great Recession included the infamous Troubled Asset Relief Program (or TARP) of 2008 and the Emergency Economic Stabilization Act of 2008 which provided government bailouts for financial services companies and car manufacturers (GM and Chrysler). These policies were *socialistic* only in the sense that they increased government intervention in the private sector economy. But the bailouts were not socialistic in the sense that they were not aimed at promoting greater economic equality: critics called them Wall Street bailouts that Main Street would have to pay for. The key to identifying socialist policies that result in big government, as opposed to non-socialist policies that result in big government, is the social policies promote egalitarianism: economic equality.

Communism can be understood as an extreme version of socialism. It takes the socialist ideal of equality, and the government's responsibility to achieve it in the economic, political, and social sectors to the point where there is no distinction between a private sector and the public sector. Communism is *totalitarian* in the sense that it advocates **total** government power over society. Indeed, the word *totalitarian* means total control with no distinction between the public sector and the private sector. In a totalitarian system, the government is authorized to use its powers and laws to regulate individual behavior, family policy, business and labor, as well as all aspects of social life.

9.62 | Anarchism

In terms of the size of government, anarchism is at the opposite end of the ideological spectrum from communism. The key to understanding anarchism is the fact that the Greek origin of the term means "without rulers." Anarchists oppose all forms of government because governments by definition have the power to coerce individuals to join a community or require obedience to laws. Government use force—even the force of law—to ensure compliance rather than merely allowing individuals to freely, voluntarily join a political community. Anarchists believe that government is not necessary because people can use their capacity for reasoning to decide whether to freely and voluntarily agree to live in orderly and just societies without government requiring them to do so. Anarchists have a basically positive view of human nature which contrasts with Thomas Hobbes who believed that humans were by nature selfish, and the strong would take advantage of the weak. Anarchists believe that people will learn from experience that some rules are necessary for peaceful and prosperous coexistence and therefore will voluntarily accept rules that provide good order and justice without the force of law. Anarchists consider government power to compel individuals to obey the law illegitimate because it violates an individual's inherent right to be free from coercion by others. In today's political debate, anarchists are most often depicted as violent radicals who oppose government policies promoting international trade and globalism.

Think About It!
The "Sheep, Wolves, and Sheepdog" scene from the 2014 film *American Sniper*
https://youtu.be/uxZ0UZf0mkk

9.63 | Populism

The term populism refers to "of the people." Populists identify with or advocate on behalf of the common person, who they depict as being unfairly treated by the rich, the powerful, or some other privileged elites who are working against them. In modern American politics, populist movements are essentially anti-establishment protests on behalf of the average American, the blue-collar workers, the middle-class, the silent majority, the forgotten person, or even the poor. Charles Barkley, a member of the National Basketball Association (NBA) Hall of Fame, expressed populist sentiment when he said that "all politics is rich people screwing poor people."

Some of the Founders worried a great deal about what is today called populism. In *Federalist No. 1*, Alexander Hamilton warned about popular leaders who, behind the "mask of zeal for the rights of the people," courted the people, became demagogues, and then ended up as tyrants. And Aaron Burr famously told the Senate that if the Constitution ever expired by the "sacrilegious hands of the demagogue or the usurper" it agonies would be witnessed on the floor of the Senate. But American ideas about democracy and popular sovereignty have made populism a recurring theme in the American political experience. President Andrew Jackson was a populist who worked to bring the average person into a political process that was controlled by "the better sorts" of society. In the latter 19th and early 20th Century, agrarian populists defended rural/agrarian interests from the urbanization and industrialization that occurred with the Industrial Revolution.

Populism often emerges as a reaction against major social, economic, or cultural changes (e.g., immigration) or economic crises (e.g., panics, depressions, or recessions). The cultural revolution of the 1960s spawned right wing populists such as George Wallace, the Governor of Alabama and third-party presidential candidate. Listen to Wallace's populist campaign message making fun of northern urban elites—including the Washington press. Because populists generally promote a more equal distribution of resources and power, the growing economic inequality in the country has fueled a rise of populist sentiments. The main targets of modern left wing populism are economic elites, principally the finance industry represented by Wall Street (e.g., Moveon.org) and the multinational corporate interests that have promoted globalization and the interests of management rather than labor. Today's right wing populism includes opposition to immigration, or at least the demand that the federal government defend the country's borders and enforce immigration laws, and opposition to efforts to change the traditional definition of marriage as a union between one man and one woman. The Tea Party Movement's rallying cry, "Take back the Constitution," is a populist protest against the establishment elites.

9.64 | *FEMINISM*

Feminism is a social or political movement that strives for equal rights for women. It is multi-faceted movement that has political, economic, social, legal, and cultural components. The *Stanford Encyclopedia of Philosophy* defines feminism and describes it by paying special attention to its various dimensions. Feminist theory describes and analyzes gender differences (and similarities) in order to better understand gender differences and gender inequality. From the perspective of political science, feminist theory is an attempt to explain relevant facts, include gender behavior, sexuality, and inequality. One relevant fact is the different gender political power relations. Feminism describes and critiques these political power relations. As such, feminist theory often promotes women's rights. The subjects of study include discrimination, stereotypes, objectification, and patriarchy. Women's Studies is a multidisciplinary academic field that includes anthropology, communications, economics, history, philosophy, political science, and sociology.

9.65 | ENVIRONMENTALISM

Environmentalism is a movement whose members advocate protecting the natural environment. Environmentalism is an example of modern issue politics advanced by individuals—policy entrepreneurs who take up a cause—and organizations (interest groups). The environmental movement began to have an impact on national politics in the 1960s and 1970s when they put the environment on the government's agenda. Senator Gaylord Nelson founded Earth Day on April 22, 1970. The Environmental Protection Agency also was created in 1970. The EPA is the primary federal government agency responsible for providing clean air and clean water. Why is the environmental movement political? Why is it controversial to provide clean air and clean water? Because doing so involves the allocation of scarce resources. Protecting the environment costs money and entails government regulation of business and consumer behavior. This explains the debate over global warming. Global warming is an example of an environmental issue that has become controversial because addressing it will require governmental regulation.

9.66 | FUNDAMENTALISM

Fundamentalism is not usually considered an ideology the way conservatism, liberalism, and libertarianism are ideologies. However, fundamentalism is an idea which has an important impact on modern American politics and the politics of other countries. Fundamentalism is usually defined as a movement within a religious denomination—a movement that reacts against modernity by advocating a return to the basics or the fundamentals of a particular faith. Religious fundamentalism is evident in most of the major religions of the world today. Christian, Islamic, and Judaic fundamentalists advocate a return to basic articles of faith, particularly those tenets of faith that are expressed or revealed in sacred texts such as the Bible or Koran.

Fundamentalism is not limited to religious movements. It can be secular as well. From a social science perspective, fundamentalism is a reaction against modernity, particularly science, secularism, and value relativism. **Secularism** is the belief that government and politics should be separate from religion, that religion is appropriate for the private (social) sphere, not the public (governmental) sphere. In the U.S., secularism is reflected in the idea that there should be a "wall of separation" between church and state. **Relativism** is the belief that values are subjective and conditional rather than universal and objectively true. Fundamentalists advocate restoring the traditional or fundamental belief that morals and values are universal truths that are not subject to evolving standards of modernity.

In the U.S., political fundamentalists advocate returning to the nation's founding values, political principles, and founding documents. Legal or constitutional fundamentalists advocate Originalism, the belief that judges should decide cases based on the original intentions of those who wrote the words of the Constitution rather than their interpretation of the words or the modern meanings of the words. Religious fundamentalists and secular fundamentalists tend to be conservative insofar as they work to return to or restore the values of the founding era.

9.67 | Terrorism

Terrorism is hard to define in a way that is universally accepted or which differentiates between acceptable and unacceptable uses of political violence. The old saying that one person's freedom fighter is another person's terrorist still applies to contemporary analyses of political violence. A basic definition of terrorism is the use of violence or the threat of violence to intimidate or coerce a people, principally for political purposes. Terrorism creates a climate of fear in a population in order to achieve a particular political objective.

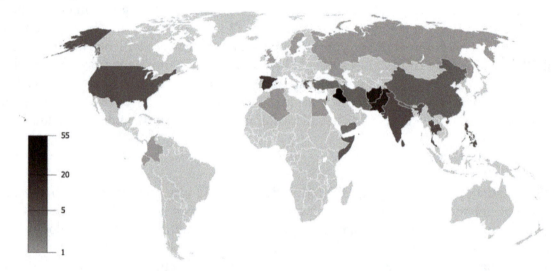

Number of terrorist incidents, by country, in 2009

U.S. law does define terrorism. Title 118 of the U.S. Code defines international terrorism as violent acts that "appear to be intended to" "intimidate or coerce a civilian population;" "to influence the policy of a government by intimidation or coercion," or to "affect the conduct of a government by mass destruction, assassination, or kidnapping."[4] It defines domestic terrorism as activities that "involve acts dangerous to human life that are a violation of the criminal laws of the United States or of any State;" "appear to be intended" to "intimidate or coerce a civilian population; to influence the policy of a government by intimidation or coercion; or to affect the conduct of a government by mass destruction, assassination, or kidnapping…"; and "occur primarily within the territorial jurisdiction of the United States."

An extremely broad range of individuals, political organizations, and movements have used terrorism: leftist and rightist; conservative and liberal; nationalistic and internationalist movements; religious and secular; defenders of the status quo and revolutionaries; populists and elitists; and even governments (though state institutions such as armies, intelligence services, and the police). Since the terrorist attacks of 9/11, the government has devoted a great deal of attention to terrorism. In fact, the Federal Bureau of Investigation describes protecting against terrorism its top priority.

Terrorism involves the use of political violence but not all political violence is terrorism. It is important to differentiate between legitimate and illegitimate uses of political violence. During the colonial era, mob actions were part of the American political experience with direct, participatory democracy. The Boston Tea Party in December 1773 was direct action intended to protest against British policies and to intimidate the British. Shays' Rebellion in the winter of 1786 and 1787 was an armed uprising by citizenry who demanded that the government be more responsive to the economic problems of average Americans who facing mortgage foreclosures.

The Tea Party movement played an important role in the 2010 mid-term elections. Conservatives and Republican candidates for national and state offices did very well. One controversy surrounding the Tea Party movement is the fact that individual members of the movement and Tea Party groups either implied or explicitly stated that the American political tradition includes demanding change through means other than the ballot box and regular elections. These alternative methods include violence and the threat of violence. The references to "Second Amendment" remedies for political problems are a reminder that the American political tradition includes famous examples of when political violence was accepted as a legitimate way to achieve political change or to oppose advocates of political change. Members of the Tea Party movement and advocates of gun rights, such as the National Rifle Association, remind the American public and government officials that the Declaration of Independence explained why individuals or organizations can take up arms when the government is tyrannical, exceeds its authority, or is not responsive to demands.[5]

9.60 | Why only two major ideologies in the U.S.?

Individual freedom of choice is a powerful idea in American culture. In economics, freedom of choice means a preference for a free marketplace of goods and services where consumers choose what to buy based on their preferences. The government does not decide what goods and services are available in the marketplace. It is considered a good thing for economic consumers to have a broad range of options from which to choose when purchasing a car, a house, health care, an insurance plan, or any other good or service. Having lots of consumer choice is also believed to create competition to continually improve products and services. Americans consider economic choice a good thing. And today's economic consumers certainly have a great variety of goods and services from which to choose. At one time, television viewers had only three broadcast networks to watch: CBS, NBC, and ABC. Now there is a seemingly endless menu of viewing choices. At one time, car buyers were mainly limited to the big three American automobile manufacturers: Chevrolet, Ford, and Chrysler. Today car buyers can also choose from many foreign manufacturers. Why is there so much more economic consumer freedom of choice than political freedom of choice? Why are economic consumers presented with so many choices of goods and services, but political consumers are for all practical purposes limited to choosing either a conservative or a liberal, a Republican or Democrat? Must individuals, issues, and parties be either conservative or a liberal? In a nation of more than 300 million people, is it possible to fit everyone into only two boxes?

9.61 | *WHAT ARE YOU?*

Two-dimensional frameworks for thinking about ideologies and political parties are useful because they help organize and simplify the political world by sorting or categorizing information. But simplifying the political world by labeling everything as either conservative or liberal can also be a simplification that distorts political reality. The political world is actually multi-dimensional, not two-dimensional. The limitations of the conservative and liberal framework have prompted searches for ways of thinking about ideology that provide for more than two options. One alternative framework that provides more than two categories is the World's Smallest Political Quiz. It makes a distinction between views on economic issues and views on personal issues. Take the quiz to see which of four ideological labels best describes you. What do you think of the quiz? Do you think the results accurately label you? Do you think the quiz is biased toward a particular ideology? The Pew Research Center has also developed a "Political Typology" quiz that provides more political colors than red and blue. Do you think the results accurately label you?

Another familiar two-dimensional framework for simplifying American politics is the *Red State* (conservative and Republican) and *Blue State* (liberal and Democratic) framework. It describes states and regions of the country based on voting behavior and public policies. These ideological frameworks are scientific in the sense that they are based on social science. Cognitive scientists have also made important contributions to understanding thinking about politics. For instance, George Lakoff's *Moral Politics* (2016) explains thinking about politics by contrasting *strict father morality* with *feel-good liberalism*. Individuals who identify with the strict father morality believe that hierarchical authority is important whereas individuals who identify with feel-good liberalism value egalitarian toleration. Table 9.61 below describes Lakoff's understanding of the conservative hierarchy of value preferences. Lakoff, who predicted Donald Trump's victory in the 2016 election, explains "your brain on Trump." According to Lakoff, liberals (that is, progressives and Democrats) think of human behavior in terms of logic and reason. Therefore they study political science, law, economic theory (but not business), and public policy. Conservatives think of human behavior in terms of emotion, clear images of right and wrong, and compelling narratives. Therefore conservatives study marketing. Donald Trump, the master of marketing and branding knew what he was doing when he repeatedly told the American public: "When I was young, we were always winning things in this country. We'd win with trade, we'd win with wars." There's going to be so much winning, you're gonna be sick and tired of winning." The appeal of Donald Trump's campaign narrative, like the appeal of Ronald Reagan's campaign narrative in 1984, was more emotional and narrative than logical reasoning. But both proved to be winning campaign strategies because their emotion and narrative appeal reinforced some conservative hierarchies of values.

Table 9.61: Lakoff's Hierarchy of Conservative Values

Right over Wrong	God over Man
Man over Nature	Strong over Weak
Rich over Poor	Employers over Employees
America over Other Countries	Western Christian Civilization over Non-Western Civilizations
Men over Women	White over Non-white

9.70 | Is Ideology A Good Influence or A Bad Influence?

It is not easy to provide simple definitions of complex terms such as conservatism and liberalism and describe their role in American government and politics. It is even harder to assess whether their role is positive or negative, whether ideologies are good or bad influences on government and politics. It is hard to objectively—that is, neutrally or without bias—assess an ideology's role because ideologies are prescriptive rather than descriptive terms. A **prescriptive** term is a normative or value-laden term. A prescriptive term is one that has a value judgment about its worth, whether it is desirable or undesirable, whether it is good or bad. A **descriptive** term is not a normative or value-laden term. The following illustrates descriptive and prescriptive statements that are (mostly) familiar to politics.

Descriptive Statements

Democracy is government of the people, by the people, and for the people.
Freedom is the right to do what you want.
Equality means treating everyone the same.
Conservatism is an ideology that values social order more than individual liberty.
Liberalism is an ideology that values individual liberty more than social order.
Socialism is an ideology that values equality.
Terrorism is the political use of violence.

Prescriptive Statements

Democracy is a good form of government.
Freedom is preferable to slavery.
Chocolate is better than vanilla.
Conservatism is preferable to liberalism.
Liberalism is preferable to conservatism.
Capitalism is a good economic system.
Socialism threatens freedom.
Violence is not a legitimate means to a political end.
Terrorism is unacceptable.

There are too many lawyers and laws in modern American society.

It is hard to *objectively* assess conservatism and liberalism because ideologies are commonly considered prescriptive rather than descriptive terms. A prescriptive term is a normative or value-laden term. A descriptive term defines or explains without making a value judgment about worth. However, people think of conservative or liberal or socialist in prescriptive terms, as good or bad rather than merely as labels that describe *different* sets of beliefs and programs for acting on them. As a result, candidates for public office, government officials, public policies, and political events are viewed through prescriptive, ideological lenses. Capitalism and democracy are considered good; other economic and political systems are considered bad. Similarly, the Republican and Democratic parties are not merely described, they are assessed as good or bad based on ideological or policy preferences.

Prescriptive terms are biased ***either for or against something***. This makes it harder to study them objectively. This is particularly the case with terrorism. Studying terrorism is complicated because terrorism is a prescriptive, value-laden term. To call a person a terrorist, or to describe an action as terrorism, is to condemn the person or the action. A descriptive definition of democracy is that it is a political system where people control their government through elections or other means. But democracy is commonly used in a prescriptive sense: "Democracy is a good (or bad) form of government." To say that democracy is a good form of government is a positive normative statement. To say that democracy is a bad form of government is a negative normative statement. Attaching prescriptive labels to political terms sometimes makes it harder, not easier, to understand what is being described. The fact that the terms liberal and conservative, which are so important for understanding American politics and government, are so often used as prescriptive labels that are attached to individuals, parties, or policies can make it harder to understand American government and politics. When thinking about ideology, it is important to try to separate the descriptive thinking about the terms from the prescriptive or normative assessment of whether the ideology is good or bad. Doing so will increase the likelihood that ideology—the systems of beliefs and policies for acting on them—can increase understanding of government and politics and the public policies that emerge from the process.

Take the 20 question "Political Typology" quiz and then think about it! Are your Red or Blue?
http://people-press.org/typology/quiz/

> **Think About It!**
> One way to think about *the government*, the *size* of government, and *big* government, is by looking at the number of government employees. The <u>Office of Personnel Management</u> employment data indicate that the federal government has about 2.7 million civilian employees and that in 2017 there were 21.8 million total government employees. The following are the U.S. executive departments with the largest number of employees in 2014. What do they suggest about what the federal government does?
>
> | The Department of Defense | 723,000 |
> | The Department of Veterans Affairs | 340,000 |
> | The Department of Homeland Security | 186,000 |
> | The Department of Justice | 114,000 |

9.80 | Summary

An ideology is a set of beliefs (or values) and a plan for acting on them. Ideologies can be useful because they provide a way for people to try to makes sense of the political world. Ideologies can increase understanding of politics, government, and public policy by simplifying the political world. For instance, individuals and ideas and public policies can be organized as either conservative or liberal. This simplifies the world of politics. Ideology can also inspire or motivate people to organize to act together to achieve desirable goals. In this sense, ideologies unite individuals with shared beliefs. But ideologies can also complicate politics. Ideologies divide people and create an "us" versus "them" framework that can make it harder for government to do what governments are created to do: solve the problems that the people put on the government agenda. Ideologies also complicate the world by strengthening the tendency to hold tightly to closely held beliefs despite empirical evidence to the contrary.

Chapter 9: Key Terms

Ideology
Traditional conservatism
Modern conservatism
Liberal
Classical liberalism
Terrorism
Libertarianism
Socialism
Communism
Anarchism
Feminism
Environmentalism
Fundamentalism

Chapter 9: Study Questions
1. What is the role of religion in ideology?
2. What is ideology?
3. How do liberalism, conservatism, and libertarianism likely influence thinking about stem cell research?
4. Briefly discuss the problems with the conservative and liberal labels.
5. Is ideology good or bad?
6. Describe some of the differences between conservatism and libertarianism.

9.9 | Additional Resources

The Center for Voting and Democracy has links to articles related to elections and democracy including voter turnout, links to organizations and ideas related to reforming the electoral system, and analysis of electoral returns. www.fairvote.org/

The World's smallest political quiz uses ten questions to place a person on the economic and social ideological spectrums. http://www.theadvocates.org/quiz

The Gallup Organization provides historical and current information about American public opinion. www.gallup.com

9.91 | In the Library

Carey, George W., et al. 1998. *Freedom & Virtue: The Conservative Libertarian Debate.* Intercollegiate Studies Institute.

Erikson, Robert. 2006. *American Public Opinion: Its Origins, Content, and Impact.* Longman.

Flanigan, William. 2006. *Political Behavior of the American Electorate.* Washington, D.C.: CQ Press.

Goddard, Taegan D. 1998. *You Won - Now What? How Americans Can Make Democracy Work from City Hall to the White House.* Scribner.

Lakoff, George. 2016. *Moral Politics: How Liberals and Conservatives Think.* 3rd Edition. Chicago: University of Chicago Press.

Mara. Gerald M. 2008. *The Civic Conversations of Thucydides and Plato: Classical Political Philosophy and the Limits of Democracy.* State University of New York Press.

Meese. Edwin. 2005. *The Heritage Guide to the Constitution.* Regnery Publishing.

Stone, Deborah. 2008. *The Samaritan's Dilemma: Should Government Help Your Neighbor?* Nation Books.

Zinn, Howard. 2001. *A People's History of the United States: 1492 to Present.* Harper.

---

[1] Kenneth M. Dolbeare and Linda J. Medcalf. 1988. *American Ideologies Today.* New York: Random House, Inc. p.3.

[2] http://teachingamericanhistory.org/library/document/jefferson-to-thomas-law/

---

[3] In *The Emerging Republican Majority* (New Rochelle, NY: Arlington House, 1969), Kevin P. Phillips predicted the rightward movement in American national politics based on his experience working with President Nixon's 1968 campaign.

[4] http://www.law.cornell.edu/uscode/uscode18/usc_sup_01_18_10_I_20_118.html

[5] See http://blogs.abcnews.com/thenote/2010/06/what-are-sharron-angles-2nd-amendment-remedies-to-reids-oppression.html

Tea Party Protest, Washington, D.C., September 12, 2009

10.0 | Political Participation

The above image of a large public demonstration in Washington, D.C., is part of a great tradition of mass public participation in politics that goes back to the colonial days. Do you participate in politics? If so, how have you participated in politics? Political participation in a democracy includes voting—but also much more than just voting. One of the ironies of modern American politics is that it is easier than ever to participate in politics in the digital age, but there are also worries that the public is becoming more disengaged or disillusioned about civic engagement in politics as a way to solve the kinds of problems that people expect government to solve.

> **Think About It!**
> What does taking the electronic pulse of civic engagement indicate about the health of American democracy?
> http://www.pewinternet.org/2013/04/25/civic-engagement-in-the-digital-age/

Stated in the most basic terms, the power problem is about government authority over individuals: why can the government, the *community*, or the *majority* tell someone that they can and cannot do—and punish them if they disobey the law? Democratic theory answers this question by describing democracy as a form of *self-government*—people agree to govern themselves as an act of self-restraint or self-control. Government of, by, and for the people requires the participation of an informed, active, and engaged citizenry. The term civics education refers to a movement to increase public information about the Constitution, the way the political system works, the way government works, and civil discourse—the ways to talk about divisive or controversial issues that emphasize working toward the formulation of solutions. This chapter examines how voting, elections, and campaigns organize participation in politics and government. Political participation is not limited to voting in elections. It includes a broad range of individual and collective action. The term **civic engagement** refers to a public that is actively engaged in politics and government. It includes voting, participating in campaigns, volunteerism, writing letters to editors, and contacting government officials or working with local government advisory boards. The chapter begins with voting and other forms of political participation. It concludes by providing resources for "getting" civics education and by providing examples of how to "do" civic engagement. The belief in American Exceptionalism is not limited to conservatives. The National Council for the Social Studies is an organization whose mission is "Preparing Students for College, Career, and Civic Life." It issued a 2007 report that seeks to perpetuate "An Idea Called America" by promoting civic competence, active citizenry, and participatory democracy through public education about the content, skills, and values associated with American civic engagement.[1]

10.1 | Voting

Voting is just one form of political participation. There are many other ways to participate in politics: writing a letter to a newspaper; posting to a Web site; making a campaign contribution; contacting a legislator; running for office; campaigning for a candidate; or lobbying government. But voting is the form of political participation that is most closely associated with meeting the responsibilities of citizenship because voting is an act of self-government. Voters select government officials to represent them and cast votes for or against issues that are on the ballot. There are many other forms of political participation: running for office, making campaign contributions, working for a party or candidate or issue, lobbying, or contacting government officials about an issue or problem which interests you. Even non-voting—the intentional refusal to participate in an election as a protest against the political system or the candidate or party choices that are available— can be a form of political participation. All these forms of participation are components of political science measures of how democratic a political system is.

10.11 | *Expanding the right to vote*

One of the most important developments in the American system of government has been the expansion of the right to vote. Over time, politics has become much more democratic. The Founders provided for a rather limited right to vote because they were skeptical of direct democracy and the ability of the masses to make good decisions about public policy or government leaders. In fact, the Founders were divided on how much political participation, including voting, was desirable. The Federalists generally advocated limited participation where only white male property owners could vote. A leading Federalist, Alexander Hamilton, advocated a system of representative government that resembled "a natural aristocracy" that was run by "gentlemen of fortune and ability."[2]

The Anti-federalists advocated broader participation. The Anti-federalist author writing under the name *The Federal Farmer* defined democratic participation as full and equal representation: "full and equal representation is that in which the interests, feelings, opinions, and views of the people are collected, in such a manner as they would be were all the people assembled." The Anti-federalist *Republicus* advocated an American democracy that provided for "fair and equal representation," which he defined as a condition where "every member of the union have a freedom of suffrage and that every equal number of people have an equal number of representatives."

Over time the right to vote was greatly expanded and the political system became much more democratic. Abraham Lincoln's *Gettysburg Address* is a memorable political speech because of what it said about democracy and equality. Lincoln famously defined democracy as government *of* the people, government *by* the people, and government *for* the people. He also brought equality back into American political rhetoric by emphasizing the political importance of equality that was first stated so memorably in the Declaration of Independence. The Declaration of Independence asserted that all men were created equal and endowed with unalienable rights. The Constitution did not include equality as a political value. It provided for slavery and allowed the states to limit the right to vote. The right to vote was expanded by constitutional amendments and by legislation. The constitutional changes included the following amendments:

> "The vote is the most powerful instrument ever devised by man for breaking down injustice and destroying the terrible walls which imprison men because they are different from other men."
>
> Lyndon B. Johnson
>
> "Always vote for principle, though you may vote alone, and you may cherish the sweetest reflection that your vote is never lost."
>
> John Quincy Adams

- The 14th Amendment (1868) prohibited states from denying to any person with their jurisdiction the equal protection of the laws.

- The 15th Amendment (1870) prohibited states from denying the right to vote on the basis of race.
- The 17th Amendment (1913) provided for direct election of Senators.
- The 19th Amendment (1920) gave women the right to vote.
- The 24th Amendment (1964) eliminated the Poll Tax.
- The 26th Amendment (1971) lowered voting age to 18.

One of the most important *statutory* expansions of the right to vote is the Voting Rights Act of 1965. It made racial discrimination in voting a violation of federal law; specifically, outlawing the use of literacy tests to qualify to register to vote, and providing for federal registration of voters in areas that had less than 50% of eligible minority voters registered. The Act also provided for Department of Justice oversight of registration, and required the Department to approve any change in voting law in districts that had used a "device" to limit voting and in which less than 50% of the population was registered to vote in 1964. The Civil Rights Act of 1964 is a landmark civil rights statute that also expanded the right to vote by limiting racial discrimination in voting.

In addition to these government actions, the political system also developed in ways that expanded the right to vote and made the system more democratic. The emergence of political parties fundamentally changed the American political system. Political parties changed the way the president is chosen by effectively making the popular vote, not the Electoral College, determine who wins the presidency. There have been notable exceptions to the rule that the candidate who receives the most popular votes wins the election (the presidential elections of 1824, 1876, 1888) and 2000), but modern political culture includes the expectation that the people select the president.

10.12 | *How democratic Is the United States?*

Democracy is a widely accepted value in the U.S. and elsewhere in the world. As more nations adopt democratic political systems, political scientists are paying attention to *whether* a country's political system is democratic as well as *how democratic* the political system is. Democracy is not an either/or value. There are degrees of democracy: a political system can be more or less democratic. Non-governmental organizations such as Freedom House and publications such as *The Economist* have developed comparative measures of how democratic a country's political system is. *The Economist* ranks the U.S. as 17th in the world.[3] This is a surprisingly low ranking for a nation that extols the value of democracy and promotes it worldwide. The low ranking on democracy is due to several factors:

- Voter Turnout. The U.S. has comparatively low rates of voter turn-out. European countries, for example, have much higher rates of voting.
- A Presidential System. The U.S. has developed into a system of presidential governance system where executive power is dominant rather than the more democratic legislative or parliamentary systems.
- National Security. The U.S. has developed extensive provisions for secrecy and national security and emergency powers which are hard to reconcile with democratic values.

10.13 | *Voter Turnout*

Voter turnout is the proportion of the voting-age public that participates in an election. Voter turnout is a function of a number of *individual* factors and *institutional* factors. Voter turnout is low in the United States. What does low mean? In many elections, less than half of the eligible voters participate in the election. The graph below shows the turnout rate for presidential elections from 1960 to 2008.

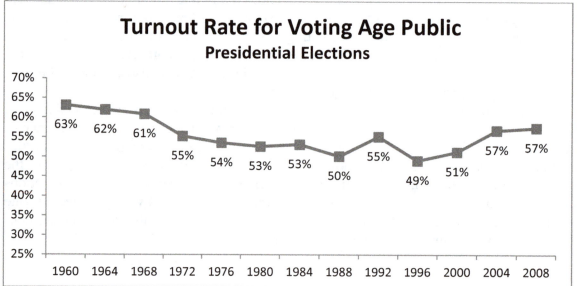

Think About It!

Should the U.S. try to increase voter turnout by either paying people to vote or by fining (or otherwise sanctioning) eligible voters who do not vote?

Voter turnout is also low compared to other western industrial democracies. Why is U.S. voter turnout low in absolute numbers (less than half) and comparatively? Some of the explanations focus on the individual while others focus on the electoral system.

10.14 | *Individual Explanations*

The individual explanations focus on an individual's motivations. The two main models of individual explanations for voting behavior are the rational choice model and the civic duty model.

The **rational choice** model of voting was developed by Anthony Downs, who argued that individuals are self-interested actors who use a cost-benefit analysis to determine whether it is in their self-interest to vote.[4] According to the rational choice model, a person's decision whether to vote is based on an individual's assessment of whether the vote will affect the outcome of the election, the expected benefit of voting and not voting, and the sense of civic duty (the personal gratification or satisfaction from voting. The rational choice model is based on the assumptions in economic models of human behavior.

The **civic duty** model describes non-material, non-rational incentives for voting. According to the civic duty model, a person votes out of a sense of responsibility to the political unit, or a commitment to democratic government and the obligations and duties as well as the rights of citizens to maintain self-government. Patriotic values and the commitment to the community or society are familiar expressions of civic duty.

In order to vote, the probability of voting, times the benefit of vote, plus the sense of duty to vote must outweigh the cost (in time, effort, and money) of voting. As the probability of a vote mattering in a federal election almost always approaches zero (because more than 100,000,000 votes are cast), duty becomes the most important element in motivating people to vote. According to the rational choice model, a person will vote if they think it is worth it; a person will not vote if they think it is not worth it. According to this cost-benefit ratio, it may be rational not to vote. An individual with a greater commitment to civic duty or responsibility will weigh the relative costs differently and may conclude that voting is worth it.

The concept of political efficacy is central to understanding voting behavior. **Political efficacy** is the belief that one's participation matters, that one's decision to vote really makes a difference. What is the likelihood that one vote will matter in a presidential election where more than 100, 000,000 votes are cast? The rational choice model suggests that voter turnout in the United States is low because individuals have thought about whether or not to vote and simply concluded that it is not worth their time and effort and money to vote.

Demographic factors affect whether or not someone turns out to vote. Demographic factors that are related to voter turn-out include income, education, race and ethnicity, gender, and age. Wealthy citizens have higher rates of voter turnout than poor citizens. *Income* has an effect on voter turnout. Wealthy citizens have higher levels of political efficacy and believe that the political works and their votes will count. On the other hand, people that make less money and have less wealth are less likely to believe that the political system will respond to their demands as expressed in elections. *Race* is also related to voter turnout. Whites vote at higher rates than minorities. *Gender* is also related to voter turnout. Women voted at lower levels than men for many years after gaining suffrage with the passage of the 19th Amendment in 1920, but today women vote at much higher levels than men do. *Age* is also important. There is a strong relationship between age and voter turnout. Older people vote at higher levels than younger people do, which helps explain why candidates for office and government officials are so sensitive to issues that affect seniors (such as reducing spending on Social Security or Medicare).

Think About It!

What should you expect when you show up at the polls to vote?

"What to Expect Before Heading to the Polls"

http://www.npr.org/templates/story/story.php?storyId=96538073

10.15 | *System Explanations*

The system explanations focus on aspects of the political system that affect voter turnout. These system factors include voter registration laws, the fact that elections are usually held on one day during the week, the large number of elections in our federal system, and the two-party system.

Eligibility. A person's eligibility for voting is provided for in the U.S. Constitution, state constitutions, and state and federal statutes. The Constitution states that suffrage cannot be denied on grounds of race or color (Fifteenth Amendment), sex (Nineteenth Amendment) or age for citizens eighteen years or older (Twenty-sixth Amendment). Beyond these basic qualifications, the states have a great deal of authority to determine eligibility and to run elections. Some states bar convicted criminals, especially felons, from voting for a fixed period of time or indefinitely. The National Conference of State Legislatures reports on felon voting rights in the states. The Sentencing Project reports that 5.8 million Americans are disenfranchised, denied the right to vote, because of a felony conviction. State felon voting laws have a disproportionate impact on African-Americans: one out of 13 African-Americans are ineligible to vote because of a felony conviction.

Voter Registration. Voter registration is the requirement that a person check in with some central registry in order to be allowed to vote in an election. In the U.S., the individual is responsible for registering to vote—sometimes well before the actual election. Furthermore, each state has different voter registration laws and moving from one state to another state requires reregistering to vote.[5] These registration laws reduce voter turnout. In some countries, the government registers eligible voters and actually fines eligible voters who do not perform their civic duty to vote in an election.

Voter Fatigue. Voter fatigue is the term for the apathy that the electorate can experience when they are required to vote too often in too many elections. The U.S. has a large number of government units (around 90,000) and Americans elect a large number of government officials—around one for every 442 citizens. Having a large number of elections—in the U.S. there is always an election somewhere—can reduce voter turnout.

The Two-party System. Finally, the two-party system can contribute to low voter turnout by increasing the sense that an individual's vote does not matter very much. In two-party systems, the parties tend to be primarily interested in winning elections. In order to win elections, the parties tend to compete for moderate voters with middle-of-the-road appeals because most of the voters are by definition centrists rather than extremists. This can be a winning electoral strategy, but it sometimes leaves voters thinking there isn't much real difference between the two major parties which compete by "muddling in the middle." Why vote if there is no real choice between the two candidates or parties? The two major American political parties tend to be interested primarily in winning elections, and only secondarily in advocating ideologies or issues. In contrast, countries with multiple party systems are more likely to have *rational* political parties. As used here, a rational party is one whose primary goal is advancing ideas, issues, or ideology; winning an election is secondary.

Listen to Southern Democrat Huey Long's critique of the Democratic and Republican Parties in the 1940 presidential election. George C. Wallace, the former Governor of Alabama and 1968 presidential candidate of the American Independent Party, famously said of the Democratic and Republican candidates for president: there is "not a dime's worth of difference between them."[6] Does it matter whether one votes for a Republican or Democrat when there really isn't much choice in a two-party system where the major parties don't differ much on the issues?

Election Tuesday? Why does the U.S. have elections on a Tuesday? The reason for Tuesday elections goes back to the days of horses and buggies when Monday elections would require traveling on the Sabbath and Wednesday was market day. So in 1845 Congress provided for Tuesday elections. Would changing from one-weekday elections to two-day weekend elections increase voter turnout by making it easier for people to fit voting into busy family and work schedules? It has in some countries. The U.S. has comparatively low rates of voter turnout but bills to change to weekend voting die in committee in Congress. Some states now allow early voting and a significant percentage of votes are now cast before prior to the day of the election. Should technology such as electronic voting be used to increase voter turnout?

10.2 | Elections

Elections are one way for people to participate in the selection of government officials. Elections also provide a means of holding government officials accountable for the way they use their power. Participation and accountability are two of the main reasons why elections are a measure of *whether* a political system is democratic and *how democratic* it is. In most cases, it is not as useful to describe a political system as democratic or non-democratic as it is to determine how democratic it is. Many countries of the world have political systems that are more or less democratic. Some countries are more democratic than others. The existence of free, open, and competitive elections is one measure of whether a country's political system is democratic.

10.21 | *Three Main Purposes*

Elections serve three main purposes in representative democracies (or republics, like the U.S.):

- **Selecting government officials**. The most basic purpose of an election in a democratic system is to select government officials. Elections provide an opportunity for the people to choose their government officials. The fact that voters choose their representatives is one of the ways that democratic or republican systems of government solve the power problem. Voting is part of self-government.

- **Informing government officials**. Elections also provide government officials with information about what the people what, what they expect, and what they think about government. Elections provide an opportunity for the voice of the people to be expressed and heard. Elections thus serve as one of the ways to regularly measure public opinion about issues, political parties, candidates, and the way that government officials are doing their jobs.

- **Holding government accountable**. Elections provide regular or periodic mechanisms for holding elected representatives, other government officials, and even political parties accountable for their actions while in power. The Founders of the U.S. system of republican government provided for elections as part of the system of checks and balances.

The political scientists who study voting and elections describe two theories of elections. One theory is the elections are **forward looking** in the sense that an election provides government officials with information about which direction the public wants the government to go on major issues. The second theory is that elections are **backward looking** in the sense that an election provides government officials with feedback about what has been done—in effect, an election is a referendum on government officials or the political party in power.

10.22 | *Too Much of a Good Thing?*

In the U.S., voters go to the polls to elect national government officials at all levels of government: national, state, and local. Voters indirectly elect the President (through selection by the Electoral College). Voters directly elect the members of the House of Representatives and the Senate. Voters directly elect state government officials such as governors, legislators, the heads of various executive departments, and in many states judges. And voters elect local government officials such as county commissioners, school board members, mayors and city council members, and members of special governing districts such as airport authorities. In addition, most states provide for referendums, elections where voters decide ballot issues. With more than 90,000 total government units in the U.S., elections are being held somewhere for some office or for some ballot measure almost all the time. Across the whole country, more than one million elected offices are filled in every electoral cycle.

10.23 | *Initiative and Referendum*

Elections are not limited to those that involve the selection of government officials. In the U.S., many state and local governments provide for ballot initiatives and referendum. A ballot initiative is an election where the voters decide whether to support or reject a proposed law. A referendum is an election where the voters go to the polls to approve or reject a law that has been passed by the state legislature or a local government body. The people vote for or against issues such as state constitutional amendments, county charters, or city charter provisions and amendments.[7]

The increased use of initiatives and referenda in states such as California has raised questions about whether direct democracy is preferable to indirect or representative democracy. In a representative democracy, the elected representatives of the people make the laws; in a direct democracy, the people make the laws. The recent trend toward initiatives and referendum has attracted the attention of people who study American politics. One organization that monitors and reports on what is happening in the states is the Ballot Initiative Strategy Center. This Center acts as a "nerve center" for "progressive" or liberal ballot initiatives in the states. The Initiative and Referendum Institute (IRI) at the University of Southern California studies ballot initiatives and referendums in the U.S. and elsewhere in the world. Technology has made it possible to use this form of direct democracy to make the political system more democratic by allowing the public more opportunities to participate in the adoption of the laws that government them.

10.24 | *Regulating Elections*

Elections are regulated by both federal and state law. The U.S. Constitution provides some basic provisions for the conduct of elections in Articles I and II. Article I, Section Four provides that "[t]he Times, Places and Manner of holding Elections for Senators and Representatives, shall be prescribed in each State by the Legislature thereof; but the Congress may at any time by Law make or alter such Regulations, except as to the Place of Chusing Senators." The 13th, 14th, and 15th Amendments also regulate elections by prohibiting states from discriminating on the basis of race or gender. The 15th Amendment states that the "right of citizens of the United States to vote shall not be denied or abridged by the United States or by any State on account of race, color, or previous condition of servitude."

However, most aspects of electoral law are regulated by the states. State laws provide for the conduct of primary elections (which are party elections to determine who the party's nominee will be in the general election); the eligibility of voters (beyond the basic requirements established in the U.S. Constitution); the running of each state's Electoral College; and the running of state and local elections.

10.25 | *Primary and General Elections*

Election campaigns are organized efforts to persuade voters to choose one candidate over the other candidates who are competing for the same office. Effective campaigns harness resources such as volunteers; money (campaign contributions); the support of other candidates; and endorsements of other government officials, interest groups and party organizations. Effective campaigns use these resources to communicate messages to voters.

Political parties have played a central role in election campaigns for most of the nation's history. However, during the last 30 years there has been an increase in candidate-centered campaigns and, more recently, independent organizations (such as super-PACS). Candidates who used to rely on political parties for information about voter preferences and attitudes now conduct their own public opinion polls and communicate directly with the public.

Before candidates can seek election to a partisan political office, they must get the nomination of their party in the **primary election.** A campaign for a non-partisan office (one where the candidates run without a party designation on the ballot), does not require getting the party nomination. A primary election is an election to determine who will be the party's nominee for office. A general election is the election to actually determine who wins the office. A primary election is typically an intra-party election: the members of a party vote to determine who gets to run with the party label in the general election. A general election is typically an inter-party election: candidates from different parties compete to determine who wins the office. Most state and local political parties in the United States use primary elections (abet with widely varying rules and regulations) to determine the slate of candidates a party will offer in the general election. More than forty states use only primary elections to determine the nomination of candidates, and primaries play a prominent role in all the other states.

There are four basic types of primary elections: **closed primaries, open primaries, modified closed primaries,** and **modified open primaries.** Closed primaries are primary elections where voters are required to register with a specific party before the election and are only able to vote in the party's election for which they are registered. Open primary elections allow anyone who is eligible to vote in the primary election to vote for a party's selection. In modified closed primaries, the state party decides who is allowed to vote in its primary. In modified open primaries, independent voters and registered party members are allowed to vote in the nomination contest.

10.3 | National Elections

The United States has a presidential system of government. In presidential systems, the executive and the legislature are elected separately. Article I of the U.S. Constitution requires that the presidential election occur on the same day throughout the country every four years. Elections for the House of Representatives and the Senate can be held at different times. Congressional elections take place every two years. The years when there are congressional and presidential elections are called presidential election years. The congressional election years when a president is not elected are called midterm elections.

The Constitution states that members of the United States House of Representatives must be at least 25 years old, a citizen of the United States for at least seven years, and be a (legal) inhabitant of the state they represent. Senators must be at least 30 years old, a citizen of the United States for at least nine years, and be a (legal) inhabitant of the state they represent. The president must be at least 35 years old, a natural born citizen of the United States and a resident in the United States for at least fourteen years. It is the responsibility of state legislatures to regulate the qualifications for a candidate appearing on a ballot paper. "Getting on the ballot" is based on candidate's performances in previous elections.

PRESIDENT AND VICE PRESIDENT		
PRESIDENTE Y VICE PRESIDENTE		
PRESIDENT AND VICE PRESIDENT +		
PRESIDENTE Y VICE PRESIDENTE +		
(Vote for One)		
(Vote por Uno)		
John McCain Sarah Palin	REP	← ◀
Barack Obama Joe Biden	DEM	← ◀
Gloria La Riva Eugene Puryear	PSL	← ◀
Chuck Baldwin Darrell Castle	CPF	← ◀
Gene Amondson Leroy Pletten	PRO	← ◀
Bob Barr Wayne A. Root	LBT	← ◀
Thomas Robert Stevens Alden Link	OBJ	← ◀
James Harris Alyson Kennedy	SWP	← ◀
Cynthia McKinney Rosa Clemente	GRE	← ◀
Alan Keyes Brian Rohrbough	AIP	← ◀
Ralph Nader Matt Gonzalez	ECO	← ◀

2008 Presidential Ballot in Palm Beach County, Florida

10.31 | *Presidential Elections*

The president and vice-president run as a team or ticket. The team typically tries for balance. A balanced ticket is one where the president and the vice-president are chosen to achieve a politically desirable balance. The political balance can be:

- Geographical. Geographical balance is when the President and Vice-president are selected from different regions of the country—balancing north and south, or east and west—in order to appeal to voters in those regions of the country.
- Ideological. Ideological balance is when the President and Vice-president come from different ideological wings of the party. The two major parties have liberal and conservative wings, and the ideological balance broadens the appeal of the ticket.
- Experience. A ticket with balanced political experience is one that includes one candidate with extensive experience in federal government and the other a political newcomer. Sometimes political experience (being a Washington insider, for instance) is considered an advantage; sometimes it is considered a handicap. Incumbency can be a plus or a minus. Balance can try to have it both ways.
- Demographics. Demographic balance refers to having a ticket with candidates who have different age, race, gender, or religion. Once again, demographic balance is intended to broaden the ticket's appeal.

The presidential candidate for each party is selected through a **presidential primary**. Incumbent presidents can be challenged in their party's primary elections, but this is rare. The last incumbent President to not seek a second term was Lyndon B. Johnson. President Johnson was mired in the Vietnam War at a time when that war was very unpopular. The presidential primary is actually a series of staggered electoral contests in which members of a party choose delegates to attend the party's national convention which officially nominates the party's presidential candidate. Primary elections were first used to choose delegates in 1912. Prior to this, the delegates were chosen by a variety of methods, including selection by party elites. The use of primaries increased in the early decades of the 20th Century then they fell out of favor until anti-war protests at the 1968 Democratic National Convention.

Police attacking protestors at the 1968 Democratic National Convention in Chicago, IL

Currently, more than eighty percent of states use a primary election to determine delegates to the national convention. These elections do not occur on one day: the primary election process takes many months. The primary election process is long, drawn-out, complex, and has no parallel in any other nation in the world. The presidential candidates begin fundraising efforts, start campaigning, and announce their candidacy months in advance of the first primary election.

It is purely historical accident that New Hampshire and Iowa have the first primary elections and are thus the focus on candidate attention for months prior to their January elections. New Hampshire had an early primary election in 1972 and has held the place of the first primary since that time. Iowa's primary is before New Hampshire, although the state uses a **caucus** to select delegates. Generally, the Iowa caucus narrows the field of candidates by demonstrating a candidate's appeal among party supporters, while New Hampshire tests the appeal of the front-runners from each party with the general public.

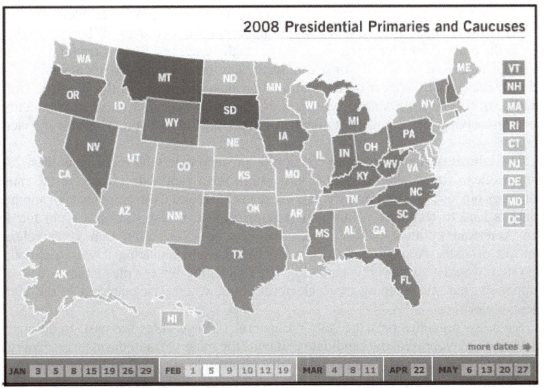

Dates of primary elections in 2008.

The unprecedented president. The unconventional president. During the campaign he broke all the rules. He ignored all the conventional wisdom about what to do and not to do to have a successful campaign. He even broke the eleventh commandment—Ronald Reagan's commandment "Thou shalt not speak ill of another Republican." And he called Americans losers?

10.32 | *The Electoral College*

The president is not directly elected by the people. The popular vote does not actually determine who wins the presidency. When the voters in a state go to the polls to cast their votes for president (and vice president), they are actually voting for members of the Electoral College. The winner of a presidential election is the candidate who receives a majority vote of the members of the Electoral College.

With the possible exception of the Federal Reserve Board, the Electoral College may be the least-understood government body in the U.S. system of government. Each member of the Electoral College cast her or his vote for a presidential and vice-presidential candidate. Each state's members of the Electoral College are chosen by the state political party at that states party convention. The state parties choose party loyalists to be the party's members of the Electoral College if that party wins the popular vote in the state. This is why the members of the Electoral College almost always vote for the presidential candidate who wins the popular vote in that state. On rare occasion, a "faithless" Elector will not vote for the candidate who won the popular vote in their state. When voters in a state go to the polls to vote for a president, they actually each cast their votes for a slate of electors that is chosen by a party or a candidate. The presidential and vice-presidential candidate names usually appear on the ballot rather than the names of the Electors. Until the passage of the Twelfth Amendment in 1804, the runner-up in a presidential election (the person receiving the second most number of Electoral College votes) became the vice-president.

The winner of the presidential election is the candidate who receives at least 270 Electoral College votes. The fact that it is possible for a candidate to receive the most popular votes but lose the election by receiving fewer Electoral College votes than another candidate is hard to reconcile with democratic principles. It also does not seem fair in modern American political culture which includes an expectation that voters chose government officials. Abolishing the Electoral College and replacing it with a national direct system would also prevent a candidate from receiving fewer votes nationwide than their opponent, but still winning more electoral votes, which last occurred in the 2000 Presidential election.

State law regulates how the state's Electoral College votes are cast. In all states except Maine and Nebraska, the candidate that wins the most votes in the state receives all its Electoral College votes (a "winner takes all" system). From 1969 in Maine, and from 1991 in Nebraska, two electoral votes are awarded based on the winner of the statewide election, and the rest (two in Maine, three in Nebraska) go to the highest vote-winner in each of the state's congressional districts.

The Electoral College is criticized for a variety of reasons:

- It is undemocratic. The people do not actually elect a president; the president is selected by the Electoral College.
- It is unequal. The number of a state's Electors is equal to the state's congressional delegation. This system gives less populous states a disproportionate vote in the Electoral College because each state has two senators regardless of population (and therefore two members of the Electoral College). The minimum number of state

Electors is three. Wyoming and California have the same number of senators. Wyoming has a population of 493,782 and 3 EC votes, 164,594 people per EC vote. California has a population of 33,871,648 and 55 EC votes, 615,848 people per EC vote.

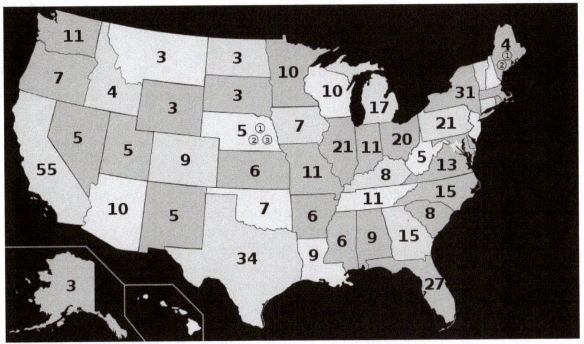

Map of Electoral College Votes

- It spotlights swing states. The Electoral College system distorts campaigning because the voters in swing states determine the outcome of the election. As a result, voters who live in states that are not competitive are ignored by the political campaigns. Abolishing the Electoral College and treating the entire country as one district for presidential elections eliminate the campaign focus on swing states.
- It is biased against national candidates. The Electoral College also works against candidates whose base of support is spread around the country rather than in a state or region of the country which would enable them to win the popular vote in one or more states. This is what happened to Ross Perot. In 1992, Perot won 18.9% of the national vote, but received no Electoral College votes because his broad appeal across the country did not include strength in one or a few state.

Despite these long-standing criticisms of the Electoral College, abolishing it is unlikely because doing so would require a constitutional amendment—and ratification of a constitutional amendment requires three-quarters of the state legislature to support it. The less populous states are not likely to support an amendment to abolish the Electoral College in favor of direct popular election of the president because doing so would decrease the voting power of the less populous states. Small states such as Wyoming and North Dakota would lose power and more populous states such as California and New York would gain power.

10.33 | *Congressional Elections*

Congressional elections take place every two years. Each member of the House of Representatives is elected for a two-year term. Each Senator is elected for a six-year term. About one-third of the Senate is elected in each congressional election. Until the Seventeenth Amendment to the United States Constitution in 1913, Senators were elected by state legislatures, not the electorate of states.

2010 Florida Senate Campaign Debate: (From L to R: Marco Rubio, Charlie Crist, Kendrick Meek)

10.34 | *House Elections*

Elections to the United States House of Representatives occur every two years on the first Tuesday after November 1 in even years. If a member dies in office or resigns before the term has been completed, a special House election is held to fill the seat. House elections are first-past-the-post elections—meaning the candidate who gets the most votes wins the election regardless of whether that person receives a majority of the votes cast in the election. The winner is the one who receives a plurality of the votes. Plurality means the most votes. It is not necessary for the winner to receive a majority (50% plus one) of the votes.

Every two years congressional elections coincide with presidential elections. Congressional elections that do not coincide with presidential elections are called mid-term elections—because they occur in the middle of a President's four-year term of office. When congressional elections occur in the same year as a presidential election, the party whose presidential candidate wins the election usually increases the number of congressional seats it holds. This is one of the unofficial linkages between presidential and congressional elections. The president and members of Congress are officially elected separately, but some voters go to the polls to vote for or against Republicans and Democrats so the president's popularity has an impact on congressional elections.

In 2010, Allen West (R) challenged incumbent and Ron Klein (D) in Florida District 22. West emphasized his military experience. A neighborhood campaign supporter produced a sign which framed the choice as "The Wimp or the Warrior."

There is a historical pattern that the incumbent president's party loses seats in mid-term elections. In mid-term elections, the president is not on the ballot. The president's party usually loses seats in mid-term elections. One reason for mid-term losses is the president's popularity has slipped during the two years in office. Another cause of mid-term election losses is the fact that voter turnout is lower in mid-term elections, and members of the president's party are less likely to vote in an election when *their* president is not on the ballot. These patterns of voting behavior illustrate the partisan linkages between congressional and presidential elections.

10.35 | *Gerrymandering*

Over time, congressional districts have become far less competitive. Congressional districts are drawn to protect individual incumbents and political parties. Another way to describe this is that congressional districts are drawn to create safe districts. A safe district is one that is not competitive; it is a safe district for the Republican Party or a safe district for the Democratic Party because the district boundaries are drawn to ensure that it contains a majority of Republicans or Democrats. One consequence of drawing safe districts is a reduction in voter choice. The Constitution requires that congressional districts be reapportioned after every census. This means that reapportionment or redistricting is done every ten years. The reapportionment is done by each state. In most cases, the political party with a majority in the state legislature controls redistricting. The fact that either one or the other major party controls the reapportionment encourages partisan gerrymandering.

Gerrymandering is drawing electoral district lines in ways that advantage one set of interests and disadvantage others. Historically, gerrymandering advantaged rural interests and disadvantaged urban interests. Voters in rural districts were over-represented and voters in urban districts were under-represented. Racial gerrymandering is done to advantage one race and to disadvantage others. Historically, racial gerrymandering over-represented white voters and under-represented Black voters. Racial gerrymandering is illegal because the Fourteenth Amendment prohibits states from denying people the equal protection of the laws. Partisan gerrymandering is drawing electoral lines to benefit the majority party and hurt the minority party. It is still practiced as a way for the majority party to use its political power.

One of the ways that the two major parties cooperate is in the creation of safe electoral districts. The Democratic and Republican parties have a vested interest in reducing the number of competitive districts and increasing the number of safe seats. The fact that more than nine out of ten Americans live in congressional districts that are not really competitive, but are safe seats for one party or the other, means that elections are not really very democratic. Redistricting to create safe seats for incumbents (those in office) gives an incumbent a great advantage over any challenger in House elections. In the typical congressional election, only a small number of incumbents lose their seat. Only a small number of seats change party control in each election. Gerrymandering to create safe districts results in fewer than 10% of all House seats actually being competitive in each election cycle—competitive meaning that a candidate of either party has a good chance of winning the seat. The lack of electorally competitive districts means that over 90% of House members are almost guaranteed reelection every two years.

"The Gerry-Mander." Boston *Gazette*, March 26, 1812.

This is a significant development because competitive elections are one measure of how democratic a political system is. The large number of safe districts makes a political system less democratic because there are fewer competitive elections. Creating safe seats for 1) Republicans and Democrats; and 2) incumbents in either party, results in conditions that resemble one-party politics in a large number of districts. If one party almost always wins a district, and the other party almost always loses, the value of political competitions is greatly diminished.

10.36 | *A Duopoly (or Shared Monopoly)*

The two major parties collude to create these political monopolies (technically they are duopolies because the two major parties control the political marketplace). The creation of a large number of safe seats makes districts more ideologically homogeneous, thereby making negotiating, bargaining, and ultimately the need to compromise less likely. A candidate who does not have to run for office in a politically diverse district is less likely to have to develop campaign strategies with broad public appeal, and once in office such a legislator is less likely to have to govern with much concern about accommodating different interests or representing different constituents.

10.4 | Campaigns

A political campaign is an organized effort to influence the decisions of an individual, group, organization, or government institution. Campaigns are one way that individuals, political parties, and organizations compete for popular support. Campaigning is political advertising that provides the public with favorable information about candidates, parties, and issues—this is positive campaigning—or unfavorable information about the opposition—this is negative campaigning. Campaigns have three elements: message, money, and machine.

10.41 | *The Message*

An effective campaign message is one that creates a strong brand that the public identifies with. Some examples of campaign messages include the following:

- John Doe is a business man, not a politician. His background in finance means he can bring fiscal discipline to state government.
- Crime is increasing and education is decreasing. We need leaders like Jane Doe who will keep our streets safe and our schools educating our children.
- Jane Doe has missed over 50 congressional votes. How can you lead if you don't show up to vote?
- Jane Doe is not a Washington politician. She remembers where she came from and won't become part of the problem in Washington.
- Jane Doe knows how to keep Americans safe from terrorism.
- John Doe is an experienced leader.
- Vote Yes on Number Four to Protect Traditional Marriage.
- Make America Great Again!

The message is one of the most important aspects of any political campaign, whether it is an individual's campaign for office or a referendum on an issue. The media (radio, television, and now the new social media such as Twitter) emphasize short, pithy, memorable phrases from campaign speeches or debates. These "sound bites" are the short campaign slogans or catchy messages that resemble bumper-stickers. Sound-bite campaigns and campaign coverage reduce political messages to slogans such as "Peace through Strength" (Ronald Reagan), "Its Morning in America" (President Reagan), and "Change We Can Believe In" (Barack Obama). The Museum of the Moving Image has archived presidential campaign ads. A memorable campaign slogan from the 1984 Democratic primary campaign was Walter Mondale's ad dismissing his main Democratic challenger, Gary Hart, with the catch phrase from a popular Wendy's commercial: "Where's the beef?" The implied charge was that the photogenic Hart lacked substance, particularly when compared to the dull but experienced Mondale. The mantra of Bill Clinton's presidential campaign in 1992 was "It's the economy stupid." This slogan stressed the importance of keeping the campaign focused on the state of the economy rather than other issues that sometimes distract Democrats. Candidate George W. Bush's campaign used the slogan "compassionate conservatism" to appeal to both conservatives and those who worried that conservatives did not care about the poor or disadvantaged.

Today's national and state campaigns are typically professional, sophisticated, carefully crafted campaigns to develop and control the image of a candidate. The marketing of political campaigns has been described as the "packaging" of a candidate and the "selling" of a candidate—even "The Selling of a President." The reference to selling a president is from Joe McGinniss's *The Selling of the President* (1968). McGinniss described how candidate Richard Nixon used Madison Avenue marketing professionals and strategies to win the White House. At the time, the idea that a political campaign could, or should, market and sell a candidate the way that beer, deodorant, and bars of soap were marketed and sold other products like beer or deodorant or a bar of soap was controversial. The idea of corporate advertising expertise being applied to democratic politics in order to influence what citizens thought of the president seemed inappropriate and threatening. Bringing marketing values to politics seemed to demean or diminish politics by treating people as consumers rather than as citizens. Political advertising also seemed threatening in the sense that it used psychology to manipulate or control what people think.

In the years since 1968, the marketing and advertising of candidates is widely accepted as the way to conduct a successful national campaign. Presidential campaigns develop a message or candidate brand. After the Watergate Scandal exposed President Nixon's dishonesty, the Jimmy Carter campaign brand was honesty: "I will not lie to you." During the Carter Administration the Soviet Union invaded Afghanistan, Americans were taken hostages during a revolution in Iran that overthrew the Shah of Iran who was an ally of the United States, and a hostage rescue mission failed. These events, coupled with the loss of the Vietnam War, allowed presidential candidate Ronald Reagan to portray President Carter, the Democrats, and liberals as weak on national defense. The Reagan campaign theme "Peace through Strength" successfully branded Carter, Democrats, and liberals as weak on national defense and Reagan, Republicans, and conservatives as strong on national defense.

The comparison of campaigning and advertising is appropriate because Madison Avenue marketing techniques and strategies have entered mainstream politics. It is no longer shocking or controversial to refer to selling candidates the way products and services are sold, or to refer to voters as consumers who have to be convinced to buy the political product. In order to be successful, national campaigns spend a great deal of money on gathering information about political consumers so that candidates and parties can craft and present a message that is appealing.

10.42 | *Money*

During the 2016 presidential Campaign, Donald Trump repeated called the political system rigged or unfair. The political system rigged or unfair in the sense that rules favor certain players and styles of play. For example, the system is rigged in favor of the two major parties—the Republican and the Democratic Parties. The system is also rigged in favor of those with money. Americans have historically been suspect of the influence of money in politics, government, and public policy. Money is associated with distorting public opinion, buying influence, and even corruption. This is why campaign finance laws are typically enacted after political scandals create political reform movements that are intended to *purify politics* or to *inoculate politicians and government officials* by regulating the amount of money in campaigns, the spending of money, and the disclosure of those who give it and who spend it. What is the problem with money?

Crime fiction is a very popular genre. Popular film and television crime stories are overwhelmingly about "ordinary" or street crime: murder, assault, robbery, and other violent crimes. White collar crime—crime in the suites as opposed to crime in the streets—is less popular. White collar crime stories are usually limited to organized crime (e.g., *The Godfather* films; the television series *The Sopranos*) where the main characters are compelling figures. What about other kinds of economic crime, such as political corruption or tax fraud? *The New York Times* article "Offshore Money, Bane of Democracy" describes the political and social damage caused by international criminal operations that move money around the world, principally via real estate investments.[8] Corporations create shell companies that make it hard for any single country to do anything about what it considers dirty money—money belonging to international criminal enterprises involved with drugs, weapons, sex trafficking, or money laundering. Even legitimate multi-national organizations present challenges for the enforcement of tax laws, for example. Dirty money is a rising high tide that distorts local markets and enabled international criminal organized enterprises that are legal only through the legal accounting. So what is the problem with money? Economic power can be used to get political power to rig the system in favor of those with the money to rig the system to further tilt the playing field.

Is there a "moneyball" strategy to level the political playing field? The term *moneyball* was coined to describe how a baseball team without a big budget could use big data analytics to assess the talents of baseball players rather than relying on the judgment of teams of seasoned baseball scouts or just buying players by signing them to big contracts. Michael Lewis described the strategy in *Moneyball: How to win in an Unfair Game* (2003). *Money* has always been called the mother's milk of politics. This is why the government adopted campaign finance regulations. The Supreme Court's decision in *Citizens United v. Federal Elections Commission* (2010) removed almost all limits on campaign contributions. One result of this deregulation of campaign finance is the decreased influence of political parties and the increased influence of very wealthy individuals, particularly billionaires who invest in candidates or fund issue campaigns. Some are liberal, and therefore Democratic, while others are conservative, and therefore Republican. As wealthy individuals, they also sometimes have libertarian streaks that include belief that individual responsibility for success (or failure) rather than government social welfare programs.

Campaign finance has become more important as campaigns have changed from traditional *retail politics* to *wholesale politics*. The term retail politics refers to campaigns where candidates actually meet voters one-on-one, in small groups or communities, at town hall meetings, or other face-to-face settings such as walking a neighborhood. The term wholesale politics refers to campaigns where candidates address large audiences often using the print and electronic mass media.

The change to wholesale politics has increased the cost of campaigning by shifting from labor-intensive campaigning—where friends and neighbors and campaign workers and volunteers canvas a district or city or make personal telephone calls to individual voters—to capital-intensive campaigns where money is used to purchase television air time or advertising. The change from campaigns as ground wars to air wars has increased the cost of campaigning.

Fundraising techniques include having the candidate call or meet with large donors, sending direct mail pleas to small donors, and courting interest groups who could end up spending millions on the race if it is significant to their interests. The financing of elections has always been controversial because money is often considered a corrupting influence on democratic politics. The perception is that the wealthy can purchase access to government officials or pay for campaigns that influence public opinion. The fact that private sources of finance make up substantial amounts of campaign contributions, especially in federal elections, contributes to the perception that money creates influence. As a result, **voluntary public funding** for candidates willing to accept spending limits was introduced in 1974 for presidential primaries and elections. The Federal Elections Commission was created in the 1970s to monitor campaign finance. The FEC is responsible for monitoring the disclosure of campaign finance information, enforcing the provisions of the law such as the limits and prohibitions on contributions, and overseeing the public funding of U.S. presidential elections.

A good source of information about money matters in American campaigns and elections is The Center for Responsive Politics. The Center tracks money in politics as part of an "open secrets project." The recommendation to "Follow the money" has become all-purpose slogan that is applicable to criminal investigations and investigations of political influence and campaign ads. The saying comes from the Hollywood film *All the President's Men* which tells the story of how Washington Post reporters investigated the Watergate scandal. A secret source named Deep Throat advised the reporters to "Follow the Money."

The National Institute on Money in State Politics is still following the money trail to determine political influence in state politics. The U.S. Supreme Court's rulings in campaign finance cases has made "Follow the money" even more relevant in today's politics. In a series of rulings, the Court has said that campaign contributions are speech that is protected by the First Amendment and that government restrictions on campaign contributions are subject to strict scrutiny—which means that the government has to show that campaign finance laws serve a compelling interest in order to be upheld. As a result, corporations can make unlimited independent campaign expenditures. Even the existing requirements that contributions be publicly disclosed are now being challenged. The Campaign Finance Information Center's mission is to help journalist follow the campaign money trail in local, state, and national politics.

10.43 | *The Machine*

The third part of a campaign is *the machine*. The campaign machine is the organization, the human capital, the foot soldiers loyal to the cause, the true believers who will carry the run by volunteer activists, the professional campaign advisers, pollsters, voter lists, political party resources, and get-out-the vote resources. Individuals need organizations to campaign successfully in national campaigns. Successful campaigns usually require a campaign manager and some staff members who make strategic and tactical decisions while volunteers and interns canvass door-to-door and make phone calls. Campaigns use all three of the above components to create a successful strategy for victory.

One continuity in American politics is that conservatives and Republicans are considered tougher on national security than liberals and Democrats. This actually creates a perverse

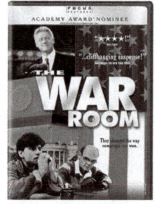

The War Room is a documentary that chronicles Bill Clinton's 1992 Presidential Campaign from an inside-look at his campaign staff.

political incentive for Republicans to increase worries about national security threats because enemies are politically useful. Does this mean that some wars are not meant to be won? Political campaigns that are described in rhetorical terms as wars (e.g., culture wars) can create a sense of alarm that motivates the public and sustains its interest. But actual wars and sustained national security threats and emergencies can also be politically useful.

10.5 | The Media

Modern campaigns for national offices—the presidency, the Senate, and the House of Representatives—are largely media campaigns. They are conducted using the print media, electronic media, and social media. Communication technology has fundamentally altered campaigns. The development of the broadcast media (radio and television) changed political campaigns from "ground wars" to "air" wars. The term ground war refers to a campaign that relies heavily on candidates and their campaign workers meeting voters and distributing campaign literature. The term air war refers to campaigns that rely heavily on the mass media.

The following two quotes from the Museum of the Moving Image archive of presidential campaign ads illustrate the change in thinking about television campaign advertising:

- "The idea that you can merchandise candidates for high office like breakfast cereal is the ultimate indignity to the democratic process."
  —Democratic presidential candidate Adlai Stevenson (1956)
- "Television is no gimmick, and nobody will ever be elected to major office again without presenting themselves well on it." —Television producer and Nixon campaign consultant (and later President of Fox News Channel) Roger Ailes (1968)

10.51 | *Who Uses Whom?*

Campaign organizations have a complicated relationship with the media. They need and use each other but they have different, sometimes conflicting needs. The media like **good visuals** and compelling personal interest stories which capture the attention of the public and turn the general public into an audience. Campaigns like to provide such visuals. But the media (and campaigns) also like to play "*gotcha*." The media consider it a good story to catch a candidate's ignorance, mistake, or gaffe—or even to ask a question that might cause a candidate to make a mistake. The mistake might be

- Misspelling a word. Vice-presidential candidate Dan Quale spelled "potato" "potatoe."
- Ignorance. Not knowing the name of a foreign leader. Presidential candidate George W. Bush did not know the name of the leader of Pakistan.
- Misrepresentation. During the presidential primary campaign, Hillary Clinton misrepresented a trip to Kosovo as one where she landed at an airport under fire to convince voters that she had the experience to be commander in chief.
- Math problems. Announcing budget numbers that do not add up.

- Ignorance. Vice-presidential candidate Sarah Palin did not know the name of any Supreme Court decision that she disagreed with.

As a candidate and early in his presidency, Trump commanded the attention of the media: the traditional press (television and radio), the Internet, and the social media. He made headlines as a compelling figure, an international celebrity, a "riveting spectacle." He started fights with the "fake" news media as a strategy that relies on continuous warfare to motivate his supporters and to force his critics and political opponents to talk about his story lines. Political analysts tended to dismiss his antics as little more than drivers rubber-necking as they pass a car crash on the side of the road. But media spectacles are not just accidents or unforced errors or gaffes or political theater. The spectacles may be a political strategy to get public attention by getting inside our heads. The erratic behavior; the unpredictable speech; the breaking of established norms; sometimes apparently almost random ideological positions; the frequency with which as strong statement is following in rather short order by another contradicting the former, may be a "variable reward schedule" analogous to the slot machine payouts that keep gamblers playing the machines. The risk is that this strategic focus on getting and keeping public attention, which is conventionally a means to public policy end, may become an end in itself. After all, presidential success is conventionally measured in terms of accomplishments, not just attention or public approval ratings. Getting "mindshare" is important because efforts to "get inside" peoples' heads typically have a goal in mind. Advertisers want to get inside peoples' heads to purchase the products being advertised. Campaigners was to get inside voters' heads to build the support for policies. "The Attention Merchants: The Struggle to Get Inside Our Heads."[9]

10.52 | *The Social Media*

Communication technology has changed national campaigns from primarily ground wars (walking the neighborhoods; kissing babies; shaking hands) to air wars (broadcast radio and television ads). Campaigns are now using social media to post material on Tumblr (videos and photos) or Spotify or Pinterest. According to Adam Fletcher, deputy press secretary for the Obama re-election campaign, "It's about authentic, two-way communication."[10] This may be true, but it may also be about a campaign strategy to try to reach people where they are: Online using social media. A presidential campaign that shares songs with the public may be less interested in actually creating two-way communication with the public than it is in establishing social connections with people by appearing to share tastes. Familiarity (with songs, photos and videos that are posted on Spotify, Flickr, Instagram, Twitter, Facebook, etc.) creates trust. Socialbakers, a social media analytics group, says the campaigns have to try to reach people wherever they are, and young people in particular are on-line more than reading newspapers or watching broadcast television networks.

10.53 | *The Age of Digital Campaigns*

The digital age is fundamentally changing campaign advertising. In the age of mass media, campaign ads that aired on the major television and radio networks were intended for the general audiences that were watching or listening to national programs. The digital age allows targeted advertising. Political intelligence companies such as Aristotle gather large files of detailed information about a person's behavior from commercial companies that keep track of consumption patterns or Internet searches, and then sell that data to campaigns. The campaigns, which then know where a person lives; what their demographics are; what they purchase; what they read; what their hobbies are; and other factors that might be related to how they think about politics, can tailor ads to very specific audiences. This digital information is very good for campaigns, but is it good for us? See the following PBS story about "How Campaigns Amass Your Personal Information to Deliver Tailored Political Ads." The digital campaigns are also developing ways to target "off the grid" voters, the voters who do not get their public affairs information from the traditional media sources (papers, television, and radio). Identifying such voters is one thing. Getting them to vote is another. Having a good ground game—people in neighborhoods, cities, districts, and states who can actually contact voters and get them out to vote—is still an important element of a successful presidential campaign strategy. President Obama's reelection campaign was successful because it combined air wars with a solid ground game in the states that it identified as the key swing states in the 2012 presidential election.

10.54 | *Campaign Fact Checking*

Think About It!
How much does a campaign know about me? See "How Campaigns Amass Your Personal Information to Deliver Tailored Political Ads."
http://www.pbs.org/newshour/bb/politics/july-dec12/frontline_10-29.html

Candidates, parties, and organizations supporting or opposing a candidate, or an issue, say things which may not meet the standard of "the truth, the whole truth, and nothing but the truth." In an age of electronic communications, it is even more likely that Mark Twain, the American humorist, was right when he said, "A lie can travel halfway around the world while the truth is still putting on its shoes." As a result, a number of organizations have developed campaign fact-checking operations to hold campaigners accountable for what they claim as facts. One of these organizations is Factcheck.org. Its Web site provides running description and analysis of inaccurate campaign statements. Some of the more interesting false statements that they fact-checked were claims that Democratic presidential candidate Barack Hussein Obama was a radical Muslim who refused to recite the Pledge of Allegiance and took the oath of office as a U.S. Senate swearing on the Koran, not the bible.

10.55 | *Political Futures Market*

One of the more innovative and interesting perspectives on the measurement of public opinion as a predictor of the outcome of an election involves the application of economic perspectives. The "political futures" markets are designed to provide an economic measure of support for a candidate as a predictor of whether the candidate will win an election. One example of this approach is The Iowa Electronic Markets. These are real-money futures markets in which contract payoffs depend on economic and political events such as elections. These markets are operated by faculty at the University of Iowa as part of their research and teaching mission.

10.6 | How to "Do" Civic Engagement

The importance of fostering civic engagement in higher education is described in *Civic Responsibility and Higher Education* (2000). Thomas Ehrlich, one of the book's editors, works to promote including civic engagement along with the traditional academic learning in the mission of universities. The American Association of Colleges and Universities stresses the role that higher education plays in developing civic learning to ensure that students become an informed, engaged, and socially responsible citizenry. These efforts emphasize the importance of connecting classroom learning with the community. The connection has two points: usable knowledge and workable skills. The emphasis on usable knowledge includes promoting social science research as problem solving. The term ***usable knowledge*** refers to knowledge that people and policy makers can apply to solve contemporary social problems. (Lindblom and Cohen) The emphasis on workable skills is even more directly related to civic engagement. Today there are many organizations that advance the cause of linking academic study and social problem solving. One of these organizations is the W. K. Kellogg Foundation. This Foundation was created by the cereal company magnate. The Foundation emphasizes the importance of developing the practical skills that will enable individuals to realize the "inherent human capacity to solve their own problems." These skills include dialogue, leadership development, and the organization of effort. In effect, civic engagement develops the practical skills that can help people help themselves. How can you "do" civic engagement?

- Contact a government official. Contact a local, state, and national government official. Ask them what they think are the major issues or problems that are on their agenda. Contacting your member of Congress is easy. (See the Chapter on Congress.)
- Attend a government meeting. Attend the public meeting of a local government: a neighborhood association; a city council meeting; a county commission meeting; a school board meeting; a school board meeting; or a state government meeting (of the legislature or an executive agency).
- Contact an organization. Contact a non-government organization to discuss an issue of your concern, community interest, or the organization's mission. These organizations, political parties, and interest groups represent business, labor, professional associations, or issues such as civil rights, property rights, the environment, immigration, religion, and education.

10.7 | Summary

One aspect of the power problem is the government's control over individuals. Laws are commands that are backed by sanctions. Individuals must obey the law or risk punishment. The government's control over individuals is legitimate if the government is based on the consent of the governed. Consent is the difference between authority and power. Democracy is a system of self-government that requires an active and engaged citizenry in order to make government control over individuals legitimate. Political participation is one of the measures of how democratic a political system is. Therefore, political participation is also a measure or indicator of government legitimacy. Voting, elections, and campaigns provide opportunities for individuals to be active and engaged citizens.

10.8 | Additional Resources

10.81 | *In the Library*

Campbell, Angus, Philip Converse, Warren Miller, and Donald Stokes. 1960. The American Voter. New York: Wiley.

Civic Responsibility and Higher Education. 2000. Thomas Ehrlich. Editor.

Downs, Anthony. 1957. *An Economic Theory of Democracy.* New York: Harper Collins.

Green, Donald P., and Alan S. Gerber. 2008. *Get Out the Vote : how to increase voter turnout.* 2nd ed. Washington, D.C.: Brookings Institution Press.

Lewis-Beck, Michael S. 2008. The American Voter Revisited. Ann Arbor: University of Michigan Press.

Lindblom, Charles E., and David K. Cohen. 1979. *Usable Knowledge.* New Haven: Yale University Press.

McGinniss, Joe. 1968. *The Selling of the President.*

Schier, Steven. 2003. *You Call This An Election? America's Peculiar Democracy.* Washington, DC: Georgetown University Press.

10.82 | *Online Resources*

Each state has primary responsibility for conducting and supervising elections. For information about Florida elections go to the My Florida Web site http://www.myflorida.com/ and click on government, then executive branch, then state agencies, then department of state, then http://election.dos.state.fl.us/. Or you can learn about Florida election laws by going directly to the Florida Department of State Web site

Key Terms:
voter fatigue
open primaries
closed primaries
presidential primary
caucus
voter turnout
rational choice model
civic duty model
political efficacy
Individual explanations
System explanations
Voter registration
"Air" campaigns

which provides information about voter registration, candidates, political parties, and constitutional amendment proposals.

Votesmart provides basic information about American politics and government. It is, in effect, American Government 101.

C-SPAN election resources are available at http://www.c-span.org/classroom/govt /campaigns.asp.

The U.S. Elections Project provides data on voting. http://www.electproject.org/home/voter-turnout/demographics

Dave Leip's *Atlas of U.S. Presidential Elections* provides interesting information about presidential elections. http://uselectionatlas.org/RESULTS/index.html

Project Vote-Smart is a nonpartisan information service funded by members and non-partisan foundations. It offers "a wealth of facts on your political leaders, including Biographies, addresses, issue positions, voting records, campaign finances, evaluations by special interests." www.vote-smart.org/

The U.S. Census Bureau has information on voter registration and turnout statistics. www.census.gov/population/www/socdemo/voting.html

C-Span produces programs that provide information about the workings of Congress and elections. www.c-span.org

10.9| STUDY QUESTIONS

1. What is the rational choice theory of voting?
2. What are the primary factors at the individual level that influence whether someone turns out to vote?
3. What are the institutional factors that depress voter turnout in the United States?

---

[1] https://www.socialstudies.org/publications/socialeducation/september2007/michael-hartoonian-richard-van-scotter-and-william-e-white

[2] Alexander Hamilton, in *The Records of the Federal Convention of 1787*, Vol. 2, ed. Max Farrand (New Haven, CT: Yale University Press, 1937), 298-299.

[3] For the methodology and results, see http://www.economist.com/markets/rankings/displaystory.cfm?story_id=8908438

[4] See Anthony Downs. 1957. *An Economic Theory of Democracy*. New York: Harper Press.

[5] Declare Yourself has information on each state and the requirements for voter registration at http://www.declareyourself.com/voting_faq/state_by_state_info_2.html

[6] George C. Wallace. Stand Up For America. New York: Doubleday, 1976:212.

[7] The National Conference of State Legislatures provides detailed information about ballot initiatives in F

[8] Oliver Bullough, "Offshore Money, Bane of Democracy, *The New York Times* (April 7, 2017). Accessed at www.nytimes.com

[9] Tim Wu, "How Trump Wins by Losing," *New York Times* (March 5, 2017), p.6

[10] Quoted in "Campaigns Use Social Media to Lure Younger Voters," Jenna Wortham, *The New York Times* (October 7, 2012). Accessed at www.nytimes.com

11.0 | Why Parties?

Why do people everywhere live, work, play, and even worship in groups? Why are large organizations—political parties, interest groups, corporations, churches, and national governments—the main actors in our social, economic, and political systems? Is there something *natural* about *social* organizations? And what is the role of the individual in political systems where groups are the dominant actors? These are some of the oldest and most interesting questions that are asked by the social scientists (political scientists, economists, sociologists, and anthropologists), political philosophers, and natural scientists that study human behavior. Natural scientists study the phenomenon of grouping in the non-human animal kingdom to learn why fish, birds, and elephants live in groups.[1] Social scientists study economic, ideological, partisan, and other groupings of the human animal.

This chapter examines political parties. Political parties exist in all modern democracies. The U.S. Constitution does not say anything about political parties because they did not exist when the Constitution was written. But parties are one of the most important features of the American system of politics and government. It is impossible to understand American politics without understanding political parties. The chapter examines two aspects of the power problem with parties. The first power problem is the tension between *democratic theory*, which values individualism, and modern *political reality*, which is politics that is dominated by large organizations. American political culture includes a strong commitment to individualism and a healthy skepticism about large, powerful organizations. The tension between individualism and organization is one reason why Americans are ambivalent about political parties. Political parties are stronger in other western democracies. In American political culture, parties are tolerated as a necessary evil because their influence on individual voters and government officials is considered suspect. Nevertheless, parties are considered essential for organizing public participation in politics, for organizing government officials to actually govern, and for holding government accountable.

The second aspect of the power problem with parties is unique to the U.S. two-party system. The Republican and Democratic Parties have a shared political monopoly—in effect, a duopoly. They are allowed to restrict access to the ballot in ways that limit the development of other parties. If the two parties were businesses, they would be guilty of violating anti-trust laws. Anti-trust laws prohibit businesses from colluding to limit economic competition and protect market share. But the Republican and Democratic Parties are allowed to control election laws in ways that protect their political market share. This chapter examines some of these aspect of party politics in the U.S.

11.1 | What is a Political Party?

A **political party** is an organization of people with shared ideas about government and politics who try to gain control of government in order to implement their ideas. Political parties usually try to gain control of government by nominating candidates for office who then compete in elections by running with the party label. Some political parties are very ideological and work hard to get their beliefs implemented in public policy. Other political parties are not as ideological because they are coalitions of different interests or they are more interested in gaining and holding power by having members win elections than strongly advocating a particular set of beliefs.

Political organizations play an important role in all systems of government. It is impossible to understand American government and politics without understanding the role of political parties and interest groups. This is ironic because American culture values individualism, but political organizations such as parties and interest groups have come to play an extremely important role in our political and economic life. Parties and interest

"I adore **political parties**. They are the only place left to us where people don't talk politics."
Oscar Wilde

"The old parties are husks, with no real soul within either, divided on artificial lines, boss-ridden and privilege-controlled, each a jumble of incongruous elements, and neither daring to speak out wisely and fearlessly on what should be said on the vital issues of the day."
Theodore Roosevelt

groups are linkage institutions. Linkage institutions are sometimes called aggregating or mediating institutions. The media are also a linkage (or mediating) institution. A linkage organization is one that links individuals to one another or the government. A linkage organization aggregates and collects individual interests. This is an important function in large scale (or mass) political systems because it is a way for individuals with shared interests to speak with a single or louder voice. Linkage organizations are also important because they mediate between individuals and government, they *mediate* between the lone (or small) individual and (increasingly) big government. The mediating role becomes more important as a country's population increases and as government get larger and larger. Intermediary organizations make it possible for individuals to think that they can have an impact on government. In this sense, political parties like other "mediating structures" actually empower people. Parties are part of **civil society**—the *non-governmental sector of public life*. Civil society includes political, economic, social, religious, cultural activities that are part of the crucial, non-governmental foundations of a political community: the family, neighborhoods, churches, and voluntary associations such as parties and interest groups. The Heritage Foundation is a conservative think tank that promotes the strengthening of these mediating structures as a way to empower individuals and to encourage civic engagement as an alternative to depending on government action. (Berger and Neuhaus) Civic engagement promotes the development of, and maintains the viability of, these traditional mediating structures.

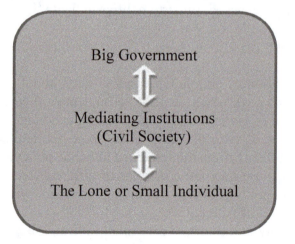

11.2 | Roles in Modern Democracies

It is hard to imagine modern democracies without political parties. The freedom to form parties and compete in the electoral process is one of the essential measures of democracy because parties are considered vital means of self-government. Political parties perform the following functions:

- Recruit and nominate candidates for office.
- Help run campaigns and elections.
- Organize and mobilize voters to participate in politics.
- Organize and operate the government.

The recruitment and nomination of candidates is one of the most important functions of political parties. In the past, party leaders exerted a great deal of control over the party's candidate for office because party leaders and activists chose their party's nominee. Today, party control over nominees has been weakened. The increased use of primary elections allows voters to choose party candidates. The deregulation of campaign finance has enabled candidates to fund and run their own campaigns. The weakened control over nominees has weakened American political parties.

Political parties also organize and mobilize voters. This function is important in large countries because it can help organize the public in ways that increase an individual's sense of political efficacy. Political efficacy is the belief that a person's participation matters, that a person's vote can make a difference. In large-scale democracies such as the United States, political parties organize individuals, gather their interests in documents such as party platforms, and then present them to the voters to make their choices. In this respect, political parties perform a unifying function. They bring individuals together with other like-minded individuals who share their thinking on government and politics.

The role of political parties is not limited to campaigns. Parties also play an important role in governance. Political parties are not officially part of the government, but they play an important role in organizing government action. The majority party in Congress organizes and runs Congress. The party whose candidate wins the presidency works with the president to organize and support policy actions. In the American two-party system, the majority party is the **Ins**, who generally advocate one set of public policies, and the **Outs**, the minority party that presents an alternative set of public policies.

Political scientists consider the above party functions vital for modern liberal democracies. But the American political tradition also includes strong skepticism of parties. The fact that about one-third of voters consider themselves Independents rather than members of either of the two major parties is evidence that Americans do not have a particularly strong attachment to parties. Independents may think parties are not essential for modern democracy, or they may think that democracies work better when voters are not attached to either party, or they consider political parties part of the problem of gridlock or bickering and infighting that prevents well-meaning representatives of the people from working together to solve problems.

11.3 | Anti-party Thinking about Politics

Parties did not exist when the Constitution was written. There were "factions" or people who shared political, economic, and regional interests, but they were not mass membership organizations competing in elections to control government. In fact, the founders considered factions harmful influences whose power needed to be checked because they pursued special interests rather than the national interest. Both George Washington and James Madison worried about the emergence of factions. Madison designed a form of government that was intended to limit the power of such special interests by a system of checks and balances.

11.31 | *George Washington*

George Washington's *Farewell Address* on September 19, 1796 is a famous statement warning against the spirit and actions of political parties. He warned against the development of state parties that created geographic divisions among Americans as well as "the baneful effects of the spirit of party generally," a spirit that was "inseparable from our nature," and existing in all forms of government, but "it is seen in its greatest rankness, and is truly their worst enemy," in popular forms of government:

> The alternate domination of one faction over another, sharpened by the spirit of revenge, natural to party dissension, which in different ages and countries has perpetrated the most horrid enormities, is itself a frightful despotism. But this leads at length to a more formal and permanent despotism. The disorders and miseries which result gradually incline the minds of men to seek security and repose in the absolute power of an individual; and sooner or later the chief of some prevailing faction, more able or more fortunate than his competitors, turns this disposition to the purposes of his own elevation, on the ruins of public liberty.
>
> ...[T]he common and continual mischiefs of the spirit of party are sufficient to make it the interest and duty of a wise people to discourage and restrain it. It serves always to distract the public councils and enfeeble the public administration. It agitates the community with ill-founded jealousies and false alarms, kindles the animosity of one part against another, foments occasionally riot and insurrection. It opens the door to foreign influence and corruption, which finds a facilitated access to the government itself through the channels of party passions. Thus the policy and the will of one country are subjected to the policy and will of another."

James Madison also considered factions a problem. But he thought than one solution—banning factions—would be a cure that was worse than the disease. He believed factions were rooted in human nature and therefore could not be eliminated. So in *Federalist Number 51* he described a political system *that made factions part of the solution to the problem of factions.* The system of checks and balances required many different factions, interests, parties, and even religions so that **no one** group could get control of government power and use it against the others. The political solution to the problem of factions was to create a system that had many factions. The way to guard against a united majority threatening the rights of the minority is to create a society with "so many separate descriptions of citizens as will render an unjust combination of a majority of the whole very improbable, if not impracticable." Madison specifically compared the problem of protecting political rights with the problem of protecting religious rights:

> "In a free government the security for civil rights must be the same as that for religious rights. It consists in the one case in the multiplicity of interests, and in the other in the multiplicity of sects. The degree of security in both cases will depend on the number of interests and sects; and this may be presumed to depend on the extent of country and number of people comprehended under the same government."

11.32 | *Parties and the Constitution*

The Founders worried that factions were divisive forces that would literally divide Americans into *parts* or parties. But the two-party system emerged in the early 1900s has not changed much for almost 200 years. The two major parties have changed a great deal, but the party system has not. Shortly after the Constitution was written, the Federalist Party and the Anti-federalist Party emerged to compete for control of the federal government. The Federalist Party supported a strong national government, a strong executive in the national government, and commercial interest. The Federalist Party's geographic base was in New England. The Anti-federalist Party supported strong state governments, legislative government, and agrarian interests. Its geographic base was strongest in the South and West. Alexander Hamilton and Chief Justice John Marshall were strong Federalists. Thomas Jefferson and James Madison were Anti-federalists (a party which came to be called the Democratic-Republicans). The election of 1800 was a presidential contest won by Jefferson, and the landmark case of *Marbury v. Madison* (1803) began as a political contest over Federalist and Anti-federalist control of government. The Jeffersonians (or Democratic-Republicans) then became the dominant party, winning seven consecutive presidential elections from 1800 to 1824.

The two major parties change because political movements and third parties have periodically arisen to demand that the government address new issues facing the nation. American political culture values individualism. Individualism makes Americans wary of political parties. But parties are also important linkage institutions that organize individuals to more effectively participate in politics. Organization increases effectiveness. The tensions between individualism and organization are reflected in a political culture that is ambivalent about parties. There is a strong tradition of declinist thinking in American politics—claims that the country is going downhill in one way or another. The declinist thinking includes thinking about political parties. Books with variations on the title *The Party is Over*[2] either celebrate or mourn the impending death of political parties. Political science research describing parties as dead or dying bring to mind Mark Twain's famous quip about a newspaper report that he had died: "The reports of my death are greatly exaggerated."

11.4 | Party Systems

Political systems are one-party systems, two-party systems, or multi-party systems. The U.S. has a two-party system.

11.41 | *One-Party Systems*

In **one-party systems**, only one political party is legally allowed to hold power. Minor parties may be allowed but they are required to accept the official party's role in governance *because* the party is usually officially part of the government. Government officials are not only members of a political party they may be party officials. There are few one-party systems in existence today but a variant, the **dominant party system**, is actually becoming more common as a global trend toward declining support for democracy continues. Declining support for democracy is related to declining support for political parties. A dominant party system is one where one party is so strong that other parties have no real chance of competing in elections to win power. Other parties are legally allowed to exist, but they are not politically viable. Dominant party systems can exist in countries with a strong democratic tradition.

 The inability of any other party to compete in elections may be due to political, social and economic circumstances, public opinion, or the dominant party's monopoly over government power, which it uses the way a business monopoly uses its market dominance to protect its dominance. The dominant party uses political patronage, voter and election fraud, gerrymandered legislative districts, and privileged access to the media, to maintain popular support. Political patronage is distributing government jobs, contracts, or other benefits to influence votes. This is why having free and fair elections is such an important component of the measure of democracy. Examples of dominant party systems include the People's Action Party in Singapore, the African National Congress in South Africa, and the Institutional Revolutionary in Mexico until the 1990s. In the United States, the South was a one-party dominant region from the 1880s until the 1970s because the Democratic Party controlled the South. The South is still a one-party dominant region but now the Republican Party is the dominant party.

11.42 | *Two-Party Systems*

A **two-party system** is one where there are two major political parties that are so strong that it is extremely difficult for a candidate from any party other than the two major parties to have a real chance to win elections. In a two-party system, a third-party is not likely to have much electoral success. The Republican and Democratic Parties are the dominant parties in the U.S. two-party system. It is difficult for any third or minor party to win elections.

 The individual states, not the federal government, primarily regulate political parties because most elections are state elections. The states organize elections for local, state, and federal offices. There are no state or federal laws that limit the *number* of political parties. The U.S. could develop a multi-party system with a Republican, Democratic, Libertarian, Socialist, Green, and even a Christian Democrat party. Third or minor parties do appear periodically on the American political landscape but they tend to be single-issue parties whose issue is often incorporated into the platform of one of the two major parties. The electoral rules also make it hard for minor parties to become major parties. For example, states have restrictive ballot access laws that make it hard for small parties to get on the ballot, win elections, and then development in strength as they broaden their appeal to voters.

In two-party systems, the electoral marketplace is typically divided into a right of center party (the conservatives) and a left of center party (the liberals). The Republican Party is right of center and the Democratic Party is left of center. Both parties are coalitions of interests. A coalition is a temporary combination or alliance of different interests that unite to achieve shared goals. The two major parties have to have broad appeal in order to win elections by capturing a majority or near majority of the votes cast in an election. The Republican Party coalition consists of four main interests: economic conservatives (primarily business interests); social conservatives (primarily the religious right); crime control conservatives (getting-tough-on crime advocates of public order); and national security conservatives. The Democratic Party coalition consists of minorities (primarily blacks but also Hispanics, women, gays and lesbians; and immigrants; economic liberals, primarily organized labor and consumers; urbanites; and young and old voters. The coalitions of interests in the two major parties do change over time.

Politics, like sports, is activity that is organized by rules that determine how the game is played and who wins. The most important rule in the electoral game is whether to use proportional representation (PR) **or single-member district plurality vote system (SMDP)**. Proportional representation is a system where each party receives a share of seats in parliament that is proportional to the popular vote that the party receives. In a single-member district plurality vote system the person who gets the most votes in an election wins the seat. It is a winner-take-all election: The person who gets the most votes (i.e., the plurality) wins the election even if he or she did not win a majority of the votes. The United States uses this single-member district plurality system. For example, in a congressional election, the candidate who gets the most votes wins the senate seat or a house seat. The Electoral College also uses this winner-take-all system. The presidential candidate that receives the most popular votes in a state gets all of that state's Electoral College votes (with the exception of Nebraska and Maine which use a system of proportional representation). The winner-take-all system is not very democratic because 49% of the voters in an election are losers! The system also disadvantages minor parties.

Election rules have a major impact on **how** the political game is played and **who** is likely to win. The winner-take-all system has the following effects on the way the political game is played:

- It tends to create and maintain a two-party system.
- It tends to make political parties more ideologically moderate because they must compete to win the most votes cast in an election or it will lose the election. Extremist or single-issue parties are unlikely to win elections.
- It increases political stability because tends the differences between the two major parties will not be as great as it would be in a political system where parties competed at the left or right extremes of the ideological spectrum. Maurice Duverger, the French sociologist described how the electoral rules had these effects on party politics.

> ## Duverger's Law is a principle that a plurality election system tends to produce a stable, two party system.

An electoral system based on proportional representation creates conditions that allow new parties to develop and smaller parties to exist. The winner-take-all plurality system marginalizes new and smaller political parties by relegating to the status of loser n elections. A small third party cannot gain legislative power if it has to compete and win in a district with a large population in order to gain a seat. Similarly, a minor party with a broad base of support that is geographically spread throughout a state or spread across the nation is unlikely to attract enough votes to actually win an election even though it has substantial public support. For example, the Libertarian Party has supporters throughout the country, and may attract a substantial number of votes, but the votes are not enough to be the majority in a single district or a single state.

Duverger also believed the SMDP vote rule produces moderation and stability. Take, for example, the following scenario. Two moderate candidates (from two moderate parties) and one radical candidate are competing for a single office in an election where there are 100,000 moderate voters and 80,000 radical voters. If each moderate voter casts a vote for a moderate candidate and each radical voter casts a vote for the radical candidate, the radical candidate would win unless one of the moderate candidates gathered less than 20,000 votes. Consequently, moderate voters seeking to defeat a radical candidate or party would be more likely to vote for the candidate that is most likely to get more votes. The political impact of the SMDP vote rule is that the two moderate parties must either merge or one moderate party must fail as the voters gravitate to the two strong parties.

A third party usually can become successful only if it can exploit the mistakes of one of the existing major parties. For example, the political chaos immediately preceding the Civil War allowed the Republican Party to replace the Whig Party as the more progressive party. Loosely united on a platform of country wide economic reform and federally funded industrialization, the decentralized Whig leadership failed to take a decisive stance on the slavery issue, effectively splitting the party along the Mason-Dixon Line. Southern rural planters, initially lured by the prospect of federal infrastructure and schools, quickly aligned themselves with the pro-slavery Democrats, while urban laborers and professionals in the northern states, threatened by the sudden shift in political and economic power and losing faith in the failing Whig candidates, flocked to the increasingly vocal anti-slave Republican Party.

In countries that use proportional representation (PR), the electoral rules make it hard to maintain a two-party system. The number of votes that a party receives determines the number of seats it wins so a new party can start small, win a local or state election, develop an electoral base of support, and then expand it. Proportional representation results in the creation of multi-party systems.

11.43 | *Multi –Party Systems*

Multi-party systems have more than two parties. The Central Intelligence Agency's *World Factbook* lists the political parties in countries. Canada and the United Kingdom have two strong parties with a third party that is strong enough to have some electoral success, may occasionally place second in elections, and presents a serious challenge to the two major parties, but the third party does not win enough votes to gain control of government. These third parties play an important role, particularly if neither of the two major parties wins a majority in the representative assembly. Then one of the major parties must try to form a coalition with the third party in order to gain a legislative majority and gain control of government. This makes the third party the "kingmaker." This occurred in the 2017 election in Britain when Prime Minister Theresa May's Conservative Party won only 318 of the 650 seats in the House of Commons, which was short of the 326 majority required to form a government. May's Conservative Party formed a coalition with a Northern Ireland Party, the Democratic Unionist Party, whose 10 seats provided the majority the Conservative Party needed to form a government. Third or minor parties also play an important role in putting problems, issues, and ideas on the government agenda. A third party may support a particular public policy that becomes popular enough for one of the two major parties to adopt it as one of their own. No party has an intellectual property right or trademark right to a particular political idea. Parties regularly steal ideas from one another.

Finland has an unusual party system. It has a three-party system in which all three parties routinely win elections and hold the top government office. It is very rare for a country to have more than three parties that are equally successful and have the same chance of gaining control of government (that is, "forming" the government or appointing the top government officials such as the prime minister). In political systems where there are numerous parties it is more common that no one party will be able to attract a majority of votes and therefore form a government, so a party will have to work with other parties to try to form a coalition government. Coalition governments, which include members of more than one party, are actually commonplace in countries such as the Republic of Ireland, Germany, and Israel.

In countries with proportional representation, the seats in a country's parliament or representative assembly would be allocated according to the popular votes the party received. The electoral districts are usually assigned several representatives. For example, assume the following distribution of the popular vote:

Party	Percent of the Popular Vote
Republican Party	36
Democratic Party	35
Libertarian Party	15
Green Party	14

The seats in the country's 100-member representative assembly would be allocated as follows:

Party	Seats in the Representative Assembly
Republican Party	36
Democratic Party	35
Libertarian Party	15
Green Party	14

Proportional representation makes it easier for smaller or minor parties to survive because they can win some seats in an election even though they never win enough votes to form a majority and control the government. Consequently, proportional representation tends to promote multi-party systems because elections do not result one winner (the candidate or party that get the most votes) and all the rest of the candidates are losers.

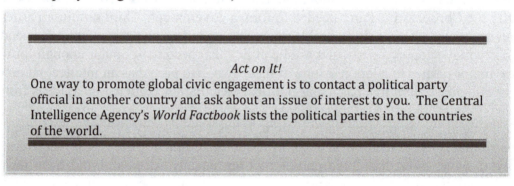

Act on It!
One way to promote global civic engagement is to contact a political party official in another country and ask about an issue of interest to you. The Central Intelligence Agency's *World Factbook* lists the political parties in the countries of the world.

11.5 | U.S. Political Parties

The U.S. has a two-party system. The two major parties are the Republican Party and the Democratic Party. The U.S. also has two well established minor parties, the Libertarian Party and the Green Party. Other smaller parties include the Constitution Party and the Socialist Party. The following table includes the largest current largest parties. Each party was on the ballot in enough states to have had a mathematical chance to win a majority of Electoral College votes in the 2008 presidential election. Project Vote Smart provides a useful list of political parties in each of the 50 states.

12.51 | *Current Largest Parties*

Party Name	Date Founded	Founder(s)	Associated Ideologies	Current Chair
Democratic Party	1792/ 1820s	Thomas Jefferson/ Andrew Jackson	Liberalism, Progressivism, Social Liberalism	Tom Perez
Republican Party	1854	Alvan E. Bovay	Conservatism, Neoconservatism, Economic Conservatism, Social Conservatism	Reince Priebus
Libertarian Party	1971	David Nolan	Libertarianism	Nicholas Sarwark (Chair of Libertarian National Committee)
Green Party US (GPUS)	1984	Howie Hawkins John Rensenbrink	Environmental Protection, Liberalism	Co-Chairs of Steering Committee of GPUS: Chris Blankenhorn, Andrea Merida Cuellar, Darlene Elias, Sandra Everette, Darryl! Moch, Tamar Yager, Bahram Zani

Act on It!
Contact a local or state party official in your state, or another state, and ask a question about the party's position on an issue that interests you.

11.6 | Political Party Eras

Political scientists have identified distinctive party eras in the U.S. party system. A party era is a time period when the two major parties took different sides on the most important issues that were facing the nation during that time period. The following describes six party eras.

11.61 | *The First Era: the 1790s until around 1824*

The election of 1796 was the first election where candidates ran as members of a political party. The Federalist Party and the Anti-Federalist Party (or Democratic Republicans) differed on the question of the power of the national government. The Federalists generally supported a strong national government and the Jeffersonian Democratic Republicans supported state government. The election of 1800 produced a number of firsts. It produced "America's first presidential campaign."[3] It marked the beginning of the end for the Federalist Party. John Adams and the Federalist Party supported England, a strong national government, industrial development, and aristocracy. Thomas Jefferson and the Republican Party supported France, decentralized state governments, and agrarian society, and egalitarian democracy. Jefferson won the election of 1800, the first transition of power from one party to the opposition party and the beginning of a party system. By 1820, the Federalist Party had gone out of existence and a Democratic Republican (James Madison) was elected president—beginning what came to be called the "Era of Good Feelings" because it was a period of one party-dominance with limited party competition.

> **Think About It!**
> What does an era of limited party politics that is called an era of good feeling imply about party politics?

11.62 | *The Second Era: from 1824 until the Civil War*

During the second era, Andrew Jackson and the Democrats were the dominant party. The Democrats advocated a populist political system that is often called **Jacksonian Democracy**. The most distinctive aspect of Jacksonian Democracy is governing based on a system of political patronage. The familiar political slogan, **"To the victor go the spoils (of office),"** describes how the candidate that won an election was entitled to give government jobs (and other benefits) to the people (including the members of his or her political party) that supported the campaign. This was the era that produced political parties as mass membership organizations rather than political parties as legislative caucuses. The most important national political issues during this era were economic matters, such as tariffs to protect manufacturing and the creation of a national bank to direct economic development, slavery, and the territorial expansion of the republic. In the years 1854 to 1856, the Republican Party emerged to replace the Whig party as the second of the major political parties of the era.

11.63 | *The Third Era: from the Civil War to 1896*

During this party era, the Republican Party and the Democratic Party were divided on two major issues: Reconstruction of the South and the Industrial Revolution. The Republican Party was a northern party that supported manufacturing, railroads, oil, and banking as part of the broader support for the Industrial Revolution. The Republican Party supported the national government's Reconstruction of the South after the Civil War. The Democratic Party was based in the South. It opposed the use of federal power, including civil rights laws, to regulate the way that Southern states treated newly freed slaves. In terms of economic policy, the Democratic Party also supported rural or agrarian interests rather than urban and industrial interests.

11.64 | *Fourth Era: from 1896 to 1932*

The Republican Party was the dominant party during the fourth party era. Its base was big business and regional strength in the northeast and the west. The Democratic Party's base was in the southern states of the old Confederacy. The early years of the fourth party era were the Progressive Era, the period from the 1890s until World War I that were notable for major reforms in politics and government. It produced the civil service system, primary elections, nonpartisan elections, and direct democracy mechanisms such as referendum, initiative, and recall. The civil service system largely replaced the spoils system of political patronage with a merit system for staffing the government. Primary and nonpartisan elections weakened political parties by giving voters more control over the selection of candidates for office any by having candidates run without party labels. These reforms were intended to get politics out of the *smoke-filled back rooms* where party bosses picked candidates for office. Referendum and initiative were two electoral reforms that expanded direct democracy by allowing the public to vote on laws proposed by state legislatures or to initiate their own laws without having to rely on state legislatures. Finally, recall was a way for voters to vote government officials out of office.

11.65 | *The Fifth Era: from the 1930s until the latter 1960s*

During this era the Democratic Party was the dominant party. The era includes the major expansions of the federal social welfare state during the New Deal programs advocated by President Franklin D. Roosevelt and the Great Society programs advocated by President Lyndon Johnson. During this era, the Democratic Party became identified with the common person, minorities, and labor, while the Republican Party became identified with business and the wealthy. The New Deal issues included the national government's response to the Depression and foreign policy matters related to World War II and the Cold War. The Great Society issues focused on the expansion of the social welfare state and civil rights and liberties. Egalitarianism is one of the values associated with New Deal/Great Society liberalism.

11.66 | *The Sixth Era: from the latter 1960s—*

This party era began as a conservative backlash against the liberalism of the New Deal and Great Society. Republicans blamed liberal Democratic policies for an increase in crime, social disorder (race riots, prison riots, and antiwar demonstrations), loss of the Vietnam War, loosening of sexual mores, school busing, affirmative action, the secularization of society, inflation—and going soft on communism! During this era, the Republican Party could be described as a four-legged stool. The four legs were

- Crime control.
- Anti-communism.
- Economic conservatism.
- Social conservatism.

Crime control meant getting tough on crime. Social conservatism meant defending and promoting traditional and family values. The term *culture wars* came to refer to the values and lifestyles conflict between liberals and conservatives. Patrick Buchanan's Address at the 1992 Republican Party Convention was a rousing speech calling for the Republican Party to fight back against liberal values. Buchanan, a traditional conservative, lost the Republican Party nomination for president but his speech inspired the social conservatives with a call to action: "There is a religious war going on in this country. It is a cultural war as critical to the kind of nation we shall be as the cold war itself—for this war is for the soul of America." Economic conservatism primarily meant de-regulation of business and opposition to taxes. Anti-communism meant an emphasis on national security that primarily focused on getting tough on the Soviet Union.

These four legs supported the Republican Party coalition that has strongly influenced the national political debates and public policy since President Nixon's election in 1968. The Republican Party won the presidency five of the six presidential elections between 1968 and 1988. And Republican President George W. Bush's party controlled both houses of Congress until the mid-term elections in 2006. When Barack Obama won the 2008 presidential election there was some speculation that the country was entering a post-party era where party politics (partisanship) would be less important than issue-based politics. This expectation was reinforced by the fact that President Obama was not a party animal! He did not enjoy, and therefore did not do much of, the familiar political backslapping and legislative deal making that was essential for building congressional support for Democratic policies. As a result, President Obama, the titular head of the Democratic Party, left the party in bad shape after his two terms in office. The Obama years were marked by intense partisan divisions that ended any speculation—or hope?—that the country was entering a post-party era of politics.

The party system is dynamic, not static. It is constantly changing. The advanced age of the current party era raises some questions about future developments in party politics. Is the sixth party era coming to an end? Does the increase in the percentage of the public that consider themselves independents indicate a major shift in the coalitions of interests in the two major parties? The political forces that shape the two major political parties are still at work: "The modern Democratic Party was shaped by the populism of the 1890s, the antibusiness reformism of the 1930s and the civil rights crusade of the 1960s.

The Republican Party was formed by abolitionism in the 1850s, anti-tax revolts in the 1970s and 1980s and the evangelical conservatism of the 1990s and 2000s."[4] The constituent elements of the two major parties change over time in response to demands that the party address contemporary problems or issues. Sometimes this results in the creation of a new dominant party era. The increase in the number of Americans who consider themselves Independents, and the ability of candidates to run for office using their own resources rather than the resources traditionally provided by a political party, has renewed speculation about the decline of political parties or even an end to the era of political parties. But partisanship has become even stronger over the last decades, so the near-term future is more likely to bring fundamental changes in the party coalitions than the end of party politics as we know it—and love to hate it!

"Are Independents Just Partisans in Disguise"
http://www.npr.org/blogs/itsallpolitics/2012/08/22/159588275/are-independents-just-partisans-in-disguise

11.7 | Political Movements and Political Parties

Understanding the long life of the U.S. two-party system requires understanding the relationship between political movements and political parties. A political movement is an organized, fairly long-term campaign to achieve a particular goal or to work for a specific **cause**. Movement can be effective because they inspire individuals to work for the cause. Movements can be organized efforts to **enact** a change in public policy OR to **stop** a proposed change. The U.S. political system has so many access points where movements can be stopped that is often easier to play defense than offense. The following is a short list of political movements:

- Abolition of slavery;
- Prohibition of alcohol;
- Pro-life or anti-abortion;
- Anti-communism;
- Civil rights;
- Feminism;
- Organized labor (unions);
- Environmentalism;
- Gay rights;
- The Tea Party;
- Property rights;
- The Religious Right; and
- The Black Lives Matter and the Blue Lives Matter Movements

Political movements have life cycles. The life cycle begins with the **identification of the cause**. The movement then develops an **organizational** or **institutional structure** to work for the cause. The movement then either **achieves** its policy goal or it **fails** to do so. Then movements tend to **fade away** whether successful or not.

Figure 11.7: The Life Cycle of Political Movements

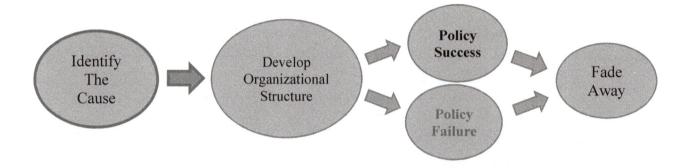

Political movements often attach themselves to one of the two major political parties in order to achieve the movement's goals. The parties are the "action arms" that help turn the ideas into public policy. The Religious Right has been an important political movement since the 1970s. It developed organizations including the Moral Majority (created by Reverend Jerry Falwell), the Christian Coalition of America, and the Faith and Freedom Coalition (both created by Ralph Reed). And the movement aligned itself with the Republican Party. Prior to and during the 2016 elections, some Christian Right leaders suggested that they should recognize that they had lost the culture wars. American culture seemed to have moved away from them: divorce was commonplace; pornography readily available; and homosexual sodomy and gay marriage were legalized. But then the movement got a new lease on life when Donald Trump won the election with the support of Evangelical Christians.

11.71 | *Major Party Coalitions*

The Republican and the Democratic Parties are coalitions of interests, some of which are political movements. The Tea Party and the Religious Right are political movements that aligned with the Republican Party to achieve their goals; the civil rights and environmental movements aligned with the Democratic Party.

The Democratic Party's coalition of interests includes racial and ethnic minorities, organized labor, consumers, urban interests (i.e., "metrosexuals") environmentalists, and more recently perhaps immigrants. This coalition began with the business reform movement of the 1930s (i.e., business regulation) and the civil rights movements of the 1950s and 1960s. The Republican Party is still identified with national security, crime control, business interests, and moral regulatory policy. The modern Republican Party is a coalition of whites, business interests, the military, and Evangelical Christians that Ronald Reagan described as a three-legged stool. The three legs were the three kinds of conservatives: national security conservatives (i.e., Cold War anti-communists); economic conservatives (anti-tax; anti-business regulation; and pro free-markets); and social values conservatives. The Republican Party is actually more accurately described as a *four-legged* stool, because crime also played a very important role in the rise of the Republican Party in the latter 1960s, and crime control continues to be an important base of conservative support.

Figure 11.71: The Republican Party Coalition

Modern Republican Party

Crime   Economics   Social   Nat. Security

> Think About It!
> The relative importance of the four legs varies from election to election. Which of the legs do you think are the widest or strongest or most important today?
> What do GOP Platforms reveal?

Political movements change political parties as the movement's ideas are incorporated into the party. As a result, party coalitions shift. The movement-party dynamic explains both **the continuity and change** in party politics. The continuity is the fact that the two-party system of Republicans and Democrats has remained the same for almost 200 years. The change is the fact that what it means to be a Republican or Democrat changes over time as movements arise to bring new issues to the political system. The dynamic of the relationship between a political party and the causes and political movements that periodically arise from within elements of a political party help explain how political change occurs within a two party system that has not changed much in 200 years in the sense that we have had the same two major parties since the early decades of the 19th Century.

11.72 | *The Just Society Belief and the Injustice of Cutting in Line*

The 2016 presidential election reveals how the party coalitions shift. Donald Trump's *hostile takeover* of the Republican Party was based on his appeal to white working class voters who had been the modern Democratic Party's base. Trump's promise to Make America Great Again resonated with these voters who believed that liberals and Democrats were allowing members of certain minority groups and even immigrants to cut ahead of them while they were standing in line to achieve the American Dream. Arlie Russell Hochschild, a journalist for a liberal publication, went to "white Louisiana" to talk to working class people about politics. He concluded that this bastion of Trump supporters believed the following conservative story about what was happening to their American Dream—and they deeply resented the unfairness of it:

"You are patiently standing in the middle of a long line stretching toward the horizon, where the American Dream awaits. But as you wait, you see people cutting in line ahead of you. Many of these line-cutters are black—beneficiaries of affirmative action or welfare. Some are career-driven women pushing into jobs they never had before. Then you see immigrants, Mexicans, Somalis, the Syrian refugees yet to come. As you wait in this unmoving line, you're being asked to feel sorry for them all. You have a good heart. But who is deciding who you should feel compassion for? Then you see President Barack Hussein Obama waving the line-cutters forward. He's on their side. In fact, isn't he a line-cutter too? How did this fatherless black guy pay for Harvard?

As you wait your turn, Obama is using the money in your pocket to help the line-cutters. He and his liberal backers have removed the shame from taking. The government has become an instrument for redistributing your money to the undeserving. It's not your government anymore; it's theirs."[5]

The above story explains how a political movement (in this case populist) and an ideology (in this case conservatism) align with a political party (in this case the Republican Party). One of the major questions about the 2016 presidential election was whether Trump voters were motivated by *economics or race*. Voting behavior is the result of many variables or factors. Political scientists try to determine the relative impact that factors have on voting. Figure 11.1 below describes seven major factors in the 2016 election.

Figure 11.1

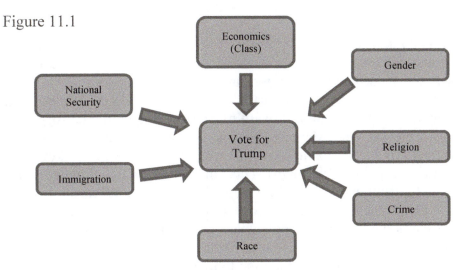

Researchers cannot simply ask people whether sensitive issues like race determine their attitudes or votes because they may think their answers are socially unacceptable evidence of prejudice. Voters are unlikely to provide honest answers to questions about whether race was a reason why they voted for Trump. In fact, conservatives and Republicans have rejected descriptions of the ideology and the party as racist, and defended positions on welfare and crime and affirmative action as principled positions reflecting beliefs about the role of government. Social scientists have developed theories of modern racism that can be applied to American National Election Studies (ANES) data in order to help answer the question whether votes for Trump were economic or racial. The concept of racial resentment captures important dimensions of modern racial animus. (Kinder and Sanders) In fact, "modern racism scales" consider racial resentment scores better predictors of attitudes toward racial policies than either ideology or racial prejudice. (Carney and Enos)

This modern racism research is relevant to the white male blue-collar voters who cast populist protest votes in the 2016 presidential election. Against whom was the populist protest vote? The "just world belief" provides an explanation. The *just world belief* shapes conservative thinking about politics (Lerner, 1980) much more than liberals—who are more likely to identify with political movements to fight injustice, to mobilize action to live up to ideals. Conservatives believe the U.S. is a basically just society where merit is recognized and rewarded. In essence, Republican voters have a post-civil rights worldview in the sense that they believe that the various civil rights movements have ended discrimination based on race and gender, for instance. Therefore they believe this is now a just world where success is determined largely by individual merit. This just world belief has the following components:

- Past racial discrimination is over. Blacks need to try harder if they want to be successful. Everyone can now enter and run the race without handicap or special benefits such as affirmative action.
- Blacks have undue influence in (democratic) politics. This influence is resented and a source of animosity.
- Immigration increases crime and immigrants take social welfare benefits that would otherwise be available for others.
- The economic stress the middle class is experiencing has been caused by the establishment's responsiveness to minorities and policies promoting diversity.

The just world believers think that Blacks, Hispanics, women, gays, and other minorities, perhaps even immigrants, are deserving special attention. In fact, in a zero sum economy, these no-longer-deserving groups are taking resources and opportunities from white working class males. These beliefs resulted not just from the liberal political parties in the U.S. and Britain. They also resulted from rightward movement of both the left-of-center parties and the right of center parties—Margaret Thatcher's Conservative Party in Britain and Reagans Republican Party in the U.S. in the 1980s with the shift toward market rather than government solutions to political problems. This "marketization" contributed to the income inequality in both countries. In the 1980s, Republican President Reagan declared that the government is the problem, not the solution. In the 1990s, Democratic President Clinton echoed the declaration by announcing that "the era of big government is over."

Some analyses of the American National Elections Study data conclude that the Trump realignment of the Republican Party coalition to include disaffected working class voters was not the result of their individual economic conditions but rather a general racial animus—*an anti-black affect*.[6] According to these analyses, the Trump vote was not about economic anxiety as much as the attitudes of white voters who angry about something much broader than their jobs and incomes. The Democratic Party enabled this affect with a campaign strategy that reinforced its already strong image as the party of racial and economic progressivism and reinforced the Republican Party's already strong image as the party of racial and economic conservatism. It is important to remember that this racial affect is best understood as broader than just race as a biological construct. The racial animus affect is similar to how 19th Century immigration policy treated race as a cultural or civilizational factor—hence the Black Irish and the treatment of Eastern and Southern Europeans as non-whites.

George Packer explains the populist revolt that erupted in both parties during the 2016 elections. For the previous several decades, elections had been fought over social issues more than economic policy. For example, even welfare reform in the 1990s was framed as more about saving morals (reducing dependency and creating initiative) more than saving money. President Clinton moved the Democratic Party rightward ideologically in 1990s by supporting welfare reform, global trade agreements, and financial capitalism.

These policies accelerated the economic and regional divides in the U.S. and other developed countries so that some individuals and some regions did very well while others did not. The political refrain from individuals and regions that did not do well was increasingly loud complaints about "[i]mmigrants, politicians, banks, criminals, the economy, and medical bills."[7]

Some *downscale whites* actually embraced the redneck and white trash labels as their own distinct identity politics that set them apart from the urban professionals with their cosmopolitan values that had become closely identified with the leadership of the Democratic Party. But this was not the typical Republican Party constituency. The term working class used to connote mainstream, main-street, Middle American values. But in *Hillbilly Elegy*, Vance (2016) laments how rural southerners became "downwardly mobile, poor, even pathological" people afflicted with the same "ills" that inhibited the black urban underclass: "intergenerational poverty, welfare, debt, bankruptcy, out-of-wedlock births, trash entertainment, addiction, jail, social distrust, political cynicism, bad health, unhappiness, early death." Rust belt cities recovered from the "inner-city decline" but now the heartland and Appalachians have been economically and socially hollowed out. According to Vance, the coastal urban elites either ignore these regions or blame individuals and their culture for their failures. He accuses the two major parties of abandoning them—thereby creating the political space for both the Trump and Sanders insurgent campaigns in 2016.

Thomas Frank's *Listen, Liberal* (2016) describes how the Democratic Party's leadership responded to popular demands for change in the 1970s, but the party replaced one set of elites (e.g., organized labor) with another set ("affluent professionals") and then failed to realize that the problems caused by growing economic inequality would be a problem for Democrats and liberals—not just for conservatives and Republicans whose economic policies had been the original cause of the inequality. President Bill Clinton's Democratic Leadership Council emphasized reinventing government (deregulating business, particularly finance), reinventing people (ending welfare and expecting the working class to rise to the professional classes in an expanding economy), and reinventing the economy (e.g., an almost religious faith in globalization as the solution to poverty among nations). In subsequent decades, it became clear that even rich nations would have losers just as there were losers within nations. Globalization reduced Global Inequality by raising poor countries, but it also made inequality much worse in rich countries. According to Frank (2016: 54), Democratic policymakers came to think of poverty as "foreign" or "black" and they misunderstood the important of nationalism because it wasn't very important to them. They, like the Republican Party establishment, grew comfortable with transnational corporations and dual citizenship and cosmopolitan urban professional values while the "other America" grew to despise these elites. In the 2016, the "other Americans" who felt neglected by the two major parties had two presidential candidates who voiced their views, and one won his party's nominations and the election.

11.73 | *The Failure of Success*

In the 1970s cities were considered centers of crime, drugs, and poverty. In 1975, for example, New York City was on the verge of bankruptcy and requested a federal bailout.

That was then. Now major cities including New York are struggling with the inequality problems created by success.

> **Think About It!**
> The PBS story "Has Urban Renewal Caused a Crisis of Success?" looks at the other side of the coin of relative economic decline in rural America. It also is a story that the two parties neglect at their peril.
> http://www.pbs.org/video/3001460660/

In fact, this version of urban renewal is part of a global problem. Economist and other social scientists describe "The Elephant Chart" to explain global trends in inequality over the last twenty years or so. The chart shows Global Income Distribution by percentage increases over twenty years from 1988 to 2008. The global income distribution has become more equal as the developing world becomes more wealth. But the chart also shows the hollowing out of the middle class in developed countries such as the U.S., Britain, and France as the developing regions of the world become wealthier in absolute and relative terms. The lower classes have gained income while the middle class incomes have been stagnant and while the top 1% has experienced steep increases in wealth. The populist protest politics in the U.S. and other western democracies has been fueled by the established, mainstream parties' failure to address these new developments in the relationship between economics and politics.

> **Think About It!**
> Paul Salman explains "The Elephant Chart" in the Making Sense segment on the PBS *Newshour*.
> http://www.pbs.org/video/3002401679/

11.74 | *Party Affiliation and Political Attitudes*

Political party identification is related to political attitudes. The origins of partisanship (the identification with a political party) have been studied extensively. There is broad agreement that a person's party identification is influenced by upbringing, ethnicity, race, geographic location, and socioeconomic status. People also identify with a party because of ideology or positions on important issues. In order to better understand all of these factors, a Gallup Panel survey asked Americans who identified themselves as Republicans or Democrats (or said they lean toward either party if they initially said they were independents) to explain in their own words just what it is about their chosen party that appeals to them most. The following Gallup Polling data describe the appeal of the two major parties.[8]

Republicans justify their allegiance to the GOP most often with reference to ideology: conservatism. Conservatism means moral regulatory policy, economic policy that prioritizes tax cuts and balanced budgets, and a generalized support for smaller government.

Republicans	Percent	Democrats	Percent
Conservative/More conservative	26	Social/Moral issue positions	18
Conservative family/moral values	15	Overall platform/ philosophy/ policies	14
Overall platform/ philosophy/ policies	12	Liberal/More liberal	11
Conservative on fiscal/economic issues	10	Help the poor	7
Favors smaller government	8	Disagree with the Republicans	5
Favors individual responsibility/self-reliance	5	Always been a Democrat	5
Always been a Republican	4	Antiwar	3
For the people/working people	3	Healthcare reform	2
Low taxes	3	Pro-environment/conservation	1
Favor strong military	3		
Pro-life on abortion	2		
More honest than the Democrats	2		
Disagree with the Democrats	2		
Other	3	Other	7
Nothing in particular (vol.)	5	Nothing in particular (vol.)	6
No opinion	6	No opinion	5

Asked of Republicans and independents who lean to the Republican Party, What is it about the Democratic Party that appeals to you most? Percentages add to more than 100% due to multiple responses.

Asked of Democrats and independents who lean to the Democratic Party) What is it about the Democratic Party that appeals to you most? Percentages add to more than 100% due to multiple responses.

Democrats are less likely to mention ideology as a reason for their partisan identity, and more likely to mention that the party's commitment to the working class, the middle class, or the *common man*. However, the 2016 presidential marked a significant change in the party's identity as disconnected from the white working class.

11.75 | *The Wired World of Party Politics*

The world is increasingly wired together by global trade, electronic communication, and travel. These connections affect politics. U.S. political parties are affected by global trends such as the current trend toward declining public confidence in established political institutions. The party systems in Europe, Britain, and the U.S. are struggling to adapt to new economic conditions, ideological coalitions, and partisan voting behavior. For example, the center-left (i.e., the social democrat) parties in Europe were expected to benefit from 1) the general trend toward globalization, secularization, and diversity; and 2) the perception that conservative parties were to blame for the Great Recession that began in 2008, the increased economic inequality, and the neoliberal public policies that rewarded individual success but failed to provide for the common or public good. But liberal parties have struggled to maintain support in the contemporary political climate, while radical, conservative populist leaders advocating nationalist policies benefited from the economic, social, religious, and political anxiety in Europe and, to a lesser extent, the U.S. Three common features of trans-Atlantic politics explain these political developments in party politics. First, the right *stole some of the left's political thunder* by adopting populist rhetoric criticizing the political establishment for ignoring the needs of the common people. Populist conservatives sounded like liberals who had been critical of the long-term trends toward increased economic and political inequality. This made it harder for liberal or left-of-center political parties to differentiate themselves from the right. For example, Donald Trump's campaign appealed to working class whites that were struggling economically and felt that they were *downwardly mobile*.

Second, over time the European left had splintered into numerous competing factions that resembled special or single-issue groups more than a liberal political party with a broad electoral appeal. Countries with multi-party systems that use proportional representation to allocate parliamentary seats fostered this splintering of interests. The 2017 general election in The Netherlands resulted in individuals from 13 political parties winning seats in the 150-member parliament. As a result, no party was able to win a majority, and a four-party coalition was necessary to get 75 seats to form a governing majority.[9] In the U.S. two-party system, the left's splintering has been primarily *intra-party* splintering that has created a Democratic Party with ideological wings. On occasion, the left's ideological splintering has resulted in major defections. In the 2000 presidential election, liberal Democrats who voted for the Green Party were a factor in George W. Bush winning the presidency despite not receiving a majority of the popular votes.

The third reason why liberal parties have not benefited from the economic crisis is the fact that *identity politics* has eroded working-class support for European social democratic parties and the American Democrats. This is a major shift in party coalitions because the working-class was the traditional base of European social democrats and the Democratic Party. As the Democratic Party became more closely identified with identity politics—blacks; ethnic minorities; gays/lesbians; immigrants; and perhaps even unions—than the economic policies that worked for the working class, they abandoned the Democrats. Frank describes this alienation in *What's the Matter with Kansas?* Donald Trump took advantage of this opportunity by campaigning as a Republican who broadened the party's appeal beyond business interests and the wealthy to include traditional democratic voters—the working class, blue-collar, middle America voters—by promising to restore jobs and values. The strength of partisanship in the electorate is evident in the fact that public opinion polls conducted in the first months of the Trump administration indicated strong support from Republicans but almost no crossover support from Democrats. The fact that the percentage of Republicans who thought the economy was good increased from 14% to 44% is evidence that partisanship determines views. As a result, both parties feel compelled to appeal to their bases of support with proposals for very different solutions for the same problem—economic insecurity.[10]

11.76 | *The Election Integrity Movement*

The election integrity movement is one of the more controversial developments in U.S. party politics over the last several election cycles. Conservatives and Republicans describe the movement as an organized campaign to protect the integrity of American elections by
- Tightening voting laws, primarily through voter identification laws;
- Tightening voter registration laws, primarily by requiring earlier registration in order to vote;
- Limiting electronic voting; and
- Restricting early voting.

The American Legislative Exchange Council (ALEC) is a conservative organization whose public policy views are closely aligned with the Republican Party. ALEC, an early supporter of the election integrity movement, created a Public Safety and Elections Task Force that developed model state laws to prevent election fraud. In 2012, ALEC ended its model policy projects on social issues, guns, voter ID, immigration, and elections after some of them became controversial.[11] Kris Kobach, the Republican who was Kansas' Secretary of State, then became the policy entrepreneur who as much as anyone else was responsible for putting ballot integrity on the agenda of the national government. The 2016 GOP platform includes a plank supporting election integrity. President Trump repeated Kobach's claims that "millions of illegals" voted in the presidential election, thereby denying Trump a majority of the popular vote. This reference to "illegals" has two meanings: illegal immigrants and citizens voting illegally. President Trump created the Advisory Commission on Election Integrity and named Kobach as vice-chair.

Kobach has linked immigration—specifically the need for extreme vetting, enforcement of immigration laws, and building a wall along the southern border—and voter fraud. Kobach was a strong supporter of a Kansas law, the Secure and Fare Election Act of 2011 (SAFE) that required presentation of a birth certificate, passport, or naturalization papers in order to register to vote. Kobach has also been a strong supporter of reducing the number of immigrants in order to preserve American national identity. He thinks the large number of Latino immigrants—particularly from Mexico—threaten American national identity. The worry that Latinos threaten American (white Protestant) national identity is based on Samuel P. Huntington's "clash of civilizations" thesis.[12] The war on terror has revived interest in Huntington's writings about the religious dimensions of the clash of civilizations after a period when liberal globalists dismissed them as Anglo-centric. The election integrity movement cannot be divorced from partisan politics because gerrymandering and restrictive voter laws are used to win elections.

> Check It Out!
> (The Kansas Voter ID Law)
> http://www.gotvoterid.com

Members of the election integrity movement investigate claims of voter fraud, prosecute illegal voters, and prevent voter fraud. Horror stories about immigrants voting, dead people voting, people voting more than once, and even dogs voting have figured prominently in justifications of the efforts to limit voting. The leaders of various state Voter Integrity Projects and the Ballot Integrity Project have taken advantage of the anti-immigration environment to claim that their efforts to prevent and prosecute illegal immigrant voting is necessary to save democracy. The stated goal of the ballot integrity movement is to prevent voter fraud. The individuals and organizations in the movement argue that restricting voting is a necessary price to pay for protection against the risk of voter fraud. It is important to understand the following issues because the intent and the effect of the ballot integrity movement is to restrict voting:

- What is vote fraud?
- What is the evidence of vote fraud?
- What is the intent of the ballot integrity movement?
- What are the effects of the ballot integrity movement?

Voter fraud is intentionally casting an illegal vote in order to affect the outcome of an election. Mistakenly casting an illegal vote is not fraud. *Claims* of voter fraud are not *evidence* of voter fraud. Conservatives and Republicans have made voter fraud an issue. Fox News programming hypes "explosive" stories about uncovering voter fraud associated with the motor voter law, for example. Rush Limbaugh, the conservative talk radio personality, regularly talks about voter fraud by Democrats: https://www.youtube.com/watch?v=KCFcle8MExw. As a candidate and as President, Trump has repeatedly warned about and claimed voter fraud and rigged elections. Conservative media frequently mention a study by Richman and Earnest, "Could Control of the Senate in 2014 Be Decided by Illegal Votes Cast by Non-Citizens?" as evidence of voter fraud. These stories and the study are not evidence of voter fraud: they are claims that voter fraud exists. The Richman and Earnest study of non-citizen voting, for example, presents a theoretical model of how much non-citizen voting might be expected to occur! Furthermore, the data they used for their model is flawed.[13]

What is Donald Trump checking (out)?

The stories of voter fraud are repeated so often that voter fraud can be considered an urban myth—a story that is told and retold and often believed but without evidence of truth. The Media Matters Electoral Studies analysis explains the difference between claims of voter fraud and evidence of it. There are actual cases of non-citizen voting. The prosecution of Rosa Maria Ortega is an interesting case. Was it voter fraud or a mistake? Did a Republican prosecute her so that the movement could have an actual case of fraud?

The intent of the election integrity movement can be inferred from the effects of its efforts. Reducing voter turnout generally favors the Republican Party. The election measures supported and adopted by the movement target liberals, younger voters, lower income voters, naturalized Hispanic voters, and blacks. For instance, members of these groups are more likely to be without the approved government-issued photo identification documents that are required by the tightened voter identification laws. Texas adopted one of the strictest photo ID laws in 2011—a law that has been repeatedly challenged in court as a violation of the Voting Rights Act of 1965 because of its effect on black and Hispanic voters. The law recognizes seven government-issued photo IDs as acceptable for voter identification: a handgun permit issued by the Texas Department of Public Safety is on the list, but student photo IDs are not. Is this because handgun owners are more likely to be Republican than college students?

Check It Out!

Texas Photo IDs
https://www.sos.state.tx.us/elections/forms/id/acceptable-forms-of-ID.pdf

Shortening voter registration time is also likely to reduce turnout of younger voters such as college students who are more likely to change residency and who are more likely to be living away from home. Laws that prohibit felons from voting, or which make it hard for felons to restore their voting rights after having served their sentences, are also likely to hurt Democrats and help Republicans. The irony of the election integrity movement is that the stated goal of increasing confidence in democracy and elections is actually undermined by the partisan efforts to use voting laws to affect the outcome of the elections. In a democracy, voters are supposed to choose government officials; government officials are not supposed to choose their voters!

The evidence supports the conclusion that the ***intent*** and the ***effect*** of the election integrity movement are to reduce the turnout of Democratic voters. Pennsylvania House Speaker Mike Turzai (Rep.) described the impact that a new state Voter ID law would likely have on the 2012 presidential election campaign between Mitt Romney (Republican) and President Obama (Democrat).

Check It Out!
https://www.youtube.com/watch?v=EuOT1bRYdK8

The federal courts have also struck down as violations of the 1965 Voting Rights Act various changes in state election laws because they diluting the votes of blacks—one of the main groups in the Democratic Party coalition.

> **Check It Out!**
> The 2016 election and the Trump administration have made fact checking a growth industry. Check out the fact checking of voter fraud claims:
> http://www.factcheck.org/2016/10/trumps-bogus-voter-fraud-claims/
> https://mediamatters.org/video/2017/01/23/cnns-jim-acosta-trumps-claim-undocumented-immigrants-cost-him-popular-vote-falsehood-full-stop/215099
> http://www.npr.org/2017/02/15/515336630/trump-claims-voter-fraud-fec-commissioner-wants-administrations-evidence

11.77 | *The Voter Fraud **Fraud***

A Brennan Center for Justice report, *The Myth of Voter Fraud and Debunking the Myth of Voter Fraud*, describes and analyzes claims of voter fraud. The Report defines voter fraud, describes the kinds of voter fraud claims, and explains why people are sometimes registered to vote in more than one place—and even why dead people sometimes vote. The Report concludes that voter fraud is a myth in the sense that investigations of voter fraud claims conclude that voter fraud (as distinct from problems with the administration of elections) is "very rare" or "almost nonexistent." There are simple reasons why immigrant voter fraud is extremely unlikely even though the rules for determining voter eligibility are complicated, and local and state government voter registration lists are notoriously error-filled. Voter fraud is a felony; it is easily detected using records of citizenship and voting records; the penalties can be severe; and voter fraud is a very inefficient way to try to influence the outcome of an election. Organized voter fraud by a candidate or political party or interest group—such as a strategy to get non-citizens (legal residents or illegal immigrants) to vote—is very inefficient and it would require getting large numbers of individuals to commit crimes. This is criminal conspiracy. It is much more logical and more efficient to try to influence the outcome of an election by 1) hacking into the electronic voting systems; or 2) by hacking into private campaign communications and releasing them to the public; or 3) by spreading fake news! Vladimir Putin operationalized plans to undermine the integrity of elections in the U.S. and Europe that relied on these methods not voter fraud.

11.8 | Summary

The U.S. two-party system provides both political continuity and change. The parties generally stabilize politics by moderating radical leftwing or rightwing ideas. The two parties create an establishment status quo. But the parties must also respond to demands for change or risk being rejected by the voters. The fact that about one-third of voters call themselves independents is evidence of some dissatisfaction with the Republican and Democratic Party labels. The 2016 presidential election challenged both the Republican and Democratic Parties. Donald Trump and Bernie Sanders ran against the Republican and

Democratic Party establishments. Trump's successful primary campaign was, in many ways, a hostile takeover of the Republican Party. His *change campaign* correctly sensed that the electorate that was dissatisfied with the status quo offered by both major parties. His general election campaign, which continued to pull the party in a new more populist direction, was successful because the Democratic Party leadership seemed out of touch with the average American on both economic issues (jobs and trade) and values (e.g., religion; diversity; gay rights). The economic and social positions that he took were also closely related to two issues that became salient during the campaign: immigration and race. Immigration policy became closely identified with national security, economics, and national identity politics. Race became closely identified with crime control politics—which has divided Republicans and Democrats, conservatives and liberals, for decades.

Independents and voters who had voted for Democrats in the past either did not vote or voted for Trump because they thought the Democratic Party was more likely to work for groups other than the white working class. Hillary Clinton was slow to recognize how the changing political dynamics were challenging the established party coalitions. She ran what had become the establishment Democratic campaign—one that appealed heavily to identity politics—despite the fact that Bernie Sanders, her primary campaign challenger, attracted strong support running as an insurgent challenging the Democratic Party establishment. During the campaign, some of Hillary Clinton's supporters warned that she was not adjusting to the changing political climate because her political instincts "are suboptimal."[14]

Pollsters, Party leaders, political analysts, have had a hard time predicting election outcomes during the recent populist politics wave in the U.S., Britain, and Europe. Populism is not just anti-establishment venting. Populists advocate for specific economic, social, and national security policies. The populist rhetoric in the 2016 U.S. elections reflects increased political polarization even while parties have become weaker political institutions. The result is a scrambling of status quo coalitions in the Republican and Democratic parties. Elections have policy consequences. The Republican victories in the state, congressional, and presidential elections in 2016 have produced major changes in the following areas of public policy:

- Criminal Justice. The Republican Party supports the crime control model of justice as part of getting tough on crime.
- Health Care. Efforts to repeal and replace Obamacare have been inspired by efforts to reduce government involvement and increase private sector insurance-based systems for providing health care.
- The Environment. The Environmental Protection Agency (EPA) is the federal agency primarily responsible for implementing environmental statutes and developing administrative regulations intended to protect the environment. Conservatives, Republicans, and President Trump have made the EPA a high-profile target for reducing government regulation.
- Economics. Conservatives, neoliberals, and Republicans generally supported free market theory that made globalization and free trade agreements centerpieces of foreign policy, and deregulation of business a centerpiece of domestic policy. The Trump administration supports both more and less government: a more statist policy as part of the make America great again goal, but a less statist policy that deregulates business from power plants to agribusiness, to pharmaceuticals, to the

Internet. This marks a change from the Democratic economic policy, which tends to supports government protection of workers and consumers while promoting economic equality. However, President Trump's initial budget proposals, tax reform proposals, and health care overall are not populist polices, but rather policies reflecting the establishment Republican priorities.

- Immigration. The Obama administration supported a comprehensive immigration reform proposal that promised to increase border security and enforcement of immigration laws by deporting individuals who committed serious crimes while in the country illegally but also offering a pathway to either legal status or citizenship. Republicans eventually adopted a political strategy of opposing immigration reform while getting tough on illegal immigration and stressing border control. President Trump's actions on immigration can be described as one of the examples of "Promises Made. Promises Kept."

Study Questions

What are the roles and functions of political parties in America? Do parties play a worthwhile role in the American political system?

1) How are political parties organized in America? What effect does this have on the political system?
2) Trace the evolution of the political parties from the founding through the New Deal. How and why did the parties change during this period?
3) What role do political parties play in elections?
4) What are the major eras in the history of American political parties?
5) Compare and contrast the platforms, strengths, weaknesses, and strategies of the Republican and Democratic Parties.

11.9 | Additional Resources

The American Presidency Project at the University of California, Santa Barbara, provides National Party Platforms, Presidential Nomination Acceptance Speeches, and Debates
http://www.presidency.ucsb.edu/platforms.php

The Republican Party Platform is available at https://www.gop.com

The Democratic Party Platform is available at
https://www.democrats.org/organization/the-democratic-national-committee

The Libertarian Party Platform is available at
https://www.lp.org/platform/

The Green Party of the U.S.: http://www.gp.org/

The Constitution Party: https://www.constitutionparty.com/

The Federal Elections Commission provides information about registering as a political party: https://www.fec.gov/help-candidates-and-committees/registering-political-party/

The Central Intelligence Agency's *World Factbook* provides a great deal of information about the party systems of the countries in the world: https://www.cia.gov/library/publications/the-world-factbook/fields/2118.html

A list of political parties is available at Gov-Spot.com: http://www.govspot.com/categories/politicalparties.htm

Yougov.com provides information about various political systems: https://today.yougov.com

11.91 | In the Library

Berger, Peter, and John Neuhaus. 1977. *To Empower People: The Role of Mediating Structures in Public Policy.*

Bibby, John F. and L. Sandy Maisel. 2002. *Two Parties—Or More?* Westview Press.

Carney, Riley K., and Ryan D. Enos. 2015. "Conservatism and Fairness in Contemporary Politics: Unpacking the Psychological Underpinnings of Modern Racism," Working Paper Presented at the Annual Meeting of the Midwest Political Science Association. Accessed at https://scholar.harvard.edu/files/rkcarney/files/carneyenos.pdf

Green, Donald, et al. 2002. *Partisan Hearts and Minds: Political Parties and the Social Identities of Voters.* Yale University Press.

Greenberg, Stanley B. 2004. *The Two Americas: Our Current Political Deadlock and How to Break It.* St. Martin's Press.

Frank, Thomas. 2004. *What's the Matter with Kansas.* New York: Henry Holt & Company.

Frank, Thomas. 2016. *Listen, Liberal: Or What Ever Happened to the Party of the People?* New York: Metropolitan Books.

Kinder, Donald R., and Lynn M. Sanders. 1996. *Divide by Color: Racial Politics and Democratic Ideals.* Chicago: University of Chicago Press.

Lerner, Melvin J. 1980. *The Belief in a Just World.* New York: Springer.

Lofgren, Michael. 2012. *The Party is Over: How Republicans Went Crazy, Democrats Became Useless, and the Middle Class Got Shafted.* New York: Viking.

Noel, Hans. 2014. *Political Ideologies and Political Parties in America*. Cambridge.

Reichley, James A. 2000. *The Life of the Parties: A History of American Political Parties*. Second Edition. Lanham, MD: Rowan & Littlefield.

Sanbonmatsu, Kira. 2004. *Democrats, Republicans, and the Politics of Women's Place*. University of Michigan Press.

Sundquist, James L. 1973. *The Dynamics of the Party System*. Washington, DC: The Brookings Institution.

Vance, J. D. 2016. *Hillbilly Elegy: A Memoir of a Family and Culture in Crisis*. New York: Harper.

---

[1] Jens Krause and Graeme D. Ruxton. 2002. *Living in Groups*. London: Oxford University Press.

[2] Mike Lofgren. 2012. The Party Is Over. New York: Viking.

[3] Edward J. Larson. 2007. *A Magnificent Catastrophe: The Tumultuous Election*

[4] Sam Tanenhaus, "Harnessing a Cause Without Yielding to It." *The New York Times* (November 9, 2008), p.3WK.

[5] Arlie Russell Hochschild, "How Donald Trump Took a Narrative of Unfairness and Twisted It to His Advantage, Mother Jones (September/October 2016). Retrieved at http://www.motherjones.com/politics/2016/08/trump-white-blue-collar-supporters/

[6] Sean McElwee and Jason McDaniel, "Economic Anxiety Didn't Make People Vote Trump, Racism Did," *The Nation* (May 8, 2017). Accessed at https://www.thenation.com/article/economic-anxiety-didnt-make-people-vote-trump-racism-did/

[7] George Packer, "Hillary Clinton and the Populist Revolt," *The New Yorker* (October 31, 2016), p.50. Accessed at http://www.newyorker.com/magazine/2016/10/31/hillary-clinton-and-the-populist-revolt

[8] http://www.gallup.com/poll/102691/Whats-Behind-Republican-Democratic-Party-ID.aspx

[9] Cynthia Kroet, "Dutch Coalition Talks on Hold After Second Attempt to Form Government Fails," *Politico* (May 23, 2017). Accessed at: http://www.politico.eu/article/dutch-coalition-talks-on-hold-after-second-attempt-to-form-government-fails-election-mark-rutte/

[10] PEW Research Center, "In First Month, Views of Trump are Already Strongly Felt, Deeply Polarized," (February, 16, 201). Accessed at http://www.people-press.org/2017/02/16/in-first-month-views-of-trump-are-already-strongly-felt-deeply-polarized/

[11] https://www.alec.org/public-affair/american-legislative-exchange-council-transparency-and-public-engagement/

[12] Ari Berman, "The Man behind Trump's Voter-Fraud Obsession," *The New York Times*, (June 13, 2017). Accessed at https://www.nytimes.com//

[13] See the NPR story for the analysis of the methodological flaws:
http://www.npr.org/2016/11/28/503628803/here-are-the-problems-with-the-trump-teams-voter-fraud-evidence

[14] John Podesta quoted in Jake Tapper "Wikileaks Seems to Reveal Top Clinton Advisers' Frustration with Clintons over Political Attacks," CNN (October 18, 2016). Accessed at
http://www.cnn.com/2016/10/18/politics/clinton-staffers-frustrated-hillary-clinton-bill-clinton-chelsea-clinton/.

Lobbyist Bob Livingston (L) and former Speaker of the House Newt Gingrich (R)

12.0 | Interest Groups

Interest groups play an extremely important role in American politics and government. In fact, it is impossible to understand American government or politics without a basic understanding of interest groups. This chapter describes interest groups and their political activities. It also explains their role in politics, government, and the public policy process. The explanation of the increased role that interest groups play in modern politics and government includes assessments of whether their role is basically good or bad, beneficial or harmful, as well as whether interest groups are too powerful. The main question about interest groups is whether they advance their special interests to the detriment of the general, public, or national interest. This question is similar to questions about the role of political parties, and it produces similar skepticism about powerful special interests. In politics as in other areas of life, organization increases effectiveness. Like parties, interest groups are mediating institutions that organize public participation in politics, function as part of the system of checks and balances, and help civil society control government power. This chapter will help you decide whether group behavior is madness or whether groups give voice to individuals.

> "MADNESS IS RARE IN INDIVIDUALS - BUT IN GROUPS, POLITICAL PARTIES, NATIONS, AND ERAS IT'S THE RULE."
>
> - FRIEDRICH NIETZSCHE
>
> "TEN PEOPLE WHO SPEAK MAKE MORE NOISE THAN TEN THOUSAND WHO ARE SILENT."
>
> NAPOLEON BONAPARTE

12.1 | What is an Interest Group?

An **interest group** is a collection of individuals or organizations that share a common interest and advocate or work for public policies on behalf of the members' shared interests. For these reasons, interest groups are also called advocacy groups, lobbying groups, pressure groups, or even special interest groups. What is the difference between an interest group and a political party? It is not size—although in the U.S. interest groups are smaller than the Republican and Democratic Parties. An interest group can have more or fewer members than a political party. A large organization such as The Association for the advancement of Retired People (AARP) has more members than some minor political parties.

The major difference between an interest group and a political party is that parties try to achieve their policy goals by running candidates for office in order to control government but interest groups usually do not. Both political parties and interest groups take positions on important public policy issues and work on behalf of their members' goals. But interest groups advocate for policies without actually running candidates in elections in order to try to take control of government. Interest groups typically lobby the government to adopt their positions. Lobbyists are the individuals who represent and advocate on behalf of an interest group.   Political scientists agree that interest groups play an important role in American politics, but they do not agree on what exactly defines an interest group. One definition of an interest group focuses on membership: a group must have a significant number of members in order to be officially recognized as an interest group. Another definition focuses on efforts to influence public policy, not membership itself, so that an interest group is defined as any non-government group that tries to affect policy. The term interest group is sometimes used generically to refer to any segment of a society that shares similar political opinions on an issue or group of issues (e.g. seniors, the poor, consumers, etc.) even if they are not necessarily part of an organized group.

12.12 | *Types of Interest Groups*

There are many types of interest groups. Interest groups represent or advocate on behalf of almost every imaginable organized interest from A (abortion; airlines; agriculture) to Z (zoning and zoos). One major distinction between types of interest groups is the difference between public and private interest groups. A **public interest group** is one that advocates for an issue that benefits society as a whole. A **private interest group** is one that advocates for an issue that primarily benefits the members of the group. There are some overlaps between these two types because it is not always possible to separate public and private interests.

Common Cause, founded by Ralph Nader, was one of the first public interest groups. It promotes responsible government generally but it has a primarily liberal orientation. Three prominent public interest groups in the field of public health are the American Heart Association, the American Cancer Society, and the American Lung Association. A related type of public interest group is The Public Interest Research Group (PIRG), but it is a primarily liberal advocate on issues such as the environment, public transportation, and education. Groups whose primary purpose is advancing the economic interests of their members are private interest groups. The Indoor Tanning Association, for example, is a trade group that advocates for a specific industry. It lobbies to protect an industry from increased government regulation during a time when there is increased concern about skin cancer. During the protracted health care reform debates of 2009 that eventually resulted in the passage of the Patient Protection and Affordable Care Act (Obamacare), Congress considered proposals to pay for the expanded health with a "Botax," a tax on elective, cosmetic surgery. Doctors successfully lobbied against the Botax in the Senate health care reform bill, so a "tantax" was substituted—a tax on indoor sun tanning services. The Indoor Tanning Association opposed the proposed Tantax. In fact, the tanning industry has a broader lobbying and public information campaign to ease public concerns about the adverse health effects of tanning and thereby avoid further taxation and regulation. This campaign is a good example of a defensive strategy, one that is intended to prevent public policy actions that are adverse to a group's interests. The U.S. political system has many veto points where legislation can be stopped.

The number of organized interest groups began increasing in the post-World War II era, with group formation surging since the 1960s. The increased size of the federal government also meant that many of the interest groups went national in the sense that they focused their activities on Washington, DC.[1]

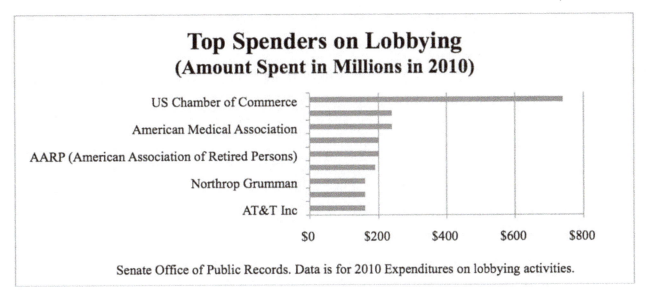

Top Spenders on Lobbying
(Amount Spent in Millions in 2010)

Senate Office of Public Records. Data is for 2010 Expenditures on lobbying activities.

The following illustrate the types of interest groups and interest group activities:

- Business Groups. A corporation such as an aerospace manufacturer or a health care company that lobbies to win a government contract to buy airplanes or provide health care services. Corporations often hire a lobbying firm to advocate for their interests.
- Trade or Professional Associations. An employers' organization or trade or professional association that represents the interests of an entire industry (e.g., manufacturers or health care or insurance or legal services). An interest group that represents an entire sector of the economy might lobby for favorable tax policies or favorable regulatory policies.
- Labor Groups. Labor unions that represent organized labor and other employee rights groups advocate for public policies that benefit workers, such as minimum wage laws or workplace safety laws or health care. These groups can represent private sector workers or public sector workers.
- Demographic Groups. These are organizations that represent specific demographic segments of society such as senior citizens; racial, ethnic, or religious minorities; veterans; persons with disabilities; and immigrants. These groups typically lobby for retirement benefits, laws protecting against discrimination, pension benefits, handicap accessibility, religious freedoms and public support, and favorable immigration policies.
- Single Issue Groups. These are groups that were created specifically to advocate for a single-issue. Single-issue groups include those that advocate for women's rights, the environment, or advocate for or against abortion or gay rights.
- Ideological Groups. Ideological groups include organizations that advocate for conservatism, liberalism, or libertarianism, for example. Ideological groups also include think tanks, the research and policy organizations that often have a

particular ideological perspective or a particular economic theory that informs their policy analysis and advocacy.

- Religious Organizations. Church Groups or organizations active on religious issues lobbying government for exemptions from zoning laws, tax laws, or employment rules and regulations.

12.13 | *Economic Interest Groups*

The greatest number of interest groups is economic interest groups including business, trade and other associations, labor, and professional associations.

- **Business**. Businesses such as General Motors, Microsoft, and Boeing lobby to influence public policy regarding employment, workplace safety, the environment, taxes, and trade policy, among others. In this era of cooperative federalism, where both the national and state governments regulate business and economic activity, corporations typically have a Public Affairs or Public Relations or Government Affairs division to conduct public relations campaigns, to make campaign contributions on behalf of candidates they support, and to lobby on behalf of the business' interests.

- **Trade Associations**. Businesses with a similar interest sometimes join trade associations to advocate on behalf of the entire industry or sector of the economy. The U.S. Chamber of Commerce, the National Federation of Independent Businesses, and the National Association of Manufacturers are trade associations. They are interest groups that represent business generally, or small business specifically, or the manufacturing sector specifically. The number of such business groups and their local, state, and national influence make them one of the more important political forces in U.S. politics. Business groups are generally members of the Republican Party coalition.

- **Labor**. Interest groups representing workers include labor unions that represent individuals who work on farms or the agricultural sector, manufacturing such as steel and auto manufacturing), and individuals who work in the service sector. Union membership in the U.S. is low, particularly compared with membership in other industrial democracies. Two of the oldest and most powerful labor unions are the AFL-CIO (The American Federation of Labor and Congress of Industrial

Organizations) and the Teamsters. The influence of organized labor has greatly diminished over the past decades. One reason for their decline is the American economy has moved away from industry and manufacturing, which were the sectors of the economy where unions were strongest, toward an information and service sector economy, where unions were not organized. Industrial and manufacturing unions represented blue-collar workers. White-collar workers have not been heavily unionized. As the economy shifted toward the service sector, a labor union was created specifically to represent these "pink collar" workers. The Service Employees International Union (SEICU), which calls itself the largest and fastest growing union, organizes on behalf of health care and hospitality industry workers. Labor Unions are traditionally members of the Democratic Party coalition.

- **Professional Associations**. Professionals have organized themselves into some of the most influential interest groups in the U.S. These include such well known professional associations as the American Medical Association; the American Bar Association; the National Education Association; the National Association of Realtors; and engineering associations—the National Society of Professional Engineers and the American Engineering Association. The AEA's mission is to make the AEA "an AMA for engineers." The above "Top Spenders on Lobbying" graph shows that professional associations are the top spenders on lobbying. Each state controls occupational licensure. That is, a state licenses professionals to operate in the state. Therefore there are 50 state medical associations and state bar associations. Medicine, law, and engineering are among the most prestigious professions. Their professional associations can exert considerable influence over government regulation of their professions, including the licensing standards that determine access to the profession. One power question about these professional associations is whether they use their influence to protect the public/consumers (from untrained or unscrupulous doctors, engineers, lawyers, or financial advisors) or whether they use their political power to protect their members.

Act on It!
Civic engagement includes interacting with organizations that are such an important part of civil society. Contact an interest group to ask about an issue that you are interested in or an issue that the group supports.

12.14 | *Ideological Groups*

Ideological groups are organized to advocate for a particular set of political beliefs. Ideological groups are harder to identify than economic groups. The American Conservative Union calls itself the oldest membership-based conservative organization in the U.S. One of its most widely known actions is the rating of elected government officials. The American Civil Liberties Union might be considered an ideological organization but its advocacy of civil liberties is sometimes liberal and sometimes conservative. The Americans for Democratic Action calls itself the oldest independent liberal organization in the U.S. There is a large number of radical or fringe organizations that are active in American politics, if sometimes only on the Internet. One such radical right organization is the Guardians of the Free Republic.

12.15 | *Think Tanks*

Think tanks are organizations that are primarily interested in researching and promoting ideas. It is appropriate to think of think tanks as "think-and-do" tanks because they are interested in thought that produces action. Think tanks research and advocate public policies that are based on the ideas they support. The American Action Network is a conservative think tank. A former director of the Congressional Budget Office described its purpose, and the purpose of other think tanks: "Having good ideas is not enough. You actually have to sell them to the Congress, the president, the citizens." [2] Two prominent think tanks are the Brookings Institution, a think tank with a generally liberal orientation, and the American Enterprise Institute, a think tank with a generally conservative orientation.

12.2 | **Incentives to join**

Why do political groups exist? Why do people join groups? The Political Scientist James Q. Wilson identified three types of incentives to join a group: solidarity, material, and purposive.[3] Some interest groups provide more than one of these incentives for membership, but the different categories are useful for understanding the different kinds of interest groups.

12.21 | *Solidarity*

Solidarity incentives for a person to join a group are essentially social reasons. Individuals decide to join a group because they want to associate with others with similar interests, backgrounds, or points of view. The old saying, Birds of a Feather Flock Together, describes solidarity incentives. Church groups, civic groups such as the Elks Club, and groups whose members have shared ethnic backgrounds, are examples of groups whose members are motivated primarily by associational or shared interests.

12.22 | *Material*

Material incentives are essentially economic motives for membership. Membership is motivated by a tangible benefit. An individual who joins the Association for the Advancement of Retired People (AARP) to get motel, restaurant, or car rental discounts is motivated by a material incentive to join. A company that becomes a member of a trade association such as the Chamber of Commerce or the National Association of Manufacturers in order to benefit from the trade association's lobbying is motivated by a material incentive. A study of interest groups in the United States and other countries found that a great majority (almost three-quarters) represents professional or occupational interests. The main motivation of such professional or occupational groups is economic or material interests.[4]

12.23 | *Purposive*

Purpose incentives are those that appeal to an individual's commitment to advancing the groups' social or political aims. Purposive groups attract members who join for reasons other than merely associating with others who share their interests, or solely because they want to obtain material benefits. Some of these purposive or issue advocacy groups are ideological. Ideological purposive groups advocate on behalf of ideas (e.g., conservative; liberal; libertarian) or causes (right-to-life; civil liberties; property rights; the environment; religious freedom). Purposive groups include the American Conservative Union, the American Civil Liberties Union, the Sierra Club, and the two major interest groups who take different sides in the debate over abortion policy: The National Right to Life and the National Abortion Rights Action League (NARAL).

12.3 | **What Do Interest Groups Do?**

Much of what interest groups do falls under the large umbrella of lobbying. Lobbying is a broad term for an interest group's activities that seek to persuade political leaders and government officials to support a particular position. Lobbying occurs at all levels of government (local, state, national, and international), in all three branches of government (although technically groups do not lobby the courts), and in non-governmental settings. Interest group lobbying includes testifying at government hearings, contacting legislators, providing information to politicians, filing lawsuits or funding lawsuits or submit amicus curiae briefs with a court, and public campaigns to change public opinion or to rally members of the group to contact public officials.

12.31 | *Lobby Congress*

Congress, committee members, and individual members of congress are frequent targets of lobbying campaigns. Interest groups might lobby in the congressional setting by providing testimony at a committee or subcommittee meeting, contributing to an individual congressional representative's campaign fund, or organizing a letter or phone-call campaign by members of the interest to convince a particular representative of the public support for a policy.

12.32 | *Lobby the Executive Branch*

Although the executive branch does not actually make the laws, interest groups target the executive branch in order to influence the formation of public policy or its implementation. Lobbying the executive branch may include contacting the president, members of the president's staff (including the chief of staff or policy advisors), cabinet level officials, or other high-ranking members of the executive departments (the political appointees that make policies). Interest groups also lobby the independent regulatory commissions. These agencies have rule making authority. The rule making process includes taking public comments about proposed regulations. Interest groups participate in this process in order to influence regulatory policy that affects them. Officials in the executive departments also play an important role in the development of the federal budget, so interest groups lobby them to support programs that the groups supports and oppose programs that the group is opposed to. Agricultural interests, food processors, and consumer groups lobby members of the Department of Agriculture, which plays an important role in congressional and administration food policy. Health care providers, insurance companies, and patient rights groups lobby officials in the Department of Health and Human Services, which play an important role in formulating and implementing health care policy (including Medicare and Medicaid). The telecommunications industry, consumer rights groups, and citizen groups interested in the content of broadcast programming lobby the Federal Communications Commission. The FCC is an independent regulatory agency that licenses broadcast companies and has some authority to regulate the content of broadcast programming and other aspect of the telecommunication industry.

Interest Groups are an important part of the policymaking process. They are one of the three major members of what political scientists call Issue Networks. The term Issue Network describes the patterns of interactions among three sets of participants in the policy making process: a congressional committee; an Executive Department; and interest groups. Each area of public policy has an Issue Network. Interest groups link the government—that is congressional committees and the executive departments or independent regulatory commissions—and the civil society (the interest groups). The following figure describes the Issue Network for defense policy. The arrows describe the mutual benefits the participants provide. Interest groups provide information to the legislative committees and executive departments that make public policy in their area of interest. Congressional committees provide budgets for programs that an interest groups supports. And executive departments support programs that interest groups support.

Figure 12.3   Issue Networks: Defense Policy

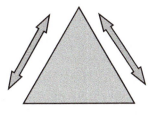

Congressional Committees
Senate Armed Services Committee
House Armed Services Committee

Executive Departments
The Department of Defense

Interest Groups
(Aerospace and Defense Industries)

12.33 | *"Lobbying" the Courts*

In an effort to maintain some separation of law and politics, it is considered inappropriate for interest groups to lobby the courts the way they lobby congress and the executive branch. Interest group efforts to influence the courts take two forms. The first is political litigation. Political litigation is using a lawsuit primarily to change public policy. An interest group may file a lawsuit on behalf of its members. The Sierra Club may file a lawsuit challenging a policy allowing development  of a natural environment. The National Federation of Independent Businesses challenged the constitutionality of the Patient Protection and Affordable Care Act (Obamacare). A second way that an interest group can lobby the courts is by filing an *amicus curiae* brief (that is, a friend of the court brief) that advocates for one of the two sides in a case that is before the court. The major cases that the Supreme Court agrees to decide typically have a large number of amicus curiae briefs submitted for both sides. A third way that interest groups attempt to influence the courts is by sponsoring a lawsuit, providing legal resources for the actual parties. Taking a case all the way to the Supreme Court requires a great deal of time and money.

A good example of political litigation is the efforts of The National Association for the Advancement of Colored People (NAACP) to support lawsuits challenging the constitutionality of segregated public schools. The landmark Supreme Court ruling in

School Segregation Banned, the *Topeka State Journal*. *Courtesy Kansas State Historical Society*

STATE THE TOPEKA **JOURNAL** Home Edition

FOLKS AND THINGS
By 2054 This Bill Should Be Terrific

SCHOOL SEGREGATION BANNED

Supreme Court Refutes Doctrine of Separate but Equal Education

High Tribunal Fails to Specify When Practice of Dual Schools Must Be Dropped by States

"Today, education is perhaps the most important function of state and local government. Compulsory school attendance laws and the great expenditures for education both demonstrate our recognition of the importance of education to our democratic society... WE CONCLUDE THAT IN THE FIELD OF PUBLIC EDUCATION THE DOCTRINE OF 'SEPARATE BUT EQUAL' HAS NO PLACE. SEPARATE EDUCATIONAL FACILITIES ARE INHERENTLY UNEQUAL. "

Oliver L. Brown, et al. vs Board of Education of Topeka, Kansas, United States Supreme Court, May 17, 1954.

Brown v. Board of Education was the result of an organized campaign to use the courts to change public policy. In fact, the various civil rights revolutions of the period 1940s-1960s relied heavily on political litigation. In the 1950s and 1960s, liberal public interest groups relied heavily on political litigation to change public policies related to prisoner rights, racial equality, freedom of expression, the right to privacy, and environmentalism. In the 1970s conservative public interest groups used political litigation to change public policies on abortion, property rights, freedom of religion, affirmative action, business and employer rights, and gun rights.

Today there are many conservative organizations that have adopted a legal strategy to achieve conservative policy goals:

- The Pacific Legal Foundation was created to challenge environmental regulations.
- The U.S. Chamber of Commerce established a National Chamber Litigation Center and the Institute for Legal Reform to advocate pro-business legal policies.
- The Christian Legal Society advocates against the separation of church and state.
- The Cato Institute advocates libertarian positions.
- The National Rifle Association advocates for gun rights.

The tort reform movement is an example of business groups going to court to change legal policies relating to torts—wrongful injuries such as medical malpractice and product liability. "Judicial Hellholes," "Jackpot Justice," "Looney Lawsuits," and "Wacky Warning Labels Contest" are terms that have entered everyday vocabulary about civil law in modern American society. The American Tort Reform Association has even trademarked the epithet "Judicial Hellholes." The National Federation of Independent Businesses has created a Small Business Legal Center

specifically to advocate in the courts: "The Legal Center is the advocate for small business in the courts. We do what federal and state NFIB lobbyists do, but instead of lobbying legislatures we lobby judges through briefs and oral arguments in court. We tell judges how the decision they make in a given case will impact small businesses nationwide."[5]

The American Tort Reform Association's membership and funding come from the American Medical Association and the Council of Engineering Companies. The National Association of Manufacturers uses political litigation to change policies that it considers anti-business, such as product liability laws and campaign finance laws that limit campaign contributions. The U.S. Chamber of Commerce has established an Institute for

Legal Reform which specializes in political litigation to advance pro-business legal

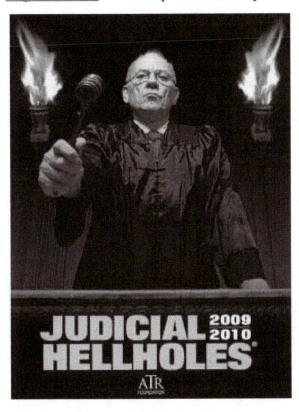

policies. Whose side are the lawyers on? In criminal justice, the defense bar represents suspects who have been accused of a crime. In civil justice issues such as product liability and medical malpractice, the plaintiff bar generally represents consumers, employees, or patients. Lawyers for Civil Justice is a national organization of corporate counsel and defense lawyers advocating for tort reform. The Florida Chamber of Commerce created the Florida Justice Reform Institute to reform what it calls a wasteful civil justice system. Other business organizations advocating tort reform include America's Health Insurance Plans, American Hospital Association, Pharmaceutical Research and Manufacturing Association, and the National Federation of Independent Businesses.

12.34 | *Grassroots Lobbying and Protests*

Interest groups also engage in **grassroots lobbying**. Grassroots lobbying is a term for efforts to mobilize local support for an issue position the group has taken. Grassroots lobbying is usually contrasted with Washington lobbying. Washington lobbying is sometimes criticized as "inside-the-beltway" activity that focuses on the Washington political establishment to the neglect of the average American or Mainstreet America. Grass roots lobbying has an "outside-the-

beltway" focus and therefore a reputation for being a more genuine reflection of public

opinion that Washington lobbying campaigns. Grassroots lobbying consists of interest groups contacting citizens and urging them to contact government officials rather than having the interest group directly contact government officials.

The political appeal of appearing to be a grass-roots organization whose members come from the community has created the phenomenon called "astroturf" lobbying. Astroturf lobbying is where an interest group without a large membership portrays itself as having roots in the community. The membership is artificial, however, which is why the grassroots are called astroturf. In today's media age and celebrity culture, grassroots campaigns can use influential media personalities (such as Rachel Maddow or Glen Beck) to encourage their listeners or viewers to take action, thereby linking the national and electronic communities to the local or grassroots. The more extreme version of grassroots lobbying is organizing or supporting protests and demonstrations. Many national organizations have a day where they bring members to Washington, D.C. to call attention to their issues, whether advocating to put an issue on the policy agenda or to protest a change in public policy.

12.35 | *Lobbyists*

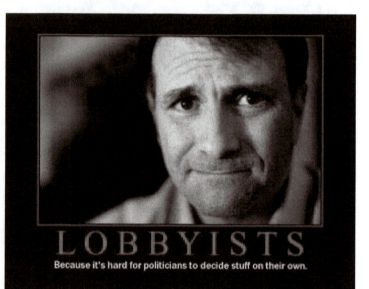

Interest groups frequently pay professional lobbyists to represent the organization to the public and the government. Professional lobbyists can either work directly for the interest group or they can be employees of public relations or law firms who are hired by the group for a specific campaign. One of the most seriously funny depictions of interest group efforts to influence public opinion and public policy, and the image of lobbyists is the Hollywood film *Thank You For Smoking*. The fictional film describes the efforts of the tobacco lobby, the alcohol lobby, and gun lobby, which IN THE FILM are called the "MOD Squad: Merchants of Death." The *Youtube* video clip is available at: http://www.youtube.com/watch?v=iBELC_vxqhI

12.36 | *Campaigns and Elections*

Interest groups also participate in campaigns and elections. In elections of government officials, interest group activity includes the following:

- Candidate recruitment. Groups recruit candidates with specific views on political issues to support for office.
- Campaign contributions. Interest groups provide funding to support campaigns.
- Campaign resources. Interest groups with large memberships provide campaign workers.
- Public information. Interest groups rate candidates (e.g., on conservatism or liberalism) to provide information to voters about where a candidate stands on the issues).

- Get out the vote efforts. Groups can rally their members to go to the polls to vote for a particular candidate.

Of course, money is the mother's milk of politics. Money has become more important as politics has moved away from the grass roots **retail politics** (one-to-one or personal relationships) toward **wholesale politics** (mass appeal campaigns). Wholesale politics is more likely to be "air war" campaigns that are conducted on television, radio, and the Internet. One of the main ways that groups participate in elections is by providing money— raising and spending money on behalf of a campaign or political cause. There are a number of organizations that are created specifically to provide money for campaigns. A **Political Action Committee (PAC)** is a political arm of a business, labor, trade, professional, or other group. PACS are legally authorized to raise voluntary funds from employees or members of the group to contribute to a party or candidate. Many interest groups have PACs. Realtors have RPAC; doctors have AMPAC; supporters of abortion rights have NARAL-PAC and pro-life advocates have Right to Life PAC.

Political action committees (PAC) allow interest groups pool resources from group members and contribute to political campaigns and politicians. Under federal law, an organization automatically becomes a PAC by either receiving contributions or making expenditures more than $1000 for the purpose of influencing a federal election. Individual contributions to federal PACs are limited to $5,000 per year. However, the whole system of campaign finance law is currently in an unsettled state because the Supreme Court has ruled that campaign spending is a form of free speech that is protected by the First Amendment. As a result, the federal laws limiting the amount of money that an individual could spend on his or her own campaign were struck down. And in *Citizens United v Federal Election Commission* (2010) the Court ruled that corporate campaign contributions that were independent of a candidate's campaign could not be limited by the government. This ruling resulted in the creation of Superpacs. In addition, organizations that are listed under section 527 of the tax code as social welfare organizations can also engage in more campaign activity without regulation.

Not all campaigns are conducted to elect government officials. Some campaigns are referendums. A referendum is a political campaign where the public votes for or against an issue that is presented on the ballot. An example of a referendum election is one where the public votes whether to approve a tax increase. Interest groups are especially important players in referendum politics because groups organize public support for their side of the issue and public opposition for the side they oppose.

12.37 | *Providing Information*

Interest groups and lobbyists typically describe their function as providing useful information to the public and government officials. The general public and even members of Congress are usually not experts on an issue that they will be voting on. Lobbyists provide technical information about their fields of interest or expertise. Lobbyists for the American Medical Association provide information about health care and lobbyists for health insurance companies provide information

about insurance. In this sense, lobbyists describe their role in the political process as an educative role: explaining technical or specialized matters to generalists. Lobbyists who represent large membership groups also "educate" members of Congress or the administration about how the general public or the group's members feel about a particular issue, bill, or law. This is also a representational role.

An interest group's strategy may also include conducting a public opinion campaign. Public opinion campaigns are efforts to change public opinion about an issue. Issue advocacy campaigns are political advertising campaigns to shape public opinion, to persuade the public to think about an issue the way that the group thinks about an issue. Oil companies that are worried about their public image can hire advertising companies to design campaigns that portray oil companies as "energy companies" that are deeply concerned about the environment, global warming, conservation, jobs, and the socially responsible production of energy. Oil spills such as the Exxon Valdez spill in Alaska and the British Petroleum oil well spill in the Gulf of Mexico in 2010 prompted extensive public relations campaigns to portray the two companies as good stewards of the environment. These kinds of well-financed public relations campaigns conducted by major corporations raise questions about the nature of public opinion in a democracy. Is public opinion the cause of public policy, or is public opinion made by these campaigns. Most interest groups today rely to some extent on direct mail, the use of computerized mailing lists to contact individuals who might share their interests.

12.38 | *Agenda Building*

Agenda building is the process by which new issues are brought to the attention of political decision-makers. There is a seemingly unlimited supply of problems or issues that someone or some group thinks the government should do something about. But public officials have limited resources (time, political capital, information, and money). Politics is the allocation of these scarce resources. Public officials must concentrate on a few important issues. Interest groups can convince politicians to put a new issue on the government's agenda.

12.39 | *Program Monitoring*

Program monitoring is when individuals or groups keep track of the government's actions to determine whether and how a bureaucracy or other administrative agency is implementing legislation. A group that monitors a program may find that a program or policy they supported is not being implemented as intended or is not being implemented well. Interest groups play a role in the policy process by monitoring policies.

12.4 | Playing Offense or Defense?

Sometime interest groups lobby *for* changes in public policy. They want to pass health care reform, make abortion illegal, increase regulation of Wall Street companies, enact policies to address global warming, or increase government support for religious activity. Sometimes interest groups lobby *against* change in public policy. They want to stop health care reform, maintain legal abortions, stop government regulation, or prevent the passage of laws that provide more government support for religious activities.

Health care policy illustrates how some interest groups play offense (they support change) and others play defense (they oppose change). There are interest groups that are working hard to change the current employment-based health care system in favor of a public or national health care policy. The groups playing offense include organized labor unions, the American Association of Retired Persons (AARP), and even the American Medical Association, which has historically opposed the creation of public health care as a form of socialized medicine. The groups playing defense include health care providers, insurance companies, and organizations representing business such as the U.S. Chamber of Commerce. The high economic stakes—health care accounts for around 17 percent of the country's gross domestic product—make it hard to make any major changes in health care. For decades the interest group battles over health care reform have been a clash of titans—a conflict among big, powerful interest groups with a great deal at stake in the outcome: groups representing doctors, hospitals and other health care providers, insurance companies, and other business groups. Interest groups devote a great deal of money, time, and other resources to such conflicts. The debate over the health care reform proposed by the Obama administration attracted an unprecedented amount of money. For a description of the large sums of money spent on health care reform see "Exploring the Big Money Behind Health Care Reform."

Is it easier to play offense or defense? The political system makes it easier to play defense than offense. It is easier to prevent the government from acting than to prompt it to act.

- The separation of powers. Passing a federal law requires working with both the legislative and executive branches.
- Bicameralism. In order for a bill to become a law it must pass both houses of Congress.
- The committee system in Congress. The committee system is a functional division of labor that creates natural contact points for interest groups to participate in the policymaking process. Interest groups can lobby a committee to "kill the bill."
- Party politics. The "OUT" party often has a vested interest in opposing a bill proposed by the "IN" party.
- Federalism. The geographic division of power between the national and state governments is part of the system of checks and balances.

All of these attributes of the political system create many veto points at which an individual or organization can try to stop action. The multiple veto points make it easier to stop action than to successfully propose it and interest groups are important players in the defensive contests to stop change that they oppose.

12.5 | The Free Rider Problem

A large, active, and committed membership is a valuable resource. Candidates for office and elected government officials tend to listen to lobbyists that represent groups with large and active membership—particularly when the membership includes voters in the individual's district or state. The American Association of Retired Persons (AARP) is an influential demographic group because it has over 40 million members—and because older people have higher rates of voter turnout than younger people. But attracting and maintaining membership can be challenging.

One of the most important challenges to forming a membership-based group is the **free-rider problem**. The free-rider problem occurs when a person can benefit from an interest group's actions without having to pay for the costs of those actions. This creates an incentive to be a free rider, to receive benefits without paying costs. Free riders get what is for them a free lunch. The free-rider problem creates membership problems for groups that rely on material or purposive incentives for members to join their group. In fact, the free-rider problem is one reason why the government requires everyone to pay taxes that are used to provide certain goods and services.

A **private good** is something of value whose benefits can be limited to those who have paid for it. A private good is divisible in the sense that it can be provided to those who have paid for it but not to those who have not paid for it. Cars, computers, and phones are divisible goods. Health care, legal advice, and education are divisible services. A **public good** is something of value whose benefits cannot be limited to those individuals who have actually paid for it. In this sense, a **public good** is an indivisible good because once it is available its benefits cannot be limited to those who have actually paid for it. For these reasons, private goods are available for purchase in the marketplace based on the ability to pay while the government provides public goods. Safe streets, public order, peace, national security, and clean air or clear water are commonly considered public goods because they are indivisible: once provided, it is hard to limit national security or clean air to those who have paid for them.

Political debates about the role and size of government can often be reduced to arguments about whether some goods or services should be considered private goods, and available in the marketplace based on the ability to pay, or public goods that are provided by the government. Is education a public or private good? Does it depend on whether the education is primary or secondary education, or a college or professional education? Is health care a private or public good? The answers to these questions are political because they answer the age-old questions about what government should be doing.

12.6 | Are Interest Groups Harmful or Helpful?

Concern about the influence of interest groups is as old as the republic and as new as the coverage of health care reform. The Founders worried about factions. In *Federalist No. 10*, Madison worried about the apparently natural tendency of individuals to organize themselves into groups that advocate for their special or self-interest rather than the general or public interest. Madison believed that the most common source of factions was "the unequal distribution of property." He did not think that the "mischiefs of faction" could be eliminated; he thought they could be controlled if there were so many different factions that no one or two could dominate politics and use government and politics for their narrow self-interest and against the minority interests.

It is not easy to determine whether interest groups play a harmful or helpful role in modern American government and politics. It is easy to criticize special interests for working against the public interest. But there is often disagreement about what the public interest is. And it is not easy to measure the influence of groups. The Center for Responsive Politics[6] studies the activities and the influence of groups, with a special emphasis on political contributions and their influence on public policy. It is easier to measure activity (e.g., campaign contributions) than influence.

It is not simply that large groups are more influential than small groups, or that money is the sole determinant of influence. Money and numbers are important. But familiar game of **rock, scissors, paper** can help explain the relationships among the major kinds of resources that groups can mobilize. Interest group resources include numbers (the size of the membership), money (financial resources), and intensity (the members' commitment to the cause). If size alone—the number of members—were the sole determinant of influence, then consumers and workers would be much more influential than business interests because there are more of consumers and workers. And the poor would be much more influential than the rich. But size can be trumped by money. The U.S. Chamber of Commerce has less than 10% of the membership of the AARP but the financial resources of the Chamber's members make it an influential interest group. Money is a resource that is used to influence decision makers by making campaign contributions or by public relations campaigns that shape the way people think about an individual, issue, or party. So money can trump numbers. And finally, intensity of interest can trump numbers and money. An organization with a small number of members who are intensely interested or committed to their cause can trump numbers or money. Intensity is one of the keys to explaining the political

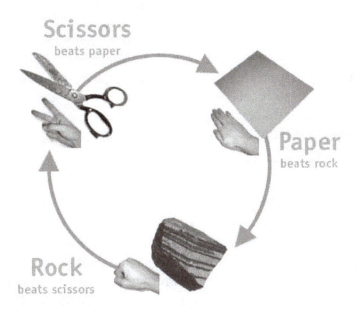

Scissors
beats paper

Paper
beats rock

Rock
beats scissors

influence of the National Rifle Association. NRA members are famously committed to the cause of advocating gun rights.

Globalization has increased the number and type of organizations that are interested in foreign policy and international trade. Some of these interest groups are private interest groups (e.g., working for the material benefits of their members), some are public interest groups (working for broad benefits to society in general), and some are organizations whose members are governments. For example, the Organisation for Economic Co-operation and Development (OECD) is an organization with 35 member countries that promotes cooperation for social, economic, and political development.

12.7 | Summary

It might be said of interest groups (and bureaucrats) that love them or hate them, we can't seem to live without them. The Founders worried about the "mischiefs" of faction, but groups have been integrated into the American political system at all levels (national, state, and local) and arenas (legislative, executive, and legal). Concerns about the power or influence of special interests remain valid, but it is not easy to determine whether groups are healthy or harmful. Members of Congress rely on interest groups to provide them with information about subjects being considered for legislation. Legislative committees take testimony from interest groups during committee hearings. Groups do provide a great deal of information to the public and to policymakers in both the legislative and executive branches of government. And like political parties, interest groups are linkage organizations that can increase political efficacy, the individual sense that participation matters, that participation can make a difference, that membership in a group increases citizen control over public policy in a democracy.

12.8 | Additional Resources

In order to get an idea of the number and type of interest groups see the list of some of the more important interest groups in the U.S., a list that is organized by the issues they represent or the public policy areas in which they lobby: "Political Advocacy Groups: A Directory of United States Lobbyists." http://www.vancouver.wsu.edu/fac/kfountain/

American Civil Liberties Union (ACLU) offers information on the entire Bill of Rights including racial profiling, women's rights, privacy issues, prisons, drugs, etc. Includes links to other sites dealing with the same issues. www.aclu.org

AFL-CIO is the largest trade union organization in America. Its Web site offers policy statements, news, workplace issues, and labor strategies. www.aflcio.org

Richard Kimber's Worldwide Index of Political Parties, Interest Groups, and Other Social Movements www.psr.keele.ac.uk/parties.htm

Mexican American Legal Defense and Education Fund (MALDEF) Web site offers information on Census 2000, scholarships, job opportunities, legal programs, regional offices information, and more. www.maldef.org

Native American Rights Fund (NARF) Web site offers profiles of issues, an archive, resources, a tribal directory, and treaty information, as well as a lot of other information. www.narf.org

The National Association for the Advancement of Colored People (NAACP) Web site offers information about the organization, membership, and issues of interest to proponents of civil rights. It also has sections on the Supreme Court, Census 2000, and the Education Summit and includes links to other Web sites. www.naacp.org

The National Rifle Association (NRA) offers information on gun ownership, gun laws, and coverage of legislation on associated issues. www.nra.org

National Organization of Women (NOW) Web site offers information on the organization and its issues/activities including women in the military, economic equity, and reproductive rights. It offers an e-mail action list and the ability to join NOW online. There is also a page with links to related sites. www.now.org

12.81 | *In the Library*

Berry, Jeffrey and Clyde Wilcox. 2008. *The Interest Group Society*. Longman.

Biersack, Robert. 2000. *After the Revolution: PAC's, Lobbies, and the Republican Congress*. Addison Wesley.

Birnbaum, Jeffrey. 2000. *The Money Men*. Times Books.

Broder, David S. 2000. *Democracy Derailed*. Harcourt Brace.

Cigler, Allan J. and Burdett A. Loomis (Eds). 2006. *Interest Group Politics*. CQ Press.

Dekieffer, Donald E. 2007. *The Citizen's Guide to Lobbying Congress*. Chicago Review Press.

Gray, Virginia and David Lowery. 2001. *The Population Ecology of Interest Representation: Lobbying Communities in the American States*. University of Michigan Press.

Hernnson, Paul S. 2004. *Interest Group Connection: Electioneering, Lobbying, and Policymaking in Washington*. Congressional Quarterly, Inc.

Keck, Margaret and Kathryn Sikkink. 1998. *Activists beyond Borders*. Cornell University Press.

Rosenthal, Alan. 2001. *Third House: Lobbyists and Lobbying in the States*. Congressional Quarterly, Inc.

Strolovitch, Dara Z. 2007. *Affirmative Advocacy: Race, Class, and Gender in Interest Group Politics*. University of Chicago Press.

STUDY QUESTIONS

1. What factors make an interest group successful? Provide examples.
2. Discuss and provide examples of how interest groups attempt to influence election outcomes.
3. Should there be additional limits on interest group participation in American politics?
4. What do interest groups do?
5. What are the different types of interest groups?
6. Should interest groups be protected under the First Amendment? Why or why not?

---

[1] See Allan J. Cigler and Burdett A. Loomis. 2007. *Interest Group Politics*. Seventh Edition. Washington, D.C.: CQ Press.

[2] Quoted in Jackie Calmes. "G.O.P. Group to Promote Conservative Ideas." *The New York Times*. (February 3, 2010). Available at http://www.nytimes.com/2010/02/04/us/politics/04conservative.html

[3] Chapter three of James Q. Wilson. 1973. *Political Organizations*. New York: Basic Books.

[4] See http://www.worldadvocacy.com/

[5] http://www.nfib.com/small-business-legal-center/about-the-legal-center/

[6] http://www.opensecrets.org/

Key Terms:
Interest group
Lobbyist
Public interest group
Economic interest group
Grassroots lobbying
Political Action Committee (PAC)
Agenda building
Program monitoring

13.0 | Public Policy

The previous chapters examined public opinion and congressional and presidential decision-making. This chapter describes the stages of the public policy process, explains the different types of public policies, and uses health care, environmental, and immigration policy as case studies that illustrate the politics of public policy.

13.1 | What is Public Policy?

A **policy** is an official position on an issue or a plan of action that is intended to achieve certain results. It is a position or plan of action taken by a government body, a business, a not-for-profit organization, or even an individual. The following are examples of policies:

- A statute that makes it a crime for individuals to provide material support for an organization that the government labels a terrorist organization.
- An executive order that defers deportation of certain undocumented immigrants who are by law eligible for deportation, or one that restricts entry of certain people from certain countries.
- Workplace safety rules and regulations.
- Corporate marketing practices for advertising tobacco or alcohol products to children.
- A company's personnel employment practices for hiring, firing, and promotion.
- An interest group's position on the environment or crime or some other issue.
- A non-profit organization's hiring practices.
- A church's budget priorities or community outreach.
- A university's academic integrity code.
- A professor's grading of coursework.

Public **policy** refers to governmental programs, rules, and courses of action. Public policies are in statutes, executive orders, administrative regulations, judicial rulings, treaties and executive agreements, Federal Reserve Board decisions (monetary policy), and budgets (fiscal policy). The study of public policy includes decision-making (*who* makes decisions and *how* they are made), substance (*what* the official position is), and analysis of impact (implementation and effectiveness). Public policy is both an academic discipline and a profession. The professional association of public policy practitioners, researchers, scholars, and students is the Association for Public Policy Analysis and Management. The academic discipline of public policy includes a broad range of social science fields including political science, economics, sociology, and public administration.

Public policy includes both government action and inaction. A government decision **not** to take action on climate change, health care, poverty, or housing is a public policy. Politics

> "...POLICY IS MORE LIKE AN ENDLESS GAME OF MONOPOLY THAN A BICYCLE REPAIR"
> - DEBORAH STONE. 2001. *POLICY PARADOX: THE ART OF POLITICAL DECISION MAKING,* PAGE 261.

includes efforts to get the government to act and efforts to stop government action. The U.S. political system has so many veto points that it is usually easier to play defense—to stop proposed action—than to play offense—to take action. Advocates of gun control historically played offense and advocates of gun rights played defense, but the success of the gun rights movement has enabled it to play offense to remove gun control laws.

The public policy process has three main stages, and politics occurs at all stages of the process:

- Identifying a problem and putting it on the government agenda;
- Making or formulating a policy and then adopting it; and
- Implementing and evaluating the policy.

13.2 | Identifying a Problem and Getting it on the Government Agenda

The first stage is individuals, interest groups, or even government officials identify a problem and put it on the government agenda. The problem might be pollution, taxes, inflation, food or drug safety, crime, terrorism, health care, immigration, bad roads, or bad schools. **Agenda setting** is putting the problem on the government agenda for action. It is easy to get some issues on the government's "to-do" list. It is easier to get maintaining safe streets, providing economic stability and prosperity, and providing national security on the government agenda because these are core government functions. Responsibilities. It is hard to get other issues on the government agenda which is why political movements are created to mount sustained campaigns and lobbying efforts to get the government to pay attention to issues such as mass shootings, public transportation, health care, environmentalism, or workplace or consumer safety.

Politics requires convincing people that something is a problem AND that the government should do something about it. Is workplace safety a public issue? The answer often depends on whether a job is, or is perceived to be, dangerous.

Think about it!
What are the deadliest jobs in America:

http://www.npr.org/blogs/money/2013/01/08/1688971

40/the-deadliest-jobs-in-america-in-one-graphic

13.21 | *Sex and Violence in the Media and Music*

Efforts to get the government to regulate indecent or violent programming on broadcast television and radio illustrate how agenda setting works. Individuals and organizations concerned about broadcast media depictions of sex and violence, and profane music lyrics, mounted sustained lobbying efforts to convince the government to put the issues on the government's agenda. The Federal Communications Commission licenses and regulates the

broadcast media. The public, and therefore the government, is especially concerned about the impact of such materials on children.

In the 1980s, the Parents Music Resource Center and other organizations lobbied Congress to put offensive music lyrics on the federal government's agenda. Tipper Gore, at that time the wife of Senator Al Gore, bought Prince's *Purple Rain* for their daughter mistakenly thinking it was a children's album. She was offended by the explicit lyrics. In 1985, she testified before Congress that music should be labeled, primarily to protect children from an increasingly coarse culture where sex and violence were more explicit. Worries about explicit lyrics were similar to earlier worries that watching violent television programming caused violent behavior in children. Congress listened to Tipper Gore's testimony, other complaints about the lack of family values in the music industry, and the testimony of musicians such as Frank Zappa who opposed government regulation of the music industry. Congress ultimately decided not to pass a law regulating music lyrics. Instead, Congress relied on the recording industry to voluntarily label music that contained offensive lyrics. This is an example of an unsuccessful effort to put an issue on the government agenda.

However, the *media effect* is still of great public interest. The question whether watching violent television programming, playing violent video games, listening to vulgar music lyrics, or visiting offensive Internet sites has a negative impact on attitudes or behavior remains an important public policy question.

13.22 | *Indecency and the Internet*

Think About It! Should the government require labeling music and video games and television and radio programs the way the government requires labeling of food?
http://www.npr.org/templates/story/story.php?storyId=4279560

Unlike the efforts to label music, efforts to put Internet indecency on the government's agenda have been successful. Stories about children being exposed to, or accessing indecent, obscene, or other objectionable material simply by doing a Google word search prompted Congress to act. The Communications Decency Act of 1996 was intended to protect minors from harmful material on the Internet by making it a criminal offense to knowingly transmit "obscene or indecent" messages to any person under 18 years old. The American Civil Liberties Union challenged the law in court arguing that the First Amendment protected freedom of expression from such federal laws. In *Reno v. American Civil Liberties Union*, 521 U.S. 844 (1997), the Court ruled that the law was unconstitutional. The Court held that the penalty—making it a federal criminal offense to send an indecent message—was too severe, particularly considering the lack of agreement on what indecent means. For example, it was not clear whether the law made it a federal criminal offense to email or Tweet an off-color joke to a minor?

The Court's ruling did not put an end to efforts to put Internet indecency on the government's agenda, and Congress passed the Child On-line Protection Act of 1998 to protect children from Internet material that was "harmful to minors." The Court struck down this Act as a violation of the First Amendment freedom of expression so Congress than passed the Children's Internet Protection Act of 2001. The American Library Association filed a lawsuit claiming the Act was unconstitutional but the Supreme Court upheld it in *United States v. American Library Association* (2003). Parental concerns about the content of Internet materials and activities such as sexting keep the issue on the government agenda.

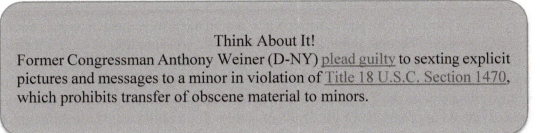

Think About It!
Former Congressman Anthony Weiner (D-NY) plead guilty to sexting explicit pictures and messages to a minor in violation of Title 18 U.S.C. Section 1470, which prohibits transfer of obscene material to minors.

13.23 | *Climate Change*

Climate change is an especially interesting case study of agenda setting. Scientists and environmental organizations use data showing temperature increases to lobby the government to take actions to reduce emissions that contribute to global warming or climate change. Business groups and conservative organizations lobby against such government action. Their initial defensive strategy was to deny the existence of climate change by claiming that temperature increases were part of natural, long-term cycles of temperature fluctuations that sometimes resulted in ice ages and sometimes resulting in warm periods. The increased scientific consensus supporting climate change required a shift in strategy, so the opponents acknowledged climate change but claimed that the evidence did not support human causes of it. In fact, climate change—like evolution—is an example of *political* science or the politicization of science related to controversial public policies. The Yale Project on Climate Change is an organization that is committed to "bridging science and society" on the matter of climate change. It includes an examination of how public opinion has been shaped by organized efforts to challenge the science.

13.24 | *Imported Goods*

Many consumer products are imported. The safety of products imported from China became an issue when media reports of goods with the "Made in China" label included stories about imported pet food and toothpaste with chemical contaminants or other harmful ingredients, dangerous toys, drugs that were not tested the way that drugs with the "Made in the U.S.A." were tested. These stories created a campaign to put consumer protection from imported products on the government agenda. The campaign included lobbying the federal government to adopt policies that increased inspection of imports. Parents who worry about imported toys with lead paint or heavy metals such as cadmium and imported dairy products contaminated with the chemical melamine can be effective advocates for putting the safety of imported products on the government agenda. The Consumer Products Safety Commission now monitors toy safety standards. The creation of the law does not end politics or the policy process. It is often necessary to lobby for funding for the agencies such as the Department of Agriculture, the Food and Drug Administration, or the Consumer Products Safety Commission, which are responsible for inspecting imports. And it is necessary to monitor whether the Consumer Products Safety Commission is actually enforcing the safety standards.

13.25 | *Food Policy*

The story of how food security and nutrition were put on the government agenda is another example of how issues become political. In one sense, the consumption of food is a classic example of a private good rather than a public good. After all, food is an item whose benefits can be limited to those who have paid for it, and kept from those who were not willing or were unable to pay for its costs. But at least certain aspects of food consumption are also considered appropriate for government action. Food policy is examined in greater detail in a separate chapter.

13.26 | *Tobacco Policy: The Tobacco Wars*

One of the early fights over health care policy was a political and legal campaign to regulate or even ban smoking and the use of other tobacco products. The term tobacco wars was coined to describe the long-running battle between the tobacco industry (primarily growers, manufacturers, and sellers) and the anti-tobacco lobby (the American Medical Association, the American Heart Association, the American Lung Association, and other consumer and public health advocates). The fight over control of tobacco policy has been waged in all political arenas: city government, state government, and the federal government; congress, the executive branch, and the courts. The consumption of tobacco was traditionally considered a private choice to use nicotine. As the adverse health consequences of tobacco use were discovered, however, an anti-smoking movement emerged to make tobacco a political issue, to put tobacco on the political agenda. The movement used political litigation (lawsuits that are intended to change public policy), administrative regulation, and legislation to produce a complicated system of tobacco regulation.

Looking at how tobacco advertisements have changed over the years reveals how much attitudes toward smoking and tobacco regulation have changed over the years. What is especially striking about many of the early tobacco ads is that they explicitly claimed or strongly implied that smoking was healthful by using doctors and nurses and science to sell cigarettes. They even used images of infants who seemed to notice that mommy was especially enjoying a particular brand of cigarettes.

13.3 | Making Policy: Policy Formulation and Adoption

Issue network have developed around specific areas of public policy. An issue network consists of the congressional committees with jurisdiction over an issue, the executive departments with jurisdiction over the issue, and the interest groups organized to advocate on matters related to the issue. Each of these three members of the issue network works to formulate public policy based on its understanding of the problem and the solution.

- Energy. Is the price of a gallon of gasoline too high or too low? Are gas price increases caused by high rates of consumption (Americans tend to drive big cars and SUVs that do not get good gas mileage!) or by decisions to not exploit all sources of energy ("Drill, baby, drill!)? Environmentalists and energy companies typically have opposing views on energy policy.

- Health Care. Is the high cost of health care caused by too much or too little access to health care? Do consumers overuse health care because their employers are paying for some of the cost of health insurance? Or are health care providers the problem? Supporters of The Patient Protection and Affordable Care Act (Obamacare) defined the problem in terms of access and coverage, while opponents defined the health care act's mandate to buy insurance as an infringement on individual freedom. Health care providers and insurance companies and groups representing consumers (patients) typically have different views on health care policy.
- Economics. Should economic policy focus on reducing taxes, budget deficits, or inflation? Or should it focus on unemployment and stagnant wages. Is unemployment caused by the lack of individual initiative or training? Management and labor typically have conflicting views on employment policy. Business interests and consumers typically have conflicting views on economic regulatory policy.
- The Environment. Energy companies and environmentalists typically have conflicting views on environmental policy. Are market forces the best way to protect the environment and conserve resources, or is government action necessary?
- Immigration. Is immigration a threat to American national identity? Do immigrants take jobs from Americans or lower wages? Is immigration policy about economics (importing a labor supply) or national security (the threat of terrorism)? Business interests have historically supported importing labor, while labor and other interests have historically worried about the effects on wages.

How an issue is framed affects the formulation of public policy. Defining the energy problem as a problem of over-consumption produces energy policy that emphasizes conservation. Defining the energy problem as inadequate supply produces policy that emphasizes production. Defining the health care problem as the need for cost control leads to health care policy that is very different than health care policy that emphasizes increased access. Each of the three components of the issue networks work hard to maintain control

over how a problem is defined in order to control the substance of the policy that is ultimately adopted.

13.31 | *Policy Adoption*

Policy adoption is the decision to officially give the policy the force of law. It usually follows public hearings to take testimony about the issue from interested or affected individuals and organizations, and to consider evidence presented. If the public policy is to promote a desirable activity such as healthy diets and conservation, then lobbying efforts focus on increasing support for government subsidizing the behavior. The U.S. system of government is an open system in the sense that there are many points and stages where supporters and opponents can participate in the process.

The policy adoption stage culminates with the passage of a law or administrative regulation that identifies the official purposes of the policy. Elected officials often publicly appear at the signing of a popular law, for example, and bureaucratic officials may support a public policy that increases the agency's budget or rule making authority over their area of expertise.

13.32 | *Implementation and Evaluation*

Implementation is what happens after a policy is adopted. A policy may not be implemented as intended due to problems with ambiguity, communication, and resistance. The *ambiguity* problem is caused by language that is vague or general. When a statute or regulation is vague or imprecise, those who are responsible for implementing the policy may not know what it requires. This problem is fairly common when Congress passes a general law that describes its goals only in very general terms, and then requires the experts or specialists in the bureaucracy to actually define what the law requires or to determine the best way to implement it.

Two examples of ambiguity are the Clean Air Act and the Clean Water Act. These federal statutes declare that it is federal policy to support clean air and clean water. But clean air and clean water are general goals that require precise definitions. The EPA is left the job of determining standards and methods of achieving them. This is why so much of the politics of  environmental policy implementation and evaluation stages. The counterterrorism debates about the use of "enhanced interrogation" are another example of ambiguity. Torture is illegal. But there are differences of opinion about what is torture. Individuals who are conducting field interrogations are sometimes left to define what treatment is torture and what is not. In fact, police officers, military police, or the FBI and CIA interrogators may not even know what the legal policy is concerning legal methods of interrogation.

Having an official or general policy against torture does not eliminate the need to define what is, and what is not, torture. All large organizations need clear *communication* of instructions throughout all levels in the organizational chain of command—from the policy makers to the policy followers—if policies are to be implemented as intended.

The third problem is *resistance*. If the individuals who are responsible for implementing the policy do not support it, the policy is unlikely to be implemented as intended. Police officers may oppose a Supreme Court ruling that the Constitution requires that individuals who are suspected of committing a crime must be notified of their rights before being questioned by the police. A public school teacher may oppose a Supreme Court ruling that that prohibits organized, spoken prayer in public schools or at school events. The political appointee on the Consumer Products Safety Commission may be opposed to further government regulation of business. The head of the Food and Drug Administration may claim that the FDA has the authority to regulate nicotine despite the tobacco lobby successfully stopped efforts to get Congress to pass a law that specifically authorized the FDA to regulate nicotine as a drug.[1] The head of the Environmental Protection Agency may be a strong critic of the agency and environmental regulatory policy. President Trump's head of the EPA, Scott Pruitt, was a strong critic of the EPA's activist agenda and sued the agency 13 times. Strongly identified with the oil and gas industry and utility companies, he sued the EPA on behalf of Oklahoma utilities challenging the increased costs of complying with the Clean Power Plan and the Waters of the U.S. rule. He also rejects the scientific consensus on human causes of climate change.

Think About It!
Compare the above description of EPA Administrator Scott Pruitt public policy actions with his official EPA biography.

Federalism and the separation of powers further complicate policy implementation: Congress creates immigration statutes, but presidents implement them; Congress passes environmental laws to protect clean air and water, and health policies such as the Affordable Care Act, but relies heavily on the states to implement the laws.

13.33 | Budgeting

Funding is essential for the implementation of most policies. Republicans continued to fight the Affordable Care Act after it was enacted into law by challenging the constitutionality of its funding and by reducing funding for it. Gun rights groups successfully lobbied Congress to effectively prohibit agencies from using health care funding to study gun violence as a public health problem. Both Congress and the president use funding to control the actions and priorities of administrative agencies. Cutting the Environmental Protection Agency's budget is one way to reduce business costs of complying with environmental regulations without actually repealing the environmental regulations or the statutes.

13.34 | Policy Evaluation

Politics does not start with government decision-making, and it does not stop with policy adoption. Politics includes what happens after a bill has become a law. **Policy evaluation** is determining whether a policy is working as intended. This can be difficult because the subject can be complex (e.g., determining the cause of crime) and because of politics. Some evaluation is based on *anecdotal evidence*. Anecdotal evidence is stories from a few people that make their way to the ears of an evaluator. Politicians often cite compelling personal stories as evidence that a policy they support is working, or as evidence that a policy they support is not working. Sometimes horror stories and success stories are cherry-picked from the data. Evaluation also sometimes relies on *public opinion*. The political assumption is that a popular policy must be a good policy and an unpopular policy must be a bad policy. But public opinion—conventional wisdom—can be mistaken. Social scientists value evaluation that is based on *empirical evidence*: the systematic analysis of data. However, policies are assessed by a variety of individuals from a variety of perspectives and with a variety of goals in mind so it is not surprising that different methods of evaluation are used.

13.35 | *Unintended Results*

Public policies frequently have unintended (unexpected) or even counterintuitive (apparently not logical) results because they apply to *complex adaptive systems*. Policies apply to complex systems such as state governments, national governments, and international governing bodies; large companies or major sectors of the economy; and even entire countries. Public policies apply to systems that are adaptive in the sense that the targets of a policy adjust (or adapt) their behavior in anticipation of public policy or as a result of the policy. Tax policy provides an example of counterintuitive adaptive behavior. Raising taxes may increase tax revenue or, depending on the size of the tax increase, may reduce tax revenue by causing capital flight or by raising the tax rate so high that people have incentives to NOT work to earn money that will be heavily taxed, or to NOT purchase a good or service. In the U.S., increasing taxes can actually reduce tax revenue because there are so many units of government. A city or a state that raises taxes can shift economic activity to another city or state where taxes are lower.

Unintended consequences happen. A good policy formulation process takes into consideration a broad range of information in order to minimize the likelihood of unintended consequences. But democratic societies and governments are complex adaptive systems so it is not possible to consider all possible effects of a particular policy. Policies are intended to affect human behavior. It makes sense to think about motivations when formulating policies intended to get people to do something. Money is a familiar motivator: individuals or companies can be paid to do things the government wants them to do (e.g., work), and fined for doing things the government does not want them to do (e.g., breaking traffic laws). But money is an imperfect motivator.[2]

A good example of unintended consequences is the public policy supporting wearing a helmet while riding a bicycle. The National Highway Traffic Safety Administration recommends that bicyclists wear helmets as a safety measure to protect against head injuries. Parents often require children to wear bicycle helmets. Should local governments require bicyclists to wear helmets while riding on bike paths? The intended result is fewer head injuries; the unintended result could be increased rates of obesity, heart disease, and diabetes if requiring helmets reduces bicycle riding (exercise). Helmet laws also present problems for the cities that adopt bike-sharing programs to increase the use of bicycles for urban transportation. When considering a law requiring bicyclists to wear helmets, the benefits of reduced head injuries should be considered against the costs of decreased bicycling.

13.36 | *Types of Policy*

Public policies are intended to affect 1) the conditions under which people live and work; and 2), the human behavior of individuals and organization. Policies affect conditions by creating safe streets, economic security, national security, and health care, for instance. Policies affect behavior by creating incentives that encourage desirable behavior and disincentives to discourage undesirable behavior. Governments accomplish these goals using distributive policy and regulatory policy.

Distributive policies provide goods and services. Distributive policies include government spending programs that provide welfare, public education, transportation systems, public safety, or other benefits as well as tax policies that provide deductions and credits. The most politically controversial distributive policies are those that redistribute income. Redistributive policy takes resources from one group of individuals or states—for example, the wealthier, the younger, the employed, or the urban—and redistributes the resources or transfers them to another group of individuals or states—for example, the poorer, older, unemployed, or rural). Social welfare programs are the most common type of redistributive policy. Money or in-kind services such as food stamps or health care (under Medicaid) are provided to individuals who cannot adequately support themselves or their families. Tax policies, particularly progressive income taxes, are redistributive policies that transfer money from wealthier to poorer individuals, states, or regions. The federal tax law that allows for deducting home mortgage interest is also redistributive. A married couple can deduct up to $1 million worth of home mortgage interest each year. This approximately $70 billion dollar tax deduction primarily benefits middle and upper income individuals and families. One of the most important social welfare policies is Social Security. The Social Security Administration (SSA) Web site provides historical information about the creation of the program and its funding, as well as current information about social security rules, regulations, and policies. The fiscal stability of Social Security has become part of contemporary political debates about entitlements in an era where the aging or greying of the American public means increased dependence on the program for income security in old age.

Regulatory policies are intended to change the behavior of individuals or organizations. Regulatory policies are usually used where there is broad consensus about what good behavior is and what bad behavior is. Regulatory policy can discourage bad behavior or encourage good behavior. Regulatory policy commonly uses fines, taxes, or sanctions to discourage bad behavior. Traffic laws enforced by fines; "sin" taxes on alcohol, tobacco, marijuana, or gambling; and even tax credits for consumers who buy hybrid vehicles or energy efficient appliances to discourage the bad behavior of consumers who buy high energy use products are all examples of regulatory policy. Most countries also have population policies that are intended to either encourage people to have more children, or to discourage people from having more children. Regulating fertility is a public policy because population policies are important components of a country's national identity—most countries want to increase the fertility rates of native residents—and national economic policy. Demographics are an important factor linked to, among other things, a country's economic development. Demographics include the age distribution of a country's population. Having a larger or smaller percentage of younger or older people has great implications for public policies. China's

> *Think about it!*
>
> *Should the government take from one group of people (or states) and give to others?*

one-child policy is an example of a national population policy whose primary objective was to control population increase. However, policies intended to solve one problem often have other, unintended consequences. China's one-child policy has controlled population growth, but it has created other problems that are just now emerging. Limiting births has serious long-term implications for a country's demographics because it affects the ratio of working age individuals to the young, elderly, and retired. Countries with aging populations such as the U.S., the Scandinavian countries, and France and Germany have used a variety of public policies to increase fertility. They have not been very effective—which is why the countries relied on immigration to import a supply of labor.

The Great Recession put government regulation of the financial services sector of the economy on the government agenda. The Obama administration proposed the creation of a Consumer Financial Protection Bureau. President Obama appointed Elizabeth Warren as a special assistant to create a Consumer Financial Protection Bureau. Her testimony (May 24, 2011) before the House of Representatives Subcommittee on TARP and Financial Services of the Committee on Oversight and Government Reform revealed the sharp partisan differences on government regulation of financial services. Democrats generally support government regulation of business to protect consumers. Republicans generally oppose such public policies because they believe the competition of the marketplace is sufficient to protect against the bad behavior that product the economic crisis. In 2012, Warren was elected as a U.S. Senator from Massachusetts.

President Obama with Elizabeth Warren, a Harvard Law Professor who participated in crafting legislation to regulate the financial industry.

Social policy includes a broad range of both redistributive and regulatory policies: social welfare policy (income or service support), health care, and education. Social policy is often distributive policy insofar as it entails taking resources from one group and providing them to another groups, or from a general population to a particular population. Because of the relationship between economic resources (income or wealth) and opportunity, social scientists study the impact of economic inequality. The relationship between income/wealth and education is particularly important because so much emphasis is placed on education as the key to economic opportunity and political equality. Studies of performance on standardized tests that are used to determine admission to colleges, for example, reveal consistent correlations between family income and performance on standardized tests.[3]

State compulsory schooling laws, testing, and taxes supporting public education are evidence of the importance of education. Is education a private good or a public good? Primary and secondary education is considered a public good because the benefits are not limited to the individual student who receives the education. The economy benefits from a trained work force; democracy benefits from having an educated citizenry. College is more complicated. Receiving a college degree is a private good in the sense that it provides an individual with certain benefits. But college is also a public good in the sense that higher education is often part of a state's economic development strategy. Recent trends in state funding of higher education, specifically reductions in tax support, reflect a nationwide shift toward thinking of college education as a private good rather than a public good. This education policy shift reflects new thinking about how to provide a trained work force for today's economy, and the wisdom of assuming that everyone should go to college. Is there an education bubble similar to the real estate bubble that played an important role in the Great Recession? Both sectors of the economy benefited from and relied on the perception that values—properties and degrees—would continue to increase? Are sub-prime mortgages, which played an important role in bringing about the Great Recession, analogous to sub-prime college degrees?

> **Think About It!**
> What is the value of a college degree?
> See the Public Broadcasting story "Assessing the Value of College Education" at
> http://video.pbs.org/video/1954954225

13.4 | Health Care Policy

Health care is important for individuals, families, and for the economy. It is an important component of social welfare policy and it is an important sector of the economy. Health care accounts for around 18% of the U.S. Gross Domestic Product (GDP). The governments of all the major industrial democracies play a role in providing health care. In the U.S., government plays a smaller and different role than the governments in other countries with similar economic and political systems. The high cost of health care in the U.S., measured as a percentage of a family's budget and as a percentage of the GDP, has put health care reform on the government agenda. However, the ideological and partisan differences of opinion about the best solution to the problems of health care have kept health care on the government agenda without consensus on policy solutions.

President Obama signed the <u>Patient Protection and Affordable Care Act</u> (commonly called the Affordable Care Act or Obamacare) into law in 2010. Republicans in Congress repeatedly tried to repeal the Act, and Republican governors filed lawsuits challenging the constitutionality of the Act. The Supreme Court upheld the Act in <u>National Federation of Independent Businesses</u> (2012). But provisions of the law were still being challenged when President Trump and the Republican majority in Congress worked on repeal and replacement with the American Health Care Act in 2017.

13.41 | *Evaluating Health Care*

Public policy analysis requires evaluating the status quo and proposed solutions. How would you diagnose the health of the U.S. health care system? Doctors routinely ask patients about pain levels and the state of their health. You be the doctor! Put a check mark in the box indicating what you think describes the health of the health care system:

■ The health care system is in Good Health.

☐ The health care system is in Fair Health.

■ The health care system is in Poor Health.

What did you use to evaluate (or diagnose) the health care system?

- Cost. Is health care affordable? The share of a person's income, a family's income, or a country's Gross Domestic Product that is spent on health care is one measure of affordability.
- Access. One measure of access is the percentage of people who have access to health care because they have, for example, insurance coverage.
- Performance. This is the measure of the bang for the health care buck! What do individuals and the national as a whole get for spending on health care? Health care performance measures include infant mortality rates, life expectancy, and quality of life.

One complication in formulating national health care policy is federalism. The states play an important role in the design and delivery of health care. The federal government cannot mandate state actions. For example, 26 Republican governors filed lawsuits challenging the constitutionality of the Affordable Care Act.

How is the health of your state's health care policy? The Kaiser Family Foundation provides data and analysis of the health care in the U.S. and other countries. It measures health care spending, quality, access and affordability, health and wellbeing. The Commonwealth Fund in an organization that promotes the creation of a more effective health care system. It provides a great deal of useful data on health care. Its State Scorecard 2014 provides an interactive map that enables a reader to quickly see where the state in which they reside ranks in terms of health care on various measures and by overall rank. It also provides Surveys and Data from states, regions, and countries.

13.42 | *COMPARATIVE APPROACHES*

Asking whether the U.S. has a good health care system often prompts not an answer but another question: Compared to what? Comparison is valuable because it provides benchmarks for evaluating policy. Health care can be studied from a number of comparative perspectives. One comparison is *historical*: comparing the current system with the past system. A second approach is *comparative*: comparing states or countries. A third way is to compare the health care sector of the American economy with other sectors of the economy.

Comparative Health Care Policy

T. R. Reid compares the health care systems in countries with political and economic systems that are similar to the U.S. and countries with different systems. The results provide valuable benchmarks for determining the performance of different health care systems:
http://www.npr.org/templates/rundowns/rundown.php?prgId=13&prgDate=8-24-2009

The comparative costs of health care are examined in this PBS story:
http://www.pbs.org/newshour/rundown/2012/10/health-costs-how-the-us-compares-with-other-countries.html

The comparisons of health care systems include the ways that health care is delivered—including the reliance on medical technology. The American practice of medicine is noted for its advanced technology. Medical technology is a mixed blessing: it produces amazing health care outcomes for some individuals but it is very expensive. The American practice of medicine's reliance on technology has made the old-fashioned physical exam—which is a low-cost diagnosis—a "dying art." Dr. Abraham Verghese, a physician at the Stanford Medical School, described the problem in a semi-serious way: "I sometimes joke that if you come to our hospital missing a finger, no one will believe you until we get a CAT scan, an MRI, and an orthopedic consult. We don't trust our senses." Dr. Verghese's comment criticizes the modern medical profession for becoming so dependent on machines to tell them about the patient (the "I-patient") that doctors do not pay very much attention to the actual patient in the hospital bed.[4]

A final comparison looks at health care relative to other sectors of the economy. The U.S. economy has various sectors: hospitality, manufacturing, agri-business, education, criminal justice, telecommunications, and even a **fast food sector**. Comparing the health care and fast food sectors may seem inappropriate because they are so different. But the fast food industry has developed and applied cost and quality control measures, as well as other organizational practices that might be applicable to the health care industry. The two sectors might seem so completely different that the one has little to say about the other, but from an organizational perspective, the attention that restaurant chains have paid to delivering a **good** (fast food) produce may be relevant to the delivery of a **service** (health care). Americans brought organizational skills to manufacturing, agriculture, and to the service sector (notably, through chain restaurants and lodging). But medicine—doctors and hospitals—have resisted the trend until recently. Doctors **were** self-employed; now three-quarters are employees. Hospitals are also becoming parts of chains. In "Big Med," Gawande describes how "[restaurant] chains have managed to combing quality control, cost control, and innovation" and asks whether their organizational principles can do the same for health care.[5]

In the U.S., health care policy developed as a series of decisions related to the regulation of hospitals, the licensing of health care providers, the creation of employer-based benefits, and the regulation of insurance companies. Health care policy is surprisingly dependent on taxes to raise money to fund government programs, to discourage certain activities (e.g., smoking), encourage certain behaviors (e.g., marriage; child rearing), and to redistribute wealth (progressive income taxes).

Think About It!
Is a tax break the best policy for subsidizing health insurance coverage?
http://www.npr.org/blogs/health/2012/12/04/166434247/the-huge-and-rarely-discussed-health-insurance-tax-break

13.5 | Environmental Policy

Environmental policy is more complicated than many other areas of public policy because so many areas of public policy—economics, transportation, energy, and food—have environmental impacts. So environmental policy includes issues such as air and pollution and the conservation of water and land and other natural resources. Like other areas of public policy, there is an environmental policy issue network consisting of congressional committees, executive agencies including the Environmental Protection Agency, and interest groups—both environmentalist groups and business groups. The EPA's mission includes a broad range of related activities. The states also play important roles in developing environmental policies and implementing federal priorities and programs. The American Council for an Energy-Efficient Economy describes what the states are doing.

For these reasons, federal environmental policy has been described as fragmented and conflicted. It is fragmented because so many units of government have authority over some aspect of environmental policy. And it is conflicted because the agency missions include both protecting natural resources and exploiting them for economic development, agricultural production, human consumption and recreation, and energy production. Water policy illustrates these issues.

Water is essential for life. Every language has a word for water. The American Museum of Natural History's "H20=Life" explains the importance of water. Historically, the major civilizations of the world developed around water, or water was considered an especially significant natural, religious, or cultural resource: the Tigris and Euphrates; the Ganges; the Nile; the Jordan. The significance of water is reflected in the central role that water plays in a country's history, economics, politics, and religion (e.g., baptism and cleansing rituals).

Today, we can engineer urban environments to make water available in arid regions, but providing a sustainable supply of water is essential for most countries. Water scarcity causes economic problems and political conflicts. In the U.S., states have been fighting water wars with neighboring states and countries (Canada and Mexico) for decades. Water is also becoming a national security issue in regions of the world such as the Middle East. There are three things to keep in mind when studying water policy in the U.S.: interstate commerce; regionalism; and federal water projects.

> U.S. national security strategy documents now describe water problems as a national security threat. Water scarcity and climate change create political problems that threaten U.S. national security interests.

Interstate Commerce. Water can be an article in interstate commerce just like other goods (cars, clothing, and electronic equipment) and services (e.g., health care or legal services). Water that moves in, involves, or affects interstate commerce comes under Congress' interstate commerce powers—whether it is lake water, river water, stream water, spring water, or underground (an aquifer). Congress has plenary (that is, total and complete) power over interstate commerce.

The federal government has complete power over interstate commerce. Article I, Sect 8 of the Constitution provides that "The Congress shall have Power To.... regulate

Commerce with foreign Nations, and among the several States, and with the Indian Tribes...." This means that any use of water that involves more than one state, or another country (e.g., international water agreements with Great Lakes states and Canada) is subject to federal regulation. **Intrastate waters**, those that are entirely within one state, can be regulated by that state. The federal government approves interstate and international water compacts because they involve interstate commerce in water.

The federal government's complete power over interstate commerce was established in an early Supreme Court case, _Gibbons v. Odgen_ (1824). The case involved a legal dispute over whether a state or the federal government could license a ferry across the Hudson River between New York City and New Jersey. The Court ruled that Congress has complete power over interstate commerce, defined as any economic activity involving or affecting more than one state. Water that affects more than one state comes under the federal government's interstate commerce power. A small lake or pond or stream that is entirely within a state is generally considered beyond the interstate commerce power of the federal government.

Regionalism. Most of the United States is blessed with an abundant supply of water for human consumption and use in agriculture, manufacturing, transportation, and the generation of electrical power. However, water is generally abundant in the eastern half of the country and generally scarce in the western half of the country. The politics of federalism requires cooperation to resolve water conflicts, and the Founders anticipated conflicts between states. The Constitution provides that the U.S. Supreme Court has original jurisdiction to hear cases where a state sues another state. These kinds of cases include legal disputes over water. Many state boundaries include rivers. Rivers change their courses, but state boundaries do not change because the river changes course. States also sue other states over the use of water from rivers, lakes, reservoirs, and aquifers.

Federal Water Projects. Federal water projects have played an important role in regional economic development. The Tennessee Valley Authority (TVA) is a major federal water and power project that increased the economic development of Appalachia. The TVA was created in the 1930s to generate electrical power. Today, the TVA website identifies "energy," "environment," and "economic development" as its purposes. Federal projects have been essential for western economic development. As the supply of clean water has become an increasingly scarce resource, water has become a contentious political issue for local, regional, state, and national government. East of the Mississippi River where water was plentiful _wasting water_ meant consuming it needlessly or using too much water. In the arid regions west of the Mississippi River, wasting water meant not using it by allowing river water to flow unimpeded and used until it eventually emptied into the ocean.

Much of western urban development—the Los Angeles, Phoenix, Las Vegas, and San Diego metropolitan area—and agricultural development was made possible by massive dams and irrigation projects that transported water over long distances and even over or around high mountains to where it was needed for thirsty people or thirsty crops. As a result, it has been said that in the American West water flows uphill—toward money. (Reissner 1986) On the Great Plains, the Ogallala (or High Plains) Aquifer that lies beneath much of the country ranging from South Dakota to Texas supports large-scale industrial agriculture. The use of this ground water can be considered **mining** as much as irrigation for **farming**.[6] Underground aquifers are mined for their water the way other minerals such as gold, copper, silver, and coal are mined.

13.51 | *Water Wars in the Dry West*

Western federal water projects have been essential for economic development, agricultural production, and urban life in major cities including Las Vegas NV, Phoenix AZ, and Los Angeles CA. California's major agricultural areas, the Central Valley and the Imperial Valley, depend on federal water projects. Western water projects have prompted the quip that in most of the world water flows downhill, but in the American West, "Water flows uphill—toward money!" It flows uphill because of projects such as the Hoover Dam, which is part of a massive western water project that is managed by the U.S. Bureau of Reclamation, "the largest wholesaler of water in the United States." The Bureau is an agency in the U.S. Department of the Interior, the agency that manages the country's "vast natural and cultural resources." The Department of Agriculture's Natural Resources Conservation Service also manages natural resources such as water. And, of course, the EPA is the primary agency responsible for administering various clean water acts. The National Oceanic and Atmospheric Association (NOAA) Centers for Environmental Information provide a map of the major river basins in the contiguous United States. In which river basin do you live?

> Check It Out!
> The American Geosciences Institute's Interactive Map of Major Streams and Rivers has a streamer app that allows you to trace any major stream upstream to its source or downstream to where it empties into the sea.

The rivers of the western U.S. have been so extensively engineered and managed that they have been transformed into **outdoor plumbing systems** that have been engineered to move water from where it is, and where it naturally flows, to where it is needed: cities, farms, and reservoirs. The Rio Grande is one such grand outdoor plumbing system. The Rio Grande Compact created in 1937 includes Colorado, New Mexico, and Texas. The Colorado River Compact includes seven states. The federal government tunneled under the Continental Divide to send Colorado River water to the Rio Grande River, which has had so much of its river flow withdrawn from the river that it no longer flows into the ocean. The Central Arizona Project (CAP) is one of these massive federal projects.

California. William Mulholland (1855-1935) was the head of the Los Angeles Department of Water and Power. He is a famous figure in the western water wars—for instance, the Owens Valley Water Wars). The western water story is told in a series *Cadillac Desert* that describes how important the development of water and waterpower was to California and the entire arid West's development. *Cadillac Desert* also provides insights into an earlier era of great confidence, the "can-do" attitude, and the belief that the

U.S. can find an engineering solution to any of its water problems. After WWII, the U.S. explored peaceful uses of its nuclear bombs. Project Plowshare was the Atomic Energy Commission's (AEC) effort to promote "peaceful nuclear explosions" for a broad range of engineering and construction purposes such as widening the Panama Canal, connecting Arizona's aquifers, and bringing water through the mountains to California's Sacramento Valley. In one sense, the AEC was providing a biblical justification for its efforts by referencing the Prophet Isaiah's belief that people would beat their swords into plowshares and their spears into pruning forks and neither study nor train for war. This also fit well with the religious belief that it was wasteful to allow river water to empty unused into the seas. The American "can-do" attitude is expressed in the Latin saying "Fiat Lux. Fiat Pluvia." [Let there be light. Let there be rain.] This is the belief that electrical light could be engineered with waterpower just as water for drinking and irrigation could be engineered with water projects.

California water utilities are on the front lines of the scarcity problem. Parkwood, a small community in California's Central Valley, is one of 28 small communities whose water systems are listed as "Critical" because it relies on a single source of water: a stream that is now becoming a dry creek. The state and local agencies that manage water include the California Environmental Protection Agency (ACWA), State Water Resources Control Board, and The Association of California Water Agencies. The fact that the ACWA was formed in 1910 is an indication of how much earlier California has been formulating water policy than states such as Florida. But California's history of local control over water resources, and the existence of "historic" water rights claims that give older users priority over newer users, results in a patchwork of water agencies that do not uniformly enforce water restrictions despite the historic drought.

The historic five-year drought in California that ended in 2016 prompted state and local rules to enact new regulations but "Historic Water Claims Mean Special Status, Despite Drought Allocation Rules." The California State Water Project is a complex and comprehensive state and local government agency that manages water resources. It includes the California Department of Water Resources. The state's fresh water policy goals include 1) providing enough water for human consumption and agriculture; and 2) preserving ecosystems. It is not easy to reconcile these goals.

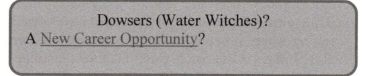

Dowsers (Water Witches)?
A New Career Opportunity?

The dam problem! In the past, major federal water projects built dams to store and then distribute water. But these dam structures are now aging, and drought and increased water usage have lowered water levels in the reservoirs. The *PBS* story "Why Dams are at the Heart of California's Water Problems" explains why One solution to the dam problem is dam repairs and proposals to solve the water shortage by building more dams that increase storage capacity. But "To Build or not to build, that's the Dam Question in Dry California" because dams are solutions that also create problems.

One alternative is to increase the supply of water by drilling more wells. But wells have already created problems. Irrigated water results in the salinization of the soil. The deeper the wells, the more chemical problems irrigated water causes in the soil and the foods (e.g., fruits and vegetables) that are grown using it. This is a major issue in the agricultural areas of California, for example. The depletion of aquifers has also caused the land to sink. Is California falling off the continental shelf? Or is it just sinking away as the increased mining of aquifers lowers the ground water levels? The "Epic Drought" that California experienced in recent years actually moved mountains—by lowering them— while the increased well drilling was lowering valley floors. In the western water wars, drilling more and deeper wells and pumping ground water at rates that lower aquifers is essentially **mining water**. It causes the land to subside. Western water comes from rain, snowmelt that fills streams and lakes and reservoirs, canals (the elaborate system water transfers across regions and states) and aquifers—from which underground water is mined.

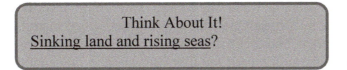

Think About It!
Sinking land and rising seas?

13.52 | *Water Wars in the Southwest*

The Red River Water Wars refers to the political and legal fights that Texas, Oklahoma, Arkansas, and Louisiana have had over the rights to use water from the Red River Basin. The Red River Compact specifies rights that are managed by a Commission. Texas and Oklahoma fight over the water from Lake Texoma. The Tarrant Regional Water District sued Oklahoma to get more rights to use water for growing cities in north Texas cities. The U.S. Supreme Court ultimately upheld a state's power to control its own natural resources rather being forced to sell them (in this case, water) to another state.

13.53 | *Water Wars in the Midwest*

The Republican River Water Wars refer to the political and legal fights among Colorado, Nebraska, and Kansas over the rights to use Republican River water. The Republican River watershed includes the three states. In 1942, the three states entered into a compact that Congress approved in 1943. The Republican River Compact stipulated each state's water rights and created the Republican River Water Compact Administration (RRCA) to administer the district. During the 1980s, Kansas began reporting that Nebraska was violating the terms of the compact by permitting groundwater wells to pump water for agricultural uses. The Compact *defined* the **virgin water supply** as the multiyear average supply of water in the Basin un-depleted by human activity; *estimated* the average water supply; and *allocated* to each state an agreed-upon share for beneficial human use. But the Compact did not provide a dispute resolution process or administrative details beyond saying that each state can appoint an administrator and the three administrators can make regulations. Non-binding arbitration resulted in a finding that Kansas 1) had suffered damages, but 2) failed to adequately prove those damages. Kansas appealed to the U.S. Supreme Court to determine if Nebraska had violated the compact and if so determine the damages. The state fights indicate that when it comes to water, we can't all just get along. The U.S. Supreme Court appointed a Special Master to gather information and make a recommendation that settled the dispute (for now) when the Supreme Court adopted the recommendations in *Kansas v. Nebraska* (2015).

These water issues also apply to mid-sized cities in the industrial north. Flint, Michigan's water woes focused attention on aging infrastructure such as lead pipes leaching into city water supplies. The City of Waukesha, Wisconsin proposed changing from well water sources to water that was piped from Lake Michigan. The city had to apply for an exception to the Great Lakes-St. Laurence River Basin Water Resources Compact and the Great Lakes-St. Laurence River Basin Sustainable Water Resource Agreement, which limited diversion of the water from the basin. The Compact Council, which consists of the governors of the eight Great Lakes states, approved the diversion. One concern with such diversions is the legal precedent that would be set by allowing water to be diverted from the basin.

The increasing value of water has caused water to be described as a kind of "blue gold." Dayton, Ohio is a Rust Belt city that was hit hard when manufacturing first left for the Sun Belt, then Mexico, and then China. Dayton is now advertising itself as a city with an abundance of fresh water vital for familiar uses such as consumption, agriculture, and manufacturing AND for new uses such as cooling computer server farms.

13.54 | Water Wars in the Southeast

The Tri-State Water Wars refer to the southeastern fights among Florida, Georgia, and Alabama, three fast-growing Sunbelt states over the rights to use water from the Apalachicola, Flint, and Chattahoochee River System. Once again, the U.S. Supreme Court is required to ultimately decide these water wars. The Southern Environmental Law Center reports on the story of this water war.

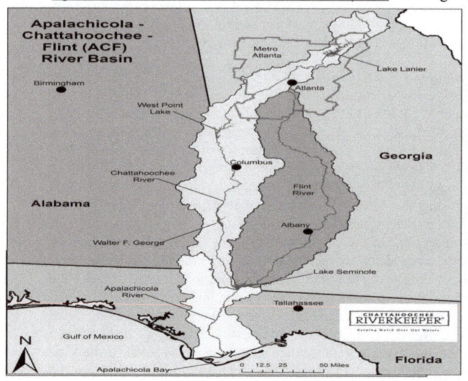

> **Think about it!**
> The "milkshake" speech from *There Will Be Blood* (2007) (at 7:20) is one of the top ten business speeches in film. What does it have to do with these water cases?
> http://www.youtube.com/watch?v=2opI3LI92Vc

13.55 | *Solutions to the Scarcity Problem*

The belief that taxes can be cut without reducing programs by increasing efficiency is similar to the belief that improved water management is the solution to the water scarcity problem. *Killing the Colorado* is the story of "Drought and Man in the West." What about conservation? Population growth in the Southwestern Sun Belt states began raising questions about whether the water scarcity problem was *too little water or too many people.* Are there too many people for too little water in the arid western states? Conservation has had an impact on behavior. The United States Geological Survey (USGS) reported a 13% decline in water usage across the nation during five-year period 2005–2010. However, little of the decline in consumption was public consumption; most of the reduction was in power plant and agricultural usage. Twelve states account for 50% of the water withdrawn from ground and surface resources: CA (11%); Texas, Idaho, Florida, Illinois, NC, ARK, CO.

> **Think About It!**
> In the academy award-winning film *The Graduate* (1967) a college graduate looking for a career is advised to get into plastics because plastics were the future. What about **getting into** water? The U.S. Geological Survey has a Water Science School.
> https://water.usgs.gov/edu/

The "supply side" solutions—drilling more wells and building more dams, reservoirs, and even de-salinization plants—do not address the "demand side" problem. Conservation attempts to address the demand side, but to date conservation measures have not ended the water wars. In fact, conservation—individuals and businesses lowering their rates of water usage—has not compensated for the higher total water usage resulting from population increases. The new western water wars are **inter-state battles** over access to Colorado River water, **intra-state battles** between urban and agricultural interests, and **regional battles** between northern California and southern California.

There also is a backlash against environmentalists. Critics accuse environmentalists of seeming more interested in protecting small creatures—a bird like the spotted owl, a mammal like a prairie dog, or a fish like the snail darter—than allowing the use of natural resources to provide people with food or water or energy or forestry products for building houses. Are tree-huggers more than people-huggers? This is in essence the point of the PBS story "Fishermen and Farmers Fight over Water in California."

13.56 | *The Water Pollution Problem*

There is extensive mining in the West. Of the approximately 500,000 abandoned mines in the country, only about 48,000 have been inventoried by the Bureau of Land Management's Abandoned Mine Lands program. The estimated cost of cleanup ranges from $20–54 billion dollars. The Clean Water Act makes mine owners responsible for controlling discharges, but owners often say that they are not responsible for cleaning up mines that stopped operating long ago. The Gold King Mine in Colorado stopped operating in 1923. In 2015, the EPA contracted with a company to plug the mine's toxic wastewater holding pond. An accident caused a three million gallon wastewater plume into the Animas River. The wastewater pond cleanup accident that polluted the Animas River was readily apparent in the color of the river water.

The alternative to plugging wastewater ponds is building a treatment plant to clean the water. Both local government officials and company officials are reluctant to support federal cleanup plans because they cost money. The Silverton area where Gold King is located was first developed after an 1872 federal mining law encouraged exploitation of western resources by allowing individuals to claim the mineral rights beneath public lands. Toxic wastewater has been left behind at many of the mining operations. The acid rock drainage pollutes watersheds with heavy metals, "stew brews" with sulfuric acid concentrations high enough to dissolve steel and to leach poisons including lead, arsenic, and cadmium out of mountainsides.

The Cuyahoga River Fire (1969) is one of the environmental disaster stories that put the environment on the national government agenda. Why were factories and cities built along waterways? One reason is rivers provided transportation. Another reason is factories and cities could literally flush some of the costs of manufacturing, and some of the costs of treating sewage, downstream or into a big body of water according to the theory that "dilution is the solution to the pollution." The story is told in an article with curious title: "Why Rivers No Longer Burn." A lot has been done to rivers. Why was the Chicago River reversed? The Chicago River used to flow eastward into Lake Michigan. Chicago was a growing metropolis that needed a sewer that did not flow right into Lake Michigan because Lake Michigan was its source of drinking water. In 1885, many people died after a heavy rainstorm washed sewage from the river—which was, in a sense, the city's sewer—into the lake where the city's water intake pipes were located. So engineers decided to reverse the flow of the river: they connected it into a "Sanitary and Ship Canal" that connects to the Illinois River, the Des Plaines River, and then flows to the Mississippi River. Today, there is a Des Plaines River watershed. The Metropolitan Water Reclamation District of Greater Chicago has authority over the waterway system. The Friends of the Chicago River opposes a plan to reverse engineer the Chicago River so that it once again flows into Lake Michigan because the river is currently "flushed" with fresh water from Lake Michigan that flows to the Mississippi.

The Great Lakes and the Great Lakes Basin are a great freshwater supply. The Great Lakes constitute 84% of North America's surface fresh water and about 21% of the world's fresh surface water. The Great Lakes are a natural resource that is subject to state, federal, and international regulation. The Great Lakes Coalition sponsors an annual Great Lakes Restoration Conference with themes such as healing our waters and caring for our drinking water.

13.57 | *Water Treatment*

The American public expects an adequate supply of clean water. This is a fairly modern expectation. The Victorian Age is remembered today mostly for being an age when people were worried about dirty books but in the Victorian Age London's filth included filthy air and water. Water systems are now integral parts of urban utility systems that provide water, electrical power, and disposal of sewage and solid waste. Water works are impressive engineering feats—especially considering the size of the urban populations they serve. But water works are victims of their own success in the sense that they have worked so well for so long that they are often taken them for granted. The *NPR* story "If a Water Main Isn't Broke, Don't Fix It (for 300 years?)" describes how years of deferred maintenance have created a stressed system. The American Water Works Association's Water Utilities Council directs its government affairs staff to sound as "the voice of water."

Think About It!
Why do people drink so much bottled water?
The Story of Bottled Water provides one explanation and the bottled water industry provides a rebuttal in The Real Story of Bottled Water.

What should be flushed down the toilet? Wipes? The fact that Wipes are flushable doesn't mean they should be flushed. Drugs? We live in a pharmaceutical age. People take lots of drugs. Where do they go? Read the NPR story "Traces of Drugs in Water?" to learn some of the impacts of drug usage. The Swedes take lots of anti-anxiety drugs—which may explain why they seem calm and generally score rather high on happiness measures. Are trace amounts of these drugs in the waters of Sweden making the fish less anxious too—and therefore making it easier for them to be eaten by other fish, and easier to be caught and eaten by people?

Think About It!
"Water, water everywhere but not a drop to drink?"
http://www.npr.org/2011/08/16/139642271/why-cleaned-wastewater-stays-dirty-in-our-minds

Public perceptions limit efforts to reuse or re-cycle water. Cognitive awareness that the wastewater has been cleaned does not completely overcome the psychological feelings about what the water had been used for and where it had been. Recycling cleaned wastewater—particularly recycling sewage water—for human consumption requires addressing the "ick" factor associated with drinking recycled toilet water. The NPR story *Water, Water Everywhere but not a Drop to Drink*? explains why people think that cleaned wastewater is still too dirty to drink. Non-profit organizations such as the WaterReuse Research Foundation conduct and promote applied research on the science of water reuse, recycling, reclamation, and desalination. Water politics is no longer just about conservation, sustainability, or being green—it is a vital resource that has national security implications.

The EPA's "History of Drinking Water Treatment" provides an overview of one aspect of water policy and technological developments. The EPA's Office of Water includes the following offices:

- Immediate Office of the Assistant Administrator for Water
- Office of Ground Water and Drinking Water
- Office of Science and Technology
- Office of Wastewater Management
- Office of Wetlands, Oceans and Watersheds

Think About It! Act on It!
Surf Your Watershed!
This is a civic engagement project:
Find out where your water comes from (not the faucet).
What watershed do you live in? Is there a special government district such as water district?
Contact a local, state, or national government official and ask them what they think is the most important water problem.

13.58 | Climate Change

Climate change—or the more controversial term global warming—presents a new set of regional water problem: rising sea levels. Rising sea level require asking which coastal cities can be defended, how they can be defended, and who should pay for the coastal defense? Hurricane Katrina's disastrous flooding of New Orleans left some people to think that New Orleans was so vulnerable to flooding that it was not worth it to try to prevent flooding considering the city's exposure to hurricanes and the high costs of flood protection. But New Orleans is not the only urban center that is vulnerable to flooding. What is the largest estuary on the west coast of the U.S.? Read "About CALFED" to learn about this surprising estuary, which includes Sacramento, a city protected by dams and dikes. Hurricane Sandy made landfall on October 29, 2012 at a barrier island north of Atlantic City. The storm water surge damaged barrier islands up the Atlantic coast and flooded New York City and the surround areas, thereby exposing the vulnerability of the entire New York City metropolitan region.

What should be the public policy goals for vulnerable coastal regions?

- Retreat from the sea? Governments could use zoning laws, flood insurance regulations, and disaster assistance funds to limit new development in flood-prone areas or even to pull back from shorelines.
- Armor the beaches? The coastal regions could be protected with sea walls and other structures as well as beach re-nourishment projects to create man-made barriers. Beach re-nourishment provides temporary protection from storms.

Congress responded to Hurricane Sandy by passing the Disaster Relief Appropriations Act of 2013, which provided around $50 billion for relief projects and programs, some of which was funding for the Army Corps of Engineers—which contracts with The Great Lakes Dredge and Dock, a company that among other things continually re-nourishes the beaches with sand dredged from offshore. Beach re-nourishment is environmentally damaging, but most of the damage is on the ocean floor in a place that is out of sight and therefore mostly out of mind.

Does the U.S. have too many governments or not enough? The argument for more governments is based on the belief that regional governments are needed to address regional environmental problems. Existing political boundaries—city borders, county lines, and state lines—are geographical and political boundaries that are not in most cases natural boundaries. Environmental problems are increasingly regional problems. Take, for instance, acidification. Air pollution from Midwestern manufacturing plants and electrical power plants is sent up smokestacks and into the jet stream, where the prevailing easterly winds drop acid rain in the northeast. The acidification of lakes and streams in the northeastern states comes from outside the region. Acid rain also causes ocean acidification. Environmentalists believe these regional and even global problems require regional or even global government action.

Libertarians disagree. Libertarians think that more government means less freedom. Therefore they look for private, non-governmental solutions to social and environmental problems. Murray Rothbard is a libertarian who thinks that government caused many of the water use conflicts therefore creating more regional governments is unlikely to be the solution to the environmental problem.

> ### Think About It!
> Do you agree with Murray Rothbard's solution to the water wars as summarized in *The American Conservative*?
> http://www.theamericanconservative.com/articles/texas-water-war/

The U.S. Army Corps of Engineers predicts that sea levels will rise 9–24 inches by 2060. Four Southeastern Florida Counties (Monroe, Miami-Dade, Broward, and Palm Beach) and 30 cities have joined the Southeast Florida Regional Climate Change Compact to coordinate responses to sea level rise, tidal flooding, and saltwater intrusion into drinking water well fields. There are many stories about it raining frogs and fish. Some are apocryphal; some are true. But cephalopods in parking lots?

An Octopus in a Miami Beach Parking Garage (in the Shade)

13.6 | Energy Policy

The U.S. is a high-consuming nation. It is not just that the U.S. uses a lot of energy—it is, after all a country with a large population. The U.S. is a high-consuming country because Americans have a high per capita use of energy. The following World Bank data compares the per capita consumption of energy in various countries.[7]

Energy use per capita

Primary energy use (before transformation to other end-use fuels) in kilograms of oil equivalent, per capita. More info »

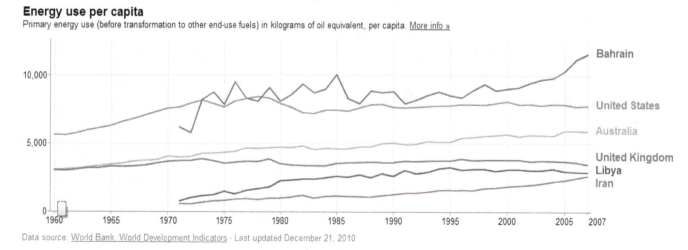

Data source: World Bank. World Development Indicators · Last updated December 21, 2010

The U.S. per person consumption of energy is high compared to other countries. U.S. dependence of foreign oil has been an issue since the 1970s Arab Oil Embargoes. The U.S. has been talking about the need for energy independence ever since then.

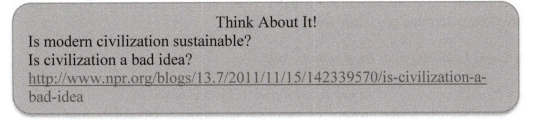

For a satirical view on political rhetoric about the importance of U.S. energy independence see The Daily Show's "An Energy-Independent Future." http://www.thedailyshow.com/watch/wed-june-16-2010/an-energy-independent-future

Energy policy has several goals: producing enough energy, conservation of resources, environmentalism, national security, and economics. The discussion of renewable energy is part of the broader discussion sustainability—whether it is energy resources, fisheries, forestry, mineral deposits, or water supplies. The discussion includes some provocative thoughts about whether modern civilization as we know it is even sustainable.

Think About It!
Is modern civilization sustainable?
Is civilization a bad idea?
http://www.npr.org/blogs/13.7/2011/11/15/142339570/is-civilization-a-bad-idea

13.61 | *Sustainability*

Sustainability is an important concept in environmental policy. Sustainable forestry practices harvest trees while keeping enough forests and healthy forests—not just tree farms, which are basically monoculture crops. Sustainable agriculture refers to farming practices that incorporate productivity with concern for maintaining water and soil quality. Marine sustainability refers to fishing practices that maintain sustainable stocks of fish and healthy natural fisheries. The Marine Stewardship Council is a global organization that works with fisheries, companies, scientists, conservation groups, and the general public to promote sustainable fisheries by labeling seafood as certified sustainable seafood. Do you care whether the fish you in the market or eat in a restaurant is obtained using sustainable fishing practices? Is the "certified sustainable" label about science or economics?

Think About It!
What Does "Sustainable" Fishing Mean?
http://www.npr.org/2013/02/12/171376617/conditions-allow-for-more-sustainable-labeled-seafood

13.7 | Immigration Policy

What are the ties that bind a people together as a political community? Is national identity based on tribe, ethnicity, race, blood, language, history, culture, religion, geography—or merely economic interests? The meaning of political identity is particularly complicated in the U.S. because Americans take pride in being a country of immigrants, but Americans also take great pride in a distinctive American national identity. The history of immigration policy reflects efforts to reconcile these two ideals. National identity politics is at the core of the tension between the ideal of the U.S. as a republic founded as an immigrant nation— famously symbolized by the Statue of Liberty which welcomes with open arms the huddled masses that come seeking a better life—and the sense that there is a distinctive American national identity that must be protected from foreign influences. Immigration policy reflects the recurring debates about whether the nation's borders should be open or closed, whether people should be pulled into the country or pushed out of the country, and whether citizenship (naturalization) should be made easier or harder to get. Immigration policy has three main components: *admission* to the country, *removal* from the country (deportation), and the rules that determine *eligibility for citizenship*.

13.71 | *The Legal Foundations of Immigration Policy*

Congress's <u>constitutional power</u> to enact immigration laws is based on
* Article I Section 8 (the power "To establish an uniform Rule of Naturalization") and Section 9 ("The Migration or Importation of such Persons as any of the States now existing shall think proper to admit, shall not be prohibited by the Congress prior to the Year one thousand eight hundred and eight, but a Tax or duty may be imposed on such Importation, not exceeding ten dollars for each Person.")*
  *This referred to slaves.

* Article VI (the Supremacy Clause provides that the Constitution, laws passed under its authority, and treaties shall be the supreme law of the land and judges in the states are bound thereby regardless of state laws.); and the
* The Plenary Power Doctrine. This is a rule that the Supreme Court created to help decide cases about who has power to make immigration policy. According to the Plenary Power Doctrine, Congress has plenary (that is, complete and unqualified) power over immigration policy.

Congress has delegated a great deal of its power to make immigration policy to the president—and the various administrative agencies such as the Department of Homeland Security and the Department of Justice). One early example of legislative delegation to the president is the <u>Alien and Sedition Acts</u> (1789). These were four laws passed during a period of worry about aliens—specifically, the French and British who were still in the country after the Revolutionary War and whose loyalty was suspect. The Naturalization Act increased the residency requirement for American citizenship from 5 to 14 years. The Alien Friends Act allowed the president to imprison or deport aliens that the president considered "dangerous to the peace and safety of the United States" at any time; and the

Alien Enemies Act authorized the president to deport any male citizen of a hostile nation, above the age of 14, during times of war.

In fact, most immigration statutes give the president a great deal of executive discretion to decide how to implement them. In 1986 Congress created the Visa Waiver Pilot Program to promote tourism and trade by allowing citizens *of certain countries* to enter the U.S. without visas, thereby bypassing the in-person interview with U.S. consulates abroad. Most of the countries were European, because Europeans were considered safer and wealthier and therefore less likely to exceed their stay in the U.S. The pilot program was made permanent in 2000, and today 30 of the 38 countries that participate in the visa waiver program are European. The rest are U.S. allies such as Japan, South Korea, and Australia. Twenty million people now travel visa-free after filing out the Department of Homeland Security's on-line application program known as the Electronic System for Travel Authorization.) One response to the 9/11 terrorist attacks on 9/11 was added security measures to the waiver program, including a requirement that participating countries share information about citizens and nationals on terrorist/security lists.

After the Republican majority in Congress stopped supporting bipartisan proposals for comprehensive immigration reform, President Obama took executive action to defer deportation of certain undocumented immigrants. In 2012, he directed the Secretary of the Department of Homeland Security to implement the Deferred Action for Childhood Arrivals (DACA) program. DACA created a process for applying for temporary deferral of deportation. Then in 2014, the Department of Homeland Security announced the Deferred Action for Parents of Americans and Lawful Permanent Residents (DAPA) program. Republicans challenged provisions of these executive actions in court. Congress also passed the Regulations from the Executive in Need of Scrutiny Act of 2017, which provides for legislative review of targeted executive actions that Republicans wanted to end, such as President Obama's immigration policies and provisions of Obamacare. These are examples of institutional struggles over control of immigration policy.

13.72 | *Early Fears of "The Other"*

A large numbers of foreign-born people—primarily British and French—lived in the U.S. in the early years of the republic people. The fear of foreigners as an internal threat to national security during the Undeclared War with France resulted in passage of four laws that were known collectively as the Alien and Sedition Acts of 1798. Threats to national security are called sedition. This early fear of political "others" has periodically made immigration controversial despite the fact that the U.S. is a "settler nation."

The U.S.—**like** Canada and Australia and **unlike** Great Britain—was a *settler nation* that recruited people from other countries to settle vast frontier lands. (Maloney) The Industrial Revolution then created additional demands for labor so immigrants were pulled into the country to provide a labor supply. But immigration was also considered a threat to the idea of a distinctive American national identity. Therefore understanding immigration policy requires understanding both the push and pull of immigrants. Some immigrants were both pushed out of their home countries and pulled into the U.S. to provide cheap labor. This is the case with the Irish, one of the first groups of immigrants, and Mexicans, one of the largest groups of immigrants. But the experiences of the two groups of immigrants are very different. The U.S. periodically pulled Mexicans into the country, the Mexican government periodically pushed them out of Mexico when the

Mexican economy was bad, and the U.S. periodically pushed Mexicans out of the country when they weren't needed.

> ### Fear of other "Others"
>
> The fear of other "Others" included Native Americans. General and President Andrew Jackson's Indian Removal Policy also provided a model for how the country responded to perceived threats to the distinctive American national identity. Read the Document Transcript to get a sense of how he saw the removal of "a few savage hunters" a sign of progress, civilization, Christian community. The removal policy of "clearing" areas of the country of Native Americans, free blacks, and fugitive slaves included Florida—the destruction of the "Negro Fort."

The story of Irish immigration is the story of the first big wave of immigrants who were both pushed out of their native country and pulled into the U.S. The *PBS* documentary, "The Irish in America: Long Journey Home*"* describes the Irish experience in America. Episode #2 "All Across America*"* describes the early Irish experiences in East coast port cities (notably Boston and New York) and New Orleans. In New Orleans, the relationship between blacks (both slaves and free persons of color) and Irish immigrants was marked by intense competition for jobs. Who fought whom, why, and who won? What do you think about the cartoon images of "the Irish" and "the black?"

Episode #3 *Up from City Streets* primarily describes how the Irish pulled themselves up from the city streets as economic and political outsiders to become economic and political insiders. They did so by developing strong political organization such as Tammany Hall in New York City that controlled votes and jobs (e.g., jobs as police officers) and government officials. These strong urban political organizations helped the Irish advance—while also raising Protestant worries about political corruption and drinking and other behaviors that were inconsistent with the distinctive American national identity.

The popular press of the day created and reinforced negative stereotypes of the Irish. Examples of these stereotypes are RF Outcault's Hogan's Alley cartoon, The Yellow Kid, *Irish Playing the Great Game of Golf*, and *Coaching an Irish Parade*. What do you think are the messages conveyed in the different images presented in the scenes below?

The first wave of Irish immigrants was primarily Irish Protestants recruited to fight Native Americans on the frontier. The "second wave" in the 19th Century was the primarily Irish Catholics who worked on the canals and railroads and in the mines and factories that created the foundation for the industrial revolution. These were the Irish that fought their way into the economic, social, and political system because they were not welcomed with open arms by the establishment insiders. The Kensington riots in Philadelphia (1844) illustrate both the outside status of the Irish and their organization to fight nativists. Eventually, urban political machines such as Tammany Hall in New York City began to recruit Irish and provide them social services. The lesson of the Irish experience is that political organization increases effectiveness. Without political organization, individuals like immigrants face struggles alone.

Nativism was one of the earliest reactions to increases in immigration, to increases in the proportion of the population that is foreign-born, and the sense that the American political culture was being threatened by foreign ideas. A positive definition of nativism is advocating for the native born citizens. A negative definition of nativism is advocating against non-natives. In the early years of the 19th Century, the Know-Nothing (or American) Party reflected nativist worries about immigrants changing American character. Anti-immigrant or pro-American movements have periodically been a backlash against immigration.

13.73 | *Development of National Immigration Policy*

Modern immigration policy (in the U.S. and elsewhere) is a function of the modern, industrial state. (Maloney) In the U.S., prior to the industrial revolution, immigration policy was primarily the concern of the **cities** where immigrants entered the U.S.—New York City and San Francisco—or cities where large numbers of immigrants settled (e.g., Boston). The development of a **comprehensive, national** immigration policy can be traced to the period 1875-1882, with passage of the 1875 Page Law (which provided for the exclusion of "undesirables"), the Immigration Act of 1882 (which restricted immigration of people "likely to become a public charge"), and the Chinese Exclusion Act of 1882. These laws mark the beginning of Congress creating immigration policy to control the composition of the citizenry: controlling the number of immigrants; restricting eligibility for citizenship; screening for "alien" or un-American ideology; and determining the composition of the workforce. Congress used immigration policy to sort individuals and groups as a social and political filter to protect American national identity.

The latter part of the 19th Century and early years of the 20th Century were periods of increases in the *number* of immigrants and changes in the *kinds* of immigrants. There were more immigrants and different immigrants—immigrants from eastern and southern Europe rather than from the British Isles and Western Europe. The result was a "panic:" a widespread fear that immigration policy threatened to erode "Americanism." This public worry about American national identity put immigration *control* on the national government agenda. The need to protect and promote Americanism is the theme of President Theodore Roosevelt's 2006 State of the Union Address. The Address devotes considerable space to the question of Americanism; the duty to manage the affairs of all the islands (the Philippines, "Porto Rico," and Hawaii) "under the American flag," including helping these people to develop so that they would eventually be prepared for citizenship. Roosevelt recommended independence for the Philippines only when (and if) they demonstrated political maturity. He recommended citizenship for residents of "Porto Rico." He recommended developing statutory immigration rights for residents of Hawaii "whenever the leaders in the various industries of those islands finally adopt our ideals and heartily join our administration in endeavoring to develop a middle class of substantial citizens."

Roosevelt also provided advice about immigration policy by reminding the nation that "[g]ood Americanism is a matter of heart, of conscience, of lofty aspirations, of sound common sense, but not of birthplace or creed." Nevertheless, an *immigration panic* resulted in passage of a broad range of laws intended to protect Americanism by limiting immigration. The Expatriation Act of 1907 required women who were U.S. citizens who married foreigners to take the nationality of their husband. This is one of the most blatantly gender-biased laws ever passed by Congress. And in 1907, Congress responded to worries about immigration by creating the U. S. Immigration Commission (The Dillingham Commission) to study the effects of immigration on American society and culture. The Dillingham Commission Reports (1911) concluded the immigration was a threat and should be greatly reduced, and Congress passed the Emergency Quota Act of 1921 and other laws in 1924 that greatly reduced immigration from eastern and southern Europe.

The Dillingham Commission Report and the subsequent laws restricting immigration were not merely based on racism. They reflected the new science of eugenics—controlled breeding to improve human populations—to sort people; old nativist political ideas about foreigners threatening American national identity; and a general bias against specific immigrant groups (e.g., Catholics; Asians) and *races*. These restrictive immigration laws created categories such as "poor physique" that were so broadly defined that they could be used to discriminate against individuals or groups. But it is also important to recognize that the Dillingham Commission's ranking of groups was based on the era's belief that scientific knowledge provided evidence that **not all men, women, races, cultures, religions, or civilizations were created equal**. This justified immigration policy that **ranked groups** in order to sort people so that the better sorts could be allowed in and the worse sorts could be kept out.

Ranking groups to sort them into desirable and undesirable immigrants remained part of immigration policy until the 1960s. The Council on Foreign Relations provides a Timeline on Post-WWII immigration policy. The Immigration and Nationality Act of 1965 fundamentally changed immigration law. Prior to the 1965 Act, most immigrants were Caucasians from Western Europe; after the 1965 Act, most came from southern and eastern Europe, Africa, Asia, and Latin America. The 1965 Act ended the historical racial and cultural assumptions about which groups should be allowed into the country and which should be excluded because they were less desirable. The national origins quota was biased in favor of Western Europe and biased against other regions, religions, races, and cultures. The 1965 Immigration and Nationality Act is a civil rights law that was part of the civil rights movement that produced the more familiar 1964 Civil Rights Act and the 1965 Voting Rights Act. The 1965 Immigration Act increased the number of immigrants admitted annually and greatly increased the country's racial and demographic diversity. In fact, the current anti-immigration mood can be considered a backlash against the effects of the 1965 immigration act.

13.74 | *Current Immigration Policy*

Immigration policy is shaped by political, economic, and legal factors. The relative influence of these three factors varies depending on the state of the economy, national security threats, and even thinking about human and civil rights.

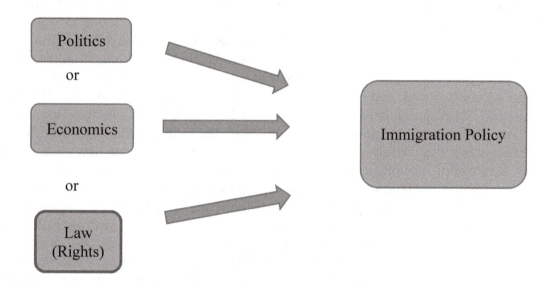

How many people get lawful permanent resident (LPR) status every year? The Department of Homeland Security provides data on the number of people who have obtained LPR status each year since 1820. The total number increased in the 1970s and since 2001 the number has averaged just over one million immigrants. The American Immigration Council provides an introductory course Immigration 101 for those who want to know the nuts and bolts of how the immigration process works.

13.75 | *Is Demography Destiny*?

Demography is the study of the structure or composition of a population—particularly vital statistics such as age, gender, race and ethnicity, and education. A country's demographics is determined by a broad range of factors including fertility rates, infant mortality rates, life expectancy, disease, accidents, and immigration policy. Immigration policy affects the structure of the body politic by determining the number of immigration admitted annually AND by *sorting* people so that **the most desirable** people are allowed to become lawful permanent residents (LPR) or naturalized citizens. *Desirable* has been defined in different ways: religion, race (broadly defined to include religion and culture and ethnicity), ethnicity, class (money), and unique professional skills and abilities (such as software engineers, fashion models, and baseball players). Demography is politically important for a number of reasons including

- Crime rates. A population with a large share of young males will likely have a higher crime rate than a population with an older and more female population;

- Education policy. Younger populations require more spending on education than older populations;
- Social Welfare policy. Older populations need more health care than younger populations. Anti-immigration politics includes opposition to immigrants using social welfare programs;
- Economic policy. A country's economic growth rate, unemployment rate, and labor force participation rate are affected by the age distribution of a population.
- National identity. A large number of immigrants and a high percentage of foreign-born in a population change the character of a political community.

The slogan *demography is destiny* reflects the belief that population trends and distributions DETERMINE a nation's future. Demography includes the total number of immigrants, the characteristics of the immigrants, and the percentage of foreign-born in the country. These demographic factors have organized anti-immigrant movements in the U.S., Britain, and Europe where the white working class and middle class worry about economics and national identity. The economic worries include worries about immigrants taking jobs, lowering wages, and straining limited social welfare programs. The claim that *demography is destiny* is about a country's *economic* destiny, *political destiny*, and *legal destiny*.

In terms of legal destiny, major human migrations have been associated with social order problems including crime waves. The criminal justice system has been used to respond to problems created by major human migrations. The political response to the crime waves that followed two major human migrations have largely defined the history of crime and punishment in the U.S. (Stuntz) The **first migration** occurred during the 70 years preceding WWI when more than 30 million Europeans came to the U.S. and settled primarily in the industrial cities of the Northeast. The **second migration** was internal. During the first two-thirds of the 20th century, around seven million blacks left the rural south and moved to northern industrial cities. The political response to these two migrations was the use of the criminal justice system to assert control over the new populations of outsiders who were considered threats to the established social order and local community identity. However, the local political establishments responded to the European immigrants by creating political machines like Tammany Hall, and the local police forces *tended* to resemble the residents of the community they policed. This is the origin of the stereotype of the Irish cop. It is significant that this did not apply to the southern black migration to northern cities. White police departments were used to control blacks. This remains a problem with police forces today. The Black Lives Matter movement exposed how police departments that are not representative of the community that they are policing create legitimacy problems.

13.76 | *National Identity: The Latino Americano Dream?*

In 2014 there were 55 million Hispanics in the U.S. The large Hispanic or Latino presence in the U.S. is one of the "harvests of empire," the result of the American military, business, and political presence in Central and South America. The Latino population is, however, a very diverse population. The PEW Research Center Hispanic Trends reports on the numbers and trends. The Latino presence resulted from the following ideas, policies, and military actions:

- Manifest Destiny—the belief that the U.S. had a right to expand all across North America—and even beyond.
- The Monroe Doctrine and the Roosevelt Corollary to the Monroe Doctrine. These doctrines declared that the U.S. had the right to act to protect public order, life, and property in the western hemisphere.
- The Mexican-American War (1846-48).
  http://www.loc.gov/rr/program/bib/mexicanwar/
  http://www.pbs.org/kera/usmexicanwar/index_flash.html
- Managing the labor supply.

The story of Mexican immigration is mostly an economic story about the *push* and *pull* of immigrant labor. The Mexican government pushed Mexicans across the U.S. border when the Mexican economy was bad. And during various periods the U.S. government actively pulled Mexicans to work in the U.S., particularly in agriculture and manufacturing. During WWI, the U.S. pulled Mexican workers into the country. But then during the Great Depression of the 1930s the U.S. Program to Repatriate Mexicans used mass roundups to deport Mexican workers. State and local government officials used vagrancy statutes that made it a crime to be idle, homeless, or without visible means of support to deport Mexican migrants. In 2006, California passed The Apology Act for its participation in the Mexican Repatriation Program.

> **The Mexican Repatriation Program**
> http://www.npr.org/templates/story/story.php?storyId=5079627
> http://www.npr.org/2015/09/10/439114563/americas-forgotten-history-of-mexican-american-repatriation

Then the U.S. government once again pulled in Mexican workers during WWII when there was a labor shortage in agriculture and manufacturing. The Bracero Program was a guest-worker program that began in 1942. It is an infamous example of the U.S. actively recruiting Mexican labor. The bad treatment of some Mexican migrant labor is one reason why people are today wary of creating a guest worker program.

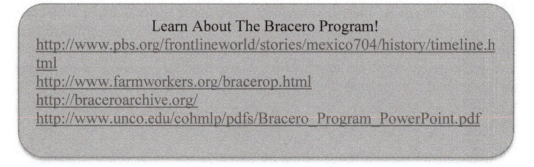

> **Learn About The Bracero Program!**
> http://www.pbs.org/frontlineworld/stories/mexico704/history/timeline.html
> http://www.farmworkers.org/bracerop.html
> http://braceroarchive.org/
> http://www.unco.edu/cohmlp/pdfs/Bracero_Program_PowerPoint.pdf

Patterns of immigration from the Caribbean and Central America also flowed form U.S. military actions. The U.S. Department of State describes how forces from the U.S. and other Western powers "entered" Haiti in 1914—and U.S. troops occupied the country until 1934. The State Department explains the <u>reasons</u> for the invasion. Haitian immigrants are one of the "harvests" of empire in the sense that it created patterns of interaction and a sense of national obligation. For example, the U.S. granted <u>Temporary Protected Status</u> for Haitians after a devastating earthquake in 2010. In 1965, the U.S. *sent in the marines* to Dominic Republic in "<u>Operation Power Pack.</u>" Is "sent in" a euphemism for invaded? In *Bitter Fruit: The Story of the American Coup in Guatemala*, Stephen Schlesinger and Stephen Kinzer describe how the 1954 CIA coup in Guatemala produced the *bitter fruit of the harvest of empire*. The extensive U.S. political, economic, and military engagement with Cuba has had a special impact on immigration policy. The PEW Hispanic Center describes Cuban immigrants as a distinctive subset of Hispanics: <u>Cubans in the U.S.</u> and <u>Hispanics of Cuban Origin in the U.S.</u>

13.77 | *Cuba Policy*

Why did a professional baseball player eat his fake passport while on an airplane flight from the Dominican Republic to Miami? Smuggling is usually associated with drugs, guns, sex trafficking, or aliens crossing the Mexican border, but it also includes smuggling baseball players into the country. The Chicago White Sox first baseman Jose Abreu left Cuba in 2013 for Haiti, where a "fixer" gave him residency status and a fake U.S. passport. He was then taken to the Dominican Republic where he got on a plane for Miami. He had to get to the U.S. because the Chicago White Sox had an oral commitment to sign him to a $68 million dollar contract if he made it into the country by October 2013. Onboard the plane, Abreu went into the bathroom, ripped out the first page of the fake passport—which had his picture and a fake name—threw away the passport, and returned to his seat where he ordered a beer (a Heineken) that he used to wash down the pieces of the first page of his fake passport as he chewed them and swallowed them. Once the plane landed in Miami, the special status of Cubans under the Cuban American Adjustment Act and the *wet foot, dry foot policy* meant that he was allowed to stay in the country.

How do we know his story? Because two Floridians—sports agent Bartolo Hernandez and trainer Julio Estrada were <u>recently tried in a federal court</u> in South Florida for smuggling alien Cuban baseball players (and their family and friends) to the U.S. Abreu testified at trial that he signed a contract to pay Estrada 20% of his earnings and Hernandez 5% of his earnings. Abreu was American League rookie of the year in 2014.

On January 12, 2017, President Obama began the process of normalizing relations with Cuba with an <u>executive action</u> that ended the *wet foot, dry foot policy* that allowed Cubans who entered the U.S. illegally to stay in the country if they were physically present in the country—that is, if they were able to actually set foot on American soil:

"Effective immediately, Cuban nationals who attempt to enter the United States illegally and do not qualify for humanitarian relief will be subject to removal, consistent with U.S. law and enforcement priorities. By taking this step, we are treating Cuban migrants the same way we treat migrants from other countries."

Ending wet foot, dry foot did not affect the immigration policy that allows around 20,000 Cuban visas for legal immigration every year, a number that is comparatively high for a country of around 11 million. But it did mean that Cuban migrants would be treated like migrants from other countries. The legislative background for the Cuba immigration policy includes the Cuban Adjustment Act of 1966—a Cold War era law that gave immigrants from Communist-governed Cuba special privileges—and the 1995 U.S.–Cuba Immigration Accord.

The special status of Cubans always created a divide within the Latino community because it provided just one group (Cubans) with special access to the country, social services, and citizenship. The Cuban Adjustment Act allowed Cubans who entered the country illegally to have their status "adjusted" to legal permanent resident (LPR; get green cards), be eligible for citizenship, and eligible for social welfare benefits that American citizens were eligible to received almost immediately upon entry. President Obama said that ending the *wet foot, dry foot policy* was for the following reasons:

- **Normalization**. Part of the administration's normalization of relations with Cuban—including opening the U.S. embassy in Havana;

- **Fairness**. Only Cubans, but not Haitians for example, were eligible for this special status despite the fact that today Cubans are economic migrants not political refugees;

- **Human rights**. Ending the program would limit the human trafficking and risky attempts to reach Florida. The administration also said it was necessary to suddenly announce the ending because Cubans, who expected that normalization would eventually mean the end of their special status, were increasingly trying to enter the U.S. using rickety boats to cross the dangerous Florida Straits or by land transit from Venezuela, through Central American countries.

Obama's normalization was not particularly controversial because of changed perceptions of the Cuban Adjustment Act of 1966. Specifically, the original Cuban migrants were considered political refugees from Communism whereas recent Cuban migrants were primarily economic refugees. Furthermore a series of investigative reports published in 2015 by a South Florida newspaper, the *Sun-Sentinel*, entitled "Plundering America: The Cuban Criminal Pipeline" described organized crime rings taking advantage of the special treatment Cubans received. The report weakened support for wet foot dry foot among Cuban-American Republicans including Florida U.S. Senator Marco Rubio. The changing politics of normalization includes changes in Cuban American demographics and Cuban American party identification that have made normalization less controversial.

13.78 | *Economic and Political Destiny*

A country's economic destiny is measured by economic growth rate, economic development, employment rate, and social welfare policy (dependency ratios). A country's *political* destiny is determined by political culture and party identity (partisanship). Studies of immigrant political behavior indicate that a person's status as an immigrant or a native citizen (nativity status) is related to politics, particularly attitudes toward government, views on public policies, and voting behavior—including party identification and voting patterns. The economic and political destiny arguments make immigration policy political in terms of both ideology and partisanship. This is the primary reason why conservatives and liberals, Republicans and Democrats, were ultimately unable to agree on comprehensive immigration reform despite the fact that all four sides agreed that the immigration system was broken and needed fixing.

The demographic composition of the country is related to the partisan composition of the country therefore proposed changes in immigration policy are likely to change the balance of Republicans and Democrats. Republican worried that large numbers of Mexican immigrants would eventually mean an increase in democratic voters if immigration reform provided a pathway to citizenship! The expectation that immigration reform would benefit one party more than the other impact was reasonable based on experience. Cuban immigrants increased the number of Latino Republicans in Florida, for example. The fear that immigration reform that provided illegal immigrants with a pathway to legal status or even citizenship would convert Latinos into Democratic voters prompted the Republican Party leaders in Congress to oppose immigration reform. The decision was good politics. It anticipated and reinforced the anti-immigration movement. Ironically, this occurred after decades of conservative and Republican support for open immigration policy in order to provide a supply of cheap labor and consistent with a broader deregulation of goods, services, and people across national borders.

The U.S. is no longer a settler nation that pulls immigrants into the country to settle a vast, largely unpopulated frontier. The U.S. is a developed country that uses immigration for other purposes including demographics. Studies of economic policy examine the relationship between two variables: economic development and the **Age Dependency Ratio**. The Age Dependency Ratio is central to public policy debates about a country's economic growth rate, wage rates, and social welfare programs. One aspect of immigration policy, admissions, determines the total number and the sorts of people to be allowed into the country every year. Conservatives and Republican have traditionally been most concerned that large numbers of immigrants would 1) change the distinctive American national identity; and 2) increase the number of people who are dependent on social welfare programs. The expansion of social welfare programs—broadly defined to include social security, Medicare, Medicaid, veterans' benefits, education and job training, food stamps, etc.—increased worries that immigrants—particularly illegal immigrants—were taking advantage of welfare programs. This is what Mitt Romney meant by his politically ill-advised 47% comment during the 2012 presidential election that 47% of the people in the country were receiving some form of government support and would not vote for him or Republicans.

There are two meanings of entitlement. One meaning is that federal statutes define who is "entitled" to received veteran's benefits, social security benefits, and food stamps, for example. The other meaning of entitlement is that some people think that they are "entitled" to government social welfare programs—and the expansion of social welfare programs increased government dependency on such programs. Conservatives and Republicans think that the one group is *deserving* of the government benefits while the other group is *undeserving*. Anti-immigrant politics includes the belief that immigrants—legal and illegal—rely heavily on social welfare programs that are paid for by taxes paid by citizens, some of whom are already experiencing financial insecurity.

Organizations such as the World Bank consider a country's dependency ratio an important measure of its economic health. The formula for determining a country's dependency ratio is to divide the number of people not of working age (young people under

14 and old people 65 and over) by the total number of people of working age (14 to 64), and then multiplying that number times 100:

Dependency Ratio (DR) = $\dfrac{\text{Total number of people aged under 14 and 65 and older}}{\text{Total number of people 14 to 64}} \times 100$

The Bureau of Labor Statistics (BLS) hires economists who measure "Labor Force Participation Rates." The media and the public generally pay attention to *the unemployment rate* as a measure of how the economy is doing but the labor force participation may be a better measure of economic performance. The Labor Force Participation Rate measures the percentage of the working age population that is actually employed. The aging of the U.S. population is a major factor in business thinking about economic policy, social welfare policy, and immigration policy. The BLS tables show a decades-long decline in labor force participation rates. The current rate is below 63%—so around 37% of the working age population is not working for one reason or another. The low labor force participation rate means that the American labor force could be more productive if more people were working. Are too many people not working because of social welfare programs such as food stamps and unemployment compensation? The recent decline in white male participation in the labor force is an especially significant development because it is one of the primary reasons for the current populist politics opposing both immigration policy and trade policy.

What is the U.S. age dependency ratio? How does it compare with other countries? The World Bank and the Central Intelligence Agency provide comparative data on the age dependency ratio, fertility rates, and other demographic data relevant to economic development. Compare the U.S. and European countries, for example, with Middle Eastern countries, African countries, or Central and South American countries. Germany used immigration policy, specifically a guest worker program, to solve the problem of a high dependency ratio and a low fertility rate. What is the relationship between economic development (low income versus high income countries) and fertility rates? The current anti-immigration politics in Germany is partly a backlash against the German policy of using immigration to import labor—economic opposition that was fueled by sudden acceptance of large numbers of refugees fleeing violence in the Middle East. Like the U.S. and France, Germany has an aging population so it was a good *economic* idea to import foreign labor until suddenly it wasn't a good *political* idea. Chancellor Angela Merkel's Christian Democratic Union Party (a center-right party) supported the policy. But German voters like American voters and French voters, are anxious about the future and angry that economic and immigration policies have primarily benefitted the wealthy and international elites. The populist, anti-immigrant backlash is fueled by worries about both economics and national identity.

> Check It Out!
> World Bank Data on Dependency Ratios and Fertility Rates:
> World Bank Data on Age Dependency Ratio (%of working age population);
> Fertility rate, Total (Births per woman)
> The Central Intelligence Agency (CIA) World Factbook comparative demographic data: media age/ranks; dependency ratios (both young and old) and ranks; birth rates/infant mortality rates/ranks; and net migration/ranks. Compare countries and regions. Do the data explain European immigration policy and the migration crisis in Europe?

13.79 | *Are there too many people, too few people, or just too many…….what?*

The New York Times series "Demography is Destiny? Teaching about Cause and Effect with Global Population Trends" reviews claims that the human population bomb was going to produce famine and disease and conflict. Were the fears wrong? Kolbert (2013) examines ways of thinking about whether the world has too many people, too few people, or just too many *of the wrong kind* of people? These are actually old questions. Thomas Malthus was a famous economist (and minister because in the good old days college education was under religious authority) whose 1798 work "*An Essay on the Principle of Population*" described the natural resource limits that constrained population growth. Over the years, the term "Malthusian" was used to describe economists or anyone else who warns about the drastic consequences of over-population—population growth beyond the limits of natural resources. The Malthusian trap or catastrophe refers to the fact that population growth is likely to outpace natural resources (e.g., food production; water; energy)—thereby resulting in an eventual catastrophe such as famine, disease, or war. Paul Ehrlich's "*The Population Bomb*" (1968) is a work in the Malthusian tradition. The environmentalist movement also reflects this Malthusian perspective on the need to control population growth to reduce strain on the environment. The Green Revolution greatly increased food production, thereby enabling population growth without subsistence living. Nitrogen-based fertilizer production greatly increased crops—and today half the world's population subsists on crops grown with nitrogen-based fertilizer. Are natural resources sufficient to sustain population projections?

Writing in *The Weekly Standard*, a conservative publication, Jonathan Last describes some of the problems created by a country where the fertility rate is so low that the population cannot sustain itself without importing people. In "Demography is Destiny: The Perils of Population Loss" (April 23, 2012), Last blames the declining fertility rates in First World countries over the last 40 years for "sputtering economies" where there aren't enough young and working age people to support the growing percentage of "old geezers." He wonders whether the First World countries will become like Florida. In "What to

Expect When No one's Expecting: America's Coming Demographic Disaster," Last also describes what he considers a problem created by differential fertility rates: black women have a "healthy rate" of 1.96 children; Hispanic women have a rate of 2.35; and white women have a 1.9 rate. Furthermore, he describes the higher birth rates of lower income women as a kind of reverse Darwinism—*survival of the least fit rather than the fittest.* These are the kinds of "sorting" problems that were part of immigration policy in the 19th and early 20th centuries. Another more religiously-conservative publication, *Human Events*, worries that Latino immigration is a special problem because "Demography is political/partisan destiny."

Steven Kramer, a professor at the National Defense University, writes about the other population bomb—the population implosion not an explosion—in "The Other Population Crisis: What Governments Can Do about Falling Birth Rates." He calls too few children (low native fertility rates) a crisis. Public policy solutions have to recognize that it is seems much easier to reduce a birth rate than to increase it. France has a broad range of pro-natalist policies that are intended to increase native French fertility rates: grants, tax deductions, and paid maternity leave. But these government subsidies seem to have a minimal impact on birth rates. Japan is facing an acute population problem (low rates of increase or even declining population) because Japanese seem uninterested in sex—which is, by the way, related to population. The government of Japan produces an annual white paper discussing ways to increase the low birth rate. Surveys indicate that large and increasing numbers of Japanese men and women are not interested in sex. So what's a country to do? Some countries use immigration policy to import people to compensate for low native fertility rates. This made political sense during times of economic growth and prosperity. However, the slow-growth economies have created a zero sum way of thinking about economics—and more natives/citizens blame immigrants for taking their jobs, undermining their economic security, and changing the country's identity. This is what Congressman Steve King (R-IA) meant when he said that the U.S. and white European Christian civilizations, like any other civilization—cannot "rebuild" or restore its civilization by relying on other people's babies.

13.8 | Additional Resources

13.81 | INTERNET RESOURCES

Congress funds the Congressional Research Service, which provides detailed descriptions and analyses of public policy issues. The Web site http://opencrs.com/
The Congressional Budget Office (CBO) Web site offers Congress's opinions on budget matters including statistics, reports, budget reviews, testimony, and more. www.cbo.gov/

The American Enterprise Institute is a conservative think tank that addresses a variety of issues. Its website offers information on their calendar of events, a variety of articles, and links: www.aei.org

The Brookings Institution is the oldest think tank in America and has the reputation of being fairly moderate. Its Web site offers policy briefings, articles, books, The Brookings Review, discussion groups, and links. www.brookings.edu

The Cato Institute is a libertarian think tank promoting free market ideas. Its Web site offers a variety of articles and links. www.cato.org

U.S. Department of Health and Human Services offers information about public policies related to health and other issues under their purview. www.hhs.gov

Almanac of Policy Issues has a wide array of information about policy related issues and has numerous links to more information. www.policyalmanac.org/social_welfare/index.shtml

13.82 | IN THE LIBRARY

Benabie, Arthur. 2003. Social Security Under the Gun. Palgrave.

Blank, Rebecca, et. al. (Eds). 2001. *The New World of Welfare*. The Brookings Institution. Bryce, Robert. 2009. *Gusher of Lies: The Dangerous Delusions of "Energy Independence."* Public Affairs.

Conkin, Paul K. 2008. *The State of the Earth: Environmental Challenges on the Road to 2100*. University Press of Kentucky.

Davis, Jack E. 2017. *The Gulf: The Making of an American Sea*. New York City: Liveright Publishing.

Diamond, Peter A. and Peter R. Orszag. 2004. *Saving Social Security: A Balanced Approach*. Brookings Institution Press.

Dinitto, Diana M., and Linda Cummins. 2004. *Social Welfare: Politics and Public Policy*. Allyn & Bacon, Inc.

Ehrenreich, Barbara. 2001. *Being Nickeled and Dimed: On (Not) Getting By in America*. Metropolitan Books.

Gilbert, Neil, and Amitai Etzioni. 2002. *Transformation of the Welfare State: The Silent Surrender of Public Responsibility*. Oxford University Press.

Katz, Michael. 2001. *The Price of Citizenship: Redefining the American Welfare State*. Metropolitan Books.

Kelly, David. 1998. A Life of One's Own: Individual Rights and the Welfare State. The Cato Institute.

Kolbert, Elizabeth. "Head Count: Fertilizer, Fertility, and the Clashes over Population Growth," *The New Yorker* (October 21, 2013: 96-99).

Kneidel, Sally. 2009. Going Green: A Wise Consumer's Guide to a Shrinking Planet. Fulcrum Publishing.

Lee, Kelly, et. al. (Eds). 2002. Health Policy in a Globalising World. Cambridge University Press.

Maloney, Deidre M. 2012. *National Insecurities: Immigrants and U.S. Deportation Policy Since 1882*. Chapel Hill: University of North Carolina Press.

Owen, David. 2017. *Where The Water Goes: Life and Death Along the Colorado River*. New York City: Riverhead Books.

Reissner, Marc. 1986. *Cadillac Desert*. New York: Viking Press.

Schram, Sanford. 2000. After Welfare: The Culture of Postindustrial Social Policy. New York University Press.

Stevens, Robert, and Rosemary Stevens. 2003. Welfare Medicine in America: A Case Study of Medicaid. Transaction Publishers.

Stuntz, William J. 2013. *The Broken Criminal Justice System*. Cambridge: Harvard University Press.

Vig, Norman J., and Michael E. Kraft. (Eds.) 2016. *Environmental Policy: New Directions for the Twenty-First Century*. Ninth Edition. Los Angeles: Sage.

White, Joseph. 2003. *False Alarm (Century Foundation Book Series): Why the Greatest Threat to Social Security and Medicare is the Campaign to Save Them*. Johns Hopkins University Press.

Zucchino, David. 1999. *Myth of the Welfare Queen*. Touchstone Books.

STUDY QUESTIONS

1. How do issues get on the political and government agendas?
2. What issues are most likely to make it onto these agendas?
3. What are the stages of the policy process?
4. What are the challenges in implementing policy?
5. Describe the problem of unintended consequences.
6. How has policymaking changed over time?

KEY   *TERMS*
Policy
Public policy
Domestic policies
Foreign policy
Agenda setting
Policy adoption
Policy evaluation
Distributive policies
Regulatory policies

---

[1] http://www.fda.gov/safety/recalls/default.htm

[2] See http://www.pbs.org/newshour/bb/business/jan-june10/makingsense_04-15.html

[3] See http://economix.blogs.nytimes.com/2009/08/27/sat-scores-and-family-income/

[4] Quoted in Richard Knox, "The Dying Art of the Physical Exam," *All Things Considered, Morning Edition,* National Public Radio (September 20, 2010). http://www.npr.org/player/v2/mediaPlayer.html?action=1&t=1&islist=false&id=129931999&m=129984296

[5] Atul Gawande, "Big Med," The New Yorker (August 13, 2012): 53-63.

[6] http://www.kgs.ku.edu/HighPlains/OHP/index.shtml

[7] See http://www.google.com/publicdata?ds=wb-wdi&met=eg_use_pcap_kg_oe&idim=country:USA&dl=en&hl=en&q=energy+consumption#met=eg_use_pcap_kg_oe&idim=country:USA:ALB:AUS:ARG:BHR:IRN to examine the energy use of additional countries. The original data is available from http://data.worldbank.org/data-catalog/world-development-indicators?cid=GPD_WDI

CHAPTER 14: ECONOMIC POLICY

14.0 | The Economy and Economic Policy

How is the economy working *for you*? How is economic *policy* working out for you? The answer to these questions increasingly depends on *who you are*. Are you young—perhaps a college student thinking about the job market, or old—maybe a retired person receiving Social Security and Medicare? Are you financially well off or not? Are you white or black, male or female? Do you live in one of the country's major metropolitan centers or a rural, low population area? The answers to these questions increasingly determine the answers to the questions about how you are doing economically. This was not always the case. The post-WWII era of prosperity has been called the *long boom* because the good economic times lasted so long. The *age of affluence* created the optimistic belief that a rising (economic) tide lifts all boats. The belief that the economy was a shared experience that lifted everyone's standard of living is hard to reconcile with today's economic conditions.

The new information and service economy works different for different people. Even before the Great Recession from 2007 to 2009, the economy and economic policy had been sorting the country into different groups of haves and the have-nots. A decades-long trend toward increasing economic inequality was sorting people by income and wealth—as well as other political and cultural and demographic factors. In *The Big Sort: How the Clustering of Like-Minded America Is Tearing Us Apart* (2008), Bill Bishop describes the negative consequences of sorting.[1] The economic fortunes of individuals (rich versus poor) and regions of the country (bit cities versus all others) continued to diverge in the years since the end of the Great Recession. As a result, today's economy and economic policy are good, fair, or bad depending on who you are and where you live. Economic conditions are much better in the major metropolitan areas of the country than rural areas.

Declining economic fortunes in rural areas have become one of the most important developments in American politics. It is not just about economics. American political culture extols rural and small town values. The values of Middle America or Main Street are considered more quintessentially American than the urban values that are associated Wall Street, Madison Avenue, and Hollywood Boulevard. But the nation's big cities are now the engines of job growth, business start-ups, and innovation. Metropolitan centers are now the hubs for the advanced industries sector of the economy. This is the high tech, high skills, and high value economy that has been prospering in recent decades. Silicon Valley may be the most familiar example of an urban region that prospered by developing the advanced industries sector, but urban centers in other regions of the country have also promoted economic development by creating research parks. This new economy prosperity has contributed to the real and perceived belief that the rural regions and rural values have been left behind.

The urban-rural sorting of economic fortunes may not interest you but what about economic sorting by age? How is the economy working for young people? Young people are more likely to have first-hand experience with how a structural change in the economy has changed the job market. During the long boom, young people who were just entering the job market could reasonably expect to get a job where they would spend their entire career working for one or two companies and then receive a pension upon retirement. This was a reasonable expectation for manufacturing jobs in the Detroit auto industry and white-collar jobs in the professional service sector. It is no longer a reasonable expectation or working life experience.

> ### Think about It!
> The term *new economy* refers to the knowledge and service economy. The new, new economy is the *sharing economy*, *gig economy*, and *side hustle economy* where more and more people hold down more than one job, change jobs frequently, and work as consultants, independent contractors, or temps rather than as full-time employees of a company. How does the economy and economic policy work for these people?

These changes are also affecting older working age people who are more likely to face layoffs or unemployment as their age, income, and health care needs increase. What about gender? The declining fortunes of white working class males became an important issue in the 2016 elections. Donald Trump's *Make America Great Again* campaign slogan was especially appealing to these workers whose loss of status as the breadwinners for their families threatened their identity and their lifestyle. The economic fortunes of men have declined relative to women, whose skill sets are more in demand in the new service economy that relies less on physical strength and more on social intelligence skills such as listening and communication. Hannah Rosin's book *The End of Men: And the Rise of Women* (2012) describes how changes in the economy have changed gender roles in ways that benefit women more than men.

So the question, how is the economy working out for you, is not limited to income or other economic measures. Income, wealth, and education are components of socioeconomic status (SES). And there are strong correlations between SES and other important factors such as political efficacy and health. Political efficacy refers to the belief that political participation matters, that people can act individually or together to make a difference, to improve their lives or the lives of others. There is a positive correlation between SES and political efficacy: the higher the SES, the higher the political efficacy. There is also a positive correlation between SES and health. Lower SES individuals tend to have worse health than higher SES individuals. The declining economic health of white working class males, and the resulting decline in medical health, was a salient issue in the 2016 elections. The connections between economic health and medical health that prompted the passage of the Patient Protection and Affordable Care Act (the Affordable Care Act or Obamacare) in 2010 also complicated Republican efforts to repeal it.

The American dream is the expectation that ability, hard work, and good behavior will be rewarded by economic prosperity. The American dream is a worker's belief in upward mobility; it is parents who believe that their children will have the opportunity to be better off than they were; and it is the belief that each generation will live longer and better. The economy is testing these elements of the American dream. Economic decline has noneconomic consequences. Economic decline in certain regions of the county—for example the loss of coal industry jobs in Appalachia—has contributed to an increase in the death rates of middle-aged white men and women. The decline in the number and quality of jobs is a factor that contributes to decreased longevity because it causes behavioral changes. The studies of American mortality and morbidity in the 21st Century document an increase in the "deaths of despair," premature deaths from alcoholism, opioids, and suicide. This pattern of dysfunctional individual behavior is actually evidence of a dysfunctional culture. The causal relationship between a bad economy, bad individual behavior, and bad cultural values is the theme of J. D. Vance's *Hillbilly Elegy: A Memoir of a Family and Culture in Crisis* (2016).

The long period of low or stagnant wage growth is one cause of growing economic inequality. The decline of labor unions, globalization, and technology are commonly cited for the low wage growth and the inequality. But public policy has also caused the increasing inequality. For instance, the federal government made the income taxes less progressive (i.e., lowered the top rates) and ended welfare "as we know it" by passage of the Personal Responsibility and Work Opportunity Reconciliation Act of 1996. The country is just beginning to discuss economic policy responses to automation, a technological development increase inequality by reducing the need for workers. One proposal is to tax robot "labor" the way wages are taxed. A person who earns $50,000 a year working for an insurance company must pay income tax and social security tax. Wages are taxed to pay for social welfare policies including unemployment compensation and worker's compensation. Bill Gates, the former head of Microsoft and current philanthropist, has proposed taxing robot labor. This novel idea seems appealing: we tax human labor (wages), so why not tax robot labor? Larry Summers, a former Secretary of the Treasury, thinks taxing robot labor would be bad economic policy, particularly if the U.S. taxed robot labor but other countries did not.[2]

However, Summers and other economists do think that the U.S. needs to begin addressing some of the social problems created by the negative effects of applying new technology in the workplace. One of these negative effects is the displacement of human labor. It is necessary to think about economic policy that addresses unemployment, underemployment, and job mobility because conventional promises to bring manufacturing or coal mining back to the U.S. are unlikely to create many jobs. Manufacturing and mining used to be labor-intensive industries, but they are now automated, capital-intensive industries that require fewer workers to be productive. One innovative approach to the inequality problems created by automation is the creation of a basic income policy whereby everyone is given periodic cash payments that are not dependent upon working. The Basic European Income Network (BEIN) was created in 1986 to advocate for adoption of the basic income policy. Why is the U.S. unlikely to adopt policies such as a basic income policy?

What does economics have to do with politics? What is the relationship between capitalism and democracy? What is economic policy and how is it made? This chapter examines three economic issues:

- The relationship between economics and politics. When studying a country's government it can be useful to examine the political system, the economic system, and the legal system. The economic and legal systems are not completely independent of the political system. In fact, they can be considered subsystems of the political system. This chapter explains how the political system and the subsystems work together in the U.S.
- The power problem. One issue for all governments is is the relationship between economic power and political power. Does economic inequality create political inequality? How does the distribution of income and wealth in the U.S. affect democracy and justice?

- Economic policy. Fiscal policy and monetary policy are the two main ways that the government makes economic policy. Fiscal policy is the taxing and spending policies that, taken together, comprise the annual budget. Monetary policy is controlling the price of money (i.e., interest rates) in order to achieve economic goals such as inflation and employment.

The close relationship between economics and politics has been evident since the colonial era. During the colonial era unarmed and armed mobs that were worried about losing their homes and businesses during bad economic times, or simply protested taxes—think of the

Boston Tea Party—marched on government to demand relief. In the 19th Century, economic downturns called Panics caused major political problems. In the 1930s, the Great Depression caused great hardship. The pattern of stagnant wages, the loss of good jobs, and the increasing inequality over the last several decades has finally caught the attention of government officials and become an issue in presidential campaigns. But the two major parties tend to propose very different solutions to the problem.

Think About it!
When someone talks about lots of things but not the most obvious thing, we ask "Why isn't anyone talking about the elephant in the room?" During the 2016 presidential campaign, all the candidates talked about creating more American jobs. But they did not talk about *the elephant in the room*: robots. Why isn't anyone talking about the robot in the room? Are American jobs going to MARS?

Machines
Analytics
Robots
Software Apps

14.1 | The Market Model and the Government Model

In terms of economic policy, one aspect of the power problem is finding the right balance between the private sector and the public sector. The market model relies primarily on the business sector to provide goods and services. Capitalist economic systems rely on the private sector to allocate scarce resources and provide good social order. The government model relies on the public sector to allocate scarce resources and provide good social order. One of the recurring themes in American politics from the earliest days of the republic is the debate about whether to rely more on business or government. Current debates about the *size* of government reflect the belief that the federal government in particular has gotten too big. Government certainly has gotten bigger relative to the private sector. In *Government versus Markets: The Changing Economic Role of the State* (2011), Vito Tanzi compares government spending as a share of a country's national income in 1870 and 2007. The numbers explain why the size of the government is an important issue.

Table 14.1

Country	Government Share of National Income by Year	
	1870	2015
U.S.	7.3%	37.7%
United Kingdom	9.4%	42.8%
Germany	10.0%	44.0%
France	12.6%	56.6%

Table 14.1, which updates Tanzi's data with Organisation for Economic Co-operation and Development (OECD) data,[3] shows the clear trend toward bigger government, as measured by the government's share of gross domestic product in western democracies. The growth of big government raises a couple of concerns. The main concern is that expanding government (that is, the public sector) will mean contracting the private sector (that is, the business sector and civil society sector). The anti-government strain in American political culture is partly based on conservative and Republican worries that expanding the public sector will shrink the private sector, that more government means the economy is less capitalist. A second concern is that the growth of government in the U.S. and other western liberal democracies occurred during a time of population increases and high rates of economic growth. But times have changed both of these conditions. These countries now face three new conditions that present economic and political challenges:

- Low rates of population growth. This is a significant development because population increases are an important component of economic growth.
- Comparatively low rates of economic growth. A growing economy has been considered an essential measure of a healthy economy. Low rates of economic growth, or even worse stagnant economies, are associated with unhealthy economic conditions and political conditions.
- Aging populations. Low population and economic growth rates produce demographic changes—changes in the age distribution of the population, specifically an aging population. An older population may have a smaller share of workers (producers) and a larger share of people who are consumers of social services such as Social Security and health care (Medicare). This can strain an economy.

Economic prosperity is strongly linked to increases in population, increases in economic productivity, and high rates of economic growth. Changing any one of these conditions changes the nature of politics. Economic growth mean that the pie was continually getting bigger and bigger. People were getting larger slices because the pie was getting bigger. This is the essence of the American dream: the expectation that people were becoming better off, that their living standards were improving, and they could expect their children to live even better than their parents. These expectations depend on continued economic growth so the emphasis on the *pie bakers*—the entrepreneurs and other creators who increase the size of the economy. Economic growth lessens conflicts over scarce resources because many peoples' slice of the economic pie is likely to be getting bigger in an expanding economy. In a low or no-growth economy, economics and politics are likely to be a zero sum game. A zero sum game is one where one player's increase (or win or gain) must come from another player's decrease (or loss). Zero sum games increase conflict as players go on offense to get more from other players or play defense to protect what they have from others. In zero sum politics, people are more likely to be worried about how the pie is being sliced to determine who the winners are and who the losers are. The term class warfare is a negative term that is often used to describe the class conflicts that arise when everyone is worried about the size of their slice of the economic pie.

14.12 | *Politics and Markets*

One indication of the importance of economics is the large number of interest groups, think tanks, policy organizations, professional associations, trade groups, and lobbyists that are active on economic issues. Economic interest groups of all kinds lobby on behalf of their members: companies, labor unions, professional associations, agribusiness, manufacturing associations, organizations representing service industries, and organizations advocating on behalf of intellectual property rights.

What is the Dow Jones Industrial Average?

The Dow Jones Industrial Average is one indicator of how the economy is doing. But the DJIA is no longer comprised of stock prices of industrial companies, as the name implies? The components of the Dow are changed every few years to reflect the breadth of the U.S. economy and to drop companies that are not doing well. In 2011, the 30 DJIA companies included four financial firms, two giant retailers, one restaurant chain, five consumer-products makers, two telecommunications firms, three drug companies, five high-tech firms and an entertainment conglomerate. It had only five traditional manufacturers— Caterpillar, Alcoa, United Technologies, 3M and General Electric — plus a couple of energy companies. The Dow is not merely a collection of the largest U.S. firms. It does not include Apple — which trades places with Exxon Mobil as the biggest company in America — or Google, which has a larger market capitalization (the number of shares outstanding multiplied by price) than Wal-Mart, which is listed on the Dow. And these companies are multinational companies that do business globally.

14.13 | *The Relationship between Politics and Economics*

The term political economy describes the close relationship of politics and economics. Economic policy refers to government positions on economic activities that are directly related to the production and distribution of goods and services. The close relationship between politics and economics is reflected in public opinion polls that regularly ask people what they think are the most important issues facing the nation. The public opinion surveys consistently identify three issues:

- **Economics** (policies to provide stability and prosperity)
- **National security** (war or threat of war; threats of terrorism)
- **Crime** (policies to provide public safety)

The ranked order of the importance of these three issues varies depending upon circumstances. During good economic times, voters consider national security or crime more important than economics. Economics is likely to be ranked number one during bad economic times (recessions, depressions, high inflation, or high unemployment). During times of war or periods of elevated national security threats, the public is most concerned about national security. People everywhere expect government to provide national security, crime control, and economic security.

14.2 | Economic History

14.21 | *The Founding Era*

When Benjamin Franklin returned to America in 1762 after spending almost five years abroad he wrote: "The expence of living is greatly advanc'd in my absence. Rent of old houses, and the value of lands…are trebled in the past six years." Franklin was complaining about an increase in the cost of living caused by a real estate *bubble*. An economic bubble occurs when a rapid increase in an asset's value, relative to other assets, that the high price cannot be sustained and ultimately collapses quickly. When the real estate bubble popped, credit was tightened, and the bad economic times contributed to the political discontent that eventually lead to the American Revolution.[4] Scholars still debate the relative importance of political ideas and economic conditions in inspiring the American Revolution. Some scholars stress the importance of the colonists' commitment to political ideas (freedom, democracy, equality, and justice) while others stress the importance of economic conditions and the economic interests of the wealthy or property owning classes. Economic conditions certainly contributed to the founding of the republic.

Shays' Rebellion is an often-told story. In the fall of 1786 and winter of 1787, Daniel Shays and other Revolutionary War veterans conducted an armed march on the capital of Massachusetts. They were protesting mortgage foreclosures of their farms and businesses due to bad economic times, and demanded debt relief from the government. Political leaders were worried that bad economic conditions were creating political unrest that included mob violence. The fear of such unrest was one of the reasons for calling the Constitutional Convention in the summer of 1787. The Constitution gave the national government new economic powers: the power to tax and spend; the exclusive power to coin money; the exclusive power to regulate interstate and foreign commerce; and the power to quell domestic disturbances such as those that arose from bad economic times.

Economic issues remained important during the early years of the republic when political debates centered on the national government's role in the economy. Differences of opinion about the government's role in the economic policy played an important role in the emergence of the first political parties. The Federalist Party supported a national government with a strong and active role in economic development. The Federalist Alexander Hamilton is still remembered as one of the greatest Secretaries of the Treasury of all time because he effectively promoted the national government's role in economic developments. The other major political party, the Jeffersonians or Democratic-Republicans, believed that the state governments, not the federal government, had primary responsibility for economic policy. The Republican and Democratic parties still take different positions on the government's role in the economy.

14.22 | *The Industrial Revolution*

The Industrial Revolution fundamentally changed the U.S. economy in the middle years of the 19th Century. It changed the economy from an agrarian and small-business economy that was dominated by landowners and small entrepreneurial craftsmen, to an industrial economy where large corporations dominated various sectors of the economy such as transportation (railroads), manufacturing (steel), energy (oil), and finance (banking). The Industrial Revolution changed the economy and caused profound social and political changes.

> Small businesses—local, independent, "mom and pop" hardware, grocery, clothing, and electronics stores, have been driven out of business long before Wal-Mart and other big box stores and corporate chains. Listen to the NPR story of "The Great A&P and the Struggle for Small Business in America."
> http://www.npr.org/player/v2/mediaPlayer.html?action=1&t=1&is list=false&id=139848775&m=139870174

14.23 | *The Progressive Era*

The Progressive Era (1890–1920) was a period of social and political reform that was inspired by efforts to solve some of the problems caused by the Industrial Revolution. Progressives were social reformers who tried to address some of the problems caused by the Industrial Revolution. *Progressives believed that big government was necessary to regulate big business.* They supported social welfare legislation to protect individuals from the economic insecurities of the marketplace. Progressive Era legislation included child labor laws, minimum wage and maximum hour laws, and workplace safety laws. The Progressive Era laid the groundwork for New Deal (1930s) and Great Society (1960s) expansion of the social welfare state.

14.24 | *The Great Depression*

In the 19th Century economic downturns were called *panics*—a descriptive term because large numbers of people rushed to banks to withdraw their money until panic ensued when the banks could not meet the depositors' demands. The 1920s were called the Roaring Twenties because of the good economic times. The good times ended with a stock market crash in late October of 1929. The Great Depression of the 1930s was actually a worldwide economic crisis that changed the relationship between government and the economy in the U.S. The American people no longer accepted the high unemployment, bank failures, factory closings, bankruptcies, home mortgage foreclosures, and a

Dorothea Lange. 1936. "Migrant Mother"

collapse of farm prices as hardships that had to be endured because they were part of the natural boom-and-bust business cycle that the government was powerless to do anything about. The Great Depression caused Americans to expect the government to do something about bad economic conditions such as unemployment, starvation, and shelter. The New Deal was the federal government's response to the public expectation that the government was responsible for managing the economy.

Nineteenth Century economic policy promoted economic development: the settling of the frontier; the expansion of the railroads; and the development of manufacturing and oil industries. Entrepreneurial risk-taking was a higher priority than protecting individuals from the economic insecurity of the business cycle, youth, old age, or infirmity. The New Deal policies of the Roosevelt administration (1933-1945) emphasized income security by providing disability benefits, unemployment insurance, and retirement benefits. Today these programs are collectively referred to as the **social welfare state**.

14.25 | *Ideology and the Role of Government in the Economy*

The Great Depression challenged the prevailing laissez faire economic theory, which held that the government should not intervene in the marketplace because market competition will naturally provide order, stability, and prosperity. An ideology is a set of beliefs. One of those beliefs is about the government's role in the economy. The following describes three theories about the size and role of government in economic affairs: the laissez fair or market model; the mixed economy model; and the government model.

Government and the Economy

The Size of Government	Small	Medium	Large
Theorist	Adam Smith	John Maynard Keynes	Karl Marx
Type of economic system	Free Market Model (Laissez faire)	Mixed Model (Regulated)	Government Model (Command)

Adam Smith's *The Wealth of Nations* (1776) is an influential work that advocated free market or laissez faire economics. It was revolutionary for its time because it challenged mercantilism, the prevailing economic theory. According to mercantilism the government directs, manages, and licenses economic activity for the good of the nation. Mercantilist policies built the British Empire. For example, the Crown licensed economic activity in the American colonies for the good of the empire. Mercantilism is a statist theory because it emphasizes government management of economic activity to achieve political goals. In *Wealth of Nations* (1776) Smith argued that the free market could produce goods and services, allocate scarce resources, and create good public order without government management or direction. Smith used the term the Invisible Hand to describe how social benefits incidentally result from individual actions without government regulation.

Smith assumed that humans were by nature self-interested that self-interest was a good thing, but self-interest needed to be held in check because greed, ambition, and the pursuit of power over others would create problems. But Smith believed that marketplace competition, not government regulation, was the best way to control individual and business behavior. Smith's ideas were very innovative. He made selfishness—which traditional religious leaders considered a human vice—an economic virtue.

> It is not from the benevolence of the butcher, the brewer, or the baker that we expect our dinner, but from their regard to their own interest. We address ourselves, not to their humanity but to their self-love, and never talk to them of our own necessities but of their advantages. [As every individual strives to use his capital and his labor to greatest advantage] he "neither intends to promote the public interest, nor knows how much he is promoting it....[H]e intends only his own gain, and he is in this, as in many other cases, led by an invisible hand to promote an end which was no part of his intention.... By pursuing his own interest he frequently promotes that of society more effectually than when he really intends to promote it. I have never known much good done by those who affected to trade for the public good. It is an affectation, indeed, not very common among merchants, and very few words need by employed in dissuading them from it.[5]

Note that Adam Smith's *Wealth of Nations* was published in 1776. James Madison made selfishness a political virtue by designing a system of government that relied on institutional selfishness for checks and balances.

> **Think About It!**
> Some new ideas in the natural sciences have crossover appeal in the social sciences. Was Charles Darwin the father of modern economics? What does the theory of natural selection have to do with economics? http://www.pbs.org/newshour/bb/business/july-dec11/makingsense_11-18.html

Adam Smith's laissez faire theory challenged mercantilism, which was the prevailing economic theory of the 18th Century. John Maynard Keynes was a British political economist who challenged laissez faire theory in the first half of the 20th Century. In *The General Theory of Employment, Interest and Money* (1936), Keynes argued that governments should use fiscal policy (the taxing and spending powers embodied in the budget) to achieve economic stability and prosperity. His theories influenced President Franklin Delano Roosevelt's New Deal programs that used fiscal policy to end the Great Depression of the 1930s and Lyndon Johnson's Great Society programs in the 1960s. Keynesian economic theory assumes that the government should intervene in the economy to 1) regulate the extremes of the boom-and-bust business cycle; 2) provide economic stability; and 3) to promote justice. The belief that Keynesian economic theory implemented during the New Deal helped the country out of the 1930s Depression made Keynesian economics the new prevailing theory of government and the economy.

14.3 | The Great Recession

The Great Recessions was a severe economic downturn that was initially considered just another stage in the regular business cycle of expansion and contraction—the boom and bust business cycle. Figure 14 below illustrates the business cycle with specific economic downturns noted, most notably the Great Depression, a severe and long-lasting economic downturn, and the Great Recession. The Great Recession officially ended with a return to economic growth, but the rate of growth has remained comparatively low, job creation has lagged behind other recoveries, and wages have remained stagnant. This is evidence that the Great Recession was not part of the normal business cycle of expansion and contraction but rather more evidence of a structural change in the American economy.

Figure 14.3
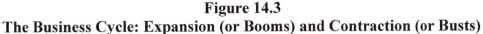
The Business Cycle: Expansion (or Booms) and Contraction (or Busts)

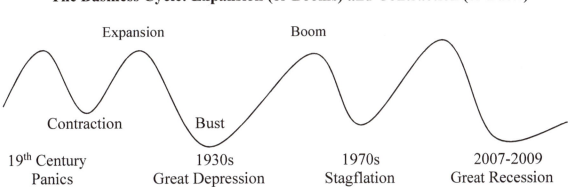

14.31 | *What's In a Name?*

What is a recession? What is a depression? And what is so great about the Great Depression and the Great Recession? In the good old days, financial crises were called "panics" because they often involved people panicking to get their money out of banks before they failed. After the Great Depression, economic downturns were called recessions partly because the word recession did not remind people of the bad memories of the 1930s. Government officials do not like to use the word recession either because it reminds voters that the economy is bad. In 1978 President Carter's economic advisor Alfred Kahn was scolded for warning that the administration's efforts to fight inflation were likely to cause a recession. President Carter did not want one of his leading economic advisors talking about a looming recession during the reelection campaign. So when Kahn spoke publicly about the likelihood that fighting inflation would cause a recession, he simply substituted the word *banana* for the word *recession*: "We're in danger of having the worst banana in 45 years."[6]

The organization that officially designates economic conditions a recession is the National Bureau of Economic Research. The National Bureau of Economic Research (NBER) defines a recession as a "significant decline in economic activity spread across the economy, normally visible in real GDP, real income, employment, industrial production, and wholesale-retail sales." The NBER's Business Cycle Dating Committee maintains a chronology of the U.S. business cycle that identifies the dates of peaks and troughs that frame economic recession or expansion. The period from a peak to a trough is a recession and the period from a trough to a peak is an expansion. According to the chronology, the most recent peak occurred in March 2001, ending a record-long expansion that began in 1991. The most recent trough occurred in November 2001, inaugurating an expansion. A recession begins just after the economy reaches a peak of activity and ends as the economy reaches its trough. Between trough and peak, the economy is in an expansion. Expansion is the normal state of the economy. Most recessions are brief and they have been rare in recent decades. The NBER reported that the Great Recession officially started in December 2007 and ended in June 2009.

14.32 | *A Structural Change in the Economy?*

The length and depth of the Great Recession increased concern that the downturn was not merely a stage of the normal business cycle but rather a structural change in the U.S. economy. A structural change is a major, long-term transformation of the economy. The Industrial Revolution was a structural change from an agrarian to an industrial/manufacturing economy. The Information Age transformed the economy into a service economy. The fact that the recovery from the Great Recession has produced disappointing job creation, continued wage stagnation, and low economic growth compared with past recoveries has reinforced the belief that the economy is undergoing a structural change.

Economists explain why technology can cause unemployment and stagnant wages in "The Great Stagnation: Why Hasn't Recent Technology Created More Jobs?" The managing director of Vista Technologies, a manufacturing company, bluntly explained why companies prefer to buy new equipment rather than hire employees.[7] He said he dreaded the hiring process: sifting through poorly written resumes; interviewing applicants; paying for drug testing and mandated safety programs; and training new employees. The Federal Reserve Board also made the cost of capital *relatively* cheaper than the cost of labor by keeping interests so low that companies could borrow money to buy equipment rather than to hire more workers or increase wages. The wage problem has been worsened by the fact that most increases in labor costs have been due to increased costs of health care not wage increases.

It is a common business strategy to control costs by buying equipment that automates production or buying software to manage personnel and customers rather than hiring new employees. This strategy is more attractive where capital costs are lower than labor costs. Purchasing equipment from foreign manufacturers compounds the negative impact on jobs. Favorable tax laws such as accelerated capital depreciation also make capital investments more cost effective than labor.

Globalization is another reason why manufacturing no longer produces the jobs that it once did. Globalization has meant that U.S. manufacturing jobs have been sent abroad to low wage countries—first to Japan and more recently to China and India and other regions of the world. Technology has meant the increased use of computer-aided industrial production. Modern factories use

> **Think about it!**
>
> *"I want to have as few people touching our products as possible. Everything should be as automated as it can be. We just can't afford to compete with countries like China on labor costs..."*
>
> *Dan Mishak, Managing Director, Vista Technologies*

robotics rather than more workers to increase production. The elimination of jobs and the resulting downward pressure on wages has had a significant impact on "the American dream" of upward mobility. In "Making It in America," Adam Davidson describes the "remnant workforce, the smaller workforce remaining in manufacturing in the U.S. He argues that this remnant workforce must be highly trained. During much of the 20th century, "simultaneous technological improvements in both agriculture and industry happened to create conditions that were favorable for people with less skill." The development of mass production "allowed low-skilled farmers to move to the city" and get jobs in highly productive factories. The change from an agricultural to an industrial economy adversely affected "the highly skilled craftsperson." The loss of manufacturing jobs is ending one of the ways that low-skilled workers could join the middle class.[8]

In spring 2017, the Bureau of Labor Statistics (BLS) reported that the economic recovery from the Great Recession reduced the unemployment rate to 4.3%, which was the lowest rate in more than a decade. The unemployment rate for blacks was just under 8%, and the unemployment rate for Hispanics was 5%. The declining unemployment rates are good news; the fact that the labor force participation rate remained steady at 62.9% was not good news.[9]

An unemployment rate below 5% is approaching what economists call full employment. Why is there so much economic anxiety if the economy is near full employment? There are a number of reasons. One reason is the fact that the unemployment rate is no longer a very good measure of how the economy is working for people. The unemployment rate does not reflect the increase in the number of jobs where the number of hours worked varies a great deal from week to week or month to month. The volatility in the number of hours worked creates increased income volatility which, in turn, creates financial uncertainty. Financial uncertainty creates financial anxiety, which creates political anxiety. Since the 1970s, steady work that pays a predictable and living wage has become increasingly difficult to find," said Jonathan Morduch, a director of the U.S. Financial Diaries project, an in-depth study of 235 low- and moderate-income households. "This shift has left many more families vulnerable to income volatility."

Stagnant wages have also undermined the meaning of the unemployment rate by people choosing not to work or look for work. The labor force participation rate in early 2017 was around 62.3%. This is the percentage of individuals in the labor force who are working or looking for work. The unemployment rate recovered from the Great Recession, but the quality of the jobs has not!

Check It Out!

The PBS *Newshour* video "It's a Slow Painful Recovery for this Former Manufacturing Town" explains why the replacement of manufacturing jobs with service sector jobs has allowed the focus on the unemployment rate to mask a deeper economic problem.
http://www.pbs.org/video/3000565563/

The displacement of manufacturing jobs by low-wage service sector jobs is also related to the gender dynamics of the 2016 elections. Hillary Clinton's campaign emphasized women's issues in a number of ways that were consistent with the gender dynamics of party politics, including promises to support health care and wage equity, which appealed to women, and promises to fight against the Republican war on women. Donald Trump's campaign was more traditionally Republican macho on economic, crime, and national security policy, which was more appealing to the blue-collar male workers in manufacturing and mining. The PBS *Newshour* story describes and explains why men are reluctant to apply for jobs in fields such as education and health care where jobs are increasing—even in regions of the country such as Appalachia and the Rust Belt that were hard hit by de-industrialization. The lower labor force participation rates for men is a development with both economic, social, political, and cultural consequences.

Think About It!
A Unisex Workforce? Traditional distinctions among white, blue, and pink collar jobs, or men's work and women's work, may not be as relevant, but the reluctance of Manly Men to apply for Girly Jobs is still an issue.
http://www.pbs.org/video/3000808015/

14.33 | *Why the U.S. Business Cycle Is So Closely Related to the Electoral Cycles*

The Great Recession is yet another example of how bad economic conditions affect politics. The first thing the federal government did was to enact a massive government bailout of businesses. The bailouts were followed by fiscal and monetary policies that were intended to stimulate the economy. The economic policies created a huge budget deficit. Voters expressed their dissatisfaction with the economic downturn by electing President Barack Obama in 2008 after he campaigned promising "Hope" and "Change." Voter anxiety then resulted in big Republican gains in the 2010 mid-term elections. Republicans gained 69 congressional seats. The political lesson of the Great Recession is that voters hold the government accountable for economic conditions—particularly during times of crisis when the public expects the national government to take decisive action to stabilize the economy.

The political impact of economic downturns is greater in the U.S. than in other western democracies because the U.S. has a smaller social welfare safety net. In the U.S., the loss of a job means the loss of income and, in many cases, the loss of health care insurance. The U.S. system of employment-based health insurance means that unemployment greatly increases income insecurity. This economic insecurity has makes the U.S. political system very sensitive to the unemployment rate. Two major parts of the social welfare system, Social Security and Medicare, are not even designed to support unemployed young people. These two programs provide income security primarily for the elderly. Taken together, these policies make the job market especially political.

The fact that the U.S. economy is a consumer economy where around two thirds of the gross domestic product comes from consumer spending further strengthens the link between the business cycle and the political cycle. The decades prior to the Great Recession were marked by high rates of consumption and debt and low savings rates. The belief that the country was undergoing a long-term structural change in the economy has stimulated interest in changing economic policy to encourage production and saving rather than consumption. This will require changing economic behavior. This explains why there has been an increase in school programs that teach children about financial literacy. **Sesame Street**, the public television children's program teaches children (and adults) about financial literacy and the importance of delaying gratification in order to increase savings rates.[10]

Count on It?
"Are U.S. Wages Enough to Live On?"
http://www.pbs.org/newshour/rundown/2012/05/are-us-wages-enough-to-live-on.html

14.4 | A Regular Business Cycle of Economic Crises

Economic problems tend to become political problems, and major economic problems become major political problems. The latter 19th Century economic panics created populist and nativist reactions that increased hostility toward immigrants, Catholics, Jews, and blacks. The worldwide economic downturn in the early 1930s resulted in totalitarian governments in Germany, Japan, and Italy. In the 1970s the U.S. suffered from two economic problems that do not usually occur together—high inflation and low growth— so a new word was coined to describe a stagnant economy with inflation: stagflation. The stagflation, which was caused by an Organization of Petroleum Exporting Countries (OPEC) oil embargo that greatly increased energy costs and decreased economic growth, decreased public confidence in American government and private sector institutions. The passage of the Troubled Asset Recovery Program and the Emergency Economic Stabilization Act of 2008 so quickly after the Great Recession began is evidence of the close relationship between economics and politics.

The Great Recession created a group of people of special concern: the formerly middle class. These were the people who achieved middle-class status at the tail end of the long economic boom, and then lost their middle class standing when they became the first ones to drop out of the middle class during the downturn caused high unemployment and steep increases in the rates of home mortgage foreclosures. A middle class that is experiencing downward mobility is likely to express its displeasure by voting against those they blame for their financial stress and their loss of status. Americans have such a strong belief in **upward mobility** that it is considered part of the American dream. It is the belief in a system where ability and hard work produce prosperity. **Downward mobility** caused by loss of a job or underemployment, loss of a home or business, a health care problem, or some other crisis, erodes confidence in the economic and political system. Downward mobility is not limited to loss of income. It includes loss of status in the community and forced changes in lifestyle. The conservative commentator David Brooks accurately predicted that the loss of social identity and the status symbols that mark the middle class's place in the social order would increase alienation and ultimately create a political protest: "If you want to know where the next big social movements will come from, I'd say the formerly middle class."[11]

The financial crisis that caused the Great Recession has renewed questions about why the U.S. experiences so many cycles of crises in the financial sector that end with government bailouts. In the 1980s, the Savings and Loan industry required a government bailout. A dot-com bubble in the high-tech sector burst in 2000. The Great Recession was caused by, among other factors, banking and investment practices that included risky behavior, corruption, scandals, and fraud. It produced emergency legislation such as the Troubled Asset Relief Program whose government bailout provisions were intended to avoid a financial meltdown. This pattern of business crises followed by government bailouts is not the normal working of the marketplace where the rise and fall of businesses is considered natural.

Why do corporate executives engage in risky or bad business practices that jeopardize their company and the economy? The first answer that comes to mind is that even smart people make some mistakes. This individual-level explanation overlooks organization-level explanations. The first organizational explanation is that some decision makers are insulated from the adverse consequences of their bad decisions. For example, the government protects bank deposits in savings accounts from bank failures through the Federal Deposit Insurance Corporation (FDIC). The FDIC insurance can actually encourage bankers to make riskier decisions—that is, to be less risk averse—by guaranteeing deposits in savings accounts.

A second organizational explanation is even more important in explaining risky corporate behavior particularly in the financial services sector of the economy: the separation of ownership and management in modern corporations. In the good old days of small business, the people who owned the business actually ran it AND they were risking their own money so they had their own skin in the game. Corporations are run by managers—and the managers of financial services companies are really playing with, or risking, other people's money (OPM). Individuals who work in financial services may be more willing to make risky decisions because they are playing with OPM. This problem was recognized *as an organizational problem* in Adolf Berle's *The Modern Corporation and Private Property* (1932).

The problems described above are examples of "the moral hazard." The moral hazard refers to situations where a decision maker does not assume all of the costs or responsibilities of a decision and is therefore likely to make riskier decisions than they would make if they knew that they would be held totally responsible for all of the negative consequences of their decisions. Some companies are considered too big or too important to fail. This means that the government will protect them from failure by bailing them out with programs such as the Toxic Asset Relief Program. In fact, the moral hazard is one explanation for the repeated pattern of financial crises and bailouts.

The recurring cycles of financial crises and government bailouts are also caused by rapid memory loss: the bad times are quickly forgotten once the good times begin again. During the Obama administration a number of regulations were enacted to prevent financial crises. One of these was the Dodd-Frank Wall Street Reform and Consumer Protection Act of 2010, which was intended to protect consumers by enhancing the power of the Commodity Futures Trading Commission. The Dodd-Frank Act created the

Consumer Financial Services Protection Bureau, a federal agency responsible for protecting consumers in the financial sector. What could get buttoned-down Wall Street bankers and lawyers dance in the streets and jump for joy? The removal of regulations that limit risky but profitable financial wheeling-and-dealing! The Wall Street Journal and Republicans support financial deregulation, including getting rid of Dodd-Frank.

This includes getting rid of laws limiting corporate tax arbitrage strategies. In economics and finance, **arbitrage** is the practice of taking advantage of price differences in different markets. **Tax arbitrage** is taking advantage of different tax rates in different markets. A corporate inversion is when an American company merges with a foreign company because that country's tax are lower than U.S. taxes. Burger King gave up its American corporate citizenship by acquiring the Canadian restaurant chain Tim Hortons as a corporate strategy to save taxes. In 2016, the drug company Pfizer bid $152 billion dollars to buy Allergen, the company that made Botox, as a corporate strategy to save taxes. As a corporate strategy, inversions are a type of **rent-seeking behavior**. Rent-seeking refers to business decisions that try to make money by taking advantage of different rules rather

> **Think About It?**
> Should we consider the recurring financial crises evidence of recidivism in the financial sector the way we think about repeat offenders in criminal law?
>
> Massachusetts Institute of Technology Finance Professor Andrew Lo discusses the recurring cycles of financial crises and government bailouts in the Public Broadcasting System story, "Evaluating and Preventing a Massive Financial Crisis."

than by focusing on making better goods or providing better services. The Obama administration issued a number of rules to reduce corporate inversions. The Trump administration proposed ending the tax regulations and the Financial Stability Oversight Council, the body that designates which financial institutions are considered "systemically important" or too-big-to-fail. The Americans for Financial Reform is a non-profit organization that was created in 2008 to advocate for the creation of what it says is a strong, stable, and ethical financial system that works for the economy and the country. It supports financial regulations that protect consumers from bad or risky financial business practices.[12]

Think About It!

Does the Moral Hazard explain why bankers become "banksters?" "Banksters" is the title of an Economist article (July 7, 2012) about British bankers illegally manipulating an important interest rate called the LIBOR (London Interbank offer rate).
http://www.economist.com/node/21558260

14.41 | *Follow the Money*

When the *Washington Post* reporters Bob Woodward and Carl Bernstein were investigating the Watergate scandal in the early 1970s, they were advised by a secret source to "follow the money." Money often leaves a telling trail. For instance, in 2008, New York State Governor Eliot Spitzer, an ambitious Democrat with a promising national career, unexpectedly resigned his office.

The media focused on the scandal angle: a high-profile political figure who paid a great deal of money to high-priced prostitutes. The story of how the government discovered the payments revealed how extensively the government monitors financial transactions. Sophisticated computer software that tracks almost all financial transactions revealed Spitzer's payments. Large cash transactions are easy to spot because banks are required to report transactions over $10,000. Computer software also tracks

small financial transactions in order to detect *pattern of suspicious activity*.[13] The ability to track almost all financial transactions raises serious questions about the use of such information in an age where more and more transactions are electronic and big data analysis allows information to be stored and retrieved for economic and political purposes.

14.5 | Government's Economic Tool Box: Fiscal Policy

Fiscal policy is the government's use of taxing and spending powers to achieve policy goals. Fiscal policy is reflected in the budget. A budget is a political document because politics can be defined as "the authoritative allocation of scarce resources." The budget is where you see policy priorities. Senator and Vice-president Joe Biden often people of his father's saying: "Don't *tell* me what you value. *Show* me what your budget is and I'll tell you what your values are." The federal government's fiscal policy is reflected in the federal government's annual budget for the fiscal year, which begins October 1st. A state's fiscal policy is reflected in the state's budget.

14.51 | *Who Makes Fiscal Policy?*

Congress and the president make fiscal policy. Until the early years of the 20th Century, Congress exerted almost complete control over fiscal policy because it has the power to tax and to spend. Congress passed the annual federal budget. Today the president plays an extremely important role in making fiscal policy. For instance, the president begins the annual budget process by introducing *the administration's* budget in Congress. Congress then holds committee hearings on the various budget proposals, debates the various provisions of the administration's budget priorities, assesses the administration's taxing and spending policies, and then adjusts the administration's priorities to reflect congressional priorities. Congress then enacts the federal budget for the fiscal year.

The politics of the budget includes debates about literally thousands of programs for law enforcement, social security, education, health care, national security and trade policy. But the most politically salient debates about the budget and fiscal policy center on the budget deficit. Deficit spending occurs when government spending exceeds revenue in a fiscal year and the year ends with red ink. If the government spends more than it taxes, the fiscal year ends with a budget deficit. The national debt is the cumulative budget deficits.

14.52 | Budget Deficits

Budget deficits are not usually accidents, mistakes, bad mathematics, or the result of incompetent accountants or emergencies. The red ink of budget deficit (spending more than tax revenue in a fiscal year) is usually intentional. Fiscal policy is the use of the taxing and spending policies to achieve public policy goals. Keynes believed that government should use fiscal policy to manage the business cycle, to moderate the extremes of expansion and contraction, to avoid the boom (the rapid economic expansion that leads to inflation) and bust (recession or depression). The term Keynesian economics refers to the government using taxing and spending policies to manage the economy. The logic of using fiscal policy to moderate the business cycle and achieve economic stability is fairly simple. During a time of rapid economic growth (a boom period), the government's fiscal policy could increase taxes and/or cut government spending. Increasing taxes and decreasing spending remove money from the economy, thereby slowing economic growth. It has a "deflationary" effect on the economy. During a downturn in the business cycle fiscal policy could decrease taxes and/or increase government spending. Cutting taxes and increasing spending puts more money into the economy, thereby stimulating economic growth. Deficit spending has an inflationary effect on the economy; austerity budgets have a recessionary effect on the economy. Fiscal policy is intended to have a counter-cyclical effect on the business cycle.

> **The Budget Deficit and the National Debt**
> http://www.pbs.org/newshour/bb/business/july-dec12/makingsense_10-25.html

14.53 | Tax Policy

What is a tax? The simplest definition is that a tax is a compulsory payment to fund government. But taxes are used for a variety of purposes:

- **Raise the Money to fund government**. The main purpose of a tax is to raise money to pay for the things that the government does. Gas taxes provide money to build roads and bridges; real estate taxes provide money for schools; and income taxes provide money for fighting crime, fighting fires, and for national security.
- **Subsidize desirable behavior.** Taxes are also used to *subsidize* behavior that the government wants to encourage or goals that it promotes. Tax policy can subsidize

marriage, having and raising children, religious and charitable contributions, or conservation of national resources by promoting green energy sources. Taxes for these purposes are primarily to subsidize behaviors rather than to raise money.

- **Regulate undesirable behavior**. Taxes are also used to discourage or regulate behavior that government wants to discourage. The term "sin" tax refers to using tax policy to decrease smoking or gambling or drinking alcohol. Carbon emission taxes are intended to reduce air pollution.
- **Redistribution**. Taxes are also used to redistribute income from some individuals or groups to others. Taxes redistribute income from richer persons or states or region to poorer persons, states, or regions. Taxes redistribute resources from younger individuals to older individuals. Redistributive taxes are used for social welfare purposes.

Good tax policy, like beauty, is in the eye of the beholder. Economists generally prefer simple tax codes that raise money to fund government programs with minimum disruption of market forces. The Tax Foundation is an organization that advocates for what it considers the principles of good tax policy: fairness; efficiency; and clarity. Efficiency and clarity are easier to measure than fairness because fairness is a subjective standard. People have different definitions of tax fairness. For example, federal tax and spending policies are redistributive. They take money from wealthier states and redistribute resources to poorer states. Is it fair for the federal government to make some states net contributors and other states net benefactors? One of the ironies of federal tax and spending policies is that the Red States, which tend to be poorer and Republican, are benefactor states while Blue States, which tend to be wealthier and Democratic, are contributor states. It is ironic that Red States benefit and Blue States pay because conservatives and Republicans are generally opposed to income redistribution as a form of welfare. Taxing and spending policies are also intended to influence individual behavior. Subsidies encourage desirable behavior—by providing rebates for buying energy efficient appliances, for instance—and taxes discourage undesirable behavior such as smoking and drinking alcohol. What do behavioral economists say about the effectiveness of taxing and spending policies that are intended to influence behavior?

The U.S. has a very complicated, expensive, and inefficient tax system. The reasons why are not very complicated. For example, the financial services sector is an increasingly important sector of the economy. Financial services include financial analysts, tax accountants, and tax preparation companies. These special interests have been very effective in lobbying Congress to provide for special tax breaks their industry. They also benefit from the public perception that taxes are too complicated for the average taxpayer to file their taxes out without professional assistance. In fact, their business model depends on it. And they benefit from the public perception that the income and other federal taxes are so complicated that the average person should not file their own taxes—and that the difficulty filing income taxes is evidence that the government cannot do anything very simply (or very well). The federal income tax system also has numerous provisions that benefit real estate developers. The average effective income tax rate for all industries is 11%. The effective rate for real estate developers is just over 1%. The real estate lobby is very effective in getting special tax breaks. President Trump is (or was?) a real estate developer. He also made income tax reform one of his administration's priorities. Reducing tax rates by simplifying the tax code will be a challenge because it will require overcoming the political power of the financial services and real estate development lobbies.

> **Think about It!**
> Why does the U.S. have such a complicated, expensive, and inefficient tax system?
> Watch T. R. Reid's comparative tax policy analysis, "What Other Countries Can Teach America about Taxes."

14.54 | *The Federal Budget Process*

Congress and the president make fiscal policy. The federal budget process is a long and complicated process whose participants include Congress (particularly the House and Senate budget committees) and the president (particularly executive agencies and The Office of Management and Budget). The Center on Budget Priorities provides a good description of the three main stages of the federal budget process: 1) the Office of Management and Budget submits the administration's proposed budget to Congress; 2) Congress adopts a budget resolution; and 3) reconciliation of the budget resolution. The process is described in greater detail in the two boxes below:

> **The Federal Budget Process**
> **As Described By**
>
> The Office of Management and Budget:
> http://www.whitehouse.gov/omb/budget
>
> The Center on Budget Priorities:
> http://www.cbpp.org/cms/?fa=view&id=155

The Federal Budget: Timelines and Participants

Early fall

The executive departments and agencies send initial budget requests to the Office of Management and Budget (OMB).

November/December/January

The OMB reviews the initial requests, modifies them, and sends them back to the agencies. The OMB hears agency appeals. The OMB resolves appeals and assembles the final budget request.

February/March

The president submits the budget request to Congress. Administration and agency officials testify in support of the budget request before the House and Senate appropriations subcommittees (House and Senate). Public witnesses also participate in the hearings.

May

The House and Senate adopt budget resolutions prepared by the budget committees. The House and Senate Appropriations Committees make 302(b) allocations—this is the section of federal law that describes how appropriations committees divide the overall level of discretionary spending provided in the Budget Resolution among thirteen subcommittees.

June

The House Appropriations Subcommittees prepare appropriations bills and the Senate Appropriations Subcommittees revise them.

July-August

The House passes spending bills and the Senate passes revised spending bills.

September

Conference committees resolve differences between the House and Senate bills and agree on final versions of spending bills. The president signs or vetoes final bills.

October 1

The start of the fiscal year. If Congress has not passed all the appropriations bills in time for the start of the fiscal year, continuing resolutions are used to maintain funding for agencies whose funding bills have not yet been passed.

14.6 | The Government's Tool Box: Monetary Policy

Monetary policy is defined as using the money supply to achieve economic goals such as controlling inflation and maintaining employment. The money supply is the amount of money in private hands. Increasing or decreasing the money supply affects the rate of inflation and the amount economic activity. Monetarists argue that monetary policy is a better way to achieve economic goals than fiscal policy. Monetary policy is based on the assumption that the price of money—that is, interest rates—is the key to economic activity because increasing interest rates will decrease economic activity, thereby lowering inflation, while decreasing interest rates will stimulate the economy. Monetarists advise increasing interest rates during boom times in order to prevent or control inflation, and decreasing interest rates to prevent a recession or to stimulate the economy to get out of one.

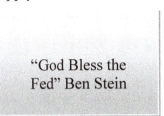

"God Bless the Fed" Ben Stein

The Federal Reserve Board (the Fed) has primary control over monetary policy. The Fed is an independent agency in the sense that Congress and the president have limited control over it. Members of the Fed are appointed for lengthy terms of office that do not coincide with presidential or congressional election cycles in order to insulate The Fed from partisan politics. The Federal Reserve Board (of Governors) consists of seven members who are appointed for 14-year terms. The Fed's Open Market Committee consists of 12 Members (seven Governors and the heads of five regional banks) is the Fed's main monetary policymaking body.

Congress created the Fed and authorized it to regulate banks and to set monetary policy. It is responsible for using monetary policy to achieve two economic objectives: price stability (controlling inflation) and maximum employment. Beginning in the fall of 2007, uncertainty in the financial markets created concern that the problems caused by sub-prime mortgage practices would turn into a full-blown nationwide or even global panic. Critics called the Troubled Asset Recovery Program (TARP) the Toxic Asset Recovery Program because the government was authorized to buy "troubled" financial assets. The Federal Reserve Board aggressively intervened in the capital markets in order bring about a measure of stability. The conservative Ben Stein reacted to the Fed's decisive action by saying, "God Bless the Fed." The sense of relief that the Chair of the Federal Reserve Board acted decisively to avert a collapse of the financial system and perhaps the entire economy is an indication of the Fed's importance. Stein also used an interesting metaphor to defend the government bailouts of banks. We had to turn to the federal government for relief from the "terrifying prospect" of financial collapse because "(t)he private sector is the patient, not the doctor."[14]

> Information about how the government measures the rate of inflation/cost of living is provided in "Why Your Salary May be Affected by the Price of Lettuce."

14.61 | *The Undemocratic Fed*

One of the basic democratic principles is that policymakers should be elected representatives of the people. In democracies, elections choose to policymakers and hold them accountable. But The Fed is a policymaking body whose members are appointed for long terms. In this respect, the Fed is an undemocratic institution. In fact, supporters of the Fed defend it *because it is not political*. The Fed is designed to insulate economics from partisan politics. The Fed is an independent agency with some insulation from direct partisan control but it is not an apolitical institution. Its views of what to do about inflation and unemployment are political. The Fed's choices about how much inflation is too much and how much unemployment is acceptable are political. The members of the Fed are bankers who bring a banking perspective to monetary policy. The Fed has faced strong political criticism since its creation. Populists think it serves the interests of big banks and Wall Street insiders rather than the common people. Libertarians are on principle opposed to government management of the economy. Former Congressman Ron Paul (Republican-Texas) and his son, Senator Rand Paul (Republican-Kentucky) are vocal critics of the Fed. What do you think of Ron Paul's comments about the Fed's role in the American system of democracy?

> **Think About It!**
> Do you agree with the Representative Ron Paul's criticism of the Federal Reserve Board? Are his views political?
> https://www.youtube.com/watch?v=OVpZtQ0ihhA

14.7 | Poor Economic Vision?

The Great Recession caught most people by surprise even though the boom and bust of the business cycle was very familiar. This raises an interesting question. Why were some of the best and brightest minds working in the financial sector of the economy so shortsighted that they failed to foresee the problem that their actions were causing? There are at least three reasons for poor economic vision (or myopia): organization incentives; ideology; and over-confidence.

14.71 | *Organizational Incentives*

The financial services industry has an incentives structure that rewards risk-taking behavior. If an industry rewards making risky loans and selling high-risk financial products because they bring higher profits than safer loans and investments, then it is rational for people who work in the financial services to engage in such riskier rather than safer economic behavior.

14.72 | *Ideology*

An ideology is a set of beliefs about how the world works. What if the beliefs are mistaken? Alan Greenspan was Chair of the Fed from 1987 until 2006. These were economic boom times. Greenspan was lionized as a great man with a deep understanding of how the financial system, monetary policy, and the economy worked. Then the Great Recession hit! Greenspan was forced to acknowledge that there were fundamental flaws in his ideological model of how the economic world worked.

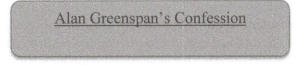

Alan Greenspan's Confession

One flaw is the *way* the financial services sector was de-regulated: bankers were allowed to make riskier investments but the government kept in place government protections against depositors losing money (i.e., the Federal Deposit Insurance Corporation). Business deregulation is considered an element of conservative and Republican economic policy, but Democratic President Carter began the federal trend toward deregulation by deregulating the airlines and natural gas in the 1970s. Then in 1980 the Monetary Control Act eliminated regulations of interest rates and usury laws. In 1982, the Garn-St. Germain Depository Institutions Act deregulated savings and loan banks. Prior to 1982, these "thrift" banks were allowed to make residential (home) loans but not riskier commercial loans. They were also prohibited from using customer deposits to invest in the stock market. The savings and loans banks lobbied Congress to change the law to allow them to use deposits for riskier and generally more profitable, investments. The ensuing savings and loan crisis of the 1980s required a massive government bailout to protect depositors from losing their money. And then in 1999 the Financial Services Modernization Act repealed the provisions of the Glass-Steagall Act, the 1933 law that separated commercial banking from investment. The problem with this deregulation is that it deregulated risk-taking while continuing insure bank deposits against loss in order to maintain public confidence in the banking system.

The movement to deregulate the economy began when conservatives and liberals supported deregulation but for very different reasons. Conservatives supported deregulation because they thought government regulation was ineffective and limited growth. Liberals supported deregulation because they thought government regulators were actually serving powerful corporate interests rather than protecting consumers or the environment.

The **Capture Theory** explains why government regulatory agencies do not do what they were created to do. According to the capture theory, regulatory agencies are created to regulate an industry but over time they come to identify with the industry that they were created to regulate. This is a variation on the Stockholm Syndrome where over time hostages over time come to identify with their captors. The capture theory works because of the revolving personnel doors between the public and private sectors. When government regulators leave their regulatory agency, they go to work in the industry the agency regulated; and regulatory agencies hire people from the industry they regulate. In effect, the players change teams. Former airlines regulators are hired by the airlines industry. Former Internal Revenue Service officials are hired by tax and accounting firms that advertise that the firm employs former IRS agents. Goldman Sachs is a multinational financial services firm that is sometimes called "Government Sachs" because presidents recruit so many former Goldman officials to work in their administrations. President Clinton's Secretary of the Treasury Robert Rubin was a Goldman official. President George W. Bush's Secretary of the Treasury Hank Paulson was a Goldman official. And President Trump's Secretary of the Treasury (Steve Mnuchin), Deputy Secretary of the Treasury, White House Chief Strategist (Steve Bannon), Director of the White House National Economic Council, and Senior Counsel for Economic Initiatives all worked for Goldman Sachs. And President Trump's nominee to head the Securities and Exchange Commission (SEC), Jay Clayton, is a corporate lawyer who represented Goldman Sachs.

> **Think about it!**
> During the presidential campaign, Donald Trump famously promised to drain the swamp if he were elected. Draining the swamp refers to lowering the water to get rid of the alligators. Did he break his campaign promise by appointing so many Wall Street people in his administration? Did he actually restock the swamp with alligators after President Obama removed some of them? Or did Trump mean he was going to drain the swamp of Washington bureaucrats by appointing Wall Street executives? Does it matter who is appointed?

The capture theory and the revolving door explain why the Securities and Exchange Commission, the Commodities Futures Trading Commission, and even The Fed grow so close to the financial services sector that it is hard to tell whether they are *regulating the industry or representing* Wall Street interests. Is this close relationship a reason why the government repeatedly bails out the industry when thing go bad?

The Federal Deposit Insurance Corporation (FDIC) provides a chronology of the Savings & Loan crisis in the latter 198s that ended with a government bailout of the industry.[15] After the crisis passed, the financial services industry developed complicated but innovative products such as securitized loans in order to increase profits. Through a combination of financial engineering and aggressive marketing, the industry offered high rates of return on financial products that were sold as low risk investments but which were actually very risky. The resulting financial crisis ended once again with government bailouts. But once again, when the immediate crisis passed, and the collapse of the financial system was averted, Wall Street went back to business as usual. The memory loss is convenient for the financial services industry because the industry essentially privatizes the profits from risky deals but socializes the costs. Are people who work in the financial services sector recidivists? The term recidivist is usually reserved for repeat offenders who break criminal laws such as robbery, burglary, or drug dealing. Paul Volcker, the chair of The Fed from 1979 to 1987 believes that financial regulation is necessary because of "Wall Street's recidivist tendencies." The lesson of the history of financial crises is that bankers will use their positions to line their pockets[16] as long as the government bailouts and subsidies such as the FDIC protect them from the financial consequences of their behavior.

14.73 | *Over-confidence*

A third reason for the cycles of economic crises is over-confidence. Modern economists and government officials assumed that our knowledge of how markets and economies work has become so advanced that technical expertise can be applied to manage the business cycle and stabilize economies. This confidence created the belief that financial expertise could be applied to make severe economic downturns like the Great Depression a thing of the past bad old days. In hindsight, over-confidence in the theories of individual rationality and market rationality blinded observers to the risks of assuming markets were self-correcting.[17]

The three main economic policy architects of the Bush administration's response to the Great Recession were Secretary of the Treasury (Hank Paulson), the Chair of the Federal Reserve Board (Ben Bernanke), and Timothy Geithner (President of the New York Federal Reserve Bank). This trio functioned as an economic SWAT team—the first responders who formulated and coordinated the emergency response to the financial crisis. The fiscal policy response included bank bailouts and the troubled asset relief program (TARP); the monetary policy response was very low interest rates. The fact that President Obama, a Democrat, basically continued the economic policies of President Bush, a Republican, was not surprising because the Obama administration's response to the Great Recession was formulated by Bernanke and Geithner, whose backgrounds provide insights into their ideas about what the government should do when facing a financial crisis.

Bernanke is an economist whose research expertise is the Great Depression of the 1930s. His study led him to conclude that the government's weak and inconsistent response to the Depression prolonged and worsened the economic crisis. The lesson he learned from the Depression is that government must act swiftly and decisively when facing a major economic crisis. He brought this background to the Bush administration's policy discussions of how to respond to the financial crisis. Geithner's public service began in 1988 as a civil servant in the Treasury Department. These were economic boom times in the United States. A long Bull Market made Wall Street and the Department of the Treasury very influential power centers for federal economic policy. Their ideas seemed to work. But Geithner's "formative experience was in figuring out how to contain the series of upheavals that swept the international financial community in the 1990s, from Japan to Mexico to Thailand to Indonesia to Russia, and threatened the boom."[18] These international financial crises revealed a new and unexpected vulnerability in the global financial system: one country's financial problems could quickly affect (or infect) countries around the world. Geithner believed that globalism increased economic efficiency and prosperity by promoting international interactions such as global free trade, but he also recognized that globalism made a country vulnerable to "infections" from abroad. His policy experience made him an institutionalist—an economist who thinks that governments and private sector institutions (non-government organizations or NGOs) play important roles in preventing financial meltdowns.

He also believed that the Great Recession was a financial crisis that required a massive government response in order to avoid a prolonged economic downturn. He blamed the Japanese government's weak response to the bursting of a real estate bubble in the early 1990s for the resulting "lost decade" of economic growth. The promotion of global trade contributed to the post-WWII "long boom," and he did not want weak economic response to the financial crisis in the U.S. to create a long bust. Geithner believed a great deal can be learned from international economic crises: "You learn much more about a country when things fall apart. When the tide recedes, you get to see all the stuff it leaves behind." One of the conclusions to be drawn from the experience of the various international financial crises that have occurred during the era of globalization is that *none* of the governments—whether in Japan or Mexico or Indonesia or the U.S.—treated the problem as an economic problem that had nothing to do with government and politics.

The current Chair of The Fed, Janet Yellen, was appointed to a four-year term in 2014. Yellen brought a perspective on using monetary policy to manage the economy that differed from her predecessors. Alan Greenspan's thinking was shaped by economic theory—particularly free market theory. Timothy Geithner's thinking was shaped by economic history—particularly financial crises. Janet Yellen's thinking is shaped by practical concerns about whether the economy is or is not working for people. During his presidential campaign, Donald Trump was very critical of The Fed and indicated that he would appoint a new Chair when Yellen's term expired. However, President Trump tempered his criticism of The Fed just as he tempered his criticism of the European Union and changed his mind about whether the North Atlantic Treaty Organization (NATO) was obsolete.

14.8 | Economic Issues

14.81 | *Globalization*

The promotion of international trade has been a central element of American foreign policy since WWII. Free trade has been considered a vital component of economic growth and development. The end of the Cold War in 1991 made free trade even more important because the threat to national security diminished. The General Agreement on Tariffs and Trade (GATT), which was in effect from 1949 until 1993, reduced tariffs to promote international trade. In 1995, GATT was replaced by the World Trade Organization (WTO), which was created to supervise and liberalize international trade. The WTO includes a framework for negotiating and formalizing trade agreements and a framework for resolving trade disputes. There are currently more than 150 countries that are members of the WTO. Historically, trade has not been a very controversial issue even though some critics thought that the trade agreements benefited business interests and the wealthy while largely neglecting the interests of labor, the environment, and human rights. Trade did become an issue in the 2016 elections. During the presidential campaign Democratic candidate Bernie Sanders and Republican candidate Donald Trump were particularly critical of the free trade agreements for not being fair trade and for not benefitting the middle class. The political controversy over free trade illustrates how globalization has blurred distinctions between foreign affairs and domestic affairs.

Globalization and the development of international trade systems have increased uniformity and leveled the economic playing field. But the populist backlash against economic globalization reveals that economic nationalism is still important because countries still have unique economic, political, and social systems. The development of a world economy is still facing political and economic fault lines or domestic pressure points where nations contact others. For example, the financial systems in some countries emphasize formal rules and regulations while others operate with informal relationships. These differences can make it difficult to understand the rules of the international trade game. In *Fault Lines: How Hidden Fractures Still Threaten the World Economy*, Raghuram G. Rajan describes how different legal regimes are now rubbing against one another in ways that will, at a minimum, prompt rethinking some of the assumptions about globalization.[19]

14.82 | *Global Economic Competitiveness*

The increase in international business and trade has increased the attention paid to comparative economic data. One of the sources of information about how the U.S. compares to other countries is the Organisation for Economic Co-operation and Development (OECD). The OECD provides basic information on how countries provide social and economic policies.

There have historically been tensions between U.S. domestic economic policy and its international trade policy. The U.S. political system responds to domestic political pressures by passing laws that benefit domestic business interests and disadvantage foreign interests. The term economic protectionism describes policies that favor domestic business over foreign business, or favor in-state business over out-of-state business. Tariffs are one common type of economic protectionism. A tariff is a tax on imports, goods that are brought into a country. One risk of import taxes is they can start trade wars, where countries retaliate against one another by passing tariffs. One amusing trade war involved a tax that France levied on chickens that were grown in the U.S. and imported to France. The U.S. then retaliated against France by taxing certain motor vehicles that were imported to the U.S. Since then, however, the auto industry has become global, and car parts are imported and vehicles are assembled in so many countries that it is sometimes hard to tell whether a car in a domestic or import. An American car company, such as Ford, has extensive foreign manufacturing plants, and it can actually be hurt by laws that place tariffs on imported vehicles or parts.

Globalization has increased the amount of attention paid to what makes a country competitive in the global economy. Where does the U.S. rank in an index of competitiveness? And what criteria are used to measure competitiveness? The World Economic Forum creates an annual Global Competitiveness Report. The 2016–17 Report ranked the U.S. third among 138 nations.[20] The decline of the American manufacturing sector, particularly steel and automobiles, is sometimes attributed to the comparatively high cost of production. The bailout of the American automobile manufacturers as part of the Troubled Asset Recovery Plan focused attention on the comparative costs of manufacturing. In a *New York Times* article, "73 Dollars and Hour: Adding it Up," David Leonhardt's comparison of auto manufacturing costs in the U.S. and other countries reveals significant differences in wage rates, benefits, and retirement costs.[21]

Globalization has meant that each nation's economy is more closely tied to others. Comparative economic policy includes comparing countries' fiscal policy. Fiscal policy in western democracies share two common features: large budget deficits and large national debt. Government budgets, deficits, and national debts are big numbers. How big is big?" A comparative perspective on national debt and deficit helps put economic data in perspectives. The National Priorities Project reports the U.S. federal budget for fiscal year 2015 was $3.8 trillion and the national debt was around $17.7 trillion. Read its "Federal Budget 101" for a more detailed way to make sense of economy policy.

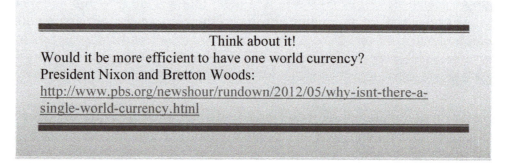

Think about it!
Would it be more efficient to have one world currency?
President Nixon and Bretton Woods:
http://www.pbs.org/newshour/rundown/2012/05/why-isnt-there-a-single-world-currency.html

14.83 | *Markets and Values*

Markets allocate scarce resources. Economists emphasize the importance of efficiency. Would it be more efficient to have one world currency? The Euro was a step away from national currencies. In capitalist countries, the market model is considered the most efficient way to determine the allocation of valuables. What about other important values such as equality and justice and human dignity? These are basic questions that are central to the long-running debates about health care policy. Critics of the Affordable Care Act (Obamacare), for example, warned that its support for rationing health care for economic reasons would inevitably lead to *death panels*.

14.84 | *Equality*

The U.S. is a democracy. Equality is a democratic value, but Americans have always accepted a great deal of economic inequality. Why does American political culture value democracy and accept inequality? Americans accept inequality if it is based on merit. A meritocracy—or natural aristocracy based on ability—is compatible with democracy while inequality based on privilege (e.g., being born rich) is harder to reconcile with democracy. Furthermore, an economic system that produces inequality is not considered unjust or unfair if it provides for economic mobility so that people can work their way up the ladder. Current debates about economic policy address issues such as economic equality and economic mobility after decades of increased inequality and decreased mobility. Until recently, liberals and Democrats calling for public policies to address growing inequality were dismissed as advocates of class warfare. Conservatives and Republicans have now joined the call to do something about the inequality problem but their solutions are different than those advocated by liberals and Democrats.

The economic policy debates have been stimulated by absolute measures of poverty and relative measures of mobility. PEW Charitable Trust's Center on the States describes family mobility and its political significance for the American dream in the wake of the Great Recession. The data from the PEW research project on mobility are discussed in the National Public Radio story, "Moving on Up More Difficult in America." Growing inequality—the increasing concentration of income and wealth—affects individuals and the aggregate economy. At some point, inequality has a negative impact on the economy, society, and politics. The high costs of inequality are examined in the PBS *Newshour* story "Inequality Hurts." One way to answer the question, how much inequality is too much, is to look at comparative data. The Central Intelligence Agency produces a great deal of comparative information about the countries of the world. One index measures equality. See the "Distribution of Family Income—the GINI Index." Where does the U.S. rank in terms of income equality? What about the historic long-term trends toward more or less inequality? The data describe patterns but do not answer important questions such as the relationship between a country's distribution of income and justice. The question, how much economic equality (or inequality) a country should have is essentially a political question. The answer causes economic policy. The economic policy, in turn, causes either more equality or more inequality.

One of the main features of the post-WWII era was Western democracies promoting free trade as the key to economic prosperity. This era appears to be over. In the U.S. and elsewhere, populist rhetoric presents economic nationalism as an alternative to globalism and the problems that it has caused. President Trump's political rhetoric, economic policy proposals, and actions are evidence that the promotion of free trade is now a lower priority than promoting the economic wellbeing of the American middle class. The Trump administration's economic priorities are fair trade AND the promotion of U.S. exports. Free trade is based on the theory that removing government trade barriers to trade increases economic prosperity and political stability. The trade barriers include tariffs or other regulations that make it harder to freely buy and sell goods and services in other countries. Free trade theory has been practiced for so long that the results of free trade policies can now be assessed to determine whom benefits and whether international trade creates winners and losers. The populist movements in Great Britain, Europe, and the U.S. have challenged the free trade theory that globalization benefits everyone. Populist movements in these countries reflect the belief that free trade and globalization have benefitted a few very wealthy cosmopolitan elites at the expense of a country's middle-class or the country as a whole. Marine Le Pen, the leader of France's National Front Party, gave voice to this populist backlash against "the wild, savage globalization."[22] Regardless of the political fortunes of individual populist leaders and parties, public policies will likely reflect new skepticism about globalization of goods, services, and people.

14.85 | *Managed Trade*

Donald Trump's campaign rhetoric was very critical of free trade agreements that he believed did not promote fair trade. This rhetoric appealed to blue-collar, working class voters who believed his promise to Make America Great Again by re-negotiating existing trade deals such as the North American Free Trade Agreement (NAFTA) to get better terms for the U.S. This campaign promise was based on his reputation as a businessman whose mastery of *The Art of the Deal* gave him a unique set of negotiating skills. Candidate Trump promised to begin making America great again by stopping losing at international trade and starting to win at it. President Trump officially withdrew from the Trans-Pacific Partnership—a multi-lateral trade agreement between the U.S. and 11 other countries. The Office of the United States Trade Representative (OTR) is within the Executive Office of the President. The Trump administration's OTR website describes the administration's "America First Trade Policy" as giving American workers "a fair shot" with better international trade agreements. The North America Free Trade Agreement (NAFTA) is another important agreement. Trump threatened to slap a 20% tariff on goods imported from Mexico (and other countries that have trade surpluses with the U.S.) unless a more favorable trade agreement can be renegotiated. Renegotiating NAFTA will be complicated. It allows the U.S., Canada, and Mexico to trade goods with each other without have to pay duties. A duty is a kind of border tax on goods entering (an import tax) or leaving (an export tax) a country. In 2016 the U.S. had a $63 billion dollar trade deficit with Mexico, the fourth highest after China, Japan, and Germany. The trade agreements have what are called ***rules of origin*** for all kinds of products: footwear, textiles, electronics, and automotive products including cars and trucks.

In 2016, the automotive industry trade deficit was $200 billion or more than a quarter of the total. The NAFTA rules for automotive products allow duty free imports and exports if at least 62% of a vehicle's value originates in one or more of the three countries that are party to NAFTA. The Trump administration's trade negotiators want to raise that percentage in order to reduce imports from China, Japan, and other non-NAFTA regions in order to increase domestic manufacturing and U.S. jobs. This is the economic and political theory of America First economic nationalism. Is it the way the business world works? Will automotive industry shift more manufacturing to the U.S.? Or with the industry shift more manufacturing to Mexico where wages are much lower than in the U.S.? This is a business investment strategy that cannot easily be controlled by a trade agreement that tilts the playing field toward one country and away from another. After all, increasing percentage of origin rule to 75%, for example, may not bring more manufacturing to the U.S. because a company could simply pay the current 2.5% duty (tax) for cars that are imported into the U.S.

There are also real practical problems with adjusting the country of origin rules. It is very hard to determine precisely the national origin of a motor vehicle's value. Cars and trucks have thousands of parts that come from supply chains that are located all over the world and sent to the assembly plant. Disassembling a car to determine the parts origin and value is hard. The task is further complicated by the fact that automotive manufacturers regularly change the sourcing of their parts. Finally, it is hard to determine the right national origin of parts percentage that will produce the intended result—to help domestic automotive manufacturing, and ultimately, American workers—without unintentionally hurting manufacturers and workers. Is 75% the right level for a national origin rule? It is hard to determine the real world effects if the U.S. trade negotiators get a 40% made in America rule of origin. The Center for Automotive Research, and automotive industry trade and lobbying groups do not think that higher rules of national origin are the solution to the problem of lost domestic manufacturing jobs. They think the problem is countries that manipulate their currency and other unfair trade practices. Matt Blount, the head of the American Automotive Policy Council, says that NAFTA current 62.5% content rule is already the highest among the 12 trade agreements, and increasing it will likely greatly disrupt the current global supply chain.

> **Think About It!**
> How did a **_chicken tax_** keep foreign truck makers out of the U.S.?

14.86 | *Morality*

One of the more interesting political aspects of economic policy is conservative and Republican support for the market model as a moral model. Is the free market the best way to preserve traditional values? Moral regulatory policy has traditionally limited freedom of choice in order to protect traditional moral values. Free markets are based on freedom of choice: consumers are free to choose what goods and services to buy largely without government regulation. The free market economist Milton Friedman famously said that greed is good, and the business of business is making money—not *being* good or *doing* good deeds. In fact, he argued that the individuals who run corporations have a legal duty—a fiduciary obligation—to maximize the profits of investors.

> **Think About It!**
> Is there a wall of separation between business and morality?
> https://www.youtube.com/watch?v=RWsx1X8PV_A

The separation of economics and morality, and the increasing concern about economic inequality in the U.S., have increased liberal and conservative criticism of free market economics. Liberals and populist conservatives support government regulation and economic management to address economic, social, and cultural problems. The prospect of some conservatives joining liberals in calling from government action initially worried some of the leading conservative organizations such as The Heritage Foundation. The Heritage Foundation is a leading conservative *think and do tank* that has for decades defended free markets AND morality. For example, it produces ideas products that explain the morality of markets. Prager University offers a series of non-credit online courses that teach the morality of markets and capitalism.[23] These are just two conservative organizations that are defending the free market in an environment where growing inequality makes the system vulnerable to criticism. Describing markets as moral insulates them from economic criticism.

One common suggestion for what ails government is the recommendation that it should be run like a business. The Trump administration is providing an experiment to see how this would work. It is a case study that reveals one business family's thinking about what it means to run government like a business. The blurring of the lines between the President's and his family's business interests has exposed flaws in a governance model that blends private profit and public service. Is it appropriate for the Kushner Companies to appeal for wealthy Chinese individuals to invest in a luxury apartment complex in New Jersey by saying that it means a great deal to the entire Kushner family? Or to have the State Department promoting Mar-a-Lago or a book by Ivanka Trump?

> **Think About It!**
> PBS Story "Kushners Put Foreign-Investor Visa Back in the Spotlight"
> http://www.pbs.org/video/3001917130/

14.87 | *Summary*

This chapter examined the relationship between economics and politics. It described the history of how economics affects politics, explained the two major components of economic policy—fiscal policy (the taxing and spending policies in the federal budget) and monetary policy (the Federal Reserve Board's efforts to manage interest rates), examined how the new service and information economy is a structural change that has created political concerns about inequality and the relationship between economics and justice. The political systems in the U.S. and other western-style democracies are currently struggling to respond to social and economic conditions that are challenging long-standing assumptions about economic policy.

14.9 | Additional Resources

14.91 | *Internet Resources*

"Fear the Boom and Bust: A Hayek vs. Keynes Rap Anthem"
http://www.youtube.com/watch?v=d0nERTFo-Sk

The von Mises Institute presents the theoretical argument for minimal government involvement in the economy: http://mises.org/etexts/ecopol.asp

President Franklin Delano Roosevelt's March 12, 1933 "Fireside Chat on Banking."
http://www.presidency.ucsb.edu/ws/index.php?pid=14540#axzz1NlGuPlqw

14.92 | *In the Library*

Baldwin, Richard. 2016. *The Great Convergence: Information Technology and the New Globalization.* Harvard University Press.

Bishop, Bill. 2008. *The Big Sort*. Houghton Mifflin Company.

Foroohar, Rana. 2016. *Makers and Takers: The Rise of Finance and the Fall of American Business*. Crown Business.
Gordon, Robert. 2016. *The Rise and Fall of American Growth*. Princeton University Press.

Isenberge, Nancy. 2016. *White Trash: The 400-Year Untold Story of Class in America.* Viking.

Mayer, Jane. 2016. *Dark Money: The Hidden History of the Billionaires Behind the Rise of the Radical Right*. Doubleday.

Rosin, Hannah. 2012. *The End of Men*. Riverhead Books.

Smith, Adam Smith. 1776. *The Wealth of Nations*.

Tanzi, Vito. 2011. *Governments Versus Markets: The Changing Economic Role of the State*. Cambridge: Cambridge University Press.

Vance, J.D. 2016. *Hillbilly Elegy: A Memoir of a Family and Culture in Crisis.*

Raghuram, Rajan G. (2010). *Fault Lines: How Hidden Fractures Still Threaten the World Economy* Princeton University Press.

KEY TERMS

The Industrial Revolution
Social welfare policies
Fiscal policy
Monetary Policy
The Business Cycle

Study Topics
1. Why are economics and politics related?
2. Define fiscal policy and monetary policy.
3. Is The Fed an undemocratic institution?
4. What is the business cycle?

[1] http://www.npr.org/templates/story/story.php?storyId=92292747

[2] Quoted in David Brancaccio, "Former Treasury Secretary Lawrence Summers Says Taxing Robots Makes No Sense," American Public Media (April 19, 2017). Accessed at https://www.marketplace.org/2017/04/19/economy/robot-proof-jobs/should-we-put-tax-on-robots-taking-jobs

[3] OECD accessed at https://data.oecd.org/gga/general-government-spending.htm

[4] Quoted in Tim Arango, "The Housing-Bubble Revolution," *The New York Times* (November 30, 2008): 5WK. http://www.nytimes.com/2008/11/30/weekinreview/30arango.html?scp=1&sq=Housing-bubble%20revolution&st=cse

[5] *Wealth of Nations*, Book 1, Chapter 2, Accessed at http://geolib.com/smith.adam/won1-02.html

[6] Quoted in "Diagnosing Depression," *The Economist* (December 30, 2008). http://www.economist.com/finance/displaystory.cfm?story_id=12852043

[7] Quoted in Catherine Rampell, "Companies Spend on Equipment, Not Workers," *The New York Times* (June 9, 2011). Accessed at http://www.nytimes.com/2011/06/10/business/10capital.html?_r=1&hp

[8] Adam Davidson, "Making It in America," *The Atlantic* January/February 2012. Accessed at https://www.theatlantic.com/magazine/archive/2012/01/making-it-in-america/308844/

[9] http://www.npr.org/sections/thetwo-way/2017/05/05/527033952/april-jobs-report-211-000-jobs-added-unemployment-at-4-4-percent

[10] http://www.sesameworkshop.org/what-we-do/our-approach-in-action/

[11] David Brooks. "The Formerly Middle Class." *The New York Times*. November 17, 2008. Accessed at http://www.nytimes.com/2008/11/18/opinion/18brooks.html?_r=1&hp

[12] http://ourfinancialsecurity.org

[13] For a good description of how monitoring occurs, listen to the following report on National Public Radio: http://www.npr.org/templates/story/story.php?storyId=88116176

[14] Ben Stein, "What if a Slowdown Is a Never-Ending Story? *The New York Times* (November 23, 2008), BU8.

[15] https://www.fdic.gov/bank/historical/sandl/

[16] John Cassidy, The Volcker Rule, *The New Yorker* 25-30, at 28 July 26, 2010.

[17] http://www.nytimes.com/2009/09/06/magazine/06Economic-t.html?_r=1&scp=2&sq=Krugman%20economists&st=cse

[18] This analysis is based on Joshua Green, "Inside Man," *The Atlantic* (April 2010): 36-51, 38.

[19] Accessed at https://data.bls.gov/pdq/SurveyOutputServlet?request_action=wh&graph_name=LN_cps bref3

[20] https://www.weforum.org/reports/the-global-competitiveness-report-2016-2017-1

[21] http://www.nytimes.com/2008/12/10/business/economy/10leonhardt.html?_r=1&hp

[22] Interview with Anderson Cooper, "France's Marine Le Pen Says She is not Waging a Religious War," *60 Minutes* (CBS) (March 5, 2017).

[23] https://www.youtube.com/user/PragerUniversity/videos

15.0 | Food Policy

Is Ketchup a vegetable? Why are around 44 million Americans getting food stamps? Is the government planning to take away my Big Gulps and other sweetened drinks? Is sugar going to be treated like tobacco products? Will the government make people eat broccoli as part of a national health care plan? These are just some of the unusual ways that we talk

"Do the food nazis want your Twinkies?"

"Should the government be the nutrition police?"

about the politics of food. In 1981 the Department of Agriculture considered a proposal to reduce federal spending by defining ketchup as a vegetable for the federally subsidized school lunch program. The proposal was widely ridiculed by food activists who were promoting children's nutrition. Stories about welfare queens using food stamps to buy sodas and candy have been told for decades by critics of the welfare state who think that a program to help the truly needy has expanded beyond its original purpose. More recently, government policies to promote nutrition and good diet in order to reduce increasing rates of obesity have prompted worries about government plans to take our Twinkies, Big Gulps, and French fries. During a 1990 press conference, President George Herbert Walker Bush confessed that he had disliked broccoli ever since he was a child and now that he was president he was not going to eat it anymore. (The statement did not make broccoli growers very happy!) Then broccoli played a surprisingly central role in the political and legal debates over the constitutionality of The Patient Protection and Affordable Care Act (better known as Obamacare).

Critics argued that argued if government could require a person to buy health insurance it could also require people to eat broccoli. In her concurring opinion in the Supreme Court ruling that upheld the constitutionality of Obamacare, Justice Ginsburg described the argument against the individual mandate as a parade of "broccoli horribles."[1]

This chapter examines the politics of food policy. Food policy is an area of federal policy that is often overlooked because the public, the political parties and interest groups, and the media pay more attention to higher profile issues such as national security, the economy, crime, and other issues such as education and health care. The government's role in ensuring food security (that is, an adequate supply of food) and food safety is not controversial. People expect the government to ensure that they have *enough* food and *safe* food. But food policy has become controversial as the government has begun to promote healthy diets by regulations that require labeling menus and limit portion sizes and proposals to tax certain items such as sweetened drinks. The chapter focuses on three aspects of food policy. First, it describes food policy. Second, it describes how diet and nutrition were put on the government agenda (i.e., the politics of food). Third, it describes the main government and non-government actors who make food policy as participants in the food issue network.

15.1 | Is Food a Private Good or a Public Good?

Why is food even a political issue? In one sense food is a classic example of a private good. Food is a divisible good (one whose benefits can be limited to those who pay for it). Private goods are available in the private sector based on the ability to pay. Food is a matter of private choice: an individual decides what to eat, how much to eat, and how much to pay for it. These decisions are based on a person's ability to pay and personal tastes. In this sense, food is provided according to the *market model* rather than the *government model*. But food is not considered a completely private good that is available *only* to those who can afford to pay for it. Food is also considered a public good that the government provides for some people regardless of their ability to pay for it. The government's food policy goals include *food security, food safety, promotion of American agriculture, and healthy food.*

During the Great Depression of the 1930s unemployment, poverty, and hunger were nationwide problems. President Franklin Delano Roosevelt captured the scope of the problem in his *Second Inaugural Address* (January 20, 1937):

> I see a great nation, upon a great continent, blessed with a great wealth of natural resources…. But here is the challenge to our democracy: In this nation I see tens of millions of its citizens—a substantial part of its whole population—who at this very moment are denied the greater part of… the necessities of life. I see millions of families trying to live on incomes so meager that the pall of family disaster hangs over them day by day. I see millions whose daily lives in city and on farm continue under conditions labeled indecent by a so-called polite society half a century ago. I see millions denied education, recreation, and the opportunity to better their lot and the lot of their children. I see millions lacking the means to buy the products of farm and factory and by their poverty denying work and productiveness to many other millions. *I see one-third of a nation ill-housed, ill-clad, ill-nourished.* [Emphasis added] It is not in despair that I paint you that picture. I paint it for you in hope—because the Nation, seeing and understanding the injustice in it, proposes to paint it out….The test of our progress is not whether we add more to the abundance of those who have much; it is whether we provide enough for those who have too little.

Freedom from want includes freedom from hunger. Today, food security is provided by the food stamp program and the Supplemental Nutrition Assistance Program (SNAP), two social welfare programs that provide food support for low-income people.

The U.S. Department of Agriculture defines **food security** as access to an adequate and safe supply of food: "access by all people at all times to enough food for an active, healthy life—in U.S. households and communities." In 2008, 85 percent of U.S. households were food-secure throughout the entire year, and 14.6 percent of households were food insecure at least some time during that year, up from 11.1 percent in 2007. This is the highest recorded rate of food insecurity since 1995 when the first national food security survey was conducted.[2]

The government also has responsibility for ensuring a safe food supply. Food is more political today than in the past because today's consumers are much more dependent upon others to provide their food. Most people are dependent on others for their food: they are consumers of food rather than producers of food. And people are not getting their food from family, friends, or neighbors; they are getting it from national and international commerce. Consumer protection is one of the functions of government. Protecting food consumers, ensuring a safe food supply, is also a government function. Unsafe, tainted, contaminated food, and outbreaks of E. coli, salmonella poisoning, and other food borne illnesses and deaths are public health issues. The Centers for Disease Control and Prevention reports on food borne illnesses in the U.S. illustrate why food safety is a political issue.

Centers for Disease Control and Prevention

"CDC Estimates of Food Borne Illness in the United States"
In 1999, 76 million ill, 325,000 hospitalized, and 5,000 deaths in the U.S. from food borne illnesses. In 2011, 48 million illnesses, 128,000 hospitalizations, and 3,000 deaths.
http://www.cdc.gov/foodborneburden/2011-foodborne-estimates.html

Food Safety News
http://www.foodsafetynews.com/2009/09/ten-of-the-most-meaningful-food-borne-illness-outbreaks-picked-out-of-so-many/

From a political science perspective, food is a public good in the sense that governments everywhere are responsible for insuring an adequate, affordable, and safe supply of food. Food is also made a political issue by events such as droughts, crop failures due to diseases, health threats from unsafe foods or food borne-illnesses, and high rates of inflation. A century ago, food consumed a large share of the typical American family's budget. In 1900, more than 40% of a family's income was spent on food.[3] But federal food policy has emphasized increasing farm production, which has resulted in cheap food. The result has been a dramatic reduction in the food share of the average American family's budget.

Today, the efficient production of an adequate food supply is not a serious problem for federal food policy. The new food issues are safety and nutrition and health.

15.12 | The Politics of Food

There is broad consensus that the federal government has a legitimate role in ensuring the safety of the food supply. But the government's role in promoting health and nutrition is much more controversial. The federal government does have a long history of promoting diet. One early government campaign promoted good diet as a patriotic contribution to the effort to win World War I.

Food and the War Effort
"Food Will Win the War: On the Homefront in WWI"
http://www.archives.gov/northeast/nyc/education/food-wwi.html

---

The Department of Agriculture also sponsored one of the earliest radio programs, "Aunt Sammy," (the domestic equivalent of Uncle Sam) as part of a government campaign to get farmwives to promote healthy diets.

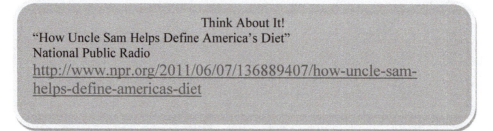

Think About It!
"How Uncle Sam Helps Define America's Diet"
National Public Radio
http://www.npr.org/2011/06/07/136889407/how-uncle-sam-helps-define-americas-diet

15.2 | The Food Issue Network

The term **issue network** describes participation in the formulation of public policy. An issue network consists of the two main government participants (the congressional committees and executive departments/agencies with authority over a particular issue) and the various non-government participants (the interest groups who are interested in a particular issue). The **food issue network** consists of the House and Senate Agriculture Committees (and subcommittees), which are the primary congressional food policy makers; the Department of Agriculture (and the Food and Drug Administration); and interest groups. The following describes the traditional and modern food issue network.

15.21 | *The Traditional Food Issue Network*

The traditional food issue network consisted of the House and Senate agriculture committees, the Department of Agriculture, and agri-business interest groups that primarily represented farmers and ranchers (the food producers).

The Traditional Food Issue Network

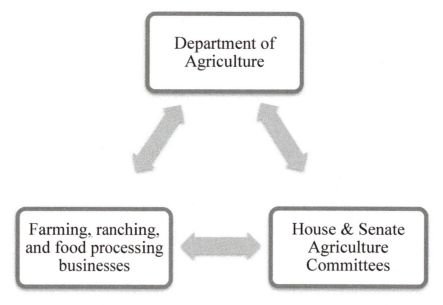

Department of Agriculture

Farming, ranching, and food processing businesses

House & Senate Agriculture Committees

15.22 | *The Modern Food Issue Network*

But today another set of interest groups have worked their way into the food issue network. In the past, food producers and food processing companies were the main private sector participants in making food policy. Today, however, consumer groups, environmentalists, and public health advocates have joined the food issue network. They provide a different perspective on the goals of federal food policy.

The Modern Food Issue Network

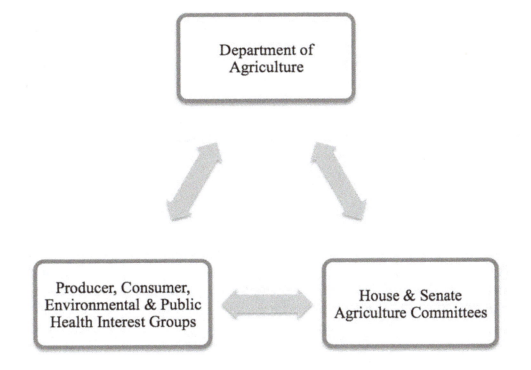

These new participants in the policy making process have made food policy more contentious because consumer, environmentalist, and public health groups have different interests than the food producers and processors. The following sections describe the three main types of participants in the modern food issue network

15.23 | *Congress: The House and Senate Agriculture Committees*

Congress makes food policy. The House of Representative Agriculture Committee (and subcommittees) and the Senate Agriculture, Nutrition and Forestry Committee (and subcommittees) have jurisdiction over bills, programs, and issues related to agriculture as well as supervision of the Department of Agriculture and other agencies with jurisdiction over food programs.

The following describes the agriculture committees and subcommittees in the 112th Congress. The House Agriculture Committee had six subcommittees, one of which was the <u>Subcommittee on Nutrition and Horticulture</u> which had jurisdiction over nutrition policy. The Senate Agriculture, Nutrition and Forestry Committee had five subcommittees, one of which was the Subcommittee on Nutrition, Specialty Crops, Food and Agricultural Research. Its legislative portfolio included provisions of the Food, Conservation and Energy Act of 2008; domestic and international nutrition and food assistance and hunger prevention; school and child nutrition programs; local and healthy food initiatives; food and agricultural research, education, economics and extension.

A letter from the ranking member of the Senate Agriculture Committee (Kansas Republican Senator Roberts) to the Secretary of Agriculture illustrates how the Senate Agriculture Committee interacts with the executive branch to advocate on behalf of agricultural interests. The October 3, 2012 letter entitled "Senator Roberts Concerned School Nutrition Programs Don't Meet Needs of Active Students" expressed concern that the Department of Agriculture was developing healthy food standards that provided insufficient calories for active students. In 2010 Congress passed the Healthy, Hunger-Free Kids Act. The Act required the Department of Agriculture's Food and Nutrition Service to revise rules for the National School Lunch Program and the School Breakfast Program to promote healthy food—in effect, to provide healthier school meals that included more vegetables and fruits and grains and fat-free or low-fat milk. Senator Roberts was concerned that the healthier food would increase student plate waste, increase costs, and not provide enough calories for active students.[4]

15.24 | *The Department of Agriculture*

The second government participant in the food issue network is the Department of Agriculture. In the U.S. and elsewhere one of the basic functions of government is to ensure that people have enough food to eat and that the food supply is safe. The origins of the federal government's food policy can be traced to President Lincoln's creation of an agricultural department in 1862. Lincoln called it "the people's department." Agriculture is sometimes called the nation's first industry; it was here before manufacturing. The department that Lincoln created eventually became one of the Cabinet agencies when the <u>Department of Agriculture</u> was created in 1889.

Historically, the United States Department of Agriculture (USDA) has functioned as a **clientele agency**. A clientele agency is an agency that is created to serve the needs or represent the interests of a specific group. The departments of Labor, Education, and Commerce are also clientele agencies that were created to represent labor, education, and business, respectively. The USDA was created to advocate for its major clientele— farmers and ranchers. In the 1920s, the USDA promoted industrial farming to increase production. The **Green Revolution** greatly increased agricultural production and in 1960 the USDA produced a video extolling the "<u>Miracles from Agriculture</u>" that made many of the amenities of modern life possible.

> The International Maize and Wheat Improvement Center (CIMMYT) played a pivotal role in the Green Revolution and continues to be a major research center working on increased productivity.
> http://www.cimmyt.org/

The Department of Agriculture's mission has been broadened beyond merely increasing production as federal food policy has expanded to include goals other than the promotion of agriculture. Today the USDA has the following areas of policy responsibility: promoting and marketing agricultural products at home and abroad; food safety and nutrition; conservation of natural resources; rural and community development; and providing job and housing assistance. However, the following short story about Pizza Politics reveals that the USDA is still a clientele agency that sees its mission as promoting American agricultural products. Domino's Pizza had falling sales. A consumer survey of national pizza chains revealed that the Domino's pizzas tied for last in taste. In order to turn the sales trends around, Domino's worked with an organization called Dairy Management to develop a pizza with 40% more cheese. Dairy Management paid for a $12 million marketing campaign. The "Pizza Turnaround" television ads that were part of the Domino's marketing campaign.

The advertising campaign for the new cheesier pizza worked. It produced double-digit sales increases. This business case study is interesting but it would be irrelevant to the study of food policy except for the fact that Dairy Management is not a private industry business consultant. Dairy Management is an organization that was created by the USDA. Dairy Management worked with other restaurant companies to increase the amount of cheese that was on restaurant menus.[5] But the USDA also sponsors a healthy diet campaign that recommended *lowering* the amount of milk fats in the American diet! The cheese story illustrates how the USDA's dual mission—to promote American agriculture (in this instance, dairy products but in other instances beef or wheat or corn) and to promote healthy diets—sometimes conflict.

15.25 | *The Food and Drug Administration*

A third main government participant in the food issue network is the Food and Drug Administration (the FDA). The FDA is an independent regulatory commission but for the purposes of issue networks it is considered an executive agency because it implements legislation. Food safety was put on the federal government's agency in the early years of the 20th Century. In 1906 Congress passed the Pure Food and Drugs Act of 1906, which prohibited companies from interstate commerce in misbranded and adulterated foods, drinks and drugs. The 1906 Act was a response to two works that focused the public's attention on problems in the nation's food supply. Upton Sinclair published *The Jungle* in 1906, and a ten-part study by Harvey Washington Wiley on additives and chemicals in the nation's food supply. *The Jungle* was a novel that exposed the terrible conditions of the meatpacking industry. It focused on the plight of workers in meatpacking plants. Sinclair had gone undercover in meatpacking plants in Chicago and wanted to expose the American public to the problems faced by blue-collar workers. But the public's attention was captured by Sinclair's prose describing the unsanitary conditions in which their food was being handled in an industrial system that they did not associate with food. Sinclair wrote:

[T]he meat would be shoveled into carts, and the man who did the shoveling would not trouble to lift out a rat even when he saw one—there were things that went into the sausage in comparison with which a poisoned rat was a tidbit. There was no place for the men to wash their hands before they ate their dinner, and so they made a practice of washing them in the water that was to be ladled into the sausage. There were the butt-ends of smoked meat, and the scraps of corned beef, and all the odds and ends of the waste of the plants, that would be dumped into old barrels in the cellar and left there. Under the system of rigid economy which the packers enforced, there were some jobs that it only paid to do once in a long time, and among these was the cleaning out of the waste barrels. Every spring they did it; and in the barrels would be dirt and rust and old nails and stale water—and cartload after cartload of it would be taken up and dumped into the hoppers with fresh meat, and sent out to the public's breakfast. *The Jungle*, Chapter 14, page 1.

A poster of the 1913 movie adaptation of Sinclair's novel

Congress created the Food and Drug Administration (the FDA) in 1930. The FDA is the primary federal regulatory agency with authority over food safety, although the Department of Agriculture also plays an important role in making federal food policy. The USDA promotes American agricultural production and sales abroad as well as ensures a safe food supply by inspecting food-processing plants. Today, the FDA has regulatory authority over about 25 cents of every dollar the consumer spends.

And of course significant portion of that dollar is spent on food consumed outside the home. The average person consumes about one-third of their calories on foods prepared outside the home.[6] As a result, the FDA has proposed new regulations that require labeling the calorie content of food served in restaurants and vending machines. The regulations would apply only to chain restaurants or vending machines companies with 20 or more locations as a concession to small businesses. The FDA's focus on food consumed outside the home reflects changes in patterns of consumption. But the FDA has not kept up with one change in where Americans get their food (and drugs). The U.S. now imports a larger share of its food. In the past, certain foods such as fruits and vegetables were only available seasonally. Today peaches and asparagus are available during the winter months in northern states because they are imported from other countries. But the FDA inspects only about 1% of imported food. Public concerns about the safety of the food supply have increased pressure to have the FDA expand its inspection of imported foods. The FDA has proposed placing more inspectors in the foreign countries from which we import food and drugs, rather than waiting until they enter the U.S., and it has opened an office in Beijing, China. But expanding the scope of the FDA's operations is controversial. It requires increasing the FDA's budget and increasing federal regulations. Addressing the food safety problem requires more than hiring more inspectors and doing more testing; it requires creating a regulatory system that works to provide food safety.

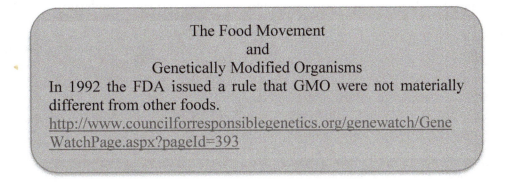

The Food Movement
and
Genetically Modified Organisms
In 1992 the FDA issued a rule that GMO were not materially different from other foods.
http://www.councilforresponsiblegenetics.org/genewatch/Gene WatchPage.aspx?pageId=393

15.26 | *Interest Groups*

The third category of issue network participants is interest groups. Traditionally, these were groups that represented farming and ranching or food processing and distributing companies. Agribusinesses such as the Archer Daniels Midland Company have a vested interest in food policy and are important participants in the food network.

Today, however, a broad range of interest groups participate in the food issue network. Take, for example, consumer groups. Consumer groups represent individual consumers (i.e., people who buy food) and business consumers (e.g., companies such as The Coca-Cola Company, PepsiCo, Mars Incorporated, and The Hershey Company) that buy commodities such as sugar and corn syrup. Two groups that take opposing positions on food issues such as labeling the caloric and nutritional content of food, limiting the size of food portions, or taxing sodas are the Center for Science in the Public Interest and the Center for Consumer Freedom. The former organization generally plays offense: it is a consumer group that advocates for more government regulation of food. The latter organization generally plays defense: it is an industry group that opposes more government regulation of food. Public health advocates also generally support more government regulation to provide consumer information and to promote public health by reducing the consumption fat, salt, and sugar. The food industry worries about the general trend toward treating sugar or fat, for example, the way that tobacco and alcohol have been treated. Tobacco and alcohol have been subjected to "sin taxes." A sin tax is a tax on a vice such as smoking or drinking. The American Beverage Association, for instance, has mobilized industry opposition to treating sweetened beverages the way that tobacco and alcohol have been treated. The policy proposals to tax sugar or certain fats as harmful are based on the belief that consumption can be discouraged by taxing and regulating consumption.

15.3 | The Farm Bill and the Food Aid Program

The Farm Bill is a major component of the federal government's food policy. The Farm Bill, which is enacted every five years, is a nearly $300 billion dollar federal program. It was originally intended to promote food production, to promote marketing of U.S. food products abroad, and to keep food prices low. Crop subsidies are one of the primary ways that these goals were achieved. The USDA has commodity programs that subsidize growing

wheat, corn, rice, cotton and a few other crops. The USDA also subsidized sugar prices and dairy prices, primarily milk price supports.

15.31 | *The Food Aid Program*

One component of the Farm Bill is the Food Aid Program. The Food Aid Program is a good example of a public policy that is both domestic policy and foreign policy. In 2007, the Food Aid Program was a $2 billion dollar program to provide food aid to other countries. The Food Aid Program began in 1954 as a way for the U.S. to dispose of surplus crops abroad. The Green Revolution, which began in the 1940s, greatly increased agricultural production. It was the result of the following developments:

- Biology. Scientific research produced more fertile and productive plants and animals.
- Chemistry. The chemical industry created more effective herbicides, pesticides, and fertilizers, which increased food production.
- Management. The industrial revolution transformed manufacturing before it reached agriculture, but eventually the agricultural sector changed from small family farms to large-scale corporate, agribusiness, or factory farming. The result was increased efficiency in growing, processing, and transporting foods.

The Green Revolution made American agriculture so productive that food policy had to address the problem of surplus, not scarcity or hunger. Food scarcity has not been the most important problem for food policy for decades. American agriculture produces far more food than can be consumed domestically. The economy of scale associated with factory farming made agriculture more efficient and more productive but it also contributed to the decline of the family farm. The "family farmer" is now analogous to the cowboy. Both are important symbols in American cultural heritage but they are no longer central figures in the economy. There are other critics of the Green Revolution. The Institute for Food and Development Policy, which is also known as Food First, advocates self-sufficiency and food sovereignty rather than dependence on international agribusiness companies.

15.32 | *Food Policy is both Domestic and Foreign Policy*

Domestic and foreign policy are often considered distinct areas of public policy. However, the food aid program is a good example of how domestic policy and foreign policy are linked. The food aid program includes provisions requiring 75% of the food aid be shipped in U.S. vessels, 25% of the food aid be shipped from Great Lakes ports, and mandating that the food aid be in the form of food (that is, American agricultural commodities such as dairy products, grain, or corn) not money. These requirements apply even when the food aid is a response to emergencies such as drought or disease. These requirements build domestic political support for the food aid program because American farmers, food processing companies, and transportation companies benefit from the program. The domestic political support is important because foreign aid is often welfare for other countries and therefore vulnerable during times of tight federal budgets and deficits. But the food aid program's requirements to buy American and ship American also create problems. One problem is that the high transportation costs of sending grain grown in the American Midwest (e.g., Kansas) to countries on the other side of the globe, and the time it takes to deliver food to where the food aid is needed, limit the effectiveness of the food aid program. A second problem is that federal corn subsidies keep the price of corn high and therefore reduce the amount of corn purchased for the food aid program. A third problem is that ethanol subsidies have resulted in corn being used for fuel rather than human or animal consumption. A Government Accounting Office (GAO) study found that it takes five months to get a new food aid to the country where it is needed. This means that the food aid may not be timely. In addition to timeliness, international food aid programs can also have a negative unintended consequence for local growers and producers. International aid can disrupt the local economy by displacing local producers when U.S. products flood the market in a country that receives foreign food aid because of a drought or other food supply problem. The food aid can solve an immediate problem but driving local companies out of business is an unintended consequence that has a negative long-term impact on a country's (or region's) ability to feed itself.

These problems of timeliness and impact on the local market have caused a new set of interest groups to participate in the creation of the food aid program in the Farm Bill. The new participants are lobbying government policy makers to pay more attention to nutrition, environmentalism, and international economic development as elements of the federal government's food policy. These new participants complicated federal food policy. The traditional food policy focused primarily on ensuring an adequate food supply in the U.S.[7] For example, CARE is a private international humanitarian organization that was created after WWII to alleviate poverty. It is one of the new participants in the food issue network that questions the effectiveness of the Food Aid Program's efforts to alleviate poverty in other countries.[8]

The United Nations Food Program and the World Bank are two international programs that provide emergency aid and economic development that is intended to help countries grow enough food to feed their own people. The United Nations Food Program provides food aid and The World Bank provides aid that will help countries achieve food self-sufficiency. In Africa, The World Bank programs have encouraged countries to eliminate fertilizer subsidies in favor of free market programs. One unintended consequence of The World Bank's program is a steep increase in fertilizer prices which can actually decrease food production. The United States Agency for International Development has also focused on promoting the private sector's role in providing fertilizer and seed, and considered government subsidies an impediment to the development of a private market in African countries such as Malawi, where famine has required extensive foreign food aid.[9] The U.S. and international aid organizations have a major impact on the way that government officials in other countries think about food policy because are associated with advanced technological and organizational skills that increase productivity.

15.33 | *International Food Policy*

The **Green Revolution** refers to the steep increase in agricultural production that began with wheat in Mexico in the 1940s. The Green Revolution contributed to economic development by making it possible for countries that were not able to produce enough food to feed their own people to produce enough food to feed their people or even surplus production to be sold abroad. Food security means producing enough food so that the government can assist during times of drought, conflict, or natural disasters in order to avert starvation. One standard way that governments achieve food security is to regulate food prices in order to ensure that producers were profitable so that they were able to stay in business. Some developing countries created food marketing boards which regulated the food industry. The boards managed the industry to stabilize commodity and food prices at levels that allowed businesses to be profitable while ensure that consumers had an affordable and adequate supply of food. The boards also bought commodities and stored them as insurance against a crop failure or inflation. These are examples of how the market model works.

15.34 | *The Marketization of Food*

Beginning in the 1980s, international aid agencies such as the World Bank and the IMF changed the goals of their programs. They strove to get countries to adopt food policies that reduced the government's role in achieving food security and increased reliance on market approaches. In effect, the international aid agencies urged countries to move away from the government model and toward the market model. This change in policy has been called the **marketization of food**.

The marketization of food is part of the broader trend toward privatization in other areas of domestic public policy. Privatization refers to the policy of returning government functions to the private sector or having services such as waste removal provided by private sector companies rather than government workers. The government model relies on regulations and subsidies to provide an adequate and safe food supply. In recent decades, the international aid community has begun to reconsider the government model which has relied on price supports; subsidies for the costs of fertilizer, herbicides, and pesticides, or high-yield crop seeds; and tariffs on imports. As economic development in general has promoted private sector activity, the international food aid community has considered the government model for food an unwise intervention in the marketplace. As a result, economic development policies have promoted market efficiency rather than government regulation.

The marketization of food meant that development aid encouraged countries to adopt policies that supported growing cash crops rather than food crops. Cash crops could be sold in the international or global marketplace. Food crops are grown primarily for domestic consumption. One result of international aid programs that emphasized marketization is that farmers grew crops like cocoa instead of staples such as maize, rice, or corn. Governments often encouraged international private investors to enter the marketplace in search of profits. Marketization and globalization are based on assumption that each country or region of the world should grow for the international marketplace what it can most efficiently produce, based on its distinctive climate or local soil. International food aid therefore emphasized economic development as measured by international trade in commodities rather than food self-sufficiency. The results are now evident in some unusual data. For instance, there has been a marked increase in the concentration of production of certain commodities. Fewer than five countries now account for around 90 percent of the corn exports and around five countries now account for around 80 percent of the world's rice exports. The increase in global efficiency has been accompanied by a global vulnerability to disruptions in trade or production. The increase in **private investment** has not entirely compensated for the **public disinvestment**. As a result, policy makers are rethinking the emphasis on market efficiency, and making food policy that encourages agricultural self-sufficiency as well as market efficiency. This will mean some government management of the agricultural sector of the economy. Food crises produce political crises (e.g., food riots) that governments are expected to respond to even if the politics does not. Some countries with rapidly growing populations and changes in patterns of food consumption are buying foreign land for growing crops to import.

> ## Think About It!
> ### How Many Earths Do We Need?
> The Global Footprint Network is an alliance of scientists who research the food supply necessary to sustain populations. The organization calculates, among other things, ***how many earths*** will be required to sustain human life at 1) current population levels and rates of consumption; and at 2) projected increases in population levels and consumption. The GFN measures consumption and waste at both individual level data and country level data.

15.4 | The Price of Food

Along with clothing and shelter, food is a basic commodity. It is one of the major items in the household budget. But the share of the average household budget that is consumed by food has steadily declined over the last half-century or so. See the following figure from U.S. Department of Agriculture data: [10]

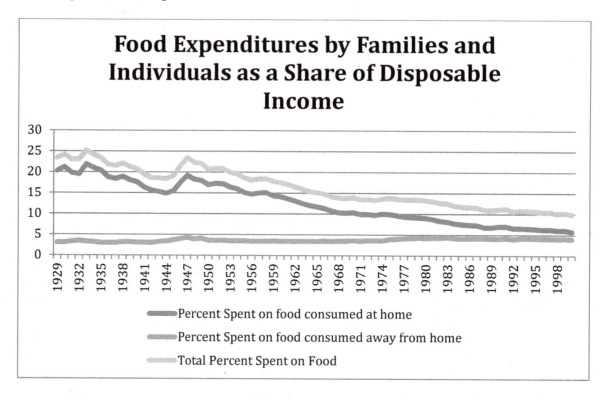

The decline in the food share of a household's disposable income explains why food security is not a high-profile issue in the U.S. However, a long-term change in food consumption patterns has made food more political: the increased share of food that is now consumed outside the home. In 1970, 26 percent of all food spending was on food away from home; by 2005, that share rose to 41 percent. A number of factors contributed to the trend of increased dining out:

- A larger share of women employed outside the home;
- More two-earner households;
- Higher incomes meant more disposable income;
- More affordable and convenient fast food outlets;
- Increased advertising and promotion by large foodservice chains; and
- The smaller size of U.S. households.

The continuation of these economic and demographic trends is expected to keep boosting the percentage of American income spent on eating outside the home.[11] Restaurants now account for almost half of the average household's food expenditures. As a result, food safety and nutrition are on the government's agenda. Consumers expect the government to inspect restaurants and food processing companies. And consumers are beginning to expect restaurants to provide consumers with more nutrition information about the items on the menu.

15.5 | Public Health Interest Groups and the Food Wars

The increase in rates of diabetes and obesity has prompted public health advocates lobby to add nutrition to the traditional emphases of federal food policy. Getting nutrition on the government's agenda has been an ongoing effort by individuals and organizations. Previously, such groups successfully lobbied the national government to make regulation of tobacco products a public issue after it was learned that nicotine was an addictive drug. Media campaigns play an important role in convincing government officials that they should act. The 2004 documentary *Super Size Me* (Directed by and starring Morgan Spurlock) called attention to the adverse health consequences of consuming fast food. http://freedocumentaries.org/film.php?id=98

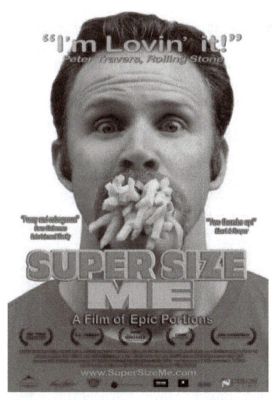

Interest groups representing the food industry, consumers, and health advocates have put food policy on the government's agenda by emphasizing two issues: food safety and public health. Food safety periodically becomes a high profile issue when outbreaks of E. coli, salmonella, botulism or some other food-related illnesses capture the public's attention. The demand for government action to ensure a safe food supply rises and falls with these episodic crises. Concerns about the health of the American population have also prompted calls for government action. The Centers for Disease Control and Prevention periodically conduct Health and Nutrition Examination Surveys.[12] The surveys show increased weight: In the early 1960s, 24 percent of American adults were overweight, defined as a body-mass index greater than 27. In 1980 the survey showed 33 percent were overweight. The weight increase presents an interesting research question: what caused the increase? The answer is essential to any policy solution. Explanations of the cause vary. Some natural scientists attribute the increased weight to biology: our brains have been developed to eat a great deal during times of plenty so that the body stores fat for lean times when the fat stores are consumed. Social scientists identify other causes. Economists blame public policies that make cheap food widely available.[13] The Green Revolution did make food cheaper relative to other goods and services that people purchase therefore people could consume more food—and chose to do so. Soft drinks, for example, are now part of daily calorie intake. Some public health advocates attribute the weight increase to addiction.

David Kessler is a former head of the Food and Drug Administration who advocated government regulation of nicotine as an addictive drug. Kessler maintains that the food industry has been reengineering food in ways that appeal to other kinds of human hunger.[14] The food industry has successfully used marketing that emphasizes "eatertainment" rather than nourishment. It produces fun products, interesting products, social products, products that are craved. Kessler calls the industry approach "conditioned hypereating." He compares the consumption of sweet and fatty foods with the conditioned response to gambling or substance abuse. McDonald's discovered that re-portioning (or super-sizing) was a very effective marketing strategy because the average consumer doesn't think in terms of calories, doesn't count calories, but rather thinks and counts in terms of the number of portions consumed. In fact, neither consumers nor food manufacturers seem to think in terms of nutrition. Most food marketing is not about nourishment—large food companies such as Pepsico, for instance, advertise the "aspirational" or lifestyle goals of consuming their product. The Pepsico Web site markets its brands as "bringing fun and refreshment to consumers for over 100 years." This is one reason why the comparison of the tobacco wars and the food wars is both appropriate and revealing.[15]

The role that large multi-national corporations play in providing food has caused some concern about their control over the food supply. After the Supreme Court ruled that life forms could be patented, companies began aggressively asserting property rights to, among other things, seeds. The documentary, _Food, Inc._, describes the role that the chemical company Monsanto has played in this movement. Monsanto now has property rights over 90% of the soybean seeds and asserts those rights in court to maintain control over the growing of soybeans.

Governments are resorting to some innovative and controversial public health approaches to regulating diet. One such approach is the use of zoning laws to limit the number of fast-food establishments. In July of 2008, the Los Angeles City Council adopted an ordinance that established a one-year moratorium on the building of new fast-food establishments in a 32-square –mile area of the city, including South Los Angeles which has around 900 restaurants (many of which are fast-food), and high rates of both adult obesity and diabetes. As more than two-thirds of American adults are fat, declaring war on junk food is politically risky; the government has to be careful about declaring war on junk food. Will the metaphorical war on junk food work like the war on drugs or the war on tobacco?

15.51 | _Is sugar the new nicotine?_

The following is based on an interview with New York City Mayor Michael Bloomberg about his portion control proposal to ban sweetened drinks in containers larger than 16 ounces.[16] Mayor Bloomberg has become famous (or infamous) for his proposals to require restaurants to provide nutrition labeling on menu items and to ban "supersized" soft drinks. A journalist asked Mayor Bloomberg about his "campaign against the sugar-industrial complex," the responsibilities of government and the responsibilities of individuals, and how he decides to pick his fights (priorities). Bloomberg replied that the government should not to ban goods; it should provide consumers with information and then let them make decisions about what to buy. He considered calorie counts and portion control two ways to provide such information about how much sugar is being consumed. Is eating like smoking? One person's weight does not hurt another person the way that one person's smoking hurts other people in the same area (second-hand smoke), but obesity does cost society which pays for health care. There is general agreement that government should prevent certain harms. Are sugary drinks like asbestos? The government would immediately pull people out of a building with an asbestos problem. The answer to the question, should the government regulate sugary drinks, is that it depends on the public-health issues. Bloomberg commented that obesity is an unusual public health problem because it is a disease that has gone from a rich person's disease to a poor person's disease: "For the first time in the history of the world, this year, more people will die from the effects of too much food than from starvation." He decided to make health an issue as mayor and for his foundation, Bloomberg Philanthropies, because he likes to tackle problems that others consider too political or too complex—guns, for instance. The portion-size question is interesting because of the correlation between the rise in obesity and the consumption of sugar. "Look, the beverage companies aren't stupid. Coca-Cola is run by a very smart guy; PepsiCo by a very smart woman. They see this train coming down the tracks at them. And that's why they're trying to get people to move over to Coke Zero or Diet Coke or Pepsi—Diet Pepsi—because down the road, the public *is* going to say "No *mas*. The cost of treating obesity is just out of control." McDonald's sued New York City when it first required the calorie now they are voluntarily providing them." The City is not proposing banning big drink it is proposing portion control: "All we're saying is that restaurants and theaters can't use cups greater than 16 ounces. So if you want to buy 32 ounces, you can buy 32 ounces, you just got to carry it back to your seat, or your table, in two cups." The public and the food industry initially opposed smoking bans. But now cities, states, and countries are creating smoke-free places.

15.6 | Environmentalism

American agriculture is extremely productive. The modern corporate, factory-farming model is very productive but it is also very energy and chemical intensive. The environmental movement has focused attention on the environmental costs of the industrial model of producing food. American agriculture requires a large amount of energy to produce crops such as corn and wheat and to produce commodities such as meat. Government crop subsidies increase food prices, increase food consumption, and increase environmental damage. The average American consumer eats 8 ounces of meat per day. About 30 percent of world's ice-free land is used directly or indirectly for livestock production, according to the United Nation's Food and Agriculture Organization. Livestock production generates 20 percent of world's greenhouse gases, which is more the greenhouse gases produced by a more familiar source of pollution: transportation. If Americans reduced meat consumption by 20 percent, the energy saved would be equivalent to their switching from a standard sedan (say a Toyota Camry) to a hybrid (say a Toyota Prius).[17]

15.7 | **Final Food for Thought**

Food is a good case study of issue transformation. Food used to be a private sector issue where individuals, families, farmers, food processors and providers made decisions about what to grow, how to provide food to consumers, and what food to buy without much government involvement. Today, food is on the government agenda and food policy is a substantial are of public policy. Changes in economic conditions, patterns of consumption, the environment, or health can prompt individuals and organizations to put food on the government's agenda. These organizations then join the food issue network as participants in making food policy. These individual policy entrepreneurs and organizations are playing offense. Other individuals and organizations play defense and work to keep food policy off the government's agenda. The American Beverage Association and the National Restaurant Association generally oppose more government regulation of their industries. But government inspections that prevent food-borne illnesses can actually protect the food industry by ensuring a safe food supply. Nutrition is another issue. The initial opposition to menu labeling has softened as public opinion has supported it. Portion control is still opposed because it raises anew the central issue in the tobacco wars and the food wars (or the food fights): —the political debates about the proper size and scope of government as much as the proper size of soft drinks.

15.8 | **Additional Resources**

Earth Policy Institute: http://www.earth-policy.org/

Behavioral Economics and Getting Children to Eat Healthy:
http://www.npr.org/templates/story/story.php?storyId=130732347

Sinclair, Upton. 1906. *The Jungle*. Available at: http://www.gutenberg.org/ebooks/140

15.12 | In the Library

Finkelstein, Eric A. and Laurie Zuckerman. 2008. *The Fattening of America How The Economy Makes Us Fat, If It Matters and What To Do About It*. New York: John Wiley & Sons
Kessler, David. 2009. *The End of Overeating: Taking Control of the Insatiable American Appetite*. New York: Rodale Books
Lindstrom, Martin. 2008. *Buyology: Truth and Lies About Why We Buy*. London: Crown Business

Key *Terms*

Food security
Modern food
policy
Clientele agency
Green Revolution
Marketization of
food

---

[1] *National Federation of Independent Businesses v. Sebelius*, 567 U.S.___(2012).

[2] See "Food Security in the United States" at http://www.ers.usda.gov/Briefing/FoodSecurity/ .

[3] Atul Gawande, "Testing, Testing," *The New Yorker* (December 14, 2009), 34-41, at 34.

[4] http://www.ag.senate.gov/newsroom/press/release/senator-roberts-concerned-school-nutrition-programs_dont-meet-needs-of-active-students. Accessed November 19, 2012.

[5] Michael Moss, "While Warning About Fat, U.S. Pushes Cheese Sales," *The New York Times*, November 6, 2010. At http://www.nytimes.com/2010/11/07/us/07fat.html?ref=dominospizzainc

[6] http://www.fda.gov/

[7] http://www.npr.org/templates/story/story.php?storyId=16053196&sc=emaf

[8] See the CARE "White Paper on Food Aid Policy," (June 6, 20006). http://www.care.org/newsroom/publications/whitepapers/food_aid_whitepaper.pdf

[9] Celia W. Dugger, "Ending Famine, Simply by Ignoring the Experts," *The New York Times* (December 2, 2007: p.1,6.

[10] http://www.ers.usda.gov/Briefing/CPIFoodAndExpenditures/Data/Expenditures_tables/table7.htm

[11] http://www.ers.usda.gov/publications/AER829/ and http://www.ers.usda.gov/Briefing/DietQuality/FAFH.htm

[12] http://www.cdc.gov/nchs/nhanes.htm

[13] Finkelstein, Eric A. and Laurie Zuckerman. 2008. *The Fattening of America How The Economy Makes Us Fat, If It Matters and What To Do About It*. New York: John Wiley & Sons

[14] 2009. *The End of Overeating: Taking Control of the Insatiable American Appetite*. New York: Rodale Books.

[15] See Martin Lindstrom. 2008. *Buyology: Truth and Lies About Why We Buy*. London: Crown Business.

[16] http://www.theatlantic.com/magazine/archive/2012/11/the-bloomberg-way/309136/ Accessed November 23, 2012.

[17] Mark Bittman, "Rethinking the Meat-Guzzler," *The New York Times* (January 27, 2008, 1WK, 4WK).

16.0 | Civil Liberties and Civil Rights: Freedom and Equality

Civil liberties and civil rights are directly related to debates about where to strike the right balance between individual freedom and government power. This chapter

- Defines civil liberties and civil rights;
- Describes the development of specific rights and liberties;
- Explains why they are controversial; and
- Uses crime policy as a case study of civil liberties and rights.

16.1 | Defining Terms

The terms *civil liberties* and *civil rights* are commonly used to mean **individual rights**, there are three differences between civil liberties and civil rights. They have different legal sources—civil liberties are provided in the Constitution while civil rights are provided in statutes. They also serve different purposes: civil liberties generally protect *freedom* while civil rights generally protect *equality*. And they present the two different sides of the power problem: civil liberties limit government power while civil rights expand government power.

**16.12 | *Civil Liberties*

In the U.S., civil liberties are **constitutional** guarantees that protect individual **freedom** from government power. The main source of civil liberties is the Bill of Rights, which are a series of *Thou Shalt Nots* that limit government power. The First Amendment declares that "Congress shall make no law...." limiting freedom of expression. The Fifth Amendment provides that "No person shall be.... deprived of life, liberty, or property without due process of law." The body of the Constitution also provides some civil liberties (e.g. the writ of habeas corpus). Finally, the 13th, 14th, 15th, and the 19th Amendments provide civil liberties.

Civil liberties cases are conflicts between individual freedom and government power. They are typically conflicts between an individual (or an organization) who claims a right to do something—such as burn a flag as a political protest, demonstrate at a funeral, obtain an abortion, view sexually explicit material on the Internet, carry a handgun or make unlimited campaign contributions—and the government which claims the power to limit that right. As part of the judiciary's dispute resolution function, courts serve as a neutral third party to settle these civil liberties disputes between individuals and the government. This is an important function in constitutional democracies such as the U.S. because civil liberties are the individual or minority rights that limit the power of the majority. The burden of proof is on the government. If the government "substantially burdens" a fundamental freedom, the government must demonstrate that it has a compelling interest in limiting the freedom *and* that it has no less restrictive means to achieve it.

Civil liberties are provided for in the 50 state constitutions, many of which were modeled on the U.S. Constitution and therefore resemble the provisions of the Bill of

Rights. Most state constitutions are, however, much longer than the U.S. Constitution so the civil liberties provisions of state constitutions are more specific. For example, Article I of The Florida State Constitution, "Declaration of Rights," provides for civil liberties including freedom of religion, speech, press, and the right of privacy. But the Florida Constitution's provision for freedom of expression is very different than the First Amendment to the U.S. Constitution, and the California State Constitution includes much more detailed and specific civil liberties provisions than the U.S. Constitution.

> Look It Up!
> What civil liberties provisions are in your state constitution?
> https://ballotpedia.org/State_constitution

16.13 | *Civil Rights*

Civil rights are legal claims that are generally provided in **statutory** law (legislation). Civil rights typically are claims to **equal treatment**—or freedom from discrimination. Civil rights laws increase government power by giving individuals a legal right to claim that an individual or an organization has discriminated against them. Civil rights laws prohibit racial, ethnic, religious, and gender-based discrimination in voting, education, employment, housing, public accommodations, and other settings. Civil rights movements have expanded equality for members of various groups (racial and ethnic and national minorities, prisoners, juveniles, women, the elderly, the handicapped, aliens, and gays and lesbians) and in various settings (employment; schools; hospitals; etc.). Civil liberties generally promote freedom by limiting government power.

16.14 | *Uncivil Liberties: Disturbing the Peace (of Mind)*

It is ironic that Americans express strong support for individual rights but are often very critical of the individuals who actually use their civil liberties. These are usually strong-willed people who stand up for their political or religious beliefs despite the threat of community hostility or government sanction. Some of these people are noble individuals who are taking a stand for a political principle; others were ignoble individuals who are merely taking advantage of a legal right. The following is a short list of some of the individuals whose convictions made them part of the American story of civil liberties.

- William Penn preaching on the streets of London and taking a stand for freedom of religion against the charge of unlawful assembly.
- Charles Schenck, the Secretary of the Socialist Party, distributing leaflets that opposed U.S. participation in WWI, which he called a capitalist enterprise to exploit workers, and compared the military draft with slavery.
- Walter Barnette objecting to a school board policy that required school children to recite the pledge of allegiance.
- Gregory Lee Johnson burning an American Flag during the 1984 Republican Party convention.

- Fred Phelps picketing at the funerals of veterans to express his belief that the veteran's death was God's punishment for American toleration of homosexuality.
- Xavier Alvarez lying about being a decorated military veteran and then claiming that he could not be prosecuted for violating the Stolen Valor Act of 2005 because the First Amendment prohibits Congress from passing laws that limit freedom of speech.

These are all examples of civil liberties cases where an individual challenged government power to limit freedom of expression. The trial of William Penn is part of the American story of religious freedom because a jury refused to convict him despite the fact that he was guilty of unlawful assembly. Charles Schenck was less fortunate. The Supreme Court upheld his conviction for distributing anti-war leaflets during WWI on the grounds that Congress can prohibit speech that presents a "clear and present danger" that it will cause evils—in this instance, refusal to comply with a military draft law—that Congress has power to prevent.

A WWII era case, West Virginia State Board of Education v. Barnette (1943), had a different outcome. During the wave of wartime patriotism, the West Virginia Board of Education adopted a policy that required all students in public schools to salute the flag as part of daily school activities. Walter Barnette was a Jehovah's Witness who argued that the policy violated his child's freedom of religion. The Supreme Court agreed. Gregory Johnson was a member of the Revolutionary Communist Youth Brigade who burned an American flag during a protest demonstration at the 1984 Republican Party National Convention in Dallas. He was convicted of violating a Texas law prohibiting desecration of the flag and fined $2,000. He appealed his conviction arguing that the First Amendment protects expressive actions such as flag burning. The Supreme Court agreed. The ruling was very unpopular with the general public and government officials. A constitutional amendment was proposed to ban flag burning but it was not adopted.

Fred Phelps continued this tradition of using freedom of expression to disturb the peace of mind in a particularly uncivil way. For more than two decades members of the Westboro Baptist Church picketed military funerals as a way to express their belief that God is punishing the United States for tolerating homosexuality. The picketing also condemned the Catholic Church for sex scandals involving its clergy. On March 10, 2006 the church's founder, Fred Phelps, and six parishioners who are relatives of Phelps picketed the funeral of Marine Lance Corporal Matthew Snyder at a Catholic Church in Maryland. Corporal Snyder was killed in Iraq in the line of duty. The picketing took place on public land about 1,000 feet from the church where the funeral was held, in accordance with rules established by local police. For about 30 minutes prior to the funeral, the picketers displayed signs that stated "Thank God for Dead Soldiers," "Fags Doom Nations," "America is Doomed," "Priests Rape Boys," and "You're Going to Hell." Matthew Snyder's father saw the tops of the picketers' signs on the way to the funeral, but he did not learn what was written on them until he watched that evening's news broadcast. He sued Phelps and his daughters, and a jury awarded Snyder more than a million dollars in compensatory and punitive damages. Phelps appealed, and the jury award was overturned on the grounds that Phelps' actions were protected by the First Amendment freedom of expression because they were comments on matters of public affairs and were not provably false. The U.S. Supreme Court ultimately agreed that the First Amendment protected even Mr. Phelps's vile speech in the case of _Snyder v. Phelps_ (2011).

Mr. Alvarez was a member of a water district board who in speeches falsely claimed to be a retired marine and recipient of the Congressional Medal of Honor. Criminal defendants have two defense strategies. They can either challenge the facts ("I did not do what the government says I did!") or they can challenge the law ("The law used to prosecute me is unconstitutional!"). Mr. Alvarez admitted making the false claims and argued that the Stolen Valor Act was unconstitutional. The Supreme Court agreed that the First Amendment protects lying. Justice Kennedy's opinion for the Court in _U.S. v. Alvarez_ (2012) begins:

> "Lying was his habit. Xavier Alvarez…lied when he said that he played hockey for the Detroit Red Wings and that he once married a starlet from Mexico. But when he lied in announcing he held the Congressional Medal of Honor, respondent ventured onto new ground; for that lie violates a federal criminal statute, the Stolen Valor Act of 2005. 18 U. S. C. §704."

So Mr. Alvarez, a person whom a Supreme Court justice described as a habitual liar, is now one of the ignoble individuals whose actions became part of the American story of civil liberties. The general public and government officials often react to court rulings that protect hateful and bigoted speech, flag burning, anti-war demonstrations, or even lying, with disappointment, disbelief, profound disagreement, or disgust.

16.2 | The First Amendment

Freedom House is an organization that compares freedom of expression in different countries. Check out the rankings of nations: http://www.freedomhouse.org/

The First Amendment guarantees freedom of expression: freedom of religion, freedom of speech, freedom of the press, and freedom to assemble and petition the government to redress grievances. Freedom of expression is today universally recognized as an essential condition for democracy and self-government. The political importance of freedom of expression is reflected in the fact that it is listed as the first of the Bill of Rights freedoms and the fact that all 50 state constitutions also guarantee freedom of expression. The following sections of this chapter describe freedom of religion and freedom of speech. Freedom of the press is examined in the media chapter.

16.21 | _Freedom of Religion_

What kind of political order did the Constitution establish? Debates about religion and moral regulatory policy are ultimately debates about the appropriate role of government. Did it establish a liberal order or a republican order? These two terms probably mean something different than you think. A **liberal order** is one where the government's role is limited to keeping the self-interested actions of individuals and organizations (including organized religion) under control. This is sometimes called the "night watchman" state because the government's role is limited to protecting people from being harmed by others. A **republican order** is one where the government's role is to protect people from harm AND to teach people how they should live a good life in a good society. In a republican order, the government functions as a kind of "schoolmaster" that instructs people on how to live a good (moral or ethical) life in a good society.

The American colonies established religions because they believed that the purpose of politics and government was to make individuals and society good. The Constitution marked a significant change in this thinking because it established a federal *republic* where the national government was prohibited from establishing religion. But we still debate the kind of political order the Constitution established. In fact, it underlies many of the *political* differences of opinion that are framed as *legal questions* in the religion cases that come before the Supreme Court.

What does the Constitution say about religion? Article VI provides that "no religious Test shall ever be required as a Qualification to any Office or public Trust under the United States." The First Amendment has two religion clauses: the **Establish Clause** and the **Free Exercise Clause**: "Congress shall make no law…respecting the establishment of religion or prohibiting the free exercise thereof." But the public, judges, and other government officials do not read the First Amendment to mean there can be *no* laws limiting freedom of religion.

16.22 | *Freedom of Religion: the Establishment Clause*

There are two interpretations of the Establishment Clause: the Wall of Separation and Accommodation. The **Wall of Separation** reading holds that the government cannot establish a religion as the official religion of the country, establish religious belief (as opposed to atheism or agnosticism) as the official position of the country, or support or oppose a particular denomination or religion in general. The Wall is a metaphor for the separation of church and state (government). The **Accommodation** reading is that the government can *accommodate* or support religions and religious beliefs as long it does not declare an official religion or help or hurt a particular religion. The Accommodation reading allows fairly extensive government support for religion (e.g., school prayer, school aid, tax credits for tuition) and public displays of religious symbols and items (e.g., the Ten Commandments, crèches, crosses and crucifixes, and other religious icons). These two readings of the First Amendment Establishment Clause have consistently divided political conservatives and political liberals as well as legal conservatives and legal liberals. Liberals tend to be secularists who support the Wall of Separation; conservatives tend to be religionists who support government involvement with religion and moral values.

The colonists explicitly believed that government and politics had explicitly religious purposes. Their founding documents such as the Mayflower Compact described government as responsible for making people morally good (as defined by the tenets of an established church) and politics as a community's efforts to make people morally good (by legislating morality). During the colonial era people came to the new world for, among other reasons, religious freedom. Colonial governments established official churches and used laws for religious purposes including church attendance and punishing blasphemy. The ratification of the Bill of Rights changed the relationship between church and state.

But studying religion and American politics reveals ongoing debates about the nature of the relationship between religion and government, debates that have been renewed by the increased religiosity in American politics over the past several decades. In fact, one dimension of the culture wars is the fight over the relationship between church and state.

The Supreme Court developed the **Lemon Test** to help guide decisions about when government support for religion violates the Establishment Clause. Lemon v. Kurtzman (1971) presented a claim that Pennsylvania and Rhode Island laws providing public support for teacher salaries, textbooks, and other instructional materials in non-public (primarily Catholic) schools violated the Establishment Clause. Chief Justice Burger upheld the laws and explained the three-pronged test to be used in such cases—a test that came to be called the Lemon Test. First, the law must have a *secular legislative purpose* (in this case, the state aid helped educate children). Second, the law must *neither help nor hurt religion.* Third, the law must *not foster excessive government entanglement* with religion. The Lemon Test is still used today. However, political conservatives are critical of the Lemon Test for being too separationist, and they advocate the Accommodation reading of the Establishment Clause. The conservative justices on the Supreme Court share this view and it possible that the Court will eliminate the Lemon Test or change its application to allow Accommodation on matters of religion and government, church and state.

Although the Establishment Clause and the Free Exercise Clause are two separate provisions of the First Amendment, they are related in the sense that government support for one religion or denomination can limit the free exercise of individuals who belong to religions other than the one or ones supported by the government.

16.23 | *Freedom of Religion: the Free Exercise Clause*

Despite the absolutist language of the First Amendment, the American public, government officials, and the courts have never read it to mean that there can be no limits on freedom of religion. The Free Exercise Clause has always been understood to mean that government can limit free exercise of religion. This apparently unusual reading of the Clause can be traced to the Supreme Court's ruling in the landmark 19th Century case *Reynolds v. U.S.* (1879).

The case arose from a law passed by Congress to prohibit the Mormon Church's practice of bigamy. The law, the Anti-Bigamy Act, made bigamy a federal offense. George Reynolds was prosecuted in the federal district court for the Territory of Utah with bigamy in violation of the Act: "Every person having a husband or wife living, who marries another, whether married or single, in a Territory, or other place over which the United States have exclusive jurisdiction, is guilty of bigamy, and shall be punished by a fine of not more than $500, and by imprisonment for a term of not more than five years." Reynolds was a Mormon who argued that church doctrine required male Mormons to practice polygamy. He asked the trial court "to instruct the jury that if they found from the evidence that he was married...in pursuance of and in conformity with what he believed at the time to be a religious duty," then the jury verdict must be "not guilty."

The Supreme Court acknowledged that Reynolds sincerely believed that this duty was of "divine origin" and that male members of the Church who did not practice polygamy would be punished by "damnation in the life to come." The Court noted that the First Amendment expressly prohibited Congress from passing a law restricting the free exercise of religion. However, it also noted that the government has always been allowed to regulate certain aspects of religious freedom. Some of the colonies and states established churches and punished certain religious beliefs and practices. In 1784 Virginia considered a bill to provide state support for "for teachers of the Christian religion." James Madison wrote *Memorial and Remonstrance* in opposition to the bill. Not only was the bill to provide for teachers of Christianity defeated, the Virginia Assembly passed Thomas Jefferson's bill "establishing religious freedom." The act described government efforts to restrain ideas because of their supposed "ill tendency" as a threat to religious liberty. Jefferson maintained that government power should be limited to "overt acts against peace and good order," that it should not have any power "in the field of opinion." According to Jefferson, beliefs are the business of the Church and actions are the business of the government. This principle separating religious beliefs and political opinions from religious and political actions remains an important principle limiting the scope of government power. A little more than a year after the passage of this Virginia statute, the members of the constitutional convention drafted the Constitution. Jefferson was disappointed that the new Constitution did not specifically guarantee freedom of religion but he supported ratification because he believed the Constitution could be improved by an amendment specifically limiting government power to restrict religious freedom. The first session of the first Congress did so by proposing the First Amendment.

In *Reynolds*, the Court quoted Jefferson's belief that religion is a private matter "solely between man and his god." Accordingly, a person is accountable only to God "for his faith or his worship." The legislative powers of government "reach actions only, and not opinions... " This distinction between faith and actions remains one of the most important rules for determining the limits of government power. According to Jefferson, the First Amendment meant that "the whole American people" declared that Congress could make no law respecting an establishment of religion or prohibiting the free exercise thereof," thereby building a wall of separation between church and state. The Reynolds Court considered Jefferson's view "an authoritative declaration of the scope and effect" of the First Amendment: "Congress was deprived of all legislative power over mere opinion, but was left free to reach actions which were in violation of social duties or subversive of good order."

Think About it!

Should the First Amendment be read to prohibit *any* law that limits the free exercise of religion? Snake handling? See the CNN video of snake handlers in Tennessee at http://www.youtube.com/watch?v=cwBVcsWYJd8

The Court then explained why polygamy was not protected by the First Amendment, why Congress could make a law prohibited polygamy: "Polygamy has always been odious among the northern and western nations of Europe, and, until the establishment of the Mormon Church, was almost exclusively a feature of the life of Asiatic and of African people. At common law, the second marriage was always void..., and from the earliest history of England polygamy has been treated as an offence against society."

Reynolds created two legal principles that are still used today to decide civil liberties cases. The first principle is that the First Amendment does not guarantee absolute freedom of religion. It guarantees absolute freedom of belief but it allows government to restrict religious practice. This distinction between religious belief and practice also applies to political expression: the government cannot restrict political ideas but it can restrict political actions. The second principle established in *Reynolds* is that government has the power to limit certain kinds of religious practices that were considered morally or socially unacceptable. Many state constitutions, for example, guarantee freedom of religion but only to those religious practices that are consistent with good moral order. The belief that state governments could prohibit certain morally or socially unacceptable practices is relevant to current debates about state laws that have traditionally defined marriage as between one man and one woman.

16.24 | *Free Exercise Today*

The Court first began reading the First Amendment to protect the free exercise of religion in the 1940s. In <u>Cantwell v. Connecticut</u> (1940), the Court ruled that the Free Exercise Clause of the First Amendment applied to the state governments, not just Congress or the federal government. This ruling signaled the Court's willingness to review state laws that historically restricted religious beliefs and practices that were considered unpopular, politically unacceptable, or immoral.

16.25 | *Defining Religion*

The Supreme Court has issued some very controversial rulings, such as the decision declaring that organized school prayer in public schools was unconstitutional, but the Court has been very wary of defining what beliefs systems constitute a religion. The definition of religion is important because there are many important legal benefits, including tax benefits that come with an organization being officially recognized as a religion. A related question is whether an individual's personal ethical or moral beliefs should be treated as the equivalent of a religion for the purposes of the First Amendment. One material benefit for an organization that is officially recognized as a religion is tax-exempt status. The legal benefit for an individual whose personal beliefs are recognized as religious beliefs, or the equivalent of religious beliefs include religious exemption from compulsory military service (the draft), religious exemptions from certain workplace rules, and religious exemptions from state drug laws for sacramental drug usage (e.g., peyote; marijuana; communion wine).

Three examples of government defining or officially recognizing religions are the "I am" movement, the Department of Veteran's Affairs policy on cemetery headstones, and the Internal Revenue Service rulings on the Church of Scientology.

Guy Ballard was a follower of the "I Am" movement. He solicited money from people for faith healing. The government accused Ballard's organization of being a business enterprise that was engaged in fraud while claiming to be a legitimate religious enterprise. Ballard maintained that his organization was a legitimate religious enterprise and took his case to the U.S. Supreme Court. The Court's reluctance to define what is and what is not a religion, and its reluctance to allow the government to define what is and what is not a religion, is evident in the 1944 case *U.S. v. Ballard*, 322 U.S. 78 (1944). The Court advised the government to be very reluctant to define what was and was not a legitimate religious activity, and to allow very broad claims of religious activity.[1]

Since 1944, the Court has broadened the definition of religion by accepting broad claims that beliefs were consistent with the concept of religion. The Court held that an individual could claim that personal "spiritual" beliefs or reasons of conscience (conscientious objector status) were legitimate reasons for religious exemption from the military draft. The claim to exemption from the military draft was not limited to identifiable religious doctrines.

There are many benefits that come with being an officially recognized religion. Must the government recognize witchcraft or humanism as religions? The Department of Veteran's Affairs had a policy to allow military families to choose any of 38 authorized images of religion that the Department would engrave on the headstones of veterans. The Department created a list of authorized headstone symbols. It included symbols for Christianity, Buddhism, Islam, Judaism, Sufism Reoriented, Eckiankar, and Seicho-No-Ie (Japanese), but not the Wiccan pentacle—a five-pointed star in a circle. The widows of two Wiccan combat veterans (approximately 1,800 active-duty service members identify themselves as Wiccan) sued the government claiming the policy that did not allow their religion's symbol on headstones violated the First Amendment. The court rulings have directed the Department of Veterans Affairs to allow the Wiccan symbol because the government should not have the power to define a legitimate or acceptable or officially recognized religion. In 2007, the Department finally agreed to allow the Wiccan pentacle to be engraved on veterans' headstones.[2]

The Church of Scientology engaged in a three decade-long political and legal battle to get the government (specifically, the Internal Revenue Service) to recognize Scientology and related organizations as a church. The government's initial denial of tax-exempt status was challenged in court. In 1993 the IRS finally recognized Scientology as a religious organization and granted it tax-exempt status as a 501(c)(3) religious or charitable organization for the purposes of the tax code.

> ### Check It Out!
> The Department of Veterans Affairs, National Cemetery Administration has an official list of "Available Emblems of Belief for Placement on Government Headstones and Markers."
> https://www.cem.va.gov/cem/hmm/emblems.asp

As organized religions adopt corporate structures that more closely resemble secular enterprises, and provide a broad range of services—education, counseling, social welfare, financial planning, day care, health care, retirement, professional seminars, communication, and media services—questions arise about religious exemptions from generally applicable laws. Can a television station be a church? The Internal Revenue Service (IRS) says, "Yes, it can."

> ### The European/German Model of Church/State
> "For Germans Religious Membership Comes at a Price"
> http://www.cbsnews.com/news/for-germans-religious-membership-comes-with-price/

16.26 | *Content Neutrality*

The court ruling striking down a Department of Veterans Administration policy that allowed some religious symbols as headstone markers but not others was based on a well-established legal principle: content neutrality. **Content Neutrality** is the principle that the government is supposed to be neutral toward political and religious beliefs. Government is not supposed to take sides in political debates by supporting some ideas but not others, or opposing some ideas but not others. Content neutrality applies broadly to freedom of expression both political and religious. It means that the government should not favor one religion over others, religious belief over non-belief, one ideology over others, or one political party over others. In effect, content neutrality means that government is not supposed to discriminate for or against ideas. If the government regulates religion, for example, the regulations should be content neutral. If the Internal Revenue Service grants religious organizations tax-exempt status, content neutrality prohibits the IRS from granting the status to some religious organizations but not others. The Department of Veterans Affairs might be able to deny all religious symbols on headstones, but the principle of content neutrality prohibited it from singling out the Wiccan symbol for exclusion. State laws that provide tax credits or vouchers for costs associated with sending children to religious schools cannot be limited to Christian schools, for example, without violating the idea of content neutrality. Content neutrality means that the government should not take sides in debates about religious or political ideas.

Of course, the government frequently and inevitably takes sides in debates about the relationship between religion and government and politics. The relationship between church and state was once very close. Most states once had Sunday closing laws which required most businesses to close on Sunday. These laws either established Sunday as the day for religious worship or merely designated Sunday as the day of rest. Today, Sunday closing laws (or laws limiting hours or the sale of certain products such as alcohol) are allowed for secular reasons, but not for religious purposes. But regardless of the reason, Sunday closing laws burden religious believers whose Sabbath did not fall on Sunday because observant Sabbatarians would have to keep their businesses closed two days a week. State and local laws can recognize Christmas as an official holiday, and even put up public displays such as crèches (nativity scenes), but that is primarily because Christmas is treated as a holiday season rather than a religious season.

State and local governments once required bible reading or organized school prayer in public schools. Legal challenges to such laws promoting religion in public schools have resulted in court rulings that they violate either the Establishment Clause or Free Exercise Clause of the First Amendment. These rulings weakened the relationship between church and state. The Supreme Court has upheld state laws that prohibit religious practices such as snake handling, and laws that require vaccinations even though an individual's religious beliefs forbid vaccinations. These laws are upheld if they serve a secular purpose (e.g., protecting public health) but struck down if they are intended to show public disapproval of a particular religious belief or practice.

States can also pass laws that are intended to discourage drug use even if they restrict freedom of religion. In *Employment Division of Oregon v. Smith* (1990) the Court upheld an Oregon law that was intended to discourage illegal drug use by denying unemployment benefits to workers who were fired drug use. Native Americans who were fired for sacramental drug use argued that the denial of unemployment benefits was unconstitutional because it restricted their freedom of religion. The Court ruled that it was reasonable for a state to pass such a law to discourage illegal drug usage, and that there was no evidence that the generally applicable law was passed to discriminate against Native Americans. Advocates of religious freedom were very critical of the ruling because the Court said that it would use the **reasonableness test** to determine whether a generally applicable law that substantially burdened freedom of religion was constitutional. Prior to this ruling, the Court used the **strict scrutiny test**, which required the government to have a compelling reason for burdening freedom of religion. Religion advocates saw the reasonableness standard as weakening constitutional protection of free exercise of religion. They lobbied Congress to pass The Religious Freedom Restoration Act of 1993 which by statute restored the strict scrutiny test.

A church in Boerne, Texas used the Religious Freedom Restoration Act to challenge the city's zoning laws that limited the church's building expansion. Zoning laws can prohibit churches in residential neighborhoods or limit remodeling and building expansion. The church was located in an historic district of Boerne, Texas. The city rejected the church's building expansion plan and the church went to court claiming the zoning restriction was a violation of freedom of religion. In _Boerne v. Flores_ (1997) the Supreme Court held that the Religious Freedom Restoration Act was unconstitutional because the Court, not the Congress, determines how to interpret the First Amendment. As a result, the courts still use the reasonableness test when determining whether a generally applicable law, a law that is intended to serve a legitimate public purpose rather than targeting specific unpopular religious practices, can limit freedom of religion. However, Congress then passed the Religious Land Use and Institutionalized Persons Act of 2000 to provide stronger protection for freedom of religion. Advocates of greater protection for religious freedom and more government support for religion challenge the secularist, Wall of Separation understanding of the relationship between church and state.

Think about it!

Should religious individuals, churches, and religious organizations be given religious exemptions from laws?

Is there currently a war on religion or a war on Christianity?

Although the Establishment Clause and the Free Exercise Clause are two different provisions of the First Amendment, they are not completely separate areas of constitutional law because government support for religion (which is an Establishment Clause matter) can limit the free exercise of religion. Some of the following cases show 1) how laws that provide spiritual support for religion can limit the free exercise of religion; and 2) how Free Exercise claims have changed over the years. Freedom of religion cases used to be brought primarily by *minorities* (e. g., religious minorities such as Mormons, Jews, Seventh-day Adventists) as well as secular minorities such as atheists). Today, Free Exercise cases are often brought by religious *majorities*. This change in freedom of religion claims is evident in conservative rhetoric about the need to fight a culture war **to take back** the country, the Constitution, and the American Judeo-Christian civilization. This rhetoric describes Christians as on the defense, fighting back against the forces of secularization, defending against those who are waging war on Christmas, or Christianity, or religion. Why are today's religion cases likely to be brought by religious majorities rather than religious minorities? Because the religious right (primarily Evangelical Christians) is a political movement that has since the 1970s adopted political and legal strategies to fight secularization. The "culture wars" include skirmishes that the religious right considers fighting back against the "war on religion" or the war on Christianity.

> John Oliver's investigation of televangelists on *This Week*

> The U.S. Department of Education documents describing freedom of religion in schools:
> http://www2.ed.gov/policy/gen/guid/religionandschools/index.html
> The Elementary and Secondary Education Act of 1965, as amended by the No Child Left Behind Act of 2001.

The conservative majority on the Rehnquist and Roberts Courts has adopted the Accommodation reading of the First Amendment. Is it relevant that the Roberts Court consisted of six Catholics and three Jews until Justice Scalia's death in 2016—when Neil Gorsuch, a Protestant joined the Court. Does religion matter? Does religion affect the way the justices read the religion clauses? Why would conservatives, including the conservative Supreme Court Justices, read the Establishment Clause **narrowly**—to allow government accommodation of religion—and read the Free Exercise Clause ***broadly***—to limit government power to restrict religious beliefs? In fact, in *Burwell v. Hobby Lobby, Inc.* (2015), the Court ruled that certain closely-held (family) corporations had First Amendment freedom of religion rights to challenge a law. The figure below portrays the different readings of the two religion clauses:

The Religion Clauses

Establishment

FREE EXERCISE

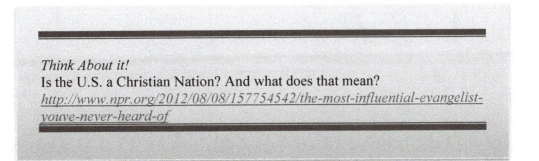

Think About it!
Is the U.S. a Christian Nation? And what does that mean?
http://www.npr.org/2012/08/08/157754542/the-most-influential-evangelist-youve-never-heard-of

16.3 | Freedom of Speech

Like freedom of religion, freedom of speech is not absolute: the government can restrict freedom of speech. Freedom of religious belief is absolute but religious action is not. Freedom of thought is absolute but action is not. Political actions are subject to a variety of *time, place, and manner* restrictions: people cannot say *whatever they want* (e.g., certain provocative words such as hate speech can be limited), *however they want* (using bullhorns or loud music or demonstrations), *wherever they want* (private property or certain public places such as residential neighborhoods or special places such as airports), or *whenever they want* (e.g., not at 4:00 in the morning). Despite these limits, there is a presumption of freedom of speech. The government bears the burden of proof to show the need to restrict freedom of expression. The U.S. is a capitalist country where the idea of a free market of goods and services has great appeal. The idea of a free marketplace of ideas is similarly appealing. The assumption is that government intervention in the political marketplace should be limited—that individuals should have freedom of choice of goods, services, and ideas.

The 50 state constitutions and virtually all of the national constitutions provide for freedom of expression. Comparing state constitutions and national constitutions can increase understanding of the First Amendment to the U.S. Constitution and the different approaches to guaranteeing freedom of expression.

Choose one or two states, or one or two countries, and compare how their constitutions provide for freedom of expression. Search state government web sites, national government web sites or sites that provide national constitutions such as http://www.constitution.org/cons/natlcons.htm

16.4 | Civil Rights

Civil liberties are constitutional protections for individual freedom. Civil rights are statutory laws that promote equality. Liberty and equality are democratic values but the relative emphasis on each value varies from country to country and over time. Democratic systems generally value individual freedom more than equality. Socialistic systems value equality more than freedom. In the U.S., equality is today a much more important value than it was when the nation was founded.

Equality *is* one of the political values extolled in the Declaration of Independence, which asserts human equality in especially memorable language:

> "We hold these truths to be self-evident, that all men are created equal, that they are endowed by their Creator with certain unalienable Rights, that among these are Life, Liberty and the pursuit of Happiness."

But the Declaration of Independence is not a governing document (the Constitution is the government document) or a legal document (it does not create any legally enforceable rights claims). Equality is not one of the political values embodied in the Constitution. The Constitution recognized slavery and did not recognize gender equality. Early statutes also recognized slavery. The Northwest Ordinance of 1787 prohibited slavery in parts of the country (western territories north of the Ohio River) but also provided that fugitive slaves could be "lawfully reclaimed." The Missouri Compromise of 1820 prohibited slavery in territories north of the parallel 36.5 degrees north of the equator. And the Fugitive Slave Law of 1793 authorized federal judges to recognize a slave owner's property rights claim to fugitive slaves.

16.41 | *Making Equality an American Value*

Equality only became an important political and legal value in the latter half of the 19th Century with the rhetoric of Abraham Lincoln, the three Civil War Amendments, and federal civil rights legislation enacted under the authority of the 14th Amendment. The Civil War Amendments were passed to guarantee the rights of newly freed slaves by limiting the power of states to discrimination on the basis of race. The 13th Amendment prohibited slavery. The Fourteenth Amendment prohibited states from making or enforcing any law that shall "deprive any person of life, liberty, or property, without due process of law; nor deny to any person within its jurisdiction the equal protection of the laws." The Fifteenth Amendment prohibited states from denying the right to vote on account of "race, color, or previous condition of servitude." Section 5 of the Fourteenth Amendment gave Congress the power to enforce "by appropriate legislation" the provisions of the Amendment.

These three Civil War Amendments became the constitutional foundation for civil rights legislation. Congress passed the Civil Rights Act of 1866 to guarantee "citizens, of every race and color…the same right, in every State and Territory…to make and enforce contracts, to sue, be parties, and give evidence, to inherit, purchase, lease, sell, hold, and convey real and personal property…" and enjoy other benefits of the laws. Congress passed the Civil Rights Act of 1875, which made it a federal offense for owners or operators of any public accommodations (including hotels, transportation, and places of amusement) to deny the enjoyment of those accommodations on account of race or religion. Innkeepers, theater owners, and a railroad company challenged the law as exceeding government power because it regulated private businesses. The Supreme Court agreed in *The Civil Rights Cases* (1883). The ruling greatly limited Congress's power to use the 14th Amendment as authority for laws promoting racial equality. As a result, matters of racial equality were left to state laws until the 1930s and 1940s. In *Brown v. Mississippi* (1936), the Supreme Court abandoned its traditional hands-off policy toward state criminal justice amid growing federal concern about racial discrimination. In *Brown* the Court unanimously held that police torture of a black suspect in order to compel a confession, questioning that was euphemistically called ***the third degree***, violated due process of law. The subsequent federal court rulings in cases involving racial administration of criminal justice were part of the broader civil rights movement in other areas of public policy.

"The law, in its majestic equality, forbids the rich as well as the poor to sleep under bridges, to beg in the streets, and to steal bread."

Anatole France,
*The Red Lily, 1894,
chapter 7*

The Civil Rights Act of 1964 and the Voting Rights Act of 1965 are major landmarks in the civil rights movement. The Civil Rights Act of 1964 expanded the federal government's power to act to eliminate a broad range of discriminatory actions. Congress passed the Act to "enforce the constitutional right to vote, to confer jurisdiction upon the district courts of the United States to provide injunctive relief against discrimination in public accommodations, to authorize the Attorney General to institute suits to protect constitutional rights in public facilities and public education, to extend the Commission on Civil Rights, to prevent discrimination in federally assisted programs, to establish a Commission on Equal Employment Opportunity, and for other purposes." The Voting Rights Act of 1965 expanded the federal government's power to remedy a specific type of racial discrimination, racial discrimination in voting, that directly affected how the democratic process worked. Section 2 of the 1965 Act provided that "No voting qualification or prerequisite to voting, or standard, practice, or procedure shall be imposed or applied by any State or political subdivision to deny or abridge the right of any citizen of the United States to vote on account of race or color."

16.42 | *Does Equality Mean Treating Everyone the Same*?

Each of the various civil liberties and rights movements that made equality a more important political value prompted debates about the meaning of equality. It turns out that equality is more complicated that it initially seems, and defining it is harder than one might expect. Equality does *not* mean treating everyone the same. This chapter began with a famous 1894 quote of the French author, Anatole France, who sarcastically praised a law that prohibited anyone, rich and poor alike, to sleep under the bridges of Paris as egalitarian. On its face, the law treated everyone equally—but of course not everyone needs to sleep under bridges. Almost all laws create categories of individuals and actions, and treat them differently. State driver's license laws treat people different based on age: very young people and sometimes very old people are treated different than middle-aged people. Food stamp programs and Medicaid are means-tested programs: they limit benefits to individuals below certain income levels. Income tax rates vary according to income levels. Laws typically limit the rights of felons to vote, possess firearms, or hold certain kinds of jobs. Some government benefits are limited to veterans while others are limited to married people. Social security is an age and income based program. Medicaid is a program that provides benefits for the poor.

Equality is a political value with social, economic, political, and legal dimensions. The Equal Protection of the Laws is generally understood to require states to provide legal equality to all persons within their jurisdiction. Legal equality means equal standing before the law, but not social or economic equality. Equality does not mean that everyone must be treated the same. Laws create classifications that treat individuals different. In one sense, then, legislation discriminates by treating individuals and actions differently. This definition of discrimination or treating people different is not what is commonly understood as discrimination. Discrimination is usually used to mean prejudice or bias against individuals or groups based on inappropriate or invalid reasons. This is the pejorative meaning of discrimination. Discrimination also has a positive meaning whereby "to discriminate" means the ability to see or make fine distinctions among individuals, objects, values, or actions. It refers to making valid distinctions or differences between individuals.

16.43 | *Expanding federal civil rights law: the constitutional revolution of 1937*

As noted in the chapter on the judiciary, 1937 is an important date in U.S. constitutional history because the Court changed from protecting business from government regulation to protecting political liberties. During the latter part of the 19th Century and into the 1930s, the Supreme Court had struck down many federal and state laws that regulated business and economic activity because the Court saw its role as protecting business from government regulation. During the Great Depression, for example, the Court struck down some of the most important provisions of the Roosevelt Administration's New Deal legislation. The result was a constitutional conflict between the president, and the Court. President Roosevelt used his "bully pulpit" to take to the radio airwaves to blame the Court for not being a team player. Roosevelt's famous March 9, 1937 Fireside scolded the Court for not being part of the three-horse team that had to pull together if the country were to get out of the Great Depression.[3] Roosevelt also took action against the Court. He proposed a court-packing plan to increase the size of the Court to a maximum of fifteen Justices, with the additional six Justices expected to support the President's views on government power to regulate the economy because the President would nominate them.

Against the background of these political pressures, the Court changed its rulings on the government's economic regulatory power. In late 1936, Justice Roberts, who had been voting with a conservative bloc of Justices who struck down the New Deal laws, changed sides and began to vote with the liberal bloc that upheld New Deal economic regulatory legislation. This was the constitutional revolution of 1937. Retirements eventually gave President Roosevelt the opportunity to change the ideological balance on the Court, and he appointed eight Justices during his terms in office. As a result, the Court changed its role from one that protected economic liberties from government regulation to one that protected political liberties. And one of the Court's special concerns was racial discrimination

16.44 | *Racial Classifications*

Dred Scott v. Sanford (1857) is a landmark Supreme Court case that is famous, or infamous, for its ruling limiting an individual slave's constitutional rights and Congress's power to limit slavery. Scott was a slave whose owner took him to Illinois and an area of the Louisiana Territory that prohibited slavery. Scott filed a lawsuit claiming that his residence in areas that prohibited slavery made him a free man. The Supreme Court ruled that Scott, as a slave, was not a citizen and could not go to court to claim that he was free. It also ruled the Missouri Compromise of 1820, which prohibited slavery in certain states, unconstitutional. The *Dred Scott* ruling made it clear that slavery was not likely to be resolved politically, and that a civil war was likely.[4]

The three constitutional amendments that were passed after the Civil War were intended to prohibit state action that discriminated against Blacks. Congress also passed civil rights statutes to promote racial equality. But in *The Civil Rights Cases* (1883), the Court greatly limited the federal government's power to regulate racial discrimination.[5] And in *Plessy v. Ferguson* (1896) the Court held that states could by law require racial segregation as long as the law did not treat one race better than another. This was the famous **Separate but Equal Doctrine** that allowed states to have racial segregation as a matter of public policy for schools, public accommodations, and other services and facilities. Justice Harlan's dissenting opinion in *Plessy* used memorable language to argue that racial segregation was unconstitutional: "Our Constitution is colorblind, and neither knows nor tolerates classes among citizens."[6] But the majority on the Court held that states could discriminate between blacks and whites, by requiring segregation, as long as the separation of the races did not include treating them unequally.

16.45 | *The Story of School Desegregation*

The story of school desegregation is a classic story of political litigation. Political litigation is the use of litigation to change public policy. Organizations such as the National Association for the Advancement of Colored People used the legal arena (courts) to get what they could not get in the political arena: desegregation of public schools. The state political systems that created racial segregation in public schools continued to support segregation despite political efforts advocating desegregation. As a result, advocates of desegregation went to the federal courts arguing that segregation violated the 14th Amendment's equal protection of the laws. The legal strategy worked. The Supreme Court began chipping away at the **Separate but Equal** doctrine. In *Missouri ex rel. Gaines v. Canada* (1938) the Court struck down a Missouri law that denied Blacks admission to the state's law school, but provided money for Blacks to attend out-of-state law schools. Then in 1950 (*Sweatt v. Painter*) the Court struck down a Texas law that created a separate law school for Blacks as a way to avoid having to admit a Black man to the University of Texas Law School. And on the same day that the Court decided, the Court decided *McLaurin v. Oklahoma State Regents* (1950) McLaurin was a Black man who was admitted to the University of Oklahoma's School of Education graduate school, but a state law required that he be segregated from other doctoral students: separate seating in the classroom; designated cafeteria table; separate library table. The Court ruled that this violated the equal protection of the laws because the treatment was separate but unequal. In these three cases the Court struck down the state segregated education policies because they did not provide separate but equal educational opportunities. The NAACP and other advocates of desegregation continued to target the separate but equal doctrine. Finally, in the landmark case of *Brown v. Board of Education of Topeka, Kansas* (1954), the Court ruled that de jure segregation in public schools, segregation by law, was unconstitutional. The separate but equal doctrine was itself unconstitutional.[7]

The *Brown* ruling was extremely controversial. Critics of Chief Justice Earl Warren put up "Save Our Republic: Impeach Earl Warren" highway billboards because Warren presided over a Court that issued a broad range of controversial rulings. It integrated public schools, and its school prayer rulings "kicked God out of" public schools. The backlash against these rulings included government officials who asserted states' rights to oppose expanded federal power over race relations. One classic statement of federalism-based states' rights opposition to *Brown v. Board* is the 1956 Southern Manifesto. Strong opposition to the *Brown* ruling prompted the Florida Legislature to pass an Interposition Resolution in 1957. Interposition is a Civil War-era doctrine that asserts that a state, as a sovereign entity in the U.S. system of federalism, has the power to "interpose" itself between the people of the state and the federal government whenever the state believes the federal action is unconstitutional. Interposition is a doctrine that gives states power to protect the people from unwarranted federal action.

At the time of the *Brown* ruling, William H. Rehnquist, who went on to become Chief Justice of the Supreme Court, served as a law clerk to Justice Jackson. Rehnquist wrote a controversial *Memorandum* to Justice Jackson which concluded that the **Separate but Equal Doctrine** was still good law and should be upheld.[8] Rehnquist's understanding of the legislative history of the intentions of the Framers of the 14th Amendment may be accurate. And requiring racial segregation while treating the races equally, for example by requiring that blacks and whites sit in alternate rows rather than requiring blacks to sit in the back of the bus, may technically meet the "equal protection of the laws" standard. However, the history of separation was inequality. And the argument that the Constitution allows racial apartheid as long as the races are treated equally is no longer considered politically acceptable.

The *Brown* ruling did not order the immediate desegregation of public schools. The Court stated that the segregated school systems had to be dismantled "With all deliberate speed." Some states took advantage of this ambiguous phrase to choose deliberation rather than speed.[9] Beginning in the latter 1960s, after more than a decade of little or no action to dismantle the system of segregated public schools, courts began to order actions to integrate public schools. These actions included court-ordered busing, judicial drawing of school attendance zones, racial quotas, and affirmative action programs.

Court rulings that ordered busing to dismantle segregated schools were always controversial, but court-ordered busing was especially controversial when it was used to remedy *de facto* racial segregation. *Brown* ruled *de jure* segregation unconstitutional. *De jure* segregation is segregation "by law." *De jure* segregation includes segregation that results from any government policy or official actions (such as drawing school attendance boundaries to produce racially segregated schools). *De facto* segregation is segregation that results "by fact." *De facto* segregation results from private actions such as housing patterns where people of one race or ethnicity or class decide to live with others of the same racial or ethnic or economic background and that just happens to result in segregation. As the country became more conservative during the latter 1970s and 1980s, public opposition to school busing and other race-based remedies for segregated schools increased. And in an interesting twist, conservatives turned to Justice Harlan's 19th Century ideal of a color blind Constitution, which he used to argue that state laws requiring racial segregation were unconstitutional, to argue that affirmative action policies, which take race into consideration when making school admissions decisions or employment decisions, are unconstitutional. Critics of affirmative action also oppose the recognition of group rights rather than individual rights. Indeed, the conservatives on the Rehnquist and Roberts

Courts have been very skeptical of affirmative action and closely scrutinize affirmative action policies to determine whether they violate equal protection of the laws.[10]

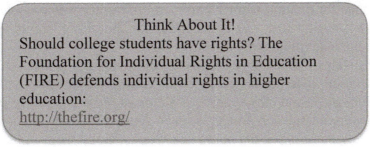

Think About It!
Should college students have rights? The Foundation for Individual Rights in Education (FIRE) defends individual rights in higher education:
http://thefire.org/

16.46 | *Employment Law*

The civil rights movements also targeted employment discrimination. Efforts to expand equal opportunity in employment focused on personnel policies related to hiring, firing, and promotion; equal pay for equal work; and awarding business contracts to minority companies. One strategy was to use affirmative action to remedy past discriminatory practices and promote equality. The use of affirmative action to produce a more diverse work force, one that reflected the racial composition of the community was very controversial. Critics called the affirmative action use of racial or gender quotas or targets in employment settings reverse discrimination. As public support for using equal rights laws to promote greater equality in the workplace decreased, the courts limited the use of affirmative action policies particularly race-based policies.

The civil rights movement to end racial discrimination had one unintended negative consequence. Efforts to end racial segregation unintentionally contributed to the breakup of black economic communities that had developed in segregated areas. The end of *de jure* racial segregation meant that members of the black community were able to live in other neighborhoods and buy goods and services outside of the black business community. This is one of the reasons for the decline in the number of black-owned businesses after desegregation.

Think About It!
"One Family's Effort to Buy Black for a Year."
http://www.pbs.org/newshour/bb/business-jan-june12-makingsense_06-19/

16.47 | *Gender*

Historically, government officials and private sector individuals (such as employers) were free to treat people differently based on gender. The Supreme Court did not examine gender-based legislative classifications until the 1970s. Prior to that time period, the Court did not consider laws that treated women different than men a violation of the Fourteenth Amendment. Gender discrimination was presumed to be constitutional. Laws that treated the "second" sex or the "weaker" sex different from the "first sex" or the "stronger" sex were presumed to reflect natural differences, social values, or public policy preferences. The policy preference for treating women and men differently was considered a matter of politics, not law, a question that was appropriate for the elected representatives of the people rather than the legal judgments of courts.

As a result, states historically used their policy making powers to pass laws that treated men and women different for purposes of voting, employment, education, social welfare benefits, jury duty, and other purposes. Some of these laws were **paternalistic** in the sense that they were intended to protect women. A good example of such a paternalistic law is the Oregon law that limited the hours that women could work in factories. The law was challenged in court but the Supreme Court upheld the law in _Muller v. Oregon_ (1908). Justice Brewer's opinion for the majority reflected the widely accepted belief that it was reasonable for a state legislature to think that women's physical constitution and the social role assigned to women in raising children might merit special protection in the workplace:

> "….That woman's physical structure and the performance of maternal functions place her at a disadvantage in the struggle for subsistence is obvious. This is especially true when the burdens of motherhood are upon her. Even when they are not, by abundant testimony of the medical fraternity, continuance for a long time on her feet at work, repeating this from day to day, tends to injurious effects upon the body, and, as healthy mothers are essential to vigorous offspring, the physical wellbeing of woman becomes an object of public interest and care in order to preserve the strength and vigor of the race. …[H]istory discloses the fact that woman has always been dependent upon man. He established his control at the outset by superior physical strength, and this control in various forms, with diminishing intensity, has continued to the present. As minors, though not to the same extent, she has been looked upon in the courts as needing especial care that her rights may be preserved…." [There are individual exceptions but women are generally not equal to men and are therefore properly placed in a class to be protected by legislation]. "It is impossible to close one's eyes to the fact that she still looks to her brother, and depends upon him. Even though all restrictions on political, personal, and contractual rights were taken away, and she stood, so far as statutes are concerned, upon an absolutely equal plane with him, it would still be true that she is so constituted that she will rest upon and look to him for protection; that her physical structure and a proper discharge of her maternal functions—having in view not merely her own health, but the wellbeing of the race— justify legislation to protect her from the greed, as well as the passion, of man. The limitations which this statute places upon her contractual powers, upon her right to agree with her employer as to the time she shall labor, are not imposed solely for her benefit, but also largely for the benefit of all."

Justice Brewer described gender protective laws as benefiting both women **and** society as a whole. This _gender difference rationale_ reflected the conventional wisdom of the day and provided the justification for a broad range of public policies that treated women different than men. For instance, states prohibited women from serving on juries.[11] Equality does not mean treating everyone the same—but it does require having good reasons for treating people different. The black civil rights movement provided inspiration and energy for the women's rights movement. Gender discrimination was put on the government's agenda by the women's rights movement. The women's rights movement challenged traditional assumptions about how public policy could treat women different

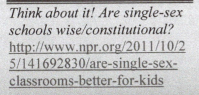

Think about it! Are single-sex schools wise/constitutional?
http://www.npr.org/2011/10/2
5/141692830/are-single-sex-
classrooms-better-for-kids

than men, lobbied for statutory laws that prohibited gender discrimination, advocated for an equal rights amendment to the U.S. Constitution, and adopted a legal strategy of political litigation that filed lawsuits that were intended to change public policy toward women.

In 1963 Congress amended the Fair Labor Standards Act to require equal pay for equal work. The Civil Rights Act of 1964 prohibited gender discrimination by employers and labor unions. Title VII of the Civil Rights Act of 1964 prohibits sexual harassment in the workplace. In 1972, the Civil Rights Act was amended to require in Title IX that all programs or activities, including educational institutions, provide equal athletic facilities and opportunities for women. Title IX had a major impact on women's opportunities. Compare the experience of Kathrine Switzer, who in 1967 was the first women to run in the Boston Marathon with women's opportunities 40 years after Title IX.

The women's movement also worked for passage of an Equal Rights Amendment. Congress proposed the ERA in 1972 but it was never ratified by the required three-quarters of the states. Only 35 of the required 38 states ratified the ERA.[12] The political litigation

The 40th Anniversary of the 1972 Title IX Amendments marked an occasion to assess its impact on educational opportunity. One aspect of the changes is discussed in the National Public Radio report, "40 Years On, Title IX Still Shapes Female Athletes."
http://www.npr.org/2012/06/22/155529815/40-years-on-title-ix-still-shapes-female-athletes

strategy was been successful. Court rulings limited gender discrimination. Women's rights advocates argued that courts should treat gender more like race when considering the enforcement of anti-discrimination laws. Doing so would make gender discrimination more like racial discrimination: a suspect classification. The Court did hold that the Fourteenth Amendment's equal protection clause applied to women, but it never accepted the argument that gender discrimination was analogous to racial discrimination. Unlike race-based legislative classifications, which are considered suspect classifications that trigger strict scrutiny, the Court has never considered gender classifications **suspect classifications** that trigger strict scrutiny.[13] But courts do closely scrutinize laws that treated people different based on gender, and fewer gender classifications are now considered constitutional. For example, in *U.S. v. Virginia* (1996) the Court ruled that it was unconstitutional for Virginia to create a separate female military institute as a remedy for a court-ordered finding that the state's male Virginia Military Institute violated the equal protection clause of the Fourteenth Amendment.

One interesting twist in the debates about racial and gender segregation in education is the recent emphasis on the quality of the education rather than racial or gender integration. Are single-sex schools wise (that is good educational policy)? Are they legal?

Gender equality is also an issue in the political and legal debates over abortion policy. The impact on women of state laws prohibiting abortion was a central issue in the decision to adopt a legal strategy to challenge abortion laws, a decision that resulted in the Roe v. Wade (1973) ruling that the right to privacy included the decision whether to continue or terminate a pregnancy.

> Think About It! Act on It!
> Can an individual make a difference by deciding to act on something they believe in? Listen to Sarah Weddington's story.
> http://www.bbc.co.uk/programmes/p0133chj

16.48 | Other Legislative classifications

Alienage? Most of the civil liberties provisions refer to "people" or "persons." The Fifth Amendment provides that no "person" shall be deprived of due process of law. The 14th Amendment prohibits states from denying "to any person" within its jurisdiction the equal protection of the laws. However, these constitutional provisions do not mean that citizens and non-citizens have the same constitutional rights. There are important differences between the rights of citizens and non-citizens because citizenship is a legal status that is relevant in many areas of law. Aliens do not have the same rights as citizens when aliens are entering the United States or when challenging the decision to be deported. Early in the nation's history, federal legislation targeted aliens, both alien enemies and alien friends. The Alien and Sedition Acts of 1798 are examples of early federal laws that not only treated aliens different than citizens but subjected aliens to harsh treatment. The Alien Act provided that in time of war or a threat against the territorial integrity of the U.S., the president could arrest and deport as "enemy aliens" any males 14 years or older who are citizens or residents of the "hostile" country.

For most of the 20th Century, immigration matters were entirely political in the sense that Congress had plenary power to determine immigration policy. However, as the various civil rights movements increased expectations of equality for more and more individuals in more and more settings, the legal protections afforded aliens expanded. In a 1971 case, *Graham v. Richardson*, the Court held that **alienage** was a suspect classification, and that an Arizona law that limited welfare benefits to citizens and created residency requirements for aliens violated the 14th Amendment provision that prohibited a state from denying to any person within its jurisdiction the equal protection of the laws. And in a 1982 case, *Plyler v. Doe*, the Court ruled that Texas could not deny public education to undocumented aliens.

But states were not required to treat aliens and non-residents the same as citizens who were residents of the state. A state can charge out-of-state individuals higher college tuition rates and higher fishing and hunting license fees for example. And states can require that individuals who hold certain public sector jobs (including teachers and police officers) be citizens. And states can restrict certain government benefits to citizens. In an interesting 2001 case dealing with a federal citizenship law that was based on both alienage and gender classification, the Court explained that the government had a valid legislative purpose when imposing different requirements for a child to become a citizen depending upon whether the citizen parent is the mother or the father. The law made it easier for a child to become a citizen if the mother was the citizen parent than if the father was the citizen parent. So public policy can make a distinction between a citizen mother and a citizen father. This is an example of how equality, and equal protection of the laws, does not mean treating everyone the same.[14]

Personhood? Constitutional rights have been expanded to corporations, which are artificial persons. Should constitutional rights be expanded to unborn persons or pre-born persons or fetuses? Pro-life groups have supported a personhood amendment which would specify that the word person in the Fourteenth Amendment includes unborn children so that they could not be denied due process or equal protection of the laws.

Class? Public policies can also treat people different based on income without violating the equal protection of the laws. Public policies that provide government benefits (social security or Medicaid or food stamps) based on income create economic classifications. Tax policies may also treat people different based on income. Progressive income tax laws treat individuals different based on their income, with lower tax rates for lower income levels and higher rates for higher income levels. The history of the federal income tax shows how this occurs. In 1861, Congress passed an income tax law that established a flat 3% tax on incomes over $800. Since then, income tax law has incorporated graduated and even progressive tax rates, and inheritance taxes typically treat estates different based on the size of the estate. What's in a name? The NPR story "How We Got from Estate Tax to 'Death Tax'" explains the importance of political rhetoric in framing the terms of political debates.

Most states have public school funding policies that rely heavily on property taxes. The result is large disparities in the amount of money available to school districts. School districts in rich communities have much more money than school districts in poor communities. Does this violate the 14th Amendment equal protection of the laws? The San Antonio Independent School District filed a lawsuit on behalf of its poorer students arguing that Texas' property tax violated the equal protection of the laws. The Supreme Court disagreed, holding that the 14th Amendment does not require exactly equal funding of districts, that some funding disparities are legal. Most states do transfer some money from wealthier communities to poorer communities in order to reduce funding disparities. These Robin Hood policies of taking from the rich and giving to the poor are generally supported by liberals more than conservatives.

16.5 | The Conservative Civil Rights Movement

The story of civil rights is usually told as the story of (primarily) liberals who used political litigation to achieve greater equality for various political minorities: blacks, women, the elderly, children, gays/lesbians, aliens, handicapped, patients, even prisoners. There is also a conservative civil rights movement that advocates for *conservative* rights: the right to life (to define an unborn child or fetus as a person); property rights; business rights; gun rights; and religious rights. Like liberal public interest groups before them, conservative public interest groups adopted political and legal strategies to achieve their public policy goals. They used political litigation to challenge campaign finance regulations, zoning laws, and gun control laws. These efforts have been very successful in changing the law. The

Supreme Court has ruled that the Second Amendment guarantees an individual right to keep and bear arms, defined campaign contributions as freedom of expression, and expanded property rights claims against government zoning and environmental regulations.

16.6 | Crime Policy

One answer to the question "Why do we have government?" is that creating and maintaining public safety is a core government function. Preventing and investigating crime, prosecuting and trying suspects, and punishing convicted offenders are basic responsibilities of governments everywhere. Public opinion polls indicate that crime is one the most important problems facing the nation.

	% Mentioning
Economy in general	31
Unemployment/Jobs	22
Dissatisfaction with government/Congress/politicians; poor leadership; corruption; abuse of power	11
Immigration/Illegal aliens	7
Poor healthcare/hospitals; high cost of healthcare	7
Natural disaster response/relief	7
Federal budget deficit/Federal debt	6
Fuel/Oil prices	5
Wars/War (nonspecific)/Fear of war	4
Lack of money	3
Ethics/Moral/Religious/Family decline; dishonesty	3
Situation/War in Afghanistan	3
Education/Poor education/Access to education	3
Situation/War in Iraq	3

Source: Gallup. July 8-11, 2010. "What do you think is the most important problem facing this country today?

The following sections have three main goals:
- Explaining ideological thinking about crime. It uses the crime control model of justice and the due process model of justice to explain conservative and liberal thinking about the causes of crime and criminal justice policies that are intended to fight crime.
- Providing basic information about criminal law. This includes constitutional law—particularly the criminal law provisions in the Bill of Rights—and statutory law.
- Describing the criminal justice system, particularly the police, the courts, and corrections.

Crime policy is central to the power problem because the government has the power to take a person's life, liberty, and property—as long as it does so after providing the person with due process of law. Americans expect government to provide safe homes, streets, subways, and parks. For most of the nation's history, criminal justice was almost exclusively the responsibility of state and local governments, but today all levels of government are involved with crime policy: local governments have police departments; state governments make and enforce criminal laws in the state; the federal government makes and enforces criminal laws for the nation; and international institutions make and enforce crime policies that target specific transnational criminal activity such as money laundering, drug dealing, and terrorism.

Elections have policy consequences. The president has a great deal of discretion to determine the criminal justice priorities of the Department of Justice. President Trump's Attorney General Jeff Session established a strong crime control record as a Republican Senator from Alabama. The Trump administration's Department of Justice has priorities that are very different than the Obama administration's Department of Justice. The Obama administration's DOJ priorities included

- Supporting a bipartisan criminal justice reform to end the mass incarceration that made the U.S. rank number one in the rate of incarceration;
- Making sentencing less punitive, particularly for low-level drug convictions such as marijuana possession;
- Establishing priorities for enforcement of immigration laws that targeted violent criminals for deportation; and
- Initiatives that investigated civil rights violations in police departments and implemented plans to reduce them by, among other things, increasing training.

Under Attorney General Sessions, the DOJ priorities were
- Stricter enforcement of immigration laws;
- Reviving the war on drugs;
- Ending the initiatives to reduce civil rights violations by police departments; and
- Emphasizing fighting street crime rather than white-collar (financial) crimes.

16.61 | *Crime Policy*

An ideology is a set of beliefs and a program for acting on them. One of the beliefs is typically about crime. Crime policy is one of the issues that over the last several decades have consistently divided liberals and conservatives, and Democrats and Republicans. There are ideological and partisan differences of opinion about the causes of crime, the best ways for criminal justice officials to fight crimes, and the purposes of punishment. Science and social science have extensively studied the causes of crime. There are two basic theories explaining the causes of crime: the human nature theory and the social theory. The **human nature theory** attributes crime to human nature generally and individually. Human nature is generally capable of evil, and individuals who commit crime have demonstrated that capacity. Accordingly, individuals should be held responsible for their criminal acts. There are actually two variations of human nature theory. The first variation is the belief that some people are simply born *bad*: they have *bad seed* or an *evil nature*. The second variation is that human beings are by nature rational actors who make choices. Criminals choose to commit a crime rather than to obey the law because they think they will gain from the illegal act. In everyday life, people calculate the costs and benefits of different courses of action, and some sometimes choose crime. They are to blame for crime.

The **social theory** of crime explains the fact of crime as caused by social circumstances, economic conditions, or cultural values. Accordingly, people are not born criminal. Criminals are made not born by social conditions such as poverty or wealth, domestic violence, racial or ethnic discrimination, neglect or abandonment or just a bad upbringing, poor education, or some other condition or

"A conservative is a liberal who has been mugged. **A liberal is a conservative who has been arrested.**" **Tom Wolfe,** *Bonfire of the Vanities* (1987)

treatment. Note that the above list includes both poverty and wealth as social causes of crime. Poverty is most often mentioned as a social cause of crime. Some crime figures are even portrayed sympathetically or even heroically because of their dire economic circumstances or their willingness to take from the rich and give to the poor. Far less attention is paid to wealth as a social cause of crime. But wealth, particularly the sense of entitlement or the opportunity to commit white-collar crimes such as fraud can be a social cause of crime.

Ideological beliefs about the causes of crime have a major impact on crime policy, particularly sentencing policies. The purposes of punishment include deterrence, incapacitation, retribution, and rehabilitation. The belief that criminals are evil justifies punishment policies that emphasize incapacitation and retribution. The belief that criminals are rational actors justifies policies that make the costs of crime higher than the benefits. The belief crime is caused by poverty or discrimination justifies punishment policy that encourages rehabilitation. The American political culture of individualism creates support for punishment policies that hold individuals responsible for their actions, including crimes.

The social theory of crime plays an interesting role in American popular culture, which includes memorable images of outlaws who are portrayed as people who were driven to their lives of crime by injustice. The social injustice (economic or political exploitation) transforms the victim into a Robin Hood figure who steals from the rich and powerful and gives to the poor and powerless. This is the mythology surrounding some of the notorious criminal figures in American history: Jesse James, Butch Cassidy and the Sundance Kid, Bonnie and Clyde (pictured), and even Al Capone. The enduring appeal of their criminal exploits is at least partly due to their images in popular culture as victims of social circumstances or outsiders who challenge a corrupt establishment.

In terms of the politics of crime, liberals generally support the social theory of crime. It has exposed liberals to the charge that they are *blame society firsters* who are soft on crime. Conservatives generally support the human nature theory. The fact that they blame individuals for their criminal acts and support punishment rather than rehabilitation has resulted in the fact that conservatives are considered tough-on-crime.

The Due Process and Crime Control Models of Justice are useful for explaining liberal and conservative thinking about crime.[15] The crime control model emphasizes effective crime fighting more than protecting individual rights. The due process model of justice emphasizes protecting individual rights by among other things providing due process of law to suspects and defendants because it is better for 100 guilty to go free than one innocent person found guilty. The two models represent the ends of a spectrum of thinking about crime. Members of the general public, government officials, and even judges are called conservative or liberal because of how much they value rights or effective crime fighting. Liberals generally support using due process rights to check the government's power while conservatives generally defend the power of police and prosecutors as key figures in the war on crime.

Incarceration (imprisonment) is not the only form of punishment, but it is certainly the one that receives the most public attention. Trials and prisons capture the public's imagination. The rate of incarceration is one of the most common measures of sentencing policy. The following describes some changes in punishment policy over roughly the last century.

Table 16.63
RATE (PER 100,000 RESIDENTS) OF SENTENCED PRISONERS IN STATE AND FEDERAL INSTITUTIONS
[*Sourcebook of Criminal Justice Statistics, 1985*; and Bureau of Justice Statistics]

Year	Rate (per 100,000 Residents)
1925	79
1930	104
1935	113
1940	131
1945	98
1950	109
1955	112
1960	117
1965	108
1970	96
1975	111
1980	138
1985	201
1990	292
2000	481
2002	702
2005	737
2010	500

The above table shows changes in the RATE of incarceration for various years. The total prison population on December 31, 2010 was 1,612,000. The increase in the rate beginning in the latter 1970s and the recent decline beginning in 2010 reveal the life cycle of the crime control model of justice.

Graph 16.63[16]

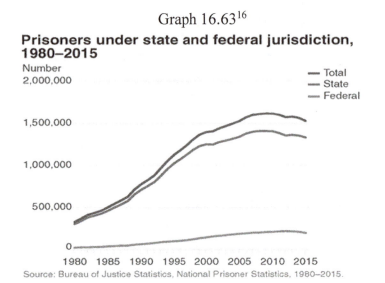

Prisoners under state and federal jurisdiction, 1980–2015

Source: Bureau of Justice Statistics, National Prisoner Statistics, 1980–2015.

    Social scientists try to explain public policies. What explains crime policy—particularly rates of incarceration? What explains the long-term increase in the rates of incarceration, and then what explains what appeared to be the recent decrease in the rate of incarceration beginning around 2010? Does the U.S. have high, medium, or low rates of incarceration? One way to determine whether the rates are high or low is to examine historical rates, look at trends, and to compare sentencing rates with other countries.

"We're Number One!" U.S. Inmate Count Dwarfs Rest of World
http://www.nytimes.com/2008/04/23/us/23prison.html?_r=1&scp=2&sq=rate+of
+incarceration&st=nyt&oref=slogin
http://www.sentencingproject.org/template/page.cfm?id=107
http://www.sentencingproject.org/doc/publications/inc_comparative_intl.pdf

It is logical to expect that there is a causal relationship between crime rates and the rate of incarceration, so that a country like the U.S. with a high crime rate would also have a high rate of incarceration. And it is logical to expect that increases in crime rates would produce increases in the rate of incarceration. But the relationship between crime and punishment is more complicated than simply changes in the rate of crime (increases or decreases) produce changes in the rate of incarceration (increases or decreases).

For example, for the past several decades the crime rate has been stable or even declining while the rate of imprisonment continued to increase. So legal scholars have studied other variables that might explain rates of incarceration:

- The Media Effect. Do media news stories and legal fiction tend to promote crime control values by focusing on crime as a public problem independent of actual crime rates?
- Ideology. Is conservative thinking about crime, specifically crime control values, a factor that explains the high rate of incarceration despite stable or even declining crime rates?
- Economics. Crime and punishment are big business. Does privatization—specifically the creation of a private, for-profit sector of the economy that makes money from imprisoning criminals and detaining immigrants create incentives for businesses to increase rates of incarceration?

When he left office, President Dwight Eisenhower warned the country about the creation of a military-industrial complex. The military-industrial complex is a term that refers to how the defense issue network works together to maintain and increase the defense budget. The congressional defense committees, the department of defense, and the aerospace and defense industries, have political and economic relationships that work together for their special interests. The term prison-industrial complex refers to the crime issue network that works together to maintain a large prison population. The issue network consists of private companies (the private, for-profit companies that build and run prisons and provide services such as food, health care, transportation, reentry programs for parolees); state and local government officials who consider prisons important to local economies; and prison guard unions that lobby to protect prison jobs.

In poorer states and rural regions, state and local government officials consider prisons part of economic development. In communities such as Walnut Grove, Mississippi, or Louisiana, a poor state with a relatively weak economy, for-profit prisons have been a growth industry. In Texas, the privatization of prisons created communities that became dependent on for-profit prisons for jobs and for taxes. The dependency was politically beneficial when the rate of incarceration was increasing but it became problematic as the rate of incarceration declined and private prison profits declined.

The Bill of Rights includes provisions that protect against unreasonable search and seizure, self-incrimination, violations of due process, and cruel and unusual punishment. It also guarantees the right to trial by jury, the assistance of counsel, and the right to confront the accuser. Why do so many of the provisions of the Bill of Rights limit the government's criminal justice powers? Were the Founders soft on crime? Were the Founders trying to protect suspects and criminals? The answer to these questions is that the Founders were very concerned about the government criminal law powers. Their concerns were rooted in their political experiences. The government's criminal law powers are indeed worth thinking about because the government can take a person's property, liberty, and even life—as long as it provides due process before it does it. The Founders had lived through the period when the English King and colonial governors used criminal law powers for political purposes—to punish opponents or critics. The political use of criminal justice powers explains why the Fourth Amendment declared that individuals had a right to be free from unreasonable searches and seizures, why the Fifth Amendment guarantees due process of law and the right against self-incrimination, why the Sixth Amendment guarantees the right to a jury trial, and why the Eighth Amendment prohibits cruel and unusual punishment. The fact that these provisions of the Bill of Right are written in such general language means that criminal cases have been such an important part of the Supreme Court's docket.

16.62 | *The Second Amendment*

Gun rights are an important part of American political culture. The Second Amendment declares, "A well regulated Militia being necessary to the security of a free State, the right to keep and bear Arms shall not be infringed." There are two readings of this Amendment: an individual rights reading and a federalism reading. For 70 years the Supreme Court read the Second Amendment as a provision of the Constitution that was intended to protect state militias from the federal government. This is the federalism reading of the Second Amendment. It holds that the Second Amendment was included in the Bill of Rights to protect the states from the federal government. The new Constitution reduced the powers of the states and greatly increased the power of the federal government by among other things, giving Congress the power to create a military. The Second Amendment protected state militias by preventing the federal government from abolishing state militias. This federalism reading of the Second Amendment is a "state's rights" reading.

Then in District of Columbia v. Heller (2008) the Court ruled that the Second Amendment guaranteed an individual right to keep, bear, and use arms. Justice Scalia's opinion for the 5–4 majority held that the right was a fundamental right that had two basic purposes. The first purpose is self-defense. Individuals have the right to keep and bear arms to fight crime. The second purpose is more explicitly political. Individuals have the right to arm themselves to fight against government tyranny. This right includes the right of racial minorities to arm themselves against a majority. Justice Scalia did acknowledge that the right to keep and bear arms was not an absolute right, and he stated that the ruling did not raise questions about existing gun control laws such as the long-standing prohibitions against felons owning guns. However, the ruling left it up to future cases to determine which gun control laws were constitutional. Because Second Amendment rights are fundamental freedoms, the government has the burden of proof to demonstrate that gun control laws serve a compelling interest. The *Heller* ruling also did not say whether the Second Amendment applied to the states (and local governments). In McDonald v. Chicago the Court ruled that it did, so now individuals can use the Second Amendment to challenge state and local gun laws. The right to use arms to fight crime is less controversial than the right to use arms to hold the government accountable.

> Think About it!
> Does the Second Amendment give individuals or groups of individuals a constitutional right to armed rebellion against the government? Read about the Stono Slave Rebellion in South Carolina in 1739.
> http://www.pbs.org/wgbh/aia/part1/1p284.html

16.63 | *The Fourth Amendment*

The meaning of the Fourth Amendment has changed over time. The Court originally interpreted the Fourth Amendment to places and things. The home and papers were given greater protection than other places and things. In *Olmstead v. U.S.* (1928) the Court ruled that the government did not have to get a search warrant before wire-tapping a suspect because a wiretap was not a physical search or an actual seizure. The Court considered wiretap technology something that enabled the government to listen to a telephone conversation without actually searching or seizing anything. Technology has greatly increased the government's power to gather information without ever physically seizing or searching anything. As a result, courts today interpret the Fourth Amendment more broadly. In Katz v. U.S. (1967) the Court held that wiretapping was a search and seizure that triggered the Fourth Amendment warrant protections.

The Fourth Amendment provides constitutional protection against unreasonable search and seizure. But it does not define what an unreasonable search is—or what a reasonable search and seizure is. The Court's case law defines these provisions of the Fourth Amendment. The general rule is that a search is reasonable if a warrant is obtained from an independent magistrate (a judicial branch official). In order to obtain a search warrant, the police must convince the magistrate that there is probable cause that search of person or place will produce evidence of the criminal activity that they are investigating. This is the rule. There also is a long list of exceptions to the rule that a reasonable search requires a search warrant:

- **Consent**—an individual can knowingly give up the right to have a warrant.
- **Stop and frisk**—a stop is not really an arrest and a frisk is not really a search so a warrant is not required for a police officer to stop and frisk a person. (*Terry v. Ohio*)
- **Plain view**—if the police officer has a right to be where he or she is, then contraband and evidence can be seized without first getting a search warrant. The plain view doctrine also applies to concept of "open fields," which includes fields, buildings, garbage put out at the curb, and material seized using technology such as helicopters, drones, and even infrared technology when used to see or otherwise detect using thermal imaging marijuana grow houses.
- **Incident to a lawful arrest**—a police officer may search the area under immediate control of a person in order to ensure officer safety or to preserve evidence.
- **Hot pursuit**—a police officer in hot pursuit of a suspect does not have to stop the chase, get a search warrant, and then resume the pursuit.
- **Motor vehicles**—the mobility of motor vehicles presents special problems so there are many circumstances where warrant-less searches are allowed. Motor vehicles, telephones, cell phones, and computers are examples of how technological developments have changed reading of the Fourth Amendment's protection of persons, houses, papers and effects from unreasonable searches.
- **Drug testing**—the government has a compelling interest in public safety, therefore certain employees such as railway workers and customs officials can be required to submit to drug tests without warrants, probable cause, or individualized suspicion.

- **Schools**—schools are special institutions, therefore the standard for justifying the search of a student's locker or backpack is merely whether the search was reasonable rather than the higher standard of probable cause that the search will produce evidence of criminal activity.
- **Administrative searches**—Fourth Amendment rights are not as strong in settings other than criminal justice, such as enforcement of game laws by searching coolers or freezers, business regulation and inspection, food safety inspections of restaurants, immigration law enforcement, and enforcement of public housing rules.
- **National security**—Fourth Amendment protections are weaker than in other areas of law. The Foreign Intelligence Surveillance Act of 1978 created a special legislative court system, the foreign intelligence surveillance court (FISC), which reviews government requests to gather intelligence without having to show probable cause. The USA PATRIOT ACT removed the "wall of separation" between intelligence gathering and criminal prosecution. The Federal Bureau of Investigation can issue National Security Letters demanding that individuals or companies produce requested information, and the National Security Agency has conducted secret intelligence surveillance.[17]

The general rule is that the Fourth Amendment requires a search warrant for a search and seizure to be constitutional. The large number of exceptions to the rule raises an interesting question. Is it still accurate to say that search warrants are required in order for a search to be constitutional? The rule is misleading. Would it be more accurate to say that there is a new rule: a warrant is not required for a search to be constitutional except under certain circumstances?

The Fourth Amendment declares a right to be free from unreasonable searches and seizures. But it does not provide a remedy for violations of that right. The Supreme Court has provided one (for violations of the Fourth Amendment or the 5th Amendment due process of law). The remedy is called the **Exclusionary Rule.** The Exclusionary Rule is a judge-created policy that evidence obtained illegally cannot be used in court to obtain a conviction. The Exclusionary Rule was first created and applied to federal courts in *Weeks v. U.S.* (1914). In *Mapp v. Ohio* (1961) the Warren Court applied the Exclusionary Rule to state courts.

Conservatives have consistently opposed the Exclusionary Rule for several reasons. First, the Exclusionary Rule is a legal policy that the Supreme Court created. As such, it is an example of judicial activism or legislating from the bench. Second, the Exclusionary Rule allows the guilty to go free on what conservatives consider legal technicalities such as the failure to get a search warrant or a warrant with a typographical error. The Exclusionary Rule does indeed sometimes allow a person to get away with murder. In those cases where a confession or a gun or a weapon is ruled inadmissible in court because the evidence was illegally obtained, a guilty person gets off on a legal technicality. Critics of the ER do not think that evidence should be given the "death penalty" merely because of the way it was obtained. Finally, conservatives oppose the Exclusionary Rule because they prefer giving police officers broad discretion to use their judgment to decide how best to go about doing their job. This difference between liberal and conservative views on how the criminal justice system should work is the reason for Tom Wolfe's quip in *The Bonfire of the Vanities,* the 1987 satirical novel about greed, race, and class in New York City, that a conservative is a liberal who was mugged (and want to get tough on crime), and a liberal is a conservative who was arrested (and quickly lawyers up). It also reflects the differences between the crime control and due process models of justice.

In fact, since the Warren Court the Court has become more conservative and significantly limited the ER by creating exceptions to the rule that illegally obtained evidence cannot be used. The exceptions include:

- **Grand jury**—illegally obtained can be presented to a grand jury.
- **Harmless error**—if the police made a harmless error the evidence can be used.
- **Civil court**—the ER does not apply to civil courts.
- **Good faith**—if the police made a good faith mistake the evidence can be used.
- **Independent source**—if the evidence could have been obtained through another source, then it can be used.
- **Inevitable discovery**—if the evidence would have been discovered inevitably, it can be used.
- **Public safety**—if the police acted illegally, but to ensure public safety, the evidence can be used.
- **Preventive detention**—the ER does not apply to decisions about whether a person should be detained in order to prevent a criminal act.
- **Parole revocation**—the ER does not apply to decisions to revoke parole.
- **Prisoners**—the ER does not apply to disciplinary hearings for inmates.
- **Impeaching a witness**—illegally obtained evidence can be used to impeach a defendant's own testimony or that of an accomplice.
- **Physical evidence**? An emerging exception is for physical evidence (e.g., a gun a bullet or a knife) as distinct from testimonial evidence (e.g. a confession)?

The growing exceptions to the Exclusionary Rule raise the same question that has been raised about the rule that a search warrant is required for a search to be reasonable: Does the long and growing list of exceptions to the ER mean that the exceptions have now become the rule? Both examples do illustrate how changes occur in the reading of the U.S. Constitution's protections for civil liberties. The words in the Constitution may not change but their meaning does—and the changed legal meanings reflect political (ideological) changes.

16.64 | *The Fifth Amendment*

The Fifth Amendment includes a number of provisions that protect individual liberties: protection against self-incrimination, protection against double jeopardy, and a guarantee of due process of law:

"No person shall be held to answer for a capital, or otherwise infamous crime, unless on a presentment or indictment of a Grand Jury, except in cases arising in the land or naval forces, or in the Militia, when in actual service in time of War or public danger; nor shall any person be subject for the same offence to be twice put in jeopardy of life or limb; nor shall be compelled in any criminal case to be a witness against himself, nor be deprived of life, liberty, or property, without due process of law; nor shall private property be taken for public use, without just compensation."

Think about it!

Should the police, soldiers, or CIA agents do whatever it takes to get information from a suspected criminal, enemy, or terrorist?

The provision protecting against self-incrimination has ancient roots in the English tradition of common law. The right is central to one of the most important and familiar features of the U.S. legal system: the assumption that a person is innocent until proven guilty. The assumption of innocence places the burden of proof on the accuser (the government). The accused does not have to prove that they are not guilty as charged. The government must prove beyond a reasonable doubt that the accused did what they were accused of doing. Why place the burden of proof on the government? It would certainly be easier to obtain convictions if the accused had to prove they were innocent. The protection against self-incrimination can be traced to the reaction against religious investigations (inquisitions) that used torture in order to obtain confessions of sin. The story of John Lambert the heretic (1537) illustrates the revulsion against using torture to obtain confessions of sin (or otherwise):

> "No man ever suffered more diabolical cruelty at the stake than this evangelical martyr, he was rather roasted than burnt to death; if the fire became stronger, or if the flame reached higher than they chose, it was removed or damped. When his legs were burnt off, and his thighs were reduced to mere stumps in the fire, they pitched his broiling body on pikes, and lacerated his flesh with their halberds. But God was with him in the midst of the flame, and supported his spirit under the anguish of expiring nature. Almost exhausted, he lifted up his hands, such as the fire had left him, and with his last breath, cried out to the people, NONE BUT CHRIST! NONE BUT CHRIST! These memorable words, spoken at such a time, and under such peculiar circumstances, were calculated to make a deeper and more lasting impression on the minds of the spectators, than could have been effected by a volume written on the subject. At last his remains were beat down into the flames, while his triumphant soul 'mocked their short arm, and, quick as thought, escaped where tyrants vex not, and the weary rest.' "[18]

The religious justification for torturing a person was to ensure that sinners confessed before meeting their maker.

The use of the "third degree" by police officers in order to obtain confessions of crime was traditionally considered a politically and legally acceptable practice. However, in *Brown v. Mississippi* (1936) the Supreme Court held that torturing suspects was unconstitutional—in a case where the police torture appeared to have produced a tainted confession by a man who simply wanted the pain to stop. The Court ruled that due process of law prohibits trial by ordeal: "The rack and torture chamber may not be substituted for the witness stand."

The Fifth Amendment provision prohibiting a person from being "compelled to be a witness against himself" is not limited to forced confessions. The Supreme Court has broadened the scope of the Fifth Amendment so that suspects have a constitutional right to be

Think about it! Conservatives think the Exclusionary Rule is an inappropriate remedy for violations of the Fourth Amendment. They recommend a tort law remedy: to sue the police for wrongful injury. Would this work?

informed of their constitutional rights prior to being questioned. This was the holding in the landmark case of *Miranda v. Arizona* (1966), which resulted in police officers reading suspects their Miranda Warnings. This decision is probably depicted in popular culture (television police shows and crime films) more than any other Court ruling[19]

> You have the right to remain silent. Anything you say can and will be used against you in a court of law. You have the right to speak to an attorney. If you cannot afford an attorney, one will be appointed for you. Do you understand these rights as they have been read to you?
> —Typical Miranda Warning

16.65 | *The Sixth Amendment*

The Sixth Amendment includes several provisions that provide rights in the criminal justice system.

> "In all criminal prosecutions, the accused shall enjoy the right to a speedy and public trial, by an impartial jury of the State and district wherein the crime shall have been committed, which district shall have been previously ascertained by law, and to be informed of the nature and cause of the accusation; to be confronted with the witnesses against him; to have compulsory process for obtaining witnesses in his favor, and to have the Assistance of Counsel for his defence."

The traditional reading of the Sixth Amendment right to the assistance of counsel was that a defendant had the right to pay for a lawyer if the defendant could afford one, but the state had no obligation to provide a defendant with a lawyer. However, in the 1930s, beginning with <u>*Powell v. Alabama*</u> (1932), the Court began to require states to provide defendants with lawyers in capital punishment cases involving special circumstances. The special circumstances included cases where there was evidence of racial hostility. Over time, number of special circumstances expanded to include cases involving very young offenders, poverty, illiteracy or a lack of education. The modern understanding of the right to the existence of counsel is that the right applies in all cases where an individual could lose his or her liberty.

16.7 | The Criminal Justice System

The criminal justice is the system of policies and institutions that are used to maintain public order, deter crime, investigate crimes, prosecute and try the accused, and punish individuals who have been convicted of crimes. Criminal justice was traditionally the responsibility of state and local governments. Beginning in the 1930s, the federal government began to make crime a national issue. The U.S. department of Justice and then the federal courts were concerned about corruption in state and local criminal justice systems, the emergence of organized crime that crossed local and state jurisdictions, and racial discrimination in law enforcement. The Warren Court's criminal justice rulings resulted in federal judicial supervision of state criminal justice policies. The liberal rulings expanded the rights of suspects and prisoners. Then, beginning in the 1960s, the media called an increase in crime a crime wave. Crime was transformed from a local/state issue into a national political issue—but for different reasons. Liberals wanted the national spotlight focused on the social causes of crime. Conservatives wanted crime control. The national political debate was shaped by conservatives who blamed liberals and judges for expanding rights in ways that made it harder for police to fight crime. The result was further "federalization" of crime, but now it was for getting tough on crime rather than providing more federal protection of the rights of suspects and prisoners in the states. The 1967 President's Commission on Law Enforcement and Administration of Justice was charged by President Johnson to develop a plan that would allow us to "banish crime."

Think about it! Is Chris Rock right about the Second Amendment and bullet control?
http://www.youtube.com/watch?v=OuX-nFmL0II

The Commission's Report, "The Challenge of Crime in a Free Society," made more than 200 recommendations as part of a comprehensive approach toward preventing and fighting crime. Some of the recommendations were included in a major new federal law, the Omnibus Crime Control and Safe Streets Act of 1968. This Act established the Law Enforcement Assistance Administration (LEAA), which provided federal grants for research on criminology, including the study of the social aspects of crime. As a result, universities created academic programs in criminology and criminal justice that eventually included sociology, psychology, and public law in departments of political science—disciplines that provided a comprehensive study of the causes of crime and the organization and operation of the criminal justice system.

The Omnibus Act recommended that the criminal justice system be made more effective by improving coordination among the three main components of the criminal justice system: police, courts, and corrections. The politics of the 1968 Omnibus Crime Control Act are very interesting. It was passed in spring of 1968 by a Democratic Congress that was worried that Democrats were going to do badly in the upcoming fall elections because they were increasing seen as soft on crime and a time when the public was becoming much more worried about street crime than police brutality. Republicans sensed the public fear of crime and took tough on crime positions while portraying Democrats as soft on crime. Republican Richard Nixon's presidential campaign used getting tough on crime rhetoric and when he took office he began implementing crime control policies.

Two criminal justice issues that divide the ideological right and left are gun control and capital punishment. Guns are an important part of American political culture therefore debates about the wisdom and the legality of using gun control to increase public safety are often heated. Liberals generally support gun control as crime control. Conservatives generally oppose gun control as crime control. The debates are partly about effectiveness: the question whether gun control affects rates of crime and levels of public safety. The debates are also about rights. The Second Amendment guarantees the right to keep and bear arms. For a seriously funny alternative to gun control as a way to reduce violence listen to comedian Chris Rock's routine recommending bullet control rather than gun control. Can the constitutional problems with gun control be avoided because the Second Amendment mentions the right "to keep and bear arms" but says nothing about the right to keep and use bullets?

16.71 | Criminal Law

Law is a system of rules that are backed by sanctions for not complying with them. Sanctions mean that compliance is not voluntary. The U.S. legal system is divided into two forms of law: civil law and criminal law. **Civil laws** are generally the rules that govern interactions between individuals or organizations. Civil law is sometimes called private law because it does not usually involve the government. Business contracts, for example, are typically private law. **Criminal laws** are the system of rules that 1) define what behaviors are considered illegal and therefore criminal; 2) the legal procedures used to investigate, prosecute, and try those who are accused of crimes; and 3) the punishments (i.e., the sentences) that are considered appropriate for convicted offenders. Criminal law is public law for two reasons. First, crimes are considered harmful to both the individual victim and society in general: crimes are offenses against the public order. Second, the government prosecutes and punishes offenders.

The primary purposes of criminal law are to protect individuals from being harmed by others and to punish those who commit crimes. All countries have criminal laws. The oldest known codified law is the Code of Hammurabi, which was established around 1760 BC in ancient Mesopotamia. Historically, criminal law was private law in the sense that individuals and groups provided their own protection and punished offenders rather than relying on government to do so. The development of professional criminal justice officials (including police, prosecutors, and judges) and a system of codified laws (to replace common law), have diminished the layperson's role in delivering justice. However, in recent years vigilantism (individuals or organizations taking the law back into their own hands) and the gun rights movement have expanded the layperson's role.

16.72 | The Criminal Justice System

The criminal justice system consists of three main parts: (1) the police (sometimes called law enforcement; (2) the courts; and (3) corrections (jails and prisons). The police (including police officers and sheriffs), judges, and corrections officials (including guards and wardens) are all part of the criminal justice system. Another important set of criminal justice officials are prosecutors, who can be considered part of the policing or law enforcement function.

16.73 | *The Police*

A police officer is the criminal justice official that the typical person is most likely to have contact with. Police officers are in the community patrolling neighborhoods, streets, and areas where people congregate. The police are also the first criminal justice officials that an offender will have contact with because it is the police who investigate crimes and make arrests. The primary functions of the police are to prevent and investigate violations of criminal laws and to maintain public order. Police officers are empowered to use force and other forms of legal coercion and legal means to effect public and social order. The word police is from the Latin *politia* ("civil administration"), which itself derives from the Ancient Greek word for *polis* ("city"). The London Metropolitan Police established in 1829 by Sir Robert Peel is considered the first modern police force. It promoted the police role in preventing and deterring urban crime and disorder rather than the tradition reactive role of investigating crimes that had already been committed. In the United States, police departments were first established in Boston in 1838 and New York City in 1844. Early police departments were not held in very high regard because they had reputations for being incompetent, corrupt, and political.

In the 1990s, the New York City Police Department developed CompStat (**Compu**ter**Stat**istics) an information-based system for tracking and mapping crime patterns and trends. CompStat is also a tool for holding police departments accountable for dealing with crime. It has been replicated in police departments across the United States and around the world, and is an example of computer information systems are applied to organizations related to policing. The <u>**Federal Bureau of Investigation**</u> is the pre-eminent

law enforcement agency in the U.S. It is responsible for investigating interstate crimes and crimes violating federal laws. Although the FBI is the most prominent police organization, it accounts for only a small portion of policing activity in the U.S. Most policing activities such as order maintenance and services such as crowd control or security are actually provided by a broad range of state and local organizations (e.g., state highway patrols; county sheriffs; city police; and school police).

16.74 | *The Courts: Criminal Trials*

The courts are examined in a separate chapter so this section provides a brief description of criminal trials. A trial is, in its simplest terms, a fact-finding process. In the U.S., the primary function of a trial court is dispute resolution. In the criminal justice system, the primary figures are the judge, the jury, the prosecutor, and the defense attorney. The courtroom work group also includes magistrates (who may perform some of the preliminary or ministerial functions of a trial), probation or parole officers, and other professionals who provide relevant information about a defendant or convicted offender. In the past, judges did not have to be lawyers. Justices of the peace were elected members of the community similar to other local leaders. Today, however, a judge in a criminal case is a lawyer. The jury, however, consists of lay people. The U.S. uses this combination of professional and lay people more than most countries, which have decreased their reliance on lay juries. It is a reminder of the close relationship between politics and law in the U.S. administration of justice.

The U.S. legal system is an **adversarial system**. An adversarial system is one where each of the two parties, the adversaries, presents its side of the case and challenges the other side's version of the facts and understanding of the law during a trial or a hearing. A neutral third party—a judge, a panel of judges (some appeals courts hear cases with panels of judges), or a jury—decides the case. The case should be decided in favor of the party who offers the most sound and compelling arguments based on the law as applied to the facts of the case.

Albert Ellery Berg, *The Universal Self-Instructor* (New York: Thomas Kelly, Publisher, 1883) 25.

The adversarial process allows each side to present its case to the judge or jury. The judge or jury is the neutral third party. Having a neutral party settle a dispute between two disputants is one of the oldest and most basic elements of justice—the belief that no one should be a judge of his or her own cause. Justice requires having a neutral third party deciding which side wins the case. In criminal justice, this means that a judge or jury determines whether a person is guilty or not guilty. In some American states, the jury verdict must be a unanimous decision; in others a majority or supermajority vote is enough to obtain a conviction. The prosecutor or district attorney is the government lawyer who brings charges against the person, persons or corporate entity accused of a crime. The prosecutor explains to the court, including the jury if it is a jury trial, what crime was committed and the evidence used to prove the charge. In the U.S. legal system, prosecutors have a great deal of discretion. They can decide whether to charge an individual with a crime, what charge to file, when to go to trial and what kinds of cases to prosecute, and what penalties to ask for upon conviction. For these reasons, prosecutors are extremely important figures in the criminal justice system. They are not merely bureaucrats who follow orders or implement the law. Prosecutorial discretion makes prosecutors powerful figures.

A defense attorney counsels the accused on the legal process, advises of the likely outcomes, and recommends legal strategies. The accused, not the lawyer, has the right to make final decisions on the most important aspects of their legal strategy, including whether to accept a plea bargain offer or go to trial, and whether to take the stand and testify at the trial. The defense attorney has a duty to represent the interests of the client, raise procedural and evidentiary issues, and hold the prosecution to its burden of proving guilt beyond a reasonable doubt. Defense counsel may challenge evidence presented by the prosecution or present exculpatory evidence and argue on behalf of their client. At trial, the defense attorney typically offers a rebuttal to the prosecutor's accusations.

The Sixth Amendment right to the assistance of counsel was originally understood to mean only that a person had a right to a lawyer if they could afford to pay for one, a right that was gradually expanded during the 20th Century. The right to a lawyer was first expanded to cases where a person could receive the death penalty (capital cases). Then the right was expanded to all cases where there were special circumstances such as very young defendants, uneducated defendants, or evidence of racial hostility. Then the right was expanded to all felony trials. And then it was further expanded to all serious cases. In the U.S. today, an accused person is entitled to a government-paid defense attorney, a public defender, if he or she cannot afford an attorney and the charge is so serious that a conviction could result in loss of life or liberty. These changes occurred primarily because judges came to consider the assistance of counsel an essential element of the administration of justice.

The vast majority of cases are settled by plea bargains, not trials. **Plea-bargaining** is when the accused pleads guilty in exchange for a reduction in the number of charges or the sentence. Ideally, a plea bargain is a deal that benefits both the prosecutor and the defense. The prosecutor saves time and money, avoids the risk of losing the case, and may include a requirement that the defendant cooperate with the police by testifying against others. The defendant typically gets a reduction in the number of charges, the severity of the charge offenses, a reduced sentence, and avoids the risk of a more serious loss of liberty or even life. Plea bargains settle over 90% of cases. Many nations do not permit the use of plea-bargaining because it can coerce innocent people to plead guilty in an attempt to avoid harsh punishment. Plea-bargaining is also controversial because it creates the public impression that criminals are getting much less punishment than they deserve. Because a plea bargain usually involves getting a sentence that is substantially less than the maximum penalty for an offense, the public tend to think of plea bargaining as evidence that the system is not as tough on crime as it might be.

Have you ever been called for jury duty? What did you think of the voir dire questioning of the jury pool?

16.75 | *Barriers to Justice*

There are a number of ways that the criminal justice system can produce unjust outcomes. The police can coerce confessions or make honest makes. Prosecutors may hide exculpatory evidence. Defense counsel can be inadequate. The judge or jury can acquit a guilty person or convict an innocent person. Or a person can be found guilty of a crime that is more or less severe than the one they actually committed. These mistakes can be intentional (misconduct) or unintentional. Bias presents an interesting case. Bias can undermine decision-making in any setting whether civil or criminal justice, employment, education, or health-care. Individuals can be biased for or against someone or something. A cognitive bias is the tendency to make systematic errors that are based on cognitive factors (what someone believes to be true) rather than the factual evidence. Cognitive biases are a common attribute of human thought, and often drastically skew the reliability of anecdotal and legal evidence. Biases can lead to discrimination. Prejudice on the part of the police, prosecutors, judges, or jurors can undermine the legitimacy and credibility of the legal process.

A **prejudice** is a prejudgment, an assumption or belief that is made about someone or something without knowledge of the facts. Prejudice is commonly thought of a preconceived judgment toward a people or a person because of race, class, gender, ethnicity, age, disability, religion, or political beliefs. A prejudice can be a positive prejudice (a favorable predisposition) or a negative prejudice (an unfavorable predisposition). Cognitive prejudice refers to what someone believes to be true. Affective

Prejudice refers to what people like and dislike (e.g., attitudes toward members of a particular class, race, ethnicity, national origin, or creed). Behavioral prejudice refers to beliefs about how people are inclined to behave. Prejudices are an extremely important issue during the selection of juries. The jury selection process includes lengthy questions about individual backgrounds and attitudes in order to get a better sense of what prejudices might be indicated. If you have ever been called for jury duty you know how important discovering attitudes and biases is in the *voir dire* process of questioning the jury pool.

Racism is a combination of racial prejudice and discrimination. It involves pre-judging a person based on their race or ethnicity. It attributes to individuals characteristics associated with members of a group. Trials are fact-finding processes that use elaborate rules of evidence partly to minimize the impacts of bias.

One additional source of problems in the criminal justice system is inequality of resources. Legal representation is expensive. The lack of adequate financial or other resources puts a person at a significant disadvantage at all stages of the criminal justice process, not just the trial. The states are required to provide public defenders for those who cannot afford legal counsel, but the state systems vary a great deal and public defenders are not paid well in some states. This is particularly troubling in death penalty cases. This is why capital punishment is jokingly explained by the quip, "If you don't have the capital, you get the punishment."

16.76 | *Corrections*

After conviction, an offender is turned over to correctional authorities for incarceration in a detention facility (for juveniles), a jail (for shorter terms, usually less than one year), or a prison. The types and purposes of punishment have changed over the years. In early civilizations, the primary forms of punishment were exile, execution, or other forms of corporal (bodily) punishment such as dismemberment (e.g., amputating the hand of a thief) or branding. Traditional societies also relied extensively on informal methods of social control. Laws are a formal method of social control that may be supplemented by other, informal methods of social control, such as religion, professional rules and ethics, or cultural mores and customs. Punishment can also be formal or informal. Shame and shunning were ways to censure individuals whose behavior the community considered inappropriate. The Puritan stocks and the scarlet letter are examples of traditional methods of informal social control. Today, however, prisons and jails are the most important methods of punishment. Formal methods of social control—prosecution for violating the law—have replaced informal methods of social control and punishment. Monetary fines are one of the oldest forms of punishment and they are still used today. These fines may be paid to the state or to the victims as a form of reparation. Probation and house arrest are also sanctions that seek to limit an offender's mobility and opportunities to commit crimes without actually placing them in a prison setting. Many jurisdictions may require some form of public service as a form of punishment for lesser offenses.

William Penn

William Penn and the Quakers initiated correctional reform in the United States in the latter part of the 17th century.[20] Pennsylvania's criminal code was revised to forbid torture and other forms of cruel punishment. Quakers advocated replacing corporal punishment with institutions where criminals could be rehabilitated or made penitent—hence the idealistic name penitentiary now more casually called the pen, which is more likely to be thought of as an enclosure.

The purposes of punishment have also changed over time. The Quaker movement is commonly credited with establishing the idea that prisons should be used to reform or rehabilitate criminals. Punishment serves four purposes: incapacitation (removing offenders from the general population; deterrence (sending a message that crime does not pay); rehabilitation (reforming offenders); and retribution ("payback"). Many societies consider punishment a form of retribution, and any harm or discomfort the prisoner suffers is just "payback" for the harm they caused their victims. A third purpose is rehabilitation or reform. One aspect of the shift from liberalism to conservatism has been the shift from liberal thinking about crime to conservative thinking about crime. Beginning in the 1970s, sentencing policy *moved away from rehabilitation and toward incapacitation, deterrence, and retribution.* This policy change has resulted in the U.S. having the highest incarceration rate in the world. The economic and social costs of maintaining such a large prison population has prompted new efforts to find out who really needs to be imprisoned. Can science be used to better predict who will commit crimes or who is really a psychopath?

Think about it! Can we develop a test to predict who is a psychopath? If so, should we use it to prevent crime? Listen to "Can a Test Really Tell Who's a Psychpath?"http://www.npr.org/2011/05/26/136619689/can-a-test-really-tell-whos-a-psychopath

---

16.77 | *Capital Punishment*

Capital punishment is probably the most controversial punishment issue. Once widely used in the U.S., it is now limited to capital crimes.[21] Concerns about wrongful convictions, inadequate legal representation, arbitrary or discriminatory application of the death penalty, and a general sense that execution is no longer consistent with the values of civilized societies, have reduced the use of the death penalty. However, efforts to declare it unconstitutional because it violates due process of law or is cruel and unusual punishment have been unsuccessful.

One current death penalty issue is who should be eligible to be sentenced to death. Should mentally handicapped individuals be eligible for the death penalty? At what point does a low IQ score make a person ineligible for the death penalty? Should minors be eligible for the death penalty? Determining the age at which children become culpable for their behavior is a controversial question. It raises political, moral, and increasingly even scientific questions. Recent advances in brain science have greatly increased the understanding of brain development and the relationship between brain development and behavior, including the kinds of youthful risk-taking behavior that include crime. Brain research has discovered that humans have a rather primitive brain, primitive in the sense that the human brain developed from a jellyfish foundation (which is characterized by primitive neural networks), then added a serpent's brain (which is characterized by simple threat response), and then added the mammal brain (the ape brain).

Think About It!
Do humans have a three ice-cream scoop brain? Lister to Jon Hamilton's story "From Primitive Parts, A Highly Evolved Brain,"
http://www.npr.org/templates/story/story.php?storyId=129027124

What does this have to do with crime policy? Brain science research has had an impact on thinking about punishment. The Supreme Court Justices tend to be empirical decision makers in the sense that they rely on evidence-based argument for or against a law. When considering the constitutionality of a law that limits television or radio broadcasts of offensive or indecent material, the Justices consider the empirical evidence of the government's interest in regulating programming. What is the evidence of harm? What percentage of the audience are children during the hours from 10:00 p.m. to 6:00 a.m.? The Justices will also take empirical evidence into consideration when deciding cases involving challenges to laws that make minors eligible for the death penalty. What does the latest brain development research say about the brains of adolescents? Should adolescents be held accountable for their violent actions in the same way that an adult is, and be tried as adults?

In recent years the Supreme Court has decided a number of cases that have limited state crime policies that govern the trial and punishment of minors. In *Eddings v. Oklahoma* (1982), the Court overturned the death sentence of a 16 year old.[22] In *Thompson v. Oklahoma* (1988), the Court ruled that it was unconstitutional to execute a person who was under age 16, In *Stanford v. Kentucky* (1989) the Court upheld state laws that provided capital punishment for juveniles who were 16 years old or older when they committed the crime.[23] Once the Court ruled that it was unconstitutional to execute minors it had to decide when someone was too young to execute. This required drawing a minimum age line. Could a person who committed a crime at 17, 16, 15, or 8 years of age be sentenced to death? Then in *Roper v. Simmons* (2005) the Court ruled that a person who was under age 18 could not be executed.

Comparative Death Penalty Policies for Juveniles
https://deathpenaltyinfo.org/execution-juveniles-us-and-other-countries

16.78 | Resources

The U.S. Department of Justice (DOJ) is one of the most valuable sources of information about crime and the federal criminal justice system. The Bureau of Justice Statistics (BJS) is one of the DOJ agencies that gathers and reports criminal and civil justice statistics. The BJS data on crime rates and rates of incarceration and prison populations provide information about a broad range of subjects including public opinion.[24] The BJS reports include the prison population, rates of imprisonment, and changes in rates of imprisonment. The BJS reports also provide information about capital punishment (i.e., "Death Penalty"). The high rate of incarceration during the years of getting tough on crime has made the U.S. the country with the highest rate of imprisonment in the world. The heavy reliance on imprisonment as punishment is a public policy issue because it is expensive to maintain prisons and because there are questions about its effectiveness.[25]

16.79 | The States

As sovereign entities in a federal system of government, the states have substantial responsibility for crime policy. Each state can create its own criminal laws and criminal justice system. As a result, crime policies vary widely. The rate of incarceration varies dramatically from state to state and region to region. The Southern states have the highest rates of incarceration. The map below indicates the number of state prison inmates per 100,000 residents

Incarceration Rates, 2006
Number of State Prison Inmates per 100,000 State Residents[26]

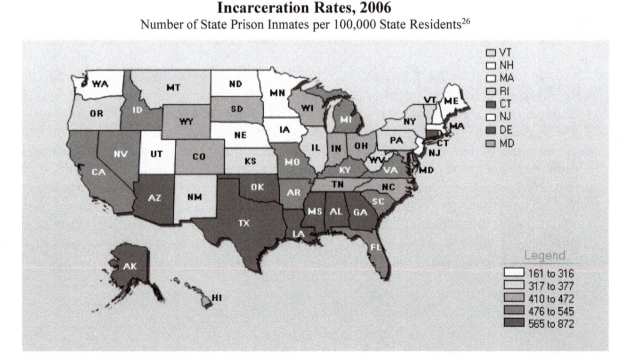

16.8 | Internet Sources

An Overview of Civil Rights: http://topics.law.cornell.edu/wex/Civil_rights

The Freedom Riders: http://video.pbs.org/video/1930441944

Photographs of the Civil Rights Movement in Florida:
http://www.floridamemory.com/OnlineClassroom/PhotoAlbum/civil_rights.cfm

The Code of Hammurabi. 1760 BC. http://www.wsu.edu/~dee/MESO/CODE.HTM

The U.S. Department of Justice gathers and reports criminal and civil justice statistics. The Bureau of Justice Statistics data on crime rates and rates of incarceration and prison populations provides important information about criminal justice policies:
http://www.ojp.usdoj.gov/bjs/

Bureau of Justice Statistics. http://bjs.ojp.usdoj.gov/

The Florida Office of the Attorney provides information about crime in Florida at http://myfloridalegal.com/.

The Florida Department of Corrections also provides information about prisons in Florida at http://www.dc.state.fl.us/.

Information about Florida's Death Row (who is on death row, or what a death row cell looks like), is available at: http://www.dc.state.fl.us/oth/deathrow/index.html

---

TERMS

The Crime Control and Due Process Models of Justice
Civil law
Criminal law
Federal Bureau of Investigation
Federalizing Crime
Rates of Incarceration
Adversarial system
Plea bargaining
Prejudice
Legal Discrimination

[1] http://religiousfreedom.lib.virginia.edu/court/us_v_ball.html

[2] See "Use of Wiccan Symbol on Veterans' Headstones Is Approved,"
http://www.nytimes.com/2007/04/24/washington/24wiccan.html

[3] Frankin D. Roosevelt's March 9, 1937 "Fireside Chat,"
http://www.presidency.ucsb.edu/ws/index.php?pid=15381#axzz1NlGuPlqw

[4] For additional information about Dred Scott, see
http://www.pbs.org/wgbh/aia/part4/4p2932.html
http://www.oyez.org/cases/1851-1900/1856/1856_0

[5] http://www.law.cornell.edu/supct/html/historics/USSC_CR_0109_0003_ZS.html
http://www.oyez.org/cases/1851-1900/1882/1882_2

[6] See http://www.oyez.org/cases/1851-1900/1895/1895_210/
http://www.law.cornell.edu/supct/html/historics/USSC_CR_0163_0537_ZS.html

[7] The Missouri case is available at:
http://en.wikipedia.org/wiki/Missouri_ex_rel._Gaines_v._Canada
http://supreme.justia.com/us/305/337/case.html
The Texas case is available at:
http://www.oyez.org/cases/1940-1949/1949/1949_44
The Oklahoma case is available at:
http://www.law.cornell.edu/supct/html/historics/USSC_CR_0339_0637_ZS.html
The Kansas case is available at:
http://www.oyez.org/cases/1950-1959/1952/1952_1/

[8] http://www.nytimes.com/2005/09/11/weekinreview/11lipt.html
http://www.gpoaccess.gov/congress/senate/judiciary/sh99-1067/324-325.pdf

[9] http://americanhistory.si.edu/brown/history/6-legacy/deliberate-speed.html

[10] For recent rulings see *Gratz v. Bollinger* (2003)
http://www.oyez.org/cases/2000-2009/2002/2002_02_516; *Grutter v. Bollinger* (2003)
http://www.oyez.org/cases/2000-2009/2002/2002_02_241; *Meredith v. Jefferson County Board of Education* (2007); and recent rulings from Kentucky and Seattle, Washington
http://www.oyez.org/cases/2000-2009/2006/2006_05_915

[11] In *Hoyt v. Florida* (1961) the Court unanimously concluded that the equal protection clause did not prohibit the State of Florida from excluding women from jury duty. See
http://www.law.cornell.edu/supct/html/historics/USSC_CR_0368_0057_ZS.html

[12] http://www.equalrightsamendment.org/
http://www.law.umkc.edu/faculty/projects/ftrials/conlaw/nineteentham.htm

[13] See *Reed v. Reed* (1971). One of the lawyers who represented Sally Reed is Ruth Bader Ginsburg, who later became a Supreme Court Justice. Her personal employment experience, and her professional legal experience representing women in court, may explain her voting record as a Justice who is sympathetic to claims of gender discrimination in the workplace.
http://www.law.cornell.edu/supct/html/historics/USSC_CR_0404_0071_ZO.html
http://law.jrank.org/pages/13163/Reed-v-Reed.html

[14] *Nyugen v. Immigration and Naturalization Service* http://www.oyez.org/cases/2000-2009/2000/2000_99_2071

[15] Packer explained the two models in *The Limits of the Criminal Sanction* (Stanford: Stanford University Press, 1968).

[16] Accessed at https://www.bjs.gov/index.cfm?ty=kfdetail&iid=488

[17] On the Foreign Intelligence Surveillance Act Courts, see
http://judgepedia.org/index.php/United_States_Foreign_Intelligence_Surveillance_Court
http://www.fas.org/irp/agency/doj/fisa/. For information about FBI National Security Letters see
http://www.u-s-history.com/pages/h1205.html Domestic military operations also raise questions of constitutional protections. See http://www.aclu.org/safefree/torture/34745res20030314.html

[18] http://www.apuritansmind.com/Reformation/MemoirsReformers/MemoirsJohnLambert.htm
[19] http://www.oyez.org/cases/1960-1969/1965/1965_759
http://www.pbs.org/wnet/supremecourt/rights/landmark_miranda.html
http://www.pbs.org/wnet/supremecourt/rights/landmark_miranda.html
[20] http://www.quaker.org/wmpenn.html
[21] See *Kennedy v. Louisiana* (2008) at http://www.law.cornell.edu/supct/html/07-343.ZO.html
[22] http://www.law.cornell.edu/supct/html/historics/USSC_CR_0455_0104_ZO.html
[23] http://www.law.cornell.edu/supct/html/historics/USSC_CR_0492_0361_ZS.html
[24] See http://www.ojp.usdoj.gov/bjs/
[25] http://www.pewcenteronthestates.org/report_detail.aspx?id=35904
[26]http://www.pewcenteronthestates.org/ttw/trends_map_data_table.aspx?trendID=11&assessment
ID=24

17.0 | Global Affairs

Presidents—and their lawyers in the Department of Justice—periodically claim that the president is the sole organ of the national in its dealings with other countries and that neither Congress nor the courts can review a president's military action as Commander-in-Chief. President Georg. W. Bush simply summarized the political and legal theory supporting these claims when he asserted that he was, in effect, *the decider-in-chief*. This phrase originates with President Bush's April 2006 rejection of calls to fire his Secretary of Defense, Donald Rumsfeld. In a rather testy tone, President Bush declared, "I hear the voices [calling for Rumsfeld's firing].... But *I am the decider*!" The reference to himself as *the decider* was widely parodied as a claim that the president is the decider of all things—or at least all things related to war powers and national security.

Listen To It!
"I am the decider"
https://www.youtube.com/watch?v=irMeHmlxE9s&list=RDirMeHmlxE9s#t=5

The statement does illustrate by the main power problem in global affairs is accountability, particularly the difficulty holding presidents politically or legally accountable for the use of power related to war and national security. The power problem in global affairs has been an issue from the founding of the republic to current debates about counterterrorism policy:

- The Constitutional Convention of 1787. The delegates to the constitutional convention extensively debated how to hold the government accountable on matters related to war powers and external (foreign) affairs.
- The early years of the republic. Accountability remained an important issue during the early years of the republic because the U.S. was surrounded by imperial powers that were ambitious to expand their sphere of influence, and because Native Americans sometimes resisted westward expansion into their lands.
- Becoming a world power. The U.S. became an economic and military power during the latter years of the 19th Century. The use of military power to acquire territory and exert influence beyond the nation's original borders was especially controversial because it conflicted with the country's identity as a republic opposed to imperial power.
- Acting as the world's policeman. The U.S. assumed the role of world policeman and leader of the free world in the early years of the 20th Century. In a democracy, projecting power abroad raises fundamental questions about legitimacy and accountability.
- The Cold War. During the Cold War (1947–1991), the emphasis on secrecy and emergency powers in the global fight against communism weakened the ordinary methods of holding government officials accountable for their actions. The epitome of congressional delegation of power to the president is the 1964 Gulf of Tonkin Resolution which stated that Congress approved the president's decision as Commander-in-Chief "to take all necessary measures to repel any armed attack against the forces of the United States and to prevent further aggression."[1] This "blank check" delegation of power greatly weakens the model of legal accountability.
- The War on Terror. On September 18, 2001, Congressional approved the Authorization for the Use of Military Force (AUMF) that granted the president the power to use "all necessary and appropriate force against the nations, organizations, or persons he determines planned, authorized, committed, or aided" the 9/11 terror attacks or "harbored such organizations or persons."[2] Al Qaeda is the organization responsible for planning and committing the attacks. President Bush claimed the AUMF authorized him to decide to invade Afghanistan and Iraq. President Obama relied on the AUMF to kill Osama bin Laden (the leader of al Qaeda), to continue the wars in Afghanistan and Iraq, and to use drone strikes, bombs, and other military actions against other terrorists and terrorist organizations such as ISIS that were not even in existence when the 9/11 attacks occurred. President Trump has claimed the AUMF grants the president power implement

counterterrorism policy that includes acts of war such as bombing Syrian government forces. The AUMF's broad language and the reluctance of either Congress or the courts to limit the AUMF to those connected to the 9/11 terror attacks illustrates how ineffective the legal model of accountability has become.

Global affairs include foreign policy, national security policy, and war powers. Foreign policy is the federal government's plans to advance national interests in dealing with other nations. National security includes the policies and actions that are intended to protect against domestic and foreign political threats to individuals, the government, and the country's territorial integrity. War powers include using military force pursuant to formal declarations of war as well as the broad range of military actions undertaken without a formal declaration of war. This chapter examines the following questions about global affairs:

- How should the U.S. engage in global affairs? The question *whether* the U.S. should engage in global affairs is simplistic because it frames the question as *either isolation or engagement*. Global affairs policy making is more accurately described as making choices about how to achieve foreign policy goals, particularly whether to use *soft power* (economics and diplomacy) or *hard power* (military force).

- What are the goals of global affairs policy? The two main theories of international relations are *realism* and *idealism*. Realism is the theory that describes nations as political actors that pursue national interest above other political values. Some realists also argue that international relations work best to maintain good order when nations pursue their national interest. Idealism is the theory that describes nations as political actors that can and should pursue national interest while also placing a high priority on political values such as democracy, human rights, justice, and the common good.

- Who should make global affairs policy? The history of global affairs is marked by institutional struggles for control over policy, primarily conflicts between Congress and the president but also conflicts between the president and the courts.

- How can presidents be held accountable for their actions, particularly the war powers and national security actions taken as Command-in-Chief?

The U.S. was founded as a republic. It won a revolutionary war for independence from an imperial power (Britain). It then assumed the role as protector of young New World (Caribbean and Central American) republics from European imperial powers—in fact, the U.S. thought of the Caribbean Sea as "an American lake" where it was free to use its military, economic, and political power to accomplish foreign policy goals. The U.S. became an imperial power. Then the U.S. assumed the role of world policeman—and the president became the leader of the free world during the Cold War. These developments were usually controversial and often debated. The war on terror has once again revived old debates about the U.S. role in global affairs. Counter-terrorism policy includes debates about using military power to export democracy, achieve regime change, and prevent or preempt national security threats.

The first question about global affairs is whether to stay out of foreign affairs as much as possible or to actively engage in foreign affairs. If the decision is to engage, the government must then determine its goals and the means to achieve them. International trade is a good example of these decisions. If the government decides to promote international trade, it must then decide what the goals of international trade policy:

- To promote free trade in general;

- To promote importing cheap goods made abroad in order to reduce consumer costs, or to promote exporting expensive good made domestically;
- To promote American agriculture, or to protect American manufacturing or intellectual property interests from foreign competition; or to
- To promote economic development abroad.

Other issues related to trade include whether the U.S. should include in international trade agreements provisions that protect labor (wages and worker rights), the environment (e.g., conservation or sustainable development), or human rights (e.g., democracy promotion). Trade and economic development policies are no longer considered unrelated to environmental, human rights, and democratic developments. Environmental issues such as global warming are increasingly recognized as global issues that are related to economic policies. The Obama administration promoted U.S. leadership in integrating economic and trade policy with environmental and human rights issues by participation in the Paris Climate Accords and the Trans-Pacific Partnership. The Trump administration's America First and economic development priorities have downplayed the integration of these issues in multi-national agreements.

Politics involves the authoritative allocation of scarce resources. Foreign policy making also requires establishing regional priorities. The U.S. has been politically, economically, and militarily engaged in the Middle East for more than half a century. Has the U.S. has achieved its goals? Working for peace in the Middle East is a laudable goal but one that has not been achieved. It also has opportunity costs. An *opportunity cost* is a potential benefit that is given up by choosing an alternate action. Spending time, energy, and resources in the Middle East means that the U.S. does not received potential benefits from pursuing foreign policy goals in other regions of the world. For instance, the Obama administration's planned *pivot to Asia*, a region of the world where rising economic and political powers presented new challenges and opportunities, was preempted by turmoil in the Middle East. Preoccupation with the Middle East also results in relative neglect of South America and large parts of Africa. China's economic expansion has made it "the world's expansionist superpower," but its expansion has been primarily economic, not military. China's massive foreign investments all over the world, but especially in economically poor but resource-rich countries, has made China the largest trading partner in more than 100 countries.[3]

The question *how* to project power abroad is usually framed as the choice between *hard power* and *soft power*. As the sole remaining military superpower, American government officials and the general public tend to think of global problems as military problem that have a military solution. The war on terror has revived the Cold War era debates about whether national security problem are political or military. The Obama administration leaned toward the liberal and Democratic approach, which frames terrorism as a political problem that requires soft power. The Trump administration leans toward the conservative and Republican approach, which frames terrorism as primarily a military threat to be confronted with military power.

The question of *who* should make policy is primarily about the relative power of Congress and the president. The fact that the modern president is in the driver's seat, with Congress riding shotgun in the passenger's seat, has greatly weakened the already weakened system of checks and balances in global affairs. The president is also much freer to act in global affairs because the interest group networks that have developed around foreign affairs are less well developed that they are in domestic affairs. The mass media pay less attention and devote few resources to investigative reporting about global affairs. The courts generally stay out of matters related to national security. And the general public pays less attention to global affairs than local or community issues. Taken together, these factors have weakened the system of checks and balances for holding presidents legally or politically accountable for their use of power abroad.

Two doctrines create special accountability problems. The first is the **Sole Organ Doctrine**. The Sole Organ Doctrine holds that the president is the sole organ of the nation in its dealings with other countries. The second doctrine is **executive discretion**. Executive discretion is defined as an executive official's power to decide upon a course of action without having that power limited by law. An example of executive discretion is commander-in-chief powers that Congress or the courts cannot limit. Another example of executive discretion is statutes that delegate the president power to do whatever the president thinks is necessary and appropriate. These broad delegations of power make it virtually impossible to hold a president legally accountable for actions because the president is given virtually unfettered discretion to decide whether to act and what to do.

17.1 | A Compromised System of Checks and Balances

Global affairs policy is political, but there are important differences between the politics of domestic affairs and global affairs. One difference is the system of checks and balances is much weaker in global affairs than domestic affairs. The model of political accountability and the model of legal accountability are not particularly effective in global affairs because the politics is distinctive. Global affairs, particularly those directly related to national security and war powers, are more likely to be framed as the kinds of issues where the normal democratic politics of negotiating, bargaining, and political compromise are considered inappropriate. In domestic affairs, policy choices typically reflect **economic** conflicts (e.g., the competing interests of business and labor), **partisan** conflict (e.g., Republicans versus Democrats), **ideological** conflict (e.g., conservative and liberal views on the size and role of government), and **institutional** conflicts among Congress, the president, the Supreme Court, or between the national and state governments. This means that global affairs have historically involved a different set of government and non-government actors than those that are typically involved with domestic affairs. For example, state and local governments and the interest group networks that participate in domestic policy making are not as prominent in global affairs.

A second difference concerns the legitimacy of government action. Democratic governments have authority over the people who live within their territorial jurisdiction. But what gives one country, whether democratic or not, the authority to use its economic, political, or military power to influence or control people in other countries? Political scientists differentiate between power and authority. Power is the ability to make someone do what you want. Authority is legitimate power. Legitimacy means that a law, a policy, or a government action is generally considered appropriate, good, legal, or just. Democracy is considered a legitimate form of government because it is based on self-government. The legitimacy problem with global affairs is projecting power abroad. Legitimacy is especially problematic in global affairs because the system for holding government officials accountable is not very effective. Political accountability is compromised because the foreign targets of the power cannot vote for or against the government officials, and legal accountability is compromised by weak commitments to the rule of law.

17.11 | *Partisanship*

The old saying that politics stops at the water's edge is based on the belief that it is not appropriate to **play politics** in foreign policy, that party politics and other political differences should be set aside so that the U.S. can present a united front when dealing with other countries. This description of non-partisan foreign policy has always been more an aspiration or hope than an actual description of foreign policy making. And globalization has blurred many of the distinctions between domestic and foreign policy so it is not surprising that the partisan divisions of opinion that characterize the ordinary politics of domestic affairs have spilled over into global affairs.

17.12 | *Separation of Powers*

The separation of powers created three co-equal branches of government in the sense each one is provided for in the Constitution. But this legal equality does mean the three branches have the same amount of power. The president is in the driver's seat because Congress generally follows the president's lead while the Supreme Court generally tries not to be a backseat driver when it comes to foreign affairs—particularly those related to national security. However, when individuals, companies, or Congress have challenged presidential actions related to foreign affairs, the Supreme Court has generally broadly interpreted presidential power.

An example of this is *U.S. v. Curtiss-Wright Export Corporation* (1936). Curtiss-Wright was a major American company that, among other things, was an international arms dealer. President Franklin Roosevelt declared an arms embargo that prohibited American companies from selling arms to two South American countries that were fighting over a disputed border region. The president issued the arms embargo because he thought that it would help bring peace to the region. The company sued, claiming the president did not have the power to issue the arms embargo. The Supreme Court ruled that the president did have the power to issue the embargo because the president the "sole organ" of the nation in its dealings with other nations. The Sole Organ Doctrine is not in the Constitution. The term came from a speech that Congressman John Marshall made on the floor of the House of Representatives. From this shaky origin, the Sole Organ Doctrine has become a powerful legal and political claim that presidents have the power to conduct foreign policy as they see fit—without Congress or the courts telling them what they can and cannot do. When presidents call for bipartisan support for their national security actions, or when they call critics of their actions un-American or unpatriotic, they are relying on the Sole Organ Doctrine to limit criticism or opposition.

17.13 | *Federalism*

The politics of global affairs is also distinctive because it is almost exclusively the responsibility of the national government. The Constitution's Supremacy Clause provides that federal laws (the Constitution, statutes, and treaties) shall be "the supreme law of the land." This means that federal laws trump state (or local) laws if the state law conflicts with federal law in an area of policy where the federal government has extensively regulated, thereby preempting state law. Take, for example, immigration policy. States located along the southern border with Mexico have comparatively high Latino populations and special interests in enforcing the border and immigration law. These states and cities can pass laws, adopt policies, or implement programs that provide resources for immigrants that the government does not provide, but the laws, policies, or programs cannot conflict with federal immigration policy. States cannot, for example, deny public education to children of illegal immigrants, deny illegal immigrants housing, or make it a crime for undocumented immigrants to seek work, or employers to offer work to undocumented immigrants. As immigration policy became more controversial, some border states (e.g., Arizona) passed anti-illegal immigration laws that purported to help the federal government enforce its own immigration laws.

The failure to provide border security was cited as one of the reasons for the failure to prevent the terrorist attacks on 9/11. As a result, the federal government was reorganized in order to provide more control over immigration. The Department of Homeland Security includes the Customs and Immigration Services Agency (CIS). The CIS combines the provision of services for immigrants and the function of enforcing immigration laws. However, the perception that the federal government was not enforcing immigration laws, or maintaining control over the southern border, caused some states to enact laws that were intended to toughen enforcement. The Arizona Legislature passed the Legal Arizona Worker's Act, which required state employers to check the immigration status of employees and provided for revoking the business license of companies that employed undocumented workers. The U.S. Chamber of Commerce challenged the law, arguing that 1) the federal government has complete power over immigration policy; and 2) the Supremacy Clause's **preemption doctrine** invalidates a state law that conflicts with a valid federal law. In Chamber of Commerce of the U.S. v. Whiting (2011), the Supreme Court upheld a state law requiring employers to check the immigration status. The Arizona legislature also passed SB1070, which made it a crime to be in the state illegally and required Arizona law enforcement officials to determine the immigration status of individuals they detained. In Arizona v. U.S. (2012) the Court struck down three of the four provisions of the state law.

Not all local governments support getting tougher on immigration. Some cities joined the sanctuary movement and announced that they are sanctuary cities that will not enforce federal immigration laws. The federal government cannot force state and local governments to help enforce federal laws, but the federal government can use financial incentives and penalties to encourage them to do so.

17.14 | *Public Opinion*

In democratic systems, public opinion is a vital essential check on government power. There are three reasons why public opinion is often a weak check on government power in global affairs. **First**, the public is not as well informed about foreign affairs as domestic affairs. The typical voter pays closer attention to domestic issues such as the condition of the schools, the economy, and the roads than foreign affairs. **Second**, the public is more dependent on the federal government for information about global affairs. The people who drive local roads and have children in local schools have direct knowledge of their condition, and know about crime rates and the local economy. But people are dependent on the government for information about most of the issues related to global affairs. This information dependency gives the government a freer hand to act independent of public opinion or even to create public opinion. **Third**, the typical initial public reaction to an international crisis or foreign threat or actual attack is to *rally around the flag*. The rally effect is an increase in patriotic support for the government. The president can expect increased public support in the immediate aftermath of a foreign crisis that touches on national security. However, the rally effect does tend to fade over time, and public support does tend to decline if a crisis continues, a hostage rescue or military action fails, or a war lingers on for a long period of time.

17.2 | The Main Traditions

The main traditions in global affairs policy are described in terms of 1) **isolationism** or **engagement** and 2) **realism** or **idealism**. *Isolationism* refers to staying out of global affairs as much as possible. *Engagement* refers to active participation in global affairs using economic, political, and military power to accomplish public policy goals. Isolationists believe that the government should place a high priority on domestic or internal affairs such as economic prosperity, political stability, and public safety. The isolationist tradition in American politics can be traced to three sources. First, the country was founded as a republic that won a revolutionary war for independence against an imperial power and came to see itself as opposed to the idea of government intervention in the political affairs of other countries. Second, the U.S. was protected from European power politics by two great oceans—the Atlantic in the east and the Pacific in the west—that allowed the young republic to focus on domestic affairs rather than trying to protect itself from foreign invasions by entangling alliances with other countries. Countries that are surrounded by other countries are more likely to have to pay more attention to global affairs. The third reason for the isolationist tradition is ideology. American political culture has elements of an "anti-statist ideology" that is wary of centralized government power.[4]

Nevertheless, the U.S. does have a strong tradition of engagement in global affairs. Supporters of engagement maintain that the U.S. should use its economic, military, and political power to strategically advance its national interests while promoting democracy abroad. In fact, one of the points of this chapter is that it is simplistic to describe U.S. policy as either isolationism or engagement because it has always had elements of both traditions. This also applies to the second set of terms commonly used to describe global policy: realism and idealism. *Realism* is the international relations theory that nations primarily pursue their national interest as the paramount goal of international relations. Some realists also think that it is appropriate for nations to pursue their national interest because an international system where each nation pursues its national self-interest is more likely to create and maintain good international order than a system that expects nations to pursue lofty, idealistic goals such as the common good. *Idealism* is the international relations theory that nations should pursue goals other than purely self-interest or power politics, that nations should also pursue goals such as democracy, human rights, conservation, the common good, and justice.

The early years of the Trump administration indicate how presidential administrations have different priorities within the main foreign policy traditions. During the campaign, Donald Trump's rhetoric was labeled isolationist because he emphasized solving domestic problems rather than global engagement—nationalism rather than globalism. However, President Trump quickly adopted internationalist or globalist positions that reflected the Republican Party's foreign policy establishment (e.g., support for the North Atlantic Treaty Organization and Middle East engagement). But during his first foreign trip, President Trump upset European allies by not explicitly committing to Article Five of the North Atlantic Treaty Organization—the collective defense article of NATO—and then returned to the U.S. to announce that he was withdrawing the U.S. from the Paris Accords, the international agreement to address global warming, in order to protect U.S. sovereignty. Protecting U.S. national sovereignty is an aspect of President Trump's America First approach.

So is the Trump administration's global policy isolationism/nationalism or engagement/globalism? David Brooks, a traditional conservative Republican, explains by citing a *Wall Street Journal* editorial written by President Trump's National Security Advisor H. R. McMaster and chief economic advisor Gary D. Cohn that provides a key insight into how President Trump thinks about global affairs. According to McMaster and Cohn, the president "embarked on his first foreign trip with a clear-eyed outlook that the world is not a 'global community' but an arena where nations, nongovernmental actors and businesses engage and compete for advantage." Brooks believes that this is an indication that the Trump administration has a Hobbesian realist view of international affairs: Hobbesian in the sense that it sees global affairs as a dog-eat-dog world of national competition for survival; realist in the sense that it describes governments as self-interested actors with little regard for idealistic goals such as cooperation in pursuit of the common good.[5]

This assessment is consistent with descriptions of President Trump and Secretary of State Rex Tillerson as transactional leaders whose business careers before government service involved making deals. And President Trump's initial foreign policy has been based on 1) personal relationships between the heads of government rather than established doctrines or official policies; 2) bi-lateral deals between the U.S. and another country rather than multilateral agreements among the governments in a particular region; and 3) deals that involve single issues such as trade, military defense, human rights, or environmental protection rather than comprehensive, multilateral agreements. Donald Trump's campaign for change was successful in part because he rejected both the Republican and Democratic establishments' support for globalism and military intervention abroad. During the campaign, this was commonly but mistakenly described as isolationism. The campaign is more accurately described as one that promised to change priorities to emphasize national interests rather than global issues. In this respect, Trump joined the growing chorus of conservative and liberal populists in the U.S. and other liberal democracies who believed that economic nationalism was the solution to problems that were created by globalism. The *Make America Great Again* and *America First* slogans made economic nationalism a viable political and economic alternative to the extremes of isolationism or globalism.

17.21 | *Isolation*

American politics has from the early years of the republic debated whether and how to be engaged in foreign affairs. President George Washington's *Farewell Address* is often remembered today as wise counsel from the father of the country warning future leaders to stay out of foreign affairs, to avoid entangling alliances and the kinds of international intrigues that made European politics a seemingly endless series of destructive wars. Washington did indeed advise the country's leaders to avoid entangling alliances, but he did not advise isolation. He did not urge the nation's leaders to look inward rather than outward. His advice was more nuanced. He advised having **commercial** (or business) relations with other nations but not political relations:

> "History and experience prove that foreign influence is one of the most baneful foes of republican government.... The great rule of conduct for us in regard to foreign nations is, in extending our commercial relations to have with them as little *political* connection as possible."

Washington thought that avoiding entangling political connections was the best way for the young republic to avoid becoming entangled in the European web of political conflicts. In effect, Washington urged the country's future leaders to be skeptical of "entangling" U.S. peace and prosperity with the European tradition of political intrigue and imperial greed. When emergencies or other situations required political connections with other countries, he recommended entering into "temporary alliances." He warned leaders to "steer clear of permanent alliances with any portion of the foreign world" because he believed that "a small or weak" country (such as the U.S.) that attached itself to a "great and powerful nation dooms the former to be the satellite of the latter."

Washington's *Farewell Address* was not limited to practical advice about how the country could pursue its national interest while avoiding war or becoming subservient to imperial powers. He advised future leaders to remain true to the nation's founding values while pursuing national self-interest. He specifically mentioned keeping good faith and justice towards all nations, promoting peace and harmony with all nations, avoiding "inveterate antipathies" against some nations and "passionate attachments" to others, and advocating trade with all nations. Washington was not an isolationist. He and other leading members of the Federalist Party, most notably Alexander Hamilton, wanted the U.S. to develop as a "commercial republic" that engaged in international trade. Some of Hamilton's contemporaries believed that the development of commercial republics would bring about a peaceful world because countries that valued international trade more than territorial expansion or national glory would be less likely to go to war with one another. But in *Federalist Number 6* Hamilton wrote that it was naïve idealism or "utopian" thinking that commercial republics would make war obsolete.

Future leaders did not heed Washington's advice about avoiding entangling alliances. In a July 4th, 1821 Independence Day speech delivered to the House of Representatives, John Q. Adams reminded the members of Congress of what America had already given mankind. America proclaimed natural rights as "the only lawful foundations of government," and "introduced the language of liberty and equality" to other countries while respecting national sovereignty and staying out of the affairs of other nations. Adams idealistically described the U.S. as a republic that assumed a leadership role in the world by serving as a model of republican government without succumbing to the temptation to "go abroad in search of monsters to destroy."

Think about it!
Was Washington right to warn the nation's leaders to stay out of foreign affairs?

Isolationists have been the strongest voices resisting the temptations of great powers to go abroad in search of monsters to destroy. Isolationists opposed U.S. participation in WWI and WWII. Charles Lindbergh was a national hero whose reputation was permanently damaged by his strong statements urging the U.S. to stay out of WWII. His 1941 *Address to the America First Committee* remains a strong statement of isolationism or non-intervention as a guiding principle for foreign and national security policy.[6]

17.22 | *Engagement*

Engagement also has roots in early American politics. The **Monroe Doctrine** (1823) declared that the U.S. sphere of influence included the entire Western Hemisphere. It put European imperial powers on notice that their efforts to colonize countries, or to interfere with Latin American efforts to gain independence from Spain, would be considered justification for American military action.

The concepts of **Manifest Destiny** and **American Exceptionalism** justified territorial expansion. Manifest Destiny is the belief that the United States was destined to expand its sphere of influence over the western territories of North America and even beyond the region. It justified westward expansion to settle the American frontier and to fight Indian Wars to remove Native Americans from their traditional lands. The Louisiana Purchase (1803) almost doubled the geographic size of the nation. Spain ceded the territory of Florida in 1819 and the U.S. annexed Texas in 1845.

Manifest Destiny justified the Mexican-American War (1846-1848) and the Spanish-American War (1898). The U.S. acquired from Mexico the vast territories that comprise California, Arizona, and New Mexico. The U.S. bought Alaska from Russia Empire in 1867 and annexed the Republic of Hawaii in 1898. The U.S. victory over Spain in the Spanish-American War gave the U.S. possession of the former Spanish colonies of the Philippines and Puerto Rico and control over Cuba. The Spanish-American War was particularly controversial because the use of military power to acquire territory abroad indicated the country was abandoning the republican ideals expressed in The Declaration of Independence and by the Revolutionary War. In "The Conquest of the U.S. By Spain" (1899), William Graham Sumner (1840-1910) argued that the U.S. paid a high price for winning the Spanish-American War because it lost its status as a republic by acquiring control over other peoples.[7]

American Exceptionalism is the belief that the U.S. is a special country with a special responsibility to use its political, economic, and military power to be a leader in global affairs. American Exceptionalism continues to justify engagement in world affairs. The Founders were wary of engaging in foreign affairs, but they did not advise isolation. The *Records of the Constitutional Convention of 1787* and the *Federalist Papers* reveal extended debates about how to deal with other nations. The Founders were acutely aware of world politics and realized that the country had to be strong enough to be secure from foreign threats. They understood that the American Revolutionary War for Independence was part of a broader, global conflict that involved the U.S., England, France, Spain, and the Netherlands. They realized that the U.S. could not isolate itself from politics outside the country. Creating a commercial republic that was actively involved with international trade made political sense because the U.S. was a struggling young nation facing economic and political challenges. Sectional differences among the north, the south, the eastern seaboard, and the frontier regions weakened national unity. The young republic was surrounded by Indian Tribes and three imperial powers (France, England, and Spain).

National identity and American sovereignty have functioned as political glue binding Americans together. Nationalism is still strong. But globalization, treaties and executive agreements, and an expanding body of international law have eroded U.S. national sovereignty. Conservative nationalists have opposed the United Nations, the International Criminal Court, and treaties that commit the U.S. to recognizing the rights of children or obligate the U.S. to take actions to address climate change. The emergence of economic nationalism in the 2016 elections, particularly Donald Trump's economic nationalist campaign, is an aspect of the resurgence of national sovereignty as a backlash against globalism.

17.23 | *Foreign Policy*

Foreign policy is defined as the set of goals and public policies that a country establishes for its interactions with other nations and, to a lesser extent, non-state actors. Foreign policies are designed to promote national interests, national security, ideology, political values, and economic prosperity. The tools of foreign policy include economic, political, social, diplomatic, technological, and military resources.

As U.S. economic and military power increased during the latter part of the 19th century, the U.S. became an increasingly important player on the global stage. This aspect of American political development marked an important, long-term shift in U.S. foreign policy that included territorial expansion, more active involvement in foreign affairs, and more engagement in international relations. In the early years of the 20th Century, U.S. foreign policy was shaped primarily by 1) promoting American business abroad; 2) worries about increased immigration from regions other than Britain and northern Europe; 3) participation in World War I; and 4) intervention in Caribbean and Central American politics. The U.S. role on the global stage continued to expand after WWII with American efforts to avoid another global conflict by bringing order to the anarchistic world of international relations. International relations were "anarchistic" in the sense that each country used power politics to pursue its national interest; military force was the primary way to settle disputes between nations; and justice reflected the principle might makes right. The U.S. interest in taking a leadership role in promoting world peace has roots in President Woodrow Wilson's ambitious plan to use American power to make the world safe for democracy. Wilson was an internationalist—today we would say a globalist—who believed that the creation of international organizations such as the League of Nations—a precursor to the United Nations— would reduce war by creating alternative ways to settle conflicts. President Wilson pleaded with the Senate to ratify the Versailles Treaty, which contained the Covenant of the League of Nations, but the Senate did not ratify the Treaty. The American political tradition of taking unilateral action, rather than joining international organization, and preserving U.S. sovereignty doomed the League of Nation.

> **Think About It!**
> "Dare we reject it [the Versailles Treaty] and break the heart of the world."
> President Woodrow Wilson, September 11, 1941
> https://www.whitehouse.gov/1600/presidents/woodrowwilson

In the years preceding WWII, the United States promoted international trade but otherwise tended to be rather isolationist. As a result, the Roosevelt administration had to overcome strong publicFF resistance to joining international efforts to confront the threats presented by Germany and Japan when they built up their military forces in the 1930s and used them against their neighbors. President Roosevelt bent the law prohibiting providing military aid to Britain by using the Lend-Lease Program to help Britain fight Nazi Germany. The U.S. then entered the war in 1941 and led the allies against Germany, Japan, and Italy. The conversion of the American economy from peacetime production to wartime production was a major factor in winning the war. The pattern of mobilizing for war and then demobilizing after war ended with WWII when, for the first time in its history, the U.S. won a war and then kept a standing peacetime army. The U.S. also made permanent some of the most important wartime institutions that were considered essential for protecting national security and ensuring military readiness. And Congress created federal agencies responsible for national defense, national security, and intelligence gathering. The federal government often responds to crises by creating government agencies to deal with them. The Great Depression of the 1930s resulted in the creation of the social welfare state. World War II and the Cold War resulted in the creation of the **warfare state**. The term warfare state refers to the

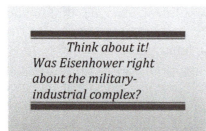

Think about it!
Was Eisenhower right
about the military-
industrial complex?

permanent national defense, national security, and intelligence agencies, including the Department of Defense, the Central Intelligence Agency, and the National Security Agency.

During the Cold War Era, the primary goal of U.S. foreign policy was national security. The end of WWII—and actual hot war—began the extended period of military and political conflict between the U.S. and the Soviet Union known as the Cold War. The foreign policy of **containment** used American military, economic, and political influence to limit the Soviet expansion of its spheres of influence in various regions of the world. In terms of economic power, the U.S. used foreign aid and other types of economic or development assistance as instruments of foreign policy to contain Soviet influence. In terms of political influence, the U.S. used diplomacy, regional treaties including the North Atlantic Treaty Organization (NATO) and the Southeast Asia Treaty Organization (SEATO), and executive agreements to counter the influence of the Soviet Union and China. In terms of military power, the U.S. used mutual defense treaties, military actions (e.g., the Korean War and the Vietnam War), proxy wars, and numerous covert or secret military or CIA operations as instruments of foreign policy. A proxy war or conflict is one where major military powers support or sponsor a smaller country's military actions because the major powers think that the fighting serves the major powers' interests.

In a famous *Farewell Address* delivered January 17, 1961, President Eisenhower warned of the dangers presented by the new national security state, and advised the public and government officials to "guard against the acquisition of unwarranted influence…by the military-industrial complex."[8] Nevertheless, military-industrial complex grew more powerful during the Cold War Era and developed into the national security state. There were expectations that the end of the Cold War with the dissolution of the Soviet Union in 1989 would produce a peace dividend—tax savings from lower defense spending—and a foreign policy that relied less on national security and placed a higher priority on international trade, human rights, and diplomacy. The 9/11 terrorist attacks ended expectations of a peace dividend or a reordering of foreign policy priorities.

17.24 | *The Modern Conservative Era*

The modern conservative era began in the latter 1960s and early 1970s when liberalism was blamed for weakening the U.S. economically and militarily. Liberalism was blamed for the following:

- Going soft on communism. Conservatives thought that American foreign policy was no longer sufficiently anti-communist, that liberal faith in peace and diplomacy and accommodation appeased the Soviet Union in ways that resembled British efforts to appease Hitler's Germany prior to WWII.
- The Vietnam Syndrome. The loss of the War in Vietnam was brought home to many American homes by television images of a chaotic withdrawal when Saigon fell in 1975. The resulting loss of confidence in the military and political leadership created doubt about American foreign policy ideals and the legitimacy of using military force abroad. Conservatives diagnosed this national malaise as the "Vietnam Syndrome." A syndrome is a medical condition that manifests with multiple symptoms. In an August 1980 presidential

campaign speech delivered at the Veterans of Foreign Wars Convention (VFW), Ronald Reagan pledged to end the Vietnam Syndrome by restoring American military power to fight effectively AND reviving the American spirit, the willingness to fight for noble causes.[9]

- Energy dependency. In the 1970s, two oil embargoes by The Organization of the Petroleum Exporting Countries (OPEC) exposed how vulnerable the American economy (and lifestyle) was because of dependence on foreign oil.

- The Iran Hostage Crisis. On November 4, 1979 Americans were taken hostage in Iran as part of a revolution against the Shah of Iran, an authoritarian ruler who had been an ally of the U.S. The taking of the hostages and a failed hostage rescue mission reinforced the perception that President Carter and the U.S. were weak.

- The Soviet invasion of Afghanistan. The Soviet Union invaded Afghanistan in December 1979. The invasion and other aggressive actions so soon after the Iran Hostage Crisis began contributed to the sense that American power was in decline. Ironically, by the time the Soviet-Afghan War ended in 1989 with a Soviet withdrawal, Afghanistan was called the *Soviet Vietnam*.

17.25 | *Declinism (Or "The Sky is Falling!")*

The dominant theme of national security debates is whether the U.S. is strong (enough), weak, or declining (going soft). The U.S. has a long history of declinist politics. Declinism refers to warnings that the country has lost its edge, has gotten weak, or is going soft. Politicians and government officials can rarely go wrong by pledging to buildup the military or promising to increase national security. In the latter 1950s and the 1960 presidential election, Democrats claimed that Republican policies created a "bomber gap" and "missile gap" that left the country vulnerable to a Soviet attack. Then Republican presidential candidate Richard Nixon's July 1967 *Address to the Bohemian Society* provided the foundations for his administration's foreign policy goals and those of Republican Presidents Reagan, George H.W. Bush, and George W. Bush. Nixon's *Address* is significant because it shows that already in the mid-1960s Republicans were

- Describing communism as a failing ideology;
- Crediting American military superiority for the post-WWII era of *Pax Americana*;
- Supporting a military buildup to keep the "Peace Through Strength;" and
- Supporting American economic power as an instrument of foreign policy to counter Soviet influence across the globe.[10]

Ronald Reagan won the 1980 presidential election partly because he promised to rebuild the military to fight Soviet communism and to restore American confidence in global leadership. After the fall of the Soviet Union, neo-conservative intellectuals argued that the U.S., as the sole remaining superpower, had a responsibility to actively engage in world leadership. In *The Case for Goliath: How America Acts as the World's Government In the Twenty-First Century* (2006), Michael Mandelbaum argued that the U.S. had become a de facto world government.

17.26 | *New Foreign Policy Issues: Trade*

The end of the Cold War in 1991 began a period where American foreign policy placed a higher priority on economics (e.g., the promotion of free trade; economic development; and global economic competition) and human rights. China, India, and the European Union emerged as major economic competitors. China is a particularly interest case because it is a Communist country whose policy of rapid economic growth and development created the second largest economy as measured by Gross Domestic Product. China's emergence as an economic competitor has raised concerns about whether China's economic power will eventually present a military and political threat to the U.S. In fact, this is the main foreign policy question about U.S. policy toward China.

The emergence of new international economic competitors has also prompted debates about what public policies the U.S. should adopt to ensure that the U.S. remains competitive in the global marketplace. The Conference Board is a "global business membership and research association" that describes itself as working to advance the public interest by providing the world's leading organizations with practical knowledge to improve their performance and to better serve society. Like many other business organizations, the Conference Board promotes public policies that encourage economic growth. It believes that the current low rates of economic growth in the U.S. have two main causes. The first is **demographics**. The U.S. and other developed countries have aging populations—an increasing percentage of older people who require more medical care and other social services. They are also less likely to be working. This means that the country has an increasing percentage of people who are consumers of services rather than producers. Immigration policies were used to import a younger labor force to offset these demographics. The Conference Board believes that the second cause of low economic growth is **educational**: stagnant educational attainment is blamed for stagnant economic growth rates. The Conference Board recommends changing immigration policy to solve the demographic problem of an aging population—specifically, changing immigration policies to allow more high-skilled workers into the country. Business interest groups generally support immigration policy as a partial solution to the problem of stagnant educational attainment or a mismatch between what employers need and employee skill sets.

Should the U.S. grant more temporary work visas for skilled foreign workers in order to meet the domestic demand for high tech workers? The H-1B Visa Program was designed to do so but employers use the program for a different purpose, as explained in the NPR story "Older Tech Workers Oppose Overhauling H-1B Visas."

Think about it!
See the British Broadcasting Corporation's "Meet China's Booming Middle Class" Aired July 2012
http://www.bbc.co.uk/news/business-18901437

Think About It!
Is immigration the solution to the problem of low economic growth?

Act on It!
Contact a government official (in the U.S. or another country), a business leader, or an interest group or political party official to see what they think is the solution to the problems with current immigration policy.

17.27 | *New Foreign Policy Issues: Globalism*

Globalism is a broad term that refers to interconnected and interdependent economies, societies, cultures, and governments. Globalization initially involved international business interests promoting international trade. It now includes issues such as human rights, environmental policy, sustainable development, and even good governance.[11] Globalism has blurred distinctions between domestic and global affairs.

Americans know much less about the people, politics, geography, and economics of other countries than people in other countries know about the U.S. American media do not provide much coverage of politics in other countries compared to other countries' media coverage of U.S. politics. Read a newspaper or magazine, watch a television news program, or go to your favorite web site to see how much news coverage is state/local, national, and international.

> Think About It!
> What do people in other countries think about U.S. presidential elections?
> Public Radio International's *The World* provides "Foreign Views on the American Presidency and the Election," (November 5, 2012).
> http://www.theworld.org/
> http://www.theworld.org/2012/11/the-world-votes-election-views-from-london/

> Act on it!
> Write a letter to the editor of one of the major newspapers of the world to see whether it gets published.

17.28 | *New Foreign Policy Issues: Human Migration and Religion*

During most of the post-WWII era, immigration policy was not very controversial in the U.S., Britain, or Europe. In fact, these countries recruited foreign workers as their populations aged and as their economic growth rates slowed. Immigration became very controversial as good jobs became harder to find, as the increased number of immigrations created worries about national identity, and as terrorism transformed immigration policy from an economic issue into a national security issue. In fact, immigration policy has become a national security issue primarily because immigration became an issue closely related to religion and American national identity. Latino immigrants, who are primarily Catholic, first raised concerns about their effect on American Protestant culture. Then radical Islamic terrorism framed immigration policy as a central element of the conflict between Christian civilization and Islamic civilization. It is ironic that religion became a threat even while foreign policy made freedom of religion a higher priority. For example, the Department of State's Office of International Religious Freedom describes its mission as promoting religious freedom as a "core objective" of foreign police. The Office provides information about the status of freedom of religion in various countries that serves as a benchmark for assessing how free a political system is.

17.3 | Instruments of Foreign and Defense Policy

Treaties and executive agreements are the two major forms of official agreements with other countries. The major difference between them is that executive agreements are less formal than treaties and they are not subject to the constitutional requirement of ratification by a two-thirds vote of the Senate.

17.31 | *Treaties*

Treaties are formal written agreements between two or more countries. The Treaty Clause of the Constitution (Article II, Section 2) provides that the President "shall have Power, by and with the Advice and Consent of the Senate, to make Treaties, provided two thirds of the Senators present concur...." The president or his advisors negotiate a treaty with another country or countries, but the Senate must ratify it in order to take effect. The Senate can reject a treaty for any reason. Senators might oppose the **substance** of the treaty: they may oppose what the treaty does the way they oppose what a law does. For example, President Wilson proposed the Treaty of Versailles after World War I, but the Senate rejected the peace treaty primarily because the **isolationist tradition** made Senators wary of U.S. participation in the League of Nation.[12]

Sovereignty and **federalism** are also reasons why Senators, state government officials, and the general public are wary of treaties. Sovereignty is defined as the supreme and independent government authority. The American commitment to preserving U.S. national sovereignty is very strong—the idea of national sovereignty is much stronger in the U.S. than in many European countries. Treaties that obligate U.S. government officials to comply with international law or treaty obligations weaken U.S. national sovereignty. Defenders of U.S. national sovereignty such as Sovereignty International, Inc., alert Americans to the threats presented by specific treaties or executive agreements as well as the general trend toward global governance. The preservation of national sovereignty is one of the reasons for opposition to the United Nations, opposition to putting U.S. troops under UN control in peacekeeping operations, and even opposition to treaties that strengthen human rights or the rights of children. Protecting children may be a laudable goal, but doing so in ways that erode national sovereignty is controversial.

Figure 17-31 below describes three levels of sovereignty: state, national, and supranational). Over time, political power has flowed upward. The Founders intended to create a state-centric system. Over time, the power of the national government expanded and the political system has become more national-centric. In fact, opposition to *big* government is often directed at the national government. Internationalist efforts to create supranational governing authorities are even more controversial than the development of a national-centric system because it involves locating sovereignty outside the U.S.

Figure 17.31: Three Levels of Sovereignty

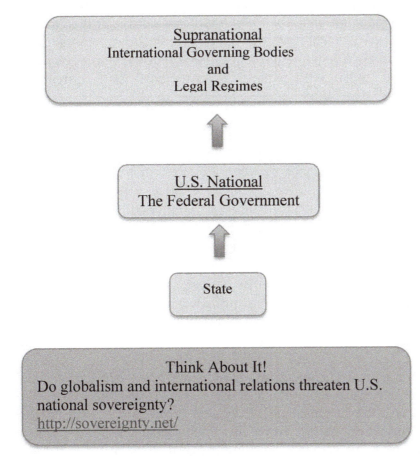

Supranational
International Governing Bodies
and
Legal Regimes

U.S. National
The Federal Government

State

Think About It!
Do globalism and international relations threaten U.S.
national sovereignty?
http://sovereignty.net/

Federalism is on reason for American wariness of treaties. Federalism complicates the legal status of treaties. Treaties (and executive agreements) are considered federal laws. Their legal effect on state law is complicated. The Supremacy Clause of the U.S. Constitution provides that federal law trumps state laws that conflict with federal law. But state government officials may be even more opposed to treaties than to ordinary federal statutes because treaties are associated with international law or organizations such as the United Nations. Can a migratory bird treaty that protects Canada Geese as they fly south from Canada to winter near the Gulf of Mexico trump state laws that allow hunting Canada Geese? Can a treaty require a state that arrests a foreign national for crime to notify that person's government that one of its citizens has been arrested? Article 36 of the Vienna Convention on the Right to Consular Access gives any foreign national who has been arrested for a crime the right to consular access. The State of Texas argued that the Vienna Convention did not obligate a state. The Supreme Court agreed in *Medellin v. Texas* (2008).

Think About It!
Why would the U.S. sign a treaty that required governments that arrest a citizen of another country to notify that country that it has arrested one of its citizens?

Where do treaties fit into the U.S. legal system? Treaties are the legal equivalent of federal statutes. The president can unilaterally reinterpret provisions of treaties. President Carter unilaterally reinterpreted the <u>Panama Canal Treaty</u> to return possession of the Panama Canal to Panama. The Supreme Court has ruled that it has the authority to declare a treaty unconstitutional, just as it has the authority to declare a statute unconstitutional, but the Court has never done so. The <u>Vienna Convention on the Law of Treaties</u> provides for the legal status of treaties. The State Department reports on treaties.[13] The following are some major treaties:

- The North Atlantic Treaty (1949) established the <u>North Atlantic Treaty Organization</u> (NATO). NATO was the major international treaty organization during the Cold War era. The Treaty created the major alliance between the Western powers that confronted the Soviet Union.
- The <u>World Trade Organization</u> (WTO) is one of the international bodies that promotes and regulates international trade with the goal of *liberalizing* international trade—that is, minimizing trade barriers. The WTO's emphasis on trade reflects the post-Cold War shift toward trade rather than national security.
- The <u>North American Free Trade Agreement</u> (NAFTA) is an example of the foreign policy emphasis on promoting free trade in regions of the world.

17.32 | *Executive Agreements*

An <u>executive agreement</u> is a formal document that is negotiated between the president and the head of another government—typically the prime minister. As such, executive agreements are not permanent agreements because they do not bind subsequent presidents the way that treaties do. Because executive agreements do not have to be ratified by the senate, presidents have relied less on treaties and more on executive agreements. The number of treaties has greatly decreased; the number of executive agreements has greatly increased. The Constitution does not mention executive agreements. But in <u>U.S. v. Belmont</u> (1937) the Supreme Court held that executive agreements were constitutional, the president had power to enter into executive agreements, and ruled that executive agreements had the same legal status as treaties. So executive agreements also have the same status as federal statutes. The president's power to enter into executive agreements is now part of the American political and legal tradition of presidential legislation in global affairs.

17.4 | Actors: Institutions and Organizations

Government and non-government actors participate in the Global Affairs policy-making process, particularly foreign policy. The following describes some of the major participants in the global affairs issue network, their roles, and their goals.

17.41 | *Congress*

Article I of the Constitution vests all the legislative power in Congress, grants Congress the power to declare war, and requires treaties—which are negotiated by the president—be ratified by the Senate. Congress also has the power of the purse. This budget power is relevant to global affairs because it means that Congress enacts the State Department's civilian budget, which is one of the main foreign policy actors, and the military budget for the Department of Defense. Congress uses its power of the purse, its budget authority, to influence foreign and national security policy.

The House Foreign Affairs Committee and the Senate Foreign Relations Committees are the primary congressional committees with jurisdiction over foreign policy—but other committees, including the defense and commerce committees, also deal with policies that are related to foreign policy. The Senate Foreign Relations Committee website describes the committee history, members, hearings, and legislation. The committee plays an important role in shaping foreign policy as well as legislative oversight of the government agencies responsible for implementing foreign policy. The Committee's website candidly acknowledged that the president, not Congress, takes the lead in foreign policy. According to the History of the Committee, the executive branch "does take the lead on nearly every aspect of foreign policy, [but] congressional committees use the power of the purse" to exert influence over the president's policies.[14] In the 113th Congress, the House Foreign Affairs Committee website (accessed February 2, 2013) described its jurisdiction as being "responsible for oversight and legislation" related to a broad range of policy responsibilities, including oversight and legislation relating to foreign assistance; the Peace Corps; national security developments affecting foreign policy; strategic planning and agreements; war powers, treaties, executive agreements, and the deployment and use of United States Armed Forces; peacekeeping, peace enforcement, and enforcement of United Nations or other international sanctions; arms control and disarmament issues; activities and policies of the State, Commerce and Defense Departments and other agencies related to the Arms Export Control Act, and the Foreign Assistance; international law; promotion of democracy; international law enforcement issues, including narcotics control programs and activities; Broadcasting Board of Governors; embassy security; international broadcasting; public diplomacy, including international communication, information policy, international education, and cultural programs; and other matters.

17.42 | *The President*

The president and the secretary of state, a presidential appointee, are the primary actors responsible for making and managing foreign policy. The importance of the president is reflected in the fact that the president's name is often attached to the administration's main foreign policy: the Monroe Doctrine; the Truman Doctrine; the Kennedy Doctrine; the Nixon Doctrine; the Reagan Doctrine; the Bush Doctrine; the Obama Doctrine; and eventually the Trump Doctrine. A doctrine typically announces the major outlines of an administration's policy. The Monroe Doctrine announced that the U.S. considered the Caribbean within its sphere of influence and would act to oppose European imperial intervention. The Truman Doctrine announced the Cold War policy: stopping Soviet expansion; supporting free people who were resisting subjugation; and negotiating regional defense treaties (the Rio Pact of 1947—Latin America; NATO in 1949); ANZUS with Australia and New Zealand; and SEATO with Southeast Asia). The Truman Doctrine greatly expanded the role of the U.S. as the world's policeman. A president's foreign policy doctrine also announces the administration's policy concerning the use of military force—particularly whether it will rely on hard power (the military) or soft power (diplomacy) to pursue national interests and resolve international conflicts.

A president who is of a different party than his predecessor is likely to announce a foreign policy doctrine that is different than the predecessor—particularly if foreign policy was an issue in the presidential campaign. For example, Republican President George W. Bush's Bush Doctrine emphasized unilateral military action to advance national interests and regime change—particularly in the Mideast. Democratic President Barack Obama's Obama Doctrine emphasized multilateral action, diplomacy, and resistance to regime change in the Mideast.

The secretary of state is the functional equivalent of the **foreign minister** in a country with a parliamentary system of government. In parliamentary systems, foreign policy is the responsibility of the prime minister, who is the head of the government. The prime minister's principal foreign policy advisor is the foreign minister, who is a political appointee of the prime minister. The secretary of state conducts diplomacy, state-to-state policy discussions, and certain interactions with the government officials of other countries. The secretary of state and ambassadors are nominated by the president and confirmed by the Senate. Congress also has power to regulate commerce with foreign nations.

It is ironic that global affairs is the president's domain because most presidents come to office with little or no experience with global affairs. Most presidents come to office with experience in domestic politics (e.g., governor; senator; vice-president) or business. The lack of experience with global affairs means that the leader of the free world must get on-the-job training. Presidents do come to office with high public expectations of the president as the leader of the free world, hosting world leaders at the White House, acting on the global stage by flying around on Air Force One, and acting as the Commander-in-Chief when deploying the military.

Congress has greatly increased presidential power over global affairs by statutorily delegating broad legislative power to the president. With the possible exception of the War Powers Resolution of 1973, the following are examples of congressional delegations of legislative power to the president on matters of national security, war powers, and emergency powers. They illustrate the problem of holding presidents *legally accountable* for the use of power because they grant the president the power to do whatever the president thinks is necessary and appropriate. The language is so vague that it is virtually impossible to hold a president legally accountable.

- Hostage Rescue Act (1868). This Act authorized the president to take "all actions necessary and proper, not amounting to war, to secure the release of hostages."
- The Gulf of Tonkin Resolution (1964). "WHEREAS, the communist regime in Vietnam....have repeatedly attacked U.S. vessels lawfully present in international waters...." RESOLVED, That the Congress approves the determination of the President "to take all necessary measures to repel any armed attack against the forces of the United States and to prevent further aggression."
- The First War Powers Act of 1941. This Act delegated broad powers to the president to organize and wage war.
- The War Powers Resolution of 1973. In order to ensure collective judgment when committing troops to hostilities or situations where hostilities are imminent, the president shall consult with Congress, report to Congress, and shall seek authorization to maintain commitments beyond specified time periods.
- International Economic Emergency Powers Act (1977). This Act authorizes the President to declare a national emergency and order embargoes, trade sanctions, asset seizures.
- Authorization for Use of Military Force Against Terrorists. (Public Law 107-40, Enacted September 18, 2001.) The AUMF authorized the President "to use all necessary and appropriate force against those nations, organizations, or persons he determines planned, authorized, committed, or aided the terrorist attacks that occurred on September 11, 2001,

or harbored such organizations or persons, in order to prevent any future acts of international terrorism against the United States by such nations, organizations or persons."

- Authorization for Use of Military Force Against Iraq Resolution. (Public Law 107-243, Enacted October 16, 2002.) This AUMF resolution began "WHEREAS, Iraq remains in material and unacceptable breach of its international obligations, [Followed by a list of 22 "whereases" listing among others the invasion of Kuwait, violations of UN cease fire terms of disarmament, weapons inspections, weapons of mass destruction, threat to the national security of the United States, 9/11 attacks and terrorists known to use Iraq, UN Sec. Council Res. 678 authorizing use of force to enforce UN Resolutions] and resolved that "The President is authorized to use the Armed Forces of the United States as he determines to be necessary and appropriate" in order to (1) defend the national security of the United States and (2) "enforce all relevant United Nations Security Council resolutions regarding Iraq."

17.43 | *The Department of State*

The State Department is the main executive branch agency responsible for developing and implementing foreign policy under the president's direction. The State Department's mission statement (for Fiscal Years 2004 – 2009) described American diplomacy as based on the belief that "our freedoms are best protected by ensuring that others are free; our prosperity depends on the prosperity of others; and our security relies on a global effort to secure the rights of others." The November 2010 Agency Financial Report described foreign policy goals as advancing freedom "for the benefit of the American people and the international community by helping to build and sustain a more democratic, secure, and prosperous world composed of well-governed states that respond to the needs of their people, reduce widespread poverty, and act responsibly within the international system."[15]

The above language reflects the State Department's and the foreign policy establishment's belief in globalism integration of governance and areas of public policy: political (democracy promotion); security (military); and economic (prosperity and development). These priorities are likely to change during the Trump administration. During the 2016 presidential campaign and as President, Donald Trump pledged to drain the (Washington) swamp. The "Drain the Swamp" slogan would be especially apt if he meant draining *Foggy Bottom*—the low-lying riverside area of Washington D.C. where the State Department moved in 1947—to rely more on the military as an instrument of foreign policy. Trump's initial budget proposal called for a 30% reduction in spending for the State Department and its foreign aid programs and diplomatic activity. This reduction and the budget increases for national defense and national security and border control reflect the shift in his administration's priorities.

> **Check it Out!**
> How much do you think the U.S. spends on foreign aid? What percentage of the federal budget do you think is spent on foreign aid? The *Congressional Research Service* describes foreign aid, the amount spent, and the share of the 2015 federal budget.
> https://fas.org/sgp/crs/row/R40213.pdf

Foreign policy has become more complicated since the end of the Cold War. During the Cold War era, global affairs were organized around a *bi-polar world* where the free Western bloc of countries confronted the communist Eastern bloc of countries. The collapse of the Soviet Union in 1991 left the U.S. as the sole remaining military superpower. The U.S. military hegemony prompted discussions about what the U.S. should do in the new, unipolar world order. One proposal was to use the peace dividend from reduced spending on defense and national security to spend on domestic affairs? The other proposal was to take advantage of the American position as the only superpower to use American military power abroad to accomplish foreign policy goals such as regime change in the Mideast. Neoconservatives, in particular, argued that the U.S. had a responsibility to use its power abroad to accomplish, among other things regime change in countries where the U.S. wanted new leadership. During both Bush administrations, neoconservatives were successful in getting the government to launch military attacks in the Mideast: the Gulf War in 1991 and the invasion of Iraq in 2003. Both were military successes, but the U.S. was unprepared for the insurgencies that developed to oppose U.S. power projection in the Mideast.

The brief *unipolar moment* of U.S. military hegemony has surprisingly quickly turned into a *multi-polar world* where there are many competing regional interests, some of which threaten peace and others where there is armed conflict. The instability of this new world dis-order has challenged U.S. policy, which has been criticized for both over-reaching (e.g., regime change in Iraq) and under-reaching (indecisive action toward the civil war in Syria). The lack of any clear guiding principles in the more chaotic world order was particularly evident in the Obama administration. Its foreign policy—which seemed to be inspired by the slogan, "Don't do stupid stuff!"—was a natural political reaction against the ongoing foreign policy failures in Afghanistan and Iraq.

The political violence and failed states in the Middle East and Africa created a migration crisis that threatens the post-WWII world order in Europe and Britain. Counter-terrorism policy that targets individuals and organizations resembles a game of *whack a mole*. And American military superiority is unlikely to solve these complicated, multidimensional problems. Which may explain why some foreign policy makers and analysts actually sound nostalgic for the Cold War era when global affairs were organized by the bi-polar conflict between the East and the West. Richard Hass, the President of the Council on Foreign Relations, describes the current state of global affairs as *The World in Disarray* (2017). The nostalgia for the Cold War *world order* is reminiscent of comments about a crime wave in the U.S. in the late 1960s and early 1970s. The federal government effectively prosecuted *organized crime* in the mid-1960s, but then the unorganized, violent street crime wave of the 1970s seemed worse than the organized crime.

Learn About Other Countries!
The Department of State's "Countries & Regions"
https://www.state.gov/p/
The CIA's World Factbook:
https://www.cia.gov/library/publications/the-world-factbook/
The Library of Congress "Country Studies" books:
https://www.loc.gov/collections/country-studies/about-this-collection/

17.44 | *The Department of Defense*

The Department of Defense (DOD) is an executive department that is headed by the Secretary of Defense, a political appointee who is usually a member of the President's **inner cabinet**—the heads of the most important agencies: State; Defense; Treasury; and Justice. The Pentagon is the building where much of the DOD policy making and business operations are headquartered.

The U.S. spends a great deal on national defense. The National Priorities Project, whose mission is to inspire action "so our federal resources prioritize peace, shared prosperity, and economic security," reports that in 2015, U.S. military spending was $598.5 billion, which is 54% of the federal government's discretionary spending and about 37% of the total $1.6 trillion in world military spending. U.S. military spending is about equal to about the next seven countries with the largest military spending combined. The assumption is that defense spending reflects the level of national security threats. However, federal budgets often reflect the priorities of special interests more than the general public. The issue network that participates in the formulation of the defense budget consists of the Department of Defense, congressional committees, and defense contractors.

Each of these three participants—government bureaucrats, elected officials, and business interests—has a vested interest in maintaining or increasing defense spending. Military contracts are distributed across states and congressional districts. The National Conference of State Legislatures provides data on defense spending in the states.

Think about it!
Why is it so hard to cut defense spending?
http://www.npr.org/2012/07/23/157243328/defense-cuts-how-do-you-buy-1-8-submarines

17.45 | *The National Security Agency*

The National Security Agency (NSA) is such a secret agency that its letters are sometimes said to refer to No Such Agency. The NSA is an intelligence agency in the Department of Defense. The Director of National Intelligence heads the NSA. The NSA's core missions are to protect U.S. national security systems and to produce foreign signals intelligence information. The Information Assurance mission protects intelligence and communications systems. The Signals Intelligence mission collects, processes, and disseminates intelligence information from foreign signals for intelligence and counterintelligence purposes and to support military operations. This Agency also enables Network Warfare operations to defeat terrorists and their organizations at home and abroad, consistent with U.S. laws and the protection of privacy and civil liberties." The NSA is responsible for collecting and analyzing foreign communications and foreign signals intelligence as well as protecting U.S. government communications and information systems.

17.46 | *The Central Intelligence Agency*

The Central Intelligence Agency website provides information about its history, organization, and mission. The CIA's mission statement describes the agency as "the nation's first line of defense," which it carries out by:
- "Collecting information that reveals the plans, intentions and capabilities of our adversaries and provides the basis for decision and action.
- Producing timely analysis that provides insight, warning and opportunity to the President and decision makers charged with protecting and advancing America's interests."

The mission statement reflects the fact that the CIA was created to be an intelligence gathering and analysis agency. But presidents have used the CIA to *conduct covert operations*. The most controversial CIA operations have been plots to assassinate foreign leaders and domestic surveillance operations. In the 1970s, the Senate Church Committee investigation uncovered illegal domestic actions and questionable foreign operations and recommended reforms to increase accountability.[16]

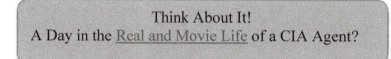

Think About It!
A Day in the Real and Movie Life of a CIA Agent?

17.47 | *The Department of Homeland Security*

The Department of Homeland Security (DHS) was created in 2003 to better coordinate anti-terrorist activities. The DHS is a huge, complicated organization that performs varied functions. It can be considered an umbrella organization because it has responsibility for a broad range of functions ranging from transportation to immigration to telecommunications. The Transportation Security Agency (TSA) is one national security policy that the average American sees (and sometimes feels!) because it conducts airport screening of passengers. The TSA's passenger screening policy is based on a strategy that involves searching for bombs rather than bombers. Passengers and luggage are searched to find materials that could be used for terrorism. The alternative strategy is to search for bombers—to look for individuals who are likely to be threatening or dangerous, to screen passengers than luggage. Screening individuals is controversial because it relies on gathering about people and making assumptions about who is likely to be a threat and who is not. Creating government data banks raises concerns about big government monitoring people and maintaining **No Fly** or other watch lists. Changing TSA policies to search individuals based on their physical appearance, name, religion, dress, nationality, or ethnicity also raises questions about profiling. Profiling is suspecting someone of criminal behavior based on his or her identity. Is profiling stereotyping or is it predicting risk based on valid information? Should profiling be used when screening airline passengers? What about when screening people who are entering the country?

The DHS is a massive federal agency responsible for aspects of immigration policy: maintaining border security, providing immigration services, and enforcing immigration laws. Counter-terrorism policies have substantially increased the size and scope of the DHS, and the agency's political profile has been raised because immigration policy has become a salient political issue during the Obama and Trump administrations. President Trump's executive orders related to immigration were just the latest occasion for debating the extensive powers of this important federal agency.

17.48 | *Non-governmental Organizations (NGOs)*

Government officials are not the only actors involved with global affairs. A large and growing body of non-governmental actors participate in making and implementing foreign policy. The interest groups are varied, with organizations advocating on behalf of economic, ideological, ethnic and national identity, religious, and other issue-based interests or causes.

The Foreign Policy Association (FPA) is a non-profit organization that was founded in 1918 to foster public knowledge of and interest in the world by providing publications, programs, and forums. The Foreign Policy Association's website describes its mission as serving "as a catalyst for developing awareness, understanding of, and providing informed opinions on global issues" and "encourage[ing] citizens to participate in the foreign policy process." One of the FPA's outreach efforts is the Great Decisions Global Affairs Education Program. Great Decisions has become the largest nonpartisan public education program on international affairs in the world. It has published a Citizen's Guide to U.S. Foreign Policy and founded the World Affairs Council of Washington, D.C.

Think tanks and public policy organizations such as the Council on Foreign Relations are also influential in the policy making process. They produce studies of various issues, they provide policy experts who testify at congressional committee hearings, and they lobby for and against specific policies and issues. These organizations are also influential because their members are recruited for government positions. When a new administration comes into office, it recruits government officials from these organizations: Republican presidents tend to recruit government officials from organizations with Republican or conservative leanings while Democratic presidents tend to recruit government officials from organizations with Democratic or liberal leanings. Think tanks and public policy organizations also provide places for policy experts to work while they, their party, or their ideas are out of government.

The Council on Foreign Relations (CFR) was established in 1921. The CFR website describes the CFR as "an independent, nonpartisan membership organization, think tank, and publisher" that serves as a resource for its members, government officials, business executives, journalists, educators and students, and civic and religious leaders.

Economic interest groups are also active lobbyists in formulating foreign policy. Business organizations such as the Chamber of Commerce and the National Association of Manufacturers, as well as labor organizations such as the AFL-CIO, lobby on behalf of international trade, commerce, and labor issues. In fact, globalization and the importance of international trade as an aspect of foreign policy have expanded the political arena in the sense that economic interest groups lobby for or against public policies in both the domestic and foreign policy arenas. Interest group politics now extends beyond the territorial boundaries of the U.S.

Business interests have a major stake in foreign and national security policy. The federal government does not manufacture military equipment. It buys military equipment from private sector companies. Consequently, the aerospace and defense industry has a vested interest in defense spending, the budget of the National Aeronautics and Space Administration (NASA), and other federal programs. The decision to end the shuttle program has had major impacts on the aerospace industry and the communities surrounding the manufacturing and launching sites. The closure of military bases also has major effects on local budgets. Privatization has increased the private sector's stake in the defense budget. The U.S. military now relies on private sector companies to provide goods and services that were once provided by members of the military. The Army and Air Force Exchange Services, which the government created to provide merchandise and services to members of the military, strives to provide American troops and their dependents with a "taste of home" wherever they are stationed across the globe. These tastes include familiar fast food franchises and other amenities. The military now contracts with food service companies to provide food that was once provided by army cooks in mess halls.

Privatization is not limited to support services such as food or amenities. Most military contractors are unarmed service providers, but the military signs logistics contracts with companies that provide armed security guards for the military and civilian support personnel. Of the more than 70,000 private sector civilians that were working in Iraq in 2011 on military contracts to provide necessities and amenities for troops in Iraq and Afghanistan, a great majority are service sector workers. Many of these employees are "third-country nationals," workers hired by foreign companies to work under service sector contracts for the military. Privatization—relying on private sector to provide public services—presents serious accountability problems. The U.S. military is responsible for its own actions. The U.S. government negotiates Status of Forces Agreements (SOFA) with countries where the military is deployed. The SOFA agreements typically include provisions that describe which country's court system will be used to try individuals who commit crimes. Who is responsible for poor or unsafe working conditions when the military contracts with companies who use subcontractors or employers or employees who are not American? Who is legally accountable when a military contractor commits a crime? Blackwater, Inc. was a U.S. company that was founded by Erik Prince. Blackwater received large government contracts to provide security services in Iraq and Afghanistan. Prince described Blackwater's mission as doing for the national security apparatus what FedEx did to the postal service.[17] When Blackwater employees were accused of criminal acts including rape, torture, and murder, the murky legal accountability presented serious problems that were highlighted during congressional hearings. Corpwatch chronicles the company's story. Today Prince runs a company called Academi, which provides private mercenary forces for countries.

> Think about it!
> Should the U.S. hire private "soldiers"? See "Private Warriors"
> http://www.pbs.org/wgbh/pages/frontline/shows/warriors/
>
> Should American companies be allowed to sell arms or provide private armies for anyone or any country?

17.5 | War (and Emergency) Powers

Striking the right balance between granting and limiting power is especially important for war and national emergencies. The Founders worried about giving the new national government too much power, and they were particularly wary of executive power which they considered monarch-like. They eased some of the worries by dividing control over war powers.

17.51 | *Divided Control of War Powers*

The war powers are divided between Congress and the president. Congress was delegated the power to declare war and the power to raise and support armies. The president was made the Commander-in-Chief of the armed forces: the president waged war as the "top general." This division of control over war powers is usually described by saying that Congress makes war (decides whether to go to war) and the president wages war (as the Commander in Chief). During the colonial era, the Founders experienced the offensive use of war powers by imperial powers. The British, French, and Spanish imperial model of government included using military power to expand the empire. The colonists' experience with offensive imperial power caused the delegates to the Constitutional Convention in 1787 to be concerned about war powers. They decided to give the new national government defensive war powers so that it could effectively defend the young republic against foreign invasion. But they nevertheless worried about war powers.

In "Political Observations" (April 20 1795), James Madison described war as the "germ" that presented the greatest threat to liberty and republican government:

"Of all the enemies of true liberty, war is, perhaps, the most to be dreaded, because it comprises and develops the germ of every other. War is the parent of armies; from these proceed debts and taxes; and armies, and debts, and taxes are the known instruments for bringing the many under the domination of the few. In war, too, the discretionary power of the Executive is extended; its influence in dealing out offices, honors and emoluments is multiplied; and all the means of seducing the minds, are added to those of subduing the force, of the people. The same malignant aspect in republicanism may be traced in the inequality of fortunes, and the opportunities of fraud, growing out of a state of war, and in the degeneracy of manner and of morals, engendered in both.

No nation can preserve its freedom in the midst of continual warfare.
War is in fact the true nurse of executive aggrandizement. In war, a physical force is to be created; and it is the executive will, which is to direct it. In war, the public treasuries are to be unlocked; and it is the executive hand which is to dispense them. In war, the honors and emoluments of office are to be multiplied; and it is the executive patronage under which they are to be enjoyed; and it is the executive brow they are to encircle.

The strongest passions and most dangerous weaknesses of the human breast; ambition, avarice, vanity, the honorable or venal love of fame, are all in conspiracy against the desire and duty of peace.
Letters and Other Writings of James Madison (Volume IV, page 491)

This is an extremely strong warning about the dangers that war powers present to republican government! Madison acknowledged that the decision to increase security by granting the government power to repel foreign invasions also increased insecurity by exposing the nation to the risk that the war powers would be used internally to threaten republican government. Is this **germ theory** of war powers accurate? As the U.S. became an economic and military power, it did use its powers to extend American influence abroad. Two notable 19th Century examples of this use of U.S. military power are the Mexican-American War and the Spanish-American War. World Wars I and II were fought primarily for reasons other than extended American power abroad, but one consequence of WWII was a greater awareness of how the U.S. could use its economic, political, and military power abroad to prevent war. This was once of the policies underlying the Cold War foreign policy. As a result military force was not limited to defensive actions but also included offensive actions. This was an important shift in thinking about national security and foreign policy. President George W. Bush declared that his administration was adopting the doctrine of preventive war, which is the use of military force for policy wars or using military force as an instrument of foreign policy. President George W. Bush's September 2002 National Security Strategy announced elements of what was unofficially called the Bush Doctrine, the set of principles that guided the Bush Administration's foreign policy. The Bush Doctrine had two main principles. First, it announced that the U.S. would unilaterally withdrawal from treaties dealing with arms control and global warming. Second, it stated that the U.S. would take unilateral military action to protect national security interests: the U.S. would act alone to use military force and it would take **preventive** military action. The Bush Doctrine of preventive military force was controversial because it declared that as a matter of policy the U.S. would not wait to use military force defensively—it would use military force preemptively in order to prevent threats to national security interests. According to the National Security Strategy document,

> "The gravest danger our Nation faces lies at the crossroads of radicalism and technology. Our enemies have openly declared that they are seeking weapons of mass destruction.... The United States will not allow these efforts to succeed. We will build defenses against ballistic missiles and other means of delivery. We will cooperate with other nations to deny, contain, and curtail our enemies' efforts to acquire dangerous technologies. And, as a matter of common sense and self-defense, America will act against such emerging threats before they are fully formed. We cannot defend America and our friends by hoping for the best. So we must be prepared to defeat our enemies' plans, using the best intelligence and proceeding with deliberation. History will judge harshly those who saw this coming danger but failed to act. In the new world we have entered, the only path to peace and security is the path of action."[18]

17.52 | *Wars: Imperfect and Perfect*

The U.S. has formally declared war upon foreign nations only five times.

- War of 1812 (1812-1814). The U.S. declared war upon the United Kingdom in 1812. The war ended with the Treaty of Ghent in 1814.
- Mexican-American War (1846-1848). The U.S. declared war upon Mexico in 1846. The war ended with the Treaty of Guadalupe Hidalgo in 1848.
- Spanish-American War (1898). The U.S. declared war upon Spain in 1898. The war ended with the Treaty of Paris 1898.
- World War I (1914-1918). The U.S. declared war upon Germany Austria-Hungary in 1917. The Great War ended with the Treaty of Berlin and the U.S.-Austrian Peace Treaty in 1921.
- World War II (1939-1945). The U.S. declared war upon Japan on December 8, 1941 and Germany on December 11th, 1941. The U.S. and the Allies fought the global war against the Axis Powers (Japan, Germany, and Italy. The war on Japan ended with the V-J Day Instrument of Surrender on September 2, 1945 and the V-E Day German Instrument of Surrender on May 8, 1945.

The U.S. has, of course, taken many more military actions than these officially declared wars. These military actions include undeclared wars, conflicts, special-forces operations, participation in United Nations police actions, hostage rescue missions, blockades of foreign ports, bomb and missile and drone attacks, and cyber-attacks. Congress or an international governing body such as the United Nations approved some of these military actions. These military actions include the following:

- The Quasi-War with France (1798–1800)
- The Indian Wars
- The Civil War (1861–1865)
- The Russian Civil War (1918)
- The Korean War (1950–1953)

- The Vietnam War (1961–1975)
- The Gulf War or Operation Desert Storm (1991–1994)
- Afghanistan War 2001–)
- Iraq War (2003–)

Two of the most prominent military conflicts (that is, undeclared wars) are the Korean War and the Vietnam War. The Vietnam War was an especially controversial war. It has had a profound and lasting impact on American politics. Long after the war was over, political debates about foreign affairs, national security, and war powers still reference Vietnam. Supporters and opponents of the Vietnam War, and supporters and opponents of contemporary military action, still refer to the war to justify their positions for or against war. The critics of military action (e.g., in Afghanistan or Iraq or Iran) appeal for "No more Vietnams." This slogan is usually meant to remind the public and government officials that the decision to use military force as an instrument of foreign policy is fraught with risks. On the other hand, those who support the use of American military power abroad urge the nation to recover from "The Vietnam Syndrome." They use the term Vietnam Syndrome to describe a condition where the nation is so worried about the use of military power that it is afraid to use U.S. military power to accomplish foreign policy objectives. The modern conservative movement's support for building up the military and the use of military force during the Republican presidencies of Ronald Reagan, George H.W. Bush, and George W. Bush, was intended to recover from the Vietnam Syndrome.

17.53 | *The War of 1812*

The War of 1812 was fought against Britain, Canadian colonists loyal to Britain, and Native Americans who were allied with the British. The U.S. declared war because it wanted to expand its national borders into the Northwest Territory, which included areas under British control; trade restrictions during Britain's war with France limited U.S. commerce; the British had impressed— that is forced—American merchant sailors to serve in the British Royal Navy; and British support for Indian tribes threatened westward expansion into frontier areas. Britain did not actively resist American westward expansion when Britain was preoccupied with the war against France. But after Napoleon was defeated, British troops captured and burned Washington, D.C. in the summer of 1814. Then in the fall and winter of 1814, U.S. forces defeated British forces in New York and New Orleans. Winning the battle of New Orleans created a renewed sense of American patriotism. The defense of Baltimore inspired the U.S. national anthem, The Star-Spangled Banner. The national pride in fighting and winning a second war against Britain produced what historians called The Era of Good Feelings—a label attached to the period from around 1816 to 1824 when partisan politics and domestic political conflict was subdued compared to the preceding era.

What a person thinks about a war depends upon which side they were on. Americans have a very different perspective on the War of 1812 than Canadians. Southerners have a different perspective on the Civil War than Northerners. And Vietnamese have a different view of the "The American War" than Americans. Writing in *The American Legion* magazine, Michael Lind describes the Vietnam war as one of the conflicts that comprised the Cold War, which he thinks is best understood as the third World War of the 20th Century—and part of that noble cause.[19]

> **Think About It!**
> Is the War of 1812 taught the same in the U.S. and Canada?
> http://www.npr.org/2012/06/18/155308632/teaching-the-war-of-1812-different-in-u-s-canada

17.54 | The Mexican-American and Spanish-American Wars

These two 19th Century wars are considered together here because they were declared for basically the same purpose: territorial expansion and global influence. The Mexican-American War was fought to expand the territory of the U.S. over the North American continent as part of the belief in Manifest Destiny and westward expansion to settle frontier areas. The Spanish-American War was fought during an era of American politics included debates about how to project the American economic, political, and military power and influence abroad. The Spanish-American War was controversial because it resulted in the U.S. acquiring territories abroad, which opponents believed transformed the U.S. from a republic, which had fought the Revolutionary War against imperial power, into an imperial power. The following image is a poster from the 1900 presidential campaign. It describes the Spanish-American War of 1898 as one that was fought for political ideals (using military power in the service of humanity) rather than for projecting American imperial power abroad.

17.55 | *The Cold War*

The Cold War was the period of almost continuous conflict between western democracies and communist countries (primarily the Soviet Union and China) from the end of World War II until the fall of the Soviet Union in 1991. In a famous 1946 "Sinews of Peace" Speech at Westminster College in Fulton, Missouri, Winston Churchill described an Iron Curtain descending across Eastern Europe along the countries that bordered the Soviet Union. The Iron Curtain metaphor captured the West's imagination about the new threat presented by the Soviet Union. In 1947, the U.S. intervened in a civil war in Greece in order to prevent Greece from falling into the Soviet sphere of influence. In 1948, the U.S. implemented the Marshall Plan—the European Recovery Program—as a comprehensive approach to rebuild Europe as a bulwark against Soviet expansion.

> Cold War Time Lines
> http://www.history-timelines.org.uk/events-timelines/03-cold-war-timeline.htm
> http://www.archives.gov/exhibits/featured_documents/marshall_plan/

The Cold War included proxy wars. A proxy war is a war where major powers use third parties—usually smaller countries or even non-state actors such as freedom fighters, revolutionaries, insurgents, or terrorists—to fight for them. The U.S. and the Soviet Union sponsored proxy wars in Korea, Vietnam, Angola, Afghanistan, and Latin America. The U.S. and its allies (including Great Britain, France, and Western Germany) confronted the Soviet Union and its satellite states (East Germany; Poland; Hungary). The Cold War competition included the space race (the first to launch a satellite; the first to put a man on the moon) and even Olympic competition.

The U.S. and Soviet militaries never directly fought one another. The Cold War conflict was expressed through mutual defense treaties, coalitions, conventional force deployments, monetary and military support, espionage, propaganda, arms races, and technological competitions such as the Space Race. The Cold War fundamentally changed American politics and government. It created the warfare state—the network of permanent national security agencies. It created the American public's acceptance the belief that life in the nuclear age meant living with an enemy that was an existential threat to the U.S. Strong government meant that power flowed from state and local governments to the national government, which had primary responsibility. It also meant that power flowed from Congress to the president.

Watching government videos that were produced to "educate" the public about the threat of nuclear war, and how to protect against it, provides good insights into how national security presented the opportunity for government to use popular culture to influence public opinion. The "Duck and Cover" videos were intended to teach children how to protect themselves in case of a nuclear attack by ducking under desks and covering themselves with whatever was available. *Target Nevada* is one of the declassified government videos of nuclear tests that were conducted in the 1950s in a Nevada valley. What do the images, the video style, the tone of the voice-over narrator, and the substantive content of these government videos, particularly *Target Nevada*, reveal about the purposes of the videos?

President Truman created the Nevada Test Site in 1950 to provide a continental nuclear test site that was cheaper than the actual test sites in the Pacific. Two of the videos are *Operation Plumbbob* and *Let's Face It*:

- The U.S. Atomic Energy Commission presents *Operation Plumbbob*, the Department of Energy Video #0800022 "Military Effects Study." *Operation Plumbbob* consisted of around 30 nuclear test explosions to measure the impacts of nuclear explosions on buildings, animals, plant life, soil and air contamination—and people, including the people who witnessed the explosions.
- The Federal Civil Defense Administration presents *Let's Face It*, U.S. Nuclear Test Film #55.

Tourists can now visit the Nevada Test Site and walk through "Doom Town" where more than 100 atomic tests were conducted. One Atomic Tourist Web site reassures potential visitors with the following statement: "Radiation badges are no longer necessary when visiting."

The Cold War
From World War to the Cold War
http://www.youtube.com/watch?v=HpYCplyBknI

17.6 | The War on Terror

The war on terror is a distinctive kind of warfare or armed conflict. *First*, it is conflict with individuals and organizations, not nations. But international law defines war as a state of armed conflict between two or more nations. The war on terror was originally against al Qaeda. Today, counterterrorism policy includes other organizations such as ISIS (Islamic State in Syria or ISIL, Islamic State in the Levant) and related offshoots and movements. *Second*, Congress did not declare war on al Qaeda. Congress passed a joint resolution (the AUMF) that authorized the president to use armed force against those responsible for the 9/11 attacks. So the AUMF granted the president power to go to war RATHER than Congress actually declaring war.

Third, the war on terror is distinctive because it is a global war without a battlefield or geographic "theater of war." It is fought in physical spaces such as Iraq and Afghanistan and Syria, cyber-space (cyber-attacks on financial systems and infrastructure), and the Internet—where terrorist organizations such as ISIS recruit supporters and rely on viral videos and other publicity to attract attention to the cause, while governments monitor social media to counter recruitment campaigns and detect and disrupt terrorist plans. *Fourth*, the war on terror is distinctive because it seems to be a war with no apparent end. In conventional warfare, there are familiar benchmarks for determining how the war is going and one side usually wins and the war is declared over. The war on terror lacks these benchmarks.

17.61 | *Political Violence*

Political violence is the use of violence to achieve a political goal. War is political violence. Terrorism is also a kind of political violence. Not all acts of political violence are terrorism. War is a kind of political violence that is not usually considered terrorism—although it may include state-sponsored terrorism. Revolutionary movements for national independence including guerrilla warfare or armed insurgencies are political violence that may or may not be terrorism.

Organized mob actions, including vigilantism, are a kind of political violence that may or may not be terrorism. Police and civilian use of deadly force to fight crime and for self-defense is a form of political violence. In fact, the American political experience includes a great deal of political violence. Political violence has been an important part of some of the nation's most important developments: the Revolutionary War founded the republic; the Civil War preserved the union and abolished slavery; the westward expansion of the country and the settling of the frontier was violent; and the U.S. used military force for territorial expansion and to extend the U.S. sphere of influence globally. Terrorism is generally defined as the inappropriate or illegal use of political violence by non-state actors. The central problem with this definition is the difficulty clearly and objectively differentiating between legitimate and illegitimate acts of political violence. This difficulty is reflected in the saying, "One person's freedom fighter is another's terrorist." Those who consider political violence appropriate for certain purposes or causes are challenged to provide principled distinctions that can be applied to actual historical or contemporary examples. It is easy to fall into the subjectivity trap: defining causes that you support as legitimate and those you oppose as illegitimate, or concluding that the ends justify the means—so that if the end is legitimate then the means are legitimate.

17.62 | *The Three Long Wars: Afghanistan, Iraq, and Terrorism*

The wars in Iraq and Afghanistan are already the longest wars in American history. The war on terror is also a distinct, ongoing but unconventional war. A conventional war is warfare between the uniformed military of two or more countries (or nation-states). Unconventional wars and conflicts involve insurgents—individuals, organizations, and movements rather than governments:

- The combatants may not be in uniform;
- The combatants may not be part of a formal military chain of command;
- The combatants may not carry arms openly;
- The combatants may be intermingled with the general population;
- There may not be a battlefield, an actual geographic place where the fighting takes place. The fighting can occur where people live and work and while they go about their daily lives.

These aspects of unconventional warfare make fighting unconventional wars difficult to fight. It is often hard to identify the enemy, whose physical appearance may be identical to civilians who are not the enemy. It is hard to limit civilian casualties. And the conflicts typically have explicitly political objectives that make military strategies of limited utility in determining who wins.

Symmetrical warfare is warfare where the combatants have roughly equal military might, kinds of power, and weapons. **Asymmetrical warfare** is warfare where one side has a great deal more military power than the other. The two sides in asymmetrical warfare are likely to use very different weaponry. The wars in Iraq and Afghanistan are asymmetrical warfare. The U.S. has vastly greater economic, military, and technological power than Iraq and Afghanistan. The U.S. uses its military and technological advantage to wage high technology warfare that relies on sophisticated weapons systems including missiles, airplane bombers, and unmanned drones that are controlled by personnel who can be stationed halfway around the world from the actual battlefield. This asymmetry does not guarantee military success. Neither the British nor the Soviets won their wars in Afghanistan. In Iraq and Afghanistan the U.S. is engaged in the kinds of asymmetrical warfare that frustrate military superpowers. The counter-insurgencies made it very difficult for the British and Soviets, two military superpowers, to *get out* of the country after invading it and experiencing initial success.

> **Think about it!**
> Is it easier for a military power to enter a country than it is to exit? Listen to the National Public Radio Broadcast, "For Invaders A Well-Worn Path Out of Afghanistan," (December 6, 2010) http://www.npr.org/2010/12/06/131788189/for-invaders-a-well-worn-path-out-of-afghanistan

The Iraq war began with the U.S. *blitzkrieg* air and ground attack that quickly overwhelmed Iraqi defenses. But then the U.S. faced resistance and conflicts that eventually became an insurgency that required a military occupation of Iraq. The Joint Chiefs of Staff initially refused to call the ongoing conflict an insurgency because 1) the word insurgency evoked memories of the U.S. being bogged down in Vietnam; 2) the military was not prepared to fight such a conflict. The U.S. Army is a large bureaucratic organization. The Army field manual still assumed that battles would be large scale "set pieces" where the armies of warring countries at war would engage one another on a battlefield. This conventional wisdom left the U.S. military unprepared for the ongoing conflict in Iraq and Afghanistan. A small band of high-ranking young officers with military experience fighting unconventional wars in Vietnam and elsewhere realized that the Army had to change in order to be prepared to fight insurgencies. One of these "insurgents" was David Petraeus. In *The Insurgents: David Petraeus and the Plot to Change the Army Way of War* (2012), Fred Kaplan describes how this "cabal" of "insurgents" forced the Army to adapt to the new unconventional warfare.

One challenge in unconventional warfare is minimizing the risks of civilian casualties, which are often euphemistically called "collateral damage." Civilian casualties are an especially serious problem in unconventional warfare because "the people are the prize" in campaigns against insurgencies. Campaigns against insurgencies are politico-military campaigns. Success usually requires paying some attention to "winning the hearts and minds of the people" so that they will not support insurgents. Innocent civilian casualties that are dismissed as collateral damage make it harder to succeed. During the Obama administration, the emphasis on military operations that minimized civilian casualties both limited military actions and stimulated efforts to reduce risks in an environment where it has often been hard to identify friend and foe. The U.S. military has the most sophisticated weapons technology available. It has also developed sophisticated information systems to help solve the problem of identifying the enemy in Iraq and Afghanistan—and more broadly as part of counterterrorism policy. The military is using social network analysis to identify insurgents who are a threat that lives and works among the general population, which is not a

> **Think about it!**
> How does the military use social network analysis to attack the network of insurgents rather than just targeting individual insurgents? Listen to the NPR report, "U.S. 'Connects the Dots' to Catch Roadside Bombers:"
> http://www.npr.org/2010/12/03/131755378/u-s-connects-the-dots-to-catch-roadside-bombers

threat. Terrorist groups such as al Qaeda and insurgencies are organized as networks of individuals or groups that work together. This networking helps identify insurgents among the civilian population. The military now uses social network analysis to attack the network of insurgents rather than merely to target individual insurgents who might plant a roadside bomb or other Improvised Explosive Device (IED).

The objective in conventional warfare may be to overwhelm the enemy by destroying its military resources and undermining popular support for continued fighting. Counterinsurgency warfare has different goals. Jingoist slogans such as "Bomb them back to the Stone Age!" or "Nuke them all and let God sort them out!" are morally, politically, and militarily problematic because "[t]he people are the prize in a counterinsurgency operation."[20] But campaign rhetoric is still likely to include tough, jingoistic language. During the presidential campaign, Donald Trump promised to take decisive action to destroy the terrorist organization ISIS saying, "I would bomb the sh**t out of them." And take their oil! Once in office, he authorized the military to drop "the mother of all bombs" on Taliban leaders hiding in caves in the mountains of Afghanistan. And on April 7, 2017, President Trump authorized launching a 59 Tomahawk cruise missile strike against a military airbase in Syria as a warning to the Syrian government.

17.63 | *War Gamers and "Air Wars"?*

Technology changes warfare AND media coverage of warfare. Vietnam War was the first television war that was brought into American living rooms. The Gulf War of 1991 (Operation Desert Storm) was presented as a *blockbuster video game war*. The U.S. military's overwhelming technological superiority produced awe-inspiring optics of real-time Cruise missiles that used GPS technology to strike targets in Baghdad that appeared in the crosshairs. Audiences could watch communications buildings, tanks, and other military equipment being destroyed and Iraqi troops being killed. Reporters announced the start of the war from the upper floors of a Baghdad hotel with the flippant comment, "I guess its show time." The television images of the nighttime strikes resembled fireworks displays, and the news coverage had story lines that made stars of General Colin Powell, General Norman Schwarzkopf, and the sophisticated military technology— particularly Patriot missiles. It is hard to imagine any reality television show that could compete for viewership with the Desert Storm TV show that the military and the media brought to American living rooms. The difference between the Vietnam, the first living room war, and Operation Desert Storm, the second living room war, could not be greater. In fact, conservatives consider Desert Storm evidence that the U.S. is finally recovering from the Vietnam Syndrome—the unwillingness to use American power abroad.

The term **air power** usually refers to missiles, bombers, jet fighters, helicopters, and now drones (unmanned aerial vehicles). The U.S. Air Force is the primary branch of the military that fights air wars and strives to maintain control over the skies. The terms *air power and air war* also refer to using the mass media or airwaves for military purposes. When Iraq invaded Kuwait in August of 1990, the Bush administration (Bush 41, George H. W. Bush) initially said the conflict was an Arab conflict to be settled by Arab states. Subsequently, however, President Bush decided to use military force to remove Iraq from Kuwait. But the administration had to convince the American public to support going to war in a distant land—a country that was disparagingly called a family-owned oil company with a seat in the United Nations! The Kuwaiti government hired the Washington DC public relations firm Hill & Knowlton to produce a political marketing campaign to sell the American public on going to war against Iraq. The campaign was so successful in *building public support* for going to war that the government then used the mass media as a force multiplier *during* the Gulf War. The media war plan included providing the public with the military's views of the war, both by releasing the dramatic, almost real time video images of American military technology and by embedding reporters with troops. The media war plan developed and maintained public support for the Gulf War.[21] Conservatives and the military blamed the media for the erosion of public support for the Vietnam War, and therefore eventually for losing the war. But the military also realized that satellite communication technology made information blackouts on troop actions completely ineffective. So the initial policy allowed reporters to cover the action as members of a pool that was required to have military escorts in the field, but also required reporters to submit stories for review prior to publication. Ultimately, the visuals of modern, high-tech warfare weaponized the media covering the Gulf War.

17.64 | *Drones*

Drones are one of the latest technologies to change warfare. The Obama administration began the extensive use of drones—unmanned aerial vehicles (UAVs)—for "targeted killings." Targeted killing presents serious political, legal, and moral questions.

- Is "targeted killing" a euphemism for assassination—which is illegal?
- Who decides who gets put on *the kill list*?
- Should the U.S. develop a legal regime governing the use of drones or simply allow the technological development and use without rules of warfare?
- What will happen when other nations or organizations develop or obtain the technology to use drones against the U.S. or its allies?

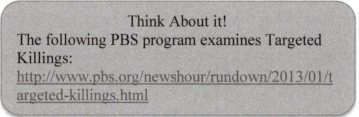

Think About it!
The following PBS program examines Targeted Killings:
http://www.pbs.org/newshour/rundown/2013/01/targeted-killings.html

The Association for Unmanned Vehicle Systems International is an organization whose mission includes supporting and advocating for unmanned systems and the robotics industry. The Association originally was closely aligned with military uses of the technology, but it now actively promotes using the unmanned vehicle technology for law enforcement.

17.65 | *The Military Law of Unintended Consequences*

The Fog of War is an unofficial post-mortem documentary that critically examines the government's decision-making during the Vietnam War. President Johnson's former Secretary of Defense Robert McNamara exposes some of the problems with fact-based decision-making during the fog of war: facts may be hard to get in the middle of a crisis; and people working in the organizational chain of command can manipulate data for political purposes. McNamara was the head of Ford Motor Company with a reputation as a modern management-by-data leader who was brought to the Department of Defense to try to get good data on how the war in Viet Nam was going. The White House wanted data to show that the U.S. was winning the war. The military got the message and provided body counts of the enemy killed in battle. The first problem with this data-driven approach to war fighting was the political pressure for data showing that the war was being won created incentives to inflate body counts. The second problem was the tendency to think that the war was being won because so many enemy fighters were being killed.

The U.S. war on terror initially focused on al Qaeda, the terrorist group responsible for the 9/11 terrorist attacks. For example, Afghanistan was invaded in 2001 because it was a safe haven for al Qaeda. But then the U.S. invaded Iraq in 2003. The original stated reasons were to accomplish regime change because the President of Iraq had weapons of mass destruction and connections with al Qaeda. Neither reason was accurate. But one unintended consequence of the Iraq War was the creation of an opportunity for a new terrorist organization even worse than al Qaeda. ISIS is currently the primary terrorist target of the global war on terror. The rise of ISIS or ISIL (Islamic State in Iraq or Islamic State in the Levant) caught Americans by surprise because it had been a major terrorist organization. The PBS Frontline Documentary *The Secret History of ISIS* explains that the U.S. overlooked ISIS even though analysts at the CIA's Counterterrorism Center gave the White House a report describing its leader, Abu Musab al-Zarqawi, as an ambitious radical leader who was a serious threat. The threat was overlooked because Vice-president Cheney wanted the CIA to provide evidence that Saddam Hussein, the President of Iraq, had connections with al Qaeda, the terrorist group responsible for the 9/11 terrorist attacks. A CIA analyst reports receiving direct calls from the Vice-president's office challenging the report describing ISIS as a threat to address because the Vice-president was focused on the al Qaeda-Hussein connection as a justification for invading Iraq. Then, after the U.S. invaded Iraq and killed Hussein, Iraq became a failed state that required a continued U.S. military occupation. The military occupation then created the opportunity for a terrorist policy entrepreneur like Zarqawi to present himself as the leader of Islamist fighters against the Westerners who had invaded and occupied Iraq after doing the same in Afghanistan.

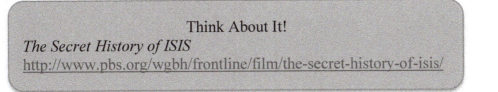

Think About It!
The Secret History of ISIS
http://www.pbs.org/wgbh/frontline/film/the-secret-history-of-isis/

17.66 | *Types of Military Action*

Table 17.66 below describes three types of military action. The first type, defensive use of military force, is not politically or legally controversial. The Constitution specifically provided for it. The second type, using military power to preempt an imminent attack is politically controversial because there are likely to be debates about whether it was actually necessary. It is not legally controversial, however, because the Supreme Court has recognized that the government can act militarily before an armed enemy that is poised to attack actually attacks. War powers can be initiated by an imminent threat of attack. The third type of military action, preventive military action, is controversial politically and legally. A preventive war is a policy war in the sense that the government simply decides to use military force to prevent a possible threat of some kind. Preventive military action is more speculative. The War in Afghanistan was a defensive war in the sense that it was fought against a country that provided a safe haven for a terrorist organization to attack the U.S. The War in Iraq was a preventive war. The Bush administration decided to use military force for regime change in Iraq. Attacking a country in order to change its government is illegal under international law, therefore the Bush administration claimed that preventive war was necessary because Saddam Hussein had contacts with al Qaeda and Iraq possessed weapons of mass destruction. In fact, the Bush administration created public support for going to war in Iraq by falsely claiming that Saddam Hussein had contacts with al Qaeda and possessed weapons of mass destruction (WMDs).

> **Think About It!**
> Can the government create public opinion about global affairs?
> http://www.youtube.com/watch?v=qxhIkzTg14M

Table 17.66: TYPES OF MILITARY ACTION

DEFENSIVE	PREEMPTIVE	PREVENTIVE
Enumerated Powers: Article I, section 8 provides that "The Congress shall have Power...To declare War...; ...suppress Insurrections and repel Invasions." Article II grants the president power as Commander-in-Chief *Implied Powers*: The government, particularly the president, has the implied power to use military force for rescue missions (such as the Mayaguez and Iranian Hostage rescue missions).	*Case Law*: Supreme Court rulings allow the government to respond to a "clear and present danger," a legal doctrine. The logic of conspiracy also means that the government does not have to wait until an armed enemy that is poised to attack actually attacks.	*Policy Wars*: The decision to use military force as an instrument of foreign policy.

17.67 | *Presidential Wars*

The U.S. now wages *presidential wars*. The personal presidency is nowhere more evident than the use of war powers, where the power problem is to find ways to hold presidents politically or legally accountable for their actions as Commander-in-Chief. The following quotes are statements that President George H. W. Bush made during the buildup to the first Iraq War—the Gulf War (1990–1991). The quotes, which are excerpted from Jean Edward Smith's *George Bush's War* (1992), illustrate the problem reconciling modern presidential thinking about war powers with the

American commitment to the rule of law:

"I've had it." News Conference, Oct 31, 1990.
"… I am getting increasingly frustrated." (News Conference November 23, 1990)
"Consider me provoked." (News Conference, November 30, 1990)
"…I am not ruling out further options…." (News Conference, November 1, 1990)
"I don't want to say what I will or will not do." (News Conference, November 8, 1990)
"And today, I am more determined than ever in my life." (Speech, November 1, 1990)
"So, I have not ruled out the use of force at all…" (News Conference, November 8, 1990)
"But I have no specific deadline in mind." (News Conference November 21, 1990)
"I will never—ever—agree to a halfway effort." (News Conference November 30, 1990)

"I have an obligation as president to conduct the foreign policy of this country as I see fit." [He then quoted the famous statement by Representative (and later, Chief Justice) John Marshall that the president is "the sole organ of the nation in its external affairs" as evidence that the Framers of the Constitution wanted the president to have such plenary power.]

I think Secretary of Defense Dick Cheney expressed it very well when he said "there is no question that the president, as commander in chief, can order the forces to engage in offensive action…" "I feel that I have the constitutional authority to" go to war.

"It was argued I can't go to war without Congress. And I was saying, I have the authority to do this."

17.7 | National Security

The term **national security** refers to a country's use of economic, political, and military power and influence to maintain its territorial integrity and political institutions. The concept of national security can be traced to the creation of nation-states, when armies were used to maintain domestic order and provide protection from foreign attacks. People create governments and form nation-states to provide for the defense of individuals and their civilization. These are basic government functions: "The most elementary function of the nation-state is the defense of the life of its citizens and of their civilization." A government that is unable to defend these values "must yield, either through peaceful transformation or violent destruction," to one that is capable of defending them.[22] Each nation develops and implements its national security policy as an attribute of national sovereignty.

17.71 | *Elements of National Security*

Hans Morgenthau was a leading figure in international relations theory, politics, and law. His classic *Politics among Nations* (1948) describes national security policy as consisting of the following elements:

- **Diplomacy**. Diplomacy is the practice of negotiating agreements between two or more nations. Diplomacy is used to build alliances and isolate threats. Professional diplomats usually conduct diplomatic relations as representatives of their nation on matters related to war and peace, trade, economics, culture, the environment, and human rights. U.S. diplomats negotiate the terms of international treaties and executive agreements prior to their endorsement by the president and, if a treaty, ratification by the Senate.

- **Emergency Preparedness.** Protecting national security includes protecting communication systems, transportation, public health systems, and the economy from attacks. The increased reliance on electronic communications in these sectors has highlighted the importance of protecting them from cyber-attacks.

- **Economic power**. Nations use their economic power to reward allies by creating favorable trade and foreign aid agreements, to build international support by such favorable treatment, and to punish threats by, for example, promoting trade sanctions or even embargoes.

- **Military force**. Nations use military force or the threat of military force to meet threats to national security interests and to prevent nations or organizations from presenting threats.

- **Domestic Legislation.** Laws that target individuals or organizations that support violence or terrorism, for example. The State Department maintains a list of terrorist nations and laws such as the PATRIOT Act give the government power to prosecute individuals or organizations that provide material aid to such groups.

- **Surveillance**. Nations use surveillance, spying, and covert operations for national security purposes. The U.S. uses its intelligence agencies to respond to threats and to prevent them. The Central Intelligence Agency, the National Security Administration, and the Defense Intelligence Agency are federal agencies that are responsible for providing surveillance related to national security (as opposed to ordinary criminal activity). The Cold War and the War on Terror have blurred some of the traditional lines between domestic surveillance and foreign surveillance.

- The FBI's mission is to protect the country from internal threats to national security or public order.

17.72 | *U.S. National Security*

During the Cold War era, U.S. national security relied heavily on military force or the threat of military force. National security became an official guiding principle of U.S. foreign policy with the enactment of the **National Security Act of 1947**. The Act created

- The National Military Establishment (which became the Department of Defense when the Act was amended in 1949);
- A Department of the Air Force from the existing Army Air Force;
- Separate military branches that were subordinated to the Secretary of Defense, which was a new cabinet level position;
- The National Security Council. The National Security Council was created to coordinate national security policy in the executive branch. The NSC is the president's main forum for considering national security and foreign policy issues.
- The Central Intelligence Agency. The CIA was the nation's first peacetime intelligence agency.
- The National Security Agency. The National Security Agency was so secretive that the letters NSA were humorously said to mean No Such Agency. The NSA Web site describes it as the home of the government's "code makers and code breakers."

For most of the 20th Century, national security was defined primarily in terms of military power—having a military strong enough to protect the country from foreign attacks or threats. WWI and WWII were armed conflict between nation-states. In WWII, the U.S. and its allies fought against countries (Germany, Japan, and Italy) that had invaded other countries. The Cold War included armed conflict between nation-states, but it primarily involved non-state actors that were supported by nation-states. Today, non-state actors including terrorist organizations and international drug cartels are considered greater threats to U.S. national security than a military attack by another country. As a result, the concept of national security has been broadened to include economic security, technology, and vital natural resources, and even environmental conditions.

During the Obama administration, the Department of State's mission statement included advancing freedom by building a more democratic, secure and prosperous world where government addressed the needs of the people—including poverty. The Trump State Department's mission statement reflects a more America First and less egalitarian mission: "The Department's mission is to shape and sustain a peaceful, prosperous, just, and democratic world and foster conditions for stability and progress for the benefit of the American people and people everywhere. This mission is shared with the USAID, ensuring we have a common path forward in partnership as we invest in the shared security and prosperity that will ultimately better prepare us for the challenges of tomorrow."

Nongovernment organizations such as The Center for New American Security define natural security to include natural resources. The broader definition of national security actually began recognition of the importance of petroleum. The world's economies are dependent on fossil fuels: oil, coal and natural gas. American dependence on imported oil is one of the reasons why the U.S. is so engaged in the Middle East. Energy independence is a goal with economic, military, and national security benefits. However, oil is not the only natural resource that is considered vital to national security.

17.73 | *Food and Water*

Governments are responsible for providing an adequate and safe food supply. Population growth and hunger are related issues that can become national security issues. The U.S. has a strategic oil reserve that is used to prevent disruptions in the energy supply. China, the world's most populous country, has a strategic pork reserve that it uses to prevent food scarcity from becoming a national security issue.

Think About It!
A Strategic Pork Reserve?
"Food for 9 Billion: Satisfying China's Growing Demand for Meat"
http://www.pbs.org/newshour/bb/world/july-dec12/china_11-13.html

Water is also a vital resource for human and other life. Access to an adequate and safe supply of fresh water is considered a component of a nation's security in a world where there is increased competition for this valuable and increasingly scarce resource. A United Nations Report "Water Scarcity" states that almost 20% of the world's population now lives in areas of physical scarcity. It provides information about and prospects for "water for life" in a world where (to quote Samuel Coleridge, Rime of the Ancient Mariner) there is "Water, water everywhere, nor any drop to drink." As nations compete for access to water, water will become a more important component of a nation's national security.

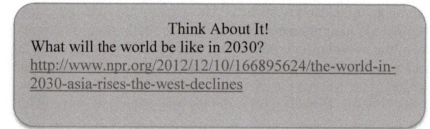

Glenn Beck's Blaze TV presents a short discussion of "War for Water."

http://www.video.theblaze.com/media/video.jsp?content_id=20256131

Every four years the National Security Council compiles a Global Trends Report that describes and analyzes developments that are likely to affect national security. The National Security Council is comprised of 17 U.S. government intelligence agencies. The 2012 Report predicted that 2030 would be "a radically transformed world." Asian countries will have surpassed the U.S. and Europe. The good news is that there will be less poverty, more democracy, more individual rights, and increased health. The bad news is that the world of 2030 is likely to include much more fighting over natural resources, particularly food and water.

Think About It!
What will the world be like in 2030?
http://www.npr.org/2012/12/10/166895624/the-world-in-2030-asia-rises-the-west-declines

17.74 | *Non-fuel minerals*

Non-fuel minerals are also important for advanced economies where rare and precious minerals used in the manufacturing and high-tech economies of the world. Non-fuel minerals are essential to manufacture of aircraft and computers and automobiles. In the information age, cell phones require tantalum, liquid crystal displays require indium, and other familiar products that are part of everyday modern life require platinum group metals. Rare earth minerals with properties such as conductivity, luminescence, and strength are very valuable for high-tech economies. Organizations such as the Center for New American Security, which identifies national security as increasingly dependent on a secure supply of natural resources, lobby for a broader perspective on national security, one that includes energy, minerals, water, land, climate change, and even biodiversity.

17.75 | *Immigration*

The U.S. proudly proclaims to be a nation of immigrants. The Statue of Liberty famously welcomes immigrants seeking opportunities for a better life and realizing the American dream of individuals and families working hard for a better life for themselves and their children. Immigration policy is usually about economic opportunity and political freedom (e.g., refugee policy) but periodically immigration becomes about national security. The post-WWII trend toward extending rights to immigrants, and making immigration policy less political and more legal, was reversed by three events:

- The War on Terror. Terrorist attacks and the threat of terrorism transformed immigration policy—particularly control of the nation's borders or border security—into national security policy. As a result, national security interests began to trump support for protecting immigrant rights by extending due process rights to them.
- Patriotism. The patriotic fervor that swept the country in the aftermath of the terrorist attacks on 9/11 revived the feeling that the U.S. needed to better protect the distinctive American national identity by limiting the number and kinds of people who were coming to the country legally or illegally. Throughout American history, immigration policy debates have periodically been shaped by worries about protecting national identity.
- The Great Recession. The Great Recession and structural changes in the American economy created a sense that economics and politics had become zero-sum. In zero-sum economics and politics, one person's (or group's) gains come from another person's (or group's) losses. This created the perception that immigrant rights were limited native-born citizens' rights, and that immigrants, particularly illegal immigrants, were taking scarce jobs from citizens, depressing wages, and consuming government benefits such as education, health care, and social welfare without paying a fair share of taxes.

17.76 | *The Trump-Russia Scandal*

Congressional investigations of Russian intervention in the 2016 U.S. elections have expanded the scope of national security beyond the terrorism-related threats that were the focus of policymakers since the 9/11 attacks. The Russian intervention in the 2016 elections was initially considered a narrowly targeted campaign against Hillary Clinton. Subsequently, however, it was apparent that the Russian campaign had far broader goals:

- First, it was considered an anti-Clinton campaign;
- Then it was considered a pro-Trump campaign;
- Then it was considered an attempt to erode confidence in American democracy;
- Then it was considered part of a campaign to erode support for NATO;
- Then it was considered part of a campaign to erode support for, or even to abolish the European Union; and finally
- It was considered, at its broadest, a campaign to erode support for western liberal democracy.

Vladimir Putin's organized campaign to undermine elections in the U.S. and other democracies was also initially assumed to be part of the effort to "Make Russia Great Again" by reviving the Cold War conflict. Subsequent analyses describe Putin as trying to initiate in a new type of conflict called non-linear warfare. The Cold War conflict was a conflict between relatively stable coalitions. Non-linear warfare is different. There is no distinction between peace and war; no actual battlefield; there are constantly shifting patterns of allies and enemies rather than stable sides; global affairs involves frenemies: friends are sometimes enemies and enemies are sometimes friends; and non-linear warfare is a new kind of total warfare in the sense that it is not all-out total are, but war is waged using economic, political, communications, and military assets and targets. Among the various federal government agencies involved with efforts to fight cyber-attacks, cyber-warfare and cyber-crime are The Department of Defense, the Central Intelligence Agency, and the Federal Bureau of Investigation.

> **Check Them Out!**
> The Department of Defense:
> https://www.defense.gov/Portals/1/features/2015/0415_cyber-strategy/Final_2015_DoD_CYBER_STRATEGY_for_web.pdf
> The Federal Bureau of Investigation describes itself as the "lead agency" for investigating cyber- attacks "by criminals, overseas adversaries, and terrorists."
> https://www.fbi.gov/investigate/cyber
> https://www.fbi.gov/wanted/cyber
> The Central Intelligence Agency's Directorate of Digital Innovation hires Cyber Operations Officers:
> https://www.cia.gov/offices-of-cia/digital-innovation/index.html

The Russian Cyber-attacks during the 2016 elections have been one of the main stories in the first year of the Trump administration. The Senate Intelligence Committee held hearings on Russian intervention in the 2016 elections, particularly on behalf of Donald Trump. The testimony of Clinton Watts (beginning at 52 minutes) explains Russia's timing of their fake news tweets. They knew when Trump was likely to re-tweet them. They also knew which states were swing states in the election and targeted them. The cyber-attack was effective mainly because Trump spread their propaganda.

> **Listen to It!**
> The testimony of former FBI agent Clinton Watts
> https://www.c-span.org/video/?c4664402/russians-play-sides-intel-committee-hears

17.8 | Comparative Politics and International Relations

17.81 | *Comparative Politics*

Comparative politics is a field of political science that relies heavily on the comparative method of studying government and politics. Comparative politics is one of the oldest fields in the study of politics. Aristotle compared the different forms of government to determine the best form of government. Today, comparative politics is generally divided into area-specialists (e.g., Africa, Latin American, Asia, or the Middle East) and scholars who use social science methods to study different political systems by comparing and contrasting different systems. Comparative politics can refer to American politics—for example, comparing state or regional government and politics within the United States—but comparative politics is primarily the study of government and politics in other countries. One way to increase understanding of U.S. government and politics is to compare it with other countries. Comparative works include Giovanni Sartori's 1976 study of party systems, Gabriel Almond and Sidney Verba's 1963 study of civil culture, and Samuel Huntington's 1968 study of developing countries. Today, global organizations describe and analyze issues such as freedom, economic development, good government, and corruption from a comparative perspective. Transparency International provides information about corruption in various countries. It defines corruption as the "abuse of entrusted power for private gain." It examines corruption related to topics such as access to information, education, humanitarian aid, and intergovernmental bodies. The organization's goal is to work toward government, politics, business, and civil society that is free of corruption.

> **Think about it!**
> When comparing countries, would a non-geographic map be useful?
> http://www.theworld.org/2012/11/frank-jacobs-and-his-strange-maps/

17.82 | *International Relations*

International relations (or international studies) is the study of relations between countries. International relations includes the study of organizations, law, and issues including national security, economic development, crime (drug, terrorism, trafficking), environmental sustainability, social welfare, and human rights. International relations examines nation-states or countries but it is not limited to governments. International relations is also the study the behavior of intergovernmental organizations such as the United Nations and the Organization of American States; non-governmental organizations; and multinational corporations. In fact, international non-governmental organizations and businesses have become very important participants in international relations. Interpol, the International Criminal Police Organization, is an international intergovernmental organization whose mission is to "Connect Police for a Safer World." The development of national and international organized criminal enterprises prompted the development of international policing efforts. With 190 countries as members, Interpol is one of the largest intergovernmental organizations. Its organizational structure includes a president, and executive committee, and a General Assembly that meets annually to discuss coordination of policing.

Historically, international law was the body of rules and principles that governing nations and their dealings with individuals of other nations. This is ***public international law*** because it deals with government bodies. International law, which included *jus gentium* (the law of nations) and *jus inter gentes* (the agreements between nations), was the body of rules of conduct that are generally accepted as binding or controlling. International law is based on the consent of the parties that are subject to it. The United Nations is the major public international law organization. Its main judicial body is the International Court of Justice. Over time, international law has extended its scope to include non-government actors. This is **private international law**—the body of rules and principles that govern individuals and non-governmental organizations. International law is a growing body of law that has been developing piecemeal, subject area by subject area, policy domain by policy domain. Trade law, intellectual property and contract law, human rights law, criminal justice law, and environmental law have been developed largely independently of one another, based on the interests and consent of the parties, rather than as a comprehensive strategy for coordinated legal development enacted by a single authoritative source. Internationalists are advocates of U.S. engagement in global affairs.

17.83 | *Realism and Idealism*

One element of a political ideology is a belief about human nature as good or bad, self-interested or public-minded. Ideological assumptions about individual behavior are also applied to thinking about the behavior of nations (which are, after all, organizations of individuals). Realism and idealism are based on different assumptions about the behavior of nations.

Realism is the theory that international relations can be best explained by the fact that nations are rational actors that primarily pursue their self-interest. Realists assume that human beings are by nature self-interested and competitive rather than benevolent and cooperative. This self-interested behavior also characterizes the behavior of nations. Accordingly, a nation's paramount self-interest is national security: survival in a Hobbesian world where nations, like individuals, pursue their self-interest without being constrained by morals or ethics or national or international governments. Realist believe that values such as democracy, equality, peace, human rights, and justice are important, but they are *secondary* to the primary goal of national self-interest. Human rights and justice can be recognized when they happen to coincide with national interest, but national interest trumps these values when they conflict with national interest.

Realists assume that the natural state of international relations is anarchy. Anarchy is a condition where governments (or individuals) are able to pursue their own interests without legal restrictions. Without a governing body or set of rules to limit the actions of nations, countries exploit power advantages over one another to achieve their national interest. Realism is therefore associated with power politics. Power politics is the belief that (national) might makes right. In other words, there is no objective understanding of justice because justice is merely whatever the stronger power (e.g., the winner of a war) says it is.

Think about it!
Do you think that it is helpful to think of the behavior of **nations** *as similar to the behavior of* **individuals***?*

The Italian political philosopher Niccolo Machiavelli (1469-1527) and the English political philosopher Thomas Hobbes (1588-1679) are classical political theorists whose views reflect realist assumptions about human and national behavior. In *The Prince*, Machiavelli argued that a political leader had to use power politics in order to accomplish the two main goals that he though all good leaders should strive for: maintaining the state (or nation) and achieving great things. Machiavelli defined **power politics** to include deception, manipulation of other actors, and the use of force—whatever means were necessary to accomplish their goals. In *Leviathan* (1651), Hobbes argued that strong government was necessary to create and maintain good order because individuals were by nature self-interested and had to be controlled. Both Machiavelli and Hobbes are considered realists in the sense that they believed that good strong leadership required a willingness to do what was effective rather than what was morally or legally right.

Idealism is the theory that international relations can be organized and conducted according to values other than, and perhaps even higher than, national self-interest. These values or higher ideals include justice, human rights, and the rule of law. In international relations, idealists believe that the behavior of nations can include actions that are motivated by political values other than national interest. In contrast to realists, idealists believe that the self-interested nature of individuals and governments can be tempered or limited by the introduction of morality, values, and law into international relations. President Woodrow Wilson (1913-1921) is perhaps the American political official who is most strongly identified with idealism. Indeed, in International

Relations idealism is sometimes referred to as Wilsonian Idealism. After the end of WWI, Wilson worked to create what he called a "Just Peace." He believed a just peace could be creating by developing an international system where individual nations were able to put aside their narrow self-interest and power politics to work for international peace and cooperation. At the Paris Peace Conference in 1919, Wilson advocated for a treaty, The Treaty of Versailles, which would commit nations to a peace plan and create the League of Nations. However, the U.S. Senate failed to ratify the Treaty partly because of the fear that U.S. national sovereignty would be compromised by legal requirements to comply with decisions of the League of Nations.

Critics of the United Nations or specific treaties still worry about weakening U.S. national sovereignty. This is one of the main reasons for opposition to U.S. signing the Rights of the Child Treaty, the United Nations Framework Convention on Climate Change (The Paris Agreement), and the Law of the Seas Treaty (LOST). The Senate has not ratified the LOST, which was negotiated during the United Nations Law of the Sea Conference from 1973–1982. Opponents worry that environmental policies to promote sustainability of marine resources and environments will require increased government regulation of business. This concern is reasonable because the Law of the Seas Treaty marks a change from the traditional law of *mare liberum*, a legal regime that allowed each nation to use resources in international waters as they saw fit, to a legal regime that regulated international waters to conserve resources and achieve sustainability. Conservative organizations such as the Heritage Foundation and the National Center for Policy Research, and libertarian organizations such as the Cato Institute, opposed ratification of the Treaty because they believed it would further erode U.S. sovereignty by requiring the United States to enforce laws that were developed to represent interests other than American interests.

> The Senate's Role in the Ratification of Treaties
> http://www.senate.gov/artandhistory/history/common/briefi ng/Treaties.htm

Debates about how the U.S. should use its power, whether the means and the ends should be idealist or realist, are not merely theoretical: they shape policy. Cold War debates about idealism or realism were framed as the question whether the U.S. should adhere to democratic values and the rule of law or adopt a "whatever it takes to win" strategy. Conservative *hawks* leaned toward realism (i.e., fighting the way the enemy fought; doing whatever was necessary to win) while liberal *doves* leaned toward idealism (i.e., playing by the rules of limited warfare). The war on terror has revived these debates. The realists in the Bush administration argued that neither the legal regime for crime nor the legal regime for conventional warfare was adequate for the war on terror, so the administration authorized the use of enhanced interrogation and special military commissions for the enemy combatants who were captured. The term illegal enemy combatants was used to differentiate detainees from prisoners of war, who were protected by established international and domestic laws. Idealists considered terms like "enhanced interrogation" a euphemism for torture—which is prohibited by domestic and international law. Idealists also defended the use of existing legal regimes—the criminal justice system and the Uniform Code of Military Justice (UCMJ)—as adequate to prosecute individuals suspected of terrorism and opposed the use of special military commissions to try them.

Think About It!

Donald Trump's *Whataboutism* strategy

Donald Trump has adopted an old Soviet tactic when faced with criticism or an uncomfortable situation. When westerners mentioned the low pay in communist countries, Soviet officials asked how much slaves were paid in the United States! Or when the leader of the free world criticized the Soviet Union for violating human rights, the Soviet Union would create a Human Rights Division and then mention that the U.S. lacked one.

Think about it!

Watch the video of the congressional investigation of the use of "coercive management techniques" for perspectives on the debate about torture, harsh interrogation, or enhanced interrogation: http://video.pbs.org/video/1629461216

17.84 | *Summary of Recent Developments*

The following are some of the most significant recent trends in global affairs:
- Terrorism. Counterterrorism policy promises to be part of a long war that shapes U.S. domestic and national security policy.
- Declining support for Democracy. The decades-long trend toward declining support for democracy, and increasing support for authoritarian government, may signal an end to the post-WWII model of governance. The Trump administration's America First approach, particularly its nationalism, marks a change in global affairs policy.
- Anti-immigration. Anti-immigration movements in the U.S., Britain, and Europe have transformed immigration (including refugee policy) from an economic issue into a national security issue. This is likely to be a long-term trend that ends the period where globalism supported human migration—freer movement of people across national borders just as freer trade made it easier for goods to move across national borders.
- Nationalism. The rise or return of nationalism—both national identity and economic nationalism—is altering basic assumptions about global governance. This includes the status of the European Union and the trans-pacific partnership between the U.S., Britain, and Europe.

Think About It!

Does the U.S. have a 1.0 Constitution for a 2.0 world order? Does the Constitution describe how government actually works in global affairs? In *The World in Disarray*, Hass says that national sovereignty was the foundation of the old world order 1.0. He supports a new world order 2.0 where a nation has an obligation to deal with the kinds of internal problems that cause global problems (disease; human migration; environmental degradation).

17.9 | Additional Resources

Almond, Gabriel, and Sidney Verba. 1963. *The Civic Culture*. Princeton: Princeton University Press.

Harvest of Empire. 2012. Dirs. Eduardo Lopez & Peter Getzels. Onyx Media Group.

Haass, Richard N. 2017. *A World in Disarray: American Foreign Policy and the Crisis of the Old Order*. New York: Penguin Books.

Huntington, Samuel. 1968. *Political Order in Changing Societies*. New Haven, CT: Yale University Press.

Madison, James. "Political Observations." In *Letters and Other Writings of James Madison*. [Philadelphia, Pennsylvania: J.B. Lippincott and Co., 1865]. Volume IV: 491-2. http://www.archive.org/stream/lettersotherwrit04madi/lettersotherwrit04madi_djvu.txt

Mandelbaum, Michael. 2006. *The Case for Goliath: How America Acts as the World's Government in the Twenty-First Century*.

Sartori, Giovanni. 1976. *Parties and Party Systems*. Cambridge: Cambridge University Press.

Smith, Hedrick.1992. *The Media and the Gulf War*. Washington, DC: Seven Locks Press.

Smith, Jean. 1992. *George Bush's War*. Henry Holt.

17.91 | *Additional Resources*

The U.S. Department of State Country and Foreign Policy Information

The United Kingdom: https://www.gov.uk/
U.S. relations with the United Kingdom: http://www.state.gov/p/eur/ci/uk/

Canada: http://www.canada.gc.ca/home.html
U.S. relations with Canada: http://www.state.gov/r/pa/ei/bgn/2089.htm

Mexico: http://en.presidencia.gob.mx/
U.S. relations with Mexico: http://www.state.gov/r/pa/ei/bgn/35749.htm

Israel: http://www.gov.il/firstgov/english
U.S. relations with Israel: http://www.state.gov/r/pa/ei/bgn/3581.htm

Germany:
http://www.bundesregierung.de/Webs/Breg/EN/Homepage/_node.html
U.S. relations with Germany: http://www.state.gov/r/pa/ei/bgn/3997.htm

Brazil: http://www.brasil.gov.br/?set_language=en
U.S. relations with Brazil: http://www.state.gov/r/pa/ei/bgn/35640.htm

Japan: http://www.mofa.go.jp/j_info/japan/government/index.html

China: http://english.gov.cn/
U.S. relations with China: http://www.state.gov/r/pa/ei/bgn/18902.htm
Saudi Arabia:
http://www.saudi.gov.sa/wps/portal/yesserRoot/home/!ut/p/b1/04_Sj9CPykssy0xP
LMnMz0vMAfGjzOId3Z2dgj1NjAz8zUMMDTxNzZ2NHU0NDd29DfWDU_P0
_Tzyc1P1C7IdFQFV9YhO/dl4/d5/L2dBISEvZ0FBIS9nQSEh/
U.S. relations with Saudi Arabia:
http://www.state.gov/j/drl/rls/hrrpt/2005/61698.htm

[1] https://www.ourdocuments.gov/doc.php?flash=false&doc=98&page=transcript

[2] https://www.congress.gov/107/plaws/publ40/PLAW-107publ40.pdf

[3] Brook Lamar, "The Expansionists," *The New York Times Magazine* (May 7, 2017, p.20–32, 78–81.

[4] Theodore J. Lowi and Benjamin Ginsberg. 1996. *American Government*. Fourth Edition (New York: W. W. Norton & Company): 689.

[5] David Brooks, "Donald Trump Poisons the World," The New York Times (June 2, 2017). Accessed at https://www.nytimes.com/.

[6] http://www.charleslindbergh.com/americanfirst/speech.asp

[7] Sumner's anti-imperialist, anti-war essay defending republican government is available at http://praxeology.net/WGS-CUS.htm

[8] Eisenhower's *Farewell Address* is available at: http://www.americanrhetoric.com/speeches/dwightdeisenhowerfarewell.html

[9] https://reaganlibrary.archives.gov/archives/reference/8.18.80.html

[10] Nixon's *Address* is available at http://www.state.gov/r/pa/ho/frus/nixon/i/20700.htm

[11] For an educational perspective on how to present globalization see http://www.cotf.edu/earthinfo/remotesens/remotesens.html

[12] https://www.senate.gov/artandhistory/history/common/generic/Feature_Homepage_TreatyVersailles.htm

[13] http://www.state.gov/g/drl/hr/treaties/

[14] http://foreignaffairs.house.gov/about.asp?sec=documents. Accessed May 15, 2011.

[15] http://www.state.gov/s/d/rm/index.htm Accessed December 22, 2010.

[16] https://www.senate.gov/artandhistory/history/common/investigations/ChurchCommittee.htm

[17] Quoted in http://www.pbs.org/moyers/journal/10192007/blackwater.html

[18] See http://www.globalsecurity.org/military/library/policy/national/nss-020920.htm

[19] https://www.legion.org/magazine/213233/why-we-went-war-vietnam

[20] Quoting Colonel Peter Masoor in "Army Focus on Counterinsurgency Debated Within," By Guy Raz, *National Public Radio*, May 6, 2008. Accessed May 10, 2008. www.npr.org

[21] See http://www.gwu.edu/%7Ensarchiv/NSAEBB/NSAEBB219/index.htm. Accessed May 15, 2011.

[22] Hans J. Morgenthau.1960. *The Purpose of American Politics* (New York: Knopf):169-170.

CPSIA information can be obtained
at www.ICGtesting.com
Printed in the USA
FSHW021814090120
65889FS